The Office

5e

PROCEDURES AND TECHNOLOGY

MARY ELLEN OLIVERIO
Lubin School of Business
Pace University
New York, New York

WILLIAM R. PASEWARK
Professor Emeritus
Texas Tech University
Office Management Consultant
Lubbock, Texas

BONNIE R. WHITE
Distinguished Professor
College of Education
Auburn University
Auburn, Alabama

Dianne Rankin, *Contributing Author*

THOMSON
™
SOUTH-WESTERN

Australia · Brazil · Canada · Mexico · Singapore · Spain · United Kingdom · United States

THOMSON

SOUTH-WESTERN

Wraparound Teacher's Edition
The Office, Procedures and Technology, 5th Edition
Mary Ellen Oliverio, William R. Pasewark, Bonnie R. White

VP/Editorial Development:
Jack W. Calhoun

VP/Editor-in-Chief:
Karen Schmohe

Contributing Author:
Dianne Rankin

Acquisitions Editor:
Jane Congdon

Project Manager:
Dr. Inell Bolls

Marketing Manager:
Michael Cloran

Marketing Coordinator:
Kelley Gilreath

**Marketing Communication
Manager:**
Elizabeth Shipp

Production Manager:
Patricia Matthews Boies

Senior Production Manager:
Kim Kusnerak

**Senior Technology Project
Manager:**
Mike Jackson

Web Coordinator:
Ed Stubenrauch

Manufacturing Coordinator:
Charlene Taylor

Production House:
Lachina Publishing Services

Printer:
Quebecor World
Dubuque, IA

Art Director:
Stacy Jenkins Shirley

Cover/Internal Design:
Grannan Graphic Design, Ltd.

Cover Images:
© Getty Images

Photo and Permissions Editor:
Darren Wright

TABLE OF CONTENTS

PART 2

Managing Information to Enhance Productivity **66**

CHAPTER 3 | Information: A Vital Business Resource **67**

Topic 3-1 Information Processing. 68
Using and Managing Information
Obstacles to Managing Information
Information Processing Activities
Information Technologies
Hardware and Software
Networks
Maintenance and Security Measures
Exercises:

Topic 3-2 Information Systems and Resources 91
Typical Information Systems
Traditional Information Resources
Electronic Resources
Intranets
The Internet
Finding and Sharing Information
E-Commerce
FOCUS ON . . . Intranets to Extranets............ 98
Exercises:

CHAPTER 4 | Communicating in Written Form **111**

Topic 4-1 Reading and Writing at Work. . 112
Reading at Work
Understanding and Following Instructions
Responding to Inquiries
Using References and Databases
Improving Reading Skills
Writing at Work
Characteristics of Effective Messages
Management of Writing Tasks
Exercises:

Topic 4-2 Business Correspondence. 128
Preparing Effective Documents
Drafting and Revising
Editing and Proofreading
Positive, Negative, and Persuasive Messages
Business Letters
Repetitive Letters
Envelopes
Memos and E-Mail
Improving Communications in Organizations
Desktop Publishing
Exercises:

Topic 4-3 Business Reports and Related Documents 150
Informational Reports
Analytical Reports
Gathering Data
Researching Information Online
Writing the Report
Report Parts and Formats
Documentation
Tables, Graphs, and Charts

To the Student

You will enter a world of work that is being transformed. This world will be a challenging and demanding one because of the rate and nature of change. Many of the changes taking place in the workplace relate to the technology. Others relate to the changing needs of businesses and their employees. The workplace is not necessarily at a specific location. For example, four individuals in four different countries may be employed by the same company with each working from a home office. Yet, the four have virtually instant communication—via telecommunications—to develop plans and make decisions.

Many office employees—executives, managers, engineers, accountants, and administrative assistants among others—are accessing databases, preparing spreadsheets, and creating presentations. No longer are information processing tasks primarily the responsibility of secretaries and administrative assistants. All workers are expected to communicate effectively; access, analyze, and share information; make decisions; and use technology to improve productivity.

The Office, Procedures and Technology, Fifth Edition is designed to help you develop skills that will be important in your career in a professional or business position. The content you study will help prepare you to enter the workforce now and to face the changes you will encounter in the future.

Objectives for the Course

As a student, you face a twofold challenge: to prepare for the initial demands of full-time employment and to acquire the skills to learn on the job and adapt to new procedures and technologies. *The Office, Procedures and Technology, Fifth Edition* has been designed to help you meet this challenge. As you study this textbook, you will:

- Develop information management, technology, and communication skills that are valuable for all types of workers
- Develop an awareness of how to learn as new technology, processes, and procedures are introduced in an organization
- Develop a comprehensive view of time management and productivity
- Reinforce and extend basic skills involving math, language, decision making, critical thinking, and teamwork
- Develop understanding of basic qualities and attitudes that are critical in the work environment
- Develop awareness of your interests, strengths, and weaknesses related to the demands of a work environment

Features of the Textbook

The Office, Procedures and Technology, Fifth Edition is organized into 5 parts and 14 chapters. Each chapter is subdivided into two or three segments called topics. The text contains features designed to help you learn the skills and concepts presented.

Part and Topic Objectives	Part and topic objectives focus on key concepts that serve as guides in becoming familiar with the content.
Workplace Connections	These feature boxes give examples and place content discussed in a workplace context.
Focus On . . .	These feature boxes highlight key topics such as disaster recovery, e-commerce, and confidentiality of business information that relate to the chapter content.
Online Resources	This feature box for each chapter provides a list of the resources available on *The Office* Web site that relate to the chapter, names of organizations that may serve as resources, and search terms related to content in the chapter. This information can be used for developing a professional reading file, researching topics for reports, or broadening the scope of the chapter.
Vocabulary Reinforcement	Terms of special importance or those that may be unfamiliar to some students are defined in the margin of the page on which the term is first introduced.
Activities	Activities to reinforce the major concepts and procedures and to provide realistic experience in working independently and in groups are included in each topic and at the end of each chapter.
Chapter Summary	Key points covered in the chapter are reviewed in this feature.
Key Terms	Key terms that students should understand after studying the chapter are listed at the end of each chapter.
Glossary	Selected terms introduced in the text are listed and defined in the glossary.

Student Activities and Simulations Workbook

The *Student Activities and Simulations* workbook designed to accompany the student textbook includes review activities for each chapter. Three workplace simulations, complete with company descriptions, instructions, documents, and other materials, are also provided in the workbook. These simulations correspond to Parts 2, 3, and 4 of the student text. A note at the end of each of these parts reminds you when to complete the simulation for that part. A *Reference Guide* is included in the workbook and provides information helpful for completing the textbook and workbook activities. The *Reference Guide* includes the following sections:

- Section A, Proofreaders' Marks
- Section B, Punctuation
- Section C, Capitalization
- Section D, Math
- Section E, Two-Letter State Abbreviations
- Section F, Alphabetic Indexing Rules
- Section G, Sample Documents

Data Files

Data files for student use in completing activities in the textbook and the *Student Activities and Simulations* workbook are provided on the *Instructor's Resource CD-ROM*. Your instructor will need to make these files available to you on disk or on your local area network. Some data files are in word processing or spreadsheet format and are to be revised or completed by the student. Other files are in PDF (Portable Document Format) and are to be printed and used as source documents or reference material. In the textbook, a data disk icon identifies applications that require a data file.

Data Disk Icon

The Office Web Site

A Web site related to this textbook is available at *http://theoffice.swlearning.com*. On this site, you can access data files, vocabulary flash cards, games that review chapter concepts, supplemental activities, and links to other Web sites. The items available for each chapter are listed in the Online Resources box at the beginning of each chapter.

For the Instructor

The Office, Procedures and Technology, Fifth Edition is appropriate for any student preparing for a career that involves office skills. The textbook and related student workbook may be adapted for completion in one semester or two semesters by selecting an appropriate mix of activities from the textbook and student workbook.

Students should be comfortable with the basic features of their word processing, spreadsheet, database, presentation, e-mail, and browser software. Students will build skills with these programs as they complete the activities in the textbook and student workbook. Students should understand how to organize and manage the files they create during this course. You may wish to direct students regarding this issue early in the course.

Electronic Test Package

Instructors can purchase a flexible, easy-to-use test bank and test generation software program that contains objective questions for each test. Test bank questions are included for 14 chapter tests and a final exam. The *ExamView®️ Pro* software enables instructors to modify questions from the test bank or add instructor-written questions to create customized tests.

The chapter tests and a final exam are also available on the *Instructor's Resource CD-ROM*. These tests may be printed and given to students. Answers to these tests are also provided on the *Instructor's Resource CD-ROM*.

Instructor's Resource Guide

The *Instructor's Resource Guide* is available to instructors who adopt the textbook for class use. The guide is a comprehensive source for practical ideas in course planning and enrichment. The guide includes teaching and grading suggestions and solutions for chapter activities, workbook review activities, and simulations.

Instructor's Resource CD-ROM

An *Instructor's Resource CD-ROM* is available to instructors who adopt the textbook for class use. The CD-ROM includes:

- Data files for use by students in completing activities for the textbook and student workbook
- Lesson plans for the instructor
- Sample solution files for selected student activities
- Electronic slides (in *Microsoft PowerPoint* format) for each chapter for use during class discussions
- Transparency masters for use in class discussions
- Tests and solutions

Wrap Instructor's Edition

A *Wrap Instructor's Edition* (WIE) is available for instructors who adopt the textbook for class use. The WIE contains the student textbook pages in a reduced size along with annotations to assist the instructor in presenting material and facilitating student learning. The annotations provide information for:

- Assessment
- Challenge Option
- Expand the Concept
- For Discussion
- Getting Started
- Points to Emphasize
- Supplemental Activity
- Teaching Tips
- Thinking Critically

The Office Web Site

A Web site related to this textbook is available at *http://theoffice.swlearning .com*. On this site, students can access data files, vocabulary flash cards, games that review chapter concepts, supplemental activities, and links to other Web sites. The items available for students for each chapter are listed in the Online Resources box at the beginning of each chapter. Additional materials are available on the Web site for instructor use. Examples of these materials are solutions to activities from the student text, transparency masters, lesson plans, and presentation slides.

A Commitment by the Authors

The Office, Procedures and Technology, Fifth Edition continues a long tradition of providing training for many types of workers who function, at least in part, in an office environment. Both industry surveys and research by private and governmental organizations make clear the need for information, technology, and teamwork skills that are emphasized in this text. We believe that students with a wide range of occupational goals can profitably study together. We are committed to providing quality learning materials that will help students develop highly portable skills relevant to today's work environment.

Mary Ellen Oliverio
William R. Pasewark
Bonnie Roe White

PART 1

The Office in the Business World

OBJECTIVES

- Describe the relationship of the office to the overall organization
- Describe typical goals and structures of businesses
- Identify the types of office competencies workers need
- Explain employer expectations and factors related to developing office competencies

Millions of Americans spend much of each workday in offices. Many changes in technology have occurred during the last decade. These changes have created a widespread need for knowledge and skills that are commonly referred to as office competencies. Whatever their fields or careers, workers share a need to know how to perform efficiently and effectively in offices. The Office in the Business World introduces you to the office as a workplace.

1

Getting Started

Discuss the Online Resources available to students for this chapter.

CHAPTER 1

The Office in a Changing Business World

Many workers in many different types of jobs perform office tasks. The recruiter in a Human Resources Department, the technician in a chemical laboratory, the curator in a museum, the buyer in a department store, and the CPA in a public accounting firm all perform a range of office tasks during a typical workweek. All office workers, regardless of their duties, must understand how office functions relate to their work and to the total organization.

In Chapter 1, you will learn about various types of offices and office workers. You will also gain an understanding of typical goals and structures of businesses, not-for-profit entities, and governmental units.

Online Resources

O *The Office* Web site:
Data Files
Vocabulary Flashcards
Beat the Clock, Organizations
Chapter 1 Supplementary
Activity
O International Association of
Virtual Office Assistants
(IAVOA)
Rt. 1 Box 275
Red Oak, OK 74563
O Search terms:
home office
mobile office
office competencies
office technology
telecommute

2

THE OFFICE TODAY

The term *office* is used in a variety of ways. An **office** is a place in which the affairs of a business or an organization are carried out. For example, you may have heard a lawyer say, "I will be out of the office during the afternoon." A teacher might say, "Come by my office." The office is a place of work for many types of workers. Accountants, marketing managers, systems analysts, human resource directors, as well as secretaries, records clerks, administrative assistants, and many others work in offices. Although each of these employees has varying duties, all of them must be knowledgeable about many office practices.

This textbook focuses on the many workers who need to understand office practices and use office skills. Regardless of what you plan for your life's work, you will benefit from studying the topics in this book and from the skills you will develop.

- O Describe various types of offices
- O Describe types of workers who use office skills
- O Explain how technology influences office practices
- O Identify common information-related office tasks

office: a place in which the affairs of a business, professional person, or organization are carried out

WORKPLACE CONNECTIONS

Carole Federman is an internal auditor for an international bank. The company headquarters are in Philadelphia. Her work requires traveling to branches throughout the United States. She visits cities such as as Paris, Milan, and Tokyo. She must write many reports to share her conclusions and recommendations. Carole composes her reports at her laptop computer. She usually completes the reports with no help from office support staff.

© LARRY LAWFER/INDEX STOCK IMAGERY

This executive prepares reports using her laptop computer.

Topic 1-1: *The Office Today*

3

information: data or facts that have been summarized or organized into a meaningful form

vendor: a seller of goods or services

Offices Are Information Driven

Information is made up of data or facts that have been organized into a meaningful form. Information is at the core of all office activities. Office workers use information in many ways. Some illustrations include:

- A manager writes the policy for sales returns.
- A stock broker accesses a database for the current price of a company's stock.
- A sales clerk enters details of a customer's order at a computer.
- A customer service rep responds by telephone to questions about installing electronic equipment.

Workers need to understand thoroughly the business or organization in which they are employed. Each task is related to the organization's purposes and goals. For example, a purchasing agent often makes telephone calls to place an order for materials or supplies. To answer questions that the **vendor** may ask, the employee needs to know the details about what is being ordered. The employee also needs to know when the item is needed, the cost of the item, and similar details.

Office Functions Are Varied

In some offices, every employee does a wide variety of tasks. In other offices, each employee's work is focused on a few tasks. Some common office tasks are shown in Figure 1-1.1 on page 5. Can you identify two activities that might be completed by a manager? Can you identify two that might be performed by an office assistant? Think of a particular career and identify two activities that might be performed by someone in that career.

WORKPLACE CONNECTIONS

Helen Serreno works as an office assistant to the director of a relatively new art gallery in Santa Fe, New Mexico. Helen talked about her job in these words:

I never know what a day will be like. I handle many office tasks as I assist the director, the art assistant, and the manager of exhibits. I do some tasks every day such as respond to e-mail messages, open and organize the mail, and handle phone calls. I have a personal computer, a photocopier, a fax machine, e-mail and Internet access, and a wide range of software programs that I use daily. I'm responsible for maintaining all the equipment, too.

4

CHAPTER 1: THE OFFICE IN A CHANGING BUSINESS WORLD

Figure **1-1.1**

KEY OFFICE ACTIVITIES

Creating/Analyzing Information
- Composing memorandums, letters, and reports
- Organizing, summarizing, and interpreting data
- Creating presentations
- Making decisions and recommendations based on information studied

Searching for Information
- Accessing databases, the Internet, and company intranets
- Requesting information from persons within the company
- Requesting information from persons outside the company
- Using reference manuals and books

Processing Information
- Editing and proofreading
- Keyboarding
- Opening and reviewing incoming communications
- Entering data in databases
- Photocopying
- Preparing outgoing communications
- Preparing checks, orders, invoices
- Preparing spreadsheets

Communicating Information
- Answering telephones
- Greeting callers
- Responding to persons within and outside the organization
- Providing instruction to coworkers
- Preparing and delivering presentations

Managing Information
- Maintaining calendars
- Maintaining databases and files
- Maintaining financial records

Workers in many jobs handle office tasks. Some workers, however, devote full time to office tasks. For example, some employees in an Accounting Department process invoices, checks, and other documents related to customer accounts. They devote all of their time to office tasks.

Expand the Concept

Students have had experience in visiting offices. Ask them to identify offices that seemed general and those that seemed specialized.

Thinking Critically

What ways of searching for information have you used as students that might be helpful at work?

5

Topic 1-1: *The Office Today*

Thinking Critically

What does "support services" mean? Give an example of a support task.

For Discussion

Some students may have had work experience where they were able to observe office activities. Ask them to describe the equipment in use where they worked.

Thinking Critically

How do good word processing skills add to efficiency and effectiveness in the preparation of reports?

The manager of a midsize manufacturing company in Lexington, Kentucky, talked about the role of office support services in these words:

The work done by the office employees in our Accounts Payable Department is vital to the success of our company. Invoices must be processed and payments made to vendors. This work must be done in a timely manner to keep materials flowing so production goals can be met. We value these workers and provide them with the most current technology.

The assistant manager in a small company is instructing a new staff member.

intranet: computer network within an organization that is meant for the use of its employees or members

Technology in Modern Offices

The use of technology is common in today's offices. An architect who designs buildings works at a computer. An executive uses the World Wide Web to find a schedule for travel to London. Sales people from several states communicate with the regional manager in Philadelphia using a company **intranet**.

Many companies use up-to-date technology in their offices to help employees be productive. Because the technology available is changing, the way work is accomplished is also changing. Workers should expect their duties, as well as the way they work, to change from time to time. The need for high productivity and quality performance means that all workers must be willing to change work methods. Office workers must be skillful learners—on their own and in more formal training and educational settings.

6

CHAPTER 1: THE OFFICE IN A CHANGING BUSINESS WORLD

Marie Ann Martinez describes what she is doing today that she was not doing just three years earlier:

Three years ago, we were a domestic company. Today we do business in 60 countries. I regularly send e-mail messages to China, Singapore, Hong Kong, Prague, and Moscow, and other places around the world. I used to prepare printed letters, place hard copies of letters in a file drawer, and conduct research by telephone. Now I send e-mail messages instead of letters in many cases. I use databases (Figure 1-1.2) and electronic files to store information. I access the Internet to research and communicate information.

	Title	First Name	Last Name	Address	City	State	Postal Code	Business Phone
	Mr.	Walt	Barker	625 Dante St.	New Orleans	LA	70118-6625	555-0117
	Mr.	John	Best	124 Granville St.	New Orleans	LA	70129-1124	555-0141
	Mrs.	Adriana	Brea	507 Loyola Ave.	New Orleans	LA	70113-5507	555-0147
	Ms.	Kim	Chassie	20 Ibis St.	New Orleans	LA	70124-0020	555-0124
	Ms.	Maria	DeOliveira	207 Chase St.	New Orleans	LA	70127-2207	555-0115
	Mr.	Jon	Gardiol	10 Bordeaux St.	New Orleans	LA	70115-0010	555-0118
	Mr.	Tu	Hewang	810 Julia St.	New Orleans	LA	70113-0810	555-0122
	Ms.	Kim	Hostilo	10 Audubon Blvd.	New Orleans	LA	70118-0118	555-0138
	Mr.	Bruce	Leski	805 Poydras St.	New Orleans	LA	70112-6805	555-0144
▶	Mr.	Daniel	Levi	20 Dorsiere St.	New Orleans	LA	70130-4420	555-0114
	Ms.	Lu	Lin	234 Foch Rd.	New Orleans	LA	70126-2234	555-0143

Record: 10 of 25

Figure 1-1.2

Many companies use database software such as Microsoft® Access to store data.

Alternative Offices

Where is the office? The office may be at headquarters, in a carrying bag, or at home. It may be a temporarily assigned workspace. No longer is the office always a particular space used for the same purpose day after day.

The typical office from earlier days is referred to as the traditional office. A traditional office is permanent and located where the company does business. In such an office, employees travel daily to a central location. They spend the working day at the same desk or in the same workspace and generally report directly to a supervisor or manager. Many businesses still use traditional offices; however, other types of work arrangements are being used more frequently.

The practice of working and communicating with others from a home office or other remote location is called telecommuting. A worker who **telecommutes** shares information with clients or coworkers using the **Internet** or an intranet. Equipment such as a computer, telephone, and fax machine makes talking and sharing data easy. These workers may work in virtual offices, mobile offices, or home offices.

telecommute: the practice of working and communicating with others from a remote location

Internet: a public, worldwide computer network made up of smaller, interconnected networks that spans the globe

Points to Emphasize

Technology has aided in expansion of business to the global community. Ask students to describe why engaging in worldwide business activity now is easier than it was a decade ago.

Challenge Option

Why are there still traditional offices in organizations?

Expand the Concept

Ask students to identify problems that might develop when workers telecommute.

7

Topic 1-1: *The Office Today*

Points to Emphasize

Technology makes virtual offices possible.

Expand the Concept

Ask students to identify the technology critical for effective and efficient telecommuting.

Thinking Critically

Why would a company choose to have nonterritorial workplaces?

Virtual Office

The term *virtual* describes something that has a conceptual form but no physical form that you can see or touch. For example, you are acquainted with your local library. It is in a physical building that contains shelves of books you can use to get information. A virtual library might be a computer station that gives you access to many libraries from your school or home. Although the virtual library has no physical form, it allows you to gather information just as a physical library does. The **virtual office**, therefore, has no physical form but allows you to perform work activities as you would in a traditional office setting.

Just as some office workers use virtual offices, some offices employ virtual assistants. A virtual assistant is a worker who performs tasks normally handled by an on-site secretary or administrative assistant. This growing field provides advantages to both the company and the virtual assistant. A virtual assistant can work from a home office. He or she can set the work schedule and work only as many hours per week as desired. Virtual assistants do not require on-site office space and are usually paid only for the hours they work. This means cost savings for the company, which can be especially important for small businesses.

virtual office: the capability to perform work activities away from a traditional office setting

WORKPLACE CONNECTIONS

Susan Gray is a successful interior designer in St. Louis. Although Susan refers to her office as a portable office, it is really a virtual office. Susan visits clients to plan and discuss projects. In her bag, she carries a digital phone; a notebook computer with wireless access to fax, e-mail, and the Internet; and a portable copier/printer. Susan can provide plans for a room, cost estimates, and a contract right in the client's living room.

Mobile Office

Mobile offices are very much like traditional offices, but they are temporarily located at a particular site or that can move from place to place

nonterritorial workspace: area not assigned to a specific person or task

hoteling: assigning temporary office workspace to workers as needed

Mobile offices are very much like traditional offices, but they are temporary. Offices set up at construction sites and manned by office staff are one type of mobile office. Another type of mobile office is the **nonterritorial workspace**. Nonterritorial workspaces are available on an assignment basis. They are not assigned to anyone permanently. This type of workspace is often found in professional organizations. For example, an accounting firm or law firm may have many staff members who work away from the company a great deal of the time. Because such personnel do not need a permanent office, they can request an office on their arrival at headquarters.

The use of nonterritorial workspace is sometimes referred to as **hoteling**. The process is similar to that of a hotel assigning a room to a guest. Computer software makes assigning space prompt and effective. Employees who generally work from a home office, for example, may be assigned office space on those occasions when they do work at the company office.

8

CHAPTER 1: THE OFFICE IN A CHANGING BUSINESS WORLD

Two architects review building plans in a mobile office.

Home Office

A space within a person's home that is used to perform office tasks is referred to as a home office. In many home offices, workers can communicate easily with others using e-mail, the Internet, an intranet, fax, and a telephone. Some people who work at home are able to take part in teleconferences with persons at other locations.

Many people who work in home offices are self-employed. Such persons are often called **freelancers**. Freelancers may occasionally meet with customers or clients in person. However, they may communicate primarily by e-mail, telephone, and mail.

freelancer: independent contractors who work for others, usually on a project-by-project basis

For Discussion

Do you know someone who works in a home office? What type of work does this person do?

Freelancers often work from home offices.

9

Topic 1-1: *The Office Today*

WORKPLACE CONNECTIONS

Ingrid Thomason owns and manages an accounting service business as a freelancer, working from her home. Having worked in the Accounting Department of a large company, she is knowledgeable about accounting systems. She decided that she would prefer to live in a small rural town. She has been successful in finding as many clients as she can handle. Her state-of-the-art computer and software programs allow clients to transmit financial information to her for processing and organizing. Her clients have online access to their financial statements on a timely basis. Ingrid notes that she has a number of clients that she has never seen in person.

Predictions Are for Further Change

Technology and procedures used in offices are changing. However, all companies do not apply change at the same rate or in the same way. Some companies monitor changes in technology. They introduce the newest equipment and software related to their work as quickly as possible. Such organizations see value in updating their operations. At the same time, other companies decide that no changes are needed.

A company may use the latest ideas and equipment. However, its workers may not be as effective as those at a company that uses more traditional methods. For example, workers who want to complete work quickly and well may be able to do so even without new equipment. They may be more productive than indifferent workers who use the latest equipment. Over time, however, new equipment and methods that aid workers tend to be used by most organizations.

10

REVIEWING THE TOPIC

1. List five information-related office tasks.
2. What kinds of employees need office competencies?
3. As you consider the office functions in Figure 1-1.1, identify at least three that you think would require skill in using equipment.
4. As you consider the office functions in Figure 1-1.1, identify at least two that you think at this point you could handle. Explain why.
5. Why might an organization have specialized offices? Give an illustration of such an office.
6. How does a traditional office differ from a virtual office, a mobile office, and a home office?
7. What makes telecommuting a feasible way of handling office work?
8. Will using the latest technology ensure that office workers are highly productive? Why or why not?

MAKING DECISIONS

Assume that you have completed your studies and are seeking your first full-time position. You have been interviewed by two companies. Each company has offered you a position. You like both companies as far as the nature of the work, the salary, and the employee benefits. But there is a difference in where you will work.

In Company A, you would be expected to come to headquarters each day. The company has current computers and other technology, and the supervisor seems very helpful and friendly. In Company B, you would be telecommuting. Company B would provide you with all the equipment and furniture for your workstation at home. You would have access to your supervisor via telecommunications. From time to time—possibly no more than once in three weeks—you would be expected to attend a training session or a team meeting at headquarters. Which position would you accept?

1. Make a list of the factors you would consider in making a decision about which job to accept.
2. Write a brief paragraph in which you discuss your decision and the basis for it.

11

Topic Review

For Discussion

Discuss alternatives for correcting the sentences with students after they complete this activity.

Teaching Tips

Assign students to the teams in which they will work to complete this activity. Discuss guidelines you expect students to follow for team projects.

REINFORCING ENGLISH SKILLS

For a group of words to be a complete sentence, it must contain both a subject and a verb. In this exercise, you will identify complete and incomplete sentences. You will change incomplete sentences into complete sentences, choosing words that make sense to you.

1. Open the *Microsoft® Word* file *CH01 English* found in the data files. Read the paragraphs, noting which sentences are complete and which are incomplete.
2. For all incomplete sentences, add a word or words to make complete sentences.
3. Save your edited sentences.

Note: Save all documents created for exercises in this textbook using meaningful filenames. Print documents or e-mail them to your instructor as your instructor directs. Keep all files for possible use in other exercises.

COMPOSITION
INTEGRATED DOCUMENT
RESEARCH
SPREADSHEET
TEAMWORK
WORD PROCESSING

Topic **1-1** ACTIVITY 1

Getting Acquainted with Local Offices

In this activity, you will become familiar with the types of offices in your own community. Work in a team with three other class members to complete this activity.

1. Develop a list of four or five major employers in your area.
2. Find answers to the following questions by visiting the company, talking with an employee, or accessing the company's Web site:
   • What is the primary product(s) or service(s) of the business or organization?
   • What percentage of the employees at this location work in offices?
   • How many workers telecommute? If there are workers who telecommute, how many of them are considered office workers?
   • What technology is being used in preparing letters and reports? for telecommunications? for records management?
   • In general, determine if the technology in use is state-of-the-art, somewhat up-to-date, or a type that does not use computers.

12

3. Prepare a written report of one to two pages in which you present the information you gathered. Use spreadsheet software to prepare a pie chart showing office use of technology that is current, somewhat current, and not current. Incorporate this pie chart in your report.

4. Participate in a discussion that summarizes what offices are like in your community.

Topic 1-1 : ACTIVITY 2

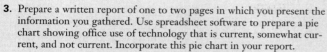

INTERNET

Accessing the Web Site for This Textbook

The publisher of this textbook maintains a Web site with information related to the textbook. *The Office* Web site contains data files, games, links, and other information that you will use as you complete the activities in this textbook. You will probably visit this site often. In this activity, you will explore the site and create a link to make visiting the site quick and easy.

1. Access the Internet. Start your Web browser such as *Microsoft® Internet Explorer*. In the Address box, enter **theoffice.swlearning.com**.

2. A Web site that contains Web pages related to your textbook should appear. Click a hyperlink, such as **Student Resources**. Quickly scan the new page to see the information that it provides. Click the **Back** button to return to the welcome page.

3. Locate and access the **Links** page on the Web site. This page contains links to other sites that you can use as you complete activities. Whenever a Web site is mentioned in an activity in the textbook, look for the link to that site on this page.

4. Return to the welcome page for this site. Add this Web site to your Favorites or Bookmarks list. Use this Favorites or Bookmarks link whenever you need to access this site for later activities.

Teaching Tips

Assist students, as needed, with finding the document online that is similar to *Publication 587* and contains information for the current year.

COMPOSITION
INTERNET
RESEARCH

Topic **1-1** ACTIVITY 3

Qualifying as a Home Office

In the United States, a person who works in a home office may be able to deduct costs related to the home office from federal income taxes. The home office and its use must meet certain requirements, however. You will learn about those requirements in this activity.

1. Open the *Word* file *CH01 Deduction* from the data files. Read the excerpt from IRS *Publication 587, Business Use of Your Home*.

2. A freelance writer uses a portion of her den for a home office. The den is also used as a family gathering place for watching TV and playing games. Does this home office qualify for a business tax deduction? Why or why not?

3. *Publication 587* was published for use in preparing year 2004 tax returns. Have the regulations changed for the current year? Access the U.S. Internal Revenue Service Web site. Search the site using the term *home office* to find current regulations.

4. Prepare a one-page report using the information you learn from this document. In the report, include a brief summary of the requirements a home office must meet to qualify for a business tax deduction. Discuss how current regulations differ from (or are the same as) those in *Publication 587* (using your research from Step 3).

14

objectives

Office tasks are related to the work of many parts of an organization. Completing office tasks often requires judgment and making decisions. Understanding the organization will help you make sound decisions in completing your work.

Understanding the Organization

Office activities are basically related to information. You will process and communicate information as you complete your work. In doing so, you will learn much about your organization. Such learning, however, is not automatic. You must make an effort to learn about the company. You will find tasks more interesting and be a more valuable employee when you understand the organization.

Learning from Your Work

The information you handle is related to your organization. You should be alert to opportunities to learn from the content of your work. Of course, you must realize at all times the information you handle may be **confidential**.

O Explain how employees develop understanding of organizations in which they work

O Describe common types of organizations

O Identify goals for different types of organizations

O Explain a common structure for personnel

O Describe the role of office employees within an organization

confidential: private or secret in nature

WORKPLACE CONNECTIONS

Fred Jansen works for a senior vice president, Mr. Roberts, in a large advertising company. Mr. Roberts is involved in buying several small advertising agencies. Fred knows that much information about possible deals is confidential. He notes for his own use, however, information from reports and other documents. He finds that his understanding of the specific deadlines, for example, can help him prioritize his work.

Learning from Resources Available

Learning about the company can help employees understand their own jobs better. Annual reports are sometimes provided to all employees. These reports can help employees understand the company's mission as well as its goals for the coming fiscal year.

Getting Started

Is there an office all students know, such as that of the guidance counselor, principal, or superintendent? If there is, such an office may be the focus for a discussion of what employees in the office need to know to do their jobs competently.

Further discussion of how the office employees become acquainted with the organization would be helpful.

Expand the Concept

What does it mean to be alert to opportunities to learn? Explain.

Thinking Critically

Why must Fred keep details of pending acquisitions confidential?

Thinking Critically

Why do managers subscribe to periodicals that deal with the industry in which their company operates?

15

Topic 1-2: *The Office in Relation to the Total Organization*

Reading trade magazines is a good way to learn about trends in your field.

Employees can read articles that appear in newspapers or magazines about the company. They may have access to Web sites that deal with the industry in which the company operates. These sites can also provide valuable information. Workers who understand the company know whom to call when they need information related to their work. They also know where to find answers to questions about the company.

Types of Organizations

In the United States, organizations are grouped into one of three categories. They may be businesses, not-for-profit entities (but not governmental), or governmental units. The goals of these organizations vary, as well their methods of operation.

Businesses

profit: monetary gain; advantage

Businesses are organizations that seek to make a **profit.** For the most part, businesses in the United States are organized as sole proprietorships, partnerships, or corporations. Sole proprietorships and partnerships can be organized without approval by any governmental body. Corporations, on the other hand, are required to secure **charters** from the states in which they incorporate. All businesses must follow the laws and regulations governing business activity.

charter: written grant of rights from a government

Sole Proprietorship

sole proprietorship: a business owned by one individual, also called single proprietorship

A business owned by one individual is a **sole proprietorship.** Such a business may or may not also be managed by the owner. Sole proprietorships may be of any size, but many of them are small. Welsh Internet Access is an example of a small business. This small company with about 1,000 customers provides Internet access for companies. They also provide consulting services for those who want to build intranets.

Partnership

A business that is not incorporated and has two or more owners is known as a **partnership**. Different types of partners may participate in a partnership. Some partners may provide funds for the business but not take part in managing it. Other partners may actively lead and manage the business. Partnerships, too, may be of any size; many are small, however.

Ramos & Saunders Graphics is an example of a partnership owned and operated by Bill Ramos and Sally Saunders. The business provides a wide range of artistic services to a variety of clients.

partnership: a business that is not incorporated and has two or more owners

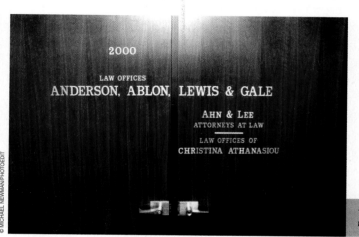

These attorneys have formed a partnership.

Corporation

A **corporation** is a business set up under the laws of a particular state. A charter must be secured for a corporation. The business may be privately or publicly owned. Owners have shares of ownership called stock certificates. Owners are called stockholders or shareholders. The corporation is considered a legal unit, separate from its shareholders. Most large companies in the United States are corporations. Publicly owned corporations are required to report information about the business to shareholders on a timely basis. Such reports become available to many others besides the stockholders.

corporation: a business organized under the laws of a particular state for which a charter was secured

Park and Son, Inc. is an example of a corporation that is privately owned. The company develops and sells software systems to individuals and companies. John Park manages the company.

Professional Service Organizations

Professionals such as lawyers, doctors, and accountants often have businesses. The business may be a sole proprietorship, partnership, or corporation. The laws and regulations governing a company of professional persons, however, are different from those that apply to other businesses.

17

Topic 1-2: The Office in Relation to the Total Organization

For Discussion

What might be some advantages of having one or more business partners? What might be some disadvantages of having business partners?

Expand the Concept

Explain that the stock of a privately owned corporation is not traded publicly, such as on the New York Stock Exchange, where anyone may buy and sell shares. All shares of a privately owned corporation are often held by a small group of people.

Point to Emphasize

More professional service organizations are being organized as an LLC or LLP to give some personal liability protection to members of the organization.

negligence: failure to use a reasonable amount of care resulting in damage

Shareholders in a corporation, for example, are generally not held responsible for the behavior of managers of the business. If the business has debts that it cannot pay, shareholders cannot be forced to pay those debts. Members of a professional service organization, however, may be legally responsible for each other's actions. They may also be responsible for the debts of the company. For example, suppose one accountant in a firm is sued for negligence in managing a client's affairs and found guilty. All members of the firm can be forced to help pay the damages awarded to the client. If the firm does not have enough money to pay the damages, members can be forced to use their personal money to pay the debt.

A professional company may choose to organize as a limited liability company (LLC) or a limited liability partnership (LLP). Both these forms offer some personal liability protection to members of the company. For example, in an LLC a member generally cannot be forced to use personal money to pay for debts of the company. Note, however, that an LLC does not protect a member from liability created by his or her own negligence or criminal activity.

Not-for-Profit Entities

Many organizations in the United States provide services without the intent of making profits. Among these organizations are associations that sponsor programs for young people, such as 4-H clubs, Girl Scouts, Boy Scouts, and the Future Business Leaders of America. Other common not-for-profit groups include centers for performing arts, museums, libraries, hospitals, and private colleges. Many hospitals and schools, however, do operate as businesses and do seek to be profitable.

© RUDI VON BRIEL/INDEX STOCK IMAGERY

This museum is a not-for-profit entity.

Not-for-profit organizations receive funds from a variety of sources. Many depend on money received from individuals and groups. They may receive money from dues and fees paid by participants. Some funds may come from government agencies at the local, state, or federal level. Often, these groups operate in what is referred to as a businesslike manner. This means that resources are carefully budgeted as though the entity were a profit-making business.

Governmental Units

Governmental units at the local, state, and national levels play a critical role in society. These units are called by different names. They may be an agency, bureau, department, or board. Each unit has specific duties related to services considered important for the citizens served. For example, the Environmental Protection Agency's (EPA) mission is to protect human health and to safeguard the natural environment. The EPA makes information available on its Web site as shown in Figure 1-2.1. Other examples include:

National	Department of the Treasury, Bureau of Labor Statistics
State or Province	Department of Commerce, Occupational Safety & Health Division
Local	Marriage License Bureau, Board of Education

Teaching Tips

Instruct students to identify local offices of state and federal agencies from the pages of the telephone book. Discuss services provided and the role of office employees in these offices.

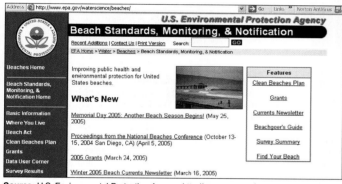

Figure 1-2.1

The EPA's mission is to protect human health and to safeguard the natural environment.

Source: U.S. Environmental Protection Agency. http://www.epa.gov/waterscience/beaches/ (accessed June 6, 2005).

Goals of Organizations

Each of the three major types of organizations has different overall goals. Businesses, including professional companies, seek to make a profit. On the other hand, not-for-profit entities and governmental units do not seek to earn profits. Their goals relate to the services they provide. These goals influence the work of the employees.

19

Topic 1-2: *The Office in Relation to the Total Organization*

Goals of Businesses

You may have heard a comment such as, "It's the bottom line that counts." Prior to the comment, a discussion may have taken place about what a business should choose to do. Various strategies for increasing profits may have been discussed. In general, strategies that will provide the most profit are selected. This increases "the bottom line"—the amount of profit shown on the bottom line of the company's profit and loss statement. Profits allow a business to expand through investment in new facilities and new equipment. Profits also provide the means to make payments (called dividends) to shareholders in a corporation.

WORKPLACE CONNECTIONS

Many tasks that workers perform relate to helping to meet the profit goals of the business. Hans Welenz works in the Customer Service Department for a company that makes personal computers. The company sells computers nationwide, primarily to businesses. Hans's main task is to understand exactly a complaint or question from a customer. He gives the information to the person in the company who can help the customer. Hans and other staff members try to answer all complaints or questions within 24 hours. Hans knows that his work aids the company in meeting profit goals. A satisfied customer will be likely to buy more computers in the future. A dissatisfied customer is likely to make future purchases from another company.

income statement: a report that details the results of business operations for a certain period of time

revenue: income, money, or other gain received

expense: financial cost; fee; charge

balance sheet: a report that presents the financial condition of a company as of a specific date

assets: goods and property owned

liabilities: debts

owner's equity: owner's share of the worth of a firm; capital

A profit and loss statement may also be called an income statement. An **income statement** details the results of business operations for a certain period of time. It answers the question, "How successful was the business during the time period?" The income statement lists the amounts and sources of **revenues**, as well as **expenses**, and the income (profit) or loss of a business for the reporting period. A net income results if revenues are greater than expenses. A net loss results if expenses are greater than revenues. Dandy's Delights' (a sole proprietorship) income statement for the recently ended fiscal year is shown in Figure 1-2.2 on page 21.

A **balance sheet** is a report that presents the financial condition of a company as of a specific date. The balance sheet reports the **assets**, **liabilities**, and **owner's equity** or capital. The assets of a company include all the goods and property owned by the firm as well as the amounts due the company from others. Liabilities are the debts of the company. The owner's equity or capital is the owner's share of the worth of the firm. This amount is the difference between assets and liabilities. On every balance sheet, the total assets must equal the total liabilities plus the owner's equity. This accounting formula applies to every balance sheet, whether the balance sheet is for a large corporation or a small, individually owned business. A balance sheet for Dandy's Delights is shown in Figure 1-2.3 on page 22.

20

CHAPTER 1: THE OFFICE IN A CHANGING BUSINESS WORLD

DANDY'S DELIGHTS
INCOME STATEMENT
For the Year Ended December 31, 20--

			% of Sales
Sales		$200,000	
Cost of Goods Sold	100,000		
Gross Profit on Sales		$100,000	50%
Operating Expenses			
Advertising Expense	500		
Delivery Expense	1,000		
Office Supplies Expense	800		
Payroll Taxes Expense	4,500		
Salaries Expense	58,200		
Utilities Expense	3,500		
Miscellaneous Expense	500		
Total Operating Expense		69,000	
Net Income from Operations		$31,000	16%
Other Income and Expenses			
Interest Expense		2,000	
Net Income Before Income Tax		$29,000	15%
Less Income Tax		8,200	
Net Income After Tax		$20,800	10%

For Discussion

What items are listed as operating expenses on this income statement?

Figure **1-2.2**

An income statement shows a company's profit or loss for a specific period of time.

21

Topic 1-2: The Office in Relation to the Total Organization

Points to Emphasize

On a balance sheet, total assets must equal total liabilities plus owner's equity.

DANDY'S DELIGHTS
BALANCE SHEET
As of December 31, 20--

Assets

Current Assets		
Cash	$12,000	
Accounts Receivable	3,500	
Baking Supplies Inventory	2,000	
Office Supplies	500	
Total Current Assets		$18,000
Fixed Assets		
Delivery Van	$7,000	
Baking Equipment	5,000	
Building and Land	95,000	
Total Fixed Assets		107,000
Total Assets		$125,000

Liabilities

Current Liabilities		
Notes Payable	$1,500	
Accounts Payable	1,000	
Salary and Wages Payable	200	
Total Current Liabilities		$2,700
Fixed Liabilities		
Long-term Note Payable	$5,000	
Mortgage Payable	35,000	
Total Fixed Liabilities		40,000
Total Liabilities		$42,700

Owner's Equity

Dan Burts, Capital			
Beginning Balance		$63,500	
Net Income for 20--	$20,800		
Less Withdrawals	2,000	18,800	
Dan Burts, Capital			
Ending Balance		82,300	
Total Liabilities and			
Owner's Equity		$125,000	

Figure **1-2.3**

A balance sheet shows a company's financial condition on a specific date.

Goals of Not-for-Profit Entities

Not-for-profit organizations, as the title states, do not seek to make a profit. The chief goal of such organizations is to provide valuable services to those who can benefit from them. Museums strive to provide interesting exhibitions of various types of art. Social agencies provide food and cleaning services for the elderly. Such organizations try to make sure all who need their services actually receive them.

WORKPLACE CONNECTIONS

Workers in not-for-profit entities perform many office tasks. Here is just one example:

Elvira Sidney works as a counselor in a not-for-profit outreach program in Apopka, Florida. Much of her time is spent helping those who come to enroll in literacy and job skills programs. Elvira realizes that many of her clients are shy and unfamiliar with offices. She is friendly, helpful, and sensitive to the need for encouragement. The outreach organization is aware of the numbers of people in the community who could benefit from the programs offered. They strive each year to increase the enrollment in their programs, which are free.

Goals of Governmental Units

Governmental units, like not-for-profit entities, do not seek to make a profit. These units are supported primarily by taxes. The overall goals of governmental units are related to providing services that citizens desire or need. For example, the government maintains a federal highway system. This system ensures ease of travel throughout the country. Such a system is an aid to commerce and to the quality of life that citizens enjoy. Many workers in government are required to handle the tasks required to meet the needs of citizens.

WORKPLACE CONNECTIONS

This brief description of the duties of one worker in a federal office will provide an idea of what is done in one governmental office:

Judy Chen works at the Federal Deposit Insurance Corporation. This federal agency regulates most insured banks in the United States. Judy's office assigns staff to examine banks and receiving reports. Attention to details and to prompt updating of all records is critical in Judy's job. She finds her work challenging and interesting. She believes she is learning much about the total banking system in the United States through her dealings with examiners and reading the reports.

For Discussion

Use the not-for-profit entities discussed earlier as a basis for a discussion of organization goals other than profit. For example, many museums and charitable organizations use volunteer office help to hold costs down while maintaining a high level of service.

Challenge Option

In a follow-up to identifying local offices of governmental units, ask students to describe the overall goal of the governmental agencies noted.

For Discussion

Discuss why giving attention to details is important in any job.

Structure of Organizations

Many different types of employees work at various levels in companies. Because they work together, they must know who is responsible for each activity. They must also know what authority each person has. Office workers, especially, find it helpful to understand the duties and authority of those with whom they work.

Knowing how a company is structured will give you a better understanding of how it operates. Many companies prepare a chart that shows positions in order of rank or authority. As you can imagine, the chart for a large company will have many pages. Figure 1-2.4 shows a partial organization chart for a small company. Note the levels of responsibility and the different titles.

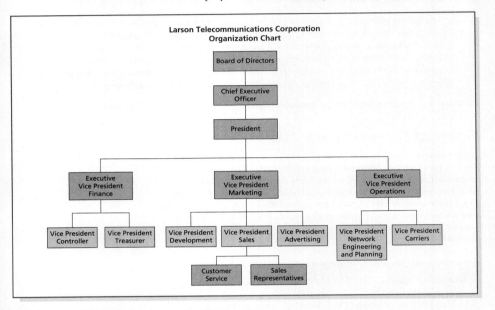

Figure 1-2.4

An organization chart shows the structure of a company.

Board of Directors

Many large corporations have a board of directors. Publicly owned corporations must have such boards. Owners elect members of the board of directors. The board establishes the policies that guide senior management in directing the company. Generally, some senior managers of the company are members of the board. The board has a number of committees that may meet more frequently than does the full board. Some members of boards of directors are not employees of the company. These directors are expected to provide guidance and to make decisions that will serve the best interests of the company. Such outside directors receive a payment for their services, which are limited to a number of meetings each year. Generally, the full board of directors may meet no more than four to five times each year.

Not-for-profit entities also have a board of directors (sometimes called a board of trustees). The board's duties are similar to those of a corporation's board.

CHAPTER 1: THE OFFICE IN A CHANGING BUSINESS WORLD

Senior Management

Persons who give direction in carrying out the policies of the board of directors are called senior management, or top management. The chief executive officer (CEO), the president, the chief operating officer (COO), and the chief financial officer (CFO) are generally included in this group. The CEO and president have overall responsibility for everything that happens in the company. In some companies, one person holds both of these positions.

Large companies are often subdivided into units. The units are organized in some manner that is appropriate for the work of the company. Often the units are called divisions or strategic business units. Divisions are usually managed by vice presidents.

Middle Management

Managers who direct the daily activities of a company are called middle management. Many companies have fewer middle managers than in the past. This type of structure is sometimes referred to as a flatter organization. Workers are allowed to make decisions without review by managers. This concept is sometimes called **employee empowerment**.

Computers help workers process and manage information. Increased use of computers has allowed companies to have fewer middle managers. In some companies, more work is done in teams with all members taking part in making decisions. This trend also reduces the need for middle managers.

employee empowerment: enabling employees to make decisions

Department Employees

The nature of a company's activities determines the types of workers that will be employed. Each type of employee has certain duties. Working together, they are expected to meet the goals of the company. In many companies, employees are organized in departments or teams that relate to the functions of the company. These functions may include finance and accounting, communications, sales and marketing, information technology, legal services, and human resources. Office workers can be found in all these areas.

Production workers are found in manufacturing companies. These workers make the products the company sells such as cars, computers, or furniture. This type of company will also have workers in departments such as research and development, inventory control, and shipping. Many companies sell or provide services rather than products. Employees such as financial counselors, legal assistants, and real estate agents who provide these services are needed in these companies.

The size of a company influences the types of workers needed. In a small company, a single person may, as is commonly stated, wear many hats. For example, one manager may determine how the company's money will be spent. He or she may approve all expenses and sign all payments for goods and services. The manager may also be present to oversee the business on a daily basis. You can imagine that an office assistant in such a company would be likely to do tasks related to communications, records management, and purchasing. In a large company, one person would probably not have the range of duties and authority that is common in a small company.

25

Topic 1-2: *The Office in Relation to the Total Organization*

25

Ask the students to describe the problems Melissa encountered in performing her job and how employee empowerment helped her overcome them.

FOCUS ON . . .

Employee Empowerment

Our employees are empowered. We couldn't function in this fast-paced world without every employee responding wisely to the changes that surround us. We rely on the common sense and wise judgment of every employee.

The president of a bank in a large North Carolina city who spoke these words is not alone in his belief in empowering all 300 of the bank's employees. He understands the value of empowerment, which is the privilege to make decisions or changes in what you do without having to get approval.

Empowerment requires that you understand your company. You learned earlier in Chapter 1 that workers need to understand thoroughly the business or organization in which they are employed. By understanding your organization, you will find every aspect of your job of greater interest. You will better understand what you are doing, and you will be able to use the privilege of empowerment successfully. Consider this example of employee empowerment:

Melissa works in a large consulting company that believes in employee empowerment. She is a new receptionist on the fourth floor, which serves as a center for meetings and conferences for employees and clients. Every day, three, four, or even more individuals would come to her desk asking: "Where is the meeting for _____?" She would have to get the name of the person responsible for the meeting, call that person's office, and get the needed information. In the meantime, others were waiting to know where they should go. Melissa realized that a problem existed due to lack of information and clear communications.

Melissa had not been told that she would need to guide individuals to the right room. When she realized this task would be a routine part of her job, however, she began to think about how she could resolve the problem. Melissa knew that conference rooms were reserved and that those assistants making arrangements submitted the details of the meeting via e-mail. She called the office that handled room assignments and asked: "Could you add my name to your list for a copy of your confirmation for a room? I will be able to direct visitors to the right room with this information." The staff member was cooperative and responded: "Melissa, that is no problem at all. We'll also keep you informed of changes in plans." In addition, Melissa decided to post a schedule for the day inside the entrance so visitors could check the time and location of the day's meetings.

Melissa remembered her orientation to the company and how she and other new employees were informed of the functions of each department of the company. She realized how that information was now helping her as she thought of better ways to handle her assignments. She enjoyed being *empowered!*

As you have learned, employees in an organization work at various levels and in many different departments. With few exceptions, you will find office workers in all areas of an organization. Even in departments such as production, office workers are needed to process information.

26

REVIEWING THE TOPIC

1. Why is it valuable for a worker to understand the business of the organization in which he or she is employed?
2. In what ways can workers learn about the organizations in which they are employed?
3. What are common forms of businesses?
4. How does a corporation, in general, differ from a sole proprietorship or a partnership?
5. What do not-for-profit entities provide?
6. What kind of services do governmental units provide?
7. Contrast the overall goal of businesses with that of not-for-profit entities and governmental units.
8. What are common titles for persons who are in top management, and what is the general nature of their responsibilities?
9. How does an organization chart aid in understanding a company?
10. At which levels in a large organization are you likely to find office workers?

INTERACTING WITH OTHERS

You were standing at a desk of a coworker when her telephone rang. This is what you heard her say:

Who do you want?

A Mr. Ted Wells? Are you sure he works for this company?

Gee, I really don't know who the executives are. I don't work for any of them. I work for the director of catering services.

Oh, you work for Johnson Corporation. Well, you know how hard it is to know your own job, let alone know what is going on in the company.

You say our operator gave you this extension? Possibly, the operator doesn't know much more about the company than I do.

If I knew the extension for the president's office, I'd transfer you because I'd guess the president's secretary knows where everyone is— but, I don't know the number offhand and I could never find my directory on this messy desk . . . Let me transfer you back to the operator. Is that okay? I so wish I could be helpful.

Just hold on. But, first where are you calling from? Why don't you call when you aren't busy, and we can have a chat. Do you have my number? It's 513-555-0192, extension 344.

Hold on. Good luck in finding Mr. Wells. Goodbye.

Teaching Tips

If the students are using the *Student Activities and Simulations* workbook, instruct them to complete the review activity for this topic.

For Discussion

Allow students to share their answers to this activity in a class discussion.

continued

1. Describe the impression you think the caller has of your coworker's knowledge of the company and of her way of working.

2. Identify what you think the coworker said that reflects positive attitudes toward others.

3. If your coworker maintained an orderly desk, what would she have done as soon as it was clear that the caller had the wrong extension? What might she have said instead of the comments shown here?

REINFORCING MATH SKILLS

As you learned in this chapter, the goal of a business is to make a profit. To judge the extent to which the profit goal is being met, businesses analyze their sales on a regular basis. Assume that you have been given the sales figures below. You have figures for actual sales four years and sales projections for three years. Create a spreadsheet or table and use formulas to analyze the sales as follows:

1. Calculate the total yearly sales by adding the U.S. and international sales.

2. Calculate the percentage U.S. sales are of the total yearly sales. Show no decimal places for all percents.

3. Calculate the percentage international sales are of the total yearly sales.

4. For U.S. sales for each year, calculate the percentage increase over 2003 sales.

5. For international sales for each year, calculate the percentage increase over 2003 sales.

6. For total sales for each year, calculate the percentage increase over 2003 sales.

7. Use appropriate column heads and format the information attractively. Add a comment below the data giving your impression of the rate of growth for this technology.

	ACTUAL AND PROJECTED SALES ($ In Millions)	
Year	**U.S. Sales**	**International Sales**
2003	70	30
2004	100	40
2005	150	50
2006	200	50
2007	240	80
2008	300	100
2009	350	170

CHAPTER 1: THE OFFICE IN A CHANGING BUSINESS WORLD

28

Teaching Tips

Encourage students to refer to Section D in the Reference Section of the *Student Activities and Simulations* workbook, if available, to review math skills.

Topic 1-2 : ACTIVITY 1

DESKTOP PUBLISHING

Organization Chart

An organization chart is often used to show the structure of an organization. Prepare an organization chart showing the management team for the World Wide Sales and Service Division of a multinational company. Refer to Figure 1-2.4 for a sample chart.

1. Begin with the company name, GLOBAL MANUFACTURING, followed by the division name, centered at the top as the chart title.

2. Place Thomas McEwen's name and title, CEO, in the top block of the chart.

3. Insert a block for Paul B. Kalis, Sr. Vice President, who is head of the division and reports to Thomas McEwen.

4. Insert blocks for the following vice presidents who report to Paul B. Kalis:

   Marco Ortiz, Vice President, Latin America

   Akira Komuro, Vice President, Asia, Pacific

   Rachel J. Kohnstamm, Vice President, Europe, Middle East, Africa

5. Insert a block for James E. Phelps, Assistant Vice President, Europe, who reports to Rachel J. Kohnstamm.

6. Insert blocks for Jean L. Lucent, Manager, France, and Howard A. Toole, Manager, Denmark, who report to James E. Phelps.

Topic 1-2 : ACTIVITY 2

SPREADSHEET

Income Statement

The goal of a business is to make a profit. Financial statements such as income statements and balance sheets report how successful a business has been in achieving this goal.

1. Use spreadsheet software to create an income statement for Holly's Crafts using the data shown below step 8. Format the income statement similar to the one shown in Figure 1-2.2. Use appropriate number formats and rules under numbers as shown in Figure 1-2.2.

2. Enter the appropriate headings and date the income statement for the year ended December 31 of the current year.

Topic Review

29

3. Enter a formula to subtract the cost of goods sold from sales to find the gross profit on sales.

4. Enter a formula to subtract the total operating expenses from the gross profit on sales to find the net income from operations.

5. Enter a formula to subtract other expenses or add other income to find net income before income tax.

6. Enter a formula to subtract income tax to find net income after income tax.

7. Enter formulas to calculate the percentage of sales for gross profit on sales, net income from operations, net income before tax, and net income after tax. (Divide each number by sales.)

8. One goal of Holly's Crafts is to have net income that is 25 percent of sales or higher. Assuming Holly's Crafts sells the same amount of merchandise and expenses and taxes remain the same, how much would the company have to increase prices to meet this goal?

Data for an income statement for the year ended December 31 of the current year:

Sales	$325,000
Cost of Goods Sold	175,000
Operating Expenses	
Advertising Expense	1,000
Delivery Expense	2,000
Office Supplies Expense	500
Payroll Taxes Expense	5,000
Salaries Expense	58,000
Utilities Expense	3,000
Miscellaneous Expense	400
Other Expense	
Interest	2,500
Income Tax	11,500

CHAPTER REVIEW 1

Summary

During your study of Chapter 1, you learned about the role of the office in today's organizations. You studied types of organizations and learned about their goals. Consider the points listed below as you reinforce your understanding of the topics in this chapter:

- Offices are found in almost all types of organizations. Many workers must perform office tasks.
- Offices are information driven.
- Modern offices are subject to rapid change as new technology is introduced.
- The office is not necessarily a place at a company's official location. Virtual offices and mobile offices can also be used.
- Understanding the total company's work helps an employee handle office activities effectively.
- Organizations are categorized as businesses, not-for-profit entities, or governmental units.
- Companies, beyond the very small, need various types of employees to help meet the company's goals.
- Many types of workers perform some office activities. The duties of office support services employees are mainly office activities.

Key Terms

assets	income statement	owner's equity
balance sheet	information	partnership
charter	Internet	profit
confidential	intranet	revenue
corporation	liabilities	sole proprietorship
employee	mobile office	telecommute
empowerment	negligence	vendor
expense	nonterritorial	virtual office
freelancer	workspace	
hoteling	office	

Teaching Tips

Have students review key points from the chapter by completing the Beat the Clock game on *The Office* Web site.

Teaching Tips

Have students review the key terms by using the Flashcards available on *The Office* Web site.

COMPOSITION
DATABASE
RESEARCH
TEAMWORK

Chapter **1** : A C T I V I T Y **1**

Organizations in Your Community

Learn more about the organizations in your community by developing a database of the organizations. Work with two classmates to complete this activity.

1. Develop a list of local organizations in your community (businesses, not-for-profit entities, and governmental units).

2. Each team member, select a different type of entity. For at least three organizations in this type of entity, obtain the information shown in step 4.

3. After obtaining the information, work as a group to design a database to record the information. Enter the data in the database. Sort the data by type of entity. If possible, post the database in a location where the information can be viewed by all members of the class.

4. Each team member, select one of the organizations from the database that you would like to consider as a place of employment. Write a brief essay in which you identify your choice. Give reasons why you think you would like to work for this type of organization.

Information about each organization:
- Type of entity
- Complete name and address of the main office
- General telephone number
- World Wide Web site address(es), if any
- Brief description of the main activity, product, or service of the organization
    - For businesses, include the form of organization
    - For not-for-profit entities, include the major sources of funds
    - For governmental units, include the level—local, state, or national
- Brief description of types of workers employed

SPREADSHEET

Chapter **1** : A C T I V I T Y **2**

Balance Sheet

You are the assistant to Holly Cooper, the owner of Holly's Crafts. Holly has asked you to create a balance sheet for Holly's Crafts.

1. Open the *Microsoft® Excel®* file *CH01 Balance Sheet* found in the data files. The data is in rough format. Format the balance sheet similar to the one shown in Figure 1-2.3. Use appropriate number formats and rules under numbers as shown in Figure 1-2.3.

2. Enter the appropriate headings and date the balance sheet as of December 31 of the current year.

CHAPTER 1: THE OFFICE IN A CHANGING BUSINESS WORLD

3. Assets: Enter a formula to add the current assets to find the total current assets. Enter a formula to add the fixed assets to find the total fixed assets. Enter a formula to add the total current assets and the total fixed assets to find the total assets.

4. Liabilities: Enter a formula to add the current liabilities to find the total current liabilities. Enter a formula to add the fixed liabilities to find the total fixed liabilities. Enter a formula to add the total current liabilities and the total fixed liabilities to find the total liabilities.

5. Owner's Equity: Enter the net income after taxes figure from the Holly's Crafts Income Statement you created earlier in this chapter as the net income. Enter a formula to subtract Holly Cooper's withdrawals from the net income. Enter a formula to add the remaining income to the capital beginning balance.

6. Enter a formula to add the total liabilities and the capital ending balance to find total liabilities and owner's equity. This number should equal the total assets.

Supplemental Activity

Have students complete the Chapter 1 Supplemental Activity, Identifying Office Tasks, available on *The Office* Web site.

Assessment

Assess student learning using the Chapter 1 test available on the *IRCD* and in *ExamView®* format.

CHAPTER 2

Office Competencies

As you learned in Chapter 1, office competencies are a requirement for many workers in performing their jobs. Whether or
not you know what you want to do as a worker, you will find
the content of this textbook valuable. You will
develop skills and understandings that have application to all types of careers and will be useful
preparation for work of any kind.

In the first topic of this chapter, you will find a brief overview
of projections to the year 2012. Next, you will be introduced to
basic office competencies. These competencies are discussed in
relation to basic skills and job opportunities. The second topic of
the chapter focuses on goals of organizations and what employers
expect from employees. A discussion of how you can plan to
develop office competencies follows.

Online Resources

O *The Office* Web site:
   Data Files
   Vocabulary Flashcards
   Sort It Out, Office
      Competencies
   Chapter 2 Supplementary
      Activity
O International Association of
   Administrative Professionals
   (IAAP)
   10502 NW Ambassador Drive
   PO Box 20404
   Kansas City, MO 64195-0404
O Search terms:
   employment outlook
   global marketplace
   information processing
   productivity
   teamwork
   total quality management

34

objectives

The business office has changed a great deal. In past years, more office support workers were needed. Companies often employed two office workers to support each executive or manager. Today, executives are not likely to have the services of office support staff as full-time assistants. **Projections** to 2012 show a strong demand for executives and managers. Yet, administrative support services jobs are not expected to increase at as high a rate as total jobs.

Many persons entering the workforce are expected to have basic office skills or competencies. These skills can be acquired through your studies while you are still a student gaining your basic education.

Much information is available about types of jobs in the United States. The U.S. Department of Labor monitors the total workforce. It provides information about the current employment situation. Also, the Department of Labor does research to predict the need for workers in the future. Such information is valuable to individuals as they plan for their future careers. Schools and universities, too, use such predictions to plan courses that prepare students for jobs.

- ○ Discuss the need for workers through the year 2012
- ○ Identify office competencies
- ○ Explain future prospects for employment where office competencies are valuable

projection: estimates or guesses about the future based on known data

© CORBIS

A purchasing manager of a large chemical company uses office skills daily.

National Overview of Employment

The U.S. Department of Labor publishes and provides **online** *The Occupational Outlook Handbook*. The *Handbook* discusses the major occupations in the country. From this book, you can learn about job prospects in a wide range of fields. The 2004–05 issue has projections to 2012. The monthly magazine *Monthly Labor Review* updates projections and provides additional information about job opportunities.

online: available in electronic format such as on the Internet or an intranet

35

Topic 2-1: *Office Competencies Needed for Employment*

Getting Started

Increasingly, the secondary school is assuming the responsibility for developing basic work skills that are important in all types of jobs and careers. The focus continues to be on the universal nature of office competencies for most jobs.

Points to Emphasize

The continually increasing capability of the PC leads to its widespread use throughout the workforce.

Points to Emphasize

You do not have to have made a decision about your future job to benefit from studying the topics in this book.

Points to Emphasize

Consider the range of types of workers in the local workforce. Surveys of local chambers of commerce will help students gain an overview of the local job market.

Employment by Major Occupational Group 2002 and Projected 2012

Occupational Group	Employment Number (Thousands of Jobs) 2002	2012	% Change 2002–2012
Total, all occupations	144,014	165,319	14.8
Management, business, and financial occupations	15,501	17,883	15.4
Professional and related occupations	27,687	34,147	23.3
Service occupations	26,569	31,905	20.1
Sales and related occupations	15,260	17,231	12.9
Office and administrative support occupations	23,851	25,464	6.8
Farming, fishing, and forestry occupations	1,072	1,107	3.3
Construction and extraction occupations	7,292	8,388	15.0
Installation, maintenance, and repair occupations	5,696	6,472	13.6
Production occupations	11,258	11,612	3.2
Transportation and material moving occupations	9,828	11,111	13.0

Source: U.S. Department of Labor, Bureau of Labor Statistics. Table III–1. Occupational Employment and Job Openings Data, 2002–12, and Worker Characteristics, 2002. http://www.bls.gov/oes/current/oes_nat.htm (accessed June 11, 2005).

Figure **2-1.1**

In projecting employment to 2012, the government's economists judged rate of increase. The overall projected rate of increase in jobs was 14.8 percent. Management, business, and financial occupations are expected to increase by 15.4 percent from 2002 to 2012. Office and administrative support occupations, which are also referred to as office support services, are expected to increase by 6.8 percent during the same period. Note the percentage of change (growth rate) projected for other occupational groups in Figure 2-1.1.

Figure 2-1.2 shows several occupations that are projected to grow in number of jobs from 2002 to 2012. Note that office competencies are needed in most of these occupations.

Outlook for Employment of Office Workers

Increased use of computers and new technology will continue to have an effect on many office support jobs. This effect is shown in the low rate of growth projected to 2012. However, many jobs will be available in this area. Many persons in this group will need to be replaced. Some workers will leave the field to enter new jobs or to retire. For example, about 4.1 million persons work as secretaries and administrative assistants.

36

36

CHAPTER 2: OFFICE COMPETENCIES

Projected Job Growth for Selected Occupations 2002 and Projected 2012

Occupation	Employment (Thousands of Jobs)		% Change
	2002	2012	2002–2012
Medical assistants	365	579	58.9
Network systems and data communications analysts	186	292	57.0
Physician assistants	63	94	48.8
Medical records and health information technicians	147	216	46.8
Computer software engineers, applications	394	573	45.5
Database administrators	110	159	44.2
Postsecondary teachers	1,581	2,184	38.1
Computer and information systems managers	284	387	36.1
Physical therapists	137	185	35.3
Personal financial advisors	126	170	34.6
Public relations specialists	158	210	32.9
Sales managers	343	448	30.5
Receptionists and information clerks	1,100	1,425	29.5
Desktop publishers	35	45	29.2
Paralegals and legal assistants	200	257	28.7
Medical and public health social workers	107	138	28.6
Agents and business managers of artists, performers, and athletes	15	19	27.8
Employment, recruitment, and placement specialists	175	223	27.3
Bill and account collectors	413	514	24.4
Customer service representatives	1,894	2,354	24.3
Hotel, motel, and resort desk clerks	178	220	23.9
Market research analysts	134	166	23.4
Tax preparers	79	98	23.2

Source: U.S. Department of Labor, Bureau of Labor Statistics. Table III–1. Occupational Employment and Job Openings Data, 2002–12, and Worker Characteristics, 2002. http://www.bls.gov/oes/current/oes_nat.htm (accessed June 11, 2005).

Figure **2-1.2**

WORKPLACE CONNECTIONS

Toula Ahara was hired nine months ago as a receptionist in a large travel agency in Boston. She acquired office skills while in high school. She completed a liberal arts program at a local community college before she accepted the job. Toula loves travel. She had taken many trips while a student. Soon after her job began, the manager asked her to assist clients. Toula enjoyed this part of her job. Just a short while ago, Toula was promoted to travel agent. She said this about her new job: "My love of travel is one key to my promotion. The other key is my skill with the personal computer—from word processing to database management."

For Discussion

What attitudes do you believe may have aided Toula in gaining a promotion?

Topic 2-1: *Office Competencies Needed for Employment*

Points to Emphasize

Electronic capabilities have made it feasible for all workers to assume many office tasks. Ask students to observe the extent that workers they encounter—delivery personnel, utilities meter readers, waiters, and waitresses—must perform some office tasks to do their jobs effectively.

Thinking Critically

Why would one company provide office support staff for employees while another company does not?

global marketplace: buying and selling of goods or services throughout the world

innovation: new method or idea

Workers Face Expanded Job Responsibilities

Office activity is increasing because of the growth of business in the **global marketplace.** A change has taken place, however, in who handles office tasks. Far more workers are doing office tasks than in the past. New technology is responsible for the shift. All types of workers can handle office tasks because of the technology available. If no **innovations** in technology had occurred during the last 20 years, about six times as many office support employees as are now employed would be needed to handle the volume of activity. Remember, though, many office support workers will continue to be employed.

WORKPLACE CONNECTIONS

Many managers now do much of their own office work. Donna Komari is a product manager in the international division of a home appliance company. She spends much time traveling. Donna works for hours during a flight from Newark to London. Using her notebook computer she writes letters, accesses databases, and creates a spreadsheet. When she reaches London, she has completed a day's work. Donna commented about her way of working: "Before we had today's technology, I would have needed a full-time secretary to do what I did alone while on the flight from Newark to London."

Executives accomplish much work while traveling.

© CORBIS

An Overview of Office Competencies

A wide range of activities make up office competencies. However, four major groups of activities based on primary skills reflect the overall nature of office work. These areas are:

- Word processing
- Data processing
- Information management and transmission
- General managing and communicating

You will now become acquainted with each of these areas. Pay attention to the basic skills needed for doing tasks effectively and efficiently.

Word Processing

Word processing is creating written documents such as letters or reports by using software programs and computers. Usually these documents are shared in printed form. However, they may also be shared and read online. Some word processing programs allow the user to save documents in HTML format. An example is shown in Figure 2-1.3. These documents can be posted and viewed on a company intranet.

Desktop publishing is producing high-quality printed documents that include both text and graphics. It is closely related to word processing and requires many of the same skills. Examples of these documents include newsletters, brochures, and forms. Basic desktop publishing can be done using word processing software such as *Microsoft Word*. Desktop publishing software programs, such as *Adobe® PageMaker®*, are used for advanced desktop publishing.

word processing: producing written documents such as letters or reports by using software programs and computers

HTML: hypertext markup language, authoring language used for World Wide Web and intranet documents

desktop publishing: producing high-quality printed documents that include both text and graphics

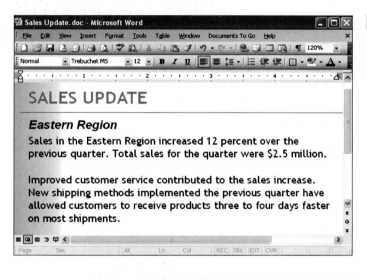

Figure **2-1.3**

Microsoft Word is a software program used to do word processing and basic desktop publishing.

Basic Competencies

The efficient use of a computer in preparing many types of documents is the goal of skill development in this area. The essential skills include:

- Keyboarding with speed and accuracy
- Knowledge and skill in use of software programs
- Skill in formatting and proofreading documents
- A large vocabulary
- **Proficiency** with grammar, punctuation, and spelling
- Ability to learn special vocabularies
- Ability to follow instructions
- Skill in preparing copy from audio recordings, if employed as a transcriptionist
- Skill in dictating text and commands if using **speech recognition software**

proficiency: ability to perform at a satisfactory level

speech recognition software: computer programs that allow the user to input text and commands by speaking into a microphone

Workers Who Need These Competencies

Word processing skills are needed by many workers. Executives in many companies spend much time writing messages. Technical personnel, such as engineers, advertising designers, architects, and public relations specialists are employees likely to use word processing and basic desktop publishing skills in their work.

Opportunities in Office Support Services

Some office support staff work full-time handling word processing and basic desktop publishing activities. Among the jobs in this category are: typist, word processor, and transcriptionist. Such workers prepare drafts as well as final copies of letters, memos, and reports. They may assist one other worker or several workers. Some word processing workers assist an entire department.

Office support workers are considered for promotions to jobs in the same category. These jobs may require more advanced skills. For example, workers who quickly learn new software may be promoted to a supervisory or training job. Workers with good writing skills may become administrative assistants.

WORKPLACE CONNECTIONS

Roberto Hernandez is a transcriptionist in a large financial services company. At the moment, Roberto is transcribing from a tape of a speech given to a group of employees. After he keys the speech, the draft will be sent to the speaker for review. When the document is considered complete, Roberto will prepare multiple copies. He will also save the file in HTML format. The file will be posted on the company's intranet so employees who missed the speech can access it easily.

Data Processing

Data processing is collecting, organizing, analyzing, and summarizing data. The data is generally in numeric form. Many jobs require such skills. This type of activity is usually done using spreadsheet or statistical computer programs. We may think of data processing as dealing with numbers and word processing as dealing with text. However, the two processes often blend with one another. The two processes together are often referred to as information processing. Many workers do this type of office activity.

data processing: collecting, organizing, analyzing, and summarizing data

Basic Competencies

Among the skills important for workers who handle data processing activities are the following:

- Proficiency with spreadsheet, database, and related software programs
- Knowledge of arithmetic processes and statistical methods
- Ability to be consistently accurate
- Knowledge of methods of organizing and analyzing data
- Ability to interpret data
- Ability to prepare reports that give information in a meaningful way
- Ability to maintain an organized workstation

© LISETTE LE BON/SUPERSTOCK INTERNATIONAL

Data processing is a basic office competency for many workers.

Workers Who Need These Competencies

Accountants, budget analysts, brokers, insurance salespersons, and many other types of workers in all kinds of organizations deal with data and prepare reports. As new software programs make processing data faster and easier, these workers must continually learn to use new programs and methods in their work.

WORKPLACE CONNECTIONS

Cathy Leitman is a budget analyst in a large company. She works at her computer much of the time. Cathy accesses information from various departments of the company. For example, she finds data about the number of product defects in some of the company's factories. She then analyzes the data and prepares reports and tables to present to the executives who must make decisions using the information. Cathy studied economics in college. When asked what prepared her for her job, Cathy said: "My college studies were of great value for what I do. The basic skills I learned in my high school office procedures class are also critical to my work every day."

Opportunities in Office Support Services

Many workers continue to be employed in the data processing category. They include specialized clerks, such as accounts payable clerk, billing clerk, order clerk, payroll clerk, and shipping clerk. Such clerks prepare and process sales, purchases, invoices, payrolls, and other types of transactions. Their work is vital to the whole organization.

aptitude: a natural ability or talent

Companies need workers who can oversee automated systems for processing data. Workers who have an **aptitude** for understanding the total operation and have learned their jobs thoroughly are good candidates for promotions.

WORKPLACE CONNECTIONS

The experience of one entry-level data processing worker reflects the opportunity for advancement. Juan Ramos began working as an order clerk in a manufacturing company when he graduated from high school. After six months, he was transferred to the controller's office where he did tasks such as enter data from invoices and create reports. The controller noted that he learned quickly and talked with Juan about his future plans. He suggested that Juan consider enrolling in a college program to study accounting. Juan liked the idea. He began night studies at a local college. He realizes that he will not complete his college studies in four years. He likes working full-time and studying part-time. Juan's long-term goal is to complete a college program and become an accountant.

information management: organizing, maintaining, and accessing records or data

Information Management and Transmission

Information management refers to organizing, maintaining, and accessing data. Transmission refers to sharing information both within and outside the organization.

Basic Competencies

The skills considered basic in this category include considerable variety:

- Ability to find the information needed
- Ability to maintain or develop an information system
- Ability to give attention to details
- Ability to use established procedures
- Knowledge of records management principles and basic filing rules
- Good keyboarding skills
- Proficiency in working with databases
- Ability to meet deadlines and solve problems
- Ability to work with others

Workers Who Need These Skills

A wide range of workers need the skills in this area. Personnel such as buyers, real estate brokers, and property managers must have well-organized information systems. The details they need to make decisions often require them to design their own systems. Often their information must be available to others, too. Following a well-designed system is the key to easy use of information.

Opportunities in Office Support Services

People who find gathering and organizing data interesting will enjoy work in this area. Work in this area involves updating and sharing data promptly. Common jobs in this category are: hotel desk clerk, mailroom clerk, records clerk, travel clerk, and communications center operator. Alert beginning employees in such jobs can learn much about the company. Such knowledge is a key to gaining promotions.

Information management is a vital function for most businesses.

Points to Emphasize

Note that workers who communicate with customers must know how to use information, but they may not be involved in developing such systems or updating them.

43

Topic 2-1: *Office Competencies Needed for Employment*

Thinking Critically

What traits or actions would you observe in a person who is a good manager?

For Discussion

What topics might be discussed at a staff meeting that relate to general management?

Thinking Critically

A major direct mail-order company has a knowledge-able staff responding to customer telephone calls. What skills must the staff have to do the job well?

General Managing and Communicating

general managing: handling work time and tasks efficiently, creating and monitoring schedules, and tracking and reporting the progress of tasks or projects

General managing and communicating are broad areas that involve handling work time and tasks efficiently. They also involve dealing with other employees and customers. Setting up schedules, meeting deadlines, and tracking the progress of tasks are aspects of general managing. Communicating with customers and coworkers is a common activity for many types of workers in a company. Reporting on the progress of tasks, projects, or budgets is also an aspect of general managing. Often, these reports are given orally and delivered with the use of a multimedia presentation.

Basic Competencies

The skills and knowledge needed to handle the activities in this category are varied. In general, they include the ability to:

priorities: a listing of items in order of importance

- Establish **priorities**
- Establish schedules and meet deadlines
- Work in teams
- Motivate others to complete work
- Use a personal computer and manage files
- Handle telephone calls effectively
- Give attention to several tasks at the same time
- Determine the time required for completion of tasks
- Communicate effectively both orally and in writing
- Interact with many types of people at all levels

Workers Who Need These Competencies

interactive: involving the user or receiver, exchanging information

General management and communication skills are critical for a wide range of employees. Executives, salespeople, and office support staff are examples of workers who need these skills. Office workers must be good managers of their own time. In addition, they must be skillful in guiding the work of any employees who report to them. They must be able to set priorities and follow schedules to complete tasks. They must communicate clearly and effectively to coworkers and customers.

WORKPLACE CONNECTIONS

Carlos Alvarez is the marketing manager of a packaged goods company. He commented about his work in these words:

Our staff of ten is hardworking. I set the pace. We have just developed a database to record far more information about product sales. We have achieved our goal: the supermarket's bar code reader and our PCs are connected. We have staff members working on various ways to connect with our customers in an interactive fashion. As I think of our progress, I realize that basic managing skills, including establishing priorities, and communicating clearly what has to be done, are critical.

Opportunities in Office Support Services

Many office workers have duties found in the general managing and communicating category. The most common jobs include administrative assistant, secretary, customer service clerk, receptionist, and general office assistant.

Some positions in this category require specialized skills. The position of secretary, for example, may require high-level information processing skills. Receptionists must be at ease in meeting and talking with all types of people. General assistants learn to handle the special needs of the offices in which they work. Then they take the **initiative** in completing tasks in the proper manner.

initiative: ability to act or think without prompting or guidance

Higher-level jobs are available to those who perform their initial tasks with success. There are many jobs in companies for those who have the ability to:

- Complete tasks with little or no supervision
- Use oral and written communication skills effectively
- Meet deadlines
- Organize tasks and work independently
- Evaluate their own performance **objectively**

objectively: in a detached manner without bias or prejudice

© LISETTE LE BON/SUPERSTOCK INTERNATIONAL

Effective communication skills are essential for office workers.

Your Future Prospects

Your education, including your study of business subjects, provides you with a background of value in many jobs. You can enter some jobs after your high school graduation. Others require further education.

Some openings for high school graduates will continue to be available. Many jobs, however, require skills and knowledge beyond those gained through high school studies. Some companies have on-the-job training to prepare employees for new tasks or new ways of doing their jobs. Business schools and colleges provide degree programs and continuing education programs. Continuing your education will add to your skills for jobs that interest you.

Topic 2-1: *Office Competencies Needed for Employment*

Thinking Critically

What kinds of tasks might a general assistant in a medical office perform?

For Discussion

Why is the ability to meet deadlines and organize tasks important for office workers?

Points to Emphasize

Further education can be gained on a part-time basis. Many companies reimburse employees who study at the college level. On-the-job experience and continuing education can help you determine career goals that match your abilities and interests.

For Discussion

What are the local institutions that provide evening part-time study for people who work full-time?

Teaching Tip

If the students are using the *Student Activities and Simulations* workbook, instruct them to complete the review activity for this topic.

For Discussion

After students have discussed the alternatives, ask them to share their thoughts with the class.

Topic Review 2-1

REVIEWING THE TOPIC

1. In what way has the computer changed the nature of employment in companies?
2. What kind of information is provided in *The Occupational Outlook Handbook*?
3. By what percentage is the entire workforce expected to increase by 2012?
4. Explain why job duties are expanding because of technological innovations.
5. Identify skills needed to handle word processing tasks.
6. Give three examples of workers who need data processing skills.
7. What are the critical skills and understandings needed to effectively perform information management and transmission tasks?
8. What are examples of good managing skills?
9. What qualifications do office support workers in entry-level positions need to be promoted?
10. What types of educational opportunities are available after graduation from secondary school?

MAKING DECISIONS

Craig is soon to be a high school senior. He needs very few courses in order to graduate at the end of the school year. He has asked you and a couple of other friends to give him your opinions about what he should do about his school program. He has listed on a sheet of paper what he believes are his options. His list has these options, which are not in order of preference:

- Take only the courses required in the mornings. Relax in the afternoon until my friends are free.
- Take some extra courses, such as accounting, business law, or office procedures. Because I think I want to work in the business world or become a lawyer after college, these courses might be helpful.
- Get a part-time job at one of the local fast-food places.
- Really learn all about the new computer at home.

1. With a group of three or four other students, discuss the alternatives Craig has outlined. Select the alternative your group believes is best for Craig.
2. As a group, write a paragraph or two that identifies the alternative you think Craig should choose. Support your choice with reasons and be prepared to share your ideas with the class.

CHAPTER 2: OFFICE COMPETENCIES

REINFORCING ENGLISH SKILLS

The following text about information and record clerks is taken from *The Occupational Outlook Handbook* online. No spelling errors were in the original copy. However, misspelled words have been introduced.

1. Key the paragraphs, correcting the spelling errors.
2. Use the spell check feature of your word processor to check for additional errors. If you are not sure about a word, check a dictionary. Remember to check for forms of words that are not used correctly such as "to" for "too."

Significant Points

- Numerus job openings should arise for most types of information and record clerks, dew to employment growth and the need to replace workers whom leave this large occupational group.
- A high school diploma or it's equivalent is the most common educational requirement.
- Because many informatin and record clerks deal directly with the public, a professional appearence and a pleasant personality are imperative.
- These occupations are well suited to flexable work schedules.

Source: U.S. Department of Labor, Bureau of Labor Statistics, *Occupational Outlook Handbook,* http://stats.bls.gov/oco/ocos131.htm (accessed July 5, 2005).

Topic 2-1 ACTIVITY 1

Jobs in Your Community

COMPOSITION
RESEARCH
TEAMWORK
WORD PROCESSING

In this activity, you will become acquainted with jobs in areas that are projected to grow from 2002 to 2012 as shown in Figure 2-1.2. Work in a group with two or three classmates to complete this activity.

1. Choose occupations from the list in Figure 2-1.2 that you would like to investigate in your own community. With your teacher's approval, you may also choose other occupations not listed in the figure. Choose twice as many occupations as there are members of the group.
2. Decide who will investigate each of the occupations listed. You may choose to work in groups of two investigating the same four occupations, or each member of the group may select two occupations to investigate.
3. Through group discussion, determine the places in the community where you are most likely to get information about the occupation. (There may be a local association of persons in an occupational field, for example.) Find answers to these questions:

47

Topic Review

For Discussion

After students have keyed the paragraphs, discuss the corrections that they should have made.

Teaching Tips

Assign students to the teams in which they will work to complete this activity. Discuss guidelines you expect students to follow for completing the project.

- In what local organizations do you find workers in this occupation?
- What are the basic educational qualifications for these workers?
- What are the key duties of persons in this occupation?
- To what extent are workers responsible for office tasks?
- What promotional opportunities exist for persons in this occupation?

4. Review the information gathered by all group members and prepare a table that presents the information. (Hint: Column headings can be the occupations. Each row can deal with the response to a question.)

5. Take part in a class discussion of job opportunities in the community for these occupations.

COMPOSITION
INTERNET
RESEARCH
WORD PROCESSING

Topic 2-1 : ACTIVITY 2

Study an Occupational Field

For this activity, choose an occupational field that interests you. Do some research to become acquainted with this field.

1. Use the Internet or the resources of your school or local community library to get information about your occupation. A reference that is likely to be helpful is *The Occupational Outlook Handbook*, which was described briefly in this chapter. A link to *The Occupational Outlook Handbook* is found on the Web site for this textbook. Find the following information for the occupation:
   - Educational requirements
   - General responsibilities
   - Employment opportunities
   - Promotional opportunities

2. Interview a person working in this occupational field. In your interview, seek answers to these questions:
   - What are the primary duties of a beginner in this occupation?
   - What do you consider your primary duties?
   - For each primary duty, would you consider education, on-the-job experience, or training the best source of preparation?
   - To what extent do you use a personal computer in completing your job tasks?
   - What office skills do you find most valuable in your work?
   - What advice would you give a student who is thinking of preparing for your field?

3. Create a report that summarizes the information you gathered. The final paragraph of your report should be your current opinion about the appeal of the occupational field as a career for you.

Teaching Tips

Assist students in accessing *The Occupational Outlook Handbook* in hard copy or online. A link to the *Handbook* online is provided on the Web site for this textbook.

objectives

- Describe issues that affect achieving company goals
- Explain the general expectations for workers
- Prepare a strategy for developing office competencies

Companies seek to hire the qualified workers who will help the company be successful. All workers are expected to help achieve company goals. In this topic, you will study issues that affect achieving company goals. Then the general expectations for employees will be described. Finally, a strategy for you to consider as you develop office skills commonly needed at work will be presented.

Goals Influence Expectations for All Employees

If you were to read a dozen annual reports of **Fortune 500 companies**, you would find information about company achievements during the past year. You would also read about goals for the future. A primary goal of most businesses is to make a profit. Companies make predictions about level of earnings, new markets, new products, or improved customer service. In some instances, goals are simply expressed as a long-term vision statement. For example, the head of one computer company declared that the company's vision was to have a computer on every workplace desk and in every home. The goals set by the company affect the work of all employees. Some companies post their goals on their company Web sites as shown in Figure 2-2.1.

Issues such as quality management, customer satisfaction, and teamwork affect how successful a company is in achieving its goals. These issues must be the concerns of all employees. The company expects all employees to be **reliable** and **cooperative** in efforts to increase productivity and meet company goals.

Fortune 500 companies: largest companies listed in *Fortune* magazine

reliable: dependable, trustworthy

cooperative: willing to act or work with others for a common purpose

Figure **2-2.1**

Some companies post their goals on their company Web sites.

About Us

Company Goals

The goals of our company are to:
- Meet the present and future needs of our customers with the highest possible standards of value, quality, and service
- Operate profitably, in a manner which is socially, ethically, and environmentally responsible
- Further research and development
- Promote the company's international presence
- Strengthen the domestic market presence in traditional and ecommerce channels
- Attract and retain quality employees by maintaining a rewarding and safe work environment with equal opportunity for promotion and success

Getting Started

Contemporary goals of companies as discussed in the business press of local newspapers can be identified for discussion.

Points to Emphasize

All employees have a stake in an organization's achievement of goals.

Teaching Tips

Annual reports of companies are a good source of information for students to learn what CEOs say about goals and plans for reaching goals.

Total Quality Management

total quality management: establishing and maintaining high standards in how work is done

The primary goal of all businesses is to make profits. In an effort to increase profits, many companies have adopted **total quality management** (TQM) plans. TQM means establishing and maintaining high standards in how work is done and in the creation and delivery of goods and services. All personnel, from the president to staff in the mailroom, are asked to view their work with an awareness of TQM.

The thrust of TQM is that managing quality is everyone's business. Quality standards apply throughout the organization. For example, in one company, all office support workers were asked to keep track of the errors in their work. Two common errors were omitting an attachment with a letter and failing to answer questions of callers. After recording such errors, the next step was to establish a new way of working so the errors would not recur.

WORKPLACE CONNECTIONS

Howard Jackson, an office employee, commented on how TQM changed his job:

It is amazing how you can maintain quality standards without feeling unreasonable pressure. Keeping track of questions I can't answer has been an eye-opener. Some questions were about issues that are not handled by my department. Many, though, were about issues someone in my department should know about. I began to learn as I worked so I understood the entire department better. Now I can answer almost any question related to the work of my department. I am so much happier than I was earlier. I confess that TQM has made my job more interesting and me far more competent.

In some companies, an executive is assigned to lead the company's efforts to improve quality. This person works with groups of employees to find out what will improve performance or products. Many companies have developed slogans such as "Quality is everybody's business" or "We want to be the best in all we do" to highlight their quality goals.

Continuous Improvement

continuous improvement: being alert at all times to ways of working more productively

Over time, the policies and procedures used by a company may become outdated or inefficient. Companies seek to avoid this problem by applying the concept of continuous improvement. **Continuous improvement** means being alert at all times to ways of working more productively. This concept overlaps the principles of TQM. All employees are encouraged to take part in continuous improvement efforts.

Because of new technology, companies are finding that many aspects of their work require changes. Continuous improvement begins with looking at the work that is done and how it is being done. Improvements are often possible. The attitude reflected in the question "Could this be done in a better way?" helps workers think creatively about improvements.

Customer Satisfaction

"We are here to serve customers" is a message that many companies send to employees. Thinking through what you do in relation to what it will mean to customers is a key focus in many companies. Many people believe that attention to customers is very important for long-term success.

WORKPLACE CONNECTIONS

The staff of a company is involved in a variety of ways in meeting the goal of customer satisfaction. One beginning worker, Kim Park, described his experiences in these words:

I serve as an assistant in our Customer Hotline office, which is open seven days a week, 24 hours a day. Among the team are members who speak English, Spanish, French, Chinese, and Japanese. Together, we are able to provide customers around the world with information about our products. We can quickly put a customer in touch with a technical person, if additional assistance is needed.

Companies often conduct surveys to see if they are delivering the value expected by customers. They study the results of such surveys and then make changes to improve customer satisfaction. An example of a customer survey is shown in Figure 2-2.2 (page 52).

Ethical Standards

Ethical standards require honesty, fairness, and justice in all business dealings. These qualities provide a foundation of trust. Company leaders should make clear their attitude toward standards of ethical behavior. Companies want to be considered trustworthy by their employees, their customers, companies with which they deal, and the public.

Companies have developed standards of conduct for their employees, called **codes of ethics** or codes of conduct. Such codes are communicated to all workers. Employees are generally informed about the code of conduct when they first join the organization.

From time to time, employees are called together to discuss what the code means in relation to specific behavior and actions. For example, all staff involved with purchasing may attend a meeting dealing with a new conflict of interest statement. This staff deals with many vendors who are eager to sell their products. The new statement makes clear that no employee is to

code of ethics: moral standards or values and related behavior; also called code of conduct

Thinking Critically

Can we apply continuous improvement to the way we are studying this subject?

For Discussion

What are ways you have observed that a company is trying to improve the way it serves customers?

For Discussion

Have you encountered office personnel that you feel do not have the proper attitude toward customers?

Thinking Critically

Why does a company strive to have honest employees?

Expand the Concept

What is the value of a company being "considered trustworthy"?

51

Topic 2-2: Developing Office Competencies

CUSTOMER SATISFACTION SURVEY

Understanding and serving your needs is our goal. Please help us improve our customer service by completing this survey.

Check the blank by your response.

1. How would you rate the overall service you have received from our company?
   - _____ Excellent
   - _____ Good
   - _____ Average
   - _____ Poor

2. How quickly did you receive a response to your most recent question or problem?
   - _____ The same day
   - _____ 1–2 days
   - _____ 3–4 days

3. Was your most recent question or problem resolved to your satisfaction?
   - _____ Yes
   - _____ Somewhat
   - _____ No

4. Did you find the customer service representative to be friendly and helpful?
   - _____ Yes
   - _____ Somewhat
   - _____ No

5. Would you recommend our company to your friends or coworkers?
   - _____ Yes
   - _____ No

Figure **2-2.2**

Companies conduct surveys to assess customer satisfaction.

accept gifts of any value from any vendor. Figure 2-2.3 shows a portion of a company's confidentiality policy that has been posted on the company intranet. This policy is part of the company's code of conduct.

Figure **2-2.3**

A portion of a company's code of conduct.

Employee Handbook

Confidentiality Policy

During your course of employment, you will handle information sensitive to our company, partner companies, and clients. All information, both written and verbal, with which you come in contact in the scope of your duties, is confidential. Please respect this trust, which our clients and customers have given us. Confidentiality is critical; communication of confidential matters may be grounds for corrective action up to and including immediate dismissal.

Thinking Critically

Why is it important for new employees to understand the company's code of ethics?

Companies also have procedures for handling violations of ethical standards. Employees found guilty of violating the code of ethics may be subject to disciplinary action. Continued or very serious violations may lead to immediate dismissal of an employee.

Responsible Teamwork

Some people work alone at the company offices or at home. Frequently, however, employees must work in teams to complete tasks. Teamwork involves combining the efforts of two or more people to accomplish a task or achieve a goal. For a team to function effectively, each team member must understand the purpose or goals of the team. Each member of the team must accept responsibility for completing his or her duties and communicate clearly with other team members. For remote teams, in which teams members may be located around the world rather than down the hall, communication is especially important.

Team members often are not from a single department. For example, customer collections were a problem in a relatively small company that makes shoes. The controller realized that those involved worked in the order entry, shipping, and billing departments. A team of several members of these departments was assigned the task of reviewing the policies and procedures involved. Through teamwork, the group recommended a new policy and related procedures. Soon thereafter, the problem was resolved to everyone's satisfaction.

Points to Emphasize

Teamwork demands a high degree of responsibility. Fairness requires that each member contribute appropriately.

Global Marketplace

The area in which a company does business is called its marketplace. In the past, many U.S. companies sold their goods or services only in the domestic marketplace, meaning within the United States. Many of these companies now produce and/or sell their products in countries around the world. Some companies have moved into the global marketplace using only traditional sales channels, such as retail stores. Other companies have expanded using **e-commerce**. These companies, sometimes called e-companies or dotcoms, sell goods and services online using a company site on the **World Wide Web**.

e-commerce: business conducted electronically, as in making purchases or selling products via the World Wide Web

World Wide Web: computers on the Internet that use and transmit HTML documents

For Discussion

In what way does modern technology encourage a global marketplace?

53

Topic 2-2: *Developing Office Competencies*

FOCUS ON . . .

Teamwork

One common question asked of prospective employees is: "How willing are you to participate in teamwork?" Interviewers are asking this question because today's business world is complex. Many of the tasks performed in any department require the skills and knowledge of several staff members. These employees must work cooperatively to assess what is to be done, how it is to be done, and who will accept responsibility for parts of the task.

Working as a team, employees bring varying experiences, observations, insights, and knowledge to determining what action should be taken and following through with those actions. A team, thinking critically, is often far more successful than an individual working alone. This belief is commonly held in successful organizations and by many successful employees.

You have probably had experience as a team member—possibly as a member of a sports team, in a science laboratory, or in an after-school club. You may enjoy teamwork or you may feel that you would rather work alone. If you have a positive view of teamwork, you will be a valuable employee. If you have a negative view of teamwork, reconsider your attitude. As an office worker, you will be expected to work in teams, and you will want to be successful in this aspect of your job. Consider these guidelines for working effectively in teams:

- Set clear goals for the team and create an action plan for achieving the goals.

- Define the responsibilities of each team member in achieving team goals.

- Identify how success will be measured. How will the team know its goals have been accomplished?

- Identify obstacles to achieving the team's goals and discuss ways to overcome the obstacles.

- Communicate clearly and often with all team members and be open to all feedback and ideas. Schedule regular meetings or reports to track the progress toward achieving team goals.

- Discuss how differences will be resolved. Understand that all members of a team may not have the same level of authority.

- Build on the strengths of individual members. Encourage all members of the team to participate in making decisions and contributing ideas. Each team member has different skills and ideas that can be valuable to the team.

- Recognize accomplishments of team members and the team as a whole.

- As an individual team member, develop your colleagues' trust by fulfilling your responsibilities, acting in a professional manner, and maintaining a positive attitude when discussing team activities.

Moving into the global marketplace affects how companies do business. Employees must travel to other countries. Company personnel who live in other countries may visit the United States. Messages used for Web sites, advertising materials, and product instructions must be available in many languages. All personnel must be sensitive to variations in cultures. They must communicate clearly with people of other nations. Employees must be acquainted with varying time zones, sources for information about travel, and places for travelers to stay and work in other countries.

Many employees travel to foreign countries as businesses operate in a global marketplace.

© CORBIS

Diversity

Diversity, as it relates to organizations, means having a workforce with people from a wide range of ethnic and cultural backgrounds. Many companies seek to have diversity at all levels. In some companies, a diversity coordinator collects data about the company's hiring and promotion policies. This person also tracks the progress of the company in achieving its diversity goals. Employees are expected to respect coworkers and customers from all backgrounds. Training programs are conducted to help employees become aware of issues related to diversity.

diversity: reflected in a workforce with people from a wide range of ethnic and cultural backgrounds

WORKPLACE CONNECTIONS

Meg works in a company where diversity is getting attention. She is one of the staff members planning diversity seminars. She was especially interested in comments from the managers who attended the seminars. They described how their evaluations of employees are now influenced by what was learned in the seminar. Her company has an awards program honoring individuals who show a respect for diversity in their work.

Points to Emphasize

In the United States, legislation has been passed to protect people from discrimination on the basis of gender, race, religion, ethnic background, or disability. The legislation is designed to provide equal employment opportunities for all.

Thinking Critically

What kinds of attitudes about people may lead to unfair evaluation of ability or job performance?

55

Topic 2-2: *Developing Office Competencies*

Employees with different backgrounds and new perspectives help businesses meet the needs of diverse customers.

© CORBIS

Thinking Critically

What motivates a reliable person to meet the requirements of a job without constant supervision?

General Expectations for Employees

A company expects the same basic work qualities in all employees. The way these qualities are shown will depend on the nature of the employee's work. Reliability, productivity, cooperativeness, and independence in learning are important qualities for all employees.

Reliability

Companies expect employees to be reliable. Reliable means dependable and trustworthy. Employers rely on employees to report to work on time. Employees are expected to devote their time on the job to completing their work. Companies expect employees to keep company business confidential and to protect the assets of the company.

WORKPLACE CONNECTIONS

A director of administrative services in a large bank commented on employee reliability:

Employees who have to be watched every minute in order to keep them doing what they should do are worthless in our bank. We must have reliable employees. One of the most common reasons for dismissal in our bank is unreliability. For example, one new employee failed to be at the office at eight o'clock on the mornings she was scheduled to open the office. The office was unattended. She didn't call to explain her lateness; she just arrived two hours later. This pattern continued in spite of several warnings. At that point, we had to dismiss her. We cannot function with such indifference to schedules.

56

CHAPTER 2: OFFICE COMPETENCIES

Productivity

Productivity is demonstrated by doing an appropriate amount of work on time and according to instructions. Employers expect workers to produce a reasonable amount of work. Often specific, measurable standards for a day's work are not practical. Managers, however, have some level of output that they believe is reasonable for an employee. Following a schedule that ensures you will complete the amount of work expected of you is important.

Valuable workers are aware of what they are accomplishing each day. They are able to evaluate their own work and make changes as needed. Some managers discuss productivity with their workers in informal ways from time to time. Other managers expect workers to decide on their own what changes are needed to improve productivity.

Managers and executives identify the following barriers to high productivity for employees:

- Talking with friends by telephone
- Chatting with coworkers for long periods of time
- Failing to maintain an organized workstation
- Failing to set priorities
- Moving from task to task before any one is completed

Cooperativeness

Most office employees work with others daily. Information must be shared, and tasks often require more than a single worker. Being cooperative is an important quality for all employees. Employees must be prepared to learn new skills and handle new tasks as circumstances change. Most office workers have job descriptions, but seldom do such descriptions fully describe everything the employee will do on the job. Employees who believe they need to do only what is outlined in their job descriptions are not effective workers.

© GETTY IMAGES/PHOTODISC

A disorganized workstation limits productivity.

Topic 2-2: *Developing Office Competencies*

One manager described an employee who was not cooperative in these words:

As long as Betty was not interrupted, she was a good worker. When I asked her to spend the next day at a conference center at midtown, however, she said she didn't understand that she would have to work in another location. She said she was hired to work in the office. Even though nothing was stated about where she would work, she was right in assuming that she would be located at headquarters. From her own observations, however, she should have realized that employees travel out of town and many employees work at conference sites. After this encounter, I became more aware of Betty's attitude, which was reflected in small ways as she worked with others. At the end of the year, Betty's performance was assessed. Her level of cooperativeness was listed as an area for improvement. She was not added to the list of persons to be considered for promotion.

For Discussion

Why is it important for each person to be an independent learner?

ezine: electronic magazine available on the World Wide Web

Independence in Learning

As you may already realize, all you need to know to be an employee will not be learned while you are a student. Companies expect their employees to learn how to use new equipment, software, and methods for completing tasks on an ongoing basis. Learning must be a lifelong activity. Professional workers, such as lawyers, doctors, and accountants, for example, must have continuing education each year. Some continuing education may be in formal programs. Much learning, however, is self-directed. Workers can learn much from what they observe at work. Many companies have resources such as databases and libraries that are available to employees.

Maintaining a professional reading file is one example of how an employee can continue to learn. Magazines, newspapers, journals, and **ezines** contain many articles and reports related to office work. Many professions and industries have associations that seek to provide current information to members. For example, the International Association of Administrative Professionals is an organization for office support staff. Many associations have magazines or journals and Web sites devoted to topics related to the profession. Many also have yearly conferences or more frequent seminars that members can attend. Current developments, new equipment or methods, and issues of concern are discussed at these meetings.

An Online Resources feature box is found on the first page of each chapter in this textbook. These feature boxes provide the names of some associations that may be of interest to office workers. Articles from a wide variety of magazines and Web sites can be found using the search terms listed in the feature boxes.

Strategy for Developing Office Competencies

You are a student. What you have experienced as a student is of great value to whatever you choose as your career. You are evaluated when you submit assignments, complete quizzes, and take examinations. You have some idea of what you are able to do, what you would like to learn, and, possibly, how you can learn. You will develop many competencies as you study and participate in the activities provided in this textbook. You can develop general and specific competencies for becoming an effective worker. These competencies will be valuable in a wide variety of jobs and careers.

Consider the competencies you have now. What skills and understandings do you have today that would be of value to an employer? You may have work experience, either paid or volunteer. This gives you an introduction to what work is like. Think about what those experiences required and the extent to which you were comfortable in doing the work.

Your education has been focused on developing critical basic competencies. Those basics included reading, writing, arithmetic, speaking, and listening. You have also studied math, literature, history, social studies, physical sciences, languages, and other subjects. Think of your educational experience. Identify your key competencies that you believe will have value at work. Competencies commonly developed in elementary and secondary school are valuable competencies for the office. Several competencies are listed in Figure 2-2.4.

Set goals for improving or developing new competencies. What do you want to accomplish this year? What skills do you want to improve? What new skills do you want to learn? Only you can make such plans. Only you can make a commitment to developing your office competencies.

COMPETENCIES FOR THE OFFICE

- Composing and formatting letters and reports
- Creating spreadsheets and charts
- Creating and maintaining databases
- Creating and giving presentations
- Keeping workstation organized
- Keyboarding and proofreading accurately
- Learning software programs
- Listening and following instructions
- Maintaining records and files
- Meeting deadlines
- Prioritizing tasks
- Speaking appropriately by telephone
- Using references such as the Internet, databases, and reference books
- Working in teams effectively

Figure **2-2.4**

Which of these competencies can you improve during this course?

For Discussion

Why is it worthwhile for someone who plans to be a sales representative, a teacher, a firefighter, a lawyer, or an automobile mechanic to develop office competencies?

Thinking Critically

Why is it important to continually evaluate your office competencies and to try to learn new skills?

59

Topic 2-2: *Developing Office Competencies*

Topic Review 2-2

REVIEWING THE TOPIC

1. Why should issues such as quality management, customer satisfaction, and teamwork be the concerns of all employees?
2. What does a company hope to achieve with a total quality management program?
3. Who is expected to participate in a program for continuous improvement?
4. Why do companies value customer satisfaction?
5. To what do ethical standards relate?
6. Why is teamwork considered important in today's world of work?
7. What changes are likely to be made in a company that shifts from being a domestic company to being a global one?
8. Why are companies interested in diversity?
9. Describe what you might observe to conclude that a worker is reliable.
10. "If it isn't in my job description, I will not do it." What does this comment imply about cooperativeness?

INTERACTING WITH OTHERS

Tanya, a manager in an advertising agency, called a meeting for three members of the staff, Jill, Dave, and Donna. Tanya explained that she had just received a telephone call about an exciting offer to submit a proposal for a new account. Tanya told them the project will require an intensive period of work, because a proposal must be submitted within two weeks.

The project is complex. Tanya believes, though, that the three of them can do the job. They will be given some help from the departmental secretary. They must research the types of advertising campaigns used in the industry. They must also gain information about what the client's goals are and what its present image is in the marketplace. After they have gathered the information, they must develop what they believe are promising campaigns. Tanya told them that they can decide among themselves how to divide the work to be done.

Jill, Dave, and Donna met immediately after leaving the supervisor's desk. Jill said: "Look, I feel rather tired and I just don't want to start work on this right away. Could I just beg off the research? Then I'll be happy to help you develop some plans for a campaign. I think I'm better in the creative part of such a project. I know that there will have to be many overtime hours during this first week of work. I just do not want to change my plans."

1. In a group with two or three other students, discuss what you would continued say to Jill if you were Dave or Donna.
2. Prepare notes on your response for use for a class discussion.

REINFORCING MATH SKILLS

Employees are planning next year's budget for the Accounts Payable Department. A study was done of how the work could be improved and costs reduced. The conclusion was that the office should operate with a supervisor and only two clerks, rather than the four clerks employed in the department last year. State-of-the-art equipment was purchased to help two clerks do the work formerly done by four clerks.

	Last Year's Expenses	Proposed Budget
Salaries	$133,000	$96,000
Supplies	4,000	3,800
Repairs and Maintenance	5,000	2,500
Depreciation	3,000	6,000
Telephone	3,500	3,900

1. Calculate the total expenses for the department using last year's figures.
2. Using last year's figures, calculate the percentage of total expenses each of the expenses items represents. Round percentages to one decimal place.
3. Using last year's figures, calculate the cost per invoice processed if 144,500 invoices were handled during the year.
4. Determine the difference in total expenses between last year's figures and the proposed budget.
5. Calculate the percentage decrease in total expenses if the proposed budget is used.

Encourage students to refer to Section D in the Reference Section of the *Student Activities and Simulations* workbook, if available, to review math skills.

Teaching Tips

Assign students to teams for completing this activity. Assist students with finding articles on the Internet if needed. Allow students to share their findings in a class discussion.

COMPOSITION
INTERNET
RESEARCH
TEAMWORK
WORD PROCESSING

Topic **2-2** : ACTIVITY 1

Checklist for Evaluating Team Projects

For this activity, work in a group of three or four students to develop a checklist for evaluating team project participation.

1. Search the Internet or other reference sources to find at least two articles about effective teamwork. Make a list of the main points of each article and share this list with the group.
2. As a group, prepare a list of factors to be included on an evaluation checklist. For example, one factor might be: Completed work on time.
3. Decide on a system to use in rating how well a student does on each factor on your list. (Hint: Should there be A, B, C grading? or 1, 2, 3, 4, 5? or Excellent, Good, Poor?)
4. Prepare a final copy of the checklist with the factors and rating scale. Use an appropriate title and format the document so it will be easy to read and use.
5. Participate in a class discussion and share the factors your team used on the checklist.

DATABASE
INTERNET
TEAMWORK

Topic **2-2** : ACTIVITY 2

Professional Reading File

Teaching Tips

Review how to create a database table and enter data. Assist students with finding articles on the Internet if needed.

Develop a database to record the source of newspaper, magazine, or online articles that will help you increase your knowledge of office work and related issues. Many articles that are published in hard copy newspapers and magazines can also be found online. Use your favorite search engine to look for articles online. Many major newspapers also have online sites where you can find some of their articles.

1. Create a new database file to store information about articles for professional development. Name the database file *Reading File*.
2. Create a table named **Articles**. Include the following fields in the database table:

Field Name	Field Type	Description
Title	Text	Title of the article
Subject	Text	Subject of the article (Sometimes the title may not clearly suggest the subject of the article.)
Author	Text	Author name
Publication	Text	Name of magazine, newspaper, or Web site
Date	Date	Date of the publication or the date you accessed the article online
Web Address	Text	For articles accessed online
Notes	Text	A place to record your brief notes about the article

3. Format the data table or create an AutoForm to make entering the data convenient.

4. Begin your reading file by finding one article related to any topic in Chapter 2. Read the article and enter the data for this article in your database.

5. Ask three classmates to share the data for the articles they have located. Enter data for the three articles in the database.

6. As you study each remaining chapter in this textbook, find at least one article related to topics studied in the chapter. Read the article and update your database.

CHAPTER REVIEW 2

Summary

Chapter 2 gave you an overview of the workforce as provided by the U.S. Department of Labor in *The Occupational Outlook Handbook*. You also learned about key categories of office competencies. Review the key points from this chapter listed below:

- The information provided by the U.S. Department of Labor is useful in learning about occupations. Projections are given through the year 2012.
- Although there will continue to be job opportunities in office occupations, the rate of increase is lower than that for some other groups.
- In many jobs, workers are expected to have office competencies. Therefore, your study of this subject is valuable for your future, regardless of your career interests.
- Office competencies are considered in four categories: word processing, data processing, information management and transmission, and general managing and communicating.
- Goals of companies influence their expectations for all employees.
- Companies focus attention on concerns such as total quality management, continuous improvement, customer satisfaction, ethical standards, responsible teamwork, global outreach, and diversity.
- Qualities considered important for employees are reliability, productivity, cooperativeness, and independence in learning.
- Planning a strategy for developing office competencies will be valuable to you no matter what you choose for your life's work.

Key Terms

aptitude	general managing	projection
code of ethics	global marketplace	reliable
continuous	HTML	speech recognition
improvement	information	software
cooperative	management	total quality
data processing	initiative	management
desktop publishing	innovation	word processing
diversity	interactive	World Wide Web
e-commerce	objectively	
ezine	online	
Fortune 500	priorities	
companies	proficiency	

Teaching Tips

Have students review key points from the chapter by completing the Sort It Out game on *The Office* Web site.

Teaching Tips

Have students review the key terms by using the Flashcards available on *The Office* Web site.

Chapter 2 : ACTIVITY 1

COMPOSITION
RESEARCH
TEAMWORK
WORD PROCESSING

Expectations of Employers

Become acquainted with workers' opinions regarding expectations employers have for employees.

1. Working with one other student, interview someone about his or her work. The purpose of the interview is to learn opinions about the importance of the employer's expectations in specific situations. Collect the following information:
   - Name and current position of the employee
   - The employee's opinion of how important each of the following qualities is to his or her employer: reliability, productivity, cooperativeness, independence in learning
   - A specific example that shows the importance of each of the qualities listed earlier

   Ask the employee to respond using these evaluation ratings:

   Very Important, Somewhat Important, Of Limited Importance, Of Little or No Importance

2. Key a report of your findings.
3. Discuss the findings in class, noting similarities and differences in responses.

Chapter 2 : ACTIVITY 2

INTEGRATED DOCUMENT
INTERNET
RESEARCH
SPREADSHEET
WORD PROCESSING

Employment Projections

Research current employment projections. Then key a report highlighting the information.

1. Open and print the PDF file *CH02 Projections* found in the data files, which contains the report. Key the report. Follow the formatting instructions written on the document. Correct any spelling or word usage errors you find in the document.

2. Use the current edition of *The Occupational Outlook Handbook* to find current employment projections. You can access the *Handbook* online at the Bureau of Labor Statistics Web site. A link to the *Handbook* is provided on the Web site for this textbook. If you do not have access to the current edition of the *Handbook*, use the information provided in the Chapter 2 text and Figure 2-1.1.

3. Create a column chart using your spreadsheet software to show the three occupational groups with the largest percentage increase. Then copy the chart into the report.

4. Proofread carefully and correct all errors before printing the report.

65

Teaching Tips

Assign students to work in a team with one other student to complete this activity. Allow students to discuss their findings with the class.

Teaching Tips

The data file for this activity is provided in a PDF (portable document format) file. Students will need a program such as *Adobe Acrobat® Reader®* to view or print the document. *Acrobat® Reader®* is provided on the *IRCD* for this textbook. Review with students how to create a column chart with spreadsheet software and copy it into the word processing document.

Supplemental Activity

Have students complete the Chapter 2 Supplemental Activity, Office Competencies Presentation, available on *The Office* Web site.

Assessment

Assess student learning using the Chapter 2 test available on the *IRCD* and in *ExamView®* format.

PART 2

Managing Information to Enhance Productivity

OBJECTIVES

- Explain the vital role that information plays in operating a business
- Describe common business information systems
- Communicate effectively in written form and in oral form
- Plan, prepare, and deliver business presentations
- Explain the purpose of common financial reports and aid in their preparation
- Process financial information such as payments, receipts, and bank reconciliations

Effectively managed information helps a company serve its customers better and operate more efficiently. Employees need accurate information for use in making decisions. This information must be shared in both visual and oral forms. In Managing Information to Enhance Productivity, you will learn about common business information systems and resources. You will have an opportunity to improve your communication and information processing skills.

66

© GETTY IMAGES/PHOTODISC

CHAPTER 3

Information: A Vital Business Resource

To prosper and grow, an organization must make sound business decisions. To do this, the organization needs accurate, up-to-date information. Information is simply facts that are organized in a meaningful and usable form. Information is a vital resource that helps an organization serve its customers and operate smoothly.

As an office worker, you will help maintain the flow of information in your organization. You will find your work more interesting and more meaningful when you understand how it relates to the total organization. As you study this chapter, you will become acquainted with common information systems and resources found in businesses. You will also develop an understanding of how technology can enhance information systems.

67

Topic 3-1

INFORMATION PROCESSING

objectives

- Define information
- Explain how businesses use information
- Describe information processing activities
- Explain how information technologies enhance information systems
- Describe local area networks and wide area networks
- List security measures for information systems

Businesses use many resources in their daily operations. They use raw materials and equipment to make products. Workers are used to process orders and build products. Computers and other equipment are used for communication. The resources used will vary from business to business. In all businesses, information is an essential resource. It affects how other resources are used and the overall success of the business.

How Businesses Use Information

Most of the work performed in offices involves the processing of information. Information starts as basic facts or raw data made up of numbers, symbols, and letters. This raw data becomes information when it is organized in a meaningful way. Consider these examples:

- A payroll manager prepares the weekly payroll checks. The raw data used includes hours worked, rates of pay, and payroll deductions. When such data is arranged for individual employees, it becomes information to use in preparing the payroll.
- An office worker in a shipping department answers a customer's inquiry about a shipping date. The basic facts used are the customer's name, the invoice number, and the shipping date. Locating the specific invoice gives the office worker the information to answer the customer's question.
- A sales associate in a real estate office prepares for a business trip. The basic facts used are travel dates, destinations, and flight numbers and times. When the sales associate arranges the facts into a meaningful form, an itinerary is created.

The most common forms of information are identified in Figure 3-1.1. These individual forms of information are often used together. Using information effectively is important in achieving success.

Figure **3-1.1**

Common Forms of Information	
Numbers	Amounts, quantities, sizes, weights, capacities, or ages organized to convey meaning, as in a table or listing
Text	Words organized to convey meaning, as in letters or reports
Image	Charts, graphs, photographs
Voice	Messages conveyed in person; messages conveyed by telephone

68

CHAPTER 3: INFORMATION: A VITAL BUSINESS RESOURCE

Information enables businesses to answer some of their most important questions:

- What do our customers want?
- How can we improve our product and deliver it faster?
- Who are our most productive employees?
- How much can we increase prices before we lose revenue?
- Where can we reduce costs?

Many businesses gather data to use in making business decisions. Consider the questions listed in Figure 3-1.2. The decisions that may be affected by the information needed are also shown.

Decisions Affected by Information

Figure **3-1.2**

Information Needed	Decisions Affected
What do our customers think of us?	Image to be built or points stressed through advertising Improvements to product quality or customer service
Who are our best customers and where are they located?	Placement of new branch locations Warehousing of goods to be shipped Areas or Web sites targeted for advertising
What are our best-selling products? Why are these products successful?	Products to keep and products to discontinue Changes for less successful products to make them more popular
Who are our best dealers? Where are our most productive sales channels?	Reward plans for dealers Strategies for improving sales in other channels—retail stores, catalog sales, Web sites
Who are our biggest competitors? What do they offer customers that we do not?	Points stressed through advertising Improvements to product quality, product features, customer service

sales channel: a method of marketing products such as through retail stores or catalogs

Managing Information

A company may process a large number of **transactions** each day. Procedures and technology are used to handle the data efficiently. Running a business can be very complex. The need for accurate information makes effective management of information essential.

transaction: a business deal or agreement, exchange of data, or sale

Complexity of Business

Operating even a small business can be quite complex. In a very small business, the owner may take care of all office activities. In many small companies, a few office workers handle all the daily work. Typically, all the information needed to operate the business is in one location, usually the business office. For a small business, good organization of information is important for success.

Well-organized information is even more important in large companies with many employees. Several workers may need to use the same information to process work or make decisions. Effective organization of information will meet the needs of workers in all areas of the company.

To be successful, a small business must manage information efficiently.

Volume of Transactions

Some companies must deal with thousands of transactions each day. Effective management of information allows these companies to run smoothly. Consider the following examples:

- Banks process thousands of checks each day. They receive thousands of deposits and pay out thousands of dollars in cash each day.
- Manufacturing companies complete the production of thousands of products each day. They ship thousands of orders and receive payments from thousands of customers each day.
- Insurance companies receive thousands of payments each day. They issue thousands of new policies and send out notices to thousands of customers each day.

Think of the problems that would occur if these companies did not manage information effectively. The volume of transactions would be overwhelming. The access and retrieval of information would be slow and tedious.

© BILL BARLEY/SUPERSTOCK INTERNATIONAL

Manufacturing companies produce (or ship) thousands of products each day.

Current and Accurate Information

For information to be valuable, it must be current and accurate. Outdated or incorrect information can be useless. Even worse, outdated information can cost a company money because poor decisions are made based on the incorrect information. Coworkers and customers expect to receive information quickly. They expect it to be accurate and up-to-date.

With the growth of e-commerce (buying and selling online), customers expect more current information. For example, a customer can buy from a traditional catalog. The customer completes an order form and mails it to the company. The customer does not know whether the item ordered is in stock or when the item will be shipped. For customers buying online, the Web site often indicates whether an item is in stock. It may also show when the item will be shipped. Many e-commerce sites provide order tracking. A customer can see the progress the order is making on the way to its destination.

WORKPLACE CONNECTIONS

Consider the value of current and accurate information in the following examples:

Airlines can provide a network of service because current data is available. Travelers can request a flight between two cities anywhere in the world. They can learn the number of seats available on the flight. Customers making reservations are not willing to wait days for a response.

A manager keeps detailed records about the company's cash-flow needs. The manager knows exactly how much cash is on hand. Cash not needed immediately is moved to short-term investments that earn money. The company benefits because accurate information is kept.

71

Topic 3-1: *Information Processing*

Thinking Critically

Ask students: Does using a computer automatically ensure that a company is accessing current and accurate information?

Points to Emphasize

Effective management of information is essential because of the complexity of business, the volume of transactions, and the need for current and accurate information.

Why would duplication of information be costly to an organization? (Example: Customers would receive duplicate mailings or duplicate invoices because the customer is in the database more than once.) Why would outdated, inaccurate, or missing information be costly? (Example: Customer moved to a new address that is not shown in the customer database.) Even if the company corrected the duplicate, outdated, or inaccurate information, how might customers' opinions of the company's reputation be affected?

Thinking Critically

How did incompatible databases make Gloria's job more difficult?

Obstacles to Managing Information

Information can help a company operate effectively. Yet, information can be difficult to manage. Data can be hard to organize and easy to lose or alter. It can be hard to locate and even incorrect. Obstacles to using information efficiently in an organization include:

incompatible: unable to work together

- Uncoordinated procedures and files
- Duplication of information
- **Incompatible** databases
- Outdated or inaccurate information
- Missing information
- Limited access to information

Office workers are often the employees best able to overcome these obstacles. Office workers gather or process information. An office worker is often the person who first recognizes that databases are incorrect or that critical information is missing.

Office workers should follow the company's procedures for reporting difficulties with using the company's data or software. If no procedures exist, a manager should be told about the problem. Include a description of the problem in your report. If a company can move quickly to correct problems with its information resources, the negative effects of these problems can be reduced.

WORKPLACE CONNECTIONS

Using incompatible databases can make sharing data difficult and may increase errors. Gloria Santana works in customer service for small company. She handles calls about the status of customer orders. She answers product questions or complaints. Before answering questions, Gloria must verify that the product was purchased from her company and when. This data is entered into a database by an employee in another department when the product is sold. Data related to product complaints or questions is stored in a different database. Because the two databases are not compatible, Gloria must also enter the customer's name, product, and purchase date when the customer calls with a question or complaint. This means that helping each customer takes longer and entering the data twice doubles the chances for errors.

Information Processing Activities

Information processing is putting facts or numbers into a meaningful and useful form. Five types of activities or operations are typically involved: input, processing, output, distribution, and storage. These operations are summarized in Figure 3-1.3.

Figure **3-1.3**

Information Processing

Operation	Example
Input: Entering data into the information system	• Taking orders by phone and keying them into an order entry system to generate shipment and billing for the order • Entering data about a new employee to activate payroll and benefits • Writing product features and benefits for an advertising brochure
Processing: Handling data to create meaningful information	• Formatting and arranging text and graphics to create a newsletter • Generating a report from a database • Calculating and sorting data in a spreadsheet
Output: Retrieving information from the system	• Viewing a list of out-of-stock items from an inventory database • Printing labels and brochures for a customer mailing
Distribution: Sending information to the appropriate people	• Faxing product updates to sales representatives • Mailing price quotes to customers • Sending a report to a coworker as an e-mail attachment • Posting a survey on the company Web site
Storage: Saving information for future use	• Filing paper documents • Saving computer files

As you perform your duties, you will often proceed directly through the input, processing, output, distribution, and storage operations. For example, you may enter numbers into a spreadsheet program, perform calculations and create a chart, print ten copies of the chart, distribute it to members of your department, and store the file and printed copy. At other times, you may complete only some of the operations. For example, you may receive a request from a coworker for another chart using some of the figures in the spreadsheet. You can proceed to the processing operation because the data has already been input earlier. Information can be stored and retrieved at any point.

Points to Emphasize

Information is raw data that has been organized in a meaningful form while *information processing* is the series of steps needed to put the raw data into a meaningful form.

For Discussion

Ask students how the obstacles to managing information (in the previous section) could make the five types of information processing activities difficult or impossible to perform.

Points to Emphasize

Understanding information processing activities will be useful to students as they study the remaining chapters in this textbook and as they take additional business courses. Students need to understand that office workers do not work in a vacuum—they rely on information from other departments just as they process and supply information to other departments.

Information Technologies

Information technology refers to the equipment and software that allow a user to create, store, and retrieve information. The information processing methods found in businesses vary according to how technology is used. The telephone is the most common piece of equipment that is found in almost all offices. Photocopiers, fax machines, and computers are becoming almost as common. Usually only small offices requiring few transactions rely heavily on manual processing methods. Technology allows for rapid processing of a huge quantity and variety of information. Some firms have enjoyed a competitive advantage by being the first to use a new technology within their industry.

WORKPLACE CONNECTIONS

Citibank was one of the first banks to use automated teller machines (ATMs). Citibank tripled its market share within the first few years after introducing ATMs. What advantages did Citibank gain? Citibank increased its number of banking transactions and earned ATM fees. It also attracted many new customers from other banks. At the same time, Citibank reduced the number of tellers and increased the accuracy and timely handling of data. Citibank held its competitive edge by using this new information to analyze customers' needs. As a result, it offered additional services based on those needs and explored new markets.

Information technologies can be used to improve communication among the staff and between companies and their suppliers and customers. Examples of common information technologies used in offices include:

electronic imaging: converting paper documents to pictures stored and displayed via computer

interactive voice response: a recorded message accessed and directed by the user to provide or record information

CD: compact disk, a type of storage device for electronic data that can be read by a computer

- Computers connected to networks, the Internet, and online services provide access to a wide range of resources.
- **Electronic imaging** and transmission of documents reduces paperwork. It saves valuable time and increases customer satisfaction.
- Electronic mail, instant messaging, online databases, and two-way video increase the flow of information and speed of responses.
- **Interactive voice response** systems reduce manual processes for sending and receiving data.
- Interactive **CD** reference media make retrieval of data quick and easy.
- Multimedia employee training programs enhance training effectiveness. Figure 3-1.4 shows an example of a multimedia training program.

Businesses must handle large amounts of information in short time spans. To be successful, they must respond quickly to customer needs and wants. Effective use of information and technologies helps businesses meet these challenges.

74

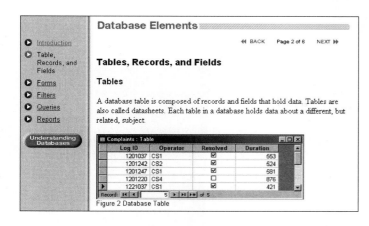

Database Elements

◀◀ BACK   Page 2 of 6   NEXT ▶▶

Tables, Records, and Fields

Tables

A database table is composed of records and fields that hold data. Tables are also called datasheets. Each table in a database holds data about a different, but related, subject.

Figure 2 Database Table

Navigation items:
- Introduction
- Table, Records, and Fields
- Forms
- Filters
- Queries
- Reports

Understanding Databases

Complaints : Table

Log ID	Operator	Resolved	Duration
1201037	CS1	☑	553
1201242	CS2	☑	524
1201247	CS1	☑	581
1201220	CS4	☐	876
1221037	CS1	☑	421

Record: 5 of 5

Figure 3-1.4

Many companies provide training seminars on the company intranet.

Computerized Processing

Computer-based systems are common in today's offices. Computerized processing relies heavily on equipment (the computer) and related software to turn data into meaningful and timely information.

Hardware

Hardware refers to the physical parts of a computer or related equipment. Although we often speak of the "the computer," many types exist. Computers can be classified by their size, speed, and processing capabilities. Mainframe computers, minicomputers, and microcomputers are three major categories of computers used in businesses.

hardware: the physical parts of a computer or related equipment

Types of Computers

Mainframe computers are large, multipurpose machines with very high processing speeds. Mainframes can handle many users and store large quantities of data. Mainframe computers use sophisticated programs to control their operation and require specially trained employees to operate the system. The mainframe computer has traditionally done tasks such as payroll, accounting, and personnel recordkeeping for large organizations.

Minicomputers are midsized computers that can support a number of users. They are less powerful than mainframe computers but can perform a wide variety of processing tasks.

Microcomputers, also called personal computers, are the small, desktop variety. The system is made up of several parts such as the central processing unit, a keyboard, mouse, and monitor. Microcomputers are designed for individual use. They are used by people at all levels of a company. Notebook and tablet computers are other forms of microcomputers. These computers can be battery powered. They are especially helpful to employees who must work on the road or at locations where desktop systems are not practical. Companies may have several types of computers to meet their processing needs.

For Discussion

Have students identify the distinguishing features of mainframe computers, minicomputers, and microcomputers.

75

Topic 3-1: *Information Processing*

75

Topic 3-1: *Information Processing*

A notebook computer is a type of microcomputer.

© CORBIS

A personal digital assistant (PDA) is a handheld computer, small enough to hold easily in one hand. A digital pen is used to input data into a PDA. PDAs allow users to complete many of the same tasks and use some of the same programs as notebook computers. Some devices combine the features of a PDA with wireless telephone features. These devices are commonly called *smart phones*. As the processing power and storage space for PDAs continue to grow, they will become even more useful.

PDAs are handheld computers used to store, process, and access information.

© MEDIOIMAGES

Ask students whether they have a PDA or a smart phone. Allow students who have these devices to describe how they are used. Ask students to describe workers they have observed using small, handheld computers. For example, an employee of a package delivery company enters data about the package into a handheld computer. The recipient may also be asked to sign for the package using the handheld computer.

Input and Output Devices

Data from business transactions often consist of handwritten, keyed, or printed facts. Before these data can be processed, however, they must be entered into the computer system. Workers use input devices to enter data into computers. An input device is hardware that allows the computer to accept the data for processing. Common input devices that you probably use regularly include the keyboard and mouse. Other input devices include touch screens, digital pens, digital tablets, and scanners. Touch screens and digital pens are used to give commands, draw, or write input directly on a screen or digital tablet. Scanners are used to input text, graphics, and photos by "reading" printed documents. Speech recognition is also a form of input.

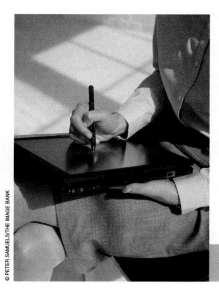

A digital pen can be used as an input device for a tablet PC.

A computer system must have at least one output device. An output device prints, displays, speaks, or records information from the computer. The most common output devices are monitors and printers. Other output forms include speakers, floppy disks, CDs, **DVDs**, **USB flash drives**, tape drives, and microfilm.

Storage Devices

The amount of primary storage in a computer is limited. Additional external storage is often needed to store data. Storage devices such as optical disks (CDs, DVDs), USB flash drives, and tapes allow large volumes of data to be stored and retrieved easily. Storage media are described in more detail in Chapter 9.

DVD: digital video disk, a type of storage device for electronic data that can be read by a computer or a player connected to a TV or stereo

USB flash drive: a magnetic storage device for electronic data that can be read by a computer

Teaching Tips

Have students find photographs of input and output devices from magazines, catalogs, and newspapers. Students should label each example and be prepared to discuss its features. Use labeled examples to prepare a bulletin board display of computer system input and output devices.

For Discussion

Discuss with students the types of external storage devices available for use in the classroom or computer lab.

CDs, DVDs, and USB flash drives are examples of external storage devices.

© GETTY IMAGES/PHOTODISC

© HEWLETT-PACKARD

software: programs containing instructions for a computer

computer virus: a destructive program loaded onto a computer and run without the user's knowledge

Software

Thousands of **software** programs are available to meet information processing needs. Software may be divided into three broad categories: operating system software, application software, and utility software. Figure 3-1.5 lists common types of software you are likely to find in an office.

Operating system software controls the basic operations of the computer. It allows the computer to communicate with devices connected to it, such as a printer. *Microsoft® Windows® XP* is an example of popular operating system software.

Application software directs the computer to carry out specific tasks. The program may perform a single task, such as word processing. Software that shares information between applications (such as word processing, database, and presentations) is known as integrated software. When these applications are packaged as one, they are commonly called a suite.

Application software can improve the way a business processes information. Software companies continue to upgrade their products and add new features. Onscreen help, tutorials, and templates make the software easy to use. With the wide selection of software available, the use of computers in offices continues to grow.

Utility software carries out "housekeeping" duties. Examples of these duties include formatting a disk, organizing files, and protecting data. Some utility programs are included with the operating system software. Many more features are available by purchasing utility software packages. As the use of computers has grown, utility software has become essential in preventing data loss.

Virus protection programs are a type of utility software. This software finds and clears files of **computer viruses**. If viruses are undetected, they can result in loss of data and computer operations. Virus protection software is generally updated regularly to keep up with the new viruses.

78

CHAPTER 3: INFORMATION: A VITAL BUSINESS RESOURCE

Software Category	Software Function
Browsers	Display HTML files such as Internet pages
Communications	**Modem** connections; fax; voice, electronic, and Internet mail; file transfers
Database management	Records creation and maintenance, records updating and editing, data querying, report creation
Desktop publishing	Page composition, use of features such as type style and fonts to product high-quality documents that contain text and graphics
Development	Tools for creating interactive applications including animations and pages for the Internet
Graphics and design	Clip-art images, photos, line art, and drawing and design tools for use in desktop publishing documents as well as computer-aided design
Finance	Checkbook, online banking, accounts receivable/payable, billing, financial reports, financial forecasting, tax planning, inventory, and job costing
Operating system	Controls the operation of the computer and communicates with devices such as printers
Network	Server performance for networks, security, management, directory services, intranets
Presentation	Multimedia shows with graphics, sound, text, and animation
Project management	Timeline schedules, calendars, appointment reminders, travel guides, address books, prioritizing and task management, and employee performance evaluations
Specialized	Software developed for specialized needs such as medical, law, and real estate offices
Spreadsheet	Number calculations using formulas, sorting, charts, "what-if" analyses
Utility	Scan and disable viruses, compress files, boost performance, recover lost files, repair disks, troubleshoot, protect, and back up data
Word processing	Document creation and editing, spelling and grammar checking, merging of text, data, and graphics into integrated documents

modem: a device that allows computer data to be transmitted via the telephone system

Teaching Tips

Computer applications are designed around the capabilities of computer systems. As technology changes and processing equipment becomes faster and less expensive, manufacturers of application software upgrade existing products and introduce new ones that use the capabilities of the hardware.

79

Topic 3-1: *Information Processing*

Networks

A computer network links two or more computers so they can share information. Networks are used to link computers and other types of hardware. Two types of networks are local area networks (LANs) and wide area networks (WANs). They help workers complete their daily tasks and share information. Use of networks is not limited to within an organization. Growth and creativity in the ways in which the Internet and the World Wide Web are being used to conduct business are affecting workers in surprising and exciting ways.

WORKPLACE CONNECTIONS

Cal-Giftorama is a national catalog-order company. It specializes in unique, handcrafted items imported from all over the world. The company has recently expanded its e-commerce activities. A B2B (business-to-business) network makes it possible to place orders with exporters located in Europe and Asia, as well as to conduct everyday business within the United States.

Thanks to its data network, the company ships 98 percent of all customer orders within 24 hours. When a customer places an order over the telephone, an employee is able to access the inventory database to see whether the ordered item is available. Within minutes, the order is processed. A packing list is printed at the distribution center. Soon the order is on its way to the customer. Without the network, it could take five or more days to process the order.

Cal-Giftorama has recently launched a Web site for B2C (business-to-consumer) sales. The site offers audio files and a live camera in the catalog showroom. Visitors to the site can view and order items from the online catalog. The company believes that selling in the virtual marketplace will help the company stay competitive in the import business.

To use a network efficiently, workers must first be trained. They must perform networking tasks such as logging on and off, exchanging files, setting password security, sending and receiving messages, managing files, and viewing network printer queues. New workers may be introduced to networks in a variety of ways. Some organizations provide hands-on training by support staff. Others assign an experienced coworker to train the new user. Still others may give the user a network procedures manual to follow.

Local Area Networks

local area network: a group of connected computers that are close to each other

A network used to link computers that are close to each other—usually within several hundred feet—is a **local area network** (LAN). With a LAN, several computer users can share data files, software, and equipment such as printers or scanners. LANs are set up as peer-to-peer networks or server-based networks.

In a peer-to-peer network, computers are connected with cables to each other. They operate as equals in the network. A computer in this type of network can access software and data stored on all the connected computers.

Individual users and the company decide which data or software files will be made public for other network users to access. All that is needed to set up a peer-to-peer network using most current computers is cabling and special software.

In a server-based network, one computer fills requests for data and program files from network users. The central computer that performs this service is called a file server. Its primary task is supplying or "serving" files to computers on the network. In this type of network, every computer to be connected must be cabled and have special software and hardware for networking.

The term *transmission carrier* refers to the cables or other equipment used to link computers in a LAN. Three types of cable that are commonly used to link computers and other equipment are twisted-pair, coaxial, and fiber-optic cables. These cables are described in Figure 3-1.6. When setting up networks, many companies use a variety of carriers to connect devices. They must consider cost, speed, efficiency, and reliability when choosing cables for use in the network.

Figure **3-1.6**

Transmission Carriers

Twisted-pair cable	• Similar to widely used, older telephone wiring • Inexpensive • Prone to interference from other electrical devices
Coaxial cable	• Widely used by cable television companies • Faster and more reliable over longer distances than twisted-pair • More expensive than twisted wire • Much less interference
Fiber-optic cable	• Made from thin glass strands • Transmits laser light pulses efficiently at very high speeds over long distances • Not affected by electrical interference

Fiber-optic cable is made from thin glass strands.

Topic 3-1: *Information Processing*

Ask your network administrator or computer technician about the types of network cable used in your school. Give this information to your students and ask them if they know what types of cable are used by local businesses they are familiar with.

Points to Emphasize

Emphasize that by using EDI a business can exchange data with many other companies, even when those companies use different computer systems. This capability is very important for e-commerce.

For Discussion

What are some advantages of using a dedicated line for data transmission? What are some advantages of using a dial-up line for data transmission?

Wireless communications are those sent without cables. For LANs, infrared light waves or radio waves can be used. Infrared light waves send data in a straight line. They require a clear path between objects. Infrared light waves are usually limited to computers, keyboards, monitors, and peripherals that are only a short distance from each other. Using radio waves is more versatile because the radio waves do not travel in a straight line. Radio waves can be used to send data between equipment in a larger area such as several rooms or a whole building.

Wide Area Networks

wide area network: a group of connected computers that are separated by long distances

A **wide area network** (WAN) links computers that are separated by long distances. A WAN for a small company may cover several cities or states. WANs for a large company may cover several countries. Wide area networks, like LANs, are used for file access, data exchange, and e-mail. Electronic data interchange (EDI) allows the exchange of data between companies that may or may not have compatible computer or network systems.

WORKPLACE CONNECTIONS

The use of wide area networks and electronic data interchange speeds business transactions. Consider this example:

A clothing manufacturer in Atlanta needs silk fabric from a supplier in Hong Kong. A purchase order is sent from a computer at the factory in Atlanta to a computer in the warehouse in Hong Kong. The order is filled, the fabric is shipped, and an electronic invoice is sent to the computer at the factory in Atlanta. No paper has been exchanged. It would take weeks for the order to be received, filled, and billed without use of electronic data interchange.

As you have learned, in a LAN data travels over cables or wireless connections. In a WAN, use of data transmission lines is purchased from a business that specializes in providing these services. When setting up a wide area network, companies choose a type of connection that will best meet their needs. A DSL (direct service line), also called a dedicated or leased line, remains connected and ready for use at all times. A dial-up line provides connections only when needed. Both provide a relatively secure, clear transmission from one computer to another.

microwave transmission: radio waves that carry data

Microwave transmissions play an important role in a WAN. Microwave dishes and towers relay signals to each other directly. You have probably noticed imposing microwave towers on hillsides. The higher the dish or tower, the further the message can be sent. Objects between the two relay stations can interfere with the signal. In a WAN, data travels by fiber-optic cable or telephone lines to the nearest microwave carrier. The data travels from carrier to carrier until it reaches the one nearest its final destination. From the last microwave carrier, the data is then sent over cables to the receiving computer. This process is illustrated in Figure 3-1.7.

82

CHAPTER 3: INFORMATION: A VITAL BUSINESS RESOURCE

Figure **3-1.7**

WANs may use fiber-optic cables or microwaves to transmit data.

For Discussion

How might the type of transmission carrier (fiber-optic, coaxial, or twisted-pair cable) used to relay signals to the microwave tower affect the speed or quality of the transmission?

In international communications, **satellites** may play a major role in sending data. Signals are sent from your computer to a satellite relay station. The satellite relay station sends the signal to an orbiting satellite. The satellite sends the message to a receiving station on Earth. From there, the signal travels over cables to your modem and computer.

satellite: a man-made object placed in orbit around the Earth containing electronic devices for relaying communications data

The use of wireless devices to connect to the Internet and then to other networks is growing. The coverage areas for wireless connections in the United States are growing. Many types of computers are able to access these wireless networks. In the future, an employee may be able to access company data at any remote location.

WORKPLACE CONNECTIONS

Connie Chan is a broker for a large real estate company. On entering a home that is about to be listed for sale, she counts rooms, measures window and doors, and notes special features of the house. She also takes some photographs. All her notes are entered on a notebook computer. The pictures are taken with a digital camera and loaded on the notebook also. Using a high-speed wireless modem in her computer, Connie sends all the information, including the photographs, to online databases. The new listing can be viewed online by potential buyers within a few minutes after she tours the house.

For Discussion

What wireless devices have you seen people using for telecommunications? What are some advantages and some disadvantages of using wireless devices?

Although WANS can be worldwide, there may be problems connecting to computers in foreign lands. Some international standards have been created. However, usage taxes are set by each nation. Many countries seek to be a part of the global economy. Some of these countries are building communications systems to attract electronic visitors to their lands.

A variety of technology is available for sharing of all types of data. Companies must evaluate their needs in order to spend their dollars wisely. One way companies share data is by using the Internet. Connecting to the Internet is discussed next. The Internet as an information resource is discussed in Topic 3-2.

83

Topic 3-1: *Information Processing*

Connecting to the Internet

Many government offices, schools, and companies have direct Internet access through their local or wide area networks. Workers can easily gain access to the Internet if their LAN or WAN is connected to it.

Internet service provider: a company that sells access to the Internet

Direct access is not the only way to get online. An **Internet service provider** (ISP) sells entry to the Internet, usually based on a monthly fee. Accessing the Internet through an ISP requires a computer with a modem, telecommunications software, and a phone line. With a dial-up access account, your computer contacts the ISP each time you want to go online. The ISP then provides you with a connection to the Internet. With a DSL (direct service line) account, your computer remains online and you can access the Internet at any time. Dial-up access is widely available. DSL service is also available in many areas. Both types of service are inexpensive and easy to set up. When selecting an ISP, evaluate the cost of the service; the company's reliability, security, and overall performance; user satisfaction; restrictions; types of services provided; and quality of customer assistance.

Maintenance and Security

Office workers are expected to be responsible users of information processing technology. They must be concerned with maintenance, security, and ethics related to information processing systems and software.

A company may use large computer networks or just a few stand-alone computers. In either case, managing the maintenance and security for the computers is important. Many companies depend heavily on technology for handling data. Disaster planning is essential to limit problems with computer service. The duties can be so demanding that some companies hire security administrators and disaster recovery coordinators. These people handle plans for protecting the system and recovering quickly if data is lost or destroyed. Read more about disaster recovery on page 365.

Maintenance

Companies use and rely on computer systems daily. Yet, a surprising number of businesses neglect to do proper maintenance on the systems. To work well, the systems must be serviced and maintained on a regular basis. Failure to maintain the equipment could result in lost data and even lost business.

WORKPLACE CONNECTIONS

Carmen received a phone call from a new customer requesting a rush delivery on an important order. She checked the inventory system. It showed that the needed items were in stock and could be delivered the same day. Little did Carmen know that the computer had been shut down for unscheduled repairs early that morning. This shutdown prevented some shipments from being entered and deducted from the inventory count. The needed items were not really in the warehouse. The company lost a customer because accurate inventory information was not available when needed.

Regular cleaning is an important part of computer maintenance.

© DAVID YOUNG-WOLFF/PHOTOEDIT

When you use a computer, follow proper maintenance procedures. Read and follow equipment operation instructions so that you do not accidentally harm the equipment. Many companies instruct employees in how to care for equipment. If you are responsible for the care of your computer, be sure you understand the procedures you are to follow.

Security

Businesses handle sensitive data daily. They depend on their computer networks to process orders and provide needed data. As a result, security is a critical issue. Security for computer systems involves protecting against loss of data and loss of service. Unauthorized access and use of data or computers is also a concern.

Loss of data can occur when a computer or network does not work properly because of hardware or software problems. To protect against loss of data, backup copies of the data are made and stored in another location. Data can also be lost through errors made by employees. For example, a file may be deleted or incorrectly updated in a customer database. Companies try to avoid losses of this nature through employee training.

Many companies have confidential data that are at risk of theft or misuse. The data gathered from customers and business partners are also at risk. Unauthorized users, called hackers, may be able to misuse or steal the data that are not protected. Companies use software and equipment called **firewalls** to prevent unauthorized access to their computer networks. Many companies use data encryption when sending data. This process helps protect data, such as a customer's credit card number or a business partner's new product design, from being stolen during transmission.

A computer virus is a destructive program loaded onto a computer and run without the user's knowledge. Viruses are dangerous because they can quickly make copies of themselves. They can cause a computer to stop working or destroy data. Some viruses can travel across networks and sneak

firewall: software and hardware designed to prevent unauthorized users from gaining access to a computer or network

85

Topic 3-1: *Information Processing*

Points to Emphasize

Companies frequently assign passwords or access codes as a security precaution. To access certain information, an office worker must enter the proper password or access code when the prompt is displayed. Review the login procedures for your school network with your students at this time.

Points to Emphasize

Companies use a combination of hardware and software referred to as a "firewall" to prevent unauthorized access to their networks. Most companies also use virus protection software to prevent viruses from entering their networks through e-mail attachments, files loaded from floppy disks by employees, or from files downloaded from the Internet. To be effective, the virus definition files must be constantly updated to detect new viruses as they appear.

past security systems. Antivirus software is used to help prevent data loss from computer viruses. *Norton AntiVirus™*, shown in Figure 3-1.8, is a popular antivirus program.

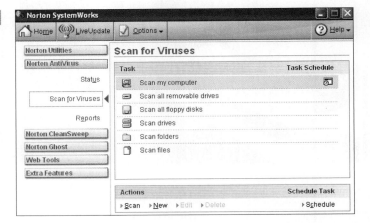

Computer viruses called Trojan horses may be used in creating distributed denial of service (DDOS) attacks. In a DDOS, hackers flood a system with so many requests for connections that the system cannot operate properly or at all. For an e-commerce site, this could mean lost sales while the site is not operating. A loss of customer confidence in using the site can also lead to lost sales in the future. DDOS attacks are illegal, but finding the person who launched the attack is very difficult. Companies can use filtering methods and adjust network settings to help protect against DDOS.

Government agencies and private organizations seek to promote awareness and prevention of computer crimes. US-CERT (United States Computer Emergency Readiness Team) was established in 2003. Its purpose is to protect the nation's Internet systems and coordinate defense against cyber attacks across the nation. The US-CERT Web site, shown in Figure 3-1.9, provides current information on computer viruses, hackers, and related security issues.

proprietary information: privately owned information, such as a design or formula, also called intellectual property

Not all security threats come from outside the company. Employee theft of **proprietary information**, such as product designs, can be costly. Theft of data from a company's information system, such as customer credit card numbers and related data, can be costly for both the company and its customers. The Computer Security Institute (CSI) regularly surveys large companies and government agencies regarding computer crime and security violations. This survey is conducted with the participation of the U.S. Federal Bureau of Investigation. The CSI surveys report that large financial losses result from theft of proprietary information.

Figure **3-1.9**

Source: U.S. Department of Homeland Security, US-CERT. http://www.us-cert.gov/ reading_room/ (accessed July 12, 2005).

Security risks are handled in a variety of ways. Figure 3-1.10 shows a list of typical security measures. All employees should follow the company's security procedures. In spite of security measures, however, companies lose millions of dollars each year to cyber crimes. Because theft of data and loss of service cannot be totally prevented, some companies purchase special insurance policies. These policies help pay for losses that result from cyber crimes. The policies may also cover losses and lawsuits arising from Internet operations.

Typical Security Measures

Figure **3-1.10**

Security Measure	Purpose
Access control	Employees limited to access information within their job responsibilities
	Outsiders prevented from accessing company networks
Identification and authentication	Use of passwords or other identification to check for authorized users
	Use of digital signatures to ensure a transmitted document has not been altered
Accuracy checks	Guard against errors and unauthorized changes
Data scans	Search for computer viruses or other software problems
Data encryption	Seeks to secure transmissions of data
Accountability	Links all activities to the user's identity
Audit trails	Maintain a log of all attempts to gain access to the system, all activity, unusual activity, and variations from established procedures

For Discussion

What types of security measures would help prevent employees from purposely destroying or copying data? Why is it important for employees to keep their passwords and access codes secret?

87

Topic 3-1: *Information Processing*

REVIEWING THE TOPIC

1. Define information.
2. What are the most common forms of information?
3. What effect might use of outdated or incorrect information have on a business?
4. List five obstacles to using information efficiently.
5. Describe the five operations involved in information processing.
6. Describe five common information technologies.
7. Name three general categories of software and describe each one.
8. Explain the difference between a peer-to-peer LAN and a server-based LAN.
9. List three types of transmission carriers used in LANs.
10. How does a WAN differ from a LAN?
11. Explain the difference between a DSL connection and a dial-up connection for WAN transmissions.
12. Why should computer systems be serviced and maintained on a regular basis?
13. List three major security concerns for computer information systems.
14. List three security measures businesses can use to help safeguard information stored in their computer systems.

INTERACTING WITH OTHERS

Kristin and Tyler work together in a small office. One of Tyler's main duties is updating customer account records. He enjoys talking with customers who call to report changes. However, he is not very prompt about updating the customer account database. Kristin's main duty is customer service. When responding to customer concerns, she accesses the customer database for information. Because Tyler failed to update the customer database promptly, Kristin did not have up-to-date information available when she responded to three different customer calls.

1. Explain why it is important for Kristin to have up-to-date information when she responds to customer calls.
2. If you were Kristin, what would you say to Tyler about this issue?

Teaching Tips

If the students are using the *Student Activities and Simulations* workbook, instruct them to complete the review activity for this topic.

For Discussion

After students have considered the alternatives, ask them to share their thoughts with the class.

REINFORCING ENGLISH SKILLS

You work for Craig-Weston Mansion, a small inn in Nova Scotia, located on a bluff above Pandora's Harbor. A member of your work team has asked you to proofread and edit some copy that is to be added to your organization's Web site. These statements contain grammar, spelling, word usage, and punctuation errors that will give a very poor impression of the organization.

1. Open the *Word* file *CH03 English* from the data files.
2. Turn on Track Changes so your team member can see the edits you make. Spell-check and proofread the document. Correct all errors.

DATABASE
RESEARCH

Topic 3-1 : ACTIVITY 1

Equipment Inventory

Office workers are often responsible for keeping an inventory of the computers, software, and other equipment used in the office. Because theft is a serious problem in some companies, having an accurate record of items purchased and assigned to the office is important. Equipment inventories are also used in scheduling equipment maintenance and upgrades. In this activity, you will complete the five operations involved in information processing as you create an inventory record. Because you probably do not currently work in an office, you will create an inventory of the hardware, software, furniture, and other equipment found in your classroom.

1. **Storage.** Create a new database file. Save the file as *Office Equipment*.
2. **Input and storage.** Create a table named **Equipment Inventory.**
   - Include the following fields: Item ID, Item, Description, Quantity, and Condition.
   - Select **AutoNumber** as the field type for the Item ID field and make this field the primary key.
   - Select **Number** as the field type for the Quantity field. Select **Text** as the field type for all other fields.
   - Enter data to create a record for each item (hardware, software, furniture, and other equipment) found in your classroom. Some items, such as software, may have no data in the Condition field.
3. **Processing and storage.** Generate a report from the data to include only the Item ID, Item, and Quantity fields. Sort the data in the report in ascending order by the Item field. Save the report as Equipment Inventory (Date). Use the current date in the name.
4. **Output.** Print the report.
5. **Distribution.** Give the report to your instructor.

Topic Review 89

After students have keyed the paragraphs, discuss the corrections that they should have made.

Assist students as needed with creating the database. Give students instructions regarding the equipment you want them to include in the database.

Teaching Tips

Students may have learned some of the information about the school's LAN from previous discussion questions. You may want to assign students to work in groups to find the answers to specific questions and then share the information with the class.

COMPOSITION
RESEARCH
WORD PROCESSING

Topic **3-1** : ACTIVITY 2

Local Area Networks

Learn about the local area network used in your school or in a local business. Find answers to the questions listed below regarding the LAN in your school. If your school does not have a LAN or if your teacher so instructs, interview someone from a local business that uses a LAN. Create a short report that gives the name of the organization you are researching and summarizes your findings.

- What physical area does the LAN cover?
- Does the LAN use peer-to-peer or server-based networking?
- What types of cabling does the LAN use (twisted pair, coaxial, fiber-optic)?
- Are any wireless connections used on the LAN? If yes, describe.
- What types of equipment (computers, printers, scanners, etc.) are connected to the LAN?
- Approximately how many computers are connected to the LAN?
- Approximately how many people use the LAN?
- Are users required to enter a password to log on to the LAN?
- What other types of security measures are used with the LAN?
- Can users access the Internet through the LAN? If yes, is firewall software used?
- What are the primary uses of the LAN (storing data files, providing users with access to programs, etc.)?

O Identify typical information systems used in
business

O Describe traditional
information resources

O Describe electronic information resources

O Describe how the Inter-
net affects the way busi-
nesses acquire, use, and
share information

Information technology refers to the computer equipment and software
used to process information. Technology is only one part of managing
information. Managing information effectively also includes people
who follow procedures to run the information technology efficiently.
An information system is composed of people, the information technology and resources, and procedures used to process information.

Typical Information Systems

Information systems help employees work efficiently. The information
systems found in a company relate to business activities such as
accounting or manufacturing. Three typical information systems are
described in the following paragraphs to help you understand how businesses use information systems. Often, the systems in a company work
together or are part of an overall system.

Accounting Information Systems

An accounting information system is used to record transactions and create
financial reports. These reports give information about many aspects of the
business such as expenses, accounts receivable, and income. The following
list gives examples of how employees in a small business would use this
information to make decisions or process work.

- A billing clerk prepares invoices and computes amounts due.
- The Credit Department manager approves credit for a customer.
- The **controller** prepares the annual budget and recommends ways
  to increase profits.

Marketing Information Systems

A marketing information system helps the business keep track of customers.
Data are recorded from an initial contact, to the point of the sale or service,
to a customer satisfaction follow-up. The data provided by marketing information systems identify whether or not:

- A particular marketing approach is successful
- A customer is satisfied with the product or service
- A customer intends to make future purchases from the company

Product Information Systems

If a business manufactures a product, it must determine the cost of goods it
sells. The activities that take place within the business to create the product
are recorded in the information system. This system contains the cost of

controller: an employee
who oversees company
finances

overhead: business costs not directly related to a product or service sold

materials, labor, and **overhead**. The information stored in this system is used to help determine the cost of the product. The following examples illustrate how different people access the information system in a manufacturing firm:

- A stock control clerk checks the inventory of raw materials and processes a purchase order to replenish stock.
- A receiving clerk scans bar code labels on incoming shipments to create a record of goods received.
- A production manager locates purchase order data for goods used to calculate production costs.
- A production worker completes an assembly operation. A part number is scanned to enter the quantity of completed products.
- An accounts payable clerk verifies invoices and receipt of goods before approving payment for purchases.
- A department manager uses prior months' financial data in creating a budget.

Bar code labels are used in creating a record of goods received.

© GETTY IMAGES/PHOTODISC

Traditional Resources

Companies can get information from many sources. Much of the information a business uses comes from within the company. You have already learned about some typical information systems. Businesses can also get information from outside sources. Some of these sources are described in the following paragraphs.

Marketing Research Firms

Marketing research firms offer data in a variety of forms for business needs. They focus on the customer and the market. Marketing research firms use questionnaires and interviews to gather information about consumer behaviors and attitudes. They also look at marketing trends and collect valuable **demographic data**. Researchers collect a variety of data. They use computers to analyze huge amounts of data and forecast market conditions.

Companies often rely on the information provided by marketing research firms. Doing market research might be too costly for a small-business owner. A large company might be able to afford to do research. However, the company could save valuable time by using the information already gathered by a research firm.

demographic data: statistics that describe a population such as age or race

Trade Publications and Associations

Many companies use trade publications, books, and journals for facts and forecasts about their industry. They provide good information about the products, service area, or industry in which the business specializes. Trade associations often conduct or sponsor research related to the industry. Association meetings and workshops provide an opportunity to talk with others who have similar interests or concerns. Conventions or trade shows provide an opportunity to view new products and services designed for the industry.

Government Agencies and Libraries

Data from government agencies are useful to many companies. Government publications often include forecasts and results from research studies. The Small Business Administration (see Figure 3-2.1) and the U.S. Census Bureau are examples of sources that provide demographics, statistics, and other data useful in making business decisions.

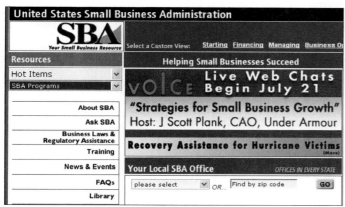

Source: United States Small Business Administration. http://www.sba.gov/ (accessed July 13, 2005).

Figure 3-2.1

The Small Business Administration provides data helpful to businesses.

WORKPLACE CONNECTIONS

A company that makes toys is interested in the demographics of a particular region. The company considers data about the number of people within a certain age range in an area. This helps the company decide whether to advertise its products in that region. If a large number of people are under the age of twelve, then toys could probably be marketed with success. On the other hand, if the number of people under the age of twelve is small, the advertising money might be better spent in another region.

University libraries are an excellent information resource. Many offer research services and specialized publications not readily available elsewhere. Some companies also have libraries. Many of these libraries also specialize in research.

Electronic Resources

With advancements in information technology come new sources of information and new ways to access the information. Electronic resources, often called online resources, are those available via a computer. Online resources are becoming more popular because of the wide range of available information and the instant access to the information.

Electronic Databases

A database is a collection of related data. Use of electronic databases has grown rapidly in the past few years. Electronic databases are available on CD, DVD, and the Internet. Online services are provided by companies such as CompuServe. These databases provide information on many topics useful to businesses. Most electronic databases have powerful search features. These features allow the user to find data quickly and easily.

Some databases support natural language searches. This means that the user simply enters a question in everyday terms. The database search feature interprets and answers the question. No special searching techniques or rules are needed. The Help feature of programs such as *Microsoft Excel*, shown in Figure 3-2.2, allows users to search in this manner.

relational database: a software program that allows the user to link data from a number of database files or tables to find information or generate reports

data mining: a process in which a software program searches for significant patterns in data

Companies often have relational databases as part of their internal information system. **Relational databases** allow the user to link data from a number of database tables to find data or generate reports. This linking capability means that data can be stored in relatively small tables that are easy to work with. Data updated in one table or file can be used to update other tables easily.

Data mining is a process that helps businesses analyze the data contained in databases. With automated data mining, the program searches for interesting and significant patterns of data in the database. The data are then

CHAPTER 3: INFORMATION: A VITAL BUSINESS RESOURCE

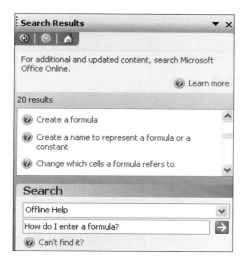

Figure **3-2.2**

The Microsoft Excel *help database supports natural language searches.*

presented in graphs, reports, and so forth. The user can look at the data from several viewpoints. The results may reveal information the user never considered. Data mining can be used to help a business target consumers and predict market trends.

Personal Digital Assistants

A personal digital assistant (PDA) provides another means for retrieving information. PDAs can be used to store a variety of data, from a list of schedules and appointments to photos to a reference text. Versions of word processing, spreadsheet, e-mail, and other application programs are available for PDAs. Figure 3-2.3 shows menu screens from a PDA. Notice the types of programs available. Some PDAs have built-in cameras or voice recorders.

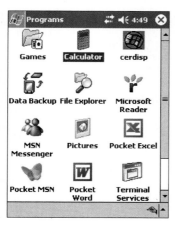

Figure **3-2.3**

Many programs are available for PDAs.

95

Topic 3-2: *Information Systems and Resources*

Consider this example of how healthcare workers use PDAs:

Healthcare workers need access to clinical data. They also refer to medical resources, decision aids, and other professional information. A PDA can be used to access this data. A small memory card that fits into the PDA can be used to provide additional information or programs. A medical calculator program can be used for standard calculations. The healthcare workers have immediate access to reference material where and when they need it.

Intranets

Intranets are internal networks based on Internet technologies and standards. The intranet may reside on a company's local area network or be part of a wide area network. An intranet is designed for users within a company and is protected by a firewall. A firewall works in two ways. First, it blocks outsiders from entering the company's intranet. Second, it allows company intranet users to access the Internet. Only those users who have registered and/or received passwords are given access to an intranet.

Intranets allow workers to share data quickly and easily. The data can be used to make decisions and serve customers effectively. An intranet can be used to keep employees informed about the company's products, procedures, and activities. An Employee Handbook screen from an intranet is shown in Figure 3-2.4.

Intranets have many uses within companies. They allow data such as production schedules to be updated quickly. They reduce the need for printed documents, which saves money. They provide quick access to data such as catalogs, price lists, product manuals, and shipping information. Job openings for which employees may apply may be posted on an intranet. Employees may be able to complete forms such as expense reports using an intranet.

The U.S. workforce is increasingly mobile. More workers than ever are on the road on a regular basis or work from home offices. With a notebook computer and modem, these workers can easily access the company intranet and interact with coworkers. Consider these examples of intranet use.

- Using an intranet, a company sends sales data daily to 400 salespeople. The data were previously sent by overnight mail.
- An import firm with offices around the world sends data on product availability to the home office via the intranet.
- A technology firm links research efforts by engineers in Europe, Asia, and the United States via the company intranet.
- Employees access training programs and find answers to frequently asked questions while away from the office via the intranet.

Figure **3-2.4**

Intranets provide cur-rent information to employees.

HUMAN RESOURCES

Employee Handbook

This Employee Handbook is an outline of your privileges and obligations as an employee and should be your primary reference. This handbook is not intended to be a comprehensive treatment of any topic or policy and is subject to change as circumstances warrant. When you have questions about policies or procedures outlined in this manual, refer them to your manager or contact the Human Resources Department.

Choose a link to learn more about the company's policies and procedures.

Attendance
At-Will Employment
Company Overview and Mission
Compensation and Employee Benefits
Confidentiality Policy
Drug and Alcohol Policy
Equal Opportunity Employment

WORKPLACE CONNECTIONS

The use of intranets has helped businesses achieve better results by making current information available. Prior to using an intranet, a national sales firm had problems with customer satisfaction. Price quotes to customers often were outdated. Items promised for immediate delivery were often not available to be shipped right away. Sales personnel had to call the home office to get current price quotes. They had to wait for faxes or returned e-mails about their customers' orders. Sales were declining.

In an effort to solve these problems, the company installed an intranet. The intranet pro-vides a central source of data for all sales associates. Location or the time of day does not affect sales quotes. Now, the sales associates have immediate access to the company's intranet for real-time price quotes, stock inventory, delivery schedules, and product details. Sales are increasing.

The technology needed to develop an intranet is getting less expensive and easier to use. In the future, more companies may make an intranet part of their information system.

The Internet

The Internet, a giant network of computers and smaller networks that spans the globe, is the world's largest information resource. Using the Internet, businesses can connect with other people, organizations, and information resources quickly and easily. The Internet is used for research, transferring files, exchanging messages, promoting organizations, advertising products and services, and buying and selling products.

For Discussion

Ask students to discuss the problems encountered by the company and how installing an intranet solved them. Also, discuss the additional benefits received by the users such as increased job satisfaction and productivity.

For Discussion

Ask students to share their experiences using the Inter-net. Ask students how they have used the Internet. Answers might include to e-mail friends, play games, use chat rooms, download music, or to research topics.

97

Topic 3-2: *Information Systems and Resources*

FOCUS ON . . .

Intranets to Extranets

Many companies use intranets to provide current information to employees. Some businesses also use an extranet. An **extranet** is an information network like an intranet, but it is partially available to select outside users. An extranet uses a firewall to provide limited access to users outside the company.

Many extranets have grown from the use of a company's intranet. For example, Federal Express began tracking the receipt and delivery of packages years ago through its mainframe system. An employee would key data to locate a package while the customer waited on the telephone. Now, Federal Express has an extranet. Customers can access it via the Internet and track their packages. Users enter their package ID number to retrieve the tracking information quickly.

Banks, insurance companies, investment firms, and schools are frequent users of extranets. In these instances, outside users look for information related to themselves. They gain access to the extranet with some form of password or ID number. The extranet can also link business partners with one another by linking their intranets. For example, a company may provide access to engineers from partner firms who are working on design projects.

By using the Internet, intranets, and extranets, companies can provide information to employees and customers. Changes can be made quickly to keep data current. Costs are lowered by reducing the number of paper documents. The use of intranets and extranets helps to keep both employees and customers better informed.

extranet: an information network like an intranet, but partially available to select outside users

The following examples describe a few ways that businesses use the Internet.

- Through electronic mail, coworkers are able to communicate with each other. Workers can send messages from their office or home or on the road.
- An office worker plans an out-of-state trip. The airline reservations are made using a travel service on the Internet.
- An investment broker accesses information on the Internet to get up-to-the-minute stock quotes.
- A small-business owner uses a Web site to sell sports items such as baseball trading cards, league pennants, autographed products, and T-shirts.
- A civic organization uses a Web site to provide information about the organization. It lists upcoming events and posts public service messages.
- A clothing maker provides product information on a company Web site. Customers can order products and track the progress of orders that have been placed.

Finding and Sharing Information

The Internet is loaded with information about many topics. Finding the specific information you need among the large amount of data available may be a challenge. Programs are available to help you search for information on the Internet. Printed directories containing popular or interesting Internet addresses may be purchased.

Web Browsers

Knowing where and how to look for information is basic to using electronic resources. With the increased use of the Internet, browser software programs have become very popular. Browsers provide navigation and search tools to help you find topics and locations on the World Wide Web.

URLs (Uniform Resource Locators) are Internet addresses that can be understood by any Web browser as it searches for **hypertext** documents on computers around the world. URL addresses start with *http://*, which stands for *HyperText Transfer Protocol*. This is a set of instructions telling computers how to send and receive hypertext data and documents. The *www* in the URL stands for *World Wide Web*. Periods in the URL are separators and are pronounced *dot*. The last letters in the URL represent the domain name. Some common domain names are *edu* for education, *org* for organization, *com* for commercial, and *gov* for government. Other parts of the URL identify sections or levels within the Web site.

hypertext: highlighted, underlined, or contrast-colored words or images that, when clicked, take the user to another location

A two-letter country code is used at the end of some addresses. Every country has its own unique geographic domain code. For example, *uk* is used for the United Kingdom and *mx* is used for Mexico. If there is no geographic code in a name, then the domain is located within your own country. Some examples of URL addresses are shown below. Can you guess the information you might find at these addresses?

- http://www.harvard.edu/admissions   (Harvard University, Admissions)
- http://www.redcross.org   (The American Red Cross)
- http://www.delta.com   (Delta Airlines)
- http://www.dol.gov   (U.S. Department of Labor)
- http://canada.gc.ca   (Government of Canada, official site)

When you want to visit a location on the Internet, you may do so by entering the URL address in your browser. Pay close attention to spelling, punctuation, symbols, and capitalization when entering the address. URLs are sensitive to the use of upper- and lowercase letters. You may also move to a different location on the Internet by clicking a hyperlink. When you use hyperlinks, the associated URLs are often invisible. You merely click on the hyperlink, and your browser takes you to the Internet address (URL) that is associated with that hyperlink.

Browsers help you locate information from several information sources. Though the programs vary in appearance, they offer many of the same features. Examples of browsers include *Netscape®* and *Microsoft® Internet Explorer. Internet Explorer* is shown in Figure 3-2.5. The lines of text shown in blue and underlined in the figure are hyperlinks.

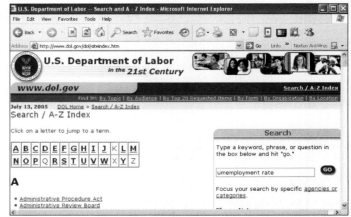

Source: U.S. Department of Labor. http://www.dol.gov/dol/siteindex.htm (accessed July 13, 2005).

Search Tools

If you are looking for information about job opportunities, doing research for work or hobbies, or planning a trip, you might need help finding Internet sites that relate to these activities. Many search tools, often referred to as search engines, can help you locate sites. You may be familiar with some widely used search engines such as Google®, AltaVista®, Lycos®, WebCrawler®, or Yahoo!®. Once you find a Web site, you can use the site's search tool to find information on the site. Search tools for the U.S. Department of Labor's Web site are shown in Figure 3-2.5.

To perform a search on most Web sites, simply identify and type two or three keywords related to the topic and then click the search button. The search tool will locate sites/documents, called "matches" or "hits," that contain these keywords. Your search may result in no matches, several matches, or thousands of matches. If your search results in a large number of matches, you may want to use more specific keywords to locate the information. On the other hand, if you receive only a few hits, you may have to broaden your search by using more general keywords. You may need to use several search tools to perform a thorough search because not all search tools look at every site that may contain the information you need.

Transferring Files

Millions of files are available on the Internet—research papers and data, software, pictures, sounds, and more. Perhaps a software vendor is offering a free update or "patch" to correct a problem for a software product. The publisher of your textbook may have a site offering student data files or special software tutorials. You may have to research a particular topic at work. You search for information about the topic with Yahoo!, Google, or other search tools. When you find sites with data you would like to use, what do you do? You can transfer or download many of these files from a distant computer to your computer by using something called file transfer protocol.

CHAPTER 3: INFORMATION: A VITAL BUSINESS RESOURCE

Teaching Tips

Continue your demonstration on using a browser by doing a search using the browser's search feature. Also do searches using some of the search engines listed in the chapter. Emphasize the importance of using appropriate search criteria—neither too broad nor too specific.

For Discussion

Ask students to share their experiences doing Web searches. Which search engines have they used, and for what type of information were they searching?

Thinking Critically

Ask students to list additional situations in which transferring files between computers might be needed.

File transfer protocol (FTP) is a powerful tool that allows a copy of the file you request from a remote computer to be copied to your computer. There are two types of FTP transfers—private and anonymous. In a private FTP transfer, you must have permission to access and download files. A private user name or account number and password are needed before you can download files (copy from) or upload files (copy to) to the remote computer. In an anonymous FTP transfer, the site can be accessed easily without privately issued user names or passwords. Thousands of anonymous sites are open to everyone.

file transfer protocol: a tool that allows files to be uploaded to or downloaded from a remote computer

E-Mail, Mailing Lists, and Newsgroups

E-mail, mailing lists, and newsgroups all provide means for communicating and sharing information via the Internet.

E-Mail

One popular use of the Internet is electronic mail, or e-mail. E-mail is the electronic transfer of messages. LANs and WANs offer e-mail to all computers that are connected, whether they are in the same office or in different countries. Users are limited to sending and receiving messages only to and from those on their network unless their network is connected to the Internet. If they are connected to the Internet, they can send and receive messages all over the world.

e-mail: the electronic transfer of messages using computers and software

E-mail messages contain text. Some programs also allow the message to contain audio and graphics. Files may be attached to an e-mail message as shown in Figure 3-2.6. These files may contain data such as research findings, corporate financial statements, or client databases. When an e-mail file

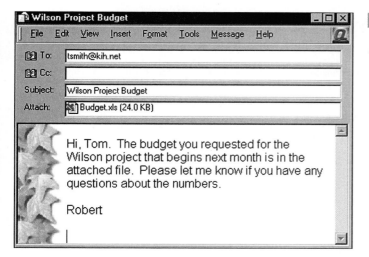

Figure **3-2.6**

This e-mail message has a file attachment.

For Discussion

What is the difference between a private and an anonymous FTP transfer?

Thinking Critically

Why has e-mail become such a vital business tool? Why is e-mail often used rather than placing a phone call or sending documents by the postal service?

Points to Emphasize

When students make attachments to e-mails they should use a file compression utility like *WinZip®* to reduce the size of the large file attachments. Large attachments can take a long time to download, and the mailboxes provided by some ISPs are not large enough to handle large attachments.

is received, it is stored in a user's electronic mailbox. An e-mail mailbox is an online computer storage space used to hold electronic messages. These messages may be read, saved for later reference, printed, or deleted. E-mail is inexpensive, fast, and easy to use for workers at all levels in organizations. You will learn more about using e-mail in Chapter 4.

Mailing Lists

mailing list: a directory of Internet user addresses

A **mailing list** is a directory of Internet user addresses. Some mailing lists are used by businesses while other lists are private. The user subscribes to the mailing list to receive messages. The messages are usually related to a certain product or topic. An option may be provided with the messages to have the user's address removed from the mailing list.

Newsgroups

newsgroup: a publication of online articles and messages related to a certain topic

When people want to share ideas and information with others on the Internet, they can do so via Usenet. Usenet, which stands for User's Network, is a collection of topically organized newsgroups. A **newsgroup** publishes online articles and messages related to a topic. Users take part in online talks about a topic by sending messages. All participants in the newsgroup can read the message. Newsgroups are available for thousands of topics.

Promoting Organizations

Many organizations are going online for promotion purposes. For example, many colleges have sites with information about their programs. Potential students visit the sites. They are able to compare courses, costs, and other aspects of campus life to help them choose a school.

Many states and cities have Web sites. The sites promote tourism and industry in the area. They typically include general information about the area and a calendar of events. Links to area hotels, restaurants, and other businesses are often included.

Civic and charitable organizations also use Web sites. The sites provide information about the mission and goals of the organization. They advertise special events and encourage contributing to the organization.

Many companies promote their products on Web sites. If the company does not sell products directly to consumers, the Web site usually gives a list of retail stores where the products may be purchased. The site may also show information such as the company's mission and goals, the history of the company, and the structure of the company.

Figure **3-2.7**

The state of Colorado promotes tourism on its Web site.

Source: State of Colorado. http://www.colorado.gov/colorado-visiting-activities/nature-outdoors.html (accessed July 13, 2005).

E-Commerce—Buying and Selling Online

Businesses are changing the ways they acquire, use, and share information. The amazing growth of the Internet is part of the reason for this change. For example, customers who buy online may provide data about themselves to the company. This data is called a customer profile. Companies may also build their store of data about online customers by using cookies. Cookies are messages exchanged by the user's Web browser and the Web server being visited. They can be used to track the user's identity and online behavior.

The data from online customers allow the business to study buying habits. Then the company can suggest related products that may be of interest to a customer. Amazon.com, one of the most successful e-commerce companies, uses this technique. When you purchase a book or movie from the company's Web site, the site suggests other titles that may be of interest to you. Using customer data to target advertising can increase sales.

Consumer trust in the company is very important in e-commerce. Companies want to build customer trust and loyalty. They offer services such as online support and order shipment tracking. Online newsletters about their products may also be offered. By using the Internet to share information with customers, they strengthen their relationships with customers.

For Discussion

Ask students to share their experiences about purchasing items online with the class. Relate your experiences to the class.

Thinking Critically

What do you think are some of the reasons for the phenomenal growth of the Internet?

Expand the Concept

When purchasing items online, students should make sure that they are keying confidential information such as bank card numbers into a secure site. Normally, a message pops up telling the customer that they will be transferred to a secure site to complete the transaction. Another indication that you are on a secure site is seeing an icon resembling a closed padlock on the status bar on your screen.

103

Topic 3-2: *Information Systems and Resources*

Figure **3-2.8**

A Web site's privacy policy discusses how customer data will be used.

THOMSON

ABOUT US
PRODUCTS & SOLUTIONS
PRESS ROOM
INVESTOR RELATIONS
CAREERS
CONTACT US

Home :

Privacy Statement

This Privacy Statement relates solely to the online information collection and use practices of our Web site located at www.thomson.com (this "Web Site"), and not to any subdomains of this Web Site. We recognize that many visitors and users of this Web Site are concerned about the information they provide to us, and how we treat that information. This Privacy Statement, which may be updated from time to time, has been developed to address those concerns.

Source: Thomson Corporation. http://www.thomson.com/corp/privacy.jsp (accessed July 13, 2005).

Privacy of customer data is an area of concern related to e-commerce. Will the company share data such as a customer's name, e-mail address, and buying habits with other companies? Many companies have privacy statements on their Web sites. A privacy statement tells how customer data will be used. These statements can reassure customers and help build their trust.

E-commerce has created a lack of geographic boundaries for many businesses. This brings new challenges in communicating and sharing information with people of many countries and cultures. Web sites must be designed to be attractive and easy to use for all customers. Product instructions, warranties, and customer support may be needed in several languages. Marketing personnel may need to study the cultures of their new customers to learn how to create appealing advertisements.

Just a few aspects of information related to e-commerce have been described in this section. As Internet use and e-commerce continue to grow, companies will need to adapt to new ways of acquiring, using, and sharing information.

For Discussion

What considerations for communicating and sharing information are associated with e-commerce?

REVIEWING THE TOPIC

1. What kinds of information does an accounting information system provide?
2. Give two examples of how people access information from a product information system.
3. List and briefly describe three traditional external resources where companies get information.
4. Describe two advantages of using a relational database.
5. What is data mining?
6. How is an intranet similar to the Internet? How is it different from the Internet?
7. List four activities for which businesses use the Internet.
8. Describe the purpose of Web browser software programs.
9. What is hypertext, and how do hypertext links work?
10. What is a URL?
11. How does a Web browser differ from a search engine?
12. What is file transfer protocol?
13. Give two examples of how organizations promote themselves using Web sites.
14. Give two examples of how an e-commerce business can use information to build consumer trust.
15. Describe how the Internet affects the way businesses acquire, use, and share information.

INTERACTING WITH OTHERS

While completing some tasks to meet a deadline, you noticed that a member of your sales team, Jeremy, was using the computer at his workstation to download copyrighted clip art. You observed him pasting the clip art into the department's online newsletter and posting it on the company's Web site. When you asked Jeremy about his activities, he shrugged and said that no one should mind because the chances of his getting caught were very slim. And besides, he was not really hurting anyone.

What should you do?

- Let the matter drop and ignore his illegal actions.
- Inform your supervisor about Jeremy's use of the Internet.
- Send an e-mail message to Jeremy condemning him for his actions.
- Talk with Jeremy again and list reasons why you think his behavior is inappropriate.

Teaching Tips

If the students are using the *Student Activities and Simulations* workbook, instruct them to complete the review activity for this topic.

For Discussion

Allow students to share their answers to this activity in a class discussion.

continued

1. Prepare a written response to each of the four suggested actions.
2. If you feel there is another action that would be more effective, describe the action.

REINFORCING MATH SKILLS

You work for an organization that gives training seminars on various topics. Recently, the company completed a series of seminars in five cities. The fee for each person at three of the seminars was $1,000. At two of the seminars (Update on Virtual Meetings and Using PDAs) the fee for each person was $500. You were given the task of e-mailing the manager of each seminar site and getting enrollment figures for the courses. The details you recorded are shown below.

1. Record the title of each of the five seminars on a separate line. Calculate and record the following:
   - The total number of participants for each seminar
   - The grand total number of participants for all seminars
   - The total revenue earned from each seminar
   - The grand total of all revenue received
   - The total number of participants in each city
2. Identify the seminar with the largest total number of participants and the seminar producing the largest total revenue.

	PARTICIPANTS				
Seminar and Date	**Boston**	**New York**	**Washington**	**Chicago**	**San Francisco**
Data Mining January 6–10	125	245	110	117	97
Managing Databases February 15–18	105	325	175	130	110
Security for the Internet March 1–4	78	110	45	72	70
Update on Virtual Meetings March 19–22	170	295	140	110	115
Using PDAs April 1–2	210	410	175	102	117

Encourage students to refer to Section D in the Reference Section of the *Student Activities and Simulations* workbook, if available, to review math skills.

Topic 3-2 : ACTIVITY 1

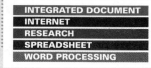

Internet Use Report

Research current Internet use numbers. Then key a report highlighting the information.

1. Open and print the PDF file *CH03 Internet Use* from the data files. This file contains the report. Follow the formatting instructions written on the document. Correct any spelling or word usage errors you find in the document.

2. Search the Internet to find current Internet use numbers. Update the reference at the end of the report to reflect your source of information. (If you do not have access to the Internet, use the numbers provided in the report.)

3. Create a pie chart using your spreadsheet software to show Internet use by language groups. Copy the chart into the report.

Topic 3-2 : ACTIVITY 2

DATABASE

Update Equipment Inventory

Update the equipment inventory database you created in Topic 3-1 Activity 1.

1. Assume the following equipment changes have been made in your classroom:
   - Two new Lexmark inkjet printers in good condition have been added.
   - Three desks have been removed.

2. Update the inventory using this information.

3. Print a new report showing the Item ID, Item, and Quantity fields for all records.

4. Create a query to find only records with "desk" in the Item field. Display all fields in the query. Print the query results.

5. Give the updated report and the query results to your instructor.

CHAPTER REVIEW 3

Teaching Tips

Have students review key points from the chapter by completing the Beat the Clock game on *The Office* Web site.

Summary

Information is important to businesses and other organizations. They use information to make decisions. Companies give a great deal of attention to managing information effectively. Businesses depend on information systems composed of people, technology, resources, and procedures for processing the information. Key points in this chapter include:

- The common types of information found in businesses are numbers, text, image, and voice.
- When information is managed effectively, organizations can operate efficiently. If information is not current or not accurate, a business may make poor decisions that could prove costly.
- Incompatible databases, duplicate or missing information, or limited access to information are examples of obstacles to using information efficiently.
- The information processing workflow consists of five operations: input, processing, output, distribution, and storage.
- Information technologies improve the workflow and communication in companies, and technology can even give a company a competitive edge.
- Computerized processing relies heavily on hardware and related software to turn data into meaningful and timely information.
- Software may be divided into three broad categories: operating system software, application software, and utility software.
- Local area networks (LANs) and wide area networks (WANs) help workers complete their daily tasks and share information.
- Office workers must be concerned with maintenance, security, and ethics related to information processing.
- Information systems found in business relate to typical business operations such as accounting or manufacturing.
- Traditional information resources include marketing research firms, trade publications and associations, and government agencies.
- Advancements in information technology provide new sources of information and new ways to access the information. Examples include electronic databases, the Internet, intranets, and extranets.
- Using the Internet, businesses can connect quickly and easily with other people, businesses, organizations, and information resources around the world.
- Tools such as Web browsers, search engines, file transfer protocol, e-mail, mailing lists, and newsgroups help workers find and share information.

■ Many organizations maintain Web sites to promote the organization or sell products or services online. As Internet use and e-commerce continue to grow, companies will need to adapt to new ways of acquiring, using, and sharing information.

Key Terms

CD	hypertext	modem
computer virus	incompatible	newsgroup
controller	information	overhead
data mining	processing	proprietary
demographic data	interactive voice	information
DVD	response	relational database
electronic imaging	Internet service	sales channel
e-mail	provider	satellite
extranet	local area network	software
file transfer protocol	mailing list	transaction
firewall	microwave	USB flash drive
hardware	transmission	wide area network

Chapter 3 : ACTIVITY 1

COMPOSITION
INTERNET
RESEARCH
TEAMWORK
WORD PROCESSING

Privacy Policies

Privacy of customer data is a concern for many consumers. Most well-established online companies post a privacy policy on the company Web site. This policy tells the user what the company will do with consumer data. Work with a classmate to explore the privacy policies of major online companies.

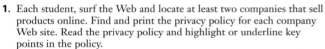

1. Each student, surf the Web and locate at least two companies that sell products online. Find and print the privacy policy for each company Web site. Read the privacy policy and highlight or underline key points in the policy.

2. As a team, discuss the key points identified by each student. Write a short report that lists the companies for which the team found privacy statements and summarizes the key points identified in the statements. In the report, discuss how the policies are similar and how they are different. List the companies to which you would be comfortable giving personal data. Then list the ones to which you would not want to give information about yourself. Explain the reasons for your choices.

109

Chapter Review

Teaching Tips

Have students review the key terms by using the Flashcards available on *The Office* Web site.

Teaching Tips

Assign students to work in a team with one other student to complete this activity. Allow students to discuss their findings with the class.

Computer Security Tips

Key a document containing computer security tips as a bulleted list that can be posted on a bulletin board or Web site.

1. Open and print the data file *CH03 Security Tips*, which contains the rough draft document.

2. Key the document with a 1.5-inch top margin and 1-inch side margins. Center and bold the title lines in all caps. Double space (DS) after the title. Key the paragraphs and then apply bullets to create bulleted paragraphs. Apply bold to the first sentence of each bulleted paragraph for emphasis. Correct errors in spelling or word usage as you key the document. Proofread carefully and correct all errors before printing the document.

© GETTY IMAGES/PHOTODISC

CHAPTER 4

Communicating in Written Form

This chapter focuses on reading and preparing written messages at work. Many business messages are in written form. Their preparation is a time-consuming task. The ability to read and understand written documents is a vital skill for all types of office workers.

In this chapter, you will learn strategies for improving your reading skills. You will also learn to create effective business documents. You will prepare effective business letters, memos, reports, and related documents.

111

Topic 4-1

objectives

- Describe the kinds of reading common at work
- Identify critical components of reading skills
- Explain common techniques for improving reading skills
- Describe the nature of writing tasks common at work
- Describe the characteristics of effective written messages
- Describe an effective procedure for managing a writing task

READING AND WRITING AT WORK

Most jobs in today's business world require reading and writing. People have different job responsibilities. A reasonable conclusion, however, is that those who work must have adequate reading and writing skills. In this topic, you will learn to improve your reading skills.

Reading at Work

On many occasions you will need to read on the job. You will find that reading is vital to understanding the total company in which you work. You will also need to read to complete your work tasks.

Learning About Your Company

Employees who want to understand how their work relates to the total company can read about the company in memos, newsletters, and other documents.

WORKPLACE CONNECTIONS

A new receptionist describes how reading helped her learn about her company:

I knew little about this company when I came here to work six months ago as a receptionist/clerk. How could I be able to answer questions of callers if I was completely uninformed about the company? We were introduced to the company and received some brochures about our products during our orientation day. That was helpful, but I wanted to know more. So I asked for copies of the last three annual reports and for any historical information available. I learned we have a small company library. When there are lulls in my work or when I am having coffee in the snack bar alone, I generally find something to read related to the company. I also read every announcement that is sent from the office of the president and other bulletins from our Department of Public Affairs.

Many policies and procedures related to your job will be available in written form. A manager may explain how a particular task is to be done or what policies are to be followed. You will find it helpful, though, to

CHAPTER 4: COMMUNICATING IN WRITTEN FORM

read the written version of what was presented. You read to have a thorough understanding of what you are to do. From time to time, memos related to ways of doing tasks or changes in policies are sent to employees. Such correspondence should be read and filed for easy reference later.

An informed employee works more effectively.

Understanding Instructions

Employees are often provided new equipment and software at work. They must read and follow the written instructions for these items. For example, an employee may need help learning to use speech recognition. The Microphone Wizard, shown in Figure 4-1.1, provides instructions regarding how to position the headset microphone properly.

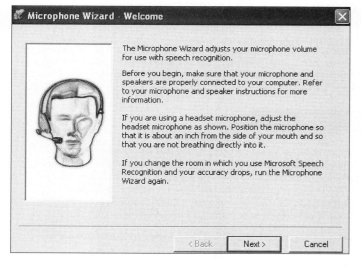

Figure **4-1.1**

Written instructions for using a headset microphone.

Why do you think it is important to learn about the company you are working for? Why is it important to read and understand the policies and procedures of your employer?

Employees who thoroughly understand the information related to their job are invaluable.

Demonstrations of new equipment are helpful. However, you can reinforce your understanding of how to use equipment by becoming familiar with the written instructions available.

113

Topic 4-1: *Reading and Writing at Work*

Businesses develop forms to use in collecting data. You will find forms for such tasks as recording telephone messages, reporting travel expenses, and submitting time reports. Reading all instructions on forms is very important. Try to provide all information requested. If some data are not needed or are not available, a comment should be added. Figure 4-1.2 shows a telephone message recorded on a form. What information did the person who recorded the message fail to add?

Figure 4-1.2

A message should include all necessary information to respond to the call.

To	Maria Perez		
Date	11/1	Time	9:15 a.m.

WHILE YOU WERE OUT

M s. Kim Yung

of Central Bank

Phone (272) 555-0134   Extension _____

Telephoned	X	Please Call	X
Called to See You		Will Call Again	
Wants to See You		**URGENT**	
Returned a Call			

Message _____
Needs additional details
_____
_____
_____

Responding to Inquiries

Many employees must respond to questions from other workers or customers. The questions will vary. Employees are not expected to know every answer from memory. Employees are expected to know where to find the answers promptly. Once the material is located, the worker needs to read quickly and accurately to find the information.

WORKPLACE CONNECTIONS

Linda works in customer services for a mail-order company that sells a variety of items related to books, such as bookcases, lamps, and reading tables. Linda often receives specific questions. For example: "I have a bookcase that is not the exact size as the one you advertise. I need a bookcase to place on top of the one I have. So I need to know what your bookcase's exact dimensions are. Can you help me?" Linda is able to access the product database quickly and provide the caller with the correct information.

114

CHAPTER 4: COMMUNICATING IN WRITTEN FORM

Using Written References/Databases

Office workers use a variety of references. References commonly found in many offices are dictionaries, atlases, telephone directories, and policy and procedures manuals. Data may be stored in databases or other electronic formats. The company may subscribe to online information services. Dictionaries and telephone directories are also available online. You will be expected to become familiar with all sources available and know where to search when requests are made. You will also want to develop references to aid you in your specific duties.

For example, an office worker who takes trips to other countries might need to know about the exchange rate for currencies. This information can be found online. Several Web sites have convenient currency calculators or converters. The office worker might create bookmarks to use in accessing such sites quickly as shown Figure 4-1.3.

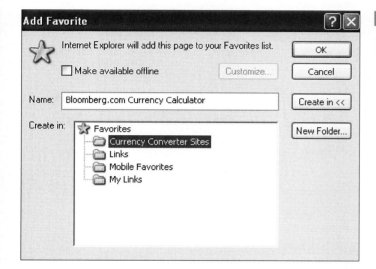

Figure **4-1.3**

Bookmark for a Web site

Improving Reading Skills

High-level reading skills will help you be more productive at work. For this reason, adopt a positive attitude toward improving your reading skills. Strive for reading skills that are so natural you need not give deliberate attention to the reading task itself. Instead, you can focus on the content of what you are reading. Critical skills for high-level reading are comprehension, vocabulary, and speed.

Thinking Critically

Why is it important to become familiar with all reference sources found in the office in which you work? Why is it important to learn how to use the reference sources?

Points to Emphasize

A positive attitude about reading and the subject matter is an important first step toward developing natural reading skills.

115

Topic 4-1: *Reading and Writing at Work*

Comprehension

comprehension: the ability to understand concepts or material that has been read

Comprehension is the ability to understand what you have read. It involves a transfer of information from the printed page or the computer screen to your memory. A simple example is keeping in mind a number that you have just found in the telephone directory. A more complex example is reading about a supplier's new product and being able to tell whether the product appears superior to the brand your company is currently using. Some techniques you may find helpful as you strive to increase reading comprehension are listed in Figure 4-1.4.

Figure **4-1.4**

Improving Reading Comprehension

Focus	Put aside anything else on your mind when you begin to read.
Identify purpose	Before you begin, ask: "What do I want to know when I have completed this reading?"
Scan	Get an overview of the page, the chapter, article, or book before you read carefully.
Summarize	Mentally summarize as you move from one paragraph to another, particularly if you are reading to gain information for handling a task.
Sequence	After reading several paragraphs, try to think of the ideas in an appropriate order.
Draw a mental picture	Attempt to imagine what it is that is being discussed.
Checkup	Determine, through a fast review of key points, whether you have learned what you expected to learn.
Reread	Begin anew to read what you have just read if you are not satisfied with your checkup process.

Vocabulary

vocabulary: a collection of words

Your **vocabulary** consists of words you know and understand how to use. A large vocabulary increases your understanding of what you read. Words that are unfamiliar to you are a barrier to your reading. Certain techniques can expand your vocabulary and help you to be an effective reader. Consider using some of these as you study the content of this book:

1. When you read an unfamiliar word, try to determine its meaning from the way it is used in the sentence. After you have a meaning you think is correct, check the dictionary. If you were right, you will now be more confident as you consider what unfamiliar words might mean.
2. When you read an unfamiliar word, try separating the word into parts to see if you can guess a meaning for one or more of the parts. You read, for example, the word *rearrange*. You know from earlier experience that *rekey* means that you must key again. You know the meaning of *arrange*. You then guess that *rearrange* means to put in a new or different order. You check the dictionary and find that your guess is right.

CHAPTER 4: COMMUNICATING IN WRITTEN FORM

3. While reading, have at hand a notepad and pencil to record words you do not know. Write down your best guess of what the word might mean. Also, record the page on which the uncertain word appears.

When you pause to reflect on what you have read, check the words on your list in a dictionary. As you read a definition, compare what you thought the meaning was with the dictionary's definition. You may want to refer back to the place where the word occurred. Reread the passage and assure yourself that you understand what is being said. If there is more than one definition provided, be sure to select the definition that fits in the context in which the word appeared. Context refers to the parts of a sentence or paragraph around a word that can help you with meaning. You may find it useful to record new words and review your list from time to time. Try using new words in your conversations as a way of reinforcing your new knowledge.

You may find a specialized vocabulary required in your work. You will want to be alert to such terms. You may have available a specialized dictionary or other reference that will help you master new words.

Practice techniques to improve your reading comprehension and vocabulary.

Speed

Another aspect of reading skill relates to speed—the time required for reading a passage. Problems with comprehension or vocabulary can slow the rate at which you read. The rate at which you read can merely be a habit. You probably can learn to read more quickly. Some strategies that can be useful in increasing reading speed are described below.

1. Focus your attention on a whole paragraph at one time. Tell yourself, "I want to read this paragraph as a single thought, and I want to know what it says." By doing so, you are forcing yourself to break a common habit of deliberately pausing at each word or each sentence as you read. When you have finished reading the paragraph, try to summarize it in a sentence or two. If you realize that you have not grasped the meaning, read it once again as quickly as possible. Again, attempt to summarize it. You are likely to improve on your second attempt.

Expand the Concept

Legal offices, medical offices, and public accounting offices are examples of places where a specialized vocabulary will be helpful.

Thinking Critically

Under what circumstances do you find it relatively easy to remember what you have read? Are you practicing any of the techniques for increasing reading comprehension?

For Discussion

How does command of an extensive vocabulary aid in reading with speed? How much time does it take to check the meaning of a word in a dictionary?

117
Topic 4-1: *Reading and Writing at Work*

2. Time your reading. Set a goal such as: "I will read this page, which has approximately 350 words, in three minutes." Check to see if you reached your goal. If you did, try the same passage with a reduced time allowance.

3. Deliberately force yourself ahead as you read. Do not set a specific time goal. Note the extent to which you return to your slower way of reading. Think about why you do not continue reading quickly.

Reading as a Single Process

The critical areas of comprehension, vocabulary, and reading speed have been highlighted separately. When you are actually reading, however, these areas interact. In some cases, a weakness in one area may be compensated for by strength in another. For example, you may comprehend well what you read. If you see an unfamiliar word, you figure out its meaning from your understanding of the rest of the sentence or paragraph. You may read rapidly, but your comprehension is limited. By reading rapidly, you have time to reread the material to improve your comprehension. Ideally, you want high skill levels in all three areas.

As you consider the variety of reading tasks you may handle at work, you will come to realize how much good skills are worth. As you complete the varied assignments in your study of office procedures, regularly assess your reading skills and think of ways to improve them.

Writing at Work

The extent and nature of your writing duties are related to the nature of your job and your own interest to assume such tasks. All office workers need strong writing skills. Among the common writing tasks are these:

- Summarizing written messages
- Writing notes of actions and decisions at meetings
- Revising others' writing and making changes
- Preparing communications for others to review
- Composing messages and revising them before they are distributed

Like most activity in business, business writing is purpose driven. A practical reason exists for all writing activity at work. Some of the most common purposes are:

- **Communicating policies and procedures.** People must be informed about the company and their work. Many written messages relate to the policies and procedures in a company.
- **Reporting on plans in progress.** Businesses know that planning for the future is important for success. Meetings are held where workers think carefully about what lies ahead. Written reports are valuable for informing everyone of plans or the progress of various projects.
- **Seeking or giving information.** Detailed data is often required to make a business decision. Messages asking for data may be sent to outsiders and employees.
- **Sending messages to customers.** Companies send messages to customers to encourage greater demand for their products and services.

CHAPTER 4: COMMUNICATING IN WRITTEN FORM

Letters, brochures, flyers, catalogs, and Web sites all require careful writing. Messages are also required to remind customers to pay over-due bills. Efforts to get payment are done in a friendly manner so that the customer will continue to buy from the company.

■ **Following up oral discussions.** Discussions may be in group meetings, person-to-person, by telephone, or by teleconferences. A written record of what was discussed is often required for those in the meetings and for others. Such a report serves as a summary of what happened and as a preview for further discussions.

© CORBIS

Written reports are valuable for communicating the plans or progress of projects.

A written record of meetings can be a very valuable tool for making sure that all meeting participants have the same understanding of what was discussed and what results or conclusions came from the meeting.

119

Topic 4-1: *Reading and Writing at Work*

Critical Thinking

When would summaries of written material be useful?

For Discussion

For what reasons might revising others' writing be an easier task than revising one's own writing?

Critical Thinking

What are some problems editors might encounter when doing their jobs?

Expand the Concept

When preparing a draft for a supervisor, knowing his or her point of view as well as facts about the subject of the draft is important.

Effective summarizing is a valuable skill. To do it well, you should understand what is important to those who will read the summary. You must listen or read attentively and identify the critical points. Write a summary as concisely as possible. Review the summary to see if it actually reflects the written communication or the meeting.

Reviewing the Writing of Others

Rewriting is often required to create an effective message. Office workers are often asked to review the messages written by others. Some executives expect their assistants to act as editors. An editor is a person who reviews what has been written to suggest changes in wording, organization, and content. Workers with editorial duties perform tasks such as those listed below.

- Identify precisely what the writer's intent is.
- Focus on the purpose of the task to ensure that the message is meeting all requirements for effectiveness.
- Make candid suggestions.
- Review their suggestions in an objective manner.

Read the message prepared by a human resources manager shown in Figure 4-1.5. Note the suggested changes made by a colleague. Consider the changes proposed. Do you think they improve the message?

Figure **4-1.5**

A paragraph marked for revision using Word's Track Changes feature.

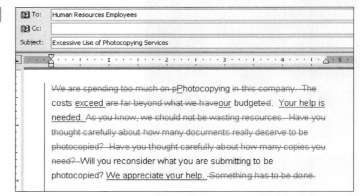

draft: a rough or preliminary version of a written message

Composing Messages

Messages may reflect the point of view of a department or the company. Often, one person is assigned to prepare a **draft**, which is then reviewed by others. Staff at all levels may participate in writing tasks.

The staff of the Human Resources Department met to discuss the company's move to a new location. The new office will be 2,000 miles away. A staff member, noted for her writing skills, was assigned the task of drafting a message to be sent by e-mail to all employees. The staff member listened carefully to what had to be included. Many employees would be disappointed with the news, so an honest, carefully worded message was needed.

In some companies, administrative assistants and secretaries read incoming messages addressed to coworkers. They prepare drafts of responses to the messages. Then the executive reads the incoming messages and the suggested response at one time. Often executives are satisfied with their assistants' suggestions. Little editing is needed. Final copies can be prepared quickly. Recipients will have responses within a relatively brief period.

You may have complete responsibility for certain writing tasks. You will want to be at ease when you write messages on your own. Little time may be available to get reviews from others and rewrite what you want to say. You will want to develop the skill of writing a message appropriately the first time so little revision is needed. When you are doing the entire job of composing and signing memos and letters, you must be your own editor. If you are objective, you will be a good editor of your own work.

Characteristics of Effective Writing

Messages written for business purposes should contain all the needed information. They should be written in a way that is easy to understand. Unlike a poem, for example, where meaning can be obscure, business writing is expected to be direct and meaningful to all who read it. Common characteristics of good business writing are listed below.

- **Clear.** A clear message is logically arranged with the information in an order that is natural for the recipient to follow. To prepare a clear message, you must know why you want to communicate, what you want to say, and who your recipient will be. A clear message eliminates the need for requests for additional comment.

- **Concise.** A concise message states what you want to say in the fewest and most direct words possible. The recipient will waste no time in reading words and thoughts that add nothing to understanding the message.

- **Courteous.** Written messages are courteous when they conform to the expected polite, considerate behavior of the business world. Expressions such as "thank you," "please," and "you are welcome" are commonly used in business correspondence. The so-called *you* approach is commonly recommended for the tone of messages.

121

Topic 4-1: *Reading and Writing at Work*

Expand the Concept

As students gain experience in composing messages in their jobs as office workers, they will be given more responsibility and more difficult assignments. Eventually, students may be given total responsibility for certain writing tasks. To be successful business writers, students will need to become experts in evaluating their own work.

Teaching Tips

Have students memorize the five Cs of effective writing and their meanings. With practice they will begin looking at all writing in relation to these characteristics.

For Discussion

How do clear messages contribute to productivity?

Expand the Concept

What does a writer have to consider when striving for a concise message? Why might executives strive to have all communications reflect the "you approach"? What knowledge of the recipient is important as the writer considers the completeness of a message?

For Discussion

Which of the five Cs did Kathy disregard when she prepared her reply to the customer?

Expand the Concept

Why are English skills considered necessary for good business communication?

- **Complete.** A complete message provides all the information needed. Think of the recipient by asking yourself: "Does this answer all the questions the recipient might raise about this matter?"
- **Correct.** A correct message is accurate and up-to-date. Details provided in messages should be verified before the final copy is prepared.

Read the two messages shown in Figure 4-1.6. Which message is clear? Which message is unclear?

Figure **4-1.6**

Example messages

Message A

Tell everybody on the team that we'll meet on Friday morning to discuss plans for the new project.

Message B

All members of the Accounting Department will meet on Friday, November 10, at 10 a.m. in Conference Room C. We will discuss plans for updating our Accounts Payable system.

WORKPLACE CONNECTIONS

Changes are common in business. Workers should take care to see that all messages have current information. Using incorrect or outdated information can cause problems. Additional messages are often required, and the goodwill of customers can be lost.

Part of Kathy's job is to answer inquiries about whether products are in stock and when they can be shipped. A customer asked whether a certain product could be shipped at four dates throughout the year. Kathy knew that the company kept good inventories. She responded by e-mail that there would be no problem in meeting the customer's order. Only after the customer sent the order with the dates for delivery did Kathy check on the items ordered. At that point, she learned that the company would stop making the item within the next two months.

Effective business writing reveals good command of the English language. To create effective messages, follow these guidelines.

- Check sentence structure and be sure all sentences are complete.
- Use proper grammar. Check grammar references as needed and use the grammar check feature of your word processing software.
- Follow rules of punctuation and capitalization. Check reference sources as needed.
- Spell words correctly. Use the spell check feature of your software and have a dictionary at hand. Remember that a spell check program does not find misused words such as "to" for "two" as shown in Figure 4-1.7.

122

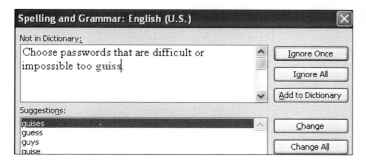

Figure **4-1.7**

A spell check program often does not find misused words.

Management of Writing Tasks

Writing tasks must be managed wisely if they are to be completed successfully and on schedule. The management of writing tasks has two aspects. One relates to the actual writing task itself. The other relates to scheduling the task properly to meet deadlines.

Managing the Task of Writing

The following steps will prove useful to you in completing a writing assignment:

1. Identify the reason for the written message.
2. Secure all the information required for the message.
3. Compose a draft of your message. Prepare an outline of what you plan to say if the message is long. Key or dictate your message directly at your computer using your outline as a guide.
4. Review your message; make corrections if needed.
5. If required, submit your draft to a colleague or manager for review and approval.
6. Prepare a revised copy of your message.
7. Proofread carefully.
8. Sign and prepare the final communication for distribution.

Managing the Schedule for Writing Tasks

In most instances, you will have a deadline for the completion of a writing task. This means that when you accept a writing task, you must review how much time is required for each aspect of the work you must do.

One strategy is to review the steps in the preceding section, noting just how much time is needed to do the task well. For example, having the required information at hand in a letter eliminates the need for time to search for information. A schedule may be needed for a major writing task to ensure that you work within the time period allowed. The time available must be scheduled so that each aspect of the task can be done properly.

123

Topic 4-1: *Reading and Writing at Work*

Expand the Concept

Even though all written communications do not need to be of the same quality, students should apply the five Cs to all written communication.

You will have many occasions during your study of office procedures to develop your writing skills. Remember that all written messages do not need to be of the same quality. For example, a message to the manager of the stockroom, whom you know personally, might be written informally and e-mailed without editing. On the other hand, a letter to thousands of customers might be rewritten several times, with others reviewing drafts to make sure the letter will attract customer attention.

With practice, you will improve your skill in preparing simple messages the first time you try. Also, you will gain a sense of what a good message should be and how to prepare one. With practice, you will develop skill in evaluating and improving your writing.

REVIEWING THE TOPIC

1. Identify several situations that require reading at work.
2. How can you determine the meaning of an unfamiliar word that you find while you are reading?
3. What are the key components of reading skill?
4. Describe a procedure to increase your comprehension of what you read.
5. What might you do to build your vocabulary through reading?
6. In what ways might the speed of reading be increased?
7. List common business writing tasks.
8. What are important skills for a person who is summarizing written messages or meetings?
9. What should a person keep in mind while reviewing a draft of a written communication?
10. Describe a situation where you would prepare a written communication to seek information.
11. For what purpose are written communications prepared after oral discussions?
12. Identify five characteristics of good business writing.

INTERACTING WITH OTHERS

Bea works as an assistant manager in the office of a warehouse facility where she interacts with a number of employees. The office is a busy place because an inventory of over 11,000 items is maintained. On several occasions, Tonia, a part-time employee, asked Bea to help her with instructions for incoming merchandise. Bea began to realize that Tonia, who was still in high school, did not understand instructions. Then Bea began to wonder if Tonia was having problems with reading. One evening after work, Bea and Tonia were leaving at the same time. The two began to talk. Tonia said to Bea: "I think I should give up this job; it is too hard for me. I guess I don't really want to work."

If you were Bea, what would you say to Tonia? Write or key your response.

If the students are using the *Student Activities and Simulations* workbook, instruct them to complete the review activity for this topic.

After students have considered the situation presented, ask them to share their thoughts with the class.

For Discussion

After students have keyed the sentences, discuss the corrections that they should have made.

Teaching Tip

After students have prepared their responses, discuss the answers with the class.

REINFORCING ENGLISH SKILLS

The following sentences have errors in noun and verb agreement. Key the sentences, correcting the errors.

Simple rules of writing applies to e-mail. This type of writing seem informal, but it is still business communications. Experts points out that brisk and brief writing are fine. Considering this type of communicating impersonal is not wise. Insensitive and discourteous statements should not be in your messages. The ease in corresponding via e-mail have led to many unclear and confusing messages. Reviews of e-mail has discovered all types of inappropriate and irrelevant material that are really clutter.

COMPOSITION
RESEARCH
WORD PROCESSING

Topic **4-1**   ACTIVITY 1

Reading to Answer Inquiries

Assume that you are an agent in the Customer Service Department of a major bank. You spend a lot of time talking with customers by telephone. One area where questions are frequent is early withdrawal costs. The bank's rules regarding early withdrawals can be accessed on the company intranet.

1. Open the PDF file *CH04 Rules* from the data files, which shows a portion of the company intranet that contains your bank's rules regarding withdrawal costs. Read this document carefully.

2. Assume that you respond to calls in which the following questions are raised. Prepare a written response to each of the customers using information you learned from reading the bank's rules.

Customer A: I have an account that has a term of 30 months, which I opened four months ago. I would like to withdraw about half of that money now. What will it cost me to do this?

Customer B: My one-year deposit will mature in eight months. Could I withdraw the money next month?

Customer C: I have an 18-month account that matures in six months. What penalty do I face if I withdraw all the money now?

Customer D: I would like to make an additional deposit to my account that I opened a year ago. May I do this?

126

CHAPTER 4: COMMUNICATING IN WRITTEN FORM

Topic 4-1 : **ACTIVITY 2**

Writing Procedures for a Task

Office workers must follow procedures for tasks such as operating equipment and using software. These procedures may need to be documented for the worker's own reference or for use in training others. Practice writing procedures for a common office task, changing a printer cartridge.

1. Write procedures for changing the printer cartridge on a printer used in your classroom. (Your instructor may need to demonstrate this process.) Title your document "Procedure for Changing Printer Cartridge."

2. Begin the document by giving the brand name, model number, and type of printer (inkjet, laser, etc.). Give the part or item number that identifies the cartridge and tell whether it is a black or color cartridge.

3. Next, include step-by-step directions for changing the printer cartridge. Review the steps to be sure they are clear, complete, and correct.

4. (Ask for your instructor's approval before completing this step.) Give your procedure to a classmate. The classmate should attempt to change the printer cartridge following your procedures. The classmate should perform only the actions in your procedures and only in the order you have listed them. Revise your procedures, if needed, using your observations of how successfully your classmate was able to complete the task following your procedures.

Teaching Tip

Tell students whether they should complete step 4 of the activity, changing the printer cartridge.

Topic 4-2

objectives

- Identify the characteristics of effective business letters, memos, and e-mail messages
- Prepare effective business correspondence
- Explain the function of business letters, memos, and e-mail messages
- Identify and use appropriately the parts of business letters, memos, and e-mail messages
- Choose appropriate formats for business letters
- List and apply guidelines for preparing documents using desktop publishing

BUSINESS CORRESPONDENCE

Office workers often compose business letters and memos or e-mail messages. Employees may prepare letters or memos for or with coworkers as well as for themselves. The ability to compose and prepare effective business messages will make you a more valuable employee. As you study this topic, you will review document parts and standard formats. You will also study some guidelines for using desktop publishing to prepare documents such as newsletters or flyers.

Preparing Effective Documents

As you learned in Topic 4-1, effective business documents are clear, concise, courteous, complete, and correct. These traits are known as the *five Cs* of business writing. They are your guidelines to preparing business documents. You can quickly check the effectiveness of your documents by considering these factors.

An effective document is planned well and prepared carefully. Preparing a document includes three stages. First, a draft of the document is written. Then the document is revised or edited as needed. The final stage is proofreading and correcting the document for final presentation.

Drafting

Your first draft of a document will probably not be your final or finished version. It is considered a rough draft. Your goal in preparing the rough draft is to record your ideas. Do not try to make each sentence perfect. You will refine your document during the editing and proofreading stages. To help focus your writing as you develop your document, ask yourself these questions:

1. What is your purpose in writing?
2. What is your message?
3. Who and where is your audience?
4. What response do you want from the reader?

Purpose

Fix the purpose of the document clearly in your mind before you begin writing. Business documents are often written to inform. For example, you may want the reader to know about a new product or a new procedure. Business documents are also written to persuade or describe. Although these purposes may overlap, you need to have a clear understanding of why you are writing the document before you attempt your first draft.

128

CHAPTER 4: COMMUNICATING IN WRITTEN FORM

This employee is creating the first draft of a letter.

Message

Determine the points you need to make. What do you need to say to get your message across? What information do you need to include to build support for your position? The **tone** of your message can be as important as the content. Keep these points in mind as you draft your message:

tone: style, manner of writing or speaking that shows a certain attitude

- Prepare an outline of the document, particularly for longer documents. An outline will help you prepare the message in a logical sequence. The better you organize your points, the easier it will be for you to write the message and for your reader to understand your message.

- Focus on the reader as you write. Avoid using too many "I" and "we" words. Instead, use "you" and "your" frequently. This technique is called the *you* approach.

- Give your message a positive tone. Avoid using negative words or a negative tone. Always be courteous. Make an effort in your writing to be helpful to the reader.

Thinking Critically

Preparing an outline saves time. Ask students to explain why this statement is true.

This employee is focusing on the reader as he drafts a letter.

129

Topic 4-2: *Business Correspondence*

Selena, an administrative assistant at a travel agency, wrote this draft:

We are happy to announce that The Traveler's Agency will now offer a full range of travel services. In addition to our regular travel services, we are now promoting three travel discount packages that we designed for the business traveler. Please contact our offices for more information. Our Web site also provides details.

Selena's manager reviewed the draft and had these comments: "This draft includes all the needed information, Selena, but the approach isn't quite right. Please revise the draft using a reader-focused approach." Selena's revision met with the manager's approval.

All your travel needs can now be met through The Traveler's Agency's full range of travel services. As a frequent business traveler, you are eligible for special travel discount packages. Three such discount packages have been designed for you, the frequent business traveler. Please return the enclosed postage-paid card to receive more information about these money-saving packages. You can find more details on the Web site.

Thinking Critically

Although Selena understood the purpose of the message she drafted, what was lacking in her original draft?

Audience

Knowing certain things about your reader(s) is important to how you develop your document. Is the reader already familiar with the topic? Knowing this will help you determine how much information to include. Is your document going to one reader or to many? Is the document for external or internal distribution? These factors may influence how formal your writing needs to be, whether confidential topics may be mentioned, or how responses may be requested.

Response

How will the reader use this document? To make a decision? To gain information? If you want a response from the reader, let the reader know the specific action you want. Make it easy for the reader to respond by stating your message and the desired response clearly.

Points to Emphasize

Review the four factors a writer should consider when drafting a document by asking students to restate each factor in their own words. Ask students to give the major points for each factor.

Revising and Editing

Many business documents are changed one or more times between the rough draft and the final document. This process of making changes to refine the document is known as editing or revising.

The primary purpose of editing is to make certain the message is accurate and says what the writer intends. In the editing stage of preparing your document, focus on the details of your writing. Read your draft carefully and consider the five Cs of effective documents. Editing is your chance to polish your writing by making changes in response to these questions:

- Can you improve your word choice?
- Are your transitions smooth, flowing logically from one topic to another?
- Should the order of your points be changed?
- Are there inconsistencies in your writing that need to be corrected?

Expand the Concept

Finding inconsistencies takes attention to the detail in your writing. Inconsistencies are difficult to spot because the item is not wrong, simply different from the other uses of the items.

130

CHAPTER 4: COMMUNICATING IN WRITTEN FORM

To make editing changes that can be understood easily by others, writers often use standard proofreaders' marks as shown in Figure 4-2.1 when editing on printed copy. Editing features of popular word processing programs allow you to edit and make comments in a document file. Once the changes are identified and marked, you can make the changes quickly using the editing features of your word processing software.

WORKPLACE CONNECTIONS

Diego works as an assistant to an engineer who prepares many reports. He has been instructed to prepare rough drafts of all reports. The engineer makes comments and indicates revisions in the document file. After the engineer gives Diego the reviewed file, Diego makes all text and formatting changes indicated. The engineer may revise complex reports several times. Diego's knowledge of word processing features allows him to make changes easily.

Proofreading

Proofreading, the third phase of preparing a document, is your careful, overall check of the document. During this process, verify that the changes you marked in the editing phase have been made correctly. Check all numbers and unusual spellings against original documents. Use a spell checker and a grammar checker if available with your software. Then complete a detailed manual proofreading. Remember that the spelling feature of your software is limited in the errors it can identify. For example, errors such as "there" for "their" will not be detected.

proofreading: checking a document carefully for errors or omissions

Teaching Tips

Discuss with students the importance of proofreading and their responsibility for proofreading. Students should be well versed in the guidelines for proofreading documents.

Figure **4-2.1**

Proofreaders' marks are used in editing printed documents.

Proofreaders' Marks

Mark	Meaning		Mark	Meaning
#	Add horizontal space		/ or *lc*	Lowercase
‖	Align			Move left
～	Bold			Move right
Cap or ≡	Capitalize			Move up
	Close up			Move down
	Delete		¶	Paragraph
∧	Insert		*sp*	Spell out
	Insert quotation marks		or *tr*	Transpose
... or *stet*	Let it stand; ignore correction			Underline or italic

Message Types

Business messages may be positive, neutral, negative, or persuasive. Each type of message has unique traits that should be considered as you prepare documents. To determine which type of message your letter contains, consider the effect the message will have on the receiver.

Positive or Neutral Messages

positive message: a communication of good news or agreement

neutral message: a communication that simply relays facts; neither positive nor negative

A reader will not be disappointed with a positive message or neutral message. For these messages, give the good news or neutral news to the reader in a direct way early in the document. Examples of positive or neutral messages include:

- Placing or confirming an order
- Placing or filling a request for information
- Filling or extending a request for credit
- Making, approving, or adjusting routine claims

To prepare good news or neutral messages, use the direct approach. Go directly to the main point of the message and give specific, complete information. Note how the message in Figure 4-2.2 follows these general guidelines.

Figure **4-2.2**

Use a direct approach to prepare a positive message.

> Dear Ms. Racine
>
> Congratulations! Your request for a car loan was approved by our loan officers this morning.
>
> Your loan for $10,000 is now being processed and will be available for your use within 24 hours. Please contact our loan officer, Jan Truong, at 555-0134 for an appointment to sign the final papers and to discuss your monthly payments.
>
> Thank you for your business. We are pleased to serve you.

Negative Messages

negative message: a communication that will be disappointing to the recipient

goodwill: friendly feeling or attitude

Negative messages typically involve a refusal or other news that the reader will find disappointing or upsetting. For this type of message, tell the reader why a request is being refused. Give reasons for the disappointing news before stating it directly. Try to keep the reader's goodwill. Examples of negative messages include:

- Refusing a request for an adjustment, a credit, or a favor
- Canceling a service
- Reporting unfavorable results

132

CHAPTER 4: COMMUNICATING IN WRITTEN FORM

Expand the Concept

Letters are sometimes referred to as "good news," "bad news," and "please" messages. Emphasize the specific strategies in each message type.

Expand the Concept

Ask students to identify the three strategy points used in preparing the good news message in Figure 4-2.2.

Negative messages require the writer to take considerable care in preparing the response. Use the indirect approach. Begin the message with a neutral statement that lets the reader know the message is your response to the request or to a situation that has arisen. Build your position by stating the reasons for your decision. State the refusal or other negative news. Close on a positive note and suggest alternatives if appropriate. Figure 4-2.3 gives an example of a negative message.

Figure **4-2.3**

Use an indirect approach to prepare a negative message.

Dear Mr. Roberts

Thank you for considering the Trust Bank for your car loan. Our loan officers met this morning to consider your loan application.

After a careful review of your application, they determined that your monthly income must be higher to support a loan of $10,000 with your current debt liability. Therefore, we cannot approve your loan at this time. Please consider resubmitting your loan application once your monthly payments of $250 on your existing loan are finished.

Your patronage is important to us, Mr. Roberts. We at Trust Bank hope you will continue to consider us for your future banking needs.

Persuasive Messages

In preparing a **persuasive message**, the writer wants to influence the reader to take a desired action. Sales letters, collection letters, and donation requests are all examples of persuasive messages. When you write a sales letter, for example, you want to influence the reader to buy your product or service. The basic steps to preparing a sales letter are as follows:

- Gain the reader's attention
- Stimulate the reader's interest and desire
- Give the reader an opportunity to act

persuasive message: a communication designed to convince the recipient

When you write a collection letter, you are trying to persuade the reader to pay his or her bill. Collection letters are typically a series of letters that move through different stages of persuasion. They begin with a reminder stage. Then they move to a strong reminder stage, an inquiry stage, and an urgency stage. If collection messages are used at your job, you will probably have sample letters available for each phase of the collection writing process.

Business Letters

A business letter is a written message to a person(s) or an organization. Letters are usually written to someone outside the company. As the writer of a business letter, you are your company's representative. Your letter helps the reader form an opinion about your company.

Expand the Concept

Ask students to identify the four strategy points used in preparing the negative message in Figure 4-2.3.

Expand the Concept

Ask students to identify the three steps used in preparing a persuasive message.

For Discussion

Ask students how business letters can be positive, negative, or persuasive.

Letters provide a long-lasting record of your message. It can be read many times and can serve different purposes. Reasons for writing business letters include:

- Requesting information or an action
- Giving information or fulfilling a request
- Being courteous or maintaining goodwill (congratulation and thank-you notes)
- Explaining or stating a position or persuading the reader
- Selling goods or services

Thinking Critically

Why would a carelessly presented letter on a smudged paper cause a reader to develop a negative attitude toward the sender?

Presentation of Business Letters

The primary purpose of a business letter is to convey a message. However, even before the message is read, the reader makes a judgment about the letter and its sender. An attractively presented letter on quality paper will encourage the recipient to read the message with care. On the other hand, a carelessly presented letter on smudged paper may fail to get close attention.

A letter makes a good first impression if it has the following characteristics:

- The margins and spacing are pleasing to the eye.
- Each letter part is correctly placed within the letter.
- Appropriate stationery is used.
- There are no obvious errors.
- The print is neat and clear.
- There are no smudges or fingerprints.

Make your letters as attractive as possible. If the appearance of the letter is pleasing to the eye, the receiver will be encouraged to read what you have written.

Letter Parts

protocol: generally accepted customs or rules

Business letters represent a form of communication within the business world that follows a standard **protocol**. That is, those who receive business letters expect to see them written using certain letter parts. In Figure 4-2.4 on page 135, you will find all the parts that could be included in a business letter. Of course, few letters will include all these parts. Some parts are included in most letters. Other parts are included only when needed. The standard letter parts that should be included in most business letters, as well as optional parts, are listed below.

Standard Letter Parts	Optional Letter Parts
Printed letterhead	Mailing notations
Date	Attention line
Letter address	Subject line
Salutation	Enclosure notation
Body	Separate cover notation
Complimentary close	Copy notation
Signature, printed name, and title	Postscript
	Reference initials
	Multiple-page heading

134
CHAPTER 4: COMMUNICATING IN WRITTEN FORM

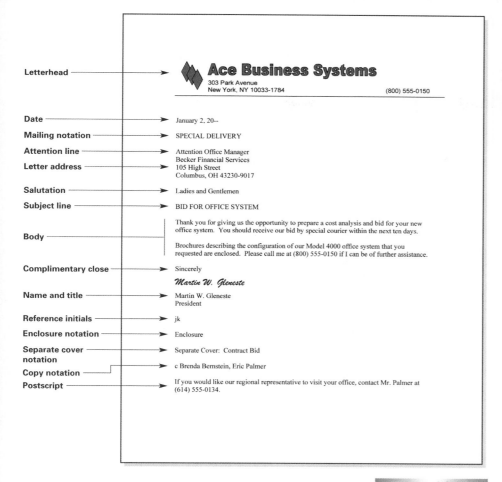

	Ace Business Systems
Letterhead	303 Park Avenue
	New York, NY 10033-1784 (800) 555-0150
Date	January 2, 20--
Mailing notation	SPECIAL DELIVERY
Attention line	Attention Office Manager
Letter address	Becker Financial Services
	105 High Street
	Columbus, OH 43230-9017
Salutation	Ladies and Gentlemen
Subject line	BID FOR OFFICE SYSTEM
Body	Thank you for giving us the opportunity to prepare a cost analysis and bid for your new office system. You should receive our bid by special courier within the next ten days.
	Brochures describing the configuration of our Model 4000 office system that you requested are enclosed. Please call me at (800) 555-0150 if I can be of further assistance.
Complimentary close	Sincerely
Name and title	*Martin W. Gleneste*
	Martin W. Gleneste
	President
Reference initials	jk
Enclosure notation	Enclosure
Separate cover notation	Separate Cover: Contract Bid
Copy notation	c Brenda Bernstein, Eric Palmer
Postscript	If you would like our regional representative to visit your office, contact Mr. Palmer at (614) 555-0134.

Occasionally, a letter will require more than one page. In such instances, a multiple-page heading is prepared to identify each page. As shown in Figure 4-2.5 on page 136, the heading includes the name of the addressee, the word *Page* and a page number, and the letter date.

Figure 4-2.4

Business letter in block format with open punctuation

Business Letter Formats

The arrangement of the letter text on the page is referred to as its **format**. Using a standard format for letters increases efficiency for both the writer and the recipient. For the writer, extra time is not needed to decide how to arrange the letter. For the recipient, the task of reading and comprehending is simplified because the format of information is familiar.

format: arrangement or layout, as of text on a page

Teaching Tips

Point out each letter part in the illustration and discuss its use.

For Discussion

Why does using a standard letter format increase efficiency in preparing letters?

Points to Emphasize

The second-page heading is blocked at the left margin in Figure 4-2.5.

1 inch

Miss Laureen DiRenna
Page 2
February 2, 20--
            DS
apply the credit toward a future purchase. Be sure to include your membership number on the account credit form provided and return the form with the questionnaire. This will ensure that your account is credited properly.

Sincerely

Figure **4-2.5**

Multipage letter heading

Many companies have procedures manuals that contain standard format instructions and examples for frequently prepared documents. If examples are not available, you will be expected to make format decisions. These decisions should reflect your desire to produce attractive, easy-to-read documents.

Writers most frequently use the block and modified block letter formats. In the block format, all lines begin at the left margin; paragraphs and other letter parts are not indented. The letter in Figure 4-2.4 is in block format. Block format is efficient because it saves time in moving from one part of the letter to another.

In modified block format, the date, complimentary close, and signature block (writer's signature, typed name, and title) begin at the horizontal center of the page rather than at the left margin. The first line of each paragraph may be indented one-half inch. The letter in Figure 4-2.6 is in modified block format.

Two punctuation styles are typically used in business letters. These styles are open punctuation and mixed punctuation. In open punctuation style, no punctuation marks are used after the salutation and the complimentary close. See Figure 4-2.4 for an example. In mixed punctuation style, a colon is placed after the salutation and a comma after the complimentary close. See Figure 4-2.6 for an example. Either punctuation style may be used with a block or modified block letter format.

Repetitive Letters

Writing in the business office often involves preparing similar messages that are used again and again. The same letters may be sent to hundreds of people. If you prepare such documents, you may want to use form letters and features of your software to speed the preparation.

For Discussion

As a review of letter formats and punctuation styles, ask students to identify how the two letter formats are similar. How do they differ? Which of the two punctuation styles is more efficient to use? Why?

For Discussion

Certain word processing features permit the writer to individualize repetitive documents. Ask students: Have you ever received a letter that you identified immediately as one that probably hundreds of others received? Did you give it much attention?

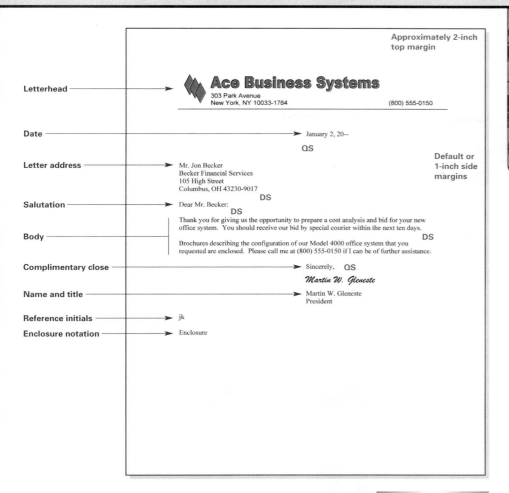

Letterhead → **Ace Business Systems**
303 Park Avenue
New York, NY 10033-1784

(800) 555-0150

Approximately 2-inch
top margin

Date → January 2, 20--

QS

Default or
1-inch side
margins

Letter address → Mr. Jon Becker
Becker Financial Services
105 High Street
Columbus, OH 43230-9017

DS

Salutation → Dear Mr. Becker:

DS

Body → Thank you for giving us the opportunity to prepare a cost analysis and bid for your new office system. You should receive our bid by special courier within the next ten days.

DS

Brochures describing the configuration of our Model 4000 office system that you requested are enclosed. Please call me at (800) 555-0150 if I can be of further assistance.

Complimentary close → Sincerely, QS

Martin W. Gleneste

Name and title → Martin W. Gleneste
President

Reference initials → jk

Enclosure notation → Enclosure

Standard text can be combined with other data to form a finished document. The writer assembles the document by using custom text (the person's name and address) with selected standard paragraphs. Standard text is also called boilerplate text. Custom text is also called variables. Once the document is assembled, it is printed and saved in the same manner as other documents. A special feature of your word processing software, often called mail merge, may allow you to combine standard text and variables automatically. See Figure 4-2.7 on page 138 for an example. The variable data may be stored in a database file such as a customer address file.

Figure 4-2.6

Business letter in modified block format with mixed punctuation

For Discussion

Why would employees prefer to have carefully written paragraphs and statements prepared in advance for use in some frequent writing tasks?

Point out the variables and the standard text in Figure 4-2.7.

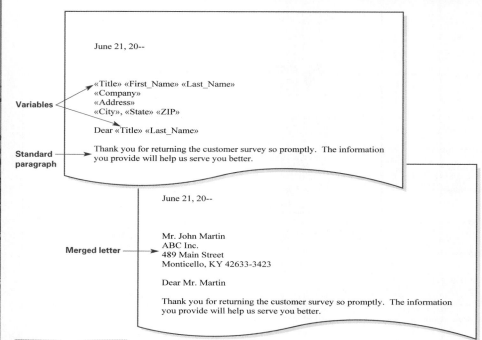

June 21, 20--

Variables → «Title» «First_Name» «Last_Name»
«Company»
«Address»
«City», «State» «ZIP»

Dear «Title» «Last_Name»

Standard paragraph → Thank you for returning the customer survey so promptly. The information you provide will help us serve you better.

June 21, 20--

Merged letter → Mr. John Martin
ABC Inc.
489 Main Street
Monticello, KY 42633-3423

Dear Mr. Martin

Thank you for returning the customer survey so promptly. The information you provide will help us serve you better.

Figure **4-2.7**

Field names from a database are entered as variables. The main document is merged with the database to create personalized letters.

WORKPLACE CONNECTIONS

Miguel often prepares mailings for groups of customers. The customer name and address information is stored in a database file. Miguel sorts the data or creates a query to find just the customers he needs, such as those in a particular city or ZIP code. He then uses the merge feature of his word processing software to create a personalized letter for each customer on the list. Using the merge feature saves a great deal of time. It also ensures that the customer addresses are accurate because the addresses do not have to be rekeyed. The merge feature can be used to create an envelope for each customer.

Envelopes

Most business letters are written to individuals outside the company. They require an envelope for mailing. The receiver begins forming an opinion of the document when he or she views the envelope. For this reason, the same care should be used in preparing envelopes as in preparing letters. The letterhead stationery and the envelope stationery should be of the same quality and color. The print should be clear, and the envelope should be free of smudges.

The envelope must be of a proper size and material acceptable to the United States Postal Service (USPS). To ensure prompt delivery, envelopes should include the following information:

- The recipient's name and address
- The sender's return address
- Special addressee notation, if any
- Special mailing notation, if any

The USPS recommends using all capital letters in the address. Omit punctuation marks except the hyphen in the ZIP code. Nonaddress data, such as a customer number or attention lines, should appear at the top of the address. Place special mailing notations, such as REGISTERED MAIL, below the stamp area as shown in Figure 4-2.8. Place special addressee notations, such as CONFIDENTIAL, just below the return address. If you have questions about addressing mail, contact your nearest Postal Business Center. You can also find help online by accessing the USPS Web site.

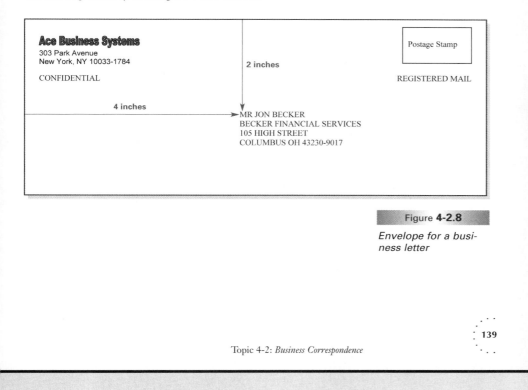

Ace Business Systems
303 Park Avenue
New York, NY 10033-1784

CONFIDENTIAL

4 inches

2 inches

Postage Stamp

REGISTERED MAIL

MR JON BECKER
BECKER FINANCIAL SERVICES
105 HIGH STREET
COLUMBUS OH 43230-9017

Figure 4-2.8

Envelope for a business letter

For Discussion

What effect has the use of e-mail had on the number of memos that are prepared in organizations?

Expand the Concept

Many office employees store memo forms or templates that include the company name and logo, heading lines, and margin settings. The form can be recalled for use each time a memo is prepared. The document is printed on plain paper.

Memos

A memo is an informal document. It is typically used to communicate with people within an organization. A memo is more formally called a memorandum. Memos are useful for giving the same information to several people. They can be used to give instructions or explain procedures. A personnel director, for example, may send memos to tell employees of holiday schedules. A credit manager may send memos to sales staff giving new credit terms for customers.

A memo may be printed on memo stationery. Plain paper with the company name and headings as part of the document can also be used. An example is shown in Figure 4-2.9. Memos can be created using a memo template or

Figure 4-2.9

A memo is used to communicate with individuals within an organization.

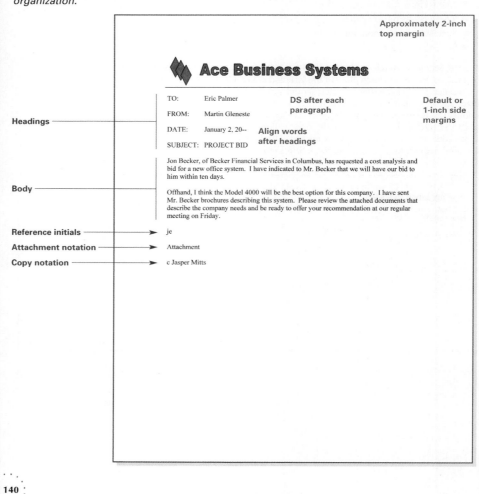

Headings

Body

Reference initials

Attachment notation

Copy notation

Approximately 2-inch top margin

Ace Business Systems

TO: Eric Palmer

FROM: Martin Gleneste

DATE: January 2, 20--

SUBJECT: PROJECT BID

DS after each paragraph

Align words after headings

Default or 1-inch side margins

Jon Becker, of Becker Financial Services in Columbus, has requested a cost analysis and bid for a new office system. I have indicated to Mr. Becker that we will have our bid to him within ten days.

Offhand, I think the Model 4000 will be the best option for this company. I have sent Mr. Becker brochures describing this system. Please review the attached documents that describe the company needs and be ready to offer your recommendation at our regular meeting on Friday.

je

Attachment

c Jasper Mitts

wizard available in word processing software. A special slogan or logo may be used on memos that provide updates on special events sponsored by the company.

The headings and body are the standard parts of a memo. Other parts, such as copy or enclosure notations, are optional. When a memo is sent to a large group of people, do not list all the recipients after the To heading. Instead, enter *Distribution List* after the To heading and list the recipients at the end of the memo under the heading Distribution List.

If the person receiving a printed memo is located nearby, the memo may be placed in the person's in-basket or mailbox. In this case, an envelope may not be needed. If the receiver is in a different location, the memo typically is sent in an interoffice envelope. A confidential document should always be placed in an envelope marked *Confidential*.

Each memo you write makes an impression on the receiver. If the memo is prepared well, the reader forms a positive image of you as an employee. When preparing a memo, follow the five Cs of effective writing and use a positive tone. Notice how the message that is written in a positive tone in Figure 4-2.10 sounds courteous while the message written in a negative tone does not.

Figure 4-2.10

The tone of a message can be positive or negative.

Message with Positive Tone

In the future, please communicate with your supervisor immediately if you see a delay developing. Early reporting of potential delays will give us time to contact an alternative supply source.

Message with Negative Tone

In the future, try not to wait so long to bring these delays to the attention of your supervisor. It is impossible to correct a situation if you cannot communicate with your supervisor in a timely fashion.

E-Mail

E-mail is a message sent electronically. Local and wide area networks can provide e-mail service to their users. Users who are connected to the Internet can send and receive messages all over the world. Workers use e-mail for routine messages with people inside and outside the company.

E-mail is appropriate for short, informal correspondence. Files containing more information may be attached to an e-mail. E-mail is inexpensive, fast, and easy to use for workers at all levels in a company. Remember, however, that e-mail messages are recorded. They may be viewed by people other than the person to whom you wrote. Your e-mail may be read by your employer or by coworkers. At work, never write an e-mail message that you would not want other employees or your supervisor to read.

141

Topic 4-2: *Business Correspondence*

Thinking Critically

What are some examples of confidential information that should not be sent by e-mail?

Expand the Concept

Ask students if they have ever received notification that an e-mail they sent could not be delivered. Was the message undeliverable because the e-mail address was keyed incorrectly? Before sending e-mail, users should proofread the address as well as the content.

Teaching Tips

Demonstrate the features of the e-mail program on your classroom computers or in the computer lab. Show students how to key and format a new e-mail; how to save a draft; how to access the In Box, Out Box, Address Book, and Deleted Items folders; how to attach a file to an e-mail; and how to delete messages.

WORKPLACE CONNECTIONS

Yoshi works in the Human Resources Department of a large company. He has access to data about employees such as salary data. Yoshi uses e-mail to send messages to managers in the company. He takes for granted that his e-mail messages will be read only by his intended recipient.

Ellen Wilson, a company employee, was being considered for a promotion. Ellen's manager, who was new to the company, sent an e-mail message to Yoshi. The message asked for Ellen's current rate of pay and the date of her last salary increase. Yoshi replied by e-mail and gave Ellen's manager the data requested. By mistake, Ellen's manager forwarded Yoshi's message to everyone in his department, including Ellen. Yoshi was called to his supervisor's office. He was reprimanded for sending confidential employee information via e-mail.

E-Mail Addresses

Before you can send and receive e-mail, you must have a unique e-mail address. E-mail addresses begin with a user ID (identification). The ID is a unique identifier such as *dsmith* (for Diane Smith). The user ID is followed by the @ sign and the domain name. To understand a domain name, read from right to left. The highest level of the domain appears at the right and identifies the type of organization. Consider the address *dsmith@eng.unlv .edu*. Starting at the right, the *edu* identifies that this address is located at an educational institution. The next section, *unlv*, identifies the specific one, such as University of Nevada, Las Vegas. The *eng* identifies the department, such as English or Engineering. The last part, *dsmith*, identifies an individual.

When you pronounce an e-mail address *Djones@cmu.com*, you would say, "d jones at c m u dot com" rather than spell out each letter. Be careful when recording an e-mail address. Addresses are often case sensitive. If you key an address incorrectly, your message will not be delivered to the intended address.

E-Mail Features

E-mail software varies somewhat in look and features from one package to another; however, certain features are found in most e-mail packages. E-mail messages contain headings and a section for the body of the message. An example is shown in Figure 4-2.11. E-mail programs allow the user to read mail, check for new messages, compose and reply to messages, delete messages, attach files to messages, and send new mail.

An e-mail address book is provided to store the user's most frequently used addresses. The Inbox collects incoming messages. A user alert, such as a tone or flashing icon, often accompanies the receipt of new mail. The Outbox holds e-mail messages to be sent to others. It may also hold messages that have already been sent, or these messages may be stored in a separate

CHAPTER 4: COMMUNICATING IN WRITTEN FORM

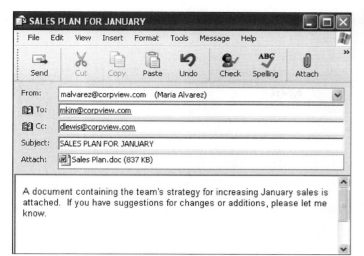

Figure **4-2.11**

E-mail makes commu-nicating fast and easy.

Sent box or folder. Because these messages are actually stored on your hard drive, you should frequently delete messages that are no longer needed. Most mail programs will allow you to prioritize an e-mail message, that is, to rank it in importance, usually from urgent or high to low.

Improving Communications in Organizations

Memos and e-mail are the most commonly used written messages within an organization. Memos should be used to provide confidential information. Memos can also be used for messages to workers who do not have access to e-mail at work, such as factory workers. E-mail is appropriate for many short, in-house messages. You should follow the same proper writing techniques for memos and e-mail as you do for your other messages.

Memos and e-mail messages should be written clearly and concisely. Often the message must be written under time pressure because of the need for prompt decisions or sharing of information. Take care to prepare an accurate, well-written message even though it is created quickly and the tone of the message is less formal than in a letter.

Consider these guidelines for improving memos and e-mail messages:

- Keep the message short. Attach a report to the message if more details are needed.
- Use a descriptive subject line so the recipient can see immediately the topic of your message.
- Follow a logical sequence in presenting the information.
- Write using a positive tone. Be tactful when expressing personal opinions in your writing. Handle sensitive situations positively.

143

Topic 4-2: *Business Correspondence*

This employee is careful to communicate effectively even when working under pressure.

© CORBIS

netiquette: guidelines for proper behavior when communicating online, derived from *network* and *etiquette*

spam: electronic junk mail, advertisements, or other messages not requested by the recipient and often sent in a mass mailing

font: a style or design for a set of type characters

- Follow the same strategies as you would for a business letter to deliver positive, neutral, negative, or persuasive messages.
- Carefully read your message, checking for application of the five Cs. Is the message clear, concise, complete, correct, and courteous?
- Use the spell check feature of your software and proofread carefully. When communicating online, observe proper **netiquette**.
- Check for messages regularly and reply to your messages promptly. Do not, however, send a message quickly in frustration or anger that you may regret later.
- Send messages only to people who really need to read the message. When replying to a message, reply only to the sender—not to everyone who received the message—unless everyone needs your answer.
- Take steps to safeguard confidential information. Never send confidential information in an e-mail message. Prepare a memo or printed report instead.
- Consider carefully before forwarding messages you receive to others. Honor others' rights of privacy. Never forward chain messages or send **spam**.

Desktop Publishing

Not all business correspondence follows standard formats as letters do. Product brochures, newsletters, and flyers may each use a unique format and design. These documents often contain graphics (clip art, photos, or other images) as well as text. They may use fancy **fonts** or banner headings to draw the reader's attention. Word processing or desktop publishing software is used to create these documents.

Desktop publishing programs, such as *QuarkXPress®* and *PageMaker*, contain features for creating complex documents with text and images. These programs allow the user to control type settings, such as **kerning**. They also allow full-color output. The text and images appear on your computer screen almost exactly as they will when printed. The images are often created or edited with programs such as *Adobe® Illustrator®*, *CorelDRAW®*, and *Adobe® Photoshop®*. They are then placed in the document using the desktop publishing program. Word processing programs usually have basic desktop publishing features. Programs such as *Word* may be used to create documents with multiple columns, text, and graphics.

kerning: adjusting the space between characters in text

Resolution

True desktop publishing results in high-resolution printed documents. Printed text and images are made up of many tiny dots of color. **Resolution** is the number of dots per inch (dpi) in a printed document. The greater the dpi, the higher the resolution and the sharper the printed image. Professional printers use around 2,400 dpi for many documents. Many businesses do not have high-resolution printers. They create the document files and send them to an outside company for printing. For in-house or informal documents, 600 dpi is considered acceptable. Many businesses have printers that can produce this resolution.

resolution: the number of dots per inch (dpi) in printed text or images

Desktop Publishing Guidelines

When creating documents to be desktop published, follow the five Cs of effective writing. Consider the purpose of the document. Is it to inform, to persuade, to request information? Also consider the audience for the document. Is in-house (probably low-resolution) printing acceptable? Should a professional printer be used? If printing will be done by a professional printer, obtain details from the printer about how the file must be created to print successfully. Use copyrighted text or images in your documents only with proper permission from the copyright holder.

Your goal is to create a document that makes a good impression. It should be attractive and deliver your message effectively. Consider these guidelines for creating desktop published documents:

- Use consistency in the design. For example, format all heads of the same level in same way. If the company logo appears on each page, place it in the same location on every page.
- Use ample **white space** to rest the eye and identify the beginning and end of sections. Effective use of white space keeps the text and images from looking cramped on the page.
- Create a pleasing balance of elements (headings, body text, and images) on the page. Documents with a balanced format (with roughly the same amount of material on each side of the page) have a formal, traditional look. Documents with an unbalanced format have a more informal look.
- Create contrast in the design by placing different objects next to each other. A graphic placed next to text, for example, creates contrast on the page.

white space: the area of a printed page that is empty, having no text or images

Topic 4-2: *Business Correspondence*

Thinking Critically

How can inappropriate artwork detract from the message or effectiveness of a document?

- Include artwork or photos that are relevant to the message. Place them near the text to which they relate. Use decorations or other artwork that are appropriate for the document. Take special care in very formal or serious documents that any artwork used is in keeping with the formal tone of the document.
- Use fonts that are easy to read. Limit the number of fonts in the document to two or three. Use bold, italic, and different sizes to vary the font appearance. Do not use font sizes that are too small to read easily.
- Use all capitals sparingly because text in all caps is hard to read.
- Avoid widow lines. Adjust the spacing or rewrite the sentence if necessary to prevent widow lines.
- Use printer's curves for apostrophes and quotes (' and " rather than ' and ").
- Avoid large horizontal spaces between words, which look unattractive. Using a ragged right margin and hyphenating words helps avoid this problem.

REVIEWING THE TOPIC

1. Describe the five characteristics of an effective document.

2. When creating the first or draft copy of a document, what four factors should you consider to help focus your writing?

3. Describe the three categories of messages common in business correspondence.

4. How can a writer use a reader-based approach in writing?

5. What reader characteristics are important for the writer to know?

6. Contrast the strategies used in preparing positive messages and negative messages.

7. What letter parts should be included in every business letter?

8. Identify the characteristics of a letter that make a good first impression.

9. Why do businesses use standard formats for their business letters and memos?

10. What is the purpose of a memo? How does it differ from a letter?

11. For what purposes are e-mail messages used?

12. List four guidelines that you think are the most important ones for improving written communications within an organization.

13. Define desktop publishing.

14. What is print resolution? How does it relate to clarity of printed material?

15. List five guidelines to follow when creating desktop published documents.

INTERACTING WITH OTHERS

Guidelines for interacting with others courteously online are called *netiquette* (derived from *network* and *etiquette*). Prepare a flyer on netiquette related to e-mail to distribute to coworkers.

1. Search the Internet or other reference sources for several articles or Web sites that provide information about netiquette. For each article or Web site, record the source information. Include the author for articles, the article or Web page name, the publication or Web site name and address, and the date of the publication or the date you view the Web site.

2. After reading about netiquette, write in your own words a list of eight to ten netiquette rules that relate to e-mail.

3. Create a one-page flyer to communicate your netiquette rules.

Teaching Tips

If the students are using the *Student Activities and Simulations* workbook, instruct them to complete the review activity for this topic.

For Discussion

After students have completed the list of netiquette rules, ask them to share their lists with the class.

continued

Follow the design guidelines found in this chapter for creating effective documents.

4. List the source information for three articles or Web sites you reviewed as sources of additional information on netiquette.

REINFORCING ENGLISH SKILLS

A coworker at Computer Corner Furniture needs your help with answering a letter to a customer. The customer has had difficulty assembling a computer workstation. The tone of the response written by your coworker is too negative.

1. Open the *Word* file *CH04 English* from the data files. Revise the excerpt from the letter to give the message a more positive tone.

2. Spell-check, proofread, and correct all errors before printing the message.

DATABASE
WORD PROCESSING

Topic **4-2**   ACTIVITY 1

Form Letters

A draft of a letter to be used as responses to routine inquiries for employment has several errors in spelling, capitalization, and word usage. These errors must be identified and corrected before the form letter is merged with the data source.

1. Open and print the PDF file *CH04 Letter* found in the data files. This file contains handwritten text to be used as standard text for a form letter.

2. Key the standard text for the form letter. Assume the letter will be printed on company letterhead. Use the current date, block letter format, and open punctuation. Add an appropriate salutation and closing. Correct errors as you key; then spell-check and proofread the message. Save the letter as *CH04 Form Letter*.

3. Create a new database file named *CH04 Contacts*. Create a table named **Contacts** that contains the following fields: Record ID, Title, First Name, Last Name, Address, City, State, ZIP Code, and Position. Make Record ID an AutoNumber field and the primary key. Make all other fields text fields.

4. Enter data for the five records as shown on the following page in the Contacts table. (The AutoNumber field data will be entered automatically.)

Mr. Tomas Perez, 298 Apple Lane, Springfield, MO 65804-1189, administrative assistant
Ms. Alice Lamson, 19 Talley Street, Englewood, CO 80111-7825, accounts payable specialist
Mrs. Mabel Jones, 339 Hogan Street, Topeka, KS 66612-1045, order entry associate
Mr. Ken Hinrichs, 809 Northsky Square, Cupertino, CA 95014-0692, customer service representative
Mrs. Emiko Yung, 56 Barrow Road, Westerville, OH 43081-2243, secretary

5. Open the standard letter (*CH04 Form Letter*). Select the *Access* file *CH04 Contacts* as the data source for a mail merge. Enter fields from the database for the variables. Complete the merge steps to create personalized letters. View the merged letters and make corrections, if needed, before printing the letters.

6. Perform a merge to create personalized envelopes for the letters. Edit the merged envelopes so the addresses are shown in all capitals. Remove all punctuation except the hyphens in the ZIP codes. Make other corrections, if needed, before printing. (Use paper cut to envelope size if envelopes are not available.)

Topic **4-2**   ACTIVITY 2

COMPOSITION
WORD PROCESSING

Standard Letter Format

Assume that you work for Western Security Systems. After several meetings, the support staff has recommended that a modified block style letter with mixed punctuation be adopted as the company standard for all business letters. You have been asked to provide a sample of the modified block letter format. You decide to use the body of the letter to describe the format and punctuation style so that everyone will understand how to prepare letters using this standard format.

1. Compose and key a sample modified block letter with mixed punctuation. Use the following information for the address and supply an appropriate salutation. The letter is from you, and your title is Administrative Assistant.

   Address:
   Customer's Name
   Street Address
   City, State ZIP

2. Create a memo form for Western Security Systems. Include the company name and heading lines to print on plain paper. Prepare a memo to all employees asking them to begin using modified block format for all letters. State in your memo that you are enclosing a sample letter as an example.

Topic Review

Topic 4-3

objectives

- Identify the characteristics of business reports
- Prepare reports in formal and informal formats
- Create visual aids used in reports
- Use software features effectively in creating and editing reports

BUSINESS REPORTS AND RELATED DOCUMENTS

Business reports are used to share information. Reports may be prepared for employees or people outside the company. The type of reports workers will prepare will depend on their job duties. In many companies, office workers write, edit, assemble, and distribute business reports.

Reports can be prepared in various formats and for various reasons. You will explore reports with different purposes in this topic. In addition, you will explore special features of reports such as tables and graphs. You will learn to gather, organize, write, and present information in a standard report format. You can easily adapt this format to other reports you may encounter on the job. Reports can be saved as Web pages and shared with others using an intranet. You will practice saving reports as Web pages.

Informational Reports

Informational reports are typically based on data gathered within the normal operations of the company. Standard report forms may be used to gather the data for such reports. The company relies on employees to complete the forms accurately and neatly. Using printed forms saves time and ensures that data are collected in the same way by all users.

WORKPLACE CONNECTIONS

Louisa Ramos works as an administrative assistant in a small insurance company. One of Louisa's duties is keeping track of the office supplies, which are stored in a central location. Every month she prepares a report for her supervisor. The report gives a summary of the supplies used and those ordered as replacements. Employees who remove supplies from storage are supposed to let Louisa know what materials have been taken. Some employees leave a note on Louisa's desk. Others send her an e-mail or voice mail message, and yet others leave a note in the supply cabinet. The messages are often incomplete. They may leave out the quantity or a clear description of the supplies removed. Louisa realized she was spending a lot of time asking employees for complete details about the supplies removed as she prepared her report each month. "This system just isn't working. There has to be a better way," Louisa thought.

Louisa created a form with spaces for an employee to record his or her name, the current date, code numbers for the supplies removed, and the quantity of the supplies removed. The forms are kept in the supplies closet. Each employee who removes supplies now completes a form and leaves it in a specially marked tray on Louisa's nearby desk. Using the information from the supplies forms, Louisa can now create the monthly report quickly.

150

CHAPTER 4: COMMUNICATING IN WRITTEN FORM

In many companies, routine reports are created on a regular basis. Procedures for gathering data needed to write these routine reports may be in place. For example, the form shown in Figure 4-3.1 is used to collect data about copier problems. A completed copier repair form is submitted each week. An employee uses the weekly reports to write a repair summary report. One of the purposes of this report is to spot high maintenance trends and to anticipate when major maintenance will be needed on a copier. The two-page memo report follows the same format each week. The similar data are summarized for each report using designated headings. The employee then adds comments at the end of the report.

Figure **4-3.1**

Informational reports are often prepared from data collected using forms.

Cory's Copier Service

Person Reporting Problem	Leslie
Date and Time	1/11/-- 9:15 a.m.
Customer Name	Amy's Hair Salon
Address	1538 South Elm
	Riverton
Copier Model	C-248
Number of Copies	235,687
Problem Reported	Lines across bottom of page
Action Needed	New Drum
Action Taken	Drum on order
Repair Person	Ryan Barnes

Some companies use handheld computers to gather data that are later used to create reports. For example, utility company workers use devices to read meters that monitor use of electricity. The data gathered are copied to a central computer. Office workers use the data in creating reports and customer bills.

When writing an informational report, follow the guidelines used for a direct message. State the purpose early and clearly. For example, use the subject line in a memo report or the title in a formal report to help focus the reader to your purpose.

Expand the Concept

Discuss with students examples of routine reports used in business.

151

Points to Emphasize

Make the report concise; do not include unnecessary information in the report. Identify your comments or interpretations to the data clearly.

For Discussion

Why do you think an analytical report might take more time to prepare than an informational report?

Points to Emphasize

Keep information organized and record complete source information as the data is gathered. Doing so will save time when writing the report.

Consider the audience in deciding how formal a report should be. Consider whether to use technical terms or confidential information. Make certain the reader knows why the report is being written. State clearly the response or action required. Provide complete and correct supporting data. Write the report in a positive tone.

Organize the report by outlining the points that should be covered. If you are expected to follow a standard format, the organization is already determined. If, however, you can develop your own reporting format, organize your thoughts around a logical way.

Present only data that relate to the topic of the report. Do not clutter the report with unnecessary data. You may be expected to add your own comments or interpretations to the data. Identify these comments clearly. Writers often use headings such as *Comments*, *Recommendations*, or *Implications* for their analysis and comments about the data.

Give attention to the formatting and final presentation of the report. The report represents you or your company. It can make a positive or negative first impression affecting how the content of the report will be received.

Analytical Reports

Analytical means involving detailed study. An analytical report is generally a longer, more complex report than an informational report. Such a report is normally prepared as a formal business report. It often requires much research and information gathering. An analytical report takes more time to write and may require in-depth analysis of situations to persuade the reader.

The data presented in an analytical report are often used to make important company decisions. Typically, an employee is asked to research a specific problem or situation. Several employees may work in a group to research and write the report. The employees gather data related to the problem. Then they write a report that presents the data they have collected. The report may also include interpretations of the data. The writers are often expected to draw conclusions and make recommendations.

Gathering Data

Reports are often completed under the pressure of deadlines. Employees are expected to gather data quickly and accurately. You may be asked to contribute to a formal business report. These guidelines will help you gather and process data quickly, accurately, and with attention to detail:

- Record complete source details for all data you locate. Include the title of the publication or Web site and address, author, publisher, date, and page.
- If information must be keyed during the data-gathering stage, key it as it is collected.
- If information must be recorded manually, use note cards to allow for ease in rearranging the data while writing the report.
- Use a scanner with **optical character recognition** (OCR) software, if available, to reduce the amount of time needed to enter large quantities

optical character recognition: reading text printed on paper and translating the images into words that can be saved in a computer file and edited

CHAPTER 4: COMMUNICATING IN WRITTEN FORM

of previously keyed data. If scanning is not possible, photocopy the material (such as tables) to be sure that the details are accurate.

- If your duties include creating many reports, consider using **speech recognition software** to speed data entry. A typical office worker might enter text using the keyboard at 50 words per minute (wpm). After a little practice using speech recognition software, the same worker could probably dictate text at 130 wpm.

- If a document has sections that are often repeated, save time by using boilerplate text.

- Use tablet PCs or handheld computers to collect data as an alternative to keying data. These devices allow the user to handwrite notes on a touch screen or scan bar codes. The handwriting can be converted to text and downloaded to a desktop computer. This process can be much faster than recording data manually on note cards or forms and then keying the data.

speech recognition software: computer programs that allow voice input, also called *voice recognition*

Scanning text and graphics can save valuable time when creating reports.

© GETTY IMAGES/PHOTODISC

WORKPLACE CONNECTIONS

Stan Bridge works for a package delivery service. He uses a handheld computer device to gather data. When each package is delivered, Stan scans the package bar code label that identifies the package and the delivery location. The customer signs for the package entering his or her signature on the touch screen of the computer device. At the end of each day, Stan places the handheld device in a unit that allows the data to be downloaded to a computer. The data are used to create a report that shows the number of deliveries Stan made that day, the number of pounds the packages weighed, and the types of items (overnight letters, small packages, large boxes) delivered.

The data collected by several drivers are also used to create reports. These reports address issues such as how long a route various drivers should be assigned. The number of drivers needed in a particular delivery area might also be discussed.

Topic 4-3: *Business Reports and Related Documents*

Expand the Concept

Explain to students that to be proficient with voice recognition software for text input, you must "train" the software to recognize your speech. Ask students: Do you think the training time required to use voice recognition software effectively is well spent?

Expand the Concept

Large volumes of information are available online and from information services. Employees who can identify the most useful source, select information relevant to the question, and organize the information into a meaningful form are highly valued.

Voice Recognition Systems

Voice recognition systems allow users to input data by simply talking to a computer. This process is also called speech recognition. As the user speaks into a microphone, the spoken words appear on the computer screen. Current software versions allow the user to speak up to 160 words per minute with 95–98 percent accuracy. This type of software has improved greatly in recent years. Voice input is now a practical alternative to keyboarding.

Using voice input helps workers be more productive. Data are input directly in one step rather than recorded on tape and then keyed later by the same or another person. This process reduces the time needed for the work to be completed.

It also reduces the need for outside transcription services.

Using voice input reduces the need for clicking a mouse. Many commands can be given by voice instead. Documents, databases, or the Internet can be searched using voice commands. This can help reduce the instances of repetitive strain injuries, such as carpal tunnel syndrome.

In the future, more programs for voice input will be developed for portable and wireless computer devices. Small, hand-held units will allow workers to use voice input when away from the office. Such upgrades will provide greater freedom and higher productivity for users.

Researching Information Online

The Internet and private information services provide access to data that can be used in reports. Many of the sources available on the Internet are free for all users. Private information services, however, usually charge a connect fee. They may also charge according to time used or the number of searches made. Many businesses find using an information service more efficient than using staff time to search for data.

By using the Internet or an information service, data can be searched quickly. Company financial profiles, investment advice, text of magazines and journals, U.S. Census data, and government regulations are a few examples of the data that can be found.

Writing the Report

When report data have been gathered, organized, and analyzed, you are ready to begin writing the report. As a writer, you will need to consider and use an appropriate tone and degree of formality in the report. If the report is for your coworkers, an informal style may be used. If the report is for a broad audience or outside the company, however, your writing style should also be more formal. Read the examples in informal and formal styles in Figure 4-3.2.

154

CHAPTER 4: COMMUNICATING IN WRITTEN FORM

Figure **4-3.2**

Use an appropriate style for each report.

Message in Informal Style

Jason, this report contains the information on the delivery routes and schedules you requested. You're right, two of the delivery schedules overlap, leaving the third route only partially covered on Tuesdays and Thursdays. No wonder we have had complaints from our customers on the third route. I'm taking immediate steps to correct this schedule.

Message in Formal Style

In July, 20--, the Board of Directors authorized a study to determine the effect of downsizing on the production capability of the Houston plant. Several additional factors were determined to contribute to the 20 percent overall production drop.

Use a formal style when the report will be read by a larger number of people or when the topic is complicated. To achieve the formal style in the second example, note that the writer

- Did not use first names (*The Board of Directors* vs. *Jason*)
- Did not use contractions (for example, *you're* or *I'm*)
- Used **passive voice** (*were determined* vs. *report contains*)

Use the general guidelines presented in Figure 4-3.3 on page 156 to begin creating the report. If several drafts of the report are required, cycle through step 4 as often as revisions are required. These steps are common to all business reports.

passive voice: a style of writing in which the subject is acted upon rather than performing the action

Distributing or Posting Reports

Once a report is completed, you may need to make one or more copies and deliver or mail the report to persons who need it. You will learn about copying documents in Chapter 10 and about mail delivery services in Chapter 11.

A report might be sent as an attachment to an e-mail message. Reports that are prepared to be used in printed form may also be posted on a company intranet. Word processing and spreadsheet programs have features and commands that allow documents to be saved as Web pages. Always preview the document in a Web browser to check the format before posting. You may need to make adjustments to the layout of documents saved as Web pages.

For Discussion

Ask students what types of reports they have accessed online.

Figure **4-3.3**

*Focus report prepara-
tions by using these
guidelines.*

For Discussion

Ask students to discuss the
similarities and differences in
the guidelines for a report
and the guidelines for letters,
memos, and e-mails dis-
cussed in Topic 4-2.

Thinking Critically

Your supervisor has asked
you to use the format from
a previous company report.
You think the format is both
confusing and inefficient.
What should you do or say
to your supervisor in this
situation?

Points to Emphasize

All margins except the left
are the same for unbound
and leftbound reports.

GUIDELINES FOR ORGANIZING AND WRITING REPORTS

1. Focus the report.
   - Identify the purpose of the report.
   - Identify your readers.
   - Determine why readers will want to read the report.
   - Identify data needed for the report.
   - Identify information resources.
2. Plan the message.
   - Identify the main topics and subtopics.
   - Prepare an outline of the report.
   - Identify potential visuals and graphics.
3. Write the first draft.
   - Write a draft of the text.
   - Develop related visuals and graphics.
4. Revise your first draft.
   - Revise the outline if necessary.
   - Edit or revise text of the first draft.
   - Verify and document sources used.
   - Finalize visuals and graphics.
5. Present your report.
   - Use a standard format.
   - Check headings and subheadings.
   - Prepare preliminary report pages.
   - Proofread the final copy.

Business Report Formats

Several acceptable formats are can be used for business reports. Your company, however, may have a preferred format. Look at previous reports or a
company procedures manual to see formats that have been used for reports.
Two common business report formats are the unbound and leftbound formats.

An unbound report is fastened in the upper left-hand corner with a paper
clip or staple. No extra space is provided in the margin for fastening the
report together. This format is useful for short reports that will be distributed internally.

In a leftbound report, the left margin contains one-half inch of extra space.
The extra space allows for binding the report at the left. All other margins
are the same as those of the unbound report. Writers use this format for
longer, more complicated reports. Leftbound format is also useful for
reports that require a formal presentation or are being sent outside the
company.

CHAPTER 4: COMMUNICATING IN WRITTEN FORM

The formats presented to you in this topic represent acceptable business report formats. Refer to Figure 4-3.4 for a summary of report formatting guidelines.

Business Reports Formats

Figure **4-3.4**

Report format guidelines

Format	Top Margin	Bottom Margin	Left Margin	Right Margin
Unbound				
First page	2 inches	1 inch	1 inch	1 inch
Other pages	1 inch	1 inch	1 inch	1 inch
Leftbound				
First page	2 inches	1 inch	1.5 inches	1 inch
Other pages	1 inch	1 inch	1.5 inches	1 inch

The body of the report is usually double-spaced, but it may be single-spaced.

Formal Business Reports

A formal business report includes standard parts. These parts help readers understand the report. A formal report generally explains the reason for the report. The report data and an explanation of their meaning follow. Conclusions or recommendations are given last. The writer also documents the sources of information used to write the report. A formal business report may contain all or some of the common report parts. Typical report parts used in a formal business report are listed in Figure 4-3.5 on page 158.

Report Pagination

Pagination is the process of dividing a document into individual pages for printing. Page breaks are set by the software as the page is filled. These breaks are called soft page breaks. When revisions are made, the page endings will change and the pages will be renumbered automatically.

The user can enter a command for a page ending. This type of page ending is called a hard page break. This page ending will not shift when edits are made to the document. A hard page break is useful for beginning a new chapter or section of a report. A hard page break can also be used to prevent paragraphs from dividing. Paragraphs divided between pages should contain at least two lines on each page. A first line of a paragraph printed by itself at the bottom of a page is called a widow line. The last line of a paragraph printed by itself at the top of a page is called an orphan line. Avoid widows and orphans by reviewing the page breaks in the report and adjusting them as needed. Your word processing software may allow you to set options that help prevent widows and orphans.

pagination: the process of dividing a document into individual pages for printing

157

Figure **4-3.5**

Report parts

Parts of a Formal Report

Title page	Contains the report title, the writer's name, the name of the organization, and the report date. The company address may also be included.
Table of contents	Contains a listing of the report headings and their corresponding page numbers. Can be created from headings marked in the body of the report in some word processing software.
Summary	Contains a brief overview of the report. The summary may also be called *executive summary* or *abstract*.
Body	Contains the text or message of the report. In long reports, the body will be divided into chapters or sections. The body may be double-spaced or single-spaced with a blank line between paragraphs.
Quotation	Material from another source that is identified in the body of the report. A quotation of more than three lines is set off from the rest of the text.
Documentation	Source information for quotations or material adapted from other sources. Two common methods are endnotes and textual citations.
References	A list of the sources used in preparing the report. The list should include the sources for direct quotes, paraphrased sources, and sources used to obtain ideas or background information. This section may also be titled *ENDNOTES, BIBLIOGRAPHY,* or *WORKS CITED.*
Appendix	Contains more detailed data (usually in the form of a chart, graph, table, or text) to support the body of the report. The appendix (or appendices if several are included) is placed at the end of the report. If more than one appendix is included, number or letter each in order.

footer: information that appears below the body text at the bottom of document pages

header: information that appears above the body text on pages of a document

Use the automatic page numbering feature of the software to number report pages. The title page of a report is considered page 1, but it should not display a page number. Pages coming before the body of the report, such as a table of contents, are numbered with lowercase Roman numerals. The numbers are centered in the page **footer**. Pages in the body of the report, the references section, and any appendices are numbered in the **header** at the right margin. See Figure 4-3.6 on pages 159 and 160 for examples of page numbers.

Report Headings

The main heading is the title of the report. Use the heading to introduce the reader to the report's topic. Give the heading a prominent position in the report by using capital letters and bold type, a slightly larger type size, or a different font style. The Title heading style of the word processing

Title Page

Center all lines

Begin title at 2 inches from the top

INTERNET USE

Begin the writer's name at 5 inches from the top

Alberto Diaz
Office Communications Consultants

Begin the date at 9 inches from the top

August 5, 20--

Title Page

Table of Contents

Top margin: 2 inches
Side margins: 1 inch or default

TABLE OF CONTENTS

Use leaders and right-align page numbers

Number the page with Roman numerals, centered in the footer

ii

Table of Contents

Figure **4-3.6**

Unbound report format examples

Expand the Concept

The heading, *TABLE OF CONTENTS,* is centered according to the format selected, unbound or left-bound. Leaders can be used to guide the reader in finding page numbers. A table of contents usually follows a title page and is numbered *ii.*

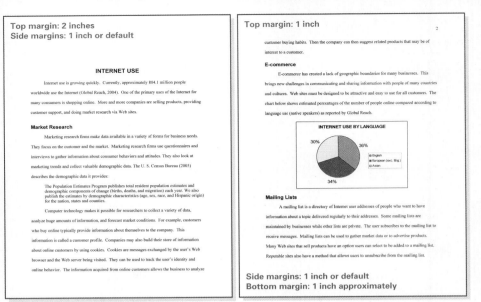

Unbound Report, Page 1   **Unbound Report, Page 2**

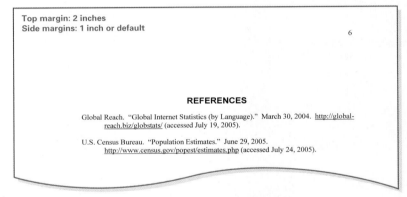

Unbound Report, References Page

Figure 4-3.6

Unbound report format examples continued

software can also be used to format the title. The secondary heading, if used, provides additional information. If a secondary heading is used, give it less prominence in your report than the main heading. Capitalize only the first letter of key words. Use the same font style, perhaps in a smaller size, as used for the main heading.

Use side headings to divide the main topic into subdivisions. Key side headings in capital and lowercase letters on a separate line beginning at the left

CHAPTER 4: COMMUNICATING IN WRITTEN FORM

margin. Insert a blank line before and after each side heading. Use bold or the different font style used for the main and secondary headings for emphasis. Default heading styles in the word processing software can be used to format report side headings. When these heading styles are used, the word processing software can generate a table of contents for the report that includes the headings.

Report Documentation

Giving credit to the sources of information you used in a report is called documentation. One common method uses endnotes. When the endnote method is used, a superior (raised) reference figure is placed at the appropriate point in the copy. The matching numbered reference is then listed at the end of the report in a section titled *ENDNOTES.*

When writing the report, credit must be given for material quoted either directly or indirectly from other sources.[1]

If using endnotes, use the footnote feature of your software to create the endnotes. If text that contains an endnote reference is moved, the endnotes will be renumbered. Endnotes numbers will also be adjusted when new endnotes are inserted.

Another common method uses textual citations. When the textual citations method is used, part of the source information is placed in parentheses within the text. This information includes author(s), date of publication, and page number(s).

When writing the report, credit must be given for material quoted either directly or indirectly from other sources (Tilton, Jackson, and Rigby, 2005, 395).

If the source is identified by name within the report copy, only the publication date and page number are used.

According to Tilton, Jackson, and Rigby, credit must be given for material quoted either directly or indirectly from other sources (2005, 395).

The matching reference is listed at the end of the report in a section titled *REFERENCES* as shown in Figure 4-3.6. The entries are listed in alphabetical order by the author's last name. Entries are single-spaced in hanging indent format with a double space between them. Each reference should provide all the data needed for the reader to locate the source. Data included will vary depending on the type of source. Consult a current reference manual for example entries. The company may identify a reference style or guide that employees should use. Examples of reference manuals include:

- *The Chicago Manual of Style*
- *How 10: A Handbook for Office Workers*
- *MLA Handbook for Writers of Research Papers*
- *Publication Manual of the American Psychological Association*

For Discussion

Under what circumstances might you use quotations, endnotes, or textual citations? Which method do you prefer and why?

Expand the Concept

List report references in alphabetic order in appropriate bibliographic format. Consult a style manual or a previously prepared report that uses an acceptable format.

161

Topic 4-3: Business Reports and Related Documents

Memo Reports

Short, informal reports are often prepared in memo format. The subject heading is used to identify the topic of the report just as the main heading is used for an unbound report. Side headings, like those used for unbound report format, may be used to identify sections of the report. Side headings are shown in Figure 4-3.7.

A memo report frequently has more than one page. In such instances, the page number is part of the heading that appears on all pages after the first page. Review multiple-page headings in Figure 4-2.5 on page 136. Use the header feature of your word processing software to automatically print the page number and the rest of the heading at the top of succeeding pages.

Figure **4-3.7**

Memo report example

Approximately 2-inch top margin

Office Communications Consultants

TO: Alma Yung, Manager

FROM: Alberto Diaz

DATE: August 5, 20--

Default or 1-inch side margins

Report subject in all caps →

SUBJECT: MARKETING AND THE INTERNET

Internet use is growing quickly. Currently, approximately 804.1 million people worldwide use the Internet. One of the primary uses of the Internet for many consumers is shopping online. More and more companies are selling products, providing customer support, and doing market research via Web sites.

Report side heading →

Market Research

Marketing research firms make data available in a variety of forms for business needs. They focus on the customer and the market. Marketing research firms use questionnaires and interviews to gather information about consumer behaviors and attitudes. They also look at marketing trends and collect valuable demographic data.

SS body, DS between paragraphs →

Computer technology makes it possible for researchers to collect a variety of data, analyze huge amounts of information, and forecast market conditions. For example, customers who buy online typically provide information about themselves to the company. This information is called a customer profile. Companies may also build their store of information about online customers by using cookies. Cookies are messages exchanged by the user's Web browser and the Web server being visited. They can be used to track the user's identity and online behavior. The information acquired from online customers allows the business to analyze customer buying habits. Then the company can suggest related products that may be of interest to a customer.

Mailing Lists

A mailing list is a directory of Internet user addresses of people who want to have information about a topic delivered regularly to their addresses. Some mailing lists are maintained by businesses while other lists are private. The user subscribes to the mailing list to receive messages. Mailing lists can be used to gather market data or to advertise products. Many Web sites that sell products have an option users can select to be added to a mailing list. Reputable sites also have a method that allows users to unsubscribe from the mailing list.

Newsgroups

Newsgroups publish online articles and messages related to a huge number of topics. Users participate in public discussions about a topic by sending messages that all participants in the newsgroup can read. Newsgroups are available for thousands of topics. Some companies sponsor newsgroups related to their products. Users can ask questions or make comments about

Approximately 1-inch bottom margin

Visual Aids

Visual aids consist of the tables, graphs, and other illustrations, such as maps, which are used to present data in a report. The purpose of using visual aids is to help make the report easy to understand. They may also reduce the amount of text needed, presenting the data in a chart or table instead.

Tables

A table contains facts, figures, and other information arranged in rows and columns. Tables can be used to summarize information and to make comparisons. When developing a table to be used in a report, be certain that it relates directly to your report. The table should have a clearly defined purpose and should focus the reader's attention on a specific aspect of the report.

A report table should be self-explanatory. That is, the reader should not have to refer to text that may accompany the table to understand the table contents. Look at the table in Figure 4-3.8. Is it self-explanatory? Which employee received the highest commission? How much were his or her total sales for the first quarter? Which employee received the lowest commission? How much were his or her total sales for the first quarter?

Figure 4-3.8 displays the standard parts of a table. Some simplified tables will not include all these parts. More complex tables will include other parts such as a source note indicating the source of the data. Ruled lines may be used to separate the data visually. Dot leaders may be used to aid in reading across the table from one column to the next.

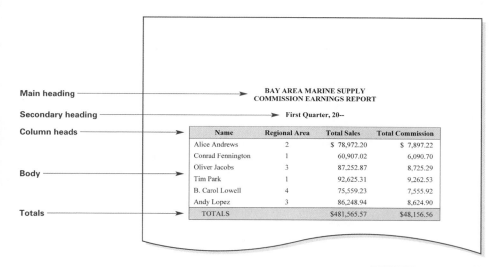

Figure **4-3.8**

Basic table format

Topic 4-3: *Business Reports and Related Documents*

Most word processing programs have a table feature that automatically determines column spacing and prepares the table layout. You may wish to start with this table layout and then make adjustments as needed. Spreadsheet software can also be used to create tables. Using spreadsheet software is best when the table contains numbers that must be totaled or used in formulas. Your goal is to create a table that is easy to read and highlights the appropriate information. The following guidelines can be used when formatting tables.

- Key the main headings in all capital letters using a 14-pt. font. Apply bold and center alignment to the title. The title may be placed as the first row in the table grid or above the table grid as shown in Figure 4-3.8. Key a secondary heading in bold a double space below the main heading.
- Key column headings in a 12-pt. font. Apply bold and center alignment to column heads.
- Key data in cells using a 12-pt. regular font. Data in cells can be aligned left, aligned right, or centered. Usually, numbers are aligned right and words are aligned left.
- Center tables horizontally on the page. Center tables vertically on a page or set a 2-inch top margin. When a table is placed in a memo or report, leave one blank line above and below the table.
- Tables can be formatted with the cell borders (gridlines) hidden, with all cell borders showing, or with selected borders showing. Shading or automatic table styles can also be used.
- The body may be either single- or double-spaced. Tables are often double-spaced for improved readability. When the table is placed within the text of a report, use the space available on the page to determine how you will space the table body. The table width should not exceed the left and right margins of the report body.
- Data in a table are often summarized or calculated with the results shown at the end of the table. *Total, Average, Maximum,* and *Minimum* are common summary lines included on tables. The last entry in a column is often underscored to separate the table data from the summary lines.

Graphs

A graph is a pictorial representation of data. Graphs make the report more interesting and informative. In many cases, data are easier to interpret in a graph than when shown in columns of figures. Graphs, therefore, are used frequently in business reports to display supporting information.

As you prepare business reports containing graphs, study previous reports from the company to determine style preferences. If the graph is half of a page or less in size, include it in the body of the text. Leave a double space before and after the graph to separate it from the text. Position the graph as near as possible to the portion of the text in which it is mentioned, ideally on the same page. If the graph is larger than half a page, place it on a separate page and include a reference to the graph's page number.

Spreadsheet programs are commonly used to prepare charts and graphs. A **pie chart** (so called because the graph wedges look like pieces of a pie) is a

pie chart: graph showing how a part contributes to the whole

Points to Emphasize

Data may be easier to interpret or understand in a graph than when shown in columns of figures or blocks of text.

For Discussion

What software have you used to create graphs? What types of graphs have you created?

Points to Emphasize

Each graph has a particular function. A pie chart shows the relationship of parts to a whole.

display of how a part contributes to the whole. The whole circle represents 100 percent, and each wedge represents a portion of the whole. Each wedge should be identified with an appropriate label, color, or pattern. A pie chart is shown in a report in Figure 4-3.6.

A bar graph is used to show comparisons, as displayed in Figure 4-3.9. Use bars of equal width and space the bars equally across the graph. If more than one set of data is included in the graph, use different colors or patterns to identify the sets of data. Stacked bars, three-dimensional bars, and gridlines may be used to make the data easier to read or understand. The number scale should be adjusted to show an appropriate range. For example, if the numbers graphed range from 75 to 103, the graph scale might begin at 70 rather than at 0. Consider carefully the point you intend to make with the graph. Adjusting the graph scale can make differences in the data appear smaller or larger.

bar graph: chart used to show comparisons

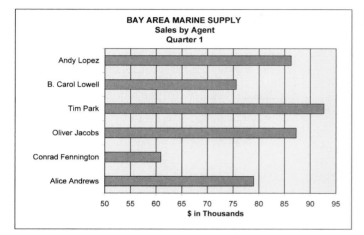

Figure **4-3.9**

Bar graphs are used to show comparisons between items.

Points to Emphasize

A bar or column graph shows comparisons.

WORKPLACE CONNECTIONS

Tina works in the Accounting Department of a small company. Her manager asked Tina to compare the costs of renting or buying a new copier for department use. Tina created a spreadsheet to include the costs of renting and the costs of buying a copier. If the copier is rented, the regular maintenance and any needed repairs will be handled by the copier rental company. The company must pay only a flat monthly fee. If a copier is purchased, however, the long-term costs will include the maintenance and any repair costs for the copier.

Tina used a spreadsheet to test various possible rent and buy scenarios. She concluded that renting a copier would be more cost-effective for the department. Tina wrote an informal report recommending that the department rent a copier and included a chart comparing the costs of the two alternatives.

line graph: chart used to display trends that emerge over a period of time

A line graph is used to display trends that emerge over a period of time. An example is shown in Figure 4-3.10. Monthly sales, for example, are frequently represented in line graph form. In preparing such a graph, place the time categories across the horizontal axis and the amounts along the vertical axis. If more than one set of data is shown on the graph, use different-colored lines to distinguish each set.

Figure **4-3.10**

Line graphs are used to display changes over a period of time.

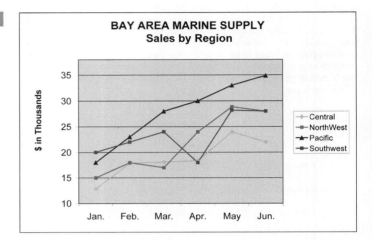

CHAPTER 4: COMMUNICATING IN WRITTEN FORM

Topic Review 4-3

REVIEWING THE TOPIC

1. What is a business report? What do all business reports have in common?
2. How does an analytical report differ from an informational report?
3. What guidelines should a writer of an informational report follow?
4. Describe three methods or technologies an office worker could use to input data for a report rather than keying the data.
5. What are the advantages of researching information online or using information services?
6. When is a formal writing style appropriate for reports?
7. How do unbound and leftbound reports differ?
8. What are the common parts of a formal business report?
9. Identify visual aids commonly used in business reports. Why are visual aids useful?
10. Describe the best uses of pie charts, bar graphs, and line graphs.

INTERACTING WITH OTHERS

You are working on a special research project with Larry Moore. He was supposed to e-mail you a lengthy attachment vital to your completion of the project. He promised to transmit it to you by noon yesterday. At 4:30 p.m., you have not heard from Larry. You are becoming very concerned because the deadline for the report is only one week away. You must study Larry's material carefully before you can complete your part of the project. By your estimate, it will take you approximately nine hours to review Larry's data.

1. Compose and key an e-mail message to Larry that is appropriate for the situation described above. If you do not have e-mail software, key the message as a memo using your word processing software. If using e-mail software, key your teacher's e-mail address after the To heading. Key an appropriate subject line in all capitals after the Subject heading. (The From and Date information will be added automatically by the e-mail program. Use your name and the current date if using word processing software.)
2. State your concerns and the action that you want Larry to take. Follow proper guidelines for preparing e-mail messages as you compose your message. Make the tone of the message positive.
3. Save and print the message. Send the message if using e-mail software.

Teaching Tips

If the students are using the *Student Activities and Simulations* workbook, instruct them to complete the review activity for this topic.

Teaching Tips

Ask some students to share their messages with the class. Discuss tactful ways to emphasize the importance of sending the needed material.

REINFORCING MATH SKILLS

You work in the Accounting Department of Black's Computers, a small retail computer store. Your supervisor, Mrs. Lowell, has sent you a file containing part of the data needed for a report. She asked you to complete the spreadsheet.

1. Open the *Excel* file *CH04 Math* from the data files, which contains the report data.
2. Enter the column headings **Total Sales, Cost of Units Sold,** and **Gross Profit** in columns F, G, and H.
3. Enter formulas to calculate the total sales for each product to Wayne Middle School for the current year.
4. Enter formulas to calculate the cost of units sold for each product. (Multiply units sold by the wholesale price.)
5. Enter formulas to calculate the gross profit for each product. (The gross profit is the difference between the total sales and the cost of units sold.) Add the gross profit column to determine the total gross profit figure. For the total gross profit amount cell, use a single top and double bottom border.
6. Save your work; you will use it in another activity.

COMPOSITION
INTEGRATED DOCUMENT
SPREADSHEET
WORD PROCESSING

Topic 4-3 : ACTIVITY 1

Memo Report with Table

Your supervisor at Black's Computers, Mrs. Lowell, has asked you to prepare a table using the spreadsheet you created earlier. The table will be included in a short memo report.

1. Create a memo form for Black's Computers that includes the company name and the appropriate memo heading lines. Address the memo to Carlos Morales, Vice President of Sales. The memo is from Mrs. Virginia Lowell, Accounting Supervisor. Use an appropriate subject heading. Date the memo using September 4 of the current year.
2. Begin the body of your memo report with the text shown on the following page. Add figures from your spreadsheet to complete the sentences. Next, inform Mr. Morales that you are including a table that shows a complete list of the products Wayne Middle School has purchased this year.
3. Refer to the spreadsheet you completed earlier. (If you did not complete the *Reinforcing Math Skills* exercise before, do so now.) Hide these columns in the spreadsheet: Product Number, Wholesale Prices, and Cost of Units Sold. Copy the spreadsheet data and paste it into the memo report. Adjust the table format, as needed, for an attractive table.

168

CHAPTER 4: COMMUNICATING IN WRITTEN FORM

The information you requested about product sales to Wayne Middle School is provided in this report. The school purchased _____ desktop computers to equip three classrooms. _____ notebook computers were purchased for staff use. One class set of _____ tablet PCs and one class set of _____ PDAs were purchased. These computers will be used in different classes at various times for specific learning units. Several printers, both inkjet and laser, and a few scanners were also purchased.

Our gross profit for this order was $_____. The three products (by product numbers) that produced the highest gross profit as part of this sale were _____ ($_____), _____ ($_____), and _____ ($_____).

Topic 4-3 : **ACTIVITY 2**

COMPOSITION
INTEGRATED DOCUMENT
SPREADSHEET
WORD PROCESSING

Memo Report with Graph

Mrs. Lowell has asked you to prepare a graph using data from the spreadsheet you created earlier. The Gross Profit column shows the dollar amount of profit on each product. Mr. Morales would like to know the markup percent this amount represents for each product.

1. Open the spreadsheet that you edited in Activity 1. Insert a new column between columns E and F. Enter **Markup Percent** for the column head.

2. Enter formulas in column F to find the markup percent for each product. (Subtract the wholesale price from the selling price and divide by the wholesale price.) Show zero decimal places in the percents.

3. Create a bar graph that compares the markup percents for all the products. (Hide columns B, C, D, and E to make creating the chart easier.) Enter **Markup Percent** for the graph title. Do not include a legend.

4. Add a paragraph at the end of the memo report you created in Activity 1. Introduce and explain what is shown in the bar graph. Tell which product has the highest markup percent. Insert the graph into the report.

5. Keep the last paragraph that introduces the graph and the graph on the same page. Add a second-page memo heading in the header on page 2.

Teaching Tips

Review how to hide columns in a spreadsheet and how to create a bar graph.

CHAPTER REVIEW 4

CHAPTER 4: COMMUNICATING IN WRITTEN FORM

Summary

Much of the communication in business is in written form. Reading and writing skills are essential for all types of office workers. In this chapter, you learned ways to improve your reading and writing skills. You also learned guidelines for preparing business documents. Review the key points from this chapter listed below:

- Employees read at work to learn about the company and understand instructions. They also read to use reference sources, complete forms, and respond to inquiries.
- Reading skills involve comprehension, vocabulary, and speed. All three areas can be improved with practice.
- All office workers need strong writing skills. Among the common writing tasks at work are summarizing messages and meetings, revising writing done by others, and preparing messages in various forms.
- Effective documents are well planned. They are clear, concise, courteous, complete, and correct.
- Using proper spelling, punctuation, and grammar are important for writing at work.
- Managing the schedule for writing tasks is important for meeting writing deadlines.
- The three stages of planning effective documents are drafting the document, revising or editing it, and proofreading it for final form.
- When writing a document, know your purpose, your message, your audience, and the response you want from your audience.
- Positive, neutral, negative, and persuasive messages are used in business documents.
- Business letters are formal documents. They are usually written to people outside the company.
- Memos are informal documents. They are generally written to people inside the company.
- Employees often individualize letters when similar letters are sent to hundreds of people.
- Memos should be used to give confidential information or for routine messages to people who do not have access to e-mail. E-mail is appropriate for most other short written messages.
- Desktop publishing is used to create high-quality printed documents. These documents usually contain text and images and often have complex formats.

Teaching Tips

Have students review key points from the chapter by completing the Sort It Out game on *The Office* Web site.

- Business reports are a source of information for making business decisions. They are basically either analytical or informational in nature. They may be in either a formal or an informal style.
- Visual aids, such as tables and graphs, are used in business reports to make a report more understandable. They add interest to the report and may reduce the text needed to explain the information.

Key Terms

appendix	negative message	quotation
bar graph	netiquette	references
comprehension	neutral message	resolution
documentation	optical character	spam
draft	recognition (OCR)	speech/voice
font	pagination	recognition
footer	passive voice	software
format	persuasive message	tone
goodwill	pie chart	vocabulary
header	positive message	white space
kerning	proofreading	
line graph	protocol	

Teaching Tips

Have students review the key terms by using the Flashcards available on *The Office* Web site.

Chapter 4 : ACTIVITY 1

COMPOSITION
TEAMWORK
WORD PROCESSING

Press Release

Assume that you are an assistant manager in the Public Information Department of Laughlin & Mead Corporation. The company's Board of Directors met yesterday. They elected Mr. T. W. Gomez to the company's new position of Vice President for Technology. The public information director has asked you to prepare a draft of a press release. The release will be sent to local newspapers as well as to business periodicals.

1. Open the PDF file *CH04 Press Release* from the data files, which contains a sample press release. Read the document to learn about writing and formatting a press release.

2. Compose and key a draft of a press release for review by the department manager. Use the current date and your name as the contact person. Other details that should be included in the release are given on page 2 of the *CH04 Press Release* file. Single-space the body of the release. It will be distributed in printed form and posted online.

Teaching Tips

Assign students to work in a team with one other student to complete this activity. Review the sample press release with students before they compose a release.

171

Chapter Review

WORD PROCESSING

Chapter 4 ⋮ ACTIVITY 2

Leftbound Report

In this activity, you will format text for a leftbound report. Review report guidelines and examples found in Topic 4-3 to help you complete this activity.

1. Open the *Word* file *CH04 Leftbound Report* found in the data files. Format the text as a leftbound report with a title page, table of contents, body, and references page.

2. Use a heading style available in your software to format the side headings. Adjust the style, if needed, so the side headings appear in a 14-pt. font.

3. Create a header to number the pages in the body of the report. The second page of the body should be page 2.

4. Generate a table of contents using the appropriate features of your software. Adjust the format of the table of contents to make the lines double-spaced. Delete any lines at the beginning of the list that are not needed, such as the report main title. Only the side headings and the References page should be listed. Change the *References* entry to initial cap to match the other entries.

172

CHAPTER 4: COMMUNICATING IN WRITTEN FORM

© DIGITAL VISION

CHAPTER 5

Communicating Orally

You will need to express yourself clearly in your speech at work so others will understand you. This is true whether you are talking with a coworker, addressing people at a meeting, or giving a presentation. In some cases, you will speak to motivate and influence people. In other cases, your spoken messages will be to inform and educate. You will also need to listen effectively so you can give appropriate feedback, answer questions, or carry out instructions.

This chapter focuses on speaking skills and their importance to your success at work. In this chapter, you will learn how to improve your listening and speaking skills for both communicating with coworkers and giving formal presentations.

173

Topic 5-1

objectives

- Describe the importance of listening
- Explain techniques that aid in active listening
- Describe what an effective speaker achieves
- Explain the factors considered in speaking

modulated: adjusted to a proper level

LISTENING AND SPEAKING

Regardless of the career you choose, you will want to be confident about your listening and speaking skills. These oral communication skills will play a role in many aspects of your responsibilities.

The Importance of Listening

Imagine you are walking along a hall in a high-rise office building downtown. You notice that many conversations are under way. You cannot hear what is being said because voices are **modulated** so that only persons nearby hear the actual words. You would undoubtedly observe persons talking by telephone and others in conference with other people. In every instance, listeners are taking part in the communication process.

Effective listening skills are vital to every office worker.

© NASI SAKURA/SUPERSTOCK INTERNATIONAL

You will need to listen at work countless times. When you listen effectively, you will be able to:

- Follow through on oral instructions correctly
- Consider the additional information as you continue your work and make decisions
- Use time productively

WORKPLACE CONNECTIONS

Helena, an assistant manager, wasn't sure what the manager told her about a task she was about to begin. She had not taken notes during their discussion of the task. When she got back to her desk, she realized she did not understand when certain information was needed from the Hong Kong and Tokyo offices. Did she have enough time to send e-mail messages or should she telephone instead? She decided that she would not bother the manager but would just send e-mail messages and trust that the information would be forwarded in time for the manager's schedule. Unfortunately, the manager called early the next morning wanting the information. Can you imagine what happened in the conversation at this point?

Later, as Helena thought about this incident, she realized what had happened. She realized her mind was elsewhere when the manager turned to her after a telephone call, which had interrupted their discussion. Helena's mind did not return to the matter at hand; however, she continued thinking about something else. Helena made a promise to herself to be a more attentive listener.

This worker is not listening effectively.

Points to Emphasize

Businesses are operating increasingly in the global community where communication is difficult.

Thinking Critically

How does listening aid productivity?

For Discussion

In what situations do you find that it is difficult to listen? Why?

175

Topic 5-1: *Listening and Speaking*

Effective Listening Strategy

Listening is required to gain an understanding of what is being said. Conversations, meetings, lectures, answering machines, and voice mail will be meaningless if you fail to listen. Listening involves a mental process as well as the physical aspects of hearing. You may hear a speaker but not actively listen to the speaker by giving your full attention to what is being said. Mental participation is the critical part of listening. The listener must think about what is being discussed. When you listen, your mind processes the information you hear through reshaping what is already known about the topic and storing the information for future use.

Poor listening may occur for a number of reasons. Some common reasons are:

- The listener feels insecure in the presence of the person who is explaining something. The listener is so fearful that it is difficult to pay attention to what is being said.
- The listener thinks he or she already knows what is being discussed.
- The listener thinks there is no value to what is about to be said.

prejudgments: conclusions reached before having full information

Think carefully about how you react when someone begins to talk with you. Notice what **prejudgments** or attitudes are influencing your own listening. The following attitudes will help you improve your listening skills:

- An attitude of openness and wanting to learn is critical to being a good listener. If you think you can learn from others, you are likely to listen with a sincere wish to know what the other person thinks. You are likely to follow up comments made by others with a closely related question or further comment.
- An attitude of respect for others is important for good listening. Remember that no two persons have had exactly the same experiences. Respecting the backgrounds of others will help you listen attentively.
- An attitude that you can contribute to the discussion will help you listen attentively. "We can all gain from this talk" is the unspoken thought of a person who is listening attentively.

Focus Attention

Have you ever heard someone—a parent, a good friend, or a teacher—say: "Please pay attention!" If you have, you may recall that the person was encouraging you to listen. Possibly, during a conversation you were asking again and again, "What did you say?" In such a situation, you were not really listening attentively to what was being said. After the plea to pay attention, you may have sharpened your focus and put aside mental distractions. Your willingness to respond aided your listening. Making an effort to think about what is being said can improve your comprehension of what you hear.

Harold worked in a busy office as an industrial engineer. At times, he had to be on the factory floor. Often he would return from the factory to find a number of messages in his voice mailbox. He would retrieve the messages. He found, however, that even though he heard the messages, he wasn't listening. He had to replay the messages two or three times. He realized he was wasting valuable time because of his failure to listen effectively. He made a promise to himself: "I will listen carefully the first time, so I do not need to repeat messages." He listened to his own promise. He was surprised at his success.

Mentally Summarize and Review

If possible, anticipate what you will hear and prepare for listening by mentally creating an outline. For example, if you know that the manager often gives you assignments, you should set up a mental outline with the following sections: What is to be done? Why must it be done? What is the deadline? At what points does my manager want to know about my progress? With such a mental outline, you can listen to your supervisor and put what is said in its proper place. A quick review of your mental outline will ensure you that you have all the information you need or help you identify what is missing.

Pause, even if momentarily, to review what you have heard. Determine whether you have clearly understood what you heard. Does it make sense? Do you have all the information you need? This review acts as a reinforcement of new information. Mentally reviewing a conversation and your notes assures you that you have gained what you needed to move ahead with your work or undertake a new assignment.

Take Notes and Ask Questions

Frequently, details are involved in talking with someone in person or by phone. Make a note of instructions, dates, figures, telephone numbers, and scheduling requirements to supplement your careful listening.

The person talking with you wants you to understand clearly what is being discussed. In most cases, he or she will welcome your questions. By listening carefully and raising questions, you can confirm that you understand the message. Your questions can also focus on points that were not clearly specified.

Teaching Tips

Ask the students to develop a mental outline for what you are going to present to them about how they are to handle an activity, for example.

Thinking Critically

What information should the students be sure to include in notes taken during a conversation?

Teaching Tips

Ask the students to raise questions about asking questions.

177

Topic 5-1: *Listening and Speaking*

Take notes about instructions to reinforce your careful listening.

Speaking Effectively

The companion skill of listening is speaking. You will have many occasions when you must speak to coworkers or customers about your work and what is to be done. On such occasions, you will want to speak with ease and confidence.

To communicate your thoughts effectively, you must show your listeners that you are interested in what you are saying. Have you ever listened to a speaker who seemed to be reading a speech with no understanding of the words? If you have heard such a speaker, do you recall whether you enjoyed what you heard or did you learn much? You probably did not.

On the other hand, you may have heard someone who seemed very interested in what was being said. Your attention was captured because of the

A speaker who is interested in the topic will capture the audience's attention.

CHAPTER 5: COMMUNICATING ORALLY

Teaching Tips

Have students describe speaking experiences they enjoyed and some they thought were unsuccessful.

Expand the Concept

An interest in communicating is helpful for effective communications. What can you do to remain attentive when you must discuss something in which you have virtually no interest?

For Discussion

Why do you enjoy hearing a speaker who seems very interested in the information being communicated?

way the person spoke as well as by the content of the message. The interest of the speaker in communicating with the listeners increased the effectiveness of the communication.

WORKPLACE CONNECTIONS

Karen was the manager of special events. She reported to the director of food services in a large company. Karen talked with people who came to the office to arrange luncheons, dinners, and other special events in the company dining rooms. The director praised Karen for her skill in working with so many different people. As the director noted: "Karen is happy to explain the menus that are available. She clearly shows her interest in being helpful and giving people all the information needed to make choices."

Express Ideas Clearly

Thinking must precede speaking, if only by a brief moment. Try asking a mental question such as: "What do I really need to say to communicate my meaning?" Consider the purpose you are trying to accomplish with your communication. You are not likely to be misunderstood if you think about what you want to say before speaking.

WORKPLACE CONNECTIONS

The supervisor asked an assistant: "What do you still have to complete for the Thompson report I gave you on Monday?" Without a pause for thought, the assistant responded: "Not much."

If the assistant had given thought to the question, the response might have been: "I have to key the conclusions, the three short appendices, and the bibliography. Then I will print the entire document." Which of the two responses is the supervisor likely to consider more satisfactory?

Speak Clearly in an Appropriate Tone

Your spoken words are worthless if the listener is unable to hear and understand them. Speaking clearly requires that you say each word carefully. This is referred to as proper **enunciation**. When you enunciate words properly, your listener is more likely to hear them correctly. Listeners have trouble understanding speech when speakers run words together and when syllables are not sounded fully. Note the examples in Figure 5-1.1.

enunciation: pronouncing words clearly

For Discussion

Someone observing Karen might say she is very patient. Why do you think she is patient in her explanations?

Expand the Concept

What are the problems, as you see them, in speaking clearly?

For Discussion

Does stating each word carefully make your speech boring to the listener?

Figure **5-1.1**

*Enunciate carefully
to avoid these
mispronunciations.*

Words and Phrases Commonly Enunciated Poorly

'preciate	for	appreciate
cam	for	calm
didya	for	did you
gimme	for	give me
gonna	for	going to
granite	for	granted
labatory	for	laboratory
libary	for	library
nothin'	for	nothing
'r	for	our
winda	for	window
winnin'	for	winning

Speaking at an appropriate volume level and using an appropriate tone are important for clear communications. Consider the situation in which you are speaking and the distance your voice must carry. Regulate the volume level of your voice so listeners can hear you clearly, but so you do not disturb others who may be working nearby. Make the tone of your voice match the message you are trying to convey. Speak in a warm and friendly tone when complimenting a coworker on a job well done. Use a questioning tone when asking for information. When giving a warning, let your tone of voice convey caution or danger. Remember that the tone of voice and expression you use in speaking can be as important as the words you say in communicating your message.

Use Standard Language

Standard language uses the words taught in English courses in schools. These words are explained in current dictionaries. However, most dictionaries also show some common terms that are not standard language.

*People who learned English
as a second language can
easily understand people
who use standard language.*

CHAPTER 5: COMMUNICATING ORALLY

Office workers should use standard language and correct grammar at work. Use of standard language helps others understand spoken messages. Increasingly, workers talk with others from around the world. Many people have learned English as a second language. For these people, using standard language helps ensure that your message will be understood.

Colloquialisms are informal words and phrases. These words are used among people who know each other well or among people from a specific geographic area. Some colloquialisms are commonly used at work among employees who know each other well and tend to speak informally. A few of these terms are shown in Figure 5-1.2.

colloquialism: informal language used among a particular group

Colloquialisms		
finish off	for	complete
get out of line	for	fail to conform
head up	for	serve as chairperson
touch bases	for	discuss a matter
walk the talk	for	carry through what you say

Figure **5-1.2**

People from a different area may not understand colloquialisms.

Slang is informal language. Discovering the meaning of slang words is difficult for those outside the group in which such words are popular. Slang expressions are often short-lived. Most of the time, slang expressions are inappropriate when communicating with others at work.

slang: informal language

Consider Your Audience

Audience is another term for listeners. Whether you are talking with a few people or a large group, you will want to consider the interests and needs of your audience. These interests will affect how you accomplish your purpose for communicating. Talking with a single person or a small group usually permits you to be more informal than when you are speaking with a large group.

audience: listeners or recipients of a message

You want to consider: (a) what your listeners want to know; (b) what they might already know; and (c) how what you are saying can be related to their experiences. You also want to be sensitive to how listeners are reacting to what you are saying. Are they looking away with lack of interest? Do they seem impatient with the length of your comments? Are they confused? Do they seem eager and attentive while you are talking? Do they seem ready to move on to another topic?

Thinking Critically

Why have colloquialisms developed? Why are they useful in environments where everyone knows those in use?

For Discussion

Why do you use slang? Where are you most likely to use it?

Expand the Concept

How can you know your audience when you have been asked to make a presentation to new employees?

181

WORKPLACE CONNECTIONS

Leon was asked to instruct a new employee, Abby, in the use of a spreadsheet software program. Leon sat at the computer with Abby, beginning the explanation as though she knew nothing about the computer.

Leon did not inquire about Abby's experience at the computer and with spreadsheets. If he had, he would have learned that Abby had considerable experience with spreadsheets, even though she didn't know the feature Leon was explaining.

Leon should have asked some questions about Abby's skills. He then would have realized that Abby was not a beginner. He could have quickly moved to the explanation specific to the features that Abby needed to learn. Also, Abby would have a more positive impression of Leon if he had been considerate of what she already knew. Both of them would have saved valuable time if the explanation were focused on what Abby needed to learn.

Be Aware of Nonverbal Communication

Communicating a message often involves more than words. Facial expressions, gestures of hands and arms, posture, and other body movements also communicate to listeners.

Nonverbal behavior can be difficult to understand. For example, glancing at a clock might mean that a person is eager to leave a meeting as quickly as possible. However, perhaps the person wants to remain until the last possible minute before going to another meeting. Making eye contact and smiling when someone comes to your workstation may show an interest in being helpful. It might also merely reveal pleasure in having an excuse to stop work and take a break.

Be aware of the nonverbal behavior that you display. Make sure it agrees with the intent of the words used. Nonverbal behavior should reinforce what is said, not distract from its meaning. Do not confuse your listeners by saying one thing and having nonverbal behavior communicate something else.

Be Interested in the Listener's Response

When speaking, allow time for interaction, if possible. Give listeners a chance to respond. One of the major advantages of oral communication is that there can be immediate feedback. When talking with others, be interested in getting questions, comments, and reactions to what you say. A skillful communicator is a good listener.

FOCUS ON . . .

Body Language

You may have heard the saying, "Actions speak louder than words." This saying can be quite true in the case of nonverbal communications. These communications are commonly called body language. Many studies have been done on nonverbal behavior. Meanings people assign to different kinds of body language vary. Non-verbal behaviors do not always speak as clearly as words. Be aware of the possible meaning of nonverbal cues. This awareness can help you understand others and deliver your messages more effectively.

Facial expressions are important nonverbal cues. A smile can convey understanding or support for what is being said. A frown, on the other hand, may indicate lack of understanding or disagreement. A smile at an inappropriate time, however, may convey smugness or insensitivity. Raised eyebrows may convey surprise or disapproval.

Eye movement can signal that you are paying attention. Making eye contact frequently shows your interest in what is being said. It implies that you are being honest or open when speaking. Letting your eyes roam around and seldom making eye contact can signal that you are not paying attention when listening or that you are being evasive when speaking.

Posture and gestures are important elements of body language. Good posture when sitting or standing shows confidence. Slouching or stooping shows an indifferent attitude or lack of self-confidence. Leaning closer or nodding conveys interest. Leaning or turning your body away conveys discomfort or disagreement with what is being discussed. Crossed arms show a defensive or unwelcome attitude. Sitting calmly with hands folded in your lap shows an openness to listen. Placing your hand to your cheek generally indicates that you are evaluating or considering. Placing your hand over your mouth generally indicates your disapproval.

Fidgeting while talking or listening shows a lack of focus. Constantly glancing at the door or at a clock while speaking with a coworker can show that you are not really interested in the discussion. This behavior may reduce the effectiveness of what you are saying.

When talking with coworkers or taking part in meetings, notice the body language of the speaker and those around you. Paying attention to body language will help you understand better what others are trying to say. When talking with coworkers or giving a formal presentation, be aware of your body language. Use your body language to reinforce the message you want to communicate. Body language that is consistent with the words you use will enhance your message.

body language: posture, body movements, gestures, and facial expressions that serve as non-verbal communication

For Discussion

What facial expressions do you find most informative when you are talking with others?

Expand the Concept

How can you be sure your nonverbal cues are matching the words you use? Can you give illustrations?

183

Topic 5-1: *Listening and Speaking*

REVIEWING THE TOPIC

1. What are possible outcomes of listening effectively?
2. In what way is listening a mental process?
3. Why is listening necessary at work?
4. What are some reasons for poor (ineffective) listening?
5. How do you mentally summarize?
6. What does it mean to have an interest in communicating?
7. What is required to speak clearly?
8. What is standard language, and why is using standard language at work important?
9. Why should you take notes and ask questions when receiving instructions?
10. What factors should a speaker consider about the audience?

INTERACTING WITH OTHERS

Three classmates were talking together after school one afternoon. One of them, Jack, said to the other two: "Listen, can I talk with you about my problem? I will confess to you that I don't want to give a talk in class next week. I'll just pretend that I am sick and not come to school for a few days. Sitting here and talking with you is fine. But I can't get up before the class. I have figured out a way to get out of doing this all through high school. I'll be honest with you. I remember having to stand before the class in the seventh grade to recite part of a poem. I was so scared that after the first two lines I couldn't remember a word. Oh, was I embarrassed. Aren't these assignments ridiculous? I'm not going to have to stand up before anyone and talk when I am out of school and earning a living. Do you agree with my scheme for next week?"

1. What would you say to Jack? What decision do you think would be best for him?
2. What tips can you give Jack to help him overcome his fear of public speaking?

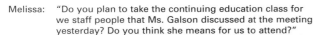

REINFORCING ENGLISH SKILLS

You overhear the following conversation between two colleagues who are standing at the photocopying machine. Both of your colleagues have made a number of errors in their use of pronouns.

1. Key a copy of the conversation between Melissa and Steve, changing all pronouns used incorrectly.

2. Underscore all the pronouns you substituted for those in error.

Melissa:	"Do you plan to take the continuing education class for we staff people that Ms. Galson discussed at the meeting yesterday? Do you think she means for us to attend?"
Steve:	"I don't know if I'll go. Both me and Earl wonder if we would be better off taking a course later in the year. The topics are interesting though, aren't it?"
Melissa:	"Well, between you and I, I think there are likely to be some good courses later; but Betsy and me have pretty much decided we will go. We believe Ms. Galson would like we to go."
Steve:	"Melissa, if you go, will you tell us what them said at the meeting?"
Melissa:	"Of course; the instructor will be good, I guess. I won't be as good as her, but I'll do my best."

Topic 5-1 : ACTIVITY 1

COMPOSITION
TEAMWORK
WORD PROCESSING

Speaking and Listening in a Meeting

Office workers must often present ideas or plans at small group meetings. Practice organizing your ideas and presenting them at a meeting in this activity.

1. Work with two classmates to complete this activity. (Read all the instructions for the activity before you begin completing the steps. You will repeat some of the steps so that each student will be a speaker, listener, and observer.)

2. As a team, create a form or checklist to use in recording notes about the effectiveness of communications during a meeting. Review Topic 5-1 and list important points for listening and speaking on the form. Also include a place to comment on the body language of both the speaker and listener.

185

Topic Review

After students have keyed the sentences, discuss the corrections that they should have made.

Review the checklists created by students. Encourage students to be honest but tactful as they comment on the talks given by classmates.

3. As the speaker, choose a topic from the following list to develop into a three- to five-minute talk. List the main points you want to convey and then place the points in logical order. Be specific and give examples or supporting information as appropriate. Present your talk to the listener as if the two of you were in a meeting. Answer your listener's questions.

Topics

Why you need new equipment or software

How you want to change a procedure and why

Why your company should sell a new product or service

Instructions for a work project the listener is to complete

4. As the listener, pay careful attention to the speaker. Using two or three minutes after the speaker finishes, note the main points of the talk. Then ask relevant questions related to the information presented.

5. As the observer, pay careful attention as your classmates role-play the meeting. Then note what you observed on the form. Discuss your observations with your classmates.

6. Repeat steps 3–5 so each person plays each role—speaker, listener, and observer. Give your teacher a copy of your notes for the talk as a speaker, notes and questions as a listener, and the form you completed as an observer.

COMPOSITION
WORD PROCESSING

Topic 5-1 : **ACTIVITY 2**

Summarize Meeting Proceedings

The ability to listen attentively and summarize what you have heard is a key skill for office workers. Practice your listening and composition skills by summarizing meeting proceedings.

1. Identify a meeting that you can attend or view on television. Examples of organizations whose meetings you might attend include school clubs, civic organizations, a local school board, and a local city or county government. Local government meetings, such as a city council meeting, are often televised in the local area.

2. Attend the meeting or watch it on television. Remember that your role is that of a guest observer. Your purpose is not to participate in the meeting, but merely to listen and watch. Write brief notes about the proceedings during the meeting.

3. After the meeting, write a one-page summary of the meeting. Include the name of the organization, the meeting place and date, the approximate number of people attending, and the main points of the items discussed or decided.

Teaching Tip

Help students identify meetings that they can attend or watch on television. Local government meetings are often televised. You may wish to record a meeting and have it available for students to watch.

objectives

- Identify the purpose of the message
- Profile the listeners
- Address the interests of the listeners
- Develop ideas for the message and organize them
- Create effective visuals and handouts
- Organize team presentations

Regardless of your job, you will need to express yourself clearly to others at work. Presentations may not be a part of your daily work. Occasionally, however, you may need to present information to others. The situation may require you to speak to a small group of your peers or to a large audience. Regardless of the size of your audience, you must keep your goals and your listeners' interests in mind as you develop your presentation.

Identify the Purpose of the Presentation

When you have an opportunity to prepare a presentation, it will likely be for one of two purposes. You will either want to motivate and influence your listeners, or you will want to inform and educate them. The message of your presentation will include the main ideas and supporting details you want to present. When you are speaking to motivate or influence, your message needs to be persuasive. Your purpose is to get your listeners to take a course of action. When you are speaking to inform, your message should be clear and concise. Your purpose is to communicate the information so your listeners can understand and use the information. Identifying the overall purpose of the presentation and the specific goals you want to accomplish is the first step in preparing a presentation.

Profile Your Listeners

Your message must be important to your audience if you are to hold their attention. Developing a **profile** of your listeners is the next step in preparing a presentation. You must determine your listeners' interests or needs. Then you can relate your message to something they want to hear about.

profile: a description or picture

To determine what is important to your listeners, you must first describe them in as much detail as possible. Put yourself in their shoes. Write down everything you know about them:

- What do the listeners like or dislike?
- What do the listeners need?
- What is the expertise of the listeners?
- What **biases** do the listeners have?
- What responsibilities do the listeners have?
- Are the listeners decision makers?

biases: prejudices

Developing a listener profile helps you identify the interests of your listeners. At first this may seem difficult, but if you try to think as they think, you should be able to do so.

187

Topic 5-2: *Planning and Preparing a Presentation*

Points to Emphasize

A speaker's goal may be to teach an audience about new ideas, to create a good feeling, to entertain an audience, to persuade an audience to accept new opinions or take certain actions, or to provide information about a topic. In all cases, the message is meant to accomplish a purpose.

Points to Emphasize

An effective speaker studies the people who will be listening to the presentation. The speaker tries to determine what may interest or excite the listeners and what might cause them to take action.

For Discussion

Even though speaking is not a part of our daily work, many of us find ourselves in situations where we are asked to make presentations. Ask students to give examples of these situations. Answers may include speaking at a graduation ceremony, making a toast to the bride and groom at a wedding reception, or addressing clubs or other organizations.

Your message must be important to your listeners.

© CORBIS

Roberto is planning a presentation for office personnel in his department. The purpose of his presentation is to tell about new office procedures that are to be used by the department. The new procedures have been adopted to help workers be more productive. However, Roberto's message to the office staff must address their concerns and interests.

Roberto knows that several workers update the customer database. As a result, some customer records are overlooked because one person assumes another employee made the updates. Workers are never sure customer records are accurate. Better procedures are needed for updating customer records. When Roberto makes his presentation, he can discuss how the procedures will affect this situation that is of interest to his audience. He will explain how the new procedures will make their jobs easier.

Develop the Message

Your ideas, or the main message of your presentation, must accomplish the purpose of the presentation. The message must also relate to your listeners' needs or interests. With the purpose clearly in mind, create a list of major points or ideas you must include to accomplish your purpose. Consider how you can relate each major point or idea to the interests of your audience.

Organize Your Ideas

After you have identified the ideas or main points to be included in the presentation, organize them in a logical way that your listener will understand. Sketching out and organizing your thoughts is called storyboarding. Storyboarding involves considering several ideas and then organizing them to create an outline and notes about the topic. The notes can be just words or phrases, or they can be complete sentences.

storyboarding: recording and organizing ideas, as for a presentation

188

CHAPTER 5: COMMUNICATING ORALLY

To create a storyboard, you can complete a worksheet page for each element or idea for your presentation. Figure 5-2.1 shows a sample of a storyboard worksheet. The worksheet helps you organize your thoughts about a specific idea. You begin by stating the purpose of the presentation. Next, you describe one of the main ideas and provide information that supports your idea. Then you identify a listener interest. You also list listener advantages. Don't be concerned right now with the worksheet box labeled "Visual Element." You'll learn about that shortly.

To complete the storyboard, you fill out a worksheet for each idea in your presentation. Once all your ideas are written down, you can improve the flow by rearranging the pages. The storyboard provides the basic organization of the presentation. Through this planning process, you organize the key concepts and define the overall presentation.

An alternative to completing storyboard worksheets is to use a software outline feature to create the storyboard pages. Create the main topics (or ideas) and then break down each main topic into subtopics. Once you key your ideas, you can edit and rearrange them quickly and easily. Be sure to include listener interests, support for your ideas, and listener advantages for each idea.

Include Supporting Details

Whenever possible, provide evidence or details that support your ideas. For example, you can state facts or offer statistics to back up a proposal. You can use examples and comparisons to confirm a need. You can use expert opinions to endorse a recommendation. You can relate a situation to personal experiences of your listeners or experiences of your own.

Storyboard Worksheet	
Purpose	Motivate and influence sales staff to increase sales during the fall campaign
Main Idea	Commission and bonus opportunities will increase
Support for Idea	Commissions on sale items raised from 10% to 15%
	$500 bonus for top ten total sales
Listener Interest	Commissions and bonuses that may be earned during the campaign
Listener Advantage	More income for the staff member
Listener Objection	Large number of clients to be handled during the sale
	Counter: The extra effort required will be rewarded with higher income
Visual Element	Growing dollar sign

Figure **5-2.1**

A storyboard worksheet helps you organize a presentation.

Points to Emphasize

A presentation should have a defined logic. If the purpose of the presentation is to inform, the information presented should be complete, explicit, and clear. If the purpose of the presentation is to persuade, the order of the reasons presented should provide support for convincing the audience to accept that opinion.

Expand the Concept

Although most speakers write their own speeches, business executives and politicians employ professional writers who help them prepare their speeches.

In a presentation on new office procedures, Roberto will describe an embarrassing situation he experienced recently. He was talking with a customer on the phone, and the information in the database was not up to date. As a result, he was not able to handle the customer's questions. Roberto's audience, the office staff, can easily identify with this problem.

Consider Listener Advantages and Objections

Once you have developed your ideas and your listener's interests, list the advantages for your listeners if they accept your ideas. If possible, prioritize these advantages in order of importance to the listeners.

objections: reasons to disapprove or reject ideas

Consider all the **objections** your listeners may have regarding your ideas. When you anticipate the listeners' objections, you can decide how to address them. You may be able to offer solutions or alternatives to what the listeners see as a problem. Your goal is to minimize the objections so the listeners no longer see them as a problem.

Choose Visuals and Audio

audio: sound that can be heard by the human ear

Images and **audio** are very powerful. Visual aids and sounds stimulate the listener and keep the listener's attention. Studies show that we remember about 10 percent of what we hear in a presentation and about 20 percent of what we see. However, we remember about 50 percent of what we both see and hear. Even in one-to-one communications, visuals are extremely effective. Not only will the visuals help you present your content, they will also make your listeners feel important because you took the time to create them.

Plan a visual for each main idea (each page in your storyboard). This will help provide direction for your presentation. Each visual you create should be designed for consistency and simplicity. Carry out the theme of the presentation in all visuals. The first visual should introduce the topic and set the tone for the presentation as shown in Figure 5-2.2. All visuals should support the overall message and should address the interests of and advantages to the listeners.

Choose the Media

media: materials or means used to communicate

The **media** you choose for your visuals will depend on your budget and the equipment you have available. Your audience and whether the presentation is formal or informal will also influence the media you use.

Flip charts are very effective for small, informal groups. They are inexpensive and easy to create and use. For one-to-one communications, desktop easels can be effective.

Points to Emphasize

Use your visuals to guide you through the presentation. If all your key ideas are presented in the visuals, you won't overlook them.

Teaching Tips

Show students examples of the various media discussed in this section. Discuss when use of each is appropriate.

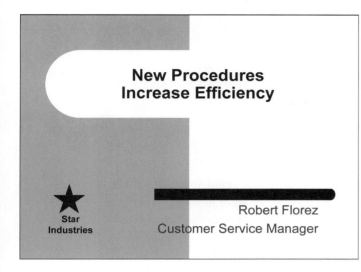

New Procedures Increase Efficiency

★ **Star Industries**

Robert Florez
Customer Service Manager

Figure **5-2.2**

This visual introduces the topic and the speaker.

© CORBIS

Flip charts are inexpensive and easy to use.

Overhead transparencies are effective for small or large groups and for formal and informal presentations. Overhead transparencies are inexpensive to create. They can be created in black and white or in color. If you have access to a copier that can handle transparency film, you can copy text, photos, and illustrations and turn them into transparencies quickly and easily. If the copier can produce color copies, you can create four-color transparencies inexpensively.

Transparencies are easy to use. If you reorganize your presentation, you can quickly and easily rearrange the order of the transparencies. You can write on them and add to them during a presentation. You can overlay them to build a concept or to add special effects or emphasis.

191

Topic 5-2: *Planning and Preparing a Presentation*

Overhead transparencies are effective for a variety of presentations.

Presentations that use electronic slides are appropriate for both large and small groups. With programs such as *Microsoft® PowerPoint®*, you can create electronic slide shows quickly and easily. Slide shows that also use sound are called multimedia presentations. If projection equipment is available, you can display slides directly through a computer. This is an effective method for presenting information.

Your needs may require you to create individual slides that are to be displayed through a slide projector. You can have individual slides created at photo centers. The slides can be produced from photos or illustrations. They can also be developed from the electronic slide shows. The cost for creating these slides varies greatly depending on the media, turnaround time for development, and the company used.

Transparencies and film slides are static images. In other words, the images don't move. If you have access to the proper software and equipment, you

Commercial software packages allow users to create professional slide shows.

CHAPTER 5: COMMUNICATING ORALLY

192

can add motion to your visuals. Most computers can display high-quality images and play sound. You can enhance a presentation by including video, animation clips, and audio.

Create the Visual Elements

Think of your favorite book. Do you remember the story with visual elements or with words? Most of us mentally picture things we remember. When we recall previous experiences, we generally remember them visually.

People remember graphics better than words. Whenever possible, use a graphic or picture instead of words or to reinforce words. Keep the graphics simple. Effective visuals help the presenter keep the listener's attention. In return, the listener can stay involved in the presentation and remember more of the message. Make sure the visual element you choose reinforces what you want to communicate. Do not use images that are unrelated to the content of the message. Use the storyboard worksheet to describe your visual element(s) as you plan and organize your presentation.

Many programs are available for working with clip art, graphs, illustrations, and photographs. However, the graphics you use in a presentation do not need to be elaborate. They can be simple creations that you draw or clip art that comes with your presentation software. For example, you can use a clock to represent "time" or an up arrow to represent "increase" as shown in Figure 5-2.3.

Design Strategies

Limit your design to one main idea per visual, and use plenty of white space. Use the same orientation (slide directions) for all of the visuals. Visuals in landscape orientation are wider than they are tall. Visuals in portrait orientation are taller than they are wide. Transparencies and slides are usually created in landscape orientation. The visual in Figure 5-2.3 is in landscape orientation.

Figure **5-2.3**

Simple graphics illustrate presentation ideas.

Customer Satisfaction

- New procedures ensure prompt updates of customer records
- Results
  - Accurate records
  - Increased customer satisfaction

Star Industries

Customer Satisfaction

Topic 5-2: *Planning and Preparing a Presentation*

Presentation programs provide some powerful design tools. Multimedia, animation, and sound options can be used to enhance presentations. However, the key to effective visuals is to keep them simple and related to the purpose of the presentation.

Why is use of ample white space important when creating visuals?

Keep the design of your visuals simple. Remember that the purpose of the visuals is to help you maintain your listeners' attention and to help your listeners remember your message. Do not make your visuals too complicated or difficult to read or understand.

Text

Limit text on visuals. If the text on a visual is crowded, it results in a confusing appearance. If you have too much text, the audience becomes involved in reading the content of the visual instead of listening to what you are saying.

Limit the use of different text styles, sizes, and colors throughout to avoid a confusing appearance. For example, you might choose to use Arial, 30-point, blue text for main points or headings and Times Roman, 24-point, black text for subheads or supporting details. Lowercase text is easier to read than all capitals. As a general rule, use all caps sparingly.

bullets: small graphics, such as circles or diamonds, used to draw attention to a line of text

Use **bullets** to help the audience follow the presentation. Bullets are effective for presenting important points and specific terminology. Indent bullets to establish a hierarchy of points or details. The visual in Figure 5-2.3 has two levels of bullets.

Make the wording on visuals parallel. On a slide, for example, begin each bullet line with same part of speech such as a verb or a noun. Use active voice. Whenever possible, make the points short and concise.

Writing on the visual as you use it in your presentation is very effective. Not only does this draw the listeners' attention to the visual, but it also enables you to create a visual memory for your audience. For example, some presentation programs allow you to underline or circle important information on a slide as you discuss the information.

Color

Use color effectively for maximum impact. Just because color is available does not mean it has to be used extensively. In fact, limiting the number of colors used is often best.

Consider the generally accepted associations of colors. For example, in business, red usually relates to cost and green usually relates to profit. In general, red draws the most attention and evokes excitement. Blues and greens are relaxing. Earth tones can be soothing but can also be dull or lack impact. A blending of colors or graduated colors instead of a solid background can help to guide the viewer's eyes to a focal point. Borders are effective for adding and using color wisely. They help to guide the viewer's attention and give the visual a professional look.

The colors you choose will depend on the media you are developing for the presentation. Transparencies are most effective with dark text on a light background. Electronic slides and film slides can be effective with a variety of background colors and textures. Choose your background color, text colors, and image colors to complement one another. You want to create a pleasing effect that will not distract your audience from the message. Some presentation programs have design templates you can use to give your visual a professional look. Coordinating colors for background, text, bullets, and other design elements are part of the template design.

CHAPTER 5: COMMUNICATING ORALLY

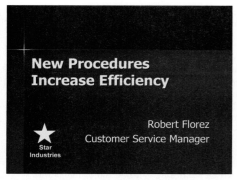

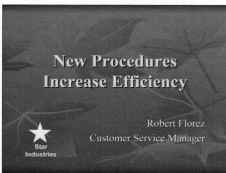
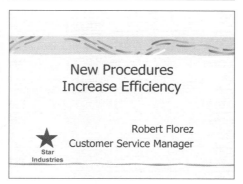

Figure **5-2.4**

The same slide takes on different looks when different design templates are used.

Use Motion

You can add motion to electronic slides in a variety of ways. Cascading bullets, transitions, video, and moving images can all be used to add interest to your electronic slides.

When creating electronic slides, bullet lines can be set to cascade or appear on screen one at a time. Using this technique is effective when you want to emphasize each point as you present it. Your listeners cannot read ahead to the next point you plan to discuss as they can when all bullets appear on screen at once. Your command (usually a mouse click or key stroke) that brings on the next bullet also signals to the audience that you are ready to move ahead to a new point.

Transitions in an electronic slide show are the motions used to move from one slide to the next. A variety of transition styles are available. You can make a slide appear to move in from one side of the screen and cover the slide that is already on screen. You can have a variety of shapes, such as boxes, circles, or diamonds, move across the screen as one slide disappears and another appears. You can also simply have one slide disappear and another appear using no transition effect. Transition effects can be set to move slowly or quickly and can be accompanied by sound in some programs.

transitions: the motions used to move from one electronic slide to the next

You can place links in electronic slides to videos you want to play during the presentation. You might include a video of a company executive who could not attend the meeting in person, for instance. You might play a video that shows technical details or operation of a piece of equipment. You might want to include videos of customers commenting on a product. A video of a warm sunny beach with swaying palm trees can set the mood for a discussion of a winter sales meeting held in Florida. As with other images, be sure the video is appropriate for the content of the message and that it is fairly short so you do not lose the attention of the audience.

Use Audio Effectively

From soft music playing as your audience gathers to resounding applause to stress a job well done, audio can enhance your presentation. Like clipart and other graphics, audio collections are readily available and contain a wide variety of music, sound effects, and common phrases. Sounds can be organized easily using programs such as *Microsoft® Clip Organizer* shown in Figure 5-2.5. If you require specific music or text, you may wish to record your own audio or have it prepared professionally.

If you add audio to your presentation, make sure it is appropriate. The audio should enhance the presentation and not be overbearing or distracting. Sound can be used effectively to introduce a topic, build excitement, or add special effects. If you decide to use sound, be sure you are not competing with it when you are talking. Like color, use sound wisely. Make sure it serves a purpose.

Create Handouts and Posters

The audience will only remember a small part of the content of your presentation. Provide **handouts** for your listeners so they can be used later for reference and as reminders of the key points in your presentation. The

handout: a printed document used to summarize or provide details, as for a presentation

Figure **5-2.5**

Audio clips can be used to add music, voice messages, or other sounds to a presentation.

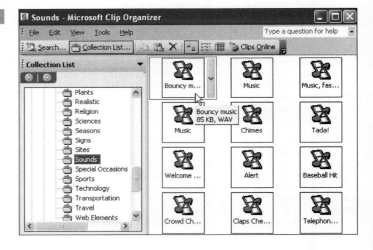

For Discussion

During what parts of a presentation might using sound be effective? When might using sound be ineffective?

For Discussion

There is nothing more embarrassing than distributing a handout that contains errors. Such mistakes reflect negatively on the credibility and image of the speaker. Ask students to give examples of handouts or other materials that contained errors and made a negative impact on them.

handouts need not be limited to text. Consider including some of the visual elements you display in your presentation. Even if they are small images, these visual elements will serve as reminders of the message you provided.

When you have several handouts to distribute, consider printing them on paper of different colors. The colored pages will make it easy for you and your listeners to refer to a certain handout. Consider using a color copier to make handouts for an important presentation. Color copies will add impact to your presentation.

Purposes of Handouts

The intent of the handouts will determine how you design them and when you give them to the audience. Handouts containing the outline of your presentation can be useful in guiding your listeners through the presentation. Distribute this type of handout at the beginning of the presentation. The outline will help your audience follow your presentation and stay involved. Throughout the presentation, the handout can be used for note taking.

Handouts can be used to supply your listeners with detailed information that is too long to place on visuals. These details or references can add credibility to your presentation. Handouts can also be used to summarize the main points of a presentation. Distribute a summary handout after you have given the presentation.

credibility: authority, reliability

WORKPLACE CONNECTIONS

In his talk on new office procedures, Roberto provided a handout containing the outline of his presentation. He removed the details of the outline and replaced them with blank lines. As he presented the new office procedures, the staff members took notes to help them remember the information.

One of the handouts contains detailed descriptions of the new office procedures. The office staff will review this information later when they begin using the new procedures.

Display Posters

Posters can be used to reinforce the content of a presentation. A slide, photo, or handout can be enlarged into a poster-size print. Display the poster to restate key points, introduce a new product, or review a visual element.

You can have posters created at photo centers. The cost will vary depending on the vendor, the poster size, and how quickly the poster must be created. Standard poster sizes include 16″ x 20″, 20″ x 30″, and 24″ x 36″. The positive impact a poster can have can justify the expense of creating it.

Thinking Critically

What are some examples of detailed information that might be provided on handouts rather than in a presentation?

Expand the Concept

Give students information regarding local photo centers or print shops that create posters. Discuss the costs for various sizes of posters. Discuss design tips for posters.

197

A poster can be effective for emphasizing important points in a presentation.

Supplemental Activity

Use some cooperative learning activities to give students additional practice working in teams. Assign some short, team presentations regarding topics familiar to the students. For example, have them make presentations to inform the class about new school policies or to persuade the class to support a club event or fundraiser.

Plan Team Presentations

Office workers often give presentations as part of a team. Different team members bring different skills and knowledge that can be used to complete the task. Working together, the team members can provide broader coverage of the topic than one person could provide.

Determine Roles of Individuals

The first step in preparing a team presentation is to select a leader. The leader will ensure that the team stays focused on accomplishing its objectives.

Each team member must have a valid role. All team members may not be involved in delivering the presentation, but each should make significant contributions. Those contributions can vary. For example, one or more team members may research and develop content for the presentation; another may create the visuals. One or more members may deliver the presentation.

Working as a Team

All members of the team should agree on the purpose or objectives of a team presentation. Everyone's efforts will be directed toward accomplishing these objectives. Team members can share ideas and develop an outline of the points to be presented.

Developing the content of a team presentation requires some special efforts. Several people may have contributed content to be covered. The team should make sure the tone and the terms used are consistent throughout the presentation. All of the content should be presented from the listeners' point of view, and it should provide clear listener advantages.

198

Individuals must work together to prepare a team presentation.

The visual aids must also be consistent in style and content. Using compatible media for visual aids can help to create a smooth transition from one presenter to another. For example, all presenters use the same template design for electronic slides.

The team should review the entire presentation to make sure all the content and visuals flow together well. Team members should be chosen to deliver each part of the content. A specific amount of time should be set for each part. As a last preparation, the team should practice giving the presentation as a group.

199

Topic 5-2: *Planning and Preparing a Presentation*

REVIEWING THE TOPIC

1. What are the two primary purposes of presentations?
2. What kind of information can you gather to profile listeners?
3. Why should you consider listener advantages and objections in planning a presentation?
4. What kinds of evidence can you use to support your ideas?
5. Describe a storyboard and its purpose.
6. List two design strategies related to text and two design strategies related to color on visuals.
7. Give two examples of how motion may be used in visuals for a presentation.
8. Explain how audio may be used effectively in a presentation.
9. Describe ways handouts may be used for a presentation.
10. What are the advantages of working in a team to prepare a presentation?

THINKING CRITICALLY

Assume that you are part of an office team assigned the task of improving the company's schedule for employee breaks and lunchtimes. The schedule was revised to prevent overcrowding in the cafeteria at various times throughout the day. The team recently submitted a proposed schedule to management and has just received approval. The new schedule will be effective the first of next month.

You have been asked to present this new schedule to the personnel in your department. You know that some people in the department are slow to accept changes. You also realize that some of the employees currently enjoy sharing their breaks and lunches with employees from other departments. Unfortunately, this may no longer be possible for some. Before you present the new schedule, you must be ready to address the concerns and needs of the personnel in your department.

1. Describe how you would introduce this new schedule with the listener in mind. What listener needs or interests would you address? What listener advantages would you present?
2. List some complaints and objections you might expect to hear from your coworkers. Explain how you would attempt to minimize these objections.

If the students are using the *Student Activities and Simulations* workbook, instruct them to complete the review activity for this topic.

After students have considered the situation presented, ask them to share their thoughts with the class.

REINFORCING ENGLISH SKILLS

Your colleague Christina Perez has asked you to review her ideas for a presentation she will give to train new employees in using the company e-mail system. She plans to create electronic slides for her presentation. A partial list of her ideas is provided below step 3.

1. Restate Christina's key ideas in short, concise phrases. Use strong, active verbs and limit the use of adjectives, adverbs, and prepositions.
2. Key the text to be contained on each slide. Use bullets to help organize the information.
3. Plan the flow of the presentation and place the material in logical order.

> This e-mail system offers many advantages that will improve your efficiency and reduce the amount of time you are online. For example, you have lots more options that you can set. You can customize these settings for your particular needs. You get faster delivery times.
>
> The features include the following: You can upload and download files. You can automatically retrieve new incoming mail and send new outgoing mail. You can also get to the address book and retrieve data quickly and easily.
>
> Let's take a close look at the address book. You can store multiple e-mail addresses within an individual record. You can sort the records in the address book in alphabetical order. Or you can organize the address book to first display the addresses you use most frequently.

COMPOSITION
PRESENTATION
WORD PROCESSING

Topic 5-2 : ACTIVITY 1

Plan and Organize a Presentation

In this activity, you will plan and organize a five-minute presentation to inform and educate your classmates. In later activities, you will prepare the visuals you plan here and give the presentation to your class.

1. Choose a hobby, sport, or activity that you really enjoy and about which you are knowledgeable. Get your teacher's approval of the topic. Plan a presentation about this topic.
2. Create a storyboard worksheet for each main idea in your topic. See Figure 5-2.1 for an example storyboard worksheet. Complete all parts of the storyboard worksheet, including ideas for the visual elements. (You will create the actual visuals in a later activity.)

Teaching Tips

After students have created titles and phrases to use on the slides, allow some students to share their work with the class. If time allows, have students create electronic slides using this information.

Teaching Tips

Remind students that this is to be a five-minute presentation. They need to be realistic about the amount of information they can present in that time.

Teaching Tips

Tell students the media options available for creating visuals for the presentation. Provide equipment for students to use in videotaping practice sessions, if possible.

COMPOSITION
PRESENTATION
WORD PROCESSING

Topic **5-2**   ACTIVITY 2

Prepare Visuals and Practice a Presentation

In this activity you will prepare visuals for the five-minute presentation you planned for Topic 5-2 Activity 1. You will also practice your presentation.

1. Choose the media you will use to create the visuals depending on the equipment and materials available. Ask your instructor for the media options available to you.

2. Create a visual for each storyboard worksheet you prepared earlier.

3. After your visuals are complete, practice your presentation in front of a mirror. If possible, videotape your practice session. Focus on using your visuals correctly so they help to emphasize the key points in your presentation. Notice your posture and gestures. Concentrate on using a pleasant voice.

objectives

- Apply methods for practicing and preparing for a presentation
- Describe appropriate personal appearance for making presentations
- Apply proper techniques for communicating with the audience
- Use visuals effectively
- Conduct question-and-answer sessions

Now that you have prepared your message, you are ready to put your ideas in motion. You may think that with all this preparation, you are ready to deliver the message. The content of your presentation may be right on target, but if you cannot communicate the content effectively, your efforts will not be rewarded. You must practice and prepare the delivery with the same care you prepared the content.

Practice and Prepare

The more experienced you become in speaking to others, the less practice you will need. If you're new at making presentations, you will definitely want to practice. You can practice before friends or colleagues, or you can rehearse the presentation on your own.

Review each of your visuals and the notes you have created to accompany them. Rehearse out loud exactly what you plan to say. Make sure you state each idea from the listeners' point of view. Also be sure to provide listener advantages.

For team presentations, each presenter must know the content he or she will present. Although each member should use his or her own style of speaking, everyone should reflect the overall theme. All team members should be present, even if some of them do not present. The team should practice the presentation as a group.

Prepare Notes

One of the best ways to ensure that you will make a successful presentation is to prepare well. The visuals you have prepared will guide you through the outline of the presentation. Use notes to remind you of the key points and the facts relevant to your presentation. You can use note cards or the notes feature of your presentation software to record details, ideas that each visual presents, content prompts, and reminders. If you have practiced at length, you will probably find you no longer need to look at your notes because you know the content and know what you plan to say. When you have done a thorough job of preparing your message, you can feel confident and remain calm during the presentation.

Videotape Your Presentation

Record your presentation on videotape if possible. Review the tape and consider ways you can improve the delivery of your message. If necessary, practice and videotape yourself again. Remember, you will most likely be much more critical of yourself than anyone in your audience will. Also, consider getting constructive criticism from friends and coworkers.

203

Topic 5-3: *Delivering a Presentation*

Points to Emphasize

Practicing the delivery of the presentation is just as important as the time and effort spent in planning the content of the presentation. Speaking before a large group can be very intimidating for students. Initially, you may wish to pair students with others they are comfortable working with or divide the class into small groups. Encourage students to first practice in front of a mirror; then have them present to their partner or their small group.

Teaching Tips

Recommend that students use index cards or the notes feature of their presentation software for their notes. Students should write brief notes as reminders of key points. If using index cards, students should number the cards so they can be quickly reorganized if they get out of order.

Teaching Tips

Videotaping is a valuable tool for teaching techniques and style. Allow students to privately review and critique their videotapes first. This will give them an opportunity to become more comfortable watching themselves. When reviewing the tape with each student, be sure to point out all the positive techniques the student demonstrates. Identify only one or two areas for the student to improve.

203

This speaker is using notes that contain detailed information.

Prepare the Meeting Room

There are many factors to consider regarding the meeting room. Make sure the seating arrangement is appropriate. A semicircular, or "U," arrangement is good for an audience that will focus on visuals at the front of the room. This arrangement also helps the presenter control the focus of the group. If the presenter is standing before the audience, a rectangular seating arrangement also works well. A circular or oval arrangement is helpful to group discussions. It does not work well, however, if the presenter will be standing to address the group.

Remember that the meeting room will grow warmer when filled with people and set the temperature accordingly.

Arrive early to set up equipment and support materials. Practice ahead of time with the specific equipment to be used in the presentation, such as a computer or projector. Even if you are familiar with operating a similar piece of equipment, make sure you practice on the one you plan to use. This will allow you to discover any differences or problems with the equipment. Test the audio equipment and get comfortable with the microphone. Know whom to call if you should need a technician.

Check the lighting in the room and determine the best light level to use for the presentation. Even though your visuals may look good in a dark room, you want the lighting sufficient so your audience can clearly see you as you speak. Also, check the room temperature. Remember that a room may become warmer as more people enter it. Setting the temperature to about 68 degrees will usually provide a comfortable environment when the room is filled with people.

Consider Your Appearance

Your appearance makes an impression on your audience and can influence how they receive your message. Dressing appropriately can help you gain their respect and hold their attention. When inappropriate, your appearance can distract your listeners.

Good grooming is important. Be neat and clean in your appearance. Get a good night's rest before the presentation so you can look and be alert. For formal presentations, business suits are appropriate. For informal presentations, your attire can be more casual depending on the audience. Dress comfortably but conservatively.

For Discussion

Ask students to collect examples of both appropriate and inappropriate appearance for speakers. Have them gather pictures from newspapers and periodicals. Discuss the pictures in class and point out the positive and negative factors of each.

205

Topic 5-3: *Delivering a Presentation*

Business attire is appropriate for formal presentations.

© AMY ETRA/PHOTOEDIT

Present Opening Remarks

In a small- or large-group presentation, another person may introduce you to your audience. You should also introduce yourself. In your opening remarks, be sure to state your purpose. Your opening remarks help to set the tone for your presentation. You may choose to use a visual for this introduction.

Always remember that your remarks should be appropriate for the occasion. For example, some people like to begin with a joke or with a note of humor. This sets a friendly tone and makes you more comfortable with your audience. Jokes should always be in good taste and appropriate for the audience. If the topic of your presentation is very serious in nature, however, a joke may not be appropriate.

Communicate With Your Audience

To deliver your message effectively, you must communicate with your audience. Although you will not be carrying on a two-way conversation with members of your audience, a sharing of ideas and information must take place. You will not be able to successfully communicate your message to your listeners until you have established a meeting of the minds. To do this, you must get your audience involved.

Your listeners will likely be involved in your presentation if you appear relaxed and comfortable. Being nervous is normal. Naturally, you want to do well, and you may experience some nervousness. Take deep breaths, concentrate on talking slowly, and think about what you're going to say next. You may think that you are talking too slowly, but that is generally not the case. The listeners will find you to be more credible because they can tell you are giving thought to what you are about to say. Maintain a positive self-image and an upbeat attitude. Remind yourself that you are well prepared and can deliver the message effectively.

For Discussion

When might using a joke to open a presentation be appropriate? When would using a joke not be appropriate?

For Discussion

Ask students to share with the class some techniques they use to control nervousness.

© CORBIS

Establishing eye contact with someone in the audience makes all your listeners feel more involved.

Maintain Eye Contact

Making eye contact with one person in the audience helps all members of the audience feel like you are talking to them. Until you become experienced, you may find it difficult to make eye contact with your listeners. If this is a problem for you, try to maintain eye contact with one individual for at least five seconds before making eye contact with another person in the audience. Maintaining eye contact helps you involve your listeners and know whether your audience is following you. You can judge their reactions to what you are saying, and your listeners will feel more involved and important.

Avoid Non-Words

Sounds or words that do not contribute to the meaning of the presentation are often called **non-words**. The use of non-words is a habit many of us need to break. Often we don't realize we say non-words such as "uhh" and "ah." Review your videotape or have a friend help you identify non-words that you use. Count the number of non-words you say throughout your presentation. You may be surprised to find how frequently you use non-words.

Usually we say non-words because we are thinking about what we want to say next, and we do not want to allow a period of silence. Actually, a non-word does not fill up much time as we speak. Having quiet pauses between our statements is preferable to using non-words. The non-words can be much more annoying to listeners than a pause with silence.

If you know you use too many non-words, videotape your presentation a second time. This time, consciously pause instead of saying a non-word. Review your videotape and count the occurrences of non-words again. Hopefully, you were able to reduce them significantly. Don't be concerned if you cannot eliminate all non-words initially. Habits are difficult to break. Consciously work on avoiding non-words in your daily communications as well. You will soon see you can speak without them.

non-words: spoken sounds such as "uhh" and "ah"

Figure **5-3.1**

Avoid the use of non-words in your presentations.

Non-Words		
ah	okay	yeah
all right	uh-huh	you know
and	well	you see
and ah		

Show Enthusiasm and Speak Convincingly

Speak with enthusiasm and conviction. A sure way to get your audience involved is to convince them that you are excited about the topic. If you believe in what you are saying, let your listeners know. Let your enthusiasm be genuine, however. Most listeners will know if you're not being honest, and that is a sure way to lose their attention.

Show a sincere interest in helping your listeners meet their needs. Use keywords that your listener wants to hear and to which they can relate. Describe experiences or examples with which your listeners can identify. In doing so, you can be very convincing as you share your ideas.

Control Your Posture and Gestures

Watching speakers who constantly pace back and forth or who shuffle their feet and shift weight from one leg to the other can be very distracting. Instead of becoming involved in your presentation, listeners start concentrating on your posture and gestures. You want them to think about your message, not your gestures.

Stand with your feet slightly apart and firmly planted, moving or shifting your weight only occasionally. Leave your hands at your sides until you use them for natural gestures that enhance your words. For example, if some-

Gestures can enhance or detract from a speaker's words.

© CORBIS

208

CHAPTER 5: COMMUNICATING ORALLY

thing is really big, show it by opening your arms really wide. If something is minor, use a gesture with your hands to show the problem is small. Make sure your gestures don't contradict your words. When your hands drop below your waist, your gestures are not effective.

Avoid other distracting gestures such as rubbing your hands together or crossing your arms. These forms of body language communicate nervousness. Your listeners will be watching your body language as they listen to you speak. Make sure your posture and gestures are not communicating something different than the message you want them to receive.

Use Good Intonation

No one likes to listen to a person speaking in a monotone. As you review your videotape, close your eyes and listen to your voice. Do you use good **intonation**? Does your voice reflect enthusiasm? Is it easy to listen to? With practice, you can learn to speak with a pleasant voice that is neither too high nor too low. Your voice should sound relaxed and have an even tone.

intonation: the rise and fall in voice pitch

Learning to relax can help you control your voice. If you are tense, your voice may sound shaky and high-pitched. Concentrate on speaking loudly enough without straining your voice or shouting. Vary your **inflection** to help you sound more interesting. Enunciate clearly and don't speak too quickly. If the meeting room and audience are large, use a microphone so you can speak normally and still be heard by everyone.

inflection: tone of voice

Keep the Audience Focused

Watch the reactions of your audience. Make sure they are focused on what you are saying. If they seem confused or distracted, back up and rephrase your point. If you sense that you are losing their attention, try to focus again on listener interests and advantages.

Do not panic, however, if the audience does seem to lose focus. Keep in mind that this topic is something that you know and understand very well. Your listeners may need more time to think about the information and ideas you are presenting.

Use Visuals Effectively

If you've prepared well, you have some great visuals to help you communicate your ideas. These visuals, however, are not the key to your presentation. You are the key element. Begin by drawing the listeners' attention to yourself. Then, when appropriate, direct their attention to the visuals to make your message more powerful.

One way visuals can make your message more powerful is by creating anticipation. Do not reveal the visual too soon. Introduce or refer to the visual before you display it.

Melita Singh gave a talk about new procedures for reporting travel expenses. She used a visual that showed data collected in a survey of staff members. To introduce the visual, Melita said, "You'll recall that last month we requested your input regarding our current travel expense reimbursement procedures. We received some interesting insights from many of you." Then Melita revealed the slide that summarizes the findings.

As you display your visuals, look at your listeners, not at your visuals. Continue to maintain eye contact. Stand to the left or right of the display of your visuals. Do not let the visuals replace you. Be sure your listeners can see you and the visuals.

Pause to allow listeners time to view and think about the visuals. You've seen them and studied them, but your listeners have not. Also use pauses to allow for listener reaction. Allow listeners time to laugh if the visual is humorous, or give them an opportunity to read and evaluate a proposed solution displayed on a visual. During this pause you can study their reactions to your visual. For example, look for nods of agreement or expressions of disagreement. If appropriate, ask for their feedback before continuing.

Answer Questions

Allow the audience time to ask questions. Question-and-answer sessions are valuable to you as well as the audience. They provide you an opportunity to hear from your listeners as they share what they are thinking.

The audience should be able to see the speaker and the visuals.

Anticipate Listener Questions

Many speakers become anxious about receiving questions from an audience. They are afraid they will not be able to answer the questions. The key to feeling calm and confident when receiving questions is preparation. Anticipate what your audience will ask you following your presentation. If you have prepared well, you have probably addressed many of their concerns in the presentation. However, you may get questions about content you have already covered. This means that the listener either did not understand or did not retain that information.

WORKPLACE CONNECTIONS

Cathy Park is preparing a talk on reassignment of sales territories. She considers anticipating questions an important part of preparing for the presentation. She knows members of the sales team will have lots of questions. They may ask about how the change will affect workloads, commissions, and follow-up on needs of customers in the territory previously assigned to a salesperson. Cathy keys each question she thinks someone is likely to ask. Then she keys a complete and concise answer to the question. Cathy will use these notes for reference if needed during the question-and-answer portion of the presentation. Preparing questions and answers in advance helps Cathy feel confident that she will be able to answer most of the questions that arise.

Perhaps when you give your audience the opportunity to ask questions, no one will raise a question. This situation happens frequently. Initially, you may think the listeners are not interested in the topic and just want to leave. If you have been effective as a speaker, they have been listening and thinking about your ideas. You have been directing their train of thought. Perhaps they have not had time to think about their own ideas and questions to ask. Just in case no one in the audience asks a question, have some questions ready. This will help to fill the time you have allotted for questions and may prompt some questions from the audience.

Restate the Question

When you receive a question from the audience, the entire group needs to hear the question. Generally, the person asking directs the question to the speaker, and the entire audience does not hear the question. Restate the question for everyone to hear. Doing so gives you time to think about the answer and lets you confirm to the listener that you understand the question.

Points to Emphasize

Anticipating listener questions is an important part of preparing for a presentation.

For Discussion

What are two reasons you should restate a question from a listener in a question-and-answer session?

211

Topic 5-3: *Delivering a Presentation*

In question-and-answer sessions, the speaker should direct the focus of the discussion.

In one-to-one situations, you may wish to rephrase a question to let the listener know you understood it. Incorporating part of the question in the beginning of your answer can also be helpful. Be careful, however, not to offend your listener by rephrasing all the questions. Instead, allow yourself time to think about the answer by making comments such as, "I can understand your concerns" and "I, too, have experienced that and this is what I've learned."

Respond to the Question

Respond to all questions in a courteous and sincere manner. Keep your answers brief to maintain the exchange between you and the audience. Direct your answer to the entire group, not just the person who asked the question. Maintain eye contact to keep the audience focused on the discussion. When appropriate, provide supporting details or evidence to back up your answer.

Be honest if you do not know the answer to a question. You will gain more credibility with your audience if you are honest than if you try to bluff your way through the answer. If appropriate, offer to find the answer and communicate it to the individual later.

Do not become frustrated if the question relates to information you have already covered. If one listener missed details or became confused, chances are that others did, too. Provide the details or explain the point again briefly. Use different words to explain the idea or data. Offer to provide more details later if appropriate.

Sometimes one individual will ask more than one question. That person may begin to dominate or take over the question-and-answer session. The other listeners often become aggravated when this happens. They can begin

Point to Emphasize

When a listener asks a question about material you have already presented, do not become frustrated. Consider this an opportunity to emphasize a point made earlier.

to feel unimportant or unnoticed. If this happens, you can quickly lose the audience's attention. If one individual begins to dominate the questions, break eye contact with the individual before he or she has an opportunity to ask another question. After giving an answer to that individual's question, establish eye contact with another person and ask, "Does anyone else have a question to ask?"

In a team presentation, the team members should decide in advance how they will handle questions from the audience. For example, they may decide that one team member will direct the questions to the appropriate person for an answer. All presenters should be included in the question-and-answer session.

Present Closing Remarks

Following the question-and-answer session, you have one last chance to get your point across. Your closing remarks should be a concise review of the major points in your presentation. Be careful, however, to word your closing so that you do not repeat exactly what you have already said. Restate the specific points. Then close the presentation, thanking your audience for listening.

Evaluate Your Presentation

After the presentation is completed, evaluate yourself. Consider the strong points of your presentation and what seemed to be effective. Think about what you could do to improve it. Did you forget to mention something? Could you have used more visuals, or did you use too many? What would you do differently the next time?

Ask for feedback from your audience by using an evaluation form. Evaluation forms are valuable tools that can help you improve your speaking skills. To be effective, though, the form has to gather appropriate information from your listeners. Be specific about the feedback you want from the audience. Figure 5-3.2 on page 214 shows a sample evaluation form. For example, ask listeners the following questions:

- Have you convinced them to take a course of action?
- Have they learned something from your presentation?
- Was the length of your presentation appropriate?
- Could they relate the content of your presentation to their personal experiences?

You will get the most accurate feedback if you ask your listeners to complete the evaluation right after the presentation. Their reactions are fresh, and their comments will be more specific.

Learn from the evaluation comments and use the information constructively to improve the content and/or the delivery of your message. Each time you speak before a group, you will grow in confidence and ability. If you have the opportunity to give the same presentation again, you can refine and improve it using the feedback you receive.

PRESENTATION EVALUATION FORM

Speaker: _____ **Date:** _____

Topic: _____

Please check one of the choices at the right for each of the statements below. Place your completed form on the table by the door on your way out. Thank you for your feedback.

	Very Much	Somewhat	Not at All
The coverage of the topic met my expectations.			
The topic was of interest to me.			
The length of the presentation was appropriate.			
The presenter addressed the topic effectively.			
The concepts were presented clearly.			
The presenter related the information to my experiences.			
The information presented will be useful to me.			
The visuals used were helpful and appropriate.			

Comments:

_____

_____

_____

Figure **5-3.2**

Evaluation forms provide valuable feedback.

REVIEWING THE TOPIC

1. What types of information should the speaker include in notes for a presentation, and how should these notes be used?
2. What seating arrangement is appropriate when the audience will be viewing visuals?
3. Describe four considerations in preparing a meeting room for a presentation.
4. What risks are involved if a speaker dresses inappropriately?
5. Why is maintaining eye contact with listeners important during the presentation?
6. What are non-words? Why do many people use them? What should speakers do instead of using non-words?
7. Describe appropriate posture and movement or gestures a speaker should use.
8. What is voice intonation, and why is appropriate use of intonation important for a speaker?
9. Describe two strategies for using visuals effectively when giving a presentation.
10. Why should a speaker anticipate questions the listeners may ask during a presentation?
11. Why should a speaker restate or rephrase a question before answering it?
12. How can a presenter discourage an individual who is beginning to dominate the question-and-answer session?

INTERACTING WITH OTHERS

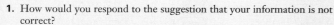

After you completed a presentation about how to operate a new copier, you asked for questions from the listeners. One person in your audience, Jason, thinks he knows this topic well. He is dominating the question-and-answer session. During one of his questions, he implies that the information you have presented is not correct.

1. How would you respond to the suggestion that your information is not correct?
2. What can you do to prevent this person from dominating the session?

Teaching Tips

If the students are using the *Student Activities and Simulations* workbook, instruct them to complete the review activity for this topic.

For Discussion

After students have considered the situation presented, ask them to share their thoughts with the class.

Teaching Tips

Encourage students to refer to Section D in the Reference Section of the *Student Activities and Simulations* workbook, if available, to review averaging numbers.

REINFORCING MATH SKILLS

At a recent presentation, you asked your listeners to complete evaluation forms. Listeners scored each item on a scale of 1 to 10. Evaluators are identified by letter because the evaluation was anonymous. Compile and average the ratings to determine an overall evaluation score.

1. Calculate the average score given by all evaluators for each item.
2. Calculate the average score given on all the items by each evaluator.
3. Find an overall evaluation score by averaging the average scores from the ten evaluators.

Evaluation Items	Evaluators									
	A	B	C	D	E	F	G	H	I	J
1. The coverage of the topic met my expectations.	8	9	7	9	10	10	9	7	8	9
2. The topic was of interest to me.	6	10	8	10	8	9	7	9	8	8
3. The length of the presentation was appropriate.	9	9	10	10	10	9	8	6	10	10
4. The presenter addressed the topic effectively.	8	9	8	9	8	9	9	7	10	10
5. The concepts were presented clearly.	8	9	8	9	8	9	9	7	10	10
6. The presenter related the information to my experiences.	6	8	9	9	7	7	7	5	8	8
7. The information presented will be useful to me.	6	8	8	8	8	7	8	6	7	9
8. The visuals used were helpful and appropriate.	9	10	9	9	8	9	8	7	10	10

Teaching Tips

Allow students to share the evaluation points they have listed on their forms with the class. Have the class agree on a common set of points to be used in evaluating class presentations.

COMPOSITION
TEAMWORK
WORD PROCESSING

Topic **5-3** | ACTIVITY 1

Create Presentation Evaluation Form

In this activity, you will create a presentation evaluation form to use in evaluating presentations given by your classmates. Work with three or four classmates to complete this assignment.

1. Review the information from this chapter related to effective speaking and presentations. Think about the information that a listener might want to comment on. Also think about the information a speaker would find useful for judging the effectiveness of the current presentation and for improving future presentations. Then create a list of evaluation points or questions to be included on the evaluation form.

216

CHAPTER 5: COMMUNICATING ORALLY

2. Key the form using a format that will be easy to use for both the evaluators and the speakers. A sample evaluation form is shown in Figure 5-3.2. Include an appropriate title for the form and blanks to record the speaker name, topic, and date of the presentation. Also include a place for the evaluator to make comments on the form.

3. Print copies of the form for use in Topic 5-3 Activity 2. You will need forms to evaluate all the other students in your group.

Topic 5-3 : ACTIVITY 2

Deliver a Presentation and Evaluate Performance

| COMPOSITION |
| PRESENTATION |
| TEAMWORK |
| WORD PROCESSING |

In this activity, you will deliver the presentation created in Topic 5-2 Activity 2 to a group of your classmates. You will also evaluate your performance and that of your classmates.

1. Work in the same group as you did for Topic 5-3 Activity 1 to complete this assignment. Take turns with the other students in your group so that all students complete steps 2 and 3.

2. Deliver your five-minute presentation to the group. Include a question-and-answer session at the end of your presentation. Ask fellow students to evaluate your presentation using the form created in Topic 5-3 Activity 1.

3. Review the evaluations of your presentation prepared by your classmates. Then write a brief self-evaluation of your presentation. Comment on your overall performance, areas where you performed particularly well, and areas where you will try to improve for future presentations.

Teaching Tips

Have students review key points from the chapter by completing the Beat the Clock game on *The Office* Web site.

Summary

Workers need to express themselves clearly in their speech at work. You may need to talk with a coworker or address others in a meeting. Some workers will also need to give a presentation. To prepare an effective presentation, you must profile your listeners and develop your presentation with them in mind. Practicing the delivery of a presentation is as important as planning and preparing the content of the presentation. The following key points will reinforce your learning from this chapter.

- When you listen effectively, you will be able to use the information you heard to complete your work correctly. You will be better able to make decisions and manage time productively.
- Listening involves a mental process as well as the physical aspects of hearing. Your prejudgments and attitudes can influence your listening.
- To listen effectively, focus your attention on what is being said. Mentally summarize and review the information. Ask questions to help you understand the information.
- To speak effectively, show a sincere interest in what you are saying. Express your ideas clearly. Use an appropriate tone of voice. Avoid using non-words and use standard language.
- Consider what your listeners want to know, what they might already know, and how what you are saying can be related to their experiences. Be aware of how nonverbal behavior can add to or detract from your message.
- When preparing a presentation, begin by identifying the purpose of your presentation. List the specific goals you wish to accomplish.
- Address the interests of your listeners as you plan the content of your presentation. Describe the advantages the listeners can gain from the information you will provide.
- Use a storyboard to help you organize ideas and plan visuals. Use a logical sequence for presenting your ideas that will help your listeners stay interested in what you have to say.
- Much of what we remember is in the form of pictures. Use visual elements to help you communicate your message.
- Handouts are effective for providing your listeners with a summary of the key points in your presentation or providing additional details.
- Practicing your presentation out loud is important. Videotaping your practice sessions can also be very helpful.
- Knowing how to communicate with your audience and keeping them involved is essential for a successful presentation.

- Question-and-answer sessions are important for both the speaker and the audience. Handling questions effectively helps you direct the focus of the session.
- Evaluations provide valuable feedback for improving your performance in future presentations.

Key Terms

audience	enunciation	objections
audio	handout	prejudgments
biases	inflection	profile
body language	intonation	slang
bullets	media	storyboarding
colloquialism	modulated	transitions
credibility	non-words	

Chapter 5   A C T I V I T Y   1

COMPOSITION
INTERNET
RESEARCH
WORD PROCESSING

Research for a Presentation

When you must prepare a presentation, the topic may be a familiar one about which you know a great deal. Often, however, you will need to do research to find the latest information or supporting details related to the topic. Practice your research skills in this activity.

1. In a later activity, you will create a presentation related to flextime. Use the Internet or other reference sources to find three articles or reports about flextime. Print or copy the articles, if possible.
2. For each article, key the name of the article and complete source information. Then compose and key a summary of the main points you learned from reading the article.

219

Chapter Review

Have students review the key terms by using the Flashcards available on *The Office* Web site.

Assist students with using the Internet or other resources to find articles about flextime. Remind students to record complete source information for the articles. Provide examples of how you want the source information arranged and formatted.

COMPOSITION
PRESENTATION
TEAMWORK
WORD PROCESSING

Chapter 5 ACTIVITY 2

Team Presentation

You work in the Accounting Department for a large insurance company. Approximately twenty-five workers are in your department. They have diverse ages and lifestyles. You and several coworkers created a plan for flextime options. Recently, management decided to test the flextime schedule with a two-month pilot program. The program will be for employees in your department only. If the pilot program is successful, the flextime options will be offered to most employees.

You and a team of coworkers have been asked to prepare and deliver a ten-minute presentation. Your goal is to motivate coworkers in your department to take part in the flextime pilot program.

1. Work with a team of three classmates to complete this assignment.
2. Open and print the PDF file *CH05 Flextime* found in the data files. This file contains specific details about the flextime program.
3. Plan the presentation. Create storyboard worksheets and develop an outline of the main points of the presentation.
4. Develop the detailed contents of the presentation. Use information found in articles from your research in Chapter 5 Activity 1 to provide supporting details. Develop the visual aids. Anticipate questions and plan sample answers.
5. Decide who will present each part of the presentation and practice with your team.
6. Deliver the presentation to your class or to another team as directed by your teacher. Include time for a question-and-answer session.
7. Ask your listeners to complete an evaluation form such as the one you developed in Topic 5-3 Activity 1. Review the evaluation forms and write a summary of how the listeners rated your presentation and what you need to improve in future presentations.

© GETTY IMAGES/PHOTODISC

CHAPTER 6

Processing and Understanding Financial Information

Sound financial information is very important to the success of a business. Many day-to-day business decisions are based on financial information. How much do we owe our suppliers? How much overtime will be needed to complete this order? Will this expense exceed our budget? Businesses need current and correct financial information to make informed decisions.

In this chapter, you will learn about procedures used in cash and banking activities. You will also study basic procedures and reports used in financial management.

221

Topic 6-1

CASH AND BANKING PROCEDURES

objectives

- Explain the value of internal control for cash handling
- Describe billing procedures
- Prepare a check voucher
- Prepare and post checks
- Prepare a bank deposit and a bank account reconciliation
- Prepare a petty cash fund report

check: a written order to a bank to make payment against the depositor's funds in that bank

debit card: a kind of bank card that allows amounts to be automatically deducted from the card-holder's bank account

forge: imitate or counterfeit for illegal purposes

internal control: a method used by a business to safeguard assets

fraud: intentional deception to cause a person or business to give up property (assets) or some lawful right

A business must keep track of cash receipts carefully to avoid losing money or recording customer payments incorrectly. A business must also make payments on time. Late payments may result in paying late charges, losing discounts, or a poor credit rating. Most businesses use procedures to help ensure that receipts and payments are handled properly.

In the business world, cash refers to currency (coins and bills), **checks**, money orders, and funds in checking accounts in banks. Some businesses accept only currency or money orders. Other companies, such as supermarkets and retail stores, handle large volumes of currency. In still other companies, almost all transactions are paid by check, credit card, **debit card**, or electronic funds transfer.

If you work in a small office, you are likely to have some duties related to cash transactions. If you work in a large company, you may work in a department where many cash transactions are processed. In either case, you should understand the safeguards for cash and procedures for processing cash transactions used in your company.

Safeguarding Cash

Cash is a valuable asset of the business. It must be safeguarded in all its forms. Currency is generally considered to be owned by the person who has it. Currency stolen from a business can be easily spent. Checks can be stolen and cashed with some ease using **forged** signatures. The overall method a business uses to safeguard assets is known as **internal control**. Internal control methods fall into three categories—preventive, detective, and corrective.

Preventive Internal Control

The goal of preventive internal controls is to reduce loss of cash due to employee error, **fraud**, or theft. Dividing the duties for handling cash among two or more employees is usually a part of this control. In Figure 6-1.1, note that tasks are given to different workers. This helps ensure that all checks received by the company are properly deposited and recorded. Accuracy checks also help prevent error. Preventive internal control is the most important category because it is designed to prevent loss of cash.

Detective Internal Control

Another type of internal controls tries to find losses that have taken place. Losses may be found by reviewing reports and customer accounts. A bank reconciliation is an example of this type of detective control. It can be used

Processing Customer Payment Checks

Mail Clerk	Cashier	Accounting Clerk
Delivers checks to cashier	1. Makes a list of checks received 2. Prepares deposit slip and makes bank deposit 3. Forwards list of checks to an accounting clerk	1. Records the customers' payments 2. Verifies that the total of customers' payments equals the total of checks listed

Figure 6-1.1

Separation of duties helps assure internal control of incoming checks.

to find missing deposits or other errors. Some companies have employees who do **audits**. Audits are done to see whether internal controls are being applied correctly. You may be expected to assist the employees who do internal audits.

audit: verify or check facts or procedures

WORKPLACE CONNECTIONS

Jill Wong, a staff member in the Internal Audit Department, was asked to determine whether the procedures for recording customer payments were being followed. Jill requested a list of the checks that were received on a particular day. She looked at the records for each customer from whom a payment was received on that date to check that the payment was recorded correctly. Jill found no differences between the list of payments and the customers' records. All the procedures were followed correctly, so the audit revealed no problems.

Corrective Internal Control

Corrective internal control is used to restore assets after a loss has occurred. For example, changing poor procedures that lead to a loss is a form of corrective internal control. Money received from insurance policies may be used to replace losses caused by employee theft. This is another type of corrective internal control.

One method used to protect cash is **bonding** employees. Bonding is insurance for financial loss due to employee theft or fraud. Bonding is effective because the company that insures bonded employees makes a search of the employee's work history and criminal record. They check with former employers and other references. This search, which is generally more thorough than that done by the company at the time employees are hired, is the major advantage of bonding.

bonding: insurance for financial loss due to employee theft or fraud

Billing Customers

Customers may pay for goods or services at the time the goods are received, or they may establish **credit** with the seller. The seller then bills the customer periodically for the goods or services. The request for payment is commonly in the form of a sales invoice or a statement of account.

credit: permission to pay later for goods or services

223

Topic 6-1: *Cash and Banking Procedures*

Expand the Concept

For what control purpose is the cashier not assigned the task of making entries in customer records?

Thinking Critically

What steps might Jill take if she did find a difference in the list of payments and the customers' records?

For Discussion

Ask students if they know any workers who are bonded. In what positions are these workers employed?

Internal audits are performed to determine the effectiveness of internal controls.

© KWAME ZIKOMO/SUPERSTOCK INTERNATIONAL

Sales Invoice

Sales invoices are usually created at the time a company ships products or performs services for a customer. An invoice can be sent with the products. It can be left with the customer after a service is performed or mailed separately to the customer. Although some invoices are handwritten, many companies use invoices printed from computer records.

Verifying that the data on an invoice are correct is very important. A sales invoice documents a customer's legal obligation to pay for products or services received. In some cases, the information on an invoice may not agree with what a customer ordered or expected to receive. In this case, the customer has the right to delay payment until any questions are settled.

A sales invoice includes information such as the invoice date, quantities and prices of items purchased, and the invoice total. The invoice in Figure 6-1.2 shows payment terms of 2/10, net 30. This means that the customer may take a 2 percent discount from the merchandise total if payment is received by the seller within ten calendar days of the invoice date. If the discount is not taken, full payment is due within 30 days of the invoice date.

Statement of Account

A statement of account is a listing of unpaid invoices as of a certain date, usually the end of a month. Many businesses mail statements of account as a courtesy to their customers. The statement provides a gentle reminder of the amounts owed. Customers can report errors if payments have not been recorded correctly. A business may prepare separate checks to pay for each invoice or one check to pay for several invoices from the same seller.

INVOICE

Shred-Rite Shredder Company
2200 New Prussia Road
Delray Beach, FL 33445-5688
(561) 555-9876

Date:	July 17, 20--
Invoice No.:	SR 107206
Customer No.:	5690
Ship Via:	UPS Ground
Terms:	2/10, net 30

Sold to:

MR HAROLD LEVITZ
LEVITZ OFFICE SUPPLY
1068 WABASHAW COURT
FERGUSON KY 42502-4664

Ship to:

Same

Item No.	Quantity	Description	Unit Price	Total
SR100	10	Personal shredder with waste receptacle	$89.00	$890.00
SR200	10	Medium duty console shredder	$399.00	$3,990.00

Subtotal	$4,880.00
Shipping & Handling	$130.00
Taxes	
Total	$5,010.00
Payment Received	$0.00
Amount Due	$5,010.00

Teaching Tips

Point out each item of information that is included on the sample sales invoice.

WORKPLACE CONNECTIONS

Paducah Builders, a company that builds houses, has several workers who pick up materials at a building supply store. When a worker picks up items at the store, the worker signs a form to show who picked up the items. He or she also receives an invoice for the items. This invoice is forwarded to the company's business office. The seller sends a statement of account at the end of the month listing all the invoices. Paducah Builders pays all the invoices for the month with one check, which is more convenient than paying the invoices separately.

A statement of account includes information such as the statement date and the seller's name and address. The customer's name and address, invoices, and the total amount due are also shown. The statement of account in Figure 6-1.3 shows four invoice amounts.

Figure **6-1.3**

*A statement of
account lists invoice
amounts for a period
of time.*

STATEMENT OF ACCOUNT

Shred-Rite Shredder Company
2200 New Prussia Road
Delray Beach, FL 33445-5688
(561) 555-9876

Date: July 31, 20--
Customer No.: 5690
Terms: 2/10, net 30

Customer:

MR HAROLD LEVITZ
LEVITZ OFFICE SUPPLY
1068 WABASHAW COURT
FERGUSON KY 42502-4664

Invoice No.	Invoice Date	Invoice Total
SR 107005	July 2, 20--	$849.32
SR 107006	July 2, 20--	$1,150.00
SR 107150	July 6, 20--	$3,090.49
SR 107206	July 17, 20--	$5,010.00
	Total Due	$10,099.81

accounts receivable:
short-term debts owed
to a company by others,
such as its customers

Receiving Payments

In some companies, employees in an **Accounts Receivable** Department
process payments. Some workers in this department handle the cash drawer.
Other workers prepare and make bank deposits.

Handling the Cash Drawer

A cash register drawer is assigned to an employee who deals with customers
in person, receiving payments and making change. When the employee is
assigned the cash drawer, it contains currency and coins to use in making
change. As transactions are completed, currency, coins, checks, and credit
card and debit card receipts from customer payments will be added to the
drawer. Each sale is recorded in the cash register, either on a paper tape or
electronically. The cash register will show the total sales made during the
time the worker used the cash drawer.

An employee issued a cash drawer is required to verify the amount of cash
in the cash drawer when he or she receives the drawer. When the drawer is
turned in, the employee must verify that the proper amount of currency,
checks, and bank card receipts are in the drawer. This procedure is known
as proving cash. To prove cash, an employee would add total sales (as shown
on the cash register for the employee's shift) to the beginning balance (the
amount in the drawer when received). This total should match the amount
in the cash drawer. In some businesses, employees may be required to list
the contents of the drawer in detail by type of item (currency, coins, checks,
and bank card receipts).

Points to Emphasize

Cash and checks are easily
transferable. Therefore, companies must depend on the
integrity of employees to be
sure cash and checks are
properly processed for company purposes.

Expand the Concept

Why is it necessary to actually count the cash in the
drawer when a cash register
report is generated?

In some companies, the employee must pay his or her own money to make up shortages when the cash drawer does not balance. Even if employees do not have to make up shortages, frequent shortages in an employee's cash drawer may lead to a poor job evaluation. These workers may not receive a promotion or even be fired if the problem continues.

Preparing Deposits

Businesses commonly deposit cash in a bank shortly after it is received. In some organizations where many payments are received, deposits may be made several times a day. In other companies, deposits may be made only a few times a month because payments are not received often.

Employees who prepare bank deposits should verify that all checks are properly endorsed. An **endorsement** is a signature or instructions, stamped or written on the back of a check. It authorizes the bank to cash or deposit the check. An endorsement is required before a check is transferred from the company or person to whom the check is written to another person, company, or bank. In many companies, office workers who prepare deposits also endorse the checks using a stamp.

Endorsements vary. Some provide more protection or instructions than others. The most commonly used forms of endorsements are *blank, restrictive,* and *special.* Look closely at Figure 6-1.4 on page 228 as you read about each form of endorsement.

Many checks have an endorsement area printed on the back of the check. Be careful to write, print, or stamp the endorsement within the area provided. If no endorsement area is indicated or the back of the check is blank, place the check face up. Grasp the left edge of the check and turn it over, keeping the same edge at the left. Carefully stamp or write an endorsement on the left edge of the check or other marked endorsement area.

For a **blank endorsement,** the signature of the **payee** is written on the back of the check. The signature must be in ink. This endorsement provides little protection because anyone who has the check can easily transfer it to another person or cash the check. Generally, use this endorsement only when you are at the bank ready to cash or deposit the check immediately.

In a **restrictive endorsement,** the purpose of the transfer of the check is indicated in the endorsement. For example, the check may be marked *For Deposit Only.* Restrictive endorsements are often made with a rubber stamp or a stamping machine.

In a **special endorsement,** the signature of the payee is placed before the name of the person or company to whom the check is being transferred. In some instances, a special endorsement is referred to as an *endorsement in full.*

endorsement: a signature on the back of a check authorizing a bank to cash or deposit the check

payee: a person to whom a check is written

Thinking Critically

Which endorsement provides the least protection? Why?

227

Topic 6-1: *Cash and Banking Procedures*

Figure **6-1.4**

Endorsements can be stamped or hand-written and provide varying levels of protection.

Endorse Here
x *Sean Burns*

Do not sign, write, or stamp below this line.
For financial institution use only.

Blank Endorsement

Endorse Here
x For Deposit Only
The Appliance Store

Do not sign, write, or stamp below this line.
For financial institution use only.

Restrictive Endorsement

Endorse Here
x *Pay to the order of*
Baylor Florist
Drew L. Westwood

Do not sign, write, or stamp below this line.
For financial institution use only.

Special Endorsement

A deposit slip is a form used to record currency, coins, and checks to be added to a bank account. On a deposit slip, *cash* refers to the total of currency and coins. When completing a deposit slip, do the following:

- Write the current date in the space provided.
- Write the amount of each item to be deposited. For each check, identify the bank on which the check is drawn. This is done by recording the bank's number, which is the upper portion of the fraction noted on each check.
- Write the amount of cash received from the deposit, if any, and sign the space to indicate that cash is received.
- Write the net deposit amount. This amount includes all checks listed on both the front and back of the deposit slip minus any cash received.

To verify the accuracy of the total deposit, add the checks and currency to be deposited. Verify that this total is exactly the same as the total listed on the deposit slip. If the totals match, the list is correct and includes all items.

WORKPLACE CONNECTIONS

One of Inez's daily tasks is preparing deposit slips for all items to be taken to a local bank. Inez works in a systematic fashion so that she makes no errors. She verifies that each deposit slip is correct by totaling the amounts carefully. Inez is proud that the bank has never sent the cashier a notice that an error had been made in a deposit she submitted.

Making Deposits

Office workers may make deposits in local banks on a regular basis. If your tasks include going to the bank with deposits, be sure all checks, currency, coins, and deposit forms are in proper order and in an envelope before you leave the office.

Deposits can be made electronically at an automated teller machine (ATM) at a bank or at other convenient locations. If you make this type of deposit, follow instructions and get a receipt. Verify that the receipt shows the amount of your deposit.

CHAPTER 6: PROCESSING AND UNDERSTANDING FINANCIAL INFORMATION

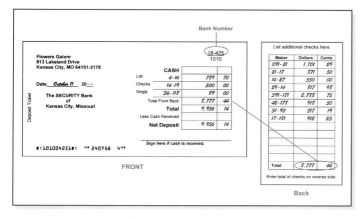

Figure **6-1.5**

On the front of the deposit slip, record the total amount of the checks listed on the back.

A company may direct customers to send payments to a lockbox address at a bank. A worker in the bank's office processes the deposit and updates the company's bank balance. The bank may transfer data electronically to the company for lockbox payments. Advantages to using a lockbox to collect payments include:

- Company employees do not have to spend as much time processing checks and preparing deposits.
- The checks received in a lockbox are processed each day by bank employees. Payments are deposited in the company's bank account right away. Funds are usually available for use at least one day sooner than when checks are deposited by company employees.
- Having the checks sent directly to the bank improves internal control by reducing the possibility of employee theft or errors.

This worker is making a deposit at an automated teller machine conveniently located near the office.

229

Topic 6-1: *Cash and Banking Procedures*

Workers in the Accounts Payable Department review documents related to company purchases.

© COMSTOCK IMAGES

Making Payments

accounts payable: short-term debts a company owes

In many firms, employees in an **Accounts Payable** Department process payments. Accounts payable are the short-term debts the company owes to others. In a small business, one person may handle all financial transactions, including receiving and making payments.

If you make payments for your company, you will be involved in several related tasks. You will review purchase-related documents, prepare vouchers, and prepare checks.

Review Documents

Companies want to be sure that payments are only made for goods or services purchased and received. Employees should review all the documents related to each purchase.

Several related documents may be generated with each purchase. The documents and their usefulness in making payments are as follows:

- A **purchase requisition** shows the items requested and an approval to make the purchase. Note the signature on the form in Figure 6-1.6.
- A **purchase order** shows exactly what was ordered and to what address it was to be shipped.
- A **receiving report** shows that goods were actually received by the company.
- An **invoice** from a vendor shows what is owed for the purchases.
- A **credit memorandum** shows any reduction in the amount owed due to return of goods or to allowance for goods not received or of poor quality.

CHAPTER 6: PROCESSING AND UNDERSTANDING FINANCIAL INFORMATION

Figure **6-1.6**

PURCHASE REQUISITION

The Lampshade Store
426 Monroe Street
Cedar Falls, IA 50613-3467

Date: October 17, 20--

Vendor of Choice	Description	Quantity	Unit Price	Total
Shred-Rite Shredder Co. 2200 New Prussia Road Delray Beach, FL 33445-5688	SR200 Medium duty console shredder	1	$399.00	$399.00
			Total	$399.00

Project No. _____

Account No. _____

Purchase Approved   **Date**

Harold Norton   10/20/--

A purchase requisition shows the items requested for purchase.

Employees should check to see if all the appropriate documents are present for each purchase. The details on all of the documents should be the same. Payment should not be made until all documents are accounted for and agree with each other. If the forms do not agree but there is a reasonable explanation for the differences, payment can be made.

Prepare Vouchers

In many offices a voucher system is used for payments. This system requires the preparation of a voucher before a check is written. A **voucher** is a document that shows the vendor name, invoice date, terms, and amount owed. The approved voucher serves as the approval to make the payment. Figure 6-1.7 on page 232 is an example of a voucher. If you have the responsibility for preparing vouchers, you should follow these general steps:

1. Check that all the documents related to the purchase are present. Often an envelope-type file folder is used to collect all the documents for a payment. A listing of collected documents is placed on the outside of the folder.
2. Prepare the voucher, checking every detail required on the form.
3. Obtain the authorized signature.
4. File the vouchers appropriately. Vouchers typically are filed by the dates on which they must be processed in order to meet the payment due dates. Filing vouchers in this way creates a **tickler file**. This file is reviewed daily for the purpose of taking action to clear the items from the file. In companies where the policy is to take all discounts allowed, the voucher is filed in the tickler file by the discount date.

voucher: a document that provides information and approval to make a payment

tickler file: notes or records arranged by date for keeping track of future actions

For Discussion

What documents support the voucher?

231

Topic 6-1: *Cash and Banking Procedures*

Figure **6-1.7**

A voucher authorizes payment on an invoice.

VOUCHER

Voucher No. 4379

The Lampshade Store
426 Monroe Street
Cedar Falls, IA 50613-3467

Date: October 17, 20--

Pay To: Just Shades
            135 Green Street
            New York, NY 10003-4689

For the following: (All supporting documents are attached.)

Invoice Date	Terms	Invoice No.	Gross Amount	Discount	Net Payable
10/17/---	2/10, net 30	5479	$4, 560.90	$91.22	$4,469.68

Payment Approved

Helen Northcut

The terms on the voucher in Figure 6-1.7 are 2/10, net 30. If the invoice is paid within ten days of the invoice date, a 2 percent discount can be taken from the invoice amount. If the invoice is paid after the 10th day and before the 30th day, the full amount of the invoice is paid. If payment is made after the 30th day, a penalty may be applied. Therefore, many businesses try to pay their bills in time to take advantage of the discount and to avoid being charged late fees.

Preparing Checks

In some offices, especially small ones, a checkbook similar to one an individual uses for personal check writing is used for checks. If you prepare checks, you should check the tickler file daily. Retrieve all vouchers for which checks are to be prepared. If you are responsible for writing checks using a checkbook, these suggestions will be helpful:

1. Read carefully the name of the company or individual to whom payment is to be made as well as the amount of the check. If you are writing a check in time to take advantage of a discount, compute the discount using a calculator.
2. Fill in the checkbook stub or the check register. (See Figure 6-1.8 for the way in which an item is listed in a check register.)
3. Prepare the check. (See Figure 6-1.8.) Note that the amount is written in numbers as well as in words. Notice how the space between the name and the dollar sign and the space between the amount in words and the word "dollars" is filled in so that changes cannot be made easily. Notice that the purpose of the payment is shown on the face of the check on the memo line.

Points to Emphasize

Companies put enormous trust in employees who write checks against company funds. This trust must be respected.

For Discussion

Why is the amount of the check written in numbers and in words? Which amount is considered to be the legal amount—the numbers or the words?

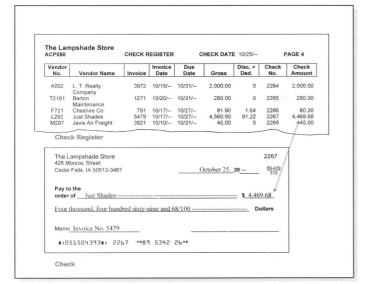

Figure **6-1.8**

Check register and completed check

The Lampshade Store
ACP050   CHECK REGISTER   CHECK DATE 10/25/--   PAGE 4

Vendor No.	Vendor Name	Invoice	Invoice Date	Due Date	Gross	Disc. + Ded.	Check No.	Check Amount
A002	L. T. Realty Company	3972	10/15/--	10/31/--	2,000.00	0	2264	2,000.00
T2161	Barton Maintenance	1271	10/20/--	10/31/--	280.00	0	2265	280.00
F721	Cheshire Co.	791	10/17/--	10/27/--	81.90	1.64	2266	80.26
L292	Just Shades	5479	10/17/--	10/27/--	4,560.90	91.22	2267	4,469.68
M297	Javis Air Freight	3921	10/10/--	10/31/--	45.00	0	2268	45.00

Check Register

The Lampshade Store   2267
426 Monroe Street
Cedar Falls, IA 50613-3467   October 25, 20 --   69-439/515

Pay to the
order of ___Just Shades-- $ 4,469.68

Four thousand, four hundred sixty-nine and 68/100 ------------------------ **Dollars**

Memo_Invoice No. 5479 _____   _____

⑆051504393⑆ 2267 ⑈89 5342 26⑈

Check

Some companies use voucher checks. Voucher checks are ordinary checks with an additional portion that gives a description of the payment. The two parts are perforated so that they can be separated easily. The voucher is detached before the check is deposited. The procedures for preparing voucher checks are the same as those for ordinary checks, except that you also fill in the voucher portion rather than merely indicating the purpose of the check.

Special Checks

From time to time, special checks that provide guarantee of payment are used by businesses.

- A **certified check** is an ordinary check that the bank marks "certified" after establishing that the funds are in the account of the party drawing the check. The funds are immediately subtracted from the depositor's account.
- A **cashier's check** is a check written by a bank on its own funds. Such a check can be purchased with cash or with an ordinary check.
- A **bank draft** is an order drawn by one bank on its deposits in another bank to pay a third party. Such a draft can be purchased with cash or with an ordinary check.

Computer-Generated Checks

Many companies use computers to prepare checks. If you prepare checks, you likely will be issued a password to access the company's accounts payable system. Security measures are taken to safeguard both the information used to prepare the checks and the printed checks.

For Discussion

Can you think of a purpose for which a business might use a certified check? A cashier's check? A bank draft?

Points to Emphasize

Although accounts payable tasks may be accomplished faster with computers, the accounting clerk must ensure that the data are accurately entered to reap the benefits of the increased processing speed.

233

Topic 6-1: *Cash and Banking Procedures*

electronic funds transfer: exchange of money by sending bank records via a computer network

bank reconciliation: a report used to compare bank and company account records

You may need to refer to the voucher and each vendor's file in the accounts payable system to obtain information needed to complete the checks. For example, you will need the vendor name and address, amount to be paid, and the purpose of payment. In automated systems, you may need to enter only a vendor number or name. Other information, such as the address, will be entered automatically by the system. Then, by selecting a menu option such as Print Checks, checks will be printed. Checks and related documents are sent to an authorized person to be signed.

Electronic Funds Transfer

Payments, as well as deposits, can be made electronically. With electronic payments or deposits, there is no physical exchange of currency or checks. **Electronic funds transfer** (EFT) is the use of a computer network to transfer funds from one party to another.

Some companies use EFT to send funds to a vendor's bank. The vendor's bank processes the deposit and credits the vendor's account. Also, many companies use EFT to deposit wage and salary payments for employees.

Reconciling a Bank Account

Companies need to be sure that receipts and payments shown in their records are reflected also in the bank's records. You may have the task of comparing these records to prepare a **bank reconciliation**. This document is prepared using a statement from the bank as well as your own company's records.

Bank Statement and Company Records

A bank statement provided by the bank shows the activity in each account on a regular basis, usually monthly. As you will note in Figure 6-1.9, a bank statement gives the following information:

- The balance as of the opening date of the statement
- Checks listed by number and amount that the bank has received and honored
- Automated teller machine transactions and miscellaneous charges
- Deposits
- The balance on the closing date of the statement

On the bank statement shown in Figure 6-1.9, the automated teller transactions are coded AW for ATM withdrawals, AC for ATM deposits and credits, and PD for preauthorized electronic deposits.

With the bank statement, the bank may return canceled checks or photocopies of canceled checks. Notices reporting increases or decreases in the bank balance will be noted. Other banks may provide only the statement. Copies of checks that have been scanned may be provided on request.

The bank statement shown in Figure 6-1.9 shows that a check deposited was returned by the bank on which it was drawn. Because the person writing the check did not have enough funds to cover the amount of the check, the check was not honored. Such checks are referred to as NSF (not sufficient funds) checks. Figure 6-1.9 shows that Adler Knitting's balance was reduced by the amount of the check that was not honored.

Figure **6-1.9**

Bank statement for Adler Knitting Manu-facturing Co.

Neches Bank
Cincinnati, Ohio

ADLER KNITTING MANUFACTURING CO
658 TEAKWOOD AVENUE
CINCINNATI OH 45224-4578

Account No.   32921-6

Statement Date   08/31/--

Balance from Previous Statement	Number of Credits	Amount of Deposits and Credits	Number of Debits	Amount of Withdrawals and Debits	Total Activity Charge	Statement Balance
22,890.75	4	26,962.10	20	29,255.96	25.00	20,596.89

Date	Code	Transaction Description	Transaction Amount	Account Balance
22-Jul	AW	0248 634	200.00	22,690.75
23-Jul		Deposit	6,790.40	29,481.15
		Check 187	3,750.00	25,731.15
		Check 189	1,890.25	23,840.90
27-Jul	AW	0248 634	2,500.00	21,340.90
28-Jul		Check 190	6,590.70	14,750.20
29-Jul	PD	Rae's Sweater Corner Deposit	7,980.70	22,730.90
3-Aug		Check 191	3,875.00	18,855.90
4-Aug		Check 192	1,870.70	16,985.20
		Check 194	580.90	16,404.30
5-Aug		Check 193	450.00	15,954.30
6-Aug	AC	ATM Deposit	4,280.90	20,235.20
9-Aug	AW	0248 634	1,000.00	19,235.20
10-Aug		Check 197	2,975.25	16,259.95
		Check 195	1,800.00	14,459.95
11-Aug		Check 196	290.20	14,169.75
12-Aug	PD	Rae's Sweater Corner Deposit	7,910.10	22,079.85
		Check 198	378.28	21,701.57
16-Aug		Check 202	150.50	21,551.07
		Check 201	95.70	21,455.37
		Check 199	110.98	21,344.39
17-Aug		Check 206	525.00	20,819.39
18-Aug		NSF Check	197.50	20,621.89
19-Aug		Service Charge	25.00	20,596.89

Generally, there are no documents included that relate to automatic teller machine (ATM) transactions. These are deposits and withdrawals made at electronic machines. Keep the slips generated at the time these transactions are made. They provide your receipt of the transaction.

To complete the reconciliation, you will need the company's checkbook or check register, which records all checks written and all deposits made. You also will need last month's reconciliation.

Purposes for Reconciliation

Cash is a valuable resource for all businesses. Knowing the exact status of the cash account, therefore, is important. By completing a bank reconciliation, you will fulfill the following purposes:

- Determine that all deposits made have been recorded by the bank, as indicated on the bank statement.

235

Topic 6-1: Cash and Banking Procedures

- Verify that all the checks that cleared the bank were written by authorized persons in the company.
- Determine which checks have not yet cleared the bank.
- Identify additional bank charges, as indicated on the bank statement, that need to be recorded in the books of the company.
- Determine the cash balance as of the date of the bank statement.

Steps in Preparing a Reconciliation

The company will have procedures for preparing bank reconciliations. You will want to learn these specific procedures. Assume that you are working in an office where a bank statement is received monthly and reconciliation is prepared at that time. The steps described here are likely to be similar to the ones you will learn on the job:

1. Compare the ending balance on last month's bank reconciliation with the beginning balance on this month's bank statement. Normally, these two balances will be the same. If there is a difference, record the two figures on a sheet of paper. Investigate any differences before completing the reconciliation.
2. Record on your reconciliation worksheet the balance in your check register as of the last day of the month. You may use pen and paper or a computer and software to prepare a bank reconciliation worksheet.
3. Record the ending balance as shown on the bank statement.
4. Compare each deposit shown on the bank statement with the deposits recorded on the check register. Put a small check mark in both places if the amount and date agree. Record on your worksheet any deposits shown in the check register that are not on the bank statement. Deposits made near the end of the month are not likely to have been processed by the bank by the date of the statement. Such deposits are referred to as deposits in transit.

Figure **6-1.10**

Bank reconciliation for Adler Knitting Manufacturing Co.

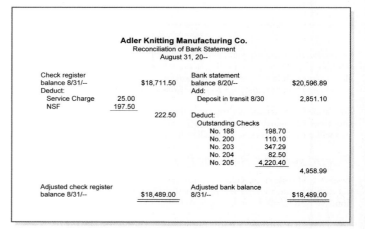

CHAPTER 6: PROCESSING AND UNDERSTANDING FINANCIAL INFORMATION

Figure **6-1.11**

One item on this
check register does
not have a check mark.
What is the status of
check #188?

Adler Knitting Manufacturing Co.
Check Register

Item No.	Date	Payment to or Deposit	Payment Amount	✓	Deposit Amount	Balance Forward
						28,681.15
187	7/17/--	Taylor Brothers	3,750.00	✓		24,931.15
188	7/16/---	Elman and Stone Co.	198.70			24,732.45
189	7/18/--	Marshall Gomez	1,890.25	✓		22,842.20
190	7/25/--	Leitz Mfg. Co.	6,590.70	✓		16,251.50
	7/29/--	Deposit		✓	7,980.70	24,232.20
191	8/1/--	Yarns, International	3,875.00	✓		20,357.20

Teaching Tips

Point out the check marks on
the check register that indicate the check has cleared.

5. Arrange in numeric order the checks returned with the bank statement.
   (Skip this step if it is not the bank's policy to return checks.)

6. Compare the amount of each check with that shown on the bank statement. Use small check marks by the items on the statement to show
   that there is agreement. Record any differences noted. Follow up on
   any differences before preparing your final reconciliation.

7. Compare each canceled check with related information in the check
   register. Place a small check mark in the register if there is agreement.
   (See Figure 6-1.11.)

8. Record on your worksheet the number, date, and amount for each check
   that was written but had not cleared as of the bank statement date.
   These checks are referred to as outstanding checks. The total of the outstanding checks will be subtracted from the bank statement balance.

9. Review last month's outstanding checks as listed on the bank reconciliation to determine which ones are still outstanding. List these on your
   worksheet also.

10. Record on your worksheet any charges shown on the statement that
    are not recorded in your company's records. For example, any checks
    returned for insufficient funds (NSF checks) must be subtracted from
    the balance in your check register. Bank charges, such as ATM fees,
    also must be subtracted.

11. Complete the calculations required on your worksheet. Note that the
    two balances are the same in the reconciliation shown in Figure 6-1.10.
    Having the same balances means that your cash account has been
    properly reconciled.

12. Prepare a clean, correct copy of the bank reconciliation. Print it on
    plain paper or use the form provided on the back of the bank statement.

When you have completed a bank reconciliation, obtain any required
approval signatures. Once the reconciliation is approved, file it so that it
can be readily retrieved. When you receive the next bank statement, you
will refer back to this one to determine which checks were outstanding
and should be in the next batch of canceled checks.

Maintaining a Petty Cash Fund

In many offices cash is needed occasionally to pay for small expenses, such as delivery services, postage due, and taxi fares. To handle such payments, departments are given a small sum of money, which is called a **petty cash** fund. Amounts in such funds can range from $20 to as much as $1,000.

WORKPLACE CONNECTIONS

The sales office of a women's clothing manufacturing company has a petty cash fund of $500. The fund is used to provide money for lunch ordered at a local coffee shop for visiting buyers. Funds are also used for late dinners when staff members must work or entertain major buyers from around the world. The fund is often used to pay for taxis and special delivery services. Wanda, the petty cashier, keeps careful records and requires receipts for all payments made from the fund.

Establishing the Fund

Company managers decide how much money will be kept in the petty cash fund. Once this amount is approved by the officer responsible for payments, a check is written payable to petty cashier, the person in charge of the petty cash fund. The petty cashier will cash the check and keep the cash in a locked cash box. Only the petty cashier has access to the key.

In some organizations, petty cash funds are kept in a separate checking account. However, the discussion here will be limited to a cash box system only.

Making Payments

The petty cashier keeps a complete and accurate record for every payment made from the petty cash fund. Petty cash receipt forms are filled out each time cash is given out. The following procedure is commonly followed in offices:

1. Ask each person who seeks payment from the petty cash fund to submit a sales receipt that shows the item purchased and the price paid. Generally, payment should not be made without some kind of receipt. Occasionally, cash payments are made even though no sales receipt is provided. On such occasions, the employee should present a brief memo giving the amount spent and describing the item or service purchased.

2. Prepare a petty cash receipt for each payment. Ask the person who will receive the cash to sign the receipt. Note the receipt shown in Figure 6-1.12. The receipt indicates the amount paid, to whom payment is made, and the purpose of the payment.

3. Attach the sales receipt or other document to the petty cash receipt and place these papers in the cash box.

For Discussion

What are the qualities needed by a petty cashier? Why is each quality important?

For Discussion

Why should a receipt be issued for each disbursement from the petty cash fund?

238

CHAPTER 6: PROCESSING AND UNDERSTANDING FINANCIAL INFORMATION

Figure **6-1.12**

PETTY CASH RECEIPT
Hardesty Security Systems

No. _42_   Date _November 17, 20--_

Amount $ _8.75_

Eight and 75/100 _____ Dollars

For _Postage_ _____

Received by _Wanda Davis_

Keeping a Record

In offices where many transactions require petty cash, an organized record is justified. In some departments, a petty cash record is kept for receipts and payments. Such a record is shown in Figure 6-1.13. Note the headings of the columns under which the payments are recorded. In each office the same types of payments are likely to occur again and again. However, the column headings for your office may be different from the ones shown here. By recording payments as they are made, the task of preparing a report at the end of the month or when you need to add money to the fund will be simplified.

You may work in an office where petty cash records are kept manually. Spreadsheet software can also be used to record petty cash transactions. In either case, attention to detail and entering all data accurately are critical when keeping petty cash records.

PETTY CASH RECORD
November, 20--

Date	Receipt No.	Balance	Books	Taxi	Office Supplies	Postage	Art Supplies	Misc.
1-Nov	Beg. Balance	250.00						
6-Nov	39	237.05	12.95					
8-Nov	40	228.55		8.50				
8-Nov	41	220.85			7.70			
11-Nov	42	210.10				10.75		
17-Nov	43	203.65						6.45
19-Nov	44	184.90	18.75					
21-Nov	45	161.90		23.00				
22-Nov	46	150.40		11.50				
24-Nov	47	120.25					30.15	
25-Nov	48	108.80				11.45		
26-Nov	49	90.30			18.50			
29-Nov	50	78.20						12.10
30-Nov	End. Balance	78.20						
		Item Totals	31.70	43.00	26.20	22.20	30.15	18.55

Figure **6-1.13**

Petty cash record

For Discussion

In the petty cash record shown in Figure 6-1.13, what category had the highest amount of expenditures reimbursed?

Thinking Critically

Why might a company direct the petty cashier to balance and replenish the petty cash fund each month, even if only a small amount of the fund has been spent?

Replenishing the Fund

From time to time, money must be added to a petty cash fund. In some offices, the fund is replenished when a certain balance is reached. In others, the fund is restored to its original amount at the end of each month regardless of the level of funds. This procedure is commonly used in offices:

1. Count the money in the cash box and total the receipts in the petty cash box.

2. Compare the petty cash box total to the petty cash receipts total. They should be the same. If they are not, determine why there is a difference. Did you fail to include a receipt in your total? Did someone fail to turn in a receipt?

3. Add the amount of the petty cash receipts to the amount of petty cash remaining in the cash box. The total should equal the amount of petty cash you had when you last balanced and/or replenished the petty cash fund.

4. Investigate any differences. Careful attention to managing the petty cash fund will result in few, if any, errors. If, after your investigation, you find that you are over or short by a few pennies, note this difference on your petty cash record. For example, if in step 2 you found only $78.00 in cash, you would indicate on your petty cash record that the fund is short $0.20.

5. Prepare a voucher for a check for the amount needed to replenish the fund. Submit your petty cash record report, the receipts, and your check voucher for approval to your department head or other designated person.

6. Once approved, follow up by sending a copy of the report to the Accounting Department and by sending the voucher to the proper office.

7. Cash the check and immediately place the cash in the cash box.

3. Consider needs in relation to the company priorities for the coming year. What new projects will your department handle that may require additional expenses? What improvements have been made that may lower expenses?

4. Collect data to support your requests. This data might be costs for new equipment or a recommended salary for a new employee who is to be hired for the department.

5. Be prepared to answer questions related to the data you helped prepare.

The company's overall goals and limited resources are considered in making a final budget for the company. Highlight or prepare a summary of the parts of the budget that relate to your department or job. Be aware that the budget may be revised at some point during the budget period. A budget is a plan for how resources will be used. You or your department may have approval to spend for certain expenses based on a budgeted amount. In many companies, however, some expenses must be approved in advance even if they are included on a budget.

Monitoring a Budget

A budget is generally a plan for a particular period of time such as a fiscal year. Budgets for shorter periods are developed from the annual budget. As the year progresses, budget reports are prepared. These reports compare the money spent in each category to the budgeted amount. Budget reports are typically prepared monthly or quarterly. If expenses in any category are too high, steps are taken to limit spending.

WORKPLACE CONNECTIONS

Johnson Company's budget included $15,000 for staff training for the year. More training than expected was needed to train employees to use the new order entry software. By August 1, $12,650 of the $15,000 budgeted amount had been spent. As a result, the manager changed the procedure for approving training. He issued a memo stating that all staff training for the remainder of the year must receive his prior approval as well as the usual approval from the department head.

A monthly or quarterly budget report is often combined with a year-to-date budget report. The year-to-date report shows the amount spent in each category from the beginning date for the budget to the date the report was prepared.

Combining both a monthly and a year-to-date report provides a better view of expenses as they relate to the entire budget time period. Some expenses, such as insurance or taxes, for example, may be paid quarterly. When the payment is made, the amount of the payment may be larger than the quarterly budgeted amount. Yet the payment may be within the total amount allotted annually. An example of a budget report for Dandy's Delights is shown in Figure 6-2.1.

For Discussion

Ask students what experiences they have had with preparing or following a budget, perhaps at home or for a school club or activity.

DANDY'S DELIGHTS
OPERATING EXPENSES BUDGET REPORT
For the Month Ending June 30, 20--

June Actual	June Budget	Variance Fav. (Unfav.)	Variance Percent	Item	Year-to-Date Actual	Year-to-Date Budget	Year-to-Date Variance Fav. (Unfav.)	Variance Percent
$4,850	$4,850	0	0.0%	Salaries	$29,100	$29,100	0	0.0%
1,125	375	(750)	-200.0%	Payroll Taxes	2,250	2,250	0	0.0%
45	42	(3)	-7.1%	Advertising	245	250	5	2.0%
210	42	(168)	-400.0%	Delivery	610	250	(360)	-144.0%
60	67	7	10.4%	Office Supplies	395	400	5	1.3%
280	333	53	15.9%	Utilities	1,400	2,000	600	30.0%
35	42	7	16.7%	Miscellaneous	255	250	(5)	-2.0%
$6,605	$5,751	($854)	-14.8%	Total Expenses	$34,255	$34,500	$245	0.7%

Figure **6-2.1**

This monthly budget report shows budgeted amounts and actual expenses.

Income Statements

An income statement is a report that shows the results of operations for a period of time. Revenues, expenses, and the income or loss for the reporting period is shown. A projected income statement is often created as part of a company's plans. It lists the revenues and expenses the company expects for the reporting period. A net income results if revenues are greater than expenses. A net loss results if expenses are greater than revenues. A projected income statement for Dandy's Delights is shown in Figure 6-2.2.

WORKPLACE CONNECTIONS

Miguel is an office assistant to Dan Burts, the owner of Dandy's Delights. The company's cookies and baked goods are sold in most local supermarkets. Mr. Burts is planning to expand soon into nearby towns. One of Miguel's duties is to prepare both actual and projected financial statements. These statements will be used to help secure funds for expansion.

DANDY'S DELIGHTS
PROJECTED INCOME STATEMENT
For the Year Ended December 31, 20--

		% of Sales
Sales	$250,000	
Cost of Goods Sold	125,000	
Gross Profit on Sales	$125,000	50%
Operating Expenses		
Advertising Expense	1,000	
Delivery Expense	1,500	
Office Supplies Expense	1,000	
Payroll Taxes Expense	4,500	
Salaries Expense	58,200	
Utilities Expense	3,800	
Miscellaneous Expense	500	
Total Operating Expense	70,500	
Net Income from Operations	$54,500	22%
Other Income and Expenses		
Interest Expense	3,000	
Net Income Before Income Tax	$51,500	21%
Less Income Tax	14,600	
Net Income After Tax	$36,900	15%

Balance Sheets

A balance sheet is a report that shows the condition of a company as of a specific date. A projected balance sheet is often created as part of a company's plans. This report shows the assets, liabilities, and owner's equity or capital projected for the end of the plan period. The assets of a company include all the goods and property owned by the firm. Amounts due to the company from others are also assets. Liabilities are the debts the company owes. The owner's equity or capital is the owner's share of the worth of the firm. This amount is the difference between assets and liabilities. A projected balance sheet for Dandy's Delights is shown in Figure 6-2.3 on page 250.

Formatting Financial Documents

When you are asked to key financial documents, study earlier copies of these documents. If possible, use the same formats as in the previous documents. Continuing to use the same formats allows easier comparison of data from year to year. Guidelines for income statements and balance sheets may be included in a company's procedures manual.

Formats for financial statements and reports may vary. Follow the format guidelines below if no company standards are given.

- Leave at least a one-inch margin at the top and bottom and on both sides.

249

Topic 6-2: *Financial Reports and Payroll*

Figure **6-2.3**

This balance sheet shows projected figures.

DANDY'S DELIGHTS
PROJECTED BALANCE SHEET
As of December 31, 20--

Assets

Current Assets		
Cash	$43,400	
Accounts Receivable	5,000	
Baking Supplies Inventory	4,000	
Office Supplies	500	
Total Current Assets		$64,900
Fixed Assets		
Delivery Van	$7,000	
Baking Equipment	5,000	
Building and Land	95,000	
Total Fixed Assets		107,000
Total Assets		$159,900

Liabilities

Current Liabilities		
Notes Payable	$5,000	
Accounts Payable	1,500	
Salary and Wages Payable	200	
Total Current Liabilities		$6,700
Fixed Liabilities		
Long-term Note Payable	$7,000	
Mortgage Payable	32,000	
Total Fixed Liabilities		39,000
Total Liabilities		$45,700

Owner's Equity

Dan Burts, Capital Beginning Balance		$82,300	
Net Income for 20--	$36,900		
Less Withdrawals	5,000	31,900	
Dan Burts, Capital Ending Balance		114,200	
Total Liabilities and Owner's Equity		$159,900	

- Center the lines in the statement heading—company name, statement name, and the date(s) covered by the statement.
- Use a single line (extending the width of the longest item in the column) keyed underneath the last figure to indicate addition or subtraction.
- Use double lines underneath a final column total.
- Use the dollar sign with the first figure of each new column of figures to be added or subtracted or with every sum or difference if the figure is keyed directly underneath a single line.

Proofread the documents carefully, even if you have used a computer to prepare the statements. Give attention to detail. If another worker is available to help you, proofreading can be made easier. One person can read aloud from the original document while the other person proofreads the prepared copy. In addition to the words and figures, the person reading aloud should indicate details such as punctuation, underscores, and dollar signs. Watch

Points to Emphasize

Proofread copy slowly and carefully. Give attention to detail. When working with numbers you calculated manually, recalculate all totals.

CHAPTER 6: PROCESSING AND UNDERSTANDING FINANCIAL INFORMATION

All financial documents must be proofread carefully.

for transposed figures (for example, 1,245 for 1,254). As a final proof, check all totals. If you are using computer software to prepare the statement, check the accuracy of any formulas used in the statement.

Payments for Wages and Salaries

A **payroll** is a list of the amount of salary, wages, or other payments for work due to employees. Payroll information must be accurate and should be kept confidential. The procedures used to handle the payroll vary depending on the size of the workforce. Common tasks related to handling a payroll include:

payroll: list of employees and amount of salary or wages due to each

- Keeping employee payroll records up to date
- Calculating **deductions** and changes in salary, commissions, or overtime
- Updating attendance, vacation, and sick leave data
- Processing, printing, and distributing paychecks
- Creating tax reports related to payroll that must be submitted to local, state, and federal agencies

deductions: items that reduce gross pay

Some companies use time and attendance recording systems. Employees register their attendance at a computer terminal. Attendance data goes directly into the company's payroll system.

Teaching Tips

Determine an amount to be paid to each student for each day spent in class. Then keep a payroll register during one week or month. Require students to sign in at the beginning of each class and sign out at the end. Issue simulated voucher checks and have students verify payments and deductions.

251

Topic 6-2: *Financial Reports and Payroll*

For Discussion

Ask students to share their experiences with e-commerce. Have their experiences been positive or negative?

FOCUS ON . . .

E-commerce and Planning Strategies

"They can have any color they want, as long as it's black."

Attributed to pioneer automaker
Henry Ford

E-commerce is changing the way businesses operate. It is creating a need for new planning strategies. Before e-commerce became established, most manufacturers used one of two basic business models. The models were either mass production or customized production. Strategies for both these business models have been well known and practiced for many years.

At the height of the Industrial Revolution, mass production allowed companies to lower costs by making large numbers of the same product. The lower costs were passed on to customers in the form of lower prices. Using a customized product business model, a product is made according to a customer's needs. In the past, customized products were often expensive to make. Few people could afford customized products of good quality.

With the advent of e-commerce, many companies sell directly to customers and buy directly from suppliers on the Web. E-commerce has made a third business model, mass customization, more widely used. Mass customization means making many products to meet customers' needs. Dell Computer Corporation is an example of a company that uses this model. Customers enter their product order on the company's Web site. Although the company makes thousands of computers each year, each one can be built for a particular customer's needs.

Companies can now offer the best of both worlds—customized products at mass-produced prices. This business model requires creative strategies for planning and budgeting. Planning is difficult because of the large number of choices customers have when ordering products. The planning process is also much more complex. Companies who use this business model rely heavily on market research to help them create forecasts for future sales and supply needs.

For Discussion

What kinds of jobs might be paid on a salary basis? On an hourly basis? On which basis would you prefer to be paid? Why?

Compensation Plans

compensated: paid

In some companies, all employees are **compensated** in the same way. In other companies, different plans may be used for different groups of workers. The typical ones include salary, hourly, commission, and combination plans.

gross salary: money earned before any deductions are made

Under a salary plan, the employee is paid a certain amount per week, month, or year. The **gross salary**, which is the salary before any deductions, is the figure quoted. A salary quoted on a yearly basis is divided into the number of pay periods per year. Thus, a person who earns $22,000 yearly and is paid twice each month will have a gross salary of $916.66 each pay period.

overtime: hours worked beyond the standard number in a workweek

In some jobs, employees are paid a wage rate per hour. The hourly rate applies to the hours considered standard. The standard workweek may be 35, 37.5, or 40 hours. When workers paid on an hourly basis work more hours than those set as their standard workweek, they generally earn a higher rate for the **overtime** hours. Overtime rates are commonly 1.5 to 2 times the standard hourly rate.

252

CHAPTER 6: PROCESSING AND UNDERSTANDING FINANCIAL INFORMATION

This salesperson is paid a commission in addition to a base salary.

Some workers' earnings are based on a percentage of the price of what they sell. This payment is called a **commission**. The percentage may vary by volume of sales. This method is commonly used for the payment of salespersons. For example, salespersons for a computer supplies company are assigned sales territories. Because their earnings depend on the sales they make, they are motivated to please customers and secure new orders. For a salesperson who earns a 10 percent commission on each sale, a $1,000 order would result in a $100 commission.

In some jobs, a combination payment plan is used. For example, a commission, referred to as a bonus, may be given to employees who are successful beyond some established standard. Such a bonus is often a percentage of additional sales or production.

commission: payment based on the price of items sold

WORKPLACE CONNECTIONS

Lauren works as a salesperson for a furniture store. She is paid according to a combination plan. She earns a weekly salary of $500 plus a 5 percent commission on weekly sales exceeding $5,000. Last week Lauren's sales were $8,000. She earned $500 in salary plus $150 ($3,000 x 5%) in commission for a total of $650. Lauren likes the combination pay plan because the weekly salary assures her of a steady, basic income. At the same time, the bonus portion of the plan rewards her for using her sales skills to make higher sales for the company.

253

Topic 6-2: *Financial Reports and Payroll*

Thinking Critically

Where would a payroll employee find the withholding tables needed to compute the deductions from gross pay? (From the IRS.)

Teaching Tips

Discuss the W-4 form shown in Figure 6-2.4 with students, pointing out the information it includes.

Deductions from Earnings

As you have learned, salaries and wages are quoted at their gross figures, which is before any deductions are considered. The earnings actually received will be less than the gross wages or salaries. Some payroll deductions are required by law; others are voluntary as requested by the employee.

Deductions Required by Law

Deductions required by law include the following:

- Federal income tax
- Federal Insurance Contributions Act tax (referred to as FICA or social security tax)
- State income tax (where applicable)
- City income tax (where applicable)

Federal income tax deductions vary depending on the gross amount of wages or salary, the employee's marital status, and the number of withholding allowances (also called exemptions) claimed. Each employee must complete an Employee's Withholding Allowance Certificate (known as a W-4 form). This form is kept on file by the company. The employee must notify the company of any changes in the number of exemptions. Figure 6-2.4 shows an example of a W-4 form.

Cut here and give Form W-4 to your employer. Keep the top part for your records.

Form **W-4**

Employee's Withholding Allowance Certificate

OMB No. 1545-0010

Department of the Treasury
Internal Revenue Service

▶ Whether you are entitled to claim a certain number of allowances or exemption from withholding is subject to review by the IRS. Your employer may be required to send a copy of this form to the IRS.

2005

1 Type or print your first name and middle initial: **Jeffrey C.** Last name: **Hunter**

2 Your social security number: **321 : 22 : 4697**

Home address (number and street or rural route): **45 Newland Place**

3 ☐ Single ☑ Married ☐ Married, but withhold at higher Single rate.
Note. If married, but legally separated, or spouse is a nonresident alien, check the "Single" box.

City or town, state, and ZIP code: **Matawan, NJ 07747-6321**

4 If your last name differs from that shown on your social security card, check here. You must call 1-800-772-1213 for a new card. ▶ ☐

5 Total number of allowances you are claiming (from line **H** above **or** from the applicable worksheet on page 2) ... **5** | **1**

6 Additional amount, if any, you want withheld from each paycheck ... **6** | $ **-0-**

7 I claim exemption from withholding for 2005, and I certify that I meet **both** of the following conditions for exemption.
- Last year I had a right to a refund of **all** federal income tax withheld because I had **no** tax liability **and**
- This year I expect a refund of **all** federal income tax withheld because I expect to have **no** tax liability.
If you meet both conditions, write "Exempt" here ... ▶ **7**

Under penalties of perjury, I declare that I have examined this certificate and to the best of my knowledge and belief, it is true, correct, and complete.

Employee's signature
(Form is not valid unless you sign it.) ▶ *Jeffrey C. Hunter*

Date ▶ *July 5, 20--*

8 Employer's name and address (Employer: Complete lines 8 and 10 only if sending to the IRS.)

9 Office code (optional)

10 Employer identification number (EIN)

For Privacy Act and Paperwork Reduction Act Notice, see page 2. Cat. No. 10220Q Form **W-4** (2005)

Figure 6-2.4

How many allowances does Jeffrey Hunter claim?

FICA deductions are a percentage of gross wages or salary, up to the maximum amount of wages or salary taxed. The employee's contribution to FICA is matched by the employer. Each year the rates are reviewed by the U.S. Congress. The rate and the maximum amount taxed are sometimes changed. Your company can provide you with the up-to-date percentages for deductions and the amount of earnings subject to FICA tax. This information also is available from your local office of the Social Security Administration.

State and local governments that tax the earnings of citizens issue instructions regarding the taxes to be withheld. The company will have this information on file for your reference.

Voluntary Deductions

Voluntary deductions are amounts taken from pay at an employee's request. In some companies, employees may choose to have money deducted for health insurance, savings plans, retirement plans, and other purposes. Employees who prepare the payroll must keep the records up to date for employees' individual deductions.

Records for Payroll

Companies maintain careful records of all payments made to employees. Employee earnings records are prepared for each pay period and for the year-to-date. The earnings records show earnings, deductions, and **net pay**. Many companies issue payroll checks that have an attached voucher showing similar information. An earnings record report and a payroll register are shown in Figure 6-2.5 on page 256.

net pay: final earnings amount after all deductions

At the end of the year, the company should give each employee a Wage and Tax Statement (commonly called a W-2 form) for the calendar year. The information needed to prepare the W-2 form is found on the payroll register. This register records all the earnings and deductions for the payroll period. The company should make weekly, monthly, or quarterly reports to government agencies of taxes withheld and taxes the employer must pay. At certain times during the year, the company makes deposits of the amounts withheld and the taxes owed.

Expand the Concept

An office worker discovers a difference between the hours reported by the supervisor and the hours reported by an employee. What might the office worker do at this point? What department typically provides employees who handle the payroll with information about salary changes?

255

Topic 6-2: *Financial Reports and Payroll*

For Discussion

In Figure 6-2.5, what percentage of Jeffrey Hunter's gross salary is deducted each year?

EMPLOYEE EARNINGS RECORD

Employee: Jeffrey Hunter
Employee No.: 3415

SS No.: 321-22-4697
Marital Status: M
No. Allowances: 1

Year Ending: December 31, 20--
Position: Data Entry Clerk
Pay per Year: $19,200

Pay Period	Ended	Regular	Total	Income Tax	FICA	State Tax	Total Tax	Health Ins.	Net Pay	Gross Acc. Earnings
1	31-Jan	$1,600.00	$1,600.00	$242.00	$122.40	$37.59	$401.99	$123.00	$1,075.01	$1,600.00
2	28-Feb	1,600.00	1,600.00	242.00	122.40	37.59	401.99	123.00	1,075.01	3,200.00
3	31-Mar	1,600.00	1,600.00	242.00	122.40	37.59	401.99	123.00	1,075.01	4,800.00
4	30-Apr	1,600.00	1,600.00	242.00	122.40	37.59	401.99	123.00	1,075.01	6,400.00
5	31-May	1,600.00	1,600.00	242.00	122.40	37.59	401.99	123.00	1,075.01	8,000.00
6	30-Jun	1,600.00	1,600.00	242.00	122.40	37.59	401.99	123.00	1,075.01	9,600.00
7	31-Jul	1,600.00	1,600.00	242.00	122.40	37.59	401.99	123.00	1,075.01	11,200.00
8	31-Aug	1,600.00	1,600.00	242.00	122.40	37.59	401.99	123.00	1,075.01	12,800.00
9	30-Sep	1,600.00	1,600.00	242.00	122.40	37.59	401.99	123.00	1,075.01	14,400.00
10	31-Oct	1,600.00	1,600.00	242.00	122.40	37.59	401.99	123.00	1,075.01	16,000.00
11	30-Nov	1,600.00	1,600.00	242.00	122.40	37.59	401.99	123.00	1,075.01	17,600.00
12	31-Dec	1,600.00	1,600.00	242.00	122.40	37.59	401.99	123.00	1,075.01	19,200.00
		$19,200.00	$19,200.00	$2,904.00	$1,468.80	$451.08	$4,823.88	$1,476.00	$12,900.12	

Figure 6-2.5

What are Jeffrey Hunter's net earnings for the year?

MODERN SOFTWARE, INC.
PAYROLL REGISTER
January 31, 20--

Employee No.	Employee Name	Regular	Overtime	Total	Income Tax	FICA	State Tax	Total Tax	Health Ins.	Net Pay
4568	Acosta, B.	$2,150.00		$2,150.00	$236.00	$164.48	$58.98	$459.46	$123.00	$1,567.54
4321	Beres, W.	1,088.00		1,088.00	131.00	83.23	19.64	233.87	123.00	731.13
3257	Cantrell, T.	2,840.00		2,840.00	635.00	217.26	103.97	956.23	76.00	1,807.77
3921	Evans, T.	2,010.00		2,010.00	249.00	153.77	55.32	458.09	76.00	1,475.91
3415	Hunter, J.	1,600.00		1,600.00	242.00	122.40	37.59	401.99	123.00	1,075.01
3401	Hutchins, W.	3,445.00		3,445.00	854.00	263.54	135.83	1,253.37	76.00	2,115.63
4563	Jacobs, S. L.	1,810.00		1,810.00	193.00	138.47	43.30	374.77	76.00	1,359.23

Payroll Check Distribution

A company may distribute checks in person or mail them to employees. Other companies use **direct deposit**. That is, they electronically deposit wage and salary payments to employees' bank accounts. The company provides the employee with a document that details the deposit. In some companies, employees may choose their payment method.

direct deposit: placing money in a bank account by electronic means rather than issuing a check

© TOM ROSENTHAL/SUPERSTOCK INTERNATIONAL

In this company, payroll checks are delivered in person.

Points to Emphasize

Direct deposit is becoming more popular with employees and companies because this method of payment is safe and convenient.

REVIEWING THE TOPIC

1. What is the purpose of a budget?
2. What suggestions will be helpful if you take part in creating a budget?
3. What information does a report used to monitor a budget typically include?
4. What is an income statement? What information does it typically include?
5. What is a balance sheet? What information does it typically include?
6. What tasks do employees who handle payroll perform?
7. How does the hourly method of payroll payment differ from the salary method?
8. How does the salary method of payroll payment differ from the commission method?
9. Name two deductions from earnings that are required by law.
10. Describe the information recorded in a payroll register.

MAKING DECISIONS

Valerie's job duties include filing invoices and purchase orders. Carmen's job duties include checking the accuracy of invoices against purchase orders. From time to time, Carmen must retrieve these documents from the files. Recently, Carmen has had difficulty in locating specific documents. Often she must search through practically an entire file drawer to find what she needs. Janie noted that others seem to be spending too much time looking through the files also.

Carmen has no authority to supervise Valerie. The supervisor has said nothing to Valerie about the matter as far as Carmen knows. "Because the supervisor doesn't use the files, the supervisor may not be aware of this problem," thinks Carmen. She believes the work of the department would be far more efficient if the filing were done carefully.

1. If you were in Carmen's position, would you discuss this situation with Valerie's supervisor? Why or why not?
2. What might be an alternative action you could take to help remedy this problem?

REINFORCING ENGLISH SKILLS

Reports and letters prepared by office workers often contain numbers. Review the following number rules. Then write or key the sentences expressing the numbers in correct form.

Number Usage Rules

- Spell numbers one through ten; use figures for numbers above ten.
- Spell a number that begins a sentence.
- Use the same style for related numbers in a sentence. If any of the numbers are above ten, use figures for all the numbers.
- Use figures and a dollar sign to express amounts of money. For money in round amounts of a million or more, the words *million* or *billion* may be used to replace the zeros ($4 million). For amounts under a dollar, use figures and the word *cents*.
- Use numbers to express measurements.

1. 15 people attended the meeting.
2. The report identifies 5 departments that are over budget.
3. The package weights two pounds 11 ounces.
4. The sales forecast for next year is 3,000,000 dollars.
5. Of the 15 companies, 7 sent executives to the training session.
6. 4 managers reported expenses totaling one thousand dollars.
7. You have been asked to purchase eighty reams of paper for use by three departments.
8. The new printer is ten inches tall and 17 inches wide.
9. The pens with red ink cost fifty cents each.
10. Last year we sold five hundred and twenty-five different types of products.

Teaching Tip

Remind students to use the payroll register shown in Figure 6-2.5 as a model for their documents.

SPREADSHEET

Topic **6-2**   ACTIVITY 1

Payroll Register

You are an office employee in Furniture Galore, a retail store in a suburban mall. You have been given a schedule of salaries to use in preparing a payroll register for the pay period November 1–15.

1. Open and print the PDF file *CH06 Salaries* from the data files. This file contains salary and other information for employees.
2. Use spreadsheet software to create a payroll register similar to the one shown in Figure 6-2.5 on page 256. Key the appropriate headings for the register. The register is being prepared two weeks after the pay period ends and should be dated November 31 of the current year. Use the heading **Bonus** rather than Overtime. Key the employee numbers and names.
3. Enter formulas to calculate the regular pay for the employees for the pay period November 1–15. The regular pay is the monthly salary divided by two.
4. Enter formulas to calculate the bonus amount for employees who receive a commission. Multiply the commission amount by the net sales for the period. Enter a formula to add the regular pay to the bonus amount, if any, to find the total gross pay.
5. Enter formulas in the spreadsheet to calculate the income tax, FICA, and state tax amounts. Use the tax rates on the printout. To find a tax amount, multiply the total gross pay by the tax percentage. Enter a formula to find the total tax for each person.
6. Enter a formula to calculate the appropriate amount for the health care deduction for each person.
7. Enter a formula to calculate the net pay for each person. To find the net pay, subtract the total tax and the health insurance amount from the total gross pay.
8. Sort the data in alphabetic order by the employee name. Print the payroll register.

Teaching Tip

Help students identify consumable items, such as file folders or pens, that will need to be purchased for the coming year. Discuss other nonconsumable items, such as staplers or paper cutters, that may not need to be purchased next year.

SPREADSHEET

Topic **6-2**   ACTIVITY 2

Supplies Budget

You are an employee in the Accounting Department at Mica Associates. You have been asked to plan a budget for office supplies for your department for the coming year.

260

CHAPTER 6: PROCESSING AND UNDERSTANDING FINANCIAL INFORMATION

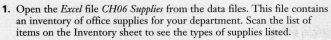

1. Open the *Excel* file *CH06 Supplies* from the data files. This file contains an inventory of office supplies for your department. Scan the list of items on the Inventory sheet to see the types of supplies listed.

2. Go to the Budget sheet. Note that this sheet also shows the items and prices in the inventory. In addition, it shows the quantity of each item purchased last year.

3. On the Budget sheet, add a column of data at the right. Key **Total Amount** for the column head. Enter a formula to multiply the price times the quantity purchased to find the total amount. Enter a formula to sum the Total Amount column to find the total amount spent for office supplies last year. Place a single line border above the column total amount.

4. In planning your budget, consider which items will need to be purchased again. For consumable items, such as file folders or pens, assume you need to purchase the same amount as for the previous year. For other items, such as staplers or paper cutters, use your judgment about how many may need to be purchased next year.

5. Add a column at the right of the worksheet. Key **Adjustments** for the column head. In this column, key amounts for items you do not plan to include in the budget this year.

6. Enter a formula to sum the Adjustments column. Place a single line border above the column total amount.

7. Enter a formula to subtract the total of the Adjustments column from the total of the Total Amount column. Place the formula in column F two rows below the total of the Adjustments column. Label this answer **Total After Adjustments** to the left of the amount.

8. Prices may increase for some items during the coming year. Key the amount **.05** in column F two rows under the cell that contains the Total After Adjustments answer. Label this amount **Allowance for Price Increases** to the left of the amount.

9. In column F two rows below the cell for Allowance for Price Increases, enter a formula to multiply the Total After Adjustments by 105 percent. Label this answer **Yearly Budget Total** to the left of the answer.

10. In column F two rows below the cell with the Yearly Budget Total amount, enter a formula to divide the Yearly Budget Total by **4**. Label this answer **Quarterly Budget Amount** to the left of the answer.

11. Format the sheet to print the column headings (in row 5) on the top of each page. Create a footer to print **Page** and the page number on each page. Format all cells with dollar amounts for currency. Make other adjustments in formatting as needed for an attractive, easy-to-read report.

12. Print the budget report. Keep this budget report file for use in a later activity.

Summary

Procedures for processing financial information may vary from company to company. However, companies should keep accurate, up-to-date records at all times. From your study of this chapter, you should be able to discuss the following key points:

- Methods used to protect assets are known as internal controls. Internal controls fall into three categories—preventive, detective, and corrective.
- Companies generally separate duties for tasks in processing cash. They may also bond employees in order to have good internal control.
- Companies bill customers for goods or services purchased on credit. The request for payment is commonly in the form of a sales invoice or a statement of account.
- Employees assist in processing cash by seeing that checks are endorsed properly and filling in deposit slips. They also prepare bank reconciliations and keep petty cash funds.
- Employees who make cash payments review documents, prepare vouchers, and prepare checks.
- Bank accounts are reconciled to be sure that receipts and payments shown in company records match the bank's records.
- The petty cash fund is used in many offices to pay for small expenses such as postage or delivery services.
- A budget is a plan that shows how the resources of a business will be used. Budgets are used for planning and monitoring spending.
- Companies design payroll procedures to ensure that employees are paid accurately and on time.
- Financial statements provide information about a company's economic resources and the results of the company's operations.

Key Terms

accounts payable	debit card	internal control
accounts receivable	deductions	net pay
audit	direct deposit	overtime
bank reconciliation	electronic funds	payee
bonding	transfer (EFT)	payroll
budget	endorsement	petty cash
check	fiscal year	tickler file
commission	forge	voucher
compensated	fraud	
credit	gross salary	

262

Chapter 6 : ACTIVITY 1

Purchasing Schedule

For this activity you will need to refer to the supplies inventory and budget information from Topic 6-2 Activity 2. The budget you prepared was based on last year's purchases and divided to calculate the quarterly budget. In this activity you will create a purchasing schedule for office supplies for each quarter. Your goal is to have items on hand when needed and to spread the purchase cost across the four quarters as evenly as possible.

1. Open the *Excel* file *CH06 Supplies* that you updated earlier. Make a copy of the Inventory sheet. Name the new sheet **Schedule.**

2. On the Schedule sheet, delete the subtitle **Office Supplies Inventory.** Key a new subtitle **Office Supplies Purchasing Schedule.** Delete the Quantity on Hand and the Totals columns.

3. Consider each item on your supplies inventory. How many of the items were purchased last year, and how many do we have on hand? Decide how to spread purchase of the items over the year. Assume most items will be used evenly over the year. If you plan to purchase only one or two of particular items, you may want to put them in your purchasing schedule in the first or second quarter even though they will be used throughout the year.

4. Enter column headings **Qty. Qtr. 1** and **Cost Qtr. 1** at the right of the sheet. Key the quantity of each item you plan to purchase in quarter 1. Enter a formula in the Cost Qtr. 1 column to multiply the price times the quantity to be purchased. Sum the Cost Qtr. 1 column. Repeat this step for quarters 2, 3, and 4.

5. Key column headings for **Total Qty.** (for the year) and **Total Cost** (for the year) at the right of the sheet. Enter formulas to calculate the total cost for the year. Sum the Total Cost column.

6. Format the spreadsheet attractively. Center the titles over all the columns. Set the column headings (in row 5) to print on each page. Create a footer to print **Page** and the page number. Format all cells with dollar amounts for currency. Place a single-line border above and a double-line border below the column totals.

7. Print a copy of your purchasing schedule in landscape orientation. Save this file for use in a later activity.

263

Chapter Review

Teaching Tips

Assist students who may have trouble deciding when to purchase items. Remind them that the goal is to have items on hand when needed and to spread the purchase cost across the four quarters as evenly as possible. Review how to copy sheets in a workbook, set the column headings to print on each page, and create a footer.

Chapter 6 ACTIVITY 2

Monitoring a Budget

In this activity, you will continue your work at Mica Associates. Assume this is the end of the second quarter of the year for which you prepared a supplies budget. You need to compare the amount you have spent for office supplies to the first- and second-quarter budgeted amounts.

1. Open the *Excel* file *CH06 Supplies* that you edited earlier. Assume you purchased all the items as planned on your purchasing schedule for quarters 1 and 2. You did not purchase any other items.

2. Determine the amount you spent for office supplies in quarters 1 and 2. Compare this amount to the amounts budgeted for quarters 1 and 2 on the office supplies budget you created earlier. Are you over or under budget and by how much? If you are over budget, what changes might you be able to make in the last two quarters to get back on budget?

3. Create a memo form for Mica Associates to include the company name and the appropriate headings. Write a memo to the department head, Freda Amosa. Use the date **July 3, 20--** and an appropriate subject line. Give Freda an update on the amount you had budgeted for office supplies for quarters 1 and 2 and the amounts you have actually spent. If you are under budget, explain why, mentioning some of the items or a strategy you used to save money. If you are over budget, explain the steps you will take in quarters 3 and 4 to stay within the yearly budget.

4. Create a bar graph to compare budgeted and actual costs for office supplies for quarters 1 and 2. Copy the graph into your memo to illustrate the data. Proofread carefully and correct all errors before printing the memo.

Chapter 6 ACTIVITY 3

Projected Income Statement

You are an office worker for Duncan's Auto Detailing. The owner, Mr. Duncan, has asked you to create two projected income statements for next year based on two different levels of potential business.

1. Open the *Excel* file *CH06 Income Statement* from the data files. This file contains last year's income statement for Duncan's Auto Detailing.

2. Make two copies of the income statement sheets in the workbook. Name the three sheets **Last Year, Best Case,** and **Worst Case.** Change the second line of the title of the Best Case and Worst Case sheets to **Projected Income Statement.** On the Best Case and Worst Case sheets, insert a row above the date and add the heading *Best Case* or *Worst Case.*

CHAPTER 6: PROCESSING AND UNDERSTANDING FINANCIAL INFORMATION

Teaching Tips

Review memo parts and format. Assist students who may need help creating the graph or copying it into the memo.

Teaching Tips

Review how to copy sheets in a workbook and how to rename sheets.

3. Make the changes Mr. Duncan projects for the best case as listed below:
   - Sales will increase 25 percent compared to last year.
   - Detailing labor will increase $20,000.
   - Supplies will increase 25 percent.
   - Advertising will increase $400.
   - Payroll taxes will increase $1,500.
   - Utilities will increase 25 percent.
   - Income tax expense will be at the same rate as last year. To find last year's rate, divide the income tax by the net income before tax on last year's sheet.

4. Make the changes Mr. Duncan projects for the worst case as listed below:
   - Sales will decrease 20 percent compared to last year.
   - Detailing labor will decrease $20,000.
   - Supplies will decrease 20 percent.
   - Payroll taxes will decrease $1,500.
   - Utilities will decrease 20 percent.
   - Income tax expense will be at the same rate as last year. To find last year's rate, divide the income tax by the net income before tax on last year's sheet.

5. Format the Best Case and Worst Case sheets to print attractively on the page. Print copies of the sheets for the best-case and worst-case projections. What were the gross profit on sales percentages for the two alternatives? How much profit or loss will Mr. Duncan have under each alternative?

After completing all the chapters in Part 2, complete the Part 2 Simulation, At Work at Maple Valley Chamber of Commerce. The simulation is found in the Student Activities and Simulations *workbook.*

Chapter Review

265

Chapter Review

Supplemental Activity

Have students complete the Chapter 6 Supplemental Activity, Sales Invoice, available on *The Office* Web site.

Assessment

Assess student learning using the Chapter 6 test available on the *IRCD* and in *ExamView®* format.

PART 3

Managing Time, Tasks, and Records

OBJECTIVES

- Manage your time; workstation; and office health, safety, and security effectively
- Plan and participate in meetings
- Make travel arrangements
- Manage paper, magnetic, and optical records and media

As an office worker, you need to use effectively the resources that support your work activities. These resources include time, reference sources, office supplies and equipment, and paper and electronic records. You need to take part in meetings with coworkers and make travel arrangements for yourself and others. You also need to be aware of the critical concerns for office health, safety, and security that affect all office workers. You will build skills in these important areas as you study Managing Time, Tasks, and Records.

266

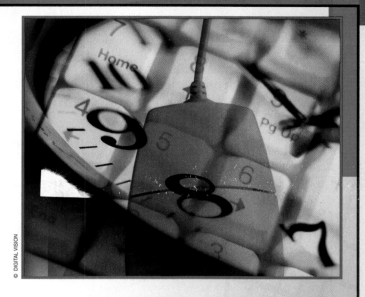

© DIGITAL VISION

CHAPTER 7

Time and Workstation Management

How you manage your actions in relation to time is important. The term *time management* refers to this process. Managing the resources used in your work is as important as managing your time wisely. Arranging furniture and equipment in your work area properly can increase your productivity. It can also make your workplace safer.

Online Resources

- *The Office* Web site:
  Data Files
  Vocabulary Flashcards
  Beat the Clock, Ergonomics
  Chapter 7 Supplementary
    Activity
- Human Factors and
    Ergonomics Society
  P.O. Box 1369
  Santa Monica, CA 90406-1369
- Search terms:
  time management
  work simplification
  personal digital assistant
    (PDA)
  ergonomics
  office health and safety
  workplace violence

In this chapter, you will learn to use your time in a productive way. You will learn about safety and security concerns that affect office workers. You also will learn about how factors such as lighting, office equipment, and furniture affect how you feel in the office environment.

267

Topic 7-1

objectives

- Identify common time-wasters
- Analyze how you spend your time
- Plan your work activities
- Use common reminder systems
- Compare and contrast manual and electronic reminder systems

time management: planning to gain control over how time is spent

TIME MANAGEMENT AND REMINDER SYSTEMS

Time management is a major factor in your productivity and effectiveness as an office worker. Managing your time at the office is a process of choosing the most effective way to do your job. The creative use of techniques to manage time will enrich your work life.

Calendar and reminder systems are helpful in bringing to mind events and tasks to be completed. These reminder systems help you schedule activities for the most efficient use of time and resources.

Manage Your Time

Time management is the process of planning your activities to gain better control over how you spend your time. Managing your time effectively is critical to your success on the job. You will want to learn how to eliminate time-wasters and handle tasks efficiently. Analyzing how you spend your time will increase your effectiveness in managing your work. One of the first steps in learning how to use your time is to recognize how it can be wasted.

Common Time-Wasters

Not all time spent at work is productive. You can waste time without realizing it. Some common time-wasters, along with suggestions for overcoming them, are discussed in the following paragraphs.

Unnecessary Telephone Conversations

The telephone can be either a time-saver or a time-waster, depending on how you use it. Often, a telephone call that could save time wastes time instead. For example, suppose an office worker takes ten minutes to verify price information by telephone. In the same call, the worker takes five minutes to discuss the latest episode of a favorite television program. A conversation that began productively ends by wasting time. If this happens two or three times a day, the time wasted can add up rapidly.

Frequent Interruptions

An interruption is a person, sound, or event that stops you from completing work. Interruptions to your work can come from many sources. Unplanned visits or questions from coworkers or customers, phone calls, and delays in receiving work or material from others are common ones. On the surface, each of these events may appear to be a time-waster. Remember, however, that working with coworkers and customers is an important part of most jobs. Questions from coworkers and customers that relate to your work are not time-wasters.

268

Excessive Socializing

Some socializing will help you keep good working relations with your coworkers. Too much socializing, however, is misuse of company time. Some workers may socialize excessively. You will be wise to avoid engaging in long conversations with them. When a coworker tries to involve you in idle conversation, offer a simple response such as: "I really must get back to work. Maybe we could discuss this at lunch." You will maintain good working relations while excusing yourself to continue your work. If you are consistent in your responses, the coworker will soon learn that you are not easily distracted from your work. Be careful to limit your lunch and breaks to the planned or approved times.

© GETTY IMAGES/PHOTODISC

Socialize with coworkers at appropriate times such as lunch or during breaks.

Ineffective Communication

As an office worker, you will receive information in both written and oral form from customers and coworkers. You also will give information in written and oral form to others. If the information that is given or received by you is inaccurate or incomplete, lost time and money can be the result of the poor communication. Be certain the information you give others is specific and accurate. Ask for feedback from those to whom you give information to be sure your message is clear and complete. Likewise, be sure that you understand any instructions or information you receive. Ask questions to verify data and to gain all the needed information.

Disorganization

Being disorganized can be a major time-waster. Searching for the paper you just had in your hands, forgetting important deadlines, and shifting unnecessarily from one project to another are all signs of a disorganized person. Take the time to organize your work area and prepare a daily plan for your work. Think through and plan complicated jobs before starting them. Group similar tasks together. Avoid jumping from one project to another before finishing the first one. Do not **procrastinate**. If unpleasant or difficult tasks are needlessly delayed, they can become problems later.

procrastinate: delay intentionally, put off

269

Topic 7-1: *Time Management and Reminder Systems*

Thinking Critically

Emphasize to students the importance of being aware of how they spend their time. Ask them: Have you ever wasted time on excessive socializing? What specifically can you do to eliminate this time-waster in the future? Describe the kind and extent of socializing that is considered appropriate in an office.

Points to Emphasize

Time on the job must be channeled to assure that time obligations are handled effectively and that time-wasters are eliminated or at least minimized.

Time Analysis Procedures

Time is a valuable resource that should be used wisely; it cannot be replaced. You have learned about common ways time can be wasted. One of the smartest things you can do is to analyze how you spend your time on the job. Time analysis aids you in determining how effectively your time is used. By keeping a written account of what you do, you can determine whether you are using your time effectively. With this information, you can then develop a plan of action to correct or redirect the use of your time.

Keep a Time Log

Start a time analysis by keeping a written record of what you do and how much time is used. Record all activities in a time-use log. Note tasks accepted and completed. Record telephone calls, meetings, discussions, receiving and responding to e-mail messages or other correspondence, and so forth.

You may choose to keep a time-use log for a day, for several days, or even a week. The longer you keep the log, the more representative it will be of how your time is spent. A partial time-use log is shown in Figure 7-1.1.

Analyze How You Spend Your Time

When you have completed your time-use log, you are ready to analyze the results. By studying your time-use patterns, you will be able to spot problem areas quickly. Be alert to the following points as you review the log:

- During what time of the day was I most productive? Least productive? Why?
- How did I lose (or waste) my time? Was it because of unnecessary interruptions, visitors/socializing, crises, telephone? Who and what was involved in each case?
- Does a pattern emerge that might show the times when most interruptions occur? Does a pattern indicate that more time is needed to handle crises or emergency tasks that may arise? Do I need more time to complete specific tasks?
- Do I think that I have used my time wisely?

Develop a Plan of Action

After you have analyzed how you spend your time, determine how well the tasks you complete contribute to meeting your work goals. Look at each activity you have listed in your time-use log. Ask yourself whether that activity helped you complete your work. If not, develop a different approach to your work that will increase the effective use of your time.

Manage Your Work

Using time efficiently requires developing an organized approach to your work. Calendars and time-management systems can help you identify busy and slow work periods. Once you know when to expect such periods, you can plan your work to allow for more productive use of your time and for a more even workload. To accommodate a busy or peak period, think ahead

270

Time-Use Log

Name Michele Fitch

Time	Monday	Tuesday	Wednesday	Thursday	Friday
8:45 a.m.	Arrived early Opened office	Arrived early Opened office	Arrived early Opened office	Arrived early Opened office	Arrived early Opened office
9:00 a.m.	Checked calendar and task list	Checked calendar and task list	Checked calendar and task list	Checked calendar and task list	Checked calendar and task list
9:15 a.m.	Met with supervisor	Met with supervisor	Keyed report	Met with supervisor	Met with supervisor
9:30 a.m.	Wrote report	Composed letter		Organized trip folder	Wrote e-mail to staff
9:45 a.m.		Took notes at meeting		Keyed new expense report form	Made copies
10:00 a.m.					
10:15 a.m.			Coffee break	Phone calls	Coffee break
10:30 a.m.	Coffee break		Keyed supplies requisition form	Coffee break	Meeting with Nancy
10:45 a.m.	Phone calls	Sorted and opened mail	Sorted and opened mail	Sorted and opened mail	Filing

Figure **7-1.1**

A time-use log will aid in determining how effectively your time is used.

to determine what jobs could be completed in advance. Then the peak period will not place undue pressure on you. Planning for the slow periods is equally important. During these times, you can catch up on those tasks that do not have deadlines but nevertheless must be done.

Plan Your Work Activities

Planning your daily work activities will help you avoid forgetting tasks that need to be completed. Take five or ten minutes either at the beginning or the close of the workday to plan the coming day's work. Prepare a task list or update an ongoing list and complete the tasks according to their order of importance or to meet deadlines. Keep the list at hand as you work. Check it frequently. This list should guide you through your daily activities. When a task is completed, indicate this on the list. Tasks not completed can be carried over to the next day's list. Be alert, however, to any item that seems to be carried over too many times. Perhaps it should be broken down into smaller segments. Perhaps you are procrastinating in completing the task.

271

Topic 7-1: Time Management and Reminder Systems

For Discussion

In Figure 7-1.1, during what time of the day was Michele most productive? Least productive? Why? Did Michele lose (or waste) time? If so, how?

Challenge Option

Emphasize to students that planning their daily activities will help them prioritize tasks and complete assignments on time. Ask them to:

1. Take five or ten minutes each day to plan their day's activities.

2. Prepare a task list similar to the one shown in Figure 7-1.2.

3. Complete the tasks according to their order of importance.

4. Cross tasks off as they are completed.

5. Carry uncompleted tasks over to the next day's list.

271

Your task list can be a simple handwritten or keyed list. If you have the software available, your list may be created using a calendar program or personal information management software. These programs allow you to manage appointments and schedule tasks as well as other functions.

Figure **7-1.2**

This task list details work or meetings for the day.

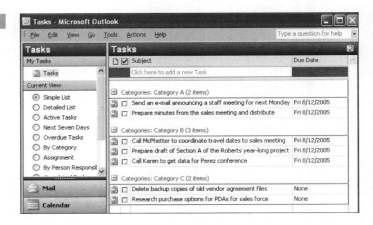

Set Priorities

Once you have identified tasks for the day, rank them on your task list and complete the most important ones first. To determine the priority of the tasks, ask yourself these questions:

- How much time will the task require?
- By what date (time) should the task be completed?
- Are others involved in completing the task?
- What will happen if this task is not completed on time?
- Do I have all of the information (or materials) I need to complete the task?

At times you may need to discuss your priorities with coworkers or a supervisor. You need to be certain that you agree on the order for doing tasks. Once you set your priorities, finish the tasks in their priority order. Remain **flexible**, however, about revising your priorities as circumstances change.

flexible: able to adapt or change as necessary

Ana Maria's task list for tomorrow is shown in Figure 7-1.2. Notice that she has identified the tasks as Category A, B, or C. The A-level tasks need immediate attention or completion. B-level tasks can be done once the A-level tasks have been completed. C-level tasks have no specific deadline but can be done when the A and B tasks have been completed. If the item is a long-term project, the portion of the task that should be finished that day is listed.

272

CHAPTER 7: TIME AND WORKSTATION MANAGEMENT

Control Large Projects

Sometimes, getting started on a large project is difficult even though it may be very important. Smaller tasks can be checked off your task list with ease; a large task may seem overwhelming. Do not let the size of a project keep you from getting organized and moving toward completion of the task. Follow these suggestions for handling a large project:

- Break the large project into smaller tasks.
- Determine the steps to be taken in each of the smaller tasks.
- Establish deadlines for each section or smaller task and meet those deadlines.
- Look for ways to improve your procedures and simplify the completion of the project.
- If the large project is one that will be repeated periodically, record your procedures for later use. Note suggestions you want to follow in the future for improvements.

Simplify Your Work

Work simplification is the process of improving the procedures for getting work done. The process often involves simplifying some steps and eliminating others. Your goal is to use the most efficient procedure for completing a task. As you complete a task, be aware of the steps you are completing. Eliminate any unnecessary steps and/or details. Consider alternative methods for completing the task. Are those methods more efficient than those you are using? Look at the task and your procedures objectively to find ways to improve your productivity.

work simplification: process of improving the procedures for doing work

---

Expand the Concept

Students may have difficulty knowing how to get started on a large project. Share with them how you plan for and complete long-range projects.

For Discussion

How can you simplify, or streamline, tasks that you are responsible for completing either at home or on the job? Do you have a large project now? Describe the procedures that will help you meet the deadline.

273

Topic 7-1: *Time Management and Reminder Systems*

Analyze the Workflow

Consider the information and work assignments you receive and those you forward to others. Ask yourself these questions:

- Does the flow of work to my desk make good use of my time and effort? Of everyone's time and effort?
- Does the flow of work provide the right information to customers or others outside the company in a timely fashion?
- Are the materials and equipment needed to complete my work readily at hand or nearby?
- Am I using the features of my office equipment and software to their fullest extent?

Your answers to these questions should provide clues to simplifying your work. Incorporate these suggestions into your workflow analysis:

- Group and complete similar tasks together. For example, if you need photocopies of the letters you are preparing, make them all at once rather than making several trips to the copier. If you have several related phone calls to make, try to make them in sequence.
- Combine tasks if doing so will increase your efficiency. For example, suppose you plan to leave a request at the records center for a series of files you need to complete a report. If the records center is near the company cafeteria, stop by the records center on your way to lunch.
- Determine how to best organize and arrange the equipment and supplies you use to complete a task. For example, do you cross a room every few minutes to retrieve pages from a printer? If yes, perhaps you can change the placement of the equipment to provide a smoother flow of work.
- Enlist the help of others when you have an important deadline to meet and the workload is overwhelming. Be sure to help other workers when the roles are reversed.

Handle Information Overload

When the amount of information you receive on a daily basis becomes overwhelming, you are experiencing information overload. You need to provide and receive information in a timely manner. You will save time (yours and others') by trying to handle each message, file, or paper just once. Take any needed action immediately if that is appropriate. Otherwise, add the task to your task list for completion at the proper time. In this way, the amount of information you receive will not become overwhelming. A good rule of thumb is to make a decision about how to handle every message, piece of paper, or file the first time you view it.

Reminder Systems

As an office worker, you must keep track of appointments, meetings, travel dates, and deadlines. Perhaps the most widely used device for keeping track of such items is a calendar. A reminder file, arranged **chronologically**, also can be helpful. This file can provide a convenient place to keep notes about tasks to be performed on specific dates.

chronologically: arranged in order of time

Manual Systems

A well-maintained desk calendar can assist you in keeping track of the many tasks and deadlines in your job. It can also be helpful to others who may have access to it. It can be used to record appointments, deadlines, meetings, or other important data.

Personal planners, also called day planners or organizers, are popular with many people. These small notebooks contain a calendar and space for recording appointments. Task lists, notes, and contacts can also be recorded. Many businesspeople find these manual aids very helpful in organizing tasks and schedules.

Wall calendars also are useful when large projects or those involving a number of people are broken into various small tasks with many deadlines. By displaying the wall calendar, you and others can keep track of deadlines.

Manual time management systems can help you plan and organize tasks.

Electronic Systems

Calendar and personal information management (PIM) programs have various features. They can be used to keep track of project deadlines, appointments, and work schedules. These programs often include task lists. For each task, related notes, deadlines, and completion dates can be entered. Some programs sound an alarm to remind users of specific tasks or deadlines. PIM programs usually include an address book where you can record contact information for coworkers, clients, and other people or companies. Programs that include more advanced features for planning large or long-term projects are sometimes called scheduling or **project management programs**.

project management programs: software with advanced features for planning large or long-term tasks

WORKPLACE CONNECTIONS

Donna uses a program to track her weekly schedule. The calendar shows an 8:30 a.m. staff meeting that the supervisor has scheduled for Monday. Several other appointments are listed as well. She can print the information, make a note regarding the meeting, or forward the message electronically to a coworker as a reminder.

275

Topic 7-1: *Time Management and Reminder Systems*

Thinking Critically

Have students compare and contrast the differences between manual and electronic calendars or scheduling systems. What is the best use for each one?

Teaching Tips

Demonstrate the features of an electronic calendar or of PIM software for students.

Personal Digital Assistants

personal digital assistant (PDA): electronic device for storing contact information and scheduling appointments and tasks

A personal digital assistant (PDA) is a handheld computer. Programs can be loaded onto a PDA to do a variety of tasks. PDAs usually come with programs for storing contact data, scheduling appointments, and creating task lists. Figure 7-1.3 shows a screen from a PDA calendar program where the user can record data related to a meeting. Other typical tasks a user can do with a PDA include:

- Use handwritten input
- Access and send e-mail messages
- Work with programs such as word processors or spreadsheets
- Do calculations such as currency conversions
- Upload data to or download data from desktop or laptop computers
- Record notes of telephone calls
- Recognize schedule conflicts
- Sound alarms as reminders of meetings or deadlines
- Search the Internet

Some PDAs can share data with calendar or PIM programs on a desktop computer. This sharing of data allows the user to coordinate schedules easily.

Figure **7-1.3**

Personal digital assistants provide a variety of calendar features.

Scheduling Appointments

Typically, you will have your own calendar to maintain. You also may make appointments and schedule meetings for coworkers. People request appointments in different ways. The request may be made in person, by telephone, by letter or memo, or by e-mail. Although the manner in which you respond to these requests may vary, the basic information you need will be the same:

Who:	Name, e-mail address, and telephone number of the individual requesting the appointment
When:	Date, time, and approximate length of appointment
Where:	Location of the appointment
Why:	Purpose of the meeting

Points to Emphasize

For every appointment to be scheduled, a worker should record the *Who, When, Where,* and *Why* or *What* information.

276

CHAPTER 7: TIME AND WORKSTATION MANAGEMENT

Responding to Appointment Requests

When you receive a request for an appointment, check the calendar to determine whether the date and time requested are available. If not, you may suggest other appointment dates and times. By knowing the purpose of the meeting, you can determine and provide all supporting materials needed. To maintain a calendar properly, clarify the following points:

- To what extent do you have authority to make appointments for others?
- When should you check with others before making appointments?
- At what regular times are appointments not to be made, such as the first half-hour of the day?
- To what extent will the manager or coworkers make appointments without checking with you?
- Does the person for whom the appointment is made want to know the purpose of each appointment you schedule?

The authority you have to make appointments will depend in great part on the nature of your job. For example, if you work in a doctor's office, most of the appointment requests would be from patients. You would be expected to schedule appointments without having to verify each one with the doctor. On the other hand, you may work in a general office where both you and your coworkers make appointments. You must agree on procedures that will allow you to operate effectively. Follow these guidelines when making appointments:

- Do not schedule overlapping appointments. Try to determine the amount of time needed for each one. Leave some time unscheduled between appointments to allow for meetings that run longer than planned, to return telephone calls, or to prepare for the next appointment.
- Keep a complete calendar. Record names, telephone numbers, e-mail addresses, and other related information.
- Use clear handwriting to record entries on handwritten calendars. Avoid crossing out and rescheduling over scratched-off entries. To make changes easily, write appointment information in pencil.
- If you make appointments for a manager or coworker, you may need to set a time for the appointment and then confirm that time with the individual. Use some symbol to indicate confirmed appointments. As appointments are confirmed, record the symbol. Commonly used symbols include a check mark, an asterisk, or an underscore of the individual's name.
- If you are responsible for keeping a calendar for others, provide a daily listing of appointments and reminders at the beginning of the workday. Show the appointments for the day in chronological order.
- Keep the previous year's appointment data. You may find it necessary to refer back to the data to find needed information. If you use an electronic calendar, print a copy of the calendar before deleting the data, or save the information in an electronic file.

Thinking Critically

Have students consider what difficulties an office worker might encounter if these points were not clarified with a manager or coworkers.

Points to Emphasize

An office calendar is a widely used reminder system for scheduling the activities and resources of a business office. Office workers often maintain office calendars and manage appointment requests.

277

Topic 7-1: *Time Management and Reminder Systems*

Entering Recurring Items

Some meetings and tasks are performed weekly, monthly, quarterly, or annually. As you set up your calendar at the beginning of the year, enter the recurring meetings and tasks. Figure 7-1.4 shows the screen for indicating a recurring meeting using *Microsoft® Outlook®*. If you block out the times for recurring events, both you and others will know what time is available for scheduling other appointments.

Figure **7-1.4**

Microsoft Outlook *allows the user to set recurring meetings.*

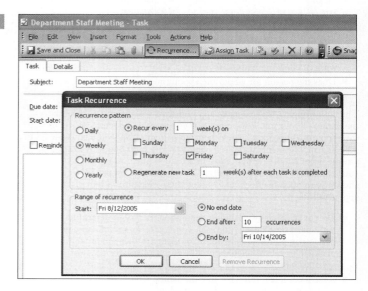

Coordinating Calendars

If both you and your coworkers schedule appointments using desk calendars, you need to coordinate appointments. Changes to schedules are usually made at the beginning or the end of the workday. Tentative appointments should be confirmed. Canceled appointments should be deleted. Materials needed for the appointments should be gathered or prepared.

You may use a calendar program for your individual schedule or to set up group activities. An electronic calendar that is on a computer network often can be updated by everyone using the calendar. Changes made are shown instantly and may be viewed by anyone using the calendar.

Points to Emphasize

Embarrassing conflicts can be avoided by coordinating and regularly updating the appointment calendar with a manager or coworkers.

278

Tickler Files

A tickler file contains notes or records arranged by date for keeping track of future actions. A paper-based tickler file is often divided into 12 monthly sections with 31 daily parts for each day of the month. Tickler files can be set up using index cards or file folders.

Reminders similar to those used in a paper tickler file also can be recorded on a computer using a PIM or database program. You enter data into the program related to a task for a particular date. With PIM software, you can set a reminder for that task to appear on your screen. A reminder for a task entered using *Microsoft Outlook* is shown in Figure 7-1.5. With database software, you would sort the records by date.

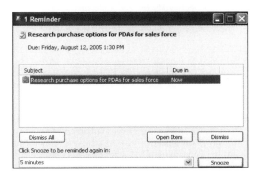

Store or record in a tickler file items requiring future action. Assume your employer says to you, "Please call the Morgan Company on Monday. Make an appointment for us to discuss our purchasing contract with them." You would prepare a reminder to make the phone call and record it under next Monday's date.

As soon as you become aware of a deadline or a detail that needs to be checked in the future, place a note in your tickler file or program under the relevant day. Check the file each morning and note those items that require attention for the current day. Complete the appropriate action for each item. Using this procedure will help your work flow smoothly.

279

Teaching Tips

If the students are using the *Student Activities and Simulations* workbook, instruct them to complete the review activity for this topic.

Teaching Tips

You may wish to lead a class discussion about how the change in the meeting date will affect the schedule before students create a revised task list.

REVIEWING THE TOPIC

1. Define *time management.* Why is time management important to office workers?
2. Identify and describe common time-wasters in the office.
3. Describe the procedures for using your time effectively.
4. Define workflow analysis. What steps can you take to complete an analysis of your workflow?
5. What are reminder systems?
6. What steps can you complete to analyze how you spend your time?
7. What is a personal digital assistant? Name some programs or features commonly found on PDAs that relate to time management.
8. What does work simplification involve?
9. What guidelines should you follow in scheduling appointments?
10. To maintain calendars effectively and efficiently, what points should be discussed with your coworkers?
11. What is the purpose of a tickler file? What types of software can be used to enter reminders electronically?

MAKING DECISIONS

Ana Maria arrived at the office a few minutes early to review the items on her task list for the day. Just as she was about to begin, her supervisor Ms. Baldwin arrived and told Ana Maria she had received a call at home last night. The national sales meeting scheduled for three weeks from today had been moved to one week from today because of an emergency. Ana Maria said to Ms. Baldwin: "This definitely changes the priorities for today." The items that Ana Maria had on her task list for today are shown below. She had not prioritized them:

- Revise sales contract for national sales meeting in three weeks
- Complete weekly sales report due in three days
- Start planning monthly sales meeting two weeks from today
- Call Tom about the Patterson report for the monthly sales meeting
- Call Lisa for lunch
- Look in tickler file
- Check e-mail messages
- Schedule room for monthly sales meeting in two weeks
- Make airline and hotel reservations for national sales meeting
- Verify travel expense vouchers
- Replenish desk supplies

1. Think about the changes Ana Maria needs to make in her task list. List the items that will be affected by the supervisor's news. Will other items be added to her task list? If yes, list them.
2. Prioritize the items to reflect the change in the date and time of the national sales meeting. Key a revised task list.

REINFORCING ENGLISH SKILLS

You work in the Human Resources Department of Raleigh Corporation, which makes modular business furniture. Your supervisor, Florita Morales, has prepared a punctuation test to be administered to job applicants. She asks you to complete the punctuation test to be sure that the instructions are clear before she has large quantities of the test printed.

1. Open the *Word* file *CH07 English* from the data files.
2. Follow the instructions to complete the test.

| COMPOSITION |
| INTEGRATED DOCUMENT |
| SPREADSHEET |
| WORD PROCESSING |

Topic 7-1 : ACTIVITY 1

Analyzing a Time Log

As you have learned in this topic, managing your time and developing an orderly approach to your work are important for your success on the job. In this activity, you will complete a daily time log. After you have charted your activities, you will use your chart to help you determine your most and least productive time periods.

1. Prepare a time-use log similar to the one shown in Figure 7-1.1 on page 271 using spreadsheet software. Use 15-minute time intervals. Prepare the chart to cover your entire waking day (for example, 6:30 a.m. until 11:00 p.m.) for one week. Print seven copies of the log, one for each day.
2. Complete your time-use log. Record your activities every 15 minutes as you progress through each day and evening. Record all your activities: studying, attending class or going to work, watching TV, talking on the telephone, eating, and so on.
3. Enter the data from your handwritten logs into your spreadsheet. Summarize your time spent by hours into categories; for example, school, work, leisure, sleep, hobbies, and so on. Use an *Other* category to group activities that occurred only once or twice for very short periods. Create a pie chart showing the percentages of time spent in each different category as part of your total time.

281

Topic Review

For Discussion

After students have completed the punctuation test, discuss the correct answers.

Teaching Tips

Remind students each day to update their time-use logs.

4. Analyze your time log. Identify the hours where you used your time most productively as well as those hours where you wasted your time. During what hours do you get the most accomplished? During what hours do you tend to waste your time?

5. Write a short report titled **TIME USE ANALYSIS** discussing your time-use log. Include the pie chart in your report. Format the report in unbound report style. Describe what you intend to do differently as a result of your time analysis.

COMPOSITION
SPREADSHEET
WORD PROCESSING

Topic **7-1** ACTIVITY 2

Long-Term Portfolio Project

As an office worker, you will need to prioritize work to fulfill duties and meet deadlines. Office work often involves planning and completing long-term projects. In this activity, you will plan, schedule, and complete a long-term project: a portfolio to display your work.

The general purpose of a portfolio is to demonstrate your skills and abilities related to work. A portfolio can contain samples of your work, awards or other recognitions, certificates or degrees related to training or education, a description of assignments or projects that have been successfully completed, and letters or recommendations related to your work abilities. A good portfolio can be helpful in getting a job.

1. This project should be completed four to six weeks from now. You and your instructor should agree on the specific timeline for this activity. Consult with your instructor to determine the deadline for completing the project.

2. List the steps to complete the portfolio. For example, define clearly the purpose for your portfolio, research portfolio layouts, schedule time to work on the portfolio, collect materials (classroom and other), and plan initial documents to go into the portfolio.

3. List the materials and resources you will need to complete the portfolio, such as folders, time, money, paper, dividers, notebooks, classroom projects, and so forth.

4. List the people you need to contact to complete the project: instructors, administrators, students, parents, businesspeople, etc.

5. Create a long-range schedule. Use spreadsheet software to list the dates and tasks to be completed by specific dates. (Hint: Key your ending date or deadline first.) Key a title and beginning date on your schedule to make it uniquely yours. Print a copy of your schedule to use as you complete your portfolio project.

282

CHAPTER 7: TIME AND WORKSTATION MANAGEMENT

Teaching Tips

Discuss a due date for this project with students. You may wish to discuss or show examples of items students might include in their portfolios.

6. Follow your plan to prepare the portfolio. Make a note of the changes that have to be made to your original schedule as you complete your project. Were your deadlines realistic? Were the people available at the times you listed? Did you find the materials and resources available when you needed them? Did you follow your schedule? If no, why not?

7. Write a short report in unbound style summarizing your experiences as you created the portfolio. Discuss the factors listed above and your own observations. Include in your summary a copy of your beginning and ending schedule for comparison purposes.

8. Display or share your portfolio with other class members. Update your portfolio periodically as you gain new skills, complete training, or produce documents that will demonstrate your skills effectively.

WORKSTATION MANAGEMENT AND OFFICE SAFETY

Office workers are managers of their time, activities, and work environment. Students should realize that being a good office worker requires more than technical skills. Discuss with them the relationship of basic job requirements to the information presented in this topic.

objectives

- Explain the importance of an organized workstation
- Identify factors related to ergonomics and their importance to the office worker
- Discuss the importance of routine maintenance and care of office equipment
- Describe significant safety and security procedures for the office
- Create a presentation about office safety

workstation: physical area in which a worker performs a job

Office workers must be able to manage work effectively to be productive. The lighting and the way materials and the work area are arranged affect your work. Most companies try to provide comfortable and safe work areas for their office employees. Employees should keep the work area well organized. They should also be aware of safety and security issues that affect workers in an office.

Workstation Management

Your workstation is a key part of your work environment. A workstation is the physical area in which a worker performs a job. A typical workstation provides a work surface and space for equipment and supplies.

Manage Your Workstation

Arrange your work area to give easy access to the items used frequently. A computer keyboard, telephone, supplies, and reference materials should be within easy reach. Many companies use modular workstations. These workstations are made up of parts that can be put together in various ways. Wall panels, storage areas, and a desktop surface are typical workstation parts. Note the workstation parts shown in Figure 7-2.1.

What factors are considered to determine the proper location of each item shown in Figure 7-2.1? Would any item be better placed in a different location? If so, where should it be placed? Why?

modular workstation: work area made up of parts that can be put together in various ways

Figure **7-2.1**

Many companies provide flexible workstations that can be arranged to meet user needs.

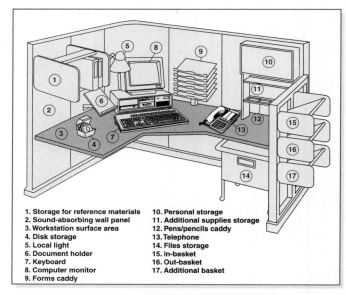

1. Storage for reference materials
2. Sound-absorbing wall panel
3. Workstation surface area
4. Disk storage
5. Local light
6. Document holder
7. Keyboard
8. Computer monitor
9. Forms caddy
10. Personal storage
11. Additional supplies storage
12. Pens/pencils caddy
13. Telephone
14. Files storage
15. In-basket
16. Out-basket
17. Additional basket

CHAPTER 7: TIME AND WORKSTATION MANAGEMENT

Desktop Area

Keep your workstation's surface clear. Clutter on the desktop can cause unnecessary delays as you search for papers or objects. Remove materials that do not relate to your current project. Put descriptive labels on file folders, and place documents in the folders when they are not needed. Place the folders in your file drawer.

Arrange your equipment and supplies to allow easy access so that you avoid making unnecessary movements. Keep frequently used supplies, such as pencils and paper clips, in a caddy on the surface of your work area. Reaching for the caddy is more efficient than opening and closing a drawer each time you need an item.

© KEN CHERNUS/TAXI

An organized desktop area will enhance productivity.

Drawers

Reserve your center drawer for frequently used supplies, such as a letter opener, scissors, and paper clips, that are not needed on the surface area. Arrange the contents of the center drawer so that the most frequently used supplies are toward the front where you can reach them easily.

The top side drawer may be used to store stationery supplies or to lay file folders containing current work so that they are at hand when you need them. You avoid cluttering the desktop by putting the file folders in a specific location in your desk. In this way, you also can protect any confidential items.

A desk also may contain either a file drawer or additional side drawers. A file drawer can be used to store files that are referred to often but are not in current use. Other drawers can be used to store supplies.

285

Topic 7-2: *Workstation Management and Office Safety*

For Discussion

Do you think the office employee who works at this workstation is organized or disorganized? Why?

Expand the Concept

A well-organized workstation increases worker productivity because time is not wasted searching for a needed item. This concept can be applied to students' personal lives as well. Ask them to arrange the items in their school lockers or in a closet at home for maximum efficiency.

Supplies are arranged neatly in this drawer.

Reference Materials

The nature of your job will determine which references you will use most often. Some items may be in print form. Others may be accessed via your computer. Reference materials that should be at your workstation may include a dictionary, telephone directories, company and office reference manuals, safety handbooks, and equipment and software manuals. Other reference items used less often may include an almanac, atlas, and vendor supply catalogues.

Supplies and Accessories

Office employees use a variety of supplies and accessories to do their jobs. The right resources help you perform your job more efficiently. What you need at your workstation will depend on your particular job. An adequately stocked workstation is essential to your productivity. If you run out of supplies in the middle of a critical task, you could lose valuable work time by stopping to gather needed supplies. Also, you run the risk of not completing the task on time. Use supplies properly for best results and to save money. Follow these guidelines:

- Select the quality of the supply according to the nature and importance of the task. For example, if you are preparing a rough draft of an important letter, don't use expensive letterhead paper. Use a lower-quality paper for the rough draft and the letterhead paper for the final copy.
- Learn to read product labels for the correct use of a product. For example, paper designed for use in a laser printer may not work well in an inkjet printer.
- Look for ways to conserve supplies. For example, reuse file folders by placing new file folder labels over the old ones. To save paper, preview documents carefully onscreen before printing.
- Do not keep more supplies than you need in your workstation. Check your workstation periodically. If you have not used a supply item in several weeks, perhaps it should be returned to the supply cabinet.

Points to Emphasize

The typical office employee uses a variety of office supplies and accessories. Correctly selecting, using, and caring for office supplies are factors in the economical use of resources. How an employee handles office supplies also demonstrates whether he or she is a good steward of a company's resources.

Teaching Tips

You may want to bring to class two or three brands of various office supplies for students to compare—such as plain paper of different weights and for different types of printers, letterhead, forms, notepads, plastic and metal paper clips, markers and pens, self-stick notes and tape flags, file folders, and so on. Cover the brand names and let students test and examine the products. Discuss the possible uses, strengths, and weaknesses of the office products.

Office Equipment

The condition of your equipment affects the quality of your work. You will want to keep your equipment in top working order. To get dependable service from your equipment, you will need to do **preventive maintenance** and give your equipment routine care. This involves servicing equipment and replacing parts while the equipment is working properly in order to prevent failure. Fewer repairs are necessary when equipment is cared for properly on a regular basis. By caring for equipment properly, you can extend the life of the equipment. Follow these maintenance guidelines:

preventive maintenance: servicing equipment and replacing parts to prevent failure

- Learn how to use and care for the equipment properly. Read and understand the manufacturer's operating instructions. Follow the care guidelines so that you are able to recognize and correct minor problems.

- Inspect and clean equipment regularly. Know the basic care routines your equipment requires. Make repairs as needed.

- Report problems right away to the appropriate person. Many minor problems can be corrected before they become serious and require costly repair.

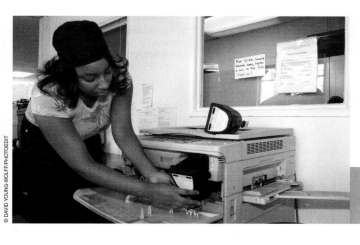

By practicing preventive maintenance, you can extend the life of office equipment.

© DAVID YOUNG-WOLFF/PHOTOEDIT

Manage Ergonomic Factors

Ergonomics is the study of the effects of the work environment on the health of workers. The way a workstation and its parts are designed can affect your physical well being. Figure 7-2.2 on page 288 shows a workstation designed to be comfortable and reduce physical stress. This workstation allows the user to adjust the chair, desk, lighting, and computer equipment.

ergonomics: the study of the effects of the work environment on the health of workers

Provide various equipment, supplies, and accessories typically found on a workstation surface or in the drawers of a workstation. Ask two students to demonstrate before the class how they would organize the workstation for maximum efficiency. Ask the class to discuss and critique the arrangement.

Points to Emphasize

Office workers are expected to learn how to use office equipment properly and to do their part in keeping it properly maintained, including anticipating and troubleshooting minor problems.

Thinking Critically

How does the work environment affect an employee's health and feelings of job satisfaction? Use Figure 7-2.2 to expand this discussion.

287

Topic 7-2: *Workstation Management and Office Safety*

Figure **7-2.2**

Ergonomic factors affect productivity.

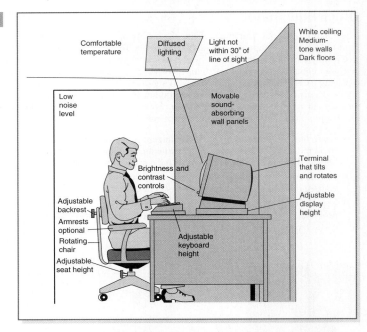

A well-designed chair is essential because many office workers spend much of their time sitting. A chair should be adjustable, like the one shown in Figure 7-2.3. Office workers should be able to adjust their chairs to fit individual physical requirements for comfort and good posture.

Figure **7-2.3**

Some experts believe a chair is the most important part of a workstation.

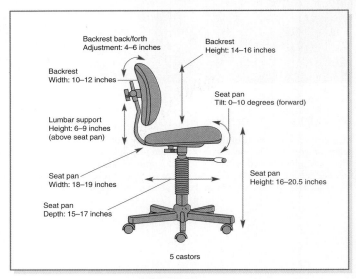

The height of the desktop should allow your elbows to be parallel to the computer keyboard and floor as shown in Figure 7-2.2. This arrangement prevents unnecessary strain on the arms and wrists. Keep the desktop clear of materials not related to the current task.

Two kinds of lighting are often found in workstations: ambient and task. Ambient lighting is provided by overhead light fixtures for the entire work area. Although you may not be able to adjust the overhead lighting, you can adjust the arrangement of your workstation. Task lighting focuses on the immediate work area and should be adjustable for your specific needs. Adjust the task lighting to prevent glare on your computer monitor or the desktop. Eliminate dark or dimly lit areas where you may have to retrieve files or work away from your desktop.

Your computer monitor should be placed at eye level, as shown in Figure 7-2.2, to help reduce eyestrain and neck pain. Glare on the monitor often contributes to eyestrain. Common symptoms of eyestrain are teary or burning eyes, blurred vision, and headaches. Glare from outside light can be prevented by placing the computer monitor so that you do not face a window or have your back to a window. Peripheral input devices, such as the mouse, should be located next to the computer keyboard. The movement of the arm from the keyboard to the input device should be natural and without strain.

Manage Your Office Health

Be aware of the physical responses your body has to your work procedures and habits. Doing so will enhance your job satisfaction, comfort, and productivity. The following guidelines may help you complete your work without feelings of strain, fatigue, or other physical discomforts:

- Learn to adjust the workstation parts for the best fit to your work habits and procedures. Follow the manufacturer's recommended work postures and practices even if at first they feel unnatural.
- Take rest breaks often—at least 15 minutes every two hours. Do not sit in front of your computer monitor or at your desk for long uninterrupted periods of time. Arrange your work so that you have to get out of your chair and walk to the copier or to the supply cabinet. If you feel yourself becoming bored, stop working and do simple breathing or relaxation exercises.
- Learn stretching exercises for your hands, wrists, arms, and fingers to relieve pressure on them. **Carpal tunnel syndrome** is a repetitive strain injury that occurs when stress is placed on the hands, wrists, or arms. It can occur while working at the computer keyboard or using the computer input device for long periods of time.
- Focus your eyes away from your computer monitor often. Remember to blink your eyes. If possible, face your computer monitor against a wall to avoid looking directly out of a window or into glare from other bright light sources. Place antiglare filters over the monitor screen. Filters reduce glare, static electricity, and dirt and smudge buildup on the screen.

carpal tunnel syndrome: a repetitive strain injury that occurs when stress is placed on the hands, wrists, or arms

For Discussion

Discuss the importance of exercise and good nutrition with students. Ask students to describe their eating and exercise habits.

FOCUS ON . . .

Workplace Wellness

Many Americans spend more hours at work than ever before. The office has become an important place for employees to understand health and wellness. Wellness includes issues such as nutrition and controlling stress. Balancing work and family life are also wellness issues.

Wellness in the workplace is now an important focus in business. Employers know that when these lifestyle factors are controlled, everyone benefits. This is why companies are consulting with wellness experts. Many companies have wellness programs that promote a healthy lifestyle. As a result, medical expenses and work time lost due to illness may decrease.

Eating healthy food, getting enough exercise, and managing one's weight are important parts of wellness. Many Americans have busy work schedules. They find making time for exercise and cooking healthy meals hard. Employers can take steps to help employees stay healthy. Some of the steps include:

- Provide purified water or juice as an alternative to soft drinks.
- Post the calories and fat grams of foods served in the company dining room.
- Encourage employees to include physical exercise in the workday. For

example, workers could use the stairs instead of the elevators. Workers might use an on-site gym for exercise before or after the workday.

Some companies provide incentives or rewards for workers who take part in wellness programs. For example, workers may earn points that can be redeemed for prizes. Other companies offer reduced rates for health insurance to employees who take part in wellness programs.

Wellness programs benefit both employers and employees. If your company has a wellness program, consider taking part in it. You can also develop your own personal plan for a healthy lifestyle. Articles related to wellness issues can be found on the Internet and in magazines and newspapers. This information can help you learn to eat properly, exercise, and manage work-related stress. For example, the U.S. government publishes *Finding Your Way to a Healthier You.** This article contains guidelines for a healthy diet. You can access this article using the link provided on *The Office* Web site.

* U.S. Department of Health and Human Services and U.S. Department of Agriculture, "Finding Your Way to a Healthier You: Based on the Dietary Guidelines for Americans," http://www.health.gov/dietaryguidelines/dga2005/document/html/brochure.htm (accessed August 16, 2005).

- Adjust the screen brightness to a contrast level that is comfortable for you. Adjust the screen angle so that it is at eye level or slightly lower. Adjust the screen display properties for comfortable viewing. Resolution and color quality settings for a system with two monitors are shown in Figure 7-2.4.
- Learn and use good posture. Keep your back straight against the back of your chair and your feet flat on the floor. Adjust your chair so that your feet do not dangle off the floor. Use a footrest if your feet don't touch the floor. Use a back pad to keep your back in a straight line and adjust your computer monitor to the right height and angle for you.

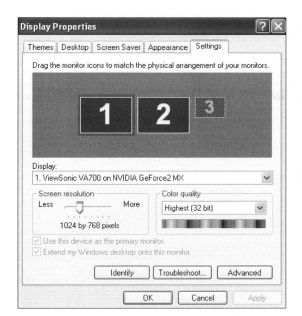

Figure **7-2.4**

The display properties can be adjusted for more comfortable viewing.

Points to Emphasize

Using the proper settings for a computer monitor helps reduce eye strain.

- Arrange your work materials so that you do not have to reach far to a telephone or supplies. Take care when lifting heavy binders or boxes or bending to reach files. Do not strain to use staplers or paper punches. Avoid repetitive motions for long periods of time without taking a break.

- Report any prolonged physical discomfort that affects your work performance to your supervisor.

WORKPLACE CONNECTIONS

Marletta Diaz works long hours at her desk and computer. In the past, she often experienced sore wrists and eyestrain. After hearing a presentation about ergonomics at a workshop, Marletta realized she could take some simple steps to help prevent these problems. Now she takes breaks from the computer keyboard frequently to give her hands, wrists, and arms a chance to relax. She drops her arms to her side and dangles them to relieve tension. She also squeezes a handgripper to strengthen and relieve tension in hands and wrists. Marletta rearranged her workstation to reduce glare on the monitor from a nearby window. These small changes in Marletta's routine and the arrangement of her workstation can make a big difference in long run.

Office Safety

Most of us think of the office as a safe place to work. Office workers are not required to use heavy equipment or power tools. They are seldom exposed to poisonous chemicals or dangerous working conditions. Yet, thousands of office workers have disabling accidents each year. Falling, tripping, or slipping account for many office accidents. Common causes of falls include drawers partially open, slippery floors, torn or loose carpeting, obstructions on stairs or in walkways, and dangling telephone or electrical cords.

Faulty or poorly maintained equipment can be a cause of accidents in the office. Falling objects and fire and electrical hazards can pose dangers. Human carelessness can also be a cause of accidents in the office. With knowledge of correct safety procedures, however, you can learn how to correct and report safety problems. Reporting problems will help prevent injury to you and your coworkers.

Accident Prevention

To many people, the office seems to hold little danger. Accidents may happen because workers do not see possible dangers. Becoming aware of safety hazards in an office is the first step to preventing accidents. Workers should develop positive safety attitudes. They should try to see potential safety problems and take steps to remove them.

WORKPLACE CONNECTIONS

Molly came around the corner with her arms full of supplies for the supply cabinet. She could not see where she was going very well because her arms were so loaded down. She should not have been trying to carry so much, but she was trying to save a few steps and not have to make a second trip.

Larry looked up from the phone to see Molly just a few feet from his open file drawer. When Larry realized that Molly could not see where she was walking, he called, "Watch out!" Too late—Molly fell with a loud crash over the bottom file drawer. X-rays showed that Molly had broken her wrist while trying to catch herself in the fall. She was unable to resume her full duties for eight weeks.

This accident could have been prevented if Molly and Larry had acted responsibly. Larry should have closed the file drawer, and Molly should have carried the supplies in two trips rather than in one.

Workstation Safety

Most office employees spend the majority of their working time at their workstations. Applying safety practices at your workstation will help prevent accidents and injuries.

292

CHAPTER 7: TIME AND WORKSTATION MANAGEMENT

Desktop Area

As you work, you will occasionally use scissors and other sharp objects. Place them away from the edge of your workstation so they will not be knocked off easily. Pencils stored on the top of your desk with the sharp points up are dangerous; they are best stored flat or with points down. Use a staple remover, rather than your fingernail, to remove staples. Never examine a jammed stapler by holding it near your eyes or testing it over your finger.

Drawers

Keep your workstation drawers neat. Do not allow papers to collect to the point of clutter. If the drawers are cluttered, your hands could easily be punctured by hidden scissors, pins, or pencils. Sharp objects such as pins and thumbtacks should be placed in closed containers.

Even with these precautions, never reach blindly into a desk drawer or file drawer. Take time to look where you are placing your hands, even if you are rushed or are talking to someone. Close workstation and file drawers by the handle. Do not push a drawer shut by placing your hand at the top or side of the drawer. You may lose a fingernail or suffer a crushed finger or hand.

Chairs/Mats/Static Control

Most office chairs have casters, which are small wheels that provide ease of movement for the worker. This same ease of movement can produce painful injury unless you look at the chair and hold onto its arms or seat as you sit down. When seated, be careful not to lean too far forward or backward to prevent falling out of the chair.

A chair mat is a vinyl pad placed underneath the chair to eliminate wear on the carpet from rolling the chair. Static control mats are designed for use on floors underneath workstations and computers. The static control mat safeguards valuable computer data and electronic equipment from possible harm from a charge of static electricity.

Chair mats and static control mats can cause you to trip, particularly if the edges are beginning to curl. Replace worn mats when they become a hazard.

Work Area Safety

In addition to your workstation, other objects in your immediate work area can add to your comfort and work productivity. They can also become a source of injury.

Office Furnishings

Learn how to use small furnishings, such as a step stool and paper cutter. In using a step stool with casters, step firmly in the middle of the stool. Never step to the side because this can cause the stool to slide out from under you. When using the paper cutter, keep your fingers away from the blade and never leave the blade up. Furniture with rough or sharp edges should be sanded or taped to prevent injury to employees and to prevent clothing from being torn. Report tears in carpets, burned-out lights, broken handles on equipment, and other potential hazards related to office furnishings to the appropriate person.

293

Topic 7-2: Workstation Management and Office Safety

Expand the Concept

Many of the suggestions for work area safety presented here can be implemented in the classroom and in the home to make those environments safer. Ask students to conduct a short safety inspection of your classroom and to offer suggestions for correcting any safety concerns they find. Also, they may want to conduct a safety inspection of their homes.

File drawers should be filled beginning with the bottom drawer of the cabinet and moving to the top drawer. They should be emptied from the top drawer down. When working with file cabinets, pull out only one drawer at a time. You do not want to change the cabinet's center of gravity and cause it to tip over. Avoid placing objects that have the potential to harm you or your coworkers on top of filing cabinets. Coffeemakers or heavy plants can slip off the cabinet and cause serious injuries.

Electrical Equipment

surge suppressor: an electrical outlet that controls unexpected sharp increases in electricity

Office workers use many pieces of equipment that require cords and cables. These cords and cables can become a safety hazard. Cables and cords should never extend into traffic areas. Do not overload electrical outlets. If necessary, purchase a power strip or **surge suppressor** made for use with multiple appliances. An extension cord should be used only to extend the position of the electrical appliance. It should not be used to increase the power load.

Extension cords often present a tripping hazard.

© DAVID YOUNG-WOLFF/PHOTOEDIT

Cords, cables, and power strips should be placed behind equipment or within the walls of the workstation. If cords must be placed where people walk, tape them down or cover them with materials made specifically for this purpose.

294

CHAPTER 7: TIME AND WORKSTATION MANAGEMENT

General Office Equipment

Office equipment can be dangerous if it is not operated properly. Keep the following safety procedures in mind when you use office equipment:

- Follow the manufacturer's directions for safe and efficient equipment use.
- Avoid other activities that will distract you from the operation of the equipment.
- If you feel a tingling sensation, notice smoke, or smell something burning while you are operating the equipment, turn it off. Investigate the problem or report it to the appropriate person immediately.
- Know where the power switches are located on the equipment in your general area. In the event of an emergency or power outage, you may need to turn off the equipment.

Emergency Procedures

Emergency procedures are steps to follow in time of trouble or danger. A fire, storm, or robbery in progress are examples of emergencies you might face at work. Learn emergency procedures as soon as you begin a new job. If your office does not have established procedures, do what you can to help initiate practices such as those described in the following paragraphs.

emergency procedures: steps to follow in time of trouble or danger

Emergency Telephone Numbers

Telephone numbers to call in times of emergency should be posted beside each telephone. The most important ones are those of the company medical and security personnel. Numbers for the local police, fire department, and paramedics should be included in the list. If your area has a general emergency number, such as 911, include it also. Emergency numbers may also be stored in each telephone's memory. The memory feature saves valuable time. You press only one or two buttons, and the number is automatically dialed.

First Aid Procedures

First aid kits should be located conveniently within the office. They should be inspected frequently and restocked whenever supplies are used from the kit. Some firms will send an employee from each floor or work group for first aid training and/or CPR (cardiopulmonary resuscitation) classes. These courses are given periodically by the American Red Cross and other organizations. Each employee should know who has completed first aid training and who is qualified to help in the critical first minutes of an emergency. First aid posters can be placed where they can easily be seen to further assist employees.

Expand the Concept

Ask students to identify emergency numbers that should be posted by their home telephone.

Challenge Option

Encourage students to attend first aid or CPR classes offered in the area. The life-saving techniques they learn will be a valuable asset in both their personal and professional lives. You might ask them to make a list for future reference of the agencies or organizations that offer first aid or CPR training in their area.

295

First aid kits should be easily accessible in office areas.

© DAVID YOUNG-WOLFF/PHOTOEDIT

Do you know the proper evacuation procedures for leaving the school building in an emergency? For leaving your home in an emergency? For leaving your workplace in an emergency?

Fires

Some companies prohibit the use of appliances, such as cup warmers and space heaters, because of their potential fire hazard. If appliances are allowed in your office, always unplug them when they are not in use and before leaving the office. Know the location of the nearest fire exit, fire alarm box, and fire extinguisher. Large office buildings generally have the fire alarm boxes and fire extinguishers in the same location patterns on each floor. Learn how to use the fire extinguisher and what type of fire it is intended to put out. Never attempt to fight a fire alone. Always have someone report it to the proper agency.

Building Evacuation Plans

evacuation: a mass departure or flight, the clearing of an area

Learn the established escape routes and evacuation procedures for your building. Emergency exit routes should be posted in noticeable places throughout the building. Employees should know their duties during a drill or evacuation. Who, for example, is responsible for checking conference rooms, restrooms, and other areas where the alarm may not be heard?

WORKPLACE CONNECTIONS

Jacob, a new employee at Park Company, was impressed when he learned that the owners are very concerned about employee safety. Jacob learned that fire evacuation routes and routes to tornado shelters are posted on every floor. The company holds fire and tornado safety drills on a monthly basis. He was also impressed to learn that the company sponsors safety classes held by the local fire department. The classes cover the use of fire extinguishers, general fire safety, first aid, and CPR.

With this clear focus on safety, Jacob knows he will be able to do his work without worrying about his personal safety.

CHAPTER 7: TIME AND WORKSTATION MANAGEMENT

CHAPTER 7: TIME AND WORKSTATION MANAGEMENT

Personal Security on the Job

Protection for yourself and your property requires continuous attention on your part. Most businesses strive to provide a safe and secure work environment for their employees. To support the company's effort in providing for your safety and security on the job, always use good common sense. A purse left at a workstation, a jacket slung over the back of a chair or left in an unoccupied office, cash left out in plain sight—all are invitations to a would-be thief. Keep personal belongings out of sight and locked in a drawer, file cabinet, employee locker, or closet. The key to this drawer or other container should be issued only to the employee who is assigned its use.

Sometimes you may find it necessary to stay late at the office or to come in early. Follow your company's procedures for being in the building during non-working hours. If no after-hours procedures exist, create your own security routine and follow it. Follow these security procedures when you work alone:

- Always work near a phone and keep emergency telephone numbers handy.
- Lock all doors to your work area. Do not open the door to anyone you are not expecting or cannot identify.
- Get to know the cleaning staff and when to expect them.
- If you use the elevator to leave the building, do not enter the elevator if anyone is in it whom you find suspicious.
- Avoid using a restroom that is located away from your work area.
- When working late, phone home before leaving the office to let someone know what time to expect you. If you live alone, call a friend before leaving the office and again when you get home to let her or him know you've arrived safely.
- Park your car near the building entrance and/or in a lighted parking lot. Check the parking lot visually before leaving the building. Have your car keys in your hand and ready to use. If security personnel are available, ask to be escorted to your car.

Building and Office Security

Many businesses take a serious approach to fulfilling building and office security needs. Discontented workers, theft, sabotage, and fire are major security concerns of a business.

Many companies have security procedures to guard against actions by employees who have been fired or who are under pressures from work. Sometimes upset workers can pose a hazard to themselves and to other workers. Be alert to changes in your coworkers' behavior. Notice statements they may make that sound like threats against employees or the company. Know the procedures for protecting yourself from these workers:

- Do not get involved in a verbal argument.
- Leave the work area if you feel threatened and go to a safe area.
- Report any unusual behavior to your supervisor and/or company security personnel.

297

Ask students how they would react in the following situation. You work in an office that is located in a large office building. You decide to work late to finish a project. Because you are alone, you lock the door to your office. You are about to "call it a day" when someone knocks on the door and says, "Open up, please. I'm with the cleaning service, and I need to get in so I can clean your office." You know the custodial staff usually cleans the offices in the building earlier in the evening. What specifically would you do in this situation?

Points to Emphasize

As an office worker, you will want to understand and abide by all security measures established by the company for which you work.

The protection of data is an issue in many companies. Entrance to secure areas where data are kept or can be accessed is carefully controlled. Employees may need access codes or passwords to enter these areas.

Controlling Outsider Access

Many companies must be open to the public to do business. However, the public does not need access to all parts of most office buildings. Businesses use varied security means to protect employees and assets.

Some companies have security personnel who make sure each visitor signs a log. The log shows the visitor's name, address, and the name of the person or office being visited. Some companies send an employee to the lobby to escort a visitor back to the office. In smaller offices, the receptionist may be present in the front office and may screen visitors.

Office security guards provide protection for workers and office property.

Controlling Employee Access

At some companies, employees must wear identification (ID) badges. These badges are used to gain entrance to parts of the building. The badge may contain the employee's photo or a fingerprint. The badge may have a magnetic code. The code may be read by a card reader to allow entrance to a room or use of equipment.

Some badge codes can be read by proximity readers. The reader automatically identifies the badge when the wearer is in a restricted area. The reader sends data to a computer. This data provides a record of who enters and leaves designated areas, the time of entry, and in some instances, the time of exit—all valuable security information.

Your cooperation in wearing your ID helps assure your personal safety and security on the job. A lost or stolen ID should be reported right away to the appropriate person.

CHAPTER 7: TIME AND WORKSTATION MANAGEMENT

For Discussion

Do you know someone who uses an identification (ID) card to gain access to buildings or grounds at his or her place of employment? Discuss the procedure this person follows.

Vikki

Foxx

© BILL ARON/PHOTOEDIT

Some companies issue photo IDs or magnetically coded access cards to their employees.

WORKPLACE CONNECTIONS

Olivia looked up to see a repairman coming through the doorway. "Hi, I'm Tim. I'm here to check your computer. Apparently, you had a large electrical surge last night. Here's the order," he said, as he flashed a copy of a repair order in front of Olivia. "This will take a few minutes—why don't you just take a short break?"

Olivia got up from her terminal, but she was puzzled. She hadn't heard that an electrical surge had occurred. "Besides," she thought, "we have surge suppressors for the equipment." Olivia felt she should check this with her supervisor, Ms. Calibre.

Ms. Calibre was not aware of an electrical surge occurring either. "Let me check on this before we do anything," she said. Olivia stepped back into her office to see the repairman disconnecting the computer.

Repairman: "Looks like I'll have to take your computer back to the shop for repairs."

Olivia: "You'll have to wait until my supervisor authorizes you to take the computer."

Repairman: "Well, I have several other computers to check. Why don't I come back after I've checked them and pick this one up."

The repairman left hurriedly, and a minute or so later Olivia's supervisor appeared at the door: "No one authorized a computer repair check. We had better report this."

Ms. Calibre called the police immediately to report the incident. She spoke to Sergeant Roberts. He told her that several businesses had recently lost computers and other equipment in this manner. "You're lucky to have an alert employee," the sergeant told Ms. Calibre. "None of the others questioned an unexpected repair check. When the employees returned from their 'short breaks,' their equipment was gone."

Would you have done what Olivia did in this situation? If not, what would you have done?

299

Topic 7-2: *Workstation Management and Office Safety*

Teaching Tips

You may want to arrange for students to visit a building that is monitored by closed-circuit television or other detection systems. Perhaps the building security guard could discuss the types of detection systems used in the building and how they operate.

Detection Systems and Alarms

detection system: devices and alarms that sense and signal a change in the condition of an area

A detection system consists of devices and alarms that sense and signal a change in the condition of an area. Some systems detect entry into an area while others detect movement in an area. An alarm sounds or is displayed on a computer screen when an intruder is detected. Such systems reduce a company's reliance on an on-site security guard. Even if a firm has security officers, they cannot be at all stations at once.

Closed-circuit television can be used to monitor corridors, entrances, or other areas. When used with a videotape recorder, closed-circuit television provides the firm with a record of events for later review.

Closed-circuit television provides continuous monitoring of the building and grounds.

© G.D.T./STONE

300

REVIEWING THE TOPIC

1. What is the guiding principle you should follow in planning the arrangement of a workstation?

2. Describe how you can organize your workstation (both desktop areas and drawers) to increase your productivity.

3. Discuss the guidelines an office worker should follow when using office equipment, supplies, and accessories.

4. Why are routine maintenance and care of office equipment important?

5. What are the safety practices you should follow in maintaining your own workstation?

6. What are the safety practices you should follow with regard to office furnishings and equipment?

7. Describe the emergency office procedures you should learn immediately upon starting a new job.

8. Describe some of the precautions you may take as an office worker to protect yourself and your personal property on the job.

9. How can you help assure your personal security when you are working alone?

10. What are some procedures businesses use to control access to their property and employees by other employees and by outsiders?

THINKING CRITICALLY

At a department meeting your manager, Mr. Joe Petersen, discusses a memo regarding company security. He shakes his head and says: "This is the second memo the managers have received about security leaks. One of our competitors has just introduced a new product, and it's identical to a product we have been working on. Apparently they discovered our plans. The president wants our thoughts on how to improve our product security. In addition to the main shredder in the copy center, he is suggesting a shredder for each office. Well, I'm just glad everyone in our department can be trusted."

As you hear this, you remember several situations you have observed in the office:

- You have seen poor photocopies—even photocopies of confidential material—discarded in the wastebasket.
- Computer printouts with product-testing results are left stacked next to the filing cabinets rather than being locked inside them.
- Workers often talk about current projects during their breaks.
- Workers have a habit of using the offices of other workers who are out of town or on vacation.

301

Topic Review

continued • Workers too freely give out unnecessary information to callers, such as telling a caller exactly where the individual is.

"Tell me," Mr. Petersen says, "do you think we need a shredder? What other measures can we take to tighten security? Please give this matter some thought and send me your ideas." How do you respond to him? What suggestions can you make for tightening office security?

1. Prepare a response to the questions Mr. Petersen asks in the form of an e-mail message. Send the message to your instructor's e-mail address (or save and print the message). Prepare a memo to Mr. Joe Petersen instead if you do not have access to e-mail.
2. In the message, include suggestions for correcting the problems discussed as well as other security measures that you think would be effective.

REINFORCING ENGLISH SKILLS

In this exercise, you will practice your writing and editing skills by preparing a letter from a rough draft.

1. Open and print the PDF file *CH07 Letter* from the data files. This file contains the rough draft letter.
2. Key the letter. Correct all grammatical, spelling, number/word usage, capitalization, and punctuation errors in the letter. Insert paragraphs and reword the letter to correct errors where appropriate. Evaluate the letter with the five Cs of effective communication in mind.
3. Assume the letter will be printed on letterhead paper. Arrange the letter in an acceptable format and add any missing letter parts. Use your name in the signature block. Print one copy and sign the letter.

INTERNET
SPREADSHEET
WORD PROCESSING

Topic 7-2 | **ACTIVITY 1**

Needs Assessment for Equipment

You work for Wayne Electronics. Your manager has received requests from several employees. They ask that the company purchase one or more multimedia projectors. Currently, employees rent a projector when it is needed.

You have been asked to do a needs assessment. Your goal is to determine whether renting or buying a projector is more cost effective for the company. A needs assessment involves gathering data about the proposed need.

302

CHAPTER 7: TIME AND WORKSTATION MANAGEMENT

For Discussion

After students have keyed the letters, discuss the corrections that they should have made. Wording of the letters will vary. Ask a few students to share their letters with the class.

Expand the Concept

Bring a projector like the one discussed in the activity to class and demonstrate it for students.

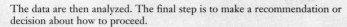

The data are then analyzed. The final step is to make a recommendation or decision about how to proceed.

1. Complete the data-gathering phase of the needs assessment. Prepare a memo form for Wayne Electronics using the appropriate headings. Compose a memo addressed to Department Heads from you. Use the current date and an appropriate subject line. Ask specific questions about projector use such as:
   - How often is a projector is used in your department?
   - What is the purpose of the presentations?
   - How many people attend the presentations?
   - What is the length of time the projector is rented for each presentation?

   Include any other questions you think are relevant. Ask the managers to include any other pertinent information they may have in their replies.

2. Analyze the information received from the other departments. Open and print the *Word* file *CH07 Projector* from the data files. This file contains replies from five departments. Use spreadsheet software to record and summarize the information in the replies. Find the estimated total spent by all departments for renting projectors for a year.

3. Analyze the use patterns for the projectors. Are they used regularly throughout the year or do several department members need a projector at the same time? Are different departments likely to need a projector at the same time?

4. Consider the sizes of the audiences for the various presentations. Will one projector be appropriate for most of the presentations? What is the maximum audience size the projector should be appropriate for?

5. Review the types of projectors available for purchase and their features by accessing office equipment Web sites or office equipment catalogs. Determine the type of projector that would be appropriate for most presentations given by employees. What is the cost of this projector and a spare bulb? How does this cost compare to the estimated annual rental cost for projectors?

6. Write a memo to your supervisor, Shawn Valdez, giving your recommendation for buying or continuing to rent projectors. Discuss how your data were collected. Summarize the information that led to your recommendation.

Points to Emphasize

Having a schedule for when routine maintenance of equipment should take place helps ensure that equipment maintenance will not be neglected.

WORD PROCESSING

Topic 7-2 ACTIVITY 2

Preventive Maintenance and Care of Equipment

You work in the Marketing Department of Robert's Distributors. One of your duties is to make sure that all preventive maintenance is done on the office equipment in your department. Preventive maintenance is usually done by a qualified repair technician to prevent equipment breakdowns and prolong the life of the equipment.

PREVENTIVE MAINTENANCE SCHEDULE

Equipment	Month Purchased	Maintenance Period
Copier, high volume	February	Every 3 months
Copier, small convenience	January	Every 6 months
Fax machine with laser printer	October	Every 4 months
Laser printer, desktop	April	Every 12 months
Laser printer, high volume	October	Every 6 months

1. Each piece of equipment was purchased last year in the month shown in the preventive maintenance schedule. Based on the schedule, which equipment will need preventive maintenance in April?

2. Will any pieces of equipment need preventive maintenance in May? If yes, which ones?

3. Assume January is the current month and the fax machine has not been serviced. How many times will the fax machine need preventive maintenance during the remainder of this year?

4. Assume March is the current month. In what month will the small convenience copier be scheduled for its next maintenance?

5. You are also responsible for routine care of all of the equipment. Because you are getting ready to leave on a two-week vacation, your supervisor has asked you to develop a set of procedures for routine care that your coworkers can follow in your absence. Open and print the PDF file *CH07 Care* from the data files. This file contains notes you have been jotting down this week about equipment care.

6. Using your notes, key a schedule for routine equipment care activities for each piece of equipment. Your notes are in rough form and incomplete sentences. Edit, correct errors, and compose as needed to create procedures that are well-written and easy to understand.

CHAPTER REVIEW 7

Summary

In this chapter, you learned the importance of managing your time and workstation effectively. Office safety and security procedures also were discussed. Consider the points listed below as you reinforce your understanding of the topics in this chapter:

- Task management is vital to your success on the job. Although what you actually do in your job will depend on the nature of your company, you will need to plan and organize your work activities, whatever they may be.
- You will need to manage effectively the resources that support your work activities. The basic resources for this are your workstation and your time. Your workstation provides the physical space for you to do your job. By correctly organizing the equipment and supplies at your workstation, you can increase your productivity.
- Your time at work must be used to assure that your job duties are handled effectively and that time-wasters are eliminated.
- Office workers use a variety of office supplies and equipment. Correctly selecting, using, and caring for office supplies help reduce costs. Office workers are expected to learn how to use office equipment properly. They must also do their part in properly maintaining it.
- Ergonomic factors related to the office affect your comfort and well-being. They can also help improve your productivity.
- Many organizations strive to maintain a safe and secure environment for their employees. As an office worker, you should follow safe practices at your workstation. You should understand and follow all security measures established by your company.

Key Terms

carpal tunnel
  syndrome
chronologically
detection system
emergency
  procedures
ergonomics

evacuation
flexible
modular workstation
personal digital
  assistant (PDA)
preventive
  maintenance

procrastinate
project management
  program
surge suppressor
time management
work simplification
workstation

Teaching Tips

Have students review key points from the chapter by completing the Beat the Clock game on *The Office* Web site.

Teaching Tips

Have students review the key terms by using the Flashcards available on *The Office* Web site.

Chapter **7** : A C T I V I T Y **1**

Prioritize and Schedule Tasks

Your manager, Mr. Wong, has asked you to plan and submit a schedule for advertising a sale of office equipment. The sale will begin two months from today. He hands you a rough draft of the inventory list of the products that will be included in the sale. Items marked with an asterisk (*) will have to be ordered from the suppliers so that they arrive in time for the sale.

1. Create a task list for the sale. Open and print the PDF file *CH07 Tasks* from the data files. This file contains a partial list.

2. Create a form that includes these columns: **Priority, Task,** and **Completed.** Place the items on the form in the Task column. Next, prioritize the items by ranking them in order of importance:

   A Most Important

   B Medium Importance

   C Least Important item

3. Key the rank in the Priority column. If an item is listed as a C item, does it need to be completed at all? If not, delete the item. Are there other items that need to be added to this list? If yes, add these items.

4. Create a schedule for preparing for the office equipment sale. Use spreadsheet software to create the schedule.

   • List tasks to be completed from your task list in order by date using the dates when a task should be begun. Start with your ending deadline and work backward to create your schedule. For example, if a task should be completed one week before the sale and the task takes two weeks to complete, then list the task on the date three weeks prior to the sale.

   • Show dates when each task should be completed.

   • Include a column to check off tasks and confirm that they have been completed on time.

Chapter **7** : A C T I V I T Y **2**

Office Safety Presentation

Your supervisor, Ms. Perez, is concerned that each employee takes an active interest in good safety practices. She would like you and the other members of the safety committee to develop a list of office safety guidelines for employees. Ms. Perez has also asked your committee to present a short presentation about office safety. The presentation will be made to your coworkers to promote office safety during the company Safety Month. Work with three other students to complete this activity.

306

CHAPTER 7: TIME AND WORKSTATION MANAGEMENT

For Discussion

After students have prioritized the tasks, allow them to share how they ranked each item with the class. Ask them to give reasons for the ranks chosen.

Teaching Tips

Encourage students to review the guidelines learned in Chapter 5 regarding planning and delivering team presentations.

1. Use your textbook, magazine articles, Web sites, or other resources to research safety as it relates to an office environment. Compose a list of 10 to 15 office safety guidelines. Arrange the items on the safety guidelines list in order of importance, with Item 1 being the most important and Item 15 being the least important. Key your guidelines in an attractive format that can be posted or distributed to office employees.

2. Plan the content and create visuals for a short presentation on office safety. Your committee may choose to include all 15 items in the safety presentation or choose to focus on the 5 most important items according to your list. Your presentation should include the major points about safety as well as art, tables, graphs, or other elements to support and enhance the presentation.

3. Decide what content each person will present and practice your presentation.

4. Deliver the presentation to another work group or to the entire class.

Supplemental Activity

Have students complete the Chapter 7 Supplemental Activity, Research Workplace Wellness, available on *The Office* Web site.

Assessment

Assess student learning using the Chapter 7 test available on the *IRCD* and in *ExamView®* format.

CHAPTER 8

Meetings and Travel

Business meetings are held for many purposes. Workers often meet to share information or solve problems. Formats for meetings can be informal or formal. Meetings can have many participants or only a few. Employees often travel to attend meetings. Travel arrangements must be made. A schedule for the trip and related documents must be prepared.

In this chapter, you will learn about planning and taking part in meetings. You will also learn about making travel arrangements and about supporting activities related to business travel.

Online Resources

O *The Office* Web site:
   Data Files
   Vocabulary Flashcards
   Sort It Out, Travel
   Chapter 8 Supplementary
     Activity
O American Institute of
   Parliamentarians
   P.O. Box 2173
   Wilmington, DE 19889-2173
O Search Terms:
   meeting planning
   parliamentary procedure
   teleconference
   travel safety
   travel planning

308

objectives

O Plan business meetings

O Prepare documents related to business meetings

O Participate effectively in meetings

Business meetings bring people together to communicate. They may meet to make decisions or solve problems. Because employees work together, many tasks are related. Meetings are an important means of communication. Without meetings, keeping up to date on company matters would be difficult for employees.

Meetings may range from an informal chat in a manager's office to a formal gathering of the board of directors. Although many meetings are held in person, technology allows people in different locations to attend meetings without leaving their offices. Well-organized meetings are necessary for businesses to run smoothly. Your role in assisting with these meetings will vary. It will depend on the degree of formality, purpose, size, and location of the meeting. In this topic, you will learn how to plan and participate in meetings.

Types of Business Meetings

Office workers should understand the differences in the nature of meetings. They should also know their roles in planning and participating in them. The nature of the organization, the duties of the department, and the purpose of the meeting will determine the size and formality of the meeting.

Informal and Small Group Meetings

Many of the meetings in which office workers are involved will be informal discussions and small group meetings. Many times, informal meetings are set up as committee meetings. These meetings address specific topics or ongoing concerns and issues, such as safety and security.

Working with customers or clients may also take the form of small group meetings. These meetings may be more formal than small group meetings with coworkers, especially if the meeting is an initial contact with a client. Follow the steps described in the following sections to plan and conduct a meeting.

This example shows how one office worker carried out her duties for setting up and taking part in a small, informal meeting.

Carla's manager sent her an e-mail as follows: "Carla, see if you can get the other four Pikesville project engineers together tomorrow at three o'clock. We need to meet for about an hour to discuss the status of the Pikesville project. See if the conference room is available." As she read through the message, Carla noted the materials she needed to bring to the meeting. She also noted the arrangements she needed to make for special equipment. Immediately after reading all the instructions, Carla checked to see if the engineers would be free through the company's electronic calendaring system. She noted that all four of the other engineers were free at that time. She added the meeting to their calendars.

Next, Carla checked the conference room schedule. Finding it free at the hour requested, she added her name as the person requesting the meeting and her telephone number as a reference. She sent an e-mail message to each of the engineers. The message noted the time, place, and approximate length of the meeting. It indicated that the meeting had been added to their electronic calendars. She then arranged for the necessary equipment and copied materials for the meeting. To follow up the request, she sent an e-mail message to the manager to confirm the arrangements. She noted the meeting on her own calendar. The next day, Carla checked the conference room before the meeting to see that everything was in order.

Informal, small group meetings are held frequently in businesses.

© CORBIS

Formal Business Meetings

A formal meeting follows a definite order of business. It involves a specific audience and requires some preparation. Many organizations set up formal staff meetings at a specific time each week or month. Other formal business

How does a formal business meeting differ from an informal business meeting?

meetings, such as conferences or quarterly sales meetings, may be planned for longer periods of time. You may be asked to help plan a meeting. You may need to prepare meeting materials and make sure that follow-up actions are noted and carried through.

Multinational Meetings

Many companies conduct meetings in which all participants do not speak the same language. All the people may not be in the same physical location. Multinational meetings for large groups are likely to be very formal. They may require detailed planning and preparation. Time differences for the different locations must be considered.

Knowledge of international and business etiquette is important for these meetings. Your role as a coordinator who arranges the meeting details will be critical. Your role may include working with hotel personnel if the meeting is held away from company offices. You may need to send the meeting plans to the people who will take part in the meeting. You may also work with equipment providers. You may need to know how to use equipment and the proper person to call for help if the equipment does not work properly.

Planning the Meeting

Regardless of the size of the meeting, documents prepared for meetings require organization and planning. Typical documents may include:

- An **agenda**, which lists the topics to be discussed during the meeting
- **Minutes**, which are the written record of the official business of a meeting
- A list of follow-up items or reminders of tasks to do following the meeting

You may have duties before, during, and after a formal meeting. You may need to prepare an agenda before the meeting. At the meeting, you may need to take the minutes. After the meeting, you may need to prepare and distribute the minutes and note the follow-up items from the minutes.

Before the Meeting

The following suggestions will be helpful to you in your planning. You may not use all the suggestions for each meeting. However, these guidelines will be helpful as you plan for most business meetings.

- **Establish a meeting folder.** Once you are aware that a meeting will take place, set up a folder for it. Use this folder to collect items related to the meeting, such as the list of attendees, the agenda, notes, and copies of materials to be distributed. Create an electronic folder on your computer to store documents related to the meeting.
- **Determine a meeting time.** You may be told the time at which a meeting is to take place, or you may have to schedule a time when all needed participants can attend. Contact each person with a couple of suggested meeting times. Ask if one of the times is convenient. This is especially important when the meeting involves clients or others from

agenda: a document that contains the information for a meeting such as the participants and topics to be discussed

minutes: written record of meeting proceedings and decisions

For Discussion

Why is knowledge of business etiquette particularly important in planning multinational business meetings?

Points to Emphasize

The person who has responsibility to complete meeting arrangements will ensure that everyone's time is used efficiently and effectively. Such arrangements typically involve procedures that must be completed before, during, and after the meeting.

311

Topic 8-1: *Planning and Participating in Meetings*

outside your company. If the participants are all from within your organization and use calendaring software, you may be able to simply check each person's calendar for a time when he or she is available.

- **Reserve a meeting room.** When you know the date, time, and location of the meeting, check to see if the desired meeting room and time are available.

- **Arrange for needed equipment.** Many times the purpose of the meeting will determine the kind of equipment that will be needed. Rooms may be equipped with overhead projectors, but electronic projection systems may be required. Special equipment may be needed if the information will be sent to an off-site location.

- **Notify the meeting participants.** Notify people as soon as possible of the time, place, approximate length, and purpose of the meeting. Identify any materials or supporting documents they should bring.

- **Use reminder systems.** Mark your and others' calendars with the meeting time and place. Use a tickler file or other reminder system to help you schedule the details. For example, if you must prepare 20 copies of a report to present at the meeting, create a reminder to do so.

- **Key an agenda.** All participants and the recording secretary should receive a copy of the agenda prior to the meeting. Topics should be stated concisely and listed in the order they will be discussed. The starting time for each agenda item may be listed, along with breaks in the program. Only the starting time for the meeting is listed if the meeting will be brief. The person who will lead the discussion or training for each topic may be listed. Other relevant information, such as meeting rooms or materials required, may also be included. An agenda typically contains many of the items shown in Figure 8-1.1 on page 314.

- **Organize meeting materials.** You may be expected to gather materials. Notepads, pencils, file folders, ID badges, and parking stickers are examples of these items. Also, organize materials and handouts such as reports or letters that will be used at the meeting. Review any material to be presented at the meeting on the equipment that is available in the meeting room.

- **Prepare the meeting room.** The room temperature should be comfortable, and the seating arranged to fit the meeting style. A room arrangement in which all participants can be seen and heard will make discussion easier. Any presentation aids should be positioned so that they are near the leader and can be seen by everyone in the room. Check to be sure that requested equipment is present and working properly.

During the Meeting

The degree to which you participate during the meeting will depend on the purpose of the meeting, where it is held, and the preplanning to be done. You may be responsible for the minutes or for leading part of the discussion.

The minutes describe the action taken by the group. They provide the reader with a concise record of what took place at the meeting. The minutes should not be a word-for-word transcript of the meeting. However, the

What information from a meeting might the acting secretary record exactly word for word?

recorder must make note of all important information. The minutes must give a clear, accurate, and complete accounting of the happenings of the meeting. Although various reporting formats are acceptable for recording minutes, the following information appears in most of them:

- Name of group, committee, organization, or business holding the meeting
- Time, date, place, and type of meeting (for example, weekly, monthly, annual, called, special)
- Name of presiding officer
- Members present and absent (In a large organization, only the number of members present must be recorded to verify that a **quorum** was present.)
- Reading and approval of the minutes from the previous meeting
- Committee or individual reports (for example, treasurer's report, standing committees, special committees)
- Unfinished business (includes discussion and action taken)
- New business (includes discussion and action taken)
- Time, date, and place of next meeting
- Time of **adjournment**
- Signature of the individual responsible for the minutes

quorum: the minimum number of members that must be present to conduct business at a meeting

adjournment: an ending or closing

The following suggestions will be helpful to you when it is your responsibility to prepare the minutes of a meeting:

1. Bring to the meeting copies of the agenda and the minutes of the previous meeting. Bring also any report or document that might be referred to during the meeting.

2. If you prepare minutes frequently, use a **parliamentary procedures** reference source (such as *Robert's Rules of Order Newly Revised*). This resource will help you better understand the meeting proceedings and the correct terms to use when taking and preparing minutes.

parliamentary procedures: guides for conducting meetings

3. Record the important points of discussion. Note the action taken or the conclusion reached.

4. Record the names of the persons making a **motion** or **seconding** a motion. Motions should be recorded word for word. A statement should be made in the minutes as to whether or not the motion was passed.

motion: a proposal formally made in a meeting

second: indicate formally the support of a motion

5. Correct minutes of the previous meeting. Sometimes at the following meeting, corrections must be made to the minutes before they can be approved. If only a few words are affected, lines may be drawn through the incorrect words and the proper insertions made above them. If more than a few words are affected, lines may be drawn through the sentences or paragraphs to be corrected and the changes written on a new page. The page number of each correction should be indicated on the original minutes. The minutes should not be rewritten after they have been read and approved at the meeting.

For Discussion

Do all of these items appear in the minutes shown in Figure 8-1.2?

Thinking Critically

Assume that a mistake has been made in the minutes in Figure 8-1.2. Under the treasurer's report, the balance in the Improvement Projects Fund is incorrect. It should have been $359,550. How should the minutes be changed to reflect this correction?

Topic 8-1: *Planning and Participating in Meetings*

313

Give the following instructions orally. Ask students to make notes of the changes they are to make to the agenda shown in Figure 8-1.1 on a plain sheet of paper before preparing a new agenda.

The last meeting of the Pikesville Improvement Council was June 30. It is now time to update the agenda for the next meeting of the Council:

1. Determine the agenda's date for the next meeting, which will be three weeks from today.

2. The new business item (under No. 7) from the June meeting should be moved to unfinished business. Unfinished business will now have two items.

3. The new business to be discussed at the coming meeting will be Funding Alternatives.

4. The date of the next meeting for item No. 8 is to be three months from the coming meeting.

2-inch top margin or center vertically

Center heading lines

AGENDA

PIKESVILLE IMPROVEMENT COUNCIL

1-inch or default side margins

June 30, 20--

The meeting will begin at 9:30 a.m in Conference Room C.

1.	Call to Order	Nancy Hollingshead, Pikesville Improvement Council Chair

DS between items

2.	Roll Call	Troy Jones, Secretary
3.	Reading of the Minutes	Troy Jones, Secretary
4.	Treasurer's Report	Sean Petersen, Treasurer
5.	Committee Report Recognitions Committee	Briana King, Chairperson
6.	Unfinished Business Telecommunications Improvement Project	
7.	New Business East Pikesville Drive Improvement Project	
8.	Date of Next Meeting	
9.	Adjournment	

Figure **8-1.1**

An agenda is a list of topics to discuss during a meeting.

314

CHAPTER 8: MEETINGS AND TRAVEL

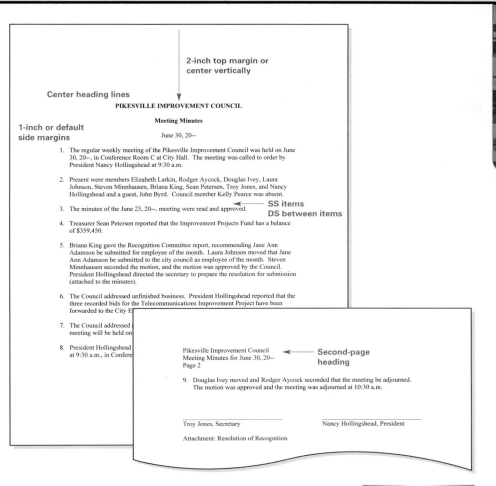

Inside the figure:

2-inch top margin or center vertically

Center heading lines

PIKESVILLE IMPROVEMENT COUNCIL

Meeting Minutes

June 30, 20--

1-inch or default side margins

1. The regular weekly meeting of the Pikesville Improvement Council was held on June 30, 20--, in Conference Room C at City Hall. The meeting was called to order by President Nancy Hollingshead at 9:30 a.m.

2. Present were members Elizabeth Larkin, Rodger Aycock, Douglas Ivey, Laura Johnson, Steven Minnhausen, Briana King, Sean Petersen, Troy Jones, and Nancy Hollingshead and a guest, John Byrd. Council member Kelly Pearce was absent.

3. The minutes of the June 23, 20--, meeting were read and approved. ← SS items

DS between items

4. Treasurer Sean Petersen reported that the Improvement Projects Fund has a balance of $359,450.

5. Briana King gave the Recognition Committee report, recommending Jane Ann Adamson be submitted for employee of the month. Laura Johnson moved that Jane Ann Adamson be submitted to the city council as employee of the month. Steven Minnhausen seconded the motion, and the motion was approved by the Council. President Hollingshead directed the secretary to prepare the resolution for submission (attached to the minutes).

6. The Council addressed unfinished business. President Hollingshead reported that the three recorded bids for the Telecommunications Improvement Project have been forwarded to the City E[...]

7. The Council addressed [...] meeting will be held on [...]

8. President Hollingshead [...] at 9:30 a.m., in Confere[...]

Pikesville Improvement Council
Meeting Minutes for June 30, 20--
Page 2

← Second-page heading

9. Douglas Ivey moved and Rodger Aycock seconded that the meeting be adjourned. The motion was approved and the meeting was adjourned at 10:30 a.m.

_____   _____
Troy Jones, Secretary   Nancy Hollingshead, President

Attachment: Resolution of Recognition

Figure 8-1.2

Minutes are the official record of a meeting.

After the Meeting

Once the meeting is over, you may need to complete follow-up activities. Make calendar or reminder notations for any item from the meeting that will require future attention. Prepare the minutes as soon as possible. Preparing the minutes will be easier when the details of the meeting are fresh in your mind. Use examples of previous minutes for appropriate format or follow the sample shown in Figure 8-1.2. Ask the chairperson of the meeting to review the minutes before they are distributed to be sure there are no omissions or errors.

Complete any correspondence related to the meeting. Write thank-you letters to speakers or resource persons. Items to be added to the agenda for the next meeting also should be noted.

Participating in Meetings

Meetings are an important part of business operations. People need to communicate with one another on a daily basis to complete the work of the organization. As an office worker, you should be prepared to lead or take part in any meeting you attend.

Leading

assertive: positive or confident in a persistent way

All employees use leadership skills in their jobs. They meet deadlines, improve how the tasks are done, and work with people to get their jobs done. These same leadership skills are important in meetings. A good meeting leader conducts the meeting in an assertive way that accomplishes the goals of the meeting. At the same time, he or she also uses a nonaggressive communication style that makes everyone feel comfortable. Follow the guidelines below to develop a nonaggressive, yet assertive communication style when leading a meeting.

- Make the objectives of the meeting clear to all participants.
- Be familiar with the background material and have relevant documents at hand.
- Offer suggestions and ask questions during the meeting.
- Always be willing to listen to others' suggestions.

consensus: common agreement or mutual understanding

- Keep the meeting on topic and moving toward a solution or a consensus.
- Ensure that all participants have an opportunity to take part in the discussion.
- Remain open to new and creative approaches.
- Summarize the decisions or plans that have been made during the meeting.
- Identify clearly the duties or tasks assigned to each group member in following up or completing plans.

Brainstorming

brainstorm: offer ideas or suggestions

Brainstorming is offering ideas or suggestions in an effort to find a solution to a problem or to create a new approach. The objective is to come up with as many ideas as possible. During the brainstorming process, the following rules are usually observed:

- All ideas are recorded, no matter how unrealistic they may appear.
- Criticism of ideas is not allowed until all ideas have been expressed. Comments such as "that will never work" or "we tried that once already" may block the flow of ideas.
- Explanations and combinations of ideas are encouraged. The value of brainstorming is that one idea may build on another.

To encourage brainstorming, a meeting leader must be willing to give time to the process and encourage everyone to take part.

316

CHAPTER 8: MEETINGS AND TRAVEL

Brainstorming in a meeting generates ideas.

WORKPLACE CONNECTIONS

The members of the Marketing Department at Bell Industries, a small manufacturing company, travel often to meet with clients and exhibit the company's products at trade shows. Currently, each department member books his or her own travel. Few rules or restrictions related to travel are in place. The department's travel expenses are over budget for the first half of the year. The department manager, Penny Ortiz, has called a meeting of department members to discuss the problem and brainstorm ideas for how to lower travel costs for the remainder of the year.

Penny: *"As you are aware, we must take steps to lower our travel costs. Starting today, I will look at each situation more closely than in the past before I approve travel for anyone in our department. Before you request travel, please consider whether you really need to make the trip. For example, can the meeting be held by phone rather than in person? Now, I need suggestions from all of you. Who has an idea on how to lower travel costs?"*

Ricardo: *"Making airline reservations at least seven days in advance will usually result in lower fares. Because we often know the dates for trade shows months in advance, we could book some flights 30 days in advance. That should save a lot of money. Of course, all air travel should be booked business class or coach—no first class fares. I think we all do that already, though."*

Kim: *"Do we sometimes fly when driving would be almost as quick? I suggest that for any destination within five hours driving time, we drive rather than fly. Driving is almost always cheaper than flying."*

Penny: *"Good suggestions, Ricardo and Kim. Anyone else? What do you think, Florence?"*

What leadership skills does Penny exhibit in this brainstorming session with coworkers?

317

Topic 8-1: *Planning and Participating in Meetings*

Florence: "Well, I know many companies set maximum amounts for certain expenses. Maybe we could do that also. For example, the maximum for hotel rooms might be $100 per day. The maximum for food might be $50 per day. The maximum for entertaining clients might be $100 per client per day. If we know ahead of time that more funds will be needed, such as for hotels in an expensive area, that expense could be approved ahead of time by Penny."

Ilena: "Speaking of expensive hotels, would anyone want to share a hotel room at trade shows? If you feel comfortable doing so, this would make the travel budget go farther."

Jordan: "What about rental cars? Let's always rent a subcompact or compact car for lower fees and use a car only when it's really necessary."

Penny: "Thanks, everyone. I have recorded all these good ideas. Think about the issue for a couple of days and let me know if you have any more suggestions. I'll create a document containing our new travel guidelines to distribute at our meeting next week."

Group Dynamics

group dynamics: the way people interact and communicate within a group

Group dynamics refers to how people interact and communicate, as in a meeting. Group dynamics can play an important part in reaching group consensus and decisions. The following sections focus on the three critical components of group dynamics.

Interactions

Interactions among group members will depend on the purpose of the meeting. In almost all meetings, communications will be improved when group members can see one another. Eye contact can be used to help gain attention or control a discussion. When all participants can see the leader and the visual aids, they can understand the discussion better. The purpose of the meeting should determine the seating arrangement.

A round table or circle may be used when the leader is seeking a true cooperative form of decision making. This format also reduces the appearance of differences in rank between the participants.

A U-shaped arrangement can be used for larger meetings—those that include 10 or 12 participants. In this arrangement, the leader may sit in the middle of the U to maintain eye contact with everyone. At the same time, all participants can see each other and are less likely to engage in side conversations.

A center table layout, with the leader at one end of the table, allows the leader to control the discussion. In this arrangement, all communication tends to flow toward the head of the table (where the leader is seated).

An appropriate seating arrangement can help accomplish the goal of the meeting.

Exchange of Information

Exchange of information can be improved by the seating arrangement and the willingness of the leader to encourage open communication. Planning by the leader before the meeting can set up the open exchange of information among group members. The leader can:

- Provide in advance materials that will be discussed.
- Arrange the room and seating to meet the needs of the meeting.
- Prepare visual aids that guide the discussion.
- Use an appropriate leadership style.

Relationships

Relationships among the group's members will affect the meeting. A good leader listens, asks questions, accepts criticism, keeps the meeting on topic, and resolves conflicts. Conflicts arise when participants have strong opinions or hidden agendas (their own private objectives). Leaders and participants should follow these guidelines to help develop mutual trust and cooperation in meetings:

- Use neutral language in the discussion
- Avoid placing blame
- Ask open-ended questions
- Use terms that all participants understand or define those that are unfamiliar
- Allow all participants to speak without interruptions
- Maintain a pleasant facial expression
- Be open to new methods and ideas

Ask students to observe the dynamics among the group members at a meeting they may attend. How were the exchanges, interactions, and relationships either encouraged or discouraged? Share with the class.

319

Topic 8-1: *Planning and Participating in Meetings*

Involving Everyone

Questions or statements, such as those listed below, may encourage group participation and give each person at the meeting the opportunity to express his or her opinion:

- What do you think about . . . ?
- What approach can we use to solve this problem?
- Jane, what do you think about Jim's idea?
- Ron, we haven't heard your ideas about. . . .
- That's an interesting question, Mary. What would be a good answer?
- Are we ready to make a decision or is there still more discussion?
- Let me summarize what we have discussed so far.

Developing an Action Plan

action plan: a description of tasks to be completed

For many meetings, developing an **action plan** to solve a problem or accomplish tasks is appropriate. A written plan of action can replace the traditional minutes of a meeting. The plan focuses on the actions to be taken after the meeting rather than simply recording the proceedings. An action plan is shown in Figure 8-1.3. The basic information about the meeting that should be included in an action plan is listed below.

- Topic of the meeting, meeting date, the chairperson's name, and the recorder's name
- Specific actions to be taken and the person(s) responsible
- Deadlines for the actions and completion dates
- Key issues discussed and the participants
- The meeting length
- Announcement of the next meeting

To arrive at a plan of action, the meeting leader should be sure that all meeting participants have input into plans and decisions. Everyone should have clear assignments to put the plan into action.

Teleconferences

teleconference: a meeting of people in different locations conducted using telecommunications equipment

A **teleconference** is a meeting of people in different locations connected by a telecommunications system. Teleconferences can be used to deliver training or exchange information. They can be held to solve problems and make decisions, just as face-to-face meetings can.

Types of Teleconferences

The meeting may be an audio conference. People taking part can speak with one another by phone or a Web connection. For a group audio conference, a room can be equipped with microphones and speakers. They are arranged on tables at certain intervals, so that all participants can talk to and hear the others.

2-inch top margin or center vertically

Center heading lines

1-inch or default side margins

SS items DS between items

PIKESVILLE IMPROVEMENT COUNCIL

ACTION PLAN

April 30, 20--

1. The purpose of the Pikesville Improvement Council meeting held on April 30, 20--, was to discuss the downtown improvement project. President Hollingshead called the meeting to order at 7:30 p.m. and declared a quorum present. Ms. Hollingshead called the members' attention to the information that was delivered to them during the week prior to the meeting.

2. Present were members Elizabeth Larkin, Rodger Aycock, Kelly Pearce, Troy Jones, Douglas Ivey, Sean Petersen, and Nancy Hollingshead. Guests present were John Byrd and Sharon Young.

3. The Council discussed the plans to acquire an additional piece of property that joins the downtown area. The property will be used for a park with an amphitheater and petting zoo for children. Mr. Byrd and Ms. Young discussed details on each piece of property under consideration:

   East Pikesville Drive (owner, Martin Victor Wolfe)
   North River Drive (owner, Hancock Industries)
   West High Street (owner, The McFaddin Family Group)

4. President Hollingshead appointed Kelly Pearce, Elizabeth Larkin, and Rodger Aycock to study each piece of property and make recommendations to the Council on which piece of property to purchase. The recommendation should be ready to present at the meeting on May 14, 20--.

5. The next meeting will be held on May 14, 20--. The meeting was adjourned at 8:30 p.m.

Troy Jones, Secretary

Nancy Hollingshead, President

Figure **8-1.3**

An action plan focuses on tasks to complete after a meeting.

321

Topic 8-1: *Planning and Participating in Meetings*

The meeting may be a video conference. This type of meeting permits people at two or more locations to hear and see each other almost as if they were in the same room. Video conferences can be held using computers equipped with cameras and microphones. A group video conference may be held in a conference room. The room is equipped with cameras, microphones, viewing monitors, and other equipment that allows the participants to see and hear one another.

Computers and electronic tablets may be used to show documents or other graphics being discussed. A speaker at one location can explain material being shown. The graphics appear on the computer screens for the participants.

In a computer conference, people communicate using private computer networks or the Internet. The conference may involve only written messages. The messages are keyed and received by the participants in real time. If the users' computers are equipped with microphones and the proper software, the participants can talk with one another rather than keying messages. If the computers also have cameras, the meeting can be a video conference.

WORKPLACE CONNECTIONS

Project team leaders of a South Carolina firm need to meet as often as six times a week to refine ideas and reach decisions on project questions. When the executive assistant is asked to set up a teleconference meeting, he first checks all team leaders' electronic calendars for an open time. He then notifies the leaders of the meeting date and time, lists a call-in telephone number and password, and provides the Web address.

On the day of the meeting, leaders dial the telephone number to be connected to the audio portion of the meeting through their speakerphones. They access a Web site via their computers to see documents. A small digital camera sits on top of each team leader's computer. The team leaders can see each other as they speak or ask questions. The company's executives feel that being able to meet and share information in this way helps them solve problems quickly and be more responsive to market changes.

Teleconferences can be conducted using computers.

322

CHAPTER 8: MEETINGS AND TRAVEL

FOCUS ON . . .

Web Conferencing

Web conferencing combines the features of video and computer conferencing. In a Web conference, participants can hear and see each other and share documents. Web conferencing is an effective and cost-saving alternative to many face-to-face meetings.

Some Web conferences may involve only a small number of people. For example, two people may meet to work on an analysis or report. Others may also involve a large number of people. For example, thousands of individuals may meet to see and hear a speaker. The equipment used depends in large part on the purpose of the meeting and the number of participants.

Teleconferencing equipment has become less expensive and easier to operate within the past few years. A small business or home office user might install a video camera and software. The user can be ready to hold a teleconference in minutes.

Teleconferencing programs are available. They provide features such as program sharing, file transfer, and text chat features. *Microsoft® NetMeeting®* conferencing software, which is a part of later versions of the *Microsoft® Windows®* operating system, offers these features in addition to video and audio.

Companies that wish to hold teleconferences may use a teleconference service provider. This type of business specializes in providing teleconferencing service to others. Some companies may choose to develop their own conference system. Special equipment and powerful software are used. Other companies may also choose to make conferencing features part of their Web site or intranet.

Web conferencing provides an effective way for people in different locations to meet and to work cooperatively. At a moment's notice, a business can have its brightest and most productive members working together to solve a problem or brainstorm new ideas.

Teaching Tips

Ask students if they have participated in a Web conference. Because cameras and other equipment needed for simple Web conferences are so reasonably priced, some students may have this equipment at home. If possible, demonstrate a Web conference for students.

Preparing for a Teleconference

Technology allows flexibility in planning, preparing for, and taking part in meetings. Teleconferencing can be expensive, so the meeting time should be used wisely. Your role in preparing for a teleconference may include the following responsibilities:

1. Reserve the conference room and necessary equipment, if a special room is to be used.
2. Notify the participants of the date, time, length, and purpose of the meeting. Include a telephone number and the name of a contact to call in the event of technical difficulties.
3. Prepare and distribute any related materials well in advance of the meeting. If several documents are to be sent, use different paper colors to copy different reports. That way, it will be easy to identify reports during the meeting.
4. Prepare and distribute an agenda well in advance of the meeting.
5. The room may be equipped with computers, an electronic tablet, or other systems for sharing documents during the meeting. Be sure these systems are operating properly.
6. If the services of a technician or coordinator are needed, arrange to have that person available or in the room during the conference. Take it on yourself to learn the less complicated details of computer teleconferencing, so that you can expand your skills and knowledge in this area.

323

Topic 8-1: *Planning and Participating in Meetings*

REVIEWING THE TOPIC

1. List three general reasons why meetings are held in business.
2. Give an example of an informal business meeting and of a formal business meeting.
3. List in brief the guidelines you should follow to prepare for a meeting.
4. What information generally appears on a meeting agenda?
5. What information generally appears in minutes of a meeting?
6. What guidelines does a good leader follow during a meeting to use an assertive, but not aggressive style?
7. Describe three types of seating arrangement that may be used for meetings and how each one may affect a meeting.
8. What are the similarities between an action plan and meeting minutes? What are the differences?
9. Describe a Web conference.
10. What preparations need to be made for a teleconference?

THINKING CRITICALLY

Mr. Burris has asked you to take charge of preparations for a meeting with union leaders and company officials on April 2. In addition, he has asked you to sit in during the meeting and take minutes. You know from the agenda that the meeting has been scheduled for his conference room.

1. Key a list of the preparations you may need to make for the conference room.
2. Key a list of questions you have for Mr. Burris regarding the meeting preparations. For example: Will there be breaks for refreshments? If yes, how many and when?
3. What items will you need to take to the meeting with you?
4. Key a list of tasks you may need to do before, during, and after the meeting.

324

CHAPTER 8: MEETINGS AND TRAVEL

REINFORCING ENGLISH SKILLS

Pronouns are words that serve as substitutes for nouns. Pronouns must agree with their antecedents (nouns for which they stand) in person, number, and gender. Write or key the following sentences, selecting the proper pronouns.

1. The executive (that, who) directed the meeting is an effective business leader.
2. Neither Jack nor Jim thinks that (his, their) itinerary should be changed.
3. The executives said that (them, they), along with a group from another company, would attend the seminar in Paris.
4. Office workers who take the minutes of meetings need a parliamentary procedures resource available to (them, they).
5. The committee has promised to have (its, their) findings ready for review at the departmental meeting next week.
6. The executives traveling on business from that office often use (its, their) company's credit cards.
7. The executive and her associate were uncertain how (she, they) should reschedule the trip.
8. The members of the group attending the meeting wanted (its, their) opinions aired before a final vote was taken.
9. The oval table (that, who) was placed in the meeting room will be there only a short time.
10. Joy and Wendy reviewed the meeting agenda before (it, they) was sent to the participants.

Topic 8-1 | ACTIVITY 1

WORD PROCESSING

Agenda for a Teleconference

You work in Atlanta for Ernest Fogg, director of the Marketing Department. Mr. Fogg is making arrangements for a teleconference with marketing vice presidents located in five different regional offices. The teleconference will originate in Atlanta. Mr. Fogg hands you an edited copy of the agenda for the teleconference. He says, "Please key this agenda in final form. Make the changes I've indicated and list the participants in alphabetic order according to city. Proofread very carefully to ensure that all numbers are correct."

325

Topic Review

Teaching Tips

After students write or key the sentences, give them the correct answers.

Teaching Tips

Remind students to refer to Figure 8-1.1 for an example agenda.

1. Open the PDF file *CH08 Agenda*. This file contains the rough draft agenda.
2. Key the final agenda following Mr. Fogg's oral and written instructions.

COMPOSITION
TEAMWORK
WORD PROCESSING

Topic 8-1 : ACTIVITY 2

Meeting and Action Plan

Work in a group with three or four classmates to apply the meeting and planning skills you learned in this topic.

1. Identify a group chairperson who will lead the meeting and a recorder who will make notes during the meeting.
2. Choose one of the problem scenarios following step 4 as the reason for your group meeting. Discuss the possible causes of the problem and related factors. Consider what you have learned about the topic in previous chapters.
3. Brainstorm ideas for solving the problem. Follow the suggestions in the *Group Dynamics* section of this topic as you participate in the meeting. Your goal is to be an active participant with an assertive, but not aggressive, communication style.
4. Create an action plan detailing the steps your group will take toward solving the problem. Assign one or more people to complete each task and set deadlines for completing the tasks. Key an action plan document using Figure 8-1.3 as a guide. Submit the action plan and the notes your recorder made during the meeting.

Scenario 1	You are employed in a small company that has five other office workers. All the office workers need help in handling office tasks such as keying reports, preparing mailings, and responding to inquiries.
Scenario 2	Your company's petty cash fund does not balance with the fund records. Cash is missing. The same situation has occurred for each of the past three months. The petty cash is kept in a small metal box in the secretary's desk. The desk is locked at night, but it is usually not locked during the day. The secretary's duties often take her away from her desk.
Scenario 3	You work for a small company that uses a local area computer network. Users can connect to the Internet via the LAN. Employees are supposed to follow procedures to log on and log off when using the network. Over the past month, computer viruses have been detected frequently on the company's computer network.

326

326

CHAPTER 8: MEETINGS AND TRAVEL

Topic 8-2

objectives

- ○ Use appropriate procedures for planning business travel
- ○ Explain procedures for getting a passport and a visa
- ○ Prepare travel documents, including an itinerary
- ○ Describe the factors involved in travel etiquette and travel safety
- ○ Complete follow-up travel activities

People travel for various business reasons. They may need to supervise company operations or meet with clients or company associates. They may attend conferences related to work. Many companies, both large and small, do business with others from around the world.

Travel arrangements are made according to company policies. Some large firms may have a travel department for this purpose. Others may rely on the services of a travel agency. In smaller firms, however, an office worker or the traveling employee may make the travel arrangements.

Preparing for Business Travel

You may have an opportunity to choose the mode of travel for a business trip. The choice of hotels may also be yours. When such choices are available, you will need to know your personal preferences. When you are making the arrangements for another person, you will need to know that person's preferences.

When you travel on business, you will want to complete your duties or tasks effectively. You should arrive at meetings on time and with the needed supporting materials. Carefully made travel plans are important to the success of a business trip.

A travel folder (or trip file) will help you organize the details of an upcoming trip. Use the folder to collect information as it becomes available. Notes on reservations, tickets, hotels, and meeting confirmations may be placed in the file. The information in the travel folder will help you prepare an **itinerary** and complete company travel documents. It can also serve as a reminder system for tasks related to the trip.

itinerary: a document giving detailed plans for a trip

As you plan the trip, set aside time to:

- Schedule meetings to be held during the trip. Shortly before the trip, contact each person with whom you plan to meet to confirm the date, time, and meeting place.
- Organize the names, titles, company names, addresses, and telephone numbers or e-mail addresses of the individuals with whom meetings are scheduled.
- Check for travel safety conditions in the destination area.
- Make reservations for transportation and overnight lodging.
- Prepare an itinerary and gather supporting materials for the trip.

327

Topic 8-2: *Arranging Travel*

Commercial Air Travel

Time is money for the busy business traveler. The popularity of air travel reflects this point. Often, the only way to manage a tight schedule is by air travel. An extensive network of airline routes is provided by national, regional, and commuter airlines. Airline schedules are available free of charge at ticket counters in airports, at airline offices in major cities, at large hotels, and from travel agents. Most airlines have Web sites that provide travel details and where tickets can be purchased. Tickets can also be purchased by telephone or in person at airports or ticket offices.

If you use several airlines, you will find the *Official Airline Guide* (OAG) a valuable source of flight information and schedules. Your company may have a copy of this publication for your reference. If not, you can access the OAG online. The online OAG is available as a subscription service. To find the site, enter the name in a search engine or follow the link on *The Office* Web site. You simply enter the departure and arrival cities and the date of travel. The flight number and airline, times, cities, number of stops, and a code that indicates the type of aircraft will be displayed.

You may make flight reservations by calling a travel agent, by calling an airline directly using a toll-free number, or by accessing various Web sites. When you purchase airline tickets online, you may receive an **electronic ticket** or a paper ticket or by mail if time allows. If not, you can pick up the ticket at the airport.

electronic ticket: document and receipt that contain ticket information received in electronic form

© GETTY IMAGES/PHOTODISC

Air travel helps busy employees maintain schedules.

If you use the services of a travel agent, your flight itinerary and an invoice may be received with the airline tickets. Each of these documents serves a specific purpose. The flight itinerary can be checked against your records and used to create the traveler's itinerary. Many travelers attach a copy of the flight itinerary to the overall itinerary for the trip. The invoice is kept to attach to the travel expense report.

Plan to arrive at the airport well ahead of your flight departure time (one to two hours). You will need time for checking in at the airline desk to receive boarding passes, check luggage, and move through security checkpoints. Be sure to have a current photo ID such as a driver's license or passport. When checking bags, verify that the luggage tag attached by the airline attendant has the correct destination code. Wait until you see your bags placed on the conveyor belt before leaving the check-in area. Do not pack money, notebook computers, or other valuable items in checked luggage. Keep these items in a carried bag instead.

Comply with all reasonable requests of security personnel. Be aware that your checked bags or carried bags, as well as your person, may be subject to search. Never leave your bags or other possessions unattended or in the care of a stranger. Never agree to carry a bag or other items from a stranger. Check with the airline for a current list of items that are not allowed in checked or carried bags. For example, knives, lighters, and strike-anywhere matches are generally not allowed in carried bags.

Other Forms of Business Travel

Rental cars and trains provide alternative forms of business travel. You may have occasion to make travel arrangements using one of these forms of transportation.

Some business trips require the use of a rental car.

329

Topic 8-2: *Arranging Travel*

Teaching Tips

Display a large map of the United States and/or the world to help students gain a sense of travel distances and times involved in traveling. Highlight the time zones on the map.

For Discussion

For businesspeople who work in the community, what towns and cities are within the range that could be reached in reasonable time by car? What cities or towns would be outside the range?

For short trips, particularly in a local area, many people prefer to rent cars. A rental car may also be suitable when you fly to a city and have appointments in outlying areas. Be sure to allow ample time to reach your destination. Rental cars are available at most airports and other convenient locations. Rental fees vary in price according to the size of the car, the length of time the car is needed, and the miles driven. Follow your company's guidelines for renting a car. Many rental car companies have Web sites where you may choose and reserve a rental car.

WORKPLACE CONNECTIONS

Joe Park rented a car on his arrival at the Kansas City International Airport. He left the car rental agency at 1 p.m. for a meeting near Kansas City scheduled for 2 p.m., giving himself ample travel time for the half-hour trip. Joe arrived at the office where the meeting was scheduled and introduced himself to the receptionist. "Oh, I'm glad you finally made it. We were concerned that something might have happened to you," the receptionist said. "I don't understand," said Joe. "The meeting is scheduled for 2 p.m. It's only 1:40." "Let's see," said the receptionist. "You traveled from Cincinnati, right? Did you remember that Kansas City is in the Central time zone?" Joe was embarrassed about being late for the meeting and promised himself to check carefully all times, including the time zone, in the future.

Train travel is popular in some sections of the country. Train stations are located in the centers of cities and can provide an alternative to air travel on certain routes. Overnight trains have sleeping and dining rooms on board. Check with a travel agent or look in the yellow pages of your telephone directory for information on the railway lines serving your area.

Amtrak, a company that provides train services in many areas of the United States, provides a Web site where customers may make reservations online. To find the site, enter the company name in a search engine or follow the link on *The Office* Web site.

Hotel/Motel Accommodations

Many business travelers must be away from home overnight and stay in a hotel or motel room. In some cases, you may be allowed to request a particular hotel. In other cases, you may rely on a travel agent or coworker to select the lodging.

Teaching Tips

If train travel is available in your area, discuss the services available with students. If not, discuss areas where train service is available and explain when a business traveler might use train service.

Thinking Critically

Have students consider what services offered by a large hotel in a major city might be of importance to a person traveling on business. Students may name airport limousine service, wake-up calls, fax/reprographic services, overnight delivery services, business services (complete with telecommunications capabilities), restaurants, meeting rooms, and physical fitness centers.

Business travelers should choose hotels that are safe and convenient to their travel destinations.

When you make reservations by telephone, use toll-free telephone numbers whenever possible. Write down the names of the persons who make and confirm reservations. Always make a note of the rates you are told. Record the **confirmation number** and repeat it to the reservation agent to make sure it is correct. The confirmation number should be included on the itinerary. A written confirmation from the hotel is helpful. Many hotels have Web sites where reservations may be made. A confirmation number is usually provided. The reservation may also be confirmed by e-mail.

confirmation number: a series of characters (often text and numbers) associated with a reservation

Reservations for hotels can also be made online. At many travel sites, information can be found about hotels in a specific area. Descriptions, prices, and dates available are shown. Many hotels or hotel chains have their own Web sites where reservations can be made.

Itinerary and Supporting Materials

Once the travel plans are set, you should prepare an itinerary. You will need to assemble travel documents and related materials for meetings or appointments. If the plans for the trip change, other arrangements may need to be made. Changes can generally be made at the time you cancel the original plans. Have your confirmation numbers and other details available when you call to change reservations or appointments.

Prepare an Itinerary

An itinerary is a detailed plan of a trip. It serves as a guide for the business traveler. Travel plans, meetings, hotel locations, and reminders or special instructions should be included. When planning a trip, allow enough travel time between meetings to avoid having to rush to make the next appointment.

Ask students: If you were making a hotel reservation directly with the hotel, what information would you need to know before you made the reservation?

Points to Emphasize

Allowing appropriate time between appointments for travel, meals, and even rest breaks is important when planning an itinerary.

331

Ali Strong is away from the office on a trip when an important client, Mr. Jobel, calls. Mr. Jobel plans to be in town on Thursday and requests a meeting with Ali. As Ali's administrative assistant, you know that Ali has been hoping to meet with Mr. Jobel, but he is not scheduled to be back in the office until Friday. You tell Mr. Jobel that Ali is out of the office right now, but you will try to arrange the meeting and call him back. Consulting Ali's detailed itinerary, you find that he is scheduled to meet with Mrs. Bridge at this time, and the itinerary includes a phone number for Mrs. Bridge's office. You hesitate to interrupt Ali's meeting with Mrs. Bridge, but decide to call her office and ask to speak to Mr. Strong. Ali seems annoyed at first when he answers your call but soon thanks you for calling. "Tell Mr. Jobel I can meet with him at any time Thursday," said Ali. "I'll reschedule my other meetings and fly home on Wednesday." You are pleased that preparing a detailed itinerary for Ali's trip has proved to be so useful.

You may need several copies of the itinerary. One hard copy should be carried with you. Another copy can be carried in the baggage. One copy should be left with a contact person at the office. You may want to give one copy to family members. The itinerary should be in an easy-to-read format that gives the day-by-day schedule for the complete trip. An electronic copy can be stored on your notebook computer or PDA and carried with you. If changes in travel plans occur during the trip, the electronic copy can be updated and e-mailed to the office and family members. A sample itinerary is shown in Figure 8-2.1.

Gather Supporting Items

Before the trip, gather the travel documents, supplies, and supporting materials, such as those listed below, that are needed for the trip.

- Itinerary
- Travel tickets
- Travel funds
- Passport, visa, health documents
- Hotel/motel and car rental confirmations
- Maps of cities or states as appropriate
- Directions to offices or other meeting locations
- Speeches, supporting correspondence, reports, or files for each appointment/meeting
- Forms for recording expenses
- Extra notepaper, pens, and business cards
- Equipment, such as a laptop computer, portable phone, or presentation projection system

Teaching Tips

Gather examples of the travel documents discussed in this section to show to students or to display on a bulletin board. You might wish to show traditional tickets and e-tickets.

ITINERARY FOR CHARLENE STANFORD

May 17 to May 19, 20--

DATE	TIME	ACTIVITY
Wednesday May 17	9:43 a.m.	Leave Hartsfield Atlanta International airport on Delta Flight 17.
	10:50 a.m.	Arrive Dallas/Ft. Worth International Airport. Pick up rental car keys at Sun Rentals counter, confirmation number 388075.
		Hotel reservations at Fairmont Hotel, 1717 W. Akard Street. Phone: 214-555-0102. Confirmation number 7K4995F.
	2:30 p.m.	Meeting with George Thatcher, Vice President of Marketing, Fabric Wholesalers, 1314 Gaston Avenue (Phone: 214-555-0196) to discuss purchase agreement.
	7:00 p.m.	Dinner with staff at hotel to review plans for Apparel Fair.
Thursday May 18	12:02 p.m.	Leave Dallas/Ft. Worth International Airport on Delta Flight 444. Drop rental car keys at Sun Rentals and take shuttle to airport.
	12:55 p.m.	Arrive at Lindbergh Field International Airport and meet Richard Stanley (Phone: 619-555-0152) at baggage claim. Travel to Naples plant with Richard, take tour, and return to hotel.
		Hotel reservations at the Seven Seas Lodge, 411 Hotel Circle South (Phone: 619-555-1300). Confirmation number 4478S84.
Friday May 19	7:55 a.m.	Leave San Diego Lindbergh Field International Airport on Delta Flight 880. Richard will meet me at my hotel at 6:45 a.m. and drive me to the airport.
	3:52 p.m.	Arrive Hartsfield Atlanta International Airport.

Figure **8-2.1**

Travel itinerary

333

Topic 8-2: *Arranging Travel*

If the supporting materials, such as a large number of handouts, will be too heavy or bulky to carry with you, arrange to have them shipped to your hotel or meeting location. Arrange for special packaging for equipment, such as computers and projection panels, to prevent damage to these items while en route. Confirm the safe arrival of supporting materials prior to or immediately on arrival and have a backup plan to follow in case items are lost or damaged. For example, you might carry one set of handouts with you so that copies can be made at your destination if necessary.

Travel Etiquette

etiquette: standards for proper behavior

U.S. companies of all sizes deal with companies in other countries. This activity is handled differently in each company. Some companies have a special division to deal with their branch offices in other countries. Your behavior as a business traveler reflects on you, your company, and your home area. Proper dress and travel **etiquette** will contribute to a successful business trip.

Dress

Remember that you represent your organization when you travel. Your dress will contribute to that most important first impression you make on others. Follow these guidelines for appropriate travel attire:

- Dress appropriately for the type of meeting or function you are attending. Many companies send employees to training sessions in which the attire is less formal than while on the job. If the meeting is to take place at another company's site, the attire may be more formal.

Dressing appropriately for a meeting will contribute to a successful business trip.

334

- Dress for travel. Many times, employees need a day to travel to a business destination. Dress in this case will be less formal on the airplane or in a car. When a short plane or car ride is all that is necessary to reach your destination, however, dress more formally to be ready to conduct business on arrival.
- Dress to impress. Consider the persons with whom you will be doing business and the impression you want to leave about your organization. Many companies may permit less formal dress while on the job. However, while on business in another city or country, more formal business dress is expected. Proper dress is especially important when traveling in foreign countries or meeting with persons from a culture different from your own. Be aware of the dress customs for the country in which you will do business and dress accordingly.

WORKPLACE CONNECTIONS

Jagu Patel looked forward to attending a conference at a popular golf resort in Florida. He carefully packed his business suits as well as casual clothes for playing golf and sight-seeing. On Monday morning, Jagu ate breakfast early and arrived on time for the first meeting session. As other people began to enter the room, he noticed that he was the only person wearing a business suit. Jagu quietly left the meeting area and went back to his room. Reviewing the conference agenda booklet again, he found that it did, indeed, indicate that business casual or resort wear would be the appropriate dress for the conference. Jagu was glad that he had packed plenty of casual clothes as he changed outfits and returned to the meeting.

Customs

Proper etiquette plays an important role in conducting business successfully, both in the United States and in foreign countries. The etiquette will vary from country to country. Various print and electronic resources are available to provide in-depth information about business and travel etiquette. For information about a specific country, consult a travel agent or someone who has lived or done business there. Consider the following customs and protocols related to business travel:

- Be on time for appointments. Arrange your schedule to allow time for unexpected delays in travel.
- Take an ample supply of business cards. Business cards are always presented by a caller and serve the purposes of introducing the person who is visiting and providing an easy future reference. Business cards should include your name, your company's name, your position, and your title. Avoid using abbreviations on the card. For international travel, have the same information printed in the local language on the reverse side of the card.

335

Topic 8-2: *Arranging Travel*

Supplemental Activity

This chapter cannot cover all of the customs that may be observed by the international business traveler. Ask students to research a specific country and share with the rest of the class the information they find about doing business in that country.

Expand the Concept

Have students practice shaking hands with fellow students in class. Stress that a handshake leaves an impression with the other person. Practice giving a firm, warm handshake. Ask students: Is it always necessary to shake hands?

- If and when appropriate, provide a gift that is company associated, such as a pen or sweatshirt with a company logo. Flowers are generally a safe and appreciated gift in almost every country.
- Paying for meals and tipping for clients is generally accepted as the role of the host—the person who set up the meeting.
- The universal business greeting in the United States is the handshake. When you offer your hand or reach out to take another's hand, be sure your grasp is firm but not painful. Make eye contact with the person at the same time.
- Know the body language and gestures that may be offensive or have different meanings in other cultures. The universal form of communication that all people recognize and appreciate is a smile. Use it often to break the ice and ease tense situations that may arise.
- Know how to pronounce the name of the person you are visiting, as well as how to address the person. Use academic or honorary titles when appropriate.
- Taste any food that is offered by the host. Many hosts will proudly present the best delicacy the area has to offer.
- Speak standard English. Avoid using slang terms. This is especially important when meeting with people for whom English is a second language.

© GETTY IMAGES/PHOTODISC

A handshake is an accepted business greeting in the United States.

336

CHAPTER 8: MEETINGS AND TRAVEL

Documents for Foreign Travel

Two documents are required for foreign travel in most countries: a passport and a visa. Other documents, such as work permits, prescriptions for medicine carried, and health records, may also be needed.

The U.S. government provides a free travel registration service for U.S. citizens who are traveling to a foreign country. The Web site is shown in Figure 8-2.2. The information you provide may help the Department of State assist you in case of an emergency. A link to the U.S. Department of State Web site is on *The Office* Web site.

Source: U.S. Department of State. https://travelregistration.state.gov/ibrs/ (accessed August 30, 2005).

Figure **8-2.2**

The U.S. Department of State Travel Registration page

Passport

A **passport** is an official document granting permission to travel. Issued by the United States Department of State, it states a person's right to protection in the foreign country. A passport is needed for travel in most foreign countries.

To secure a passport, application forms may be obtained from government offices and many travel agencies. Information about how to get a passport is available at the Passports Home page on the U.S. Department of State Web site. The site is shown in Figure 8-2.3 on page 338. You can also look in the white pages telephone directory (under "Government Agencies") to find the passport office nearest you.

The requirements to obtain a passport for the first time are listed on the passport application and on the U.S. Department of State Web site. Processing the application normally takes up to six weeks. You should allow enough lead time to avoid having to delay travel plans. Requesting *Expedited* service and paying an extra fee can speed the process to as little as two weeks. After the passport is received, it should be signed, and the information requested on the inside cover completed. To replace an expired passport, obtain a renewal application. Submit the renewal application well in advance of the expiration date for the current passport to avoid being without a current passport.

passport: official U.S. government document that grants permission to travel outside the United States

Teaching Tips

Obtain a copy of a passport application so that students can become familiar with the kinds of questions asked and the process involved in applying for a passport. Many students have traveled with parents or on tours sponsored by schools; ask them to bring their passports for demonstration purposes.

337

Topic 8-2: *Arranging Travel*

Points to Emphasize

A visa is often in the form of a stamp on a passport and usually includes specific dates when the visa is effective. Ample time should be allowed before a trip for obtaining a visa when one is required.

For Discussion

Where can a traveler learn about the vaccinations required for travel in a particular country? Ask students whether they have had to get vaccinations, documentation for prescription drugs, or other health documents before traveling abroad.

Figure **8-2.3**

The U.S. Department of State Web site offers guidelines for obtaining a passport.

Source: U.S. Department of State. http://travel.state.gov/passport/passport_1738.html (accessed August 22, 2005).

A passport should be carried or kept in a hotel security box or safe and never be left in a hotel room. Make a photocopy of the identification page so that the passport can be replaced if it is lost. Report the loss of a passport immediately to the nearest passport office. If traveling abroad, report the loss to the United States Embassy.

Visa

visa: a permit granted by a foreign government for a person to enter its country

A **visa** is a permit granted by a foreign government for a person to enter its country. The visa usually appears as a stamped notation in a passport, indicating that the person may enter the country for a certain purpose and for a specific period of time. Be sure to note the effective dates of a visa.

consulate: person appointed by a government to serve its citizens and business interests in another country

embassy: the offices of an ambassador in a foreign country

Always check to see whether you need a visa for the country in which travel is planned. Contact the **consulate** or **embassy** of the country or a travel agent before leaving the United States. Addresses and telephone numbers of consulates of most foreign countries in the United States can be found online. Search using the term *embassy*. You can also look in the yellow pages of telephone directories in major cities under *Consulates* to find phone numbers. Addresses and telephone numbers for many consulates are provided on the U.S. Department of State Web site. Again, allow lead time to obtain the visa stamp from the appropriate consulate prior to traveling to that country.

Health Documents

vaccination: injection given to produce immunity to a disease

When traveling to some countries, certain **vaccinations** may be required to protect against a variety of diseases. A country may require people entering the country to have health tests, such as testing for contagious diseases. A travel agency or the consulate of the country to be visited can supply information about required vaccinations or tests. Records of the vaccinations and tests must be signed by a doctor. They must also be validated by the local or state health officer on a specific form. The form may be obtained from a travel agent, the passport office, the local health department, or some doctors. Even if the country to be visited does not require vaccinations, a traveler should carry a written record of childhood vaccinations and booster shots.

CHAPTER 8: MEETINGS AND TRAVEL

Other health factors should be considered for international travel. Taking medicine for air sickness may make travelers more comfortable on long flights. Prescriptions from a doctor for medicines that must be taken by the traveler can be helpful. Permission to carry medicines that might not be available in the country to be visited may be required. Check with a travel agent or the country's consulate to see what arrangements must be made for these medicines.

Travel Safety

Many airlines, hotels and motels, and travel agencies provide tips for travelers. Follow these safety suggestions as you travel or make travel preparations:

- Access the U.S. Department of State Web site for travel warnings, consular information sheets, and public announcements regarding travel.
- Do not leave your luggage or other items unattended in hotel lobbies or in waiting areas in airports. Unattended luggage may be stolen or have illegal or unsafe items placed in it.
- Keep your passport and travel funds in a safe, secure place.
- Do not display cash or expensive jewelry or other items when traveling.
- Do not agree to carry items in your luggage for another person.
- Use all locking devices on doors and windows in your hotel room.
- Do not leave valuables in your car, and be sure to lock your vehicle.

© CORBIS

Never leave your luggage unattended.

For Discussion

Review the travel safety tips presented in this section. Ask students to tell which tips they think are the most important and why.

- Be aware of your surroundings, and look around before entering parking lots late at night. Always return to your hotel through the main entrance after dark.
- Protect your credit or bank card and telephone calling card numbers at all times.

Many motels and hotels place safety guidelines on specially printed cards in rooms. Read and follow their guidelines for your personal safety.

Handling Work While Away from the Office

Business travelers may depend on an office assistant to handle routine tasks and messages while away from the office. Before the traveler leaves for a business trip, the office assistant should understand how to deal with routine matters. Plans for handling crisis situations and out-of-the-ordinary situations should also be made.

During the Trip

Answers to the following questions may be helpful to the traveler in keeping work flowing and situations under control during the trip:

- Who will handle crises that may arise while you are out of the office? What kinds of emergencies or crises have occurred in the past that you need to be prepared for?
- Who will be making routine decisions for you while you are out of the office?
- What kinds of messages or documents should be forwarded to you?
- When will you be in touch with the office during the trip?
- What kinds of documents will be forwarded to the office prior to returning to the office?

To keep the office running smoothly, the following suggestions may be helpful to the office assistant:

- Keep an itemized list of incoming mail for the traveler.
- Answer routine mail or e-mail for the traveler if authorized to do so.
- Keep a log of faxes, telephone calls, and office visitors for the traveler.
- If possible, avoid making appointments for the traveler for the first day he or she will be back in the office.
- Keep notes of matters you want to discuss with the traveler on his or her return.

Staying in Touch

Technology makes it easy for travelers to stay in touch with the office or clients. Data can be sent and received using computers, networks, and mobile phones. Some hotels provide fully equipped business centers for travelers. Many hotels offer rooms with special data access phone lines designed for modem use. Airlines provide in-flight telephones and conference rooms in airports. Travelers can often complete tasks such as:

Thinking Critically

Why might a traveler want to avoid having appointments scheduled for the first day he or she is back in the office?

For Discussion

Which of the tasks listed in this section do you think a business traveler might do most often? Why?

- Send and receive business data by fax
- Access messages (voice or electronic mail)
- Participate in teleconferences
- Access the Internet for travel information
- Transfer travel expense records to an office assistant
- Check availability of products for clients
- Place orders and receive confirmation of orders placed by clients
- Access a company intranet for policy or procedural changes that occur while the traveler is out of the office

Technology will continue to play an important role in how work is handled while workers are traveling on business.

Today's technology allows travelers to complete work away from the office.

© CORBIS

Business Travel Follow-Up Activities

Certain follow-up activities should be completed as soon as possible after a trip. These activities include reporting travel expenses, writing a variety of reports, and writing letters.

Expense Reports

Typically, a company will have a form that employees use to report travel expenses. The expenses listed may include charges for items such as hotel rooms, meals, and car rentals. Other expenses, such as for entertaining

341

Topic 8-2: *Arranging Travel*

341

travel expense report: document that lists expenses to be reimbursed such as for hotels and meals

clients, may also be approved expenses. Some travelers may receive travel money in advance from the company. These funds are accounted for on the travel expense report. Receipts may be required for travel expenses. Follow company procedures to prepare expense reports. Be sure to obtain the necessary signatures or approvals of the completed forms.

Meeting Reports

Examples of meeting reports include sales summaries, client visit logs, project progress updates, and others that present the results of the business trip. The completed reports may provide a written record of decisions that were made or goals that were set. They may discuss complaints or suggestions from customers or ideas for new products or services. Reports are sent to persons who will be affected by the decisions, goals, complaints, or ideas.

Letters

Thank-you letters may be sent to people with whom you meet during the trip. The need for thank-you letters will depend on the purpose of the travel and business etiquette guidelines.

Other follow-up letters may provide a written record of agreements made during the visit. They may give details that were not available during the meeting or discuss tasks related to the meeting. When writing follow-up letters, remember to use the five Cs of effective communications to evaluate your documents.

REVIEWING THE TOPIC

1. In planning a business trip, what activities should you set aside time to complete?
2. What procedures should you follow in making hotel reservations by phone?
3. What items might be collected in a travel folder?
4. List five important travel safety tips.
5. Identify and describe three common forms of business travel.
6. Where can airline schedules be obtained?
7. What items generally appear in a travel itinerary?
8. Define travel etiquette. List five etiquette tips related to business travel.
9. Where can you obtain forms to apply for a passport? How much time should you allow for processing the passport application?
10. Describe three follow-up activities a traveler may need to complete after returning from a trip.

THINKING CRITICALLY

You are a department manager for Ellis Tools, Inc. An employee in your department has submitted a travel expense form for your approval. Your company pays employees 30 cents per mile for travel in their personal cars. The maximum amounts allowed per day for meals are: breakfast, $10; lunch, $15; and dinner, $25. Employees must submit a receipt for any expense item greater than $25. The purpose of the business trip should be clearly explained on the form. The form should include the destination, people with whom the employee met, and the purpose of the meeting.

1. Open and print the PDF file *CH08 Expenses* from the data files. This file contains a travel expense form and related receipt.
2. Verify the numbers on the form and note any needed corrections. Circle any other items on the form that are incorrect or require more information.
3. Create a memo form for Ellis Tools, Inc. to include the company name and appropriate memo headings. Write a memo to the employee indicating the changes that should be made to the form and indicate that the form is attached.

Teaching Tips

If the students are using the *Student Activities and Simulations* workbook, instruct them to complete the review activity for this topic.

Teaching Tips

Remind students to evaluate their memos using the five Cs of effective communications.

For Discussion

Why is getting competing bids from two or more companies important when planning off-site events?

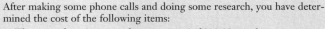

REINFORCING MATH SKILLS

Your supervisor has asked you to calculate the estimated cost of an off-site staff meeting. The meeting will take place in a conference room at a local hotel. Forty-three people will attend the meeting.

After making some phone calls and doing some research, you have determined the cost of the following items:

- The cost of renting a conference room is $900.00 per day.
- The cost of renting a video projector is $50.00 per day
- The cost of pastries and beverages for the morning break is $3.50 per person.
- The cost of a catered lunch is $6.75 per person plus a gratuity equal to 18 percent of the total.
- The cost of beverages for the afternoon break is $2.00 per person.
- The cost of pens, paper, markers, and flip chart pads is $75.00.

1. Using the information you collected, calculate the cost of each expense item for the meeting.
2. Calculate the total estimated cost of the meeting.
3. A salesperson at another hotel that you called said that she would beat any deal you get at a local hotel by 10 percent. Calculate the total estimated cost of the meeting if you use this competing hotel.

Teaching Tips

Remind students to refer to Figure 8-2.1 for a sample itinerary. Discuss with students how they might share the tasks in the activity with a teammate to accomplish the work more quickly.

COMPOSITION
RESEARCH
TEAMWORK
WORD PROCESSING

Topic 8-2 : ACTIVITY 1

Travel Reservations and Itinerary

Your manager, Miss Patti Walker, has sent you some notes for a conference she plans to attend in Orlando, Florida. She asks you to research and make reservations for the trip. You should also key an itinerary for her trip. Work with a classmate to complete this assignment.

1. Open the PDF file *CH08 Conference* from the data files. This file contains an e-mail from your manager with notes about the trip.
2. Using a printed airline guide or an airline Web site, research flights for Miss Walker's trip. You could also telephone airlines for flight information and costs. Miss Walker prefers coach nonstop flights if available. Choose the flights you think are most appropriate, considering the costs and the schedule. Pretend that you have reserved these flights for Miss Walker. Make a note of the flight information for her itinerary or print the information from the Web site if possible.
3. Miss Walker would like to stay at a hotel near the Orange County Convention Center. Use a printed hotel guide or a Web site to find a hotel

344

CHAPTER 8: MEETINGS AND TRAVEL

near the convention center and to find rooms available and rates. You could also telephone hotel reservations numbers (many are toll free) for information. Choose the room and rates you think are most appropriate. Pretend that you have reserved a room for Miss Walker. Make a note of the information for her itinerary or print the information from the Web site if possible. Use the confirmation number MH2933X2.

4. Miss Walker will need a rental car while she is in Orlando. Use a rental car Web site or call a rental car company to find the costs of a mid-size car. Pretend that you have reserved a car for Miss Walker. Make a note of the information for her itinerary or print the information from the Web site if possible. Use the confirmation number C835LX1.

5. Create an itinerary for Miss Walker. Use the itinerary in Figure 8-2.1 as an example. Attach any reservation information you have printed from Web sites for the airline, hotel, or car rental. If you did not print information, key notes about each reservation and attach the notes to the itinerary.

Topic 8-2 : ACTIVITY 2

Travel Etiquette and Safety Brochure

COMPOSITION
DESKTOP PUBLISHING
INTERNET
RESEARCH
TEAMWORK

Your manager, Antiono Alvarez, has asked your work group to create a brochure about travel etiquette and safety tips for business travelers in your company. Many managers are traveling to U.S. and foreign destinations. The brochure would be helpful to them and their office assistants. Work in a group with two classmates to complete this assignment.

1. Create a list of travel etiquette and safety tips that both domestic and international travelers need to know. Add to the information found in the textbook with information you can find from magazines or from an online search. Use search terms such as *travel etiquette, business etiquette, travel tips,* or *travel safety tips.*

2. Plan the format for your brochure. Lay out your brochure on paper before you create it on the computer. The answers to the following questions may be helpful to your group:
   • What is the name of your brochure?
   • What are the most important points you should emphasize?
   • What supporting information can you provide?
   • What kind of clip art will you need and what is available to you?
   • What software is available to you to create your brochure?

3. Use word processing or desktop publishing software to complete your brochure. Review the information on desktop publishing in Chapter 4, page 144. Your finished brochure should include bulleted items and clip art or other graphics to enhance the brochure.

Teaching Tips

Have students review key points from the chapter by completing the Sort It Out game on *The Office* Web site.

Summary

In this chapter, you discovered the important role office workers play in planning and conducting meetings. You learned about taking part in meetings, arranging travel, and doing business away from the office. You also learned about travel etiquette and travel safety. Key points in this chapter include:

- Office workers often attend meetings and travel on business. Tasks related to meetings and travel must be completed before, during, and after the event.
- Office workers attend both small and large meetings. The meeting may be formal or informal.
- Office workers may prepare a meeting agenda, minutes, and a list of follow-up or action items.
- Meetings allow workers to discuss problems, exchange information, and make decisions. As an office worker, you should be prepared to lead or take part in any meeting you attend.
- A teleconference is a meeting of people in different locations connected by a telecommunications system. Teleconferences can be used to deliver training, share data, or solve problems.
- Carefully planned travel arrangements are important to the success of a business trip. A travel folder (or trip file) will help you organize the details of an upcoming trip.
- Business trips may involve travel by airplane, train, or car and staying at hotels or motels. Reservations can be made by phone or online at company Web sites.
- An itinerary is a detailed plan of a trip. It includes travel arrangements, appointments, lodging reservations, and reminders or special instructions.
- Travelers should be aware of travel etiquette and safety guidelines. The U.S. Department of State provides travel warnings, consular information sheets, and public messages regarding travel.
- A passport and a visa are required for foreign travel in most countries. Other documents, such as work permits, prescriptions for medicine, and health records may also be needed.
- The office assistant plays a critical role in the office while coworkers travel on business trips. The activities the assistant will handle should be agreed to by both the assistant and the traveler.
- Computers, networks, and mobile phones help travelers stay in touch with the office while away.
- Thank-you notes, travel expense forms, and other documents related to the trip should be completed promptly when the traveler returns from a trip.

Key Terms

action plan	embassy	quorum
adjournment	etiquette	second
agenda	group dynamics	teleconference
assertive	itinerary	travel expense report
brainstorm	minutes	vaccination
confirmation number	motion	visa
consensus	parliamentary	
consulate	procedures	
electronic ticket	passport	

COMPOSITION
DESKTOP PUBLISHING
TEAMWORK
WORD PROCESSING

Chapter 8   ACTIVITY 1

Teleconference on Travel Etiquette and Safety

Your manager has asked your work group to plan a teleconference that will focus on international travel etiquette and safety. She indicates that the teleconference should be planned for three weeks from today. It will be held in the company's interactive teleconference room. Those who will attend the teleconference include office workers in various positions. These workers may travel to new company sites abroad. Office assistants who will help make travel arrangements will also attend. Work with two classmates to complete this assignment.

1. Decide on the date and time for the teleconference. Key a paragraph or list describing the procedures and information you would use to prepare before the meeting.

2. Choose a city and country where the company has the new branch office. Obtain the address of the U.S. consulate for the country you have chosen. You can find this information by completing an online search. For example, if the country you have chosen is Japan, you might search using the term *U.S. consulate Japan.* Write a letter to the consulate asking for information about traveling and doing business in the country.

3. Because it may take some time for your request to the consulate to be processed, also search for information from other sources. Complete an online search for customs, business etiquette, and travel safety tips for the country you have chosen. Revise the brochure on travel etiquette and safety you created earlier to include customs and etiquette guidelines and safety tips for a traveler to that country.

347

Chapter Review

4. Research the travel documents needed to travel in that country. Key a list and description of travel documents a traveler needs for the country. Obtain samples of or applications for the documents if possible.

5. Plan the topics to be discussed during the teleconference based on the information you have collected. Key an agenda for the meeting. Review the contents and format of an agenda in Figure 8-1.1.

6. Submit the following items to your instructor:
   - List describing the meeting preparations
   - Letter you have written to the consulate
   - Revised brochure describing customs, etiquette guidelines, and travel tips
   - Samples or applications for travel documents
   - Teleconference agenda

International Travel Arrangements

You are one of the office workers who attended the teleconference on international travel etiquette and safety described in Chapter 8 Activity 1. You need to make travel arrangements for a trip next month to the company's new branch office.

1. You will travel from your home city to the city and country your group chose for the company's new branch office in Activity 1. Your travel date to that city is one month from today. Your return travel date is one week later.

2. Using a printed airline guide or an airline Web site, research airline flights to that city. You could also telephone airlines for flight information and costs. (If you chose a small city for the company branch office, you may need to fly to a larger city that is nearby.) Choose the flights you think are most appropriate, considering the costs and the schedule. Pretend that you have reserved these flights. Make a note of the flight information for your itinerary or print the information from the Web site if possible.

3. Use a printed hotel guide or search the Web to find a hotel in that city. You could also telephone hotel reservations numbers (many are toll free) for information. Choose the room and rates you think are most appropriate. Pretend that you have reserved a room. Make a note of the information for your itinerary or print the information from the Web site if possible. Use the confirmation number Vl379XA.

4. A company representative, Ms. Kitty How, will meet you at the airport and provide transportation during your stay. She will take you to the airport for your return flight.

Expand the Concept

Discuss how the rules and restrictions may differ for reservations made at a general travel Web site and those made directly with a hotel or airline by phone or online. For example, the general travel Web site may have lower rates; but it may also have more restrictions on cancellations and refunds.

5. Create an itinerary for your trip to include travel details and the scheduled activities shown below. See Figure 8-2.1 for an example itinerary. Attach any reservation information you have printed from Web sites for the airline and hotel. If you did not print information, key notes about each reservation and attach the notes to the itinerary.

Day 1	Travel to destination city
Day 2	9:30 a.m. – 11:30 a.m. Tour of new office
	12 noon – 2 p.m. Lunch with branch manager, Mr. Lou
	2:30 p.m. – 4:30 p.m. Prepare meeting room and materials
Days 3, 4, and 5	9:30 a.m. – 4:30 p.m. Provide training to employees at the branch office
	(one-hour lunch break starting around noon)
Day 6	9:30 a.m. – 11:30 a.m. Meeting with department managers to discuss additional training needs
Day 7	Travel to home city

Supplemental Activity

Have students complete the Chapter 8 Supplemental Activity, Thank-You Letter, available on *The Office* Web site.

Assessment

Assess student learning using the Chapter 8 test available on the *IRCD* and in *ExamView®* format.

© GETTY IMAGES/PHOTODISC

CHAPTER 9

Records Management Systems

Information is important to the operation of a company. A system is needed for organizing, storing, and retrieving records and for removing outdated records. As an office worker, you will need to follow records management procedures carefully. These procedures include how to organize, store, retrieve, remove, and dispose of records. This series of steps is known as the record life cycle.

You will learn in this chapter that organizations keep records on a variety of media. They use paper, magnetic tapes and disks, optical disks, and micrographics. You will also learn that there are advantages and disadvantages to each. You should know about these media so that you can maintain records properly. This chapter will give you the latest information about the various media and the skills to use the most common filing systems.

Online Resources

- O *The Office* Web site:
  Data Files
  Vocabulary Flashcards
  Beat the Clock, Filing Systems
  Chapter 9 Supplementary
  Activity
- O ARMA International
  13725 W. 109th Street, Suite 101
  Lenexa, KS 66215
- O Search terms:
  records management
  records retention
  storage media
  micrographics
  imaging systems
  disaster recovery plan

350

Topic 9-1

objectives

O Explain the purposes of records management

O Identify the benefits of records management

O Describe types of media on which records are kept

O Identify the cost factors involved in a records management system

O Describe the phases of the record life cycle

O Describe the process for the removal and archiving of records

O Describe disaster recovery

O Use database software to create a retention schedule for records

An office cannot operate without records. For example, each time an item or service is purchased or sold by an organization, a record of the transaction is made and kept in the files. When you work in an office, you will keep a copy of correspondence you mail or transmit. You will also keep items that you receive from other individuals or companies, such as letters, memos, reports, and advertisements. You may even keep a written record of important telephone conversations.

Records are kept so that you and others in the office can refer to the information later or use it to complete another task. A records management system will help you store and retrieve records efficiently and keep the files current.

Overview of a Records Management System

A **record** is data in forms such as text, numbers, images, or voice that is kept for future reference. A **records management system** is a set of procedures used to organize, store, retrieve, remove, and dispose of records.

The main purpose of a records management system is to make sure records are available when needed so that a company can operate efficiently. Such a system fulfills this purpose in several ways by:

- Using storage media
- Providing proper storage equipment and supplies
- Outlining procedures for filing records
- Developing an efficient retrieval procedure
- Setting up a schedule for when records should be kept or discarded

An effective records management system benefits a company in two ways. First, workers are more productive. Second, customer goodwill is maintained.

To make wise decisions or complete a task well, workers need accurate, current information. For example, to prepare a monthly sales report, you need to have the sales figures for each sales person. Before you pay an invoice, you should check your records to be sure the charges are correct. Before you can mail a package, you need to know the recipient's complete address.

You must be able to access needed records easily and quickly. An effective records management system will help you to be more productive. You will not waste valuable time searching for information that should be easily available.

record: information kept for future reference

records management system: a set of procedures used to organize, store, retrieve, and dispose of records

Students have probably seen people locating and checking records: tellers providing balances in banks, their parents preparing for taxes, clerks looking for receipts in stores, and so on. Ask students to give their observations of how well organized the people who were seeking records seemed to be. Ask if they have ever heard someone express dismay at being unable to find a record. Why do the students think such a problem may have occurred?

An employee of a Records Department who has a good understanding of the services the department provides for the entire company and of how the records management system works may be a valuable guest speaker for your class. He or she could be asked to discuss the organization of his or her department and the responsibilities of entry-level employees.

351

Topic 9-1: *Maintaining Office Records*

This medical assistant can quickly access patient records.

© MARK ADAMS/SUPERSTOCK INTERNATIONAL

medium or media: material(s) or form(s) on or in which information may be stored

magnetic media: disks or tapes used to store documents electronically

micrographics: converts documents to very small photographs for storage on microfilm

Storage Media

A company may keep records on a variety of **media**. Paper, **magnetic media** such as computer disks or tape, and **micrographics** (documents reduced and placed on film) are used for storing records. The company must determine a combination of media that is best for its needs. As an office worker, you may be expected to work with all these media. Each **medium** has particular advantages and disadvantages, and you will learn more about these in this topic.

Storage Equipment and Supplies

Storage equipment, such as filing cabinets, should be chosen with specific storage media in mind. For example, if your records are on paper, you might use a filing cabinet. However, the same cabinet might not be appropriate for filing micrographic records. You may use supplies such as file folders to hold paper records. You would not use these folders for storing computer tapes. Chapter 10 discusses the various equipment and supplies for each type of storage medium.

Valuable records can be kept in fireproof cabinets or vaults. A good records management system includes policies that help you decide which records require special protection. For example, you may need to protect original copies of contracts by storing them in a fireproof vault.

Open shelf files are used for storing paper records in some offices.

Filing Procedures

Filing is the process of storing records in an orderly manner within an organized system. The procedure used to file records varies. It depends on the storage media used and the way the files are organized. Topic 9-2 explains the various paper filing systems. Chapter 10 presents specific filing procedures for hard copy files and electronic files.

filing: the process of storing records in an orderly manner within an organized system

Employees often remove records from the files for use in their work. Removing a record from the files and noting information about the record is called **charging out**. Company procedures should provide guidelines for charging out records. The following information is usually recorded when a record is removed from the files:

charging out: removing a record from the file and recording related information

- Name and department of the worker who is taking the record
- Date the record was retrieved
- Date the record will be returned

This information is kept in case someone else must locate the record. A retrieval procedure also should indicate whether all workers or only certain staff members have free access to the records. Chapter 10 explains retrieval procedures in more detail.

Records Retention and Disposition

A records management system should include information on how long records are kept and how they are to be disposed of. Most companies use a **retention schedule**, which lists how long each type of record should be kept. You should follow this schedule to be certain that the files are free of outdated or unnecessary records so that you can work efficiently. Proper **records disposition** can be equally important. Later in this topic, you will learn more about this aspect of records management.

retention schedule: a list of how long each type of record should be kept

records disposition: moving records to permanent storage or destroying records

Topic 9-1: *Maintaining Office Records*

Thinking Critically

Ask students: Why might a company choose to maintain some records on paper even though other storage media are available? Answers may include access in easily readable form, legal reasons, and so on.

Thinking Critically

What kinds of records would be best kept on paper? Best kept electronically? Would their answers change for a used auto parts dealer? For a medical office? Help students see that the filing system and equipment should vary based on the type of office and purposes for records.

For Discussion

Ask students to name all of the advantages and disadvantages that they can think of for storing records on magnetic media.

Storage Media for Records

Records are stored on a variety of media. The most common storage medium is paper. Paper records will remain a major part of filing systems for years to come. Many records are also stored on magnetic or optical disks and on microfilm. These records require less space to store than paper records.

Paper

Each time you print a document or complete a telephone message form, you are recording information on paper. These paper records are referred to as hard copy. The advantage of keeping paper records is that you can easily read the information they contain. With magnetic media records, such as a word processing file stored on your computer, however, you need a display screen or printer to access the information. Two disadvantages of storing records on paper are that such records take up a great deal of space and they can be easily misfiled.

The best records management system is one in which a mixture of paper and other storage media are used. Records that are vitally important may be stored in more than one medium. Records that must be seen all at once or are signed, legal documents are often stored in paper form. Records that are no longer needed daily but, perhaps, occasionally may be kept in electronic form. Whatever the needs of the office, paper records should be kept to a minimum. Follow these rules:

- Do not be a pack rat. Know what paper to save and what to throw away.
- Do not wait until you are afloat in a sea of paper or have a large number of electronic files to store or organize them. Set aside time for records management in each day.
- Keep a file directory. Maintain a written directory for files.

Paper records should be easily accessible. Topic 9-2 offers an explanation of the various filing systems used for paper records. Chapter 10 covers the equipment you will need for filing. An efficient combination of systems and equipment allows workers to find records easily. For instance, movable filing racks are great for quick access. A numeric filing system may be just right for an office in a clinic with lots of files for patients.

Magnetic Media

Magnetic media are reusable and contain information that is stored electronically. The most frequently used forms of magnetic media are hard computer disks (hard drives), flexible (floppy) disks, flash drives, and tapes. **Hard disks** are metal disks that are magnetized to hold the information put onto them. Most computers have an internal hard disk. External hard disks that connect to a computer with a cable are also available. These disks vary in storage capacity. **Floppy disks** are bendable disks placed inside a hard casing to protect them. They work in the same way as hard disks but hold less information and are less durable. Their main use is portability. Information can be placed on a floppy disk in one computer and transported by that disk to be read or used in another computer. These disks hold from 1.44 megabytes to 120 megabytes of information.

hard disk: a magnetic medium used to store electronic data that can be read by a computer

floppy disk: portable magnetic medium used to store small amounts of computer data

354

CHAPTER 9: RECORDS MANAGEMENT SYSTEMS

A **flash drive** is an external storage device that attaches to a computer. The drive consists of a small printed circuit board encased in a hard plastic covering. These devices are also called pen drives or memory sticks. Storage capacities range from 128 megabytes to several gigabytes. They may be carried in pockets or briefcases or attached to key rings. Flash drives may be used to carry files to another computer or to back up computer data.

flash drive: an external storage device for computer data

Magnetic tape is used for backing up (making a copy of the files on) hard drives and other storage needs. Tape can hold large amounts of information.

magnetic tape: a storage medium for computer and other electronic data

Using magnetic media has both advantages and disadvantages. Four major advantages to the use of magnetic media are:

- Records can be retrieved quickly and easily.
- The storage space required for housing records on magnetic media is much less than that required for paper.
- Records stay in the same order on the magnetic media even after being retrieved several times.
- Records can be organized and updated easily.

Three disadvantages to using magnetic media to store records are:

- An output device such as a monitor or printer is needed to read the records.
- Electrical power surges and failures can erase or change the data recorded on magnetic media.
- Magnetic media require special protection from extreme heat and cold and should be kept away from magnetic fields.

Optical Disks

A CD (compact disk) and a DVD (digital video disk) are optical storage media. Data are put on the disk by laser and read by a drive in the computer. These disks can hold more information than a floppy disk but not

Many records are stored on optical media.

355

Topic 9-1: *Maintaining Office Records*

For Discussion

Ask students to name all of the advantages and disadvantages that they can think of for storing records on optical media.

as much as some hard disks. The biggest advantage of optical disks over magnetic media is their ability to hold large files needed for graphic information, including moving pictures with stereo sound. The disadvantage is that some older computers only have a drive to read CDs or DVDs and cannot write (or save) information to these disks. New computers and stand-alone drives are available that write to CDs and DVDs.

CDs and DVDs should be handled carefully. Keep disks in a protective jacket or case to prevent the surface from being scratched or getting dirty. Scratches or dirt on the surface and warping, which can be caused by extreme heat, may make a disk unreadable.

WORKPLACE CONNECTIONS

When Joyce walked by Ken's workstation, she noticed that several floppy disks and a CD out of its protective jacket were lying on top of the monitor. Ken was working at the computer and seemed unconcerned about the situation:

Joyce: "Ken, did you know you could be destroying all your hard work right now?"

Ken: "What do you mean?"

Joyce: "Floppy disks are sensitive to magnetic forces such as those found in the computer and even the telephone. You should never place them on top of the monitor! And, by leaving the CD out of its jacket you risk scratching it or dropping something on it that will mar the surface and make it unreadable."

Ken: "I guess you're right." (He removes the floppy disks from the top of the monitor and places the CD in its jacket.) "I'd hate to lose everything I just worked on."

microfiche: a small rectangular sheet of microfilm that contains a series of records arranged in rows and columns

Micrographics Systems

Micrographics systems create photographs of documents that are a fraction of their original size and place them on microfilm or **microfiche**. The following steps are involved in the process:

1. Records are gathered so they can be imaged to film. (Chapter 10, Topic 10-2, describes methods of organizing microfilm records for storage.)
2. A special camera is used to take pictures of the hard copy documents.
3. The film is developed. Each record then appears as a tiny picture—a microimage—on the film. A picture of microfilm is shown on page 357.
4. A device called a reader is used to display the microimage for reading. Some readers, referred to as reader/printers, will also print a hard copy of the image.

Microfilm is used when paper or computer files would be less practical. For instance, a car dealer usually will keep parts lists for past-year vehicles on microfiche. Because the list is unchanging, keeping the data on magnetic

Roll microfilm and micro-fiche are used to store records that would be bulky in paper form.

media that can be updated is not necessary. Because the fiche is less bulky, it is easier to store and retrieve than paper records. Libraries often keep back issues of magazines and newspapers on microfilm. Storing rolls of films is much easier and less costly than storing huge stacks of periodicals.

Microforms

You may use different forms of microfilm. Collectively, they are called micro-forms. The most frequently used microforms are described in Figure 9-1.1.

Microforms	Figure **9-1.1**
Roll Microfilm	Available in different widths
	Usually a roll of 16mm or 35mm film that contains a series of images
	The most inexpensive microform
	Used to store records that are not used frequently or do not require changes
Aperture Card	Paper card that holds a piece of microfilm visible through an opening in the card
	Usually contains one microimage from 16mm or 35mm film
	Often used for large-format drawings
	Identifying information can be printed on the card
Microfiche	Small rectangular sheet of microfilm that contains a series of records arranged in rows and columns
	The 6" x 4" size is the most commonly used
	Identifying information appears at the top
	Individual records are more easily located on microfiche than on roll microfilm
Microfilm Jacket	A plastic holder for strips of 16mm or 35mm microfilm
	Strips or single microimages are inserted into sleeves or pockets
	Can be easily updated
	Space at the top of the jacket shows the contents

357

Topic 9-1: *Maintaining Office Records*

FARGO, ND-MOORHEAD, MN   (YELLOW)
CONTRACTORS-GENERAL (CONT) - LUGGAGE REPAIR
PGS. 123-210   FICHE 03 OF 05 03/93 55272

PHONEFICHE

© JEFF GREENBERG/PHOTOEDIT

A microfilm jacket holds strips of microfilm or single microimages.

For Discussion

Ask students for advantages and disadvantages of using microform storage. Advantages include reduced storage space. Disadvantages include the inability to update records in this form.

archive: keep permanently in inactive files

Advantages and Disadvantages of Using Microfilm

Storing records on microfilm has several advantages. These advantages include:

- A microimage takes up less space than a record stored on paper.
- In a microimaging system, the image is viewed but not removed from the film. The microimages are always in the same order on the same microform, regardless of how often the microform is retrieved and filed.
- Hard copies of microimages can be produced on reader/printers when needed.
- Microimaging is an inexpensive way to archive important records. Microimages are usually accepted in courts as legal evidence just as paper records are.
- Retrieval devices available for use with microfilm make it easy to access needed records.
- Microfilm can be easily duplicated and stored in a separate, protected location.

During their break, Mario and Carolyn began discussing the new microimaging system their company had recently begun using:

Mario: "At first, I wasn't sure that microimaging would be helpful. But now, I'm glad we have the system."

Carolyn: "I was looking forward to having our records on microfilm! Our file cabinets were so crowded that I had difficulty just filing and retrieving records."

Mario: "What I've enjoyed is being able to refer to a record without cluttering my workstation with more paper. But if I need a hard copy, I can make one by using the microfilm reader/printer."

Three disadvantages of storing records on microfilm are:

- The initial cost may seem high because a camera, reader/printer(s), and microfilm must be purchased to record information on film.
- Office workers must be given special training so they can operate the microimaging equipment.
- Records stored on microfilm cannot be updated or altered.

Imaging Systems

Imaging is a common method of handling information and the media on which it is kept. An **imaging system** converts all types of documents to **digitized** electronic data that can be read by a computer. The data may be stored on CDs, DVDs, or other media and can be retrieved quickly. Electronic imaging systems include:

imaging system: converts documents to electronic form

digitized: converted to a form that can be read by a computer

- A scanner to convert the paper documents to a digitized electronic form
- A processor that compresses the image
- A storage medium to retain the image
- A retrieval device to convert the image for viewing on a monitor
- A printer for creating hard copy documents

Imaging systems reduce paper processing. They speed up workflow and make files instantly accessible. The best use of imaging is in companies that have a high volume of documents, refer to files often, and require a high level of security for documents.

For Discussion

Both Mario and Carolyn have positive attitudes toward the changes taking place at their company. Ask students how Mario's and Carolyn's attitudes will help them adjust to the new microimaging system.

Teaching Tips

Demonstrate using a scanner to convert a paper document to digital format. Explain that, depending on the way the document is scanned, the resulting electronic document may be an image file or may be a text file that can be edited.

Cost Factors

Costs are involved with any records management system. The costs involve buying equipment and supplies, leasing storage space, and paying office workers to file and retrieve records.

Equipment, Supplies, and Storage

Major equipment purchases such as filing cabinets and shelves, as well as periodic purchases of filing supplies, contribute to the cost of using a records management system. Proper care of equipment and careful use of supplies by employees will help control costs.

When businesses lease office space, they lease by the square foot. The company pays for the space occupied by records every time it writes a rent check. By keeping that space to a minimum, the room available for work is increased. Using microfilm, optical disks, or magnetic media to store records is one way to reduce the amount of space required to house records.

Human Resources

Workers are a key element in an effective records management system. Efficient procedures are worthless unless they are put into practice. Thus, the salaries a company must pay its human resources (workers) to handle records are a cost factor of records management.

Human resources are a cost factor of records management.

© GETTY IMAGES/PHOTODISC

CHAPTER 9: RECORDS MANAGEMENT SYSTEMS

Large companies often have several workers to handle records management. A manager may be in charge of a Records Management Department. The staff may include an analyst, a records center supervisor, and several clerks. Because records management is a field growing in importance, many businesses are looking for workers who specialize in this area. Records management is a major career opportunity.

Destruction Costs

Several costs are associated with destroying records. Paper must be shredded and removed from the business. It should be placed in a landfill in an ecologically sound manner. Some paper records may need to be placed on other media before being destroyed. Storage of those resulting records will be an added expense. Some of the costs can be reduced. Small businesses may use commercial records centers for destruction of records. Companies can hire imaging services if imaging is needed. Large businesses may find it more cost-effective to complete these steps in-house.

Record Life Cycle

Records come from many sources. Some records, such as letters from clients, come from outside the company. Others are created within the company. Examples of these records include memos, records of sales and purchases, reports, and copies of outgoing letters. Records are categorized according to their usefulness and importance.

- **Vital records** are essential to the company. These records are often not replaceable. Examples include original copies of deeds, copyrights, and mortgages.
- **Important records** are needed for the business to operate smoothly. These records would be expensive to replace. Examples include tax returns, personnel files, and cancelled checks.
- **Useful records** are convenient to have but are replaceable. Examples include letters, purchase orders, and the names and addresses of suppliers.
- **Nonessential records** have one-time or very limited usefulness. Examples include meeting announcements and advertisements.

The usefulness of each record has a beginning and an end. Therefore, each record has a life cycle. The phases of the record life cycle are the same regardless of whether the records are kept on paper, magnetic or optical media, or micrographics. Sometimes, however, records will be stored on different types of media at different stages in their life cycle. A paper record might be converted to microfilm before being placed in inactive storage. A record life cycle is shown in Figure 9-1.2 on page 362. Refer to this figure as you read the following brief description of each phase.

1. **Creation or collection.** The cycle begins when you create or collect the records.
2. **Distribution.** During this phase, records are sent to the persons responsible for their use.
3. **Use.** Records are commonly used in decision making, for reference, in answering inquiries, or in satisfying legal requirements.

For Discussion

Discuss examples of each type of record (vital, important, useful, and nonessential) with students.

For Discussion

Ask students to name the phases of the records life cycle. Then ask them what skills an office worker needs in relation to each phase.

4. **Maintenance.** When records are kept for later use, they must be categorized and stored, retrieved as needed, and protected from damage or loss. The exact procedure you use in this phase will vary depending on whether the record is on paper, magnetic media, optical media, or micrographics. You also need to know whether the record should be filed alphabetically, numerically, or chronologically. Each record's value should be reevaluated regularly. Some records may remain in active storage while others are placed in inactive storage.

5. **Disposition.** Records are disposed of either by destroying the records or by moving them to permanent storage, often at less expensive storage sites.

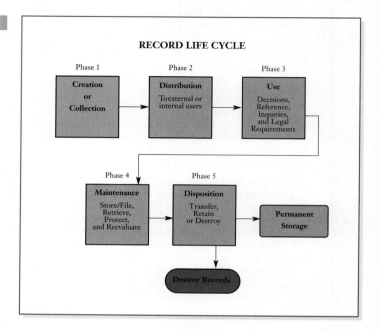

Removing Records from Active Storage

When records are outdated or seldom needed, they should be removed from the active storage area. This transfer will leave more space for active records. An effective records management system will include a policy for such removal.

Retention Schedule

A retention schedule shows how long particular types of records should be kept. An example retention schedule is shown in Figure 9-1.3. The retention schedule includes a description of the type of record. The retention period (how long the record should be kept) is given for each type of record. The retention period may be shown in total years only, or it may be divided into active and inactive storage periods. The authority who decides how long the record should be kept may also be included. Government authority dictates how long certain records, such as tax returns, should be kept. Company managers may set policies for how long to keep other records such as bank statements, expense reports, budgets, and correspondence. Therefore, retention schedules will vary from company to company.

Records Retention Schedule

Record Description	Active Storage Years	Inactive Storage Years	Total Years
ACCOUNTING RECORDS			
Accounts Payable Ledger	3	3	6
Accounts Receivable Ledger	3	3	6
Balance Sheets	3	P	P
Bank Statements	3	3	6
General Ledger Reports	3	P	P

P = Permanent

Figure 9-1.3

Can you determine from this retention schedule how long bank statements must be kept?

Inactive Storage and Commercial Records Centers

Inactive records are those that have value for the company but are not used often. Inactive records should be stored separately from active ones. For example, assume you are required to keep company bank statements for three years. You are not likely to refer often to the past years' statements. Those records can be removed from active storage. Inactive records should not occupy valuable active storage space. Retrieving and filing active records is easier when inactive records are stored in a separate location because you have fewer records to deal with on a regular basis.

Points to Emphasize

A retention schedule outlines how long particular types of records should be kept. Government authorities dictate how long some records must be kept. Company executives decide how long other records will be kept.

Points to Emphasize

Retrieving and filing active records is easier when inactive records are stored in a separate location because you have fewer records to deal with on a regular basis.

363

Many businesses, particularly small ones, store inactive records in commercial records centers. Most of these centers offer a number of services and charge on a unit-cost basis per month. These centers base the unit on a standard-sized box that fits their shelving. Customers are required to use these boxes to make the best use of storage space. Other costs may include pickup and delivery, initial storage, and destruction costs at the end of the record's life cycle.

Special records of historical value are stored apart from active records. An archive is a storage area that is dedicated to organizing and preserving such historical records. These archived records may be in the form of paper, optical media, or microimages.

Disaster Recovery

A disaster is an event that causes serious harm or damage. A disaster recovery plan provides procedures to be followed in case of such an event. Examples of disasters include events such as an earthquake, hurricane, fire, flood, or power outage. Any other situation that results in a partial or total loss of records can be considered a disaster. Plans will vary depending on the needs of the company. The plan should be reviewed periodically and updated as needed.

Many companies provide services designed to aid in disaster recovery. Trained consultants can help create a recovery plan. Secure off-site storage areas and backup locations for the business to use during recovery are examples of these services. At some sites, special below-ground vaults are used to store vital records.

For Discussion

Ask students to describe situations they know about where records have been destroyed due to some type of disaster.

FOCUS ON . . .

Disaster Recovery Plans

The terrorist attacks on the World Trade Center in New York City and destruction caused by hurricane Katrina are extreme examples of the need for disaster recovery plans. Hundreds of offices and records were destroyed in these disasters. Losses have been estimated in billions of dollars.

Every business may not be involved in a major national crisis. However, every business needs a disaster recovery plan. A disaster may be caused by natural events such as a hurricane, tornado, or earthquake. Disasters may be due to fires, computer viruses, bombs, or even human error. Disaster recovery planning can help prepare a business to deal with a crisis situation and to resume normal business operations as soon as possible.

Companies must be concerned about the disaster recovery plans of partners and suppliers. If a partner or supplier cannot operate normally, this situation can have a serious effect on a company. Companies that work closely together may coordinate their plans.

A disaster recovery plan should include steps for prevention, readiness, reaction, and recovery.

- **Prevention** involves taking action to avoid a disaster. For example, antivirus programs can prevent damage to computer data. Buildings can be checked regularly for fire hazards. Important data files can be stored in secure locations to prevent loss. Many companies use off-site records storage to limit data loss.

- **Readiness** is being prepared for a disaster. Companies must try to judge the damage that events may cause and plan to minimize the damage. The plan should be updated and tested regularly. Training for employees on putting the plan into action is an important part of readiness.

- **Reaction** is setting a disaster plan in motion. Companies may move to backup sites when a disaster happens. They may use alternate means of communication such as home e-mail addresses, pagers, and cell phones. Reaction also involves taking steps to begin recovering from the event and to prevent further damage.

- **Recovery** means getting back to normal operations. In the area of records management, recovery involves replacing data lost in a disaster. Computer data may be restored from backup copies. Computers and other office equipment may be repaired or replaced.

Many organizations and companies promote awareness and education about disaster recovery. The Disaster Recovery Institute International has a professional certification program for business continuity/disaster recovery planners.

For Discussion

Why does every business, large or small, need a disaster recovery plan? Name some types of disasters that might destroy a company's records.

Teaching Tips

If the students are using the *Student Activities and Simulations* workbook, instruct them to complete the review activity for this topic.

REVIEWING THE TOPIC

1. Why is an effective records management system vital to the smooth operation of an organization?
2. How does an effective records management system result in greater productivity by office workers?
3. List one advantage and two disadvantages of using paper to store information.
4. What are three frequently used forms of magnetic storage media? What are two frequently used forms of optical storage media?
5. Identify four types of microforms.
6. List four advantages of storing records on microfilm.
7. What are four cost factors that affect the efficiency of a records management system?
8. List the phases of the record life cycle and describe the activities in each phase.
9. What is a retention schedule?
10. What is a disaster recovery plan, and why is it important?

Teaching Tips

After students have composed responses to the alternatives offered, ask them to share their responses with the class.

INTERACTING WITH OTHERS

An important folder is missing from the central files. You discover that someone in your department has signed it out. You go to this person, who is above your level in the company, and he says that he does not have it. The folder is essential for your work. What should you do?

1. Should you confront the higher-ranking person and insist that he give you the file? Why or why not?
2. Should you go to your supervisor and ask her to help resolve the situation? Why or why not?
3. Should you attempt to do your work without the folder and make mistakes because you do not have the information you need? Why or why not?

CHAPTER 9: RECORDS MANAGEMENT SYSTEMS

REINFORCING MATH SKILLS

1. A single file drawer contains 75 folders. Documents from 15 of these folders were converted to micrographic form. The microforms were transferred to inactive storage. Of the remaining active folders, six had their contents divided into two folders each. How many active folders are now in the file drawer? What is the percentage of decrease in the number of folders in the active file?

2. Eight departments have requested additional file folders. Folders are ordered from the supply company in boxes, each containing 25 folders. The number of folders each department needs is shown below. How many folders are required to meet the needs of all the departments? How many boxes of folders should be ordered? How many folders will be left after each department has received the number of folders it requested?

Accounting	21	Production	175
Finance	48	Public Relations	100
Human Resources	99	Marketing	260
Information Systems	125	Customer Service	32

Topic 9-1 : ACTIVITY 1

DATABASE
RECORDS MANAGEMENT

Retention Schedule

Each company creates its own records retention schedule. Your manager has written some notes that you will use to create a records retention schedule for your company. In determining the retention times for each record, she considered how long the records will be used, how frequently the records will be used, the form in which the records will be kept, and laws that pertain to records retention.

1. Create a new database file named *CH09 Retention*. Create a table named **Retention Schedule** to include the following fields: Records Series, Record, Years Active, Years Inactive, and Total Years. Make all fields text fields.

2. Open and print the PDF file *CH09 Retention* found in the data files. This file contains your manager's handwritten notes.

3. Create a record in your database for each type of record listed in your manager's notes. For each record, key the series name in the Record Series field. Key the record description in the Record field. Key numbers in the Years Active, Years Inactive, and Total Years fields or key **P** for Permanent.

4. Sort the records by the Records Series field in ascending order and then by the Record field in ascending order.

5. Create and print a report to show the records retention schedule. Show all fields in the Retention Schedule table in the report. Group the records by records series. Choose **Landscape** orientation. Save the report as **Records Retention Schedule.**

6. Create a query named **Permanent Query** based on the Retention Schedule table. In the query results, show the Record Series, Record, and Total Years fields. Show only records with a *P* in the Total Years field. Sort the results first by the Record Series field and then by the Record field. Print the query results.

WORD PROCESSING

Topic 9-1 | **ACTIVITY 2**

Records Management Job Descriptions

Your supervisor, Ms. Suzuki, asks you to update the records management section of the office manual. She approaches your workstation and says: "Here is my edited draft of the updated material for the office manual. Please prepare a final copy, making the changes I've indicated on the draft. Correct any errors I may have overlooked."

1. Open and print the PDF file *CH09 RM Jobs* from the data files. This file contains the rough draft.

2. Prepare a final copy of the document and print it on plain paper.

Topic 9-2

In Topic 9-1, you learned that each record has a life cycle. In this topic, you will become acquainted with systems for organizing paper files while the records are in the storage phase of the life cycle.

Although many companies use electronic records, paper filing systems are still common. Many companies use both systems. Procedures for organizing magnetic and optical media and microfilm records are presented in Chapter 10.

In a paper filing system, records are stored in folders. These folders are organized alphabetically according to names. Names of individuals, organizations, businesses, subjects, or geographic locations may be used. Files may also be organized by numbers or by dates. As an office worker, you need to understand your company's filing system so that you can file and retrieve records efficiently. You may even have an opportunity to suggest ways to improve the system.

Paper Filing Systems

A filing system requires equipment, procedures, and supplies. You need to understand the various types of each. You also need to understand the use of guides that apply to all of the systems.

Equipment

Various types of cabinets and shelves are used to store paper records. Lateral file cabinets are used in many offices. In this topic, we will assume that all records in your organization are stored in lateral file cabinets. Chapter 10 describes other equipment used in a paper filing system.

Procedures

Before placing records in folders, you should index and code each record. **Indexing** is the process of deciding how to identify each record to be filed—either by name, subject, geographic location, number, or date. **Coding** is the process of marking a record to indicate how it was indexed. As you learned in Topic 9-1, you may retrieve and refile a record many times while it is in active storage. By coding a record, you help ensure that it will be filed correctly each time it is returned to the files. Chapter 10 explains in detail the procedures for indexing and coding.

objectives

- Identify the parts of a paper filing system
- Describe alphabetic filing systems and apply alphabetic indexing rules to arrange records
- Explain how a numeric filing system is organized
- Create an accession log and an alphabetic index for a numeric file
- Arrange records for terminal-digit and middle-digit filing systems
- Explain how a chronologic filing system is organized and arrange records in a tickler file
- Sort records for a geographic file

indexing: deciding how to identify each record to be filed

coding: marking a record to indicate how it was indexed

369

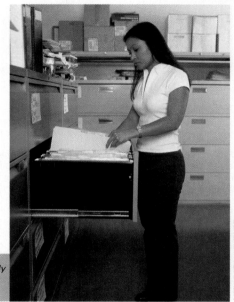

Lateral files are frequently used to store records in offices.

Ask students what kinds of
records might be stored in
lateral files.

For Discussion

Ask students what kinds of
records might be stored in
lateral files.

Teaching Tips

Collect and display samples
of various storage supplies
for paper records—such as file
folders, guides, and labels.
You may wish to take a file
drawer and set it up with the
samples in it organized properly with primary and special
guides and labeled file folders.

Points to Emphasize

No more than ten folders
should be placed behind
one guide to facilitate quick
retrieval of records.

Supplies

Each drawer in a file contains two different kinds of filing supplies: guides and file folders. The guides divide the drawer into sections and serve as signposts for quick reference. They also provide support for the folders and their contents. File folders hold the papers in an upright position in the drawer and serve as containers to keep the papers together. Labels are attached to file folders to identify the contents of each folder. Labels are also attached to file cabinet drawers to identify the contents of each drawer.

Guides

guide: heavy cardboard sheet that creates divisions in a file

caption: notation on a guide, folder, or drawer that indicates the contents

Guides are heavy cardboard sheets that are the same size as the file folders. A tab extends over the top of each guide, and a notation is marked or printed on the tab. This notation is called a **caption**. By reading the captions, you can quickly identify divisions within the file. For example, a guide may carry the caption A, which tells you that only records starting with the letter A are found between that guide and the next one.

Guides are classified as primary or special. Primary guides indicate the major divisions, such as letters of the alphabet, into which the filing system is separated. Special guides indicate subdivisions within these major divisions. Figure 9-2.4 on page 374 shows how primary and special guides are arranged in an alphabetic filing system. Behind primary guide C is a special guide, *Cooper Temporaries*. For quick retrieval of files, place no more than 10 folders behind a guide and place only about 15 to 25 guides in a file drawer.

Labels

Labels are strips of paper, usually self-adhesive, that are attached to file drawers or folders. The label has a caption that identifies the contents as shown in Figure 9-2.1. You need labels on file drawers so that you can identify the contents of each drawer without opening it. The drawer label should be specific, easy to read, and current. When the contents of a cabinet are changed in any way, the drawer label should be corrected immediately.

label: strip of paper attached to a file drawer or folder with a caption identifying the contents

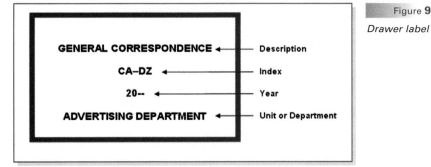

Figure **9-2.1**

Drawer label

Folder labels are attached to the folder tabs as shown in Figure 9-2.2. The caption on the label identifies the contents of the folder. The captions should be placed in a consistent manner, usually at the top, left-hand corner of the label. Labels come in standard sizes to match various tab sizes for folders. Some word processing programs have templates or other special features to format a document for these standard label sizes. Using these special features makes creating and printing labels easy. Many companies use color-coded labels to improve filing accuracy. For example, a different color might be used for each alphabetic section of the files.

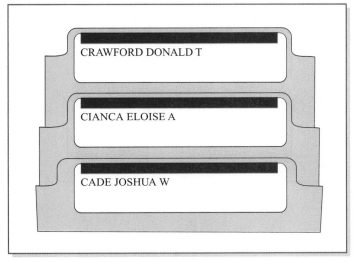

Figure **9-2.2**

Folder labels

371

Folders

folder: a durable container used to hold papers in a file

A **folder** is a container made of strong, durable paper called manila and used to hold papers in a file. Each folder is larger than the papers it contains so that it will protect the contents. Standard folder sizes are designed for papers that are $8\frac{1}{2}'' \times 11''$, $8\frac{1}{2}'' \times 13''$, or $8\frac{1}{2}'' \times 14''$.

Folder cuts are made in the back of a folder, which is higher than the front, to create a tab. Labels with captions are attached to the tabs to identify the contents. Folder tabs vary in width and position, as shown in Figure 9-2.3. Sometimes the tab is the full width of the folder. This is called a full-cut or straight-cut folder. Half-cut tabs are half the width of the folder and have two possible positions. Third-cut folders have three positions, each tab occupying a third of the width of the folder. Another standard tab has five positions and is called a fifth-cut folder. Some folders hang from metal frames placed inside the file drawer. Removable tabs can be attached to these folders at appropriate positions.

Costs

The costs related to paper filing are for items such as paper, folders, labels, and storage containers. Computers used for printing documents and printing supplies also add to the cost. The largest budget item is often for active files. The cost is ongoing because new files are added to the system regularly. New paper supplies and equipment such as storage cabinets must be purchased periodically.

Figure 9-2.3

Folder tabs vary in width and position.

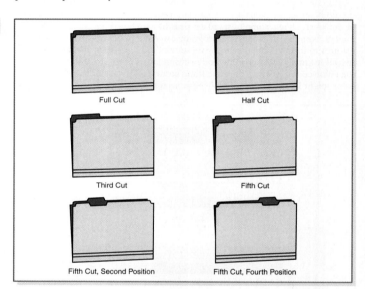

Full Cut   Half Cut

Third Cut   Fifth Cut

Fifth Cut, Second Position   Fifth Cut, Fourth Position

CHAPTER 9: RECORDS MANAGEMENT SYSTEMS

Position of Guides and Folders

A variety of filing systems are used in offices today. The positioning of guides and folders within filing systems will vary from office to office. Regardless of the system used, the guides and folders should be arranged so they are easy to see and in a logical order. You can see that the arrangement in Figure 9-2.4 on page 374 allows your eye to move easily from left to right.

Guides

When you open a file drawer to store or retrieve a document, look first for the appropriate primary guide. Because English is read from left to right, the tab on the primary guide should be at the far left, where it will be easy to locate.

Special guides are used to pinpoint the location of an individual folder. In Figure 9-2.4, special guides are located in the third position. For example, the special guide *Dorcey Electronics* was added because of frequent requests for the Dorcey Electronics folder. Using the special guide, this folder can easily be located. Sometimes a special guide is used to pinpoint the location of a series of folders relating to a specific subject. In Figure 9-2.6, on page 377, for example, the special guide *Film* marks the location of two individual folders relating to that subject.

Folders

A general folder is used for each primary guide. This general folder tab is placed in the second position and bears the same caption as the one shown on the primary guide. For example, the general folder that goes behind the primary guide *C* also will bear the caption *C*. These folders are given the name general because they are used to store records that do not justify the use of an individual folder. When you have five or more records relating to one name or subject, prepare an individual folder for those records.

Using individual folders helps you locate records more quickly. In Figure 9-2.4, individual folders are shown in the combined fourth/fifth position. Notice the width of the tabs on the individual folders. This extra width allows ample space for labeling personal, company, or subject names.

Alphabetic Filing Systems

In an **alphabetic file**, records are arranged and stored according to the letters of the alphabet. Letters and words are used as captions on the guides and folders. These words may be names, subjects, or geographic locations. Both guides and folders are arranged in alphabetic order according to the captions. ARMA International, an association for records management professionals, recommends standard filing rules. The alphabetic indexing rules shown in Figure 9-2.5 on pages 375 and 376 are written to agree with the ARMA International standards.

alphabetic file: records arranged and stored according to the letters of the alphabet

Points to Emphasize

The positioning of guides and folders within filing systems will vary from office to office. Regardless of the system used, the guides and folders should be arranged so that they are easy to see and are in a logical order.

Challenge Option

To give students practical experience with records management systems, ask them to establish a filing system for their personal records. Students will gain experience determining appropriate label captions and folder cuts for their records. You may wish to have on hand used folders, with the labels removed, in various cuts for students who cannot afford to purchase their own.

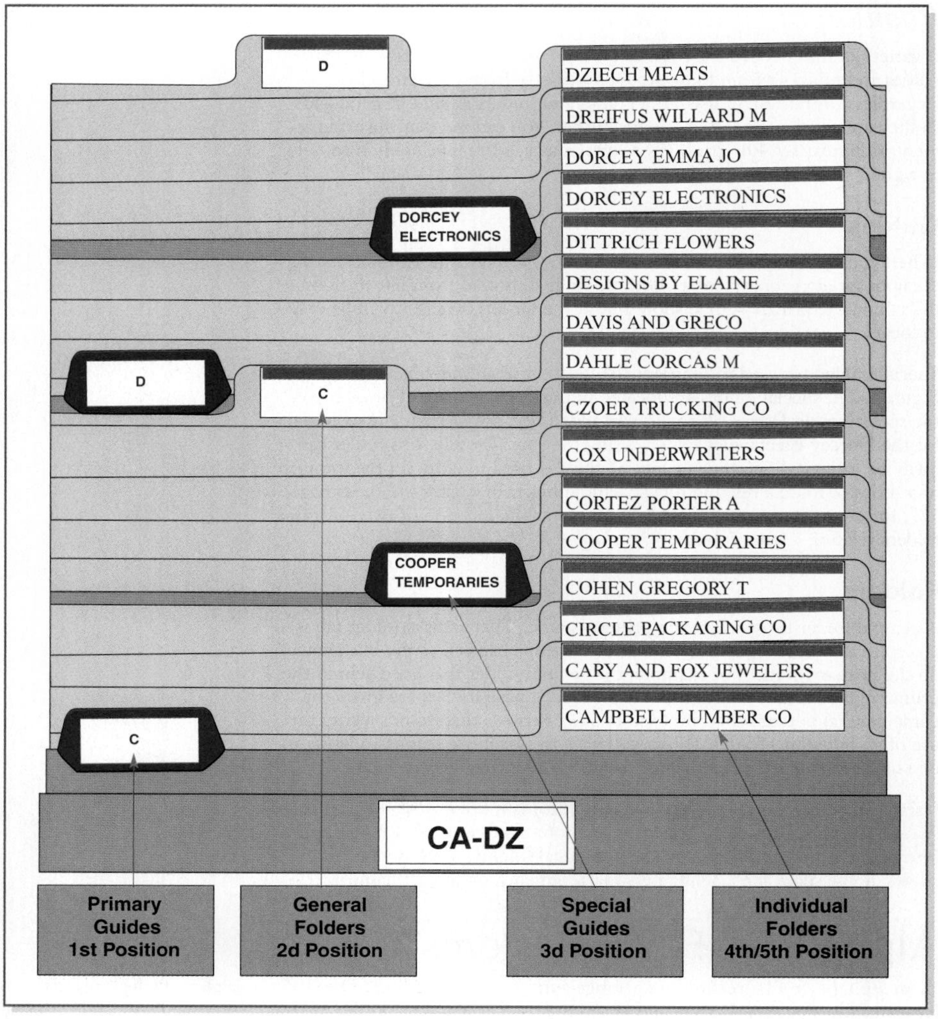
D
DZIECH MEATS
DREIFUS WILLARD M
DORCEY EMMA JO
DORCEY ELECTRONICS
DORCEY ELECTRONICS
DITTRICH FLOWERS
DESIGNS BY ELAINE
DAVIS AND GRECO
DAHLE CORCAS M
D
C
CZOER TRUCKING CO
COX UNDERWRITERS
CORTEZ PORTER A
COOPER TEMPORARIES
COOPER TEMPORARIES
COHEN GREGORY T
CIRCLE PACKAGING CO
CARY AND FOX JEWELERS
C
CAMPBELL LUMBER CO
CA-DZ
Primary Guides 1st Position
General Folders 2d Position
Special Guides 3d Position
Individual Folders 4th/5th Position

Figure **9-2.4**

Note the position of guides and folders in this portion of a name file.

Common alphabetic filing systems use names, subjects, or geographic locations. Many offices do not have enough file space for separate name and subject files. When this is true for your office, you may file name and subject folders together.

Filing by Name

If a name file is used, records are indexed according to the name of an individual or organization. The folders are arranged in alphabetic order within the file drawer. Figure 9-2.4 shows how alphabetic primary and special

Supplemental Activity

Compare retrieving records filed by name to finding names and phone numbers in a phone book. Provide each student with a telephone directory or with pages extracted from one. (Outdated directories can be used.) Give students a sheet with 20 names of local residents and/or businesses and ask them to record telephone numbers for each name. Have students raise their hands when they have all numbers recorded. Note the accuracy of the responses recorded.

Figure **9-2.5**

Alphabetic indexing rules

Rule 1 Indexing Order of Names

In a personal name, the surname (last name) is the first unit, the given name (first name) or initial is the second unit, and the middle name or initial is the third unit. Business names are indexed as written using letterheads or trademarks as guides. Each word in a business name is considered a separate indexing unit.

Rule 2 Minor Words and Symbols in Business Names

Articles, prepositions, conjunctions, and symbols are considered separate indexing units. Symbols are considered spelled in full. When the word *the* appears as the first word of a business name, it is consider the last indexing unit.

Rule 3 Punctuation and Possessives

All punctuation is disregarded when indexing personal and business names.

Rule 4 Single Letters and Abbreviations

Initials in personal names are separate indexing units. Abbreviations of personal names and nicknames are indexed as they are written. Single letters in business and organization names are indexed as written. If single letters are separated by spaces, index each letter as a separate unit. An acronym (such as AAA or FASB) is indexed as one unit regardless of spacing. Abbreviated words (Corp., Inc.) and names are indexed as one unit. Radio and television station call letters are indexed as one unit.

Rule 5 Titles and Suffixes

In personal names, a title before a name (Mrs., Dr.), a seniority suffix (II, III, Jr., Sr.) or a professional suffix (M.D., Mayor) after a name is the last indexing unit. Numeric suffixes are filed before alphabetic suffixes. If a name contains both a title and a suffix, the title is the last unit. Royal and religious titles followed by either a given name only or a surname only (Father Leo, Princess Anne) are indexed as written. Titles in business names are indexed as written.

Rule 6 Prefixes—Articles and Particles

A foreign article or particle (Mac, St., San, De, Von der) in a personal or business name is combined with the part of the name following it to form a single indexing unit. Spaces in the prefix or between the prefix and the name are disregarded.

Rule 7 Numbers in Business Names

Numbers spelled out (Seven Acres Inn) in business names are filed alphabetically. Numbers written in digits are filed in ascending order before alphabetic letters or words (7 Acres Inn comes before Seven Acres Inn). Arabic numerals (2, 3) are filed before Roman numerals (II, IV). Names with inclusive numbers (33–37 Apartments) are filed by the first digits only (33 Apartments). For numbers containing *st, d,* and *th* (1st, 2d, 4th), ignore the letter endings and consider only the digits.

Points to Emphasize

The alphabetic indexing rules presented in Figure 9-2.5 reflect the guidelines published by ARMA International. Refer to these rules while reading the text and completing certain end-of-topic and end-of-chapter activities. If the students are using the *Student Activities and Simulations* workbook, instruct them to refer to Reference Guide Section F to see examples of each rule.

Figure **9-2.5**

*Alphabetic indexing
rules continued*

Rule 8 Organizations and Institutions

Banks and other financial institutions, clubs, colleges, hospitals, hotels, magazines, motels, museums, newspapers, religious institutions, schools, unions, universities, and other organizations are indexed and filed according to the names written on their letterheads.

Rule 9 Identical Names

When personal names or names of businesses or organizations are identical, filing order is determined by the address. Compare the addresses in this order: city names, state or province names, street names (including Avenue, Boulevard, Drive, Road, or Street), house or building numbers.

Rule 10 Government Names

Government names are indexed first by the name of the governmental unit—country, state, county, or city. For example, the first indexing unit of a United States government agency name is *UNITED STATES GOVERNMENT.* Next, index the name of the department, bureau, office, or board. Rearrange the units, if necessary, so the more distinctive parts come first. For example, the name *Dept. of Public Safety, Baltimore, Maryland* would be indexed in five units: *MARYLAND, PUBLIC, SAFETY, DEPT, OF.*

To see examples of each rule, refer to *Reference Guide Section F* in the *Student Activities and Simulations* workbook.

guides are used in a name file to help you file and retrieve records efficiently. If you were looking for a folder labeled *Emma Jo Dorsey,* you would find the primary guide *D* and search for the individual folder for Emma Jo Dorsey. By using the guides, you should be able to locate the folder quickly without having to thumb through all the folders. If you do not find an individual folder for the record, file the record in the appropriate general folder.

WORKPLACE CONNECTIONS

Employees must understand proper filing procedures in order to store records in the correct folders and ensure that the records can be found later.

Carrie: "Roy, there is no folder labeled Dalton Real Estate in the file. Where do I file this letter?"

Roy: "If there is no individual folder for Dalton Real Estate, file it in the general folder behind the D guide. When we have several more letters to or from Dalton Real Estate, we'll set up an individual folder for those records."

Filing by Subject

When a **subject filing** system is used, records are arranged according to particular subjects. Marketing, office machines, and public relations are examples of topics that might be used. A subject file is used when records are requested by their contents more often than by the names of individuals or companies. Subject titles are used as captions for primary guides. In Figure 9-2.6, you can see that the primary guides are *Advertisers*, *Applications*, and *Audiovisual Equipment*.

subject file: records arranged by topic

Supplemental Activity

Have students develop the captions for a subject file you might maintain in the classroom that would be available to both the teachers and students.

For Discussion

Ask students to name the primary guides and the special guides in Figure 9-2.6. Ask them what information is included on the individual folders behind the primary guides and on those behind the special guides.

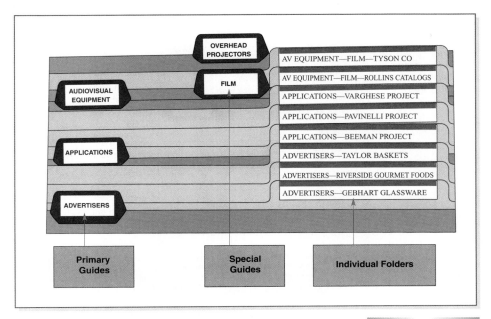

OVERHEAD PROJECTORS

FILM

AUDIOVISUAL EQUIPMENT

APPLICATIONS

ADVERTISERS

AV EQUIPMENT—FILM—TYSON CO
AV EQUIPMENT—FILM—ROLLINS CATALOGS
APPLICATIONS—VARGHESE PROJECT
APPLICATIONS—PAVINELLI PROJECT
APPLICATIONS—BEEMAN PROJECT
ADVERTISERS—TAYLOR BASKETS
ADVERTISERS—RIVERSIDE GOURMET FOODS
ADVERTISERS—GEBHART GLASSWARE

Primary Guides   **Special Guides**   **Individual Folders**

Figure 9-2.6

In subject files, the special guides identify subdivisions of the main subjects.

You may use special guides to identify subdivisions within the main subjects. In Figure 9-2.6, the main subject *Audiovisual Equipment* is divided by special guides into subdivisions of *Film* and *Overhead Projectors*. You may use names, geographic locations, numbers, or subjects as captions for special guides.

As you can see in Figure 9-2.6, the label for an individual folder behind a primary guide includes the primary guide caption (*Advertisers*, for example) and the caption for the folder (*Gebhart Glassware*, for example). The label for an individual folder behind a special guide should include:

- The primary guide caption (*AV Equipment*, for example, and note that you may abbreviate *Audiovisual* as *AV*)
- The special guide caption (*Film*, for example)
- The caption for the folder (*Rollins Catalogs*, for example)

377

Topic 9-2: *Paper Records Systems*

Expand the Concept

Ask students how a real estate agency might maintain files on properties for sale, how such a file might be organized, and why it might be useful.

For Discussion

Ask the students the names and positions of the guides and folders shown in Figure 9-2.7. Ask them to explain the components of the system.

Filing by Geographic Location

geographic file: records arranged according to locations

In a **geographic file**, records are stored according to locations. The file may use sales territories, states, or cities in a single state, for instance, as divisions. Typical users of geographic filing are publishing houses, mail-order houses, radio and television advertisers, and real estate firms. Organizations dealing with a large number of small businesses scattered over a wide area may also use this type of file. Refer to Figure 9-2.7 as you read about the parts of a geographic filing system.

Figure 9-2.7

In a geographic file, the primary guides identify the largest geographic locations within the file.

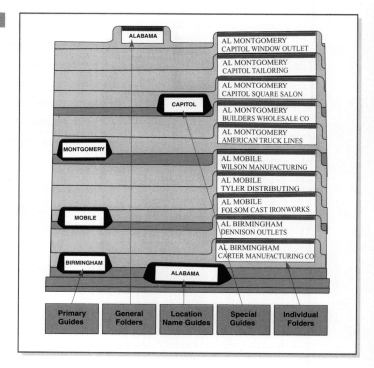

Guides and Folders

The main divisions used in a geographic file, such as states or countries, are placed on guides in the front of the file drawers. These divisions are sometimes called the *key units*. The primary guides in a geographic file are named for the largest divisions below the level of the key units. For example, in Figure 9-2.7, the primary guides are based on cities. The key unit (*Alabama*) appears on a guide placed in the center front of the file. The special guide (*Capitol*) is used to pinpoint the location of several individual folders.

A general folder is placed behind each location name guide. In the figure, the general folder and the location name guide bear the same caption (*Alabama*). When you prepare labels for individual folders, give the location on the first line (*AL Birmingham*, for example). On the second line, indicate the caption for the individual folder (*Carter Manufacturing Co*, for example). These complete labels tell you behind which primary and special guide to refile the folder.

Alphabetic Index

To retrieve a record in a geographic file, you must know the geographic location of each person or company. Because you may not remember all this information, you will need an alphabetic index. This index can be in a computer database or a printed list. The index is arranged according to the names in the file. The record for each organization or individual shows the geographic location under which records are filed.

WORKPLACE CONNECTIONS

The firm where Carlota Diaz works uses a geographic filing system based on states. This morning, her supervisor needed a record pertaining to Wonderland Toy Company. To retrieve the record, Carlota first checked the alphabetic index file. She learned the toy company was located in Richmond, Virginia. She scanned the drawer labels and opened the drawer labeled *Virginia*. She then searched through the primary guides until she came to the city of Richmond. Then locating the folder for Wonderland Toy Company was easy. Carlota's supervisor appreciated her ability to locate the record so quickly.

Numeric Filing Systems

In a **numeric file**, records are stored by number. Files arranged in simple numeric order use a consecutive numbering method. Other numbering methods, such as terminal-digit or middle-digit, are discussed later in this topic.

The numeric method of filing is often used when records are already arranged in numeric order. For example, insurance companies may arrange their records according to policy number. Utility companies often identify records by customer account number. Some companies file records by number even though they are not already numbered before the filing process. For example, a number may be assigned to each name or subject in a file. The caption on the individual folder would then be a number (for example, *3877* for *Global Security Systems* or *8551* for *West Coast Development Project*) rather than a name or a subject.

numeric file: records arranged by numbers

Points to Emphasize

An alphabetic index is needed to retrieve records in a geographic file. The index may be kept in a computer database.

Teaching Tips

Have students ask a parent, guardian, or family friend how paper records are organized at her or his place of business (alphabetically, numerically, or chronologically). Ask students to volunteer to share findings with the class. This activity will help students gain practical knowledge of paper records systems.

Guides

The guide captions in a numeric system are numbers instead of letters or words. Look at the consecutive numeric file shown in Figure 9-2.8. Notice how the numbered special guides highlight divisions within the primary guide category. Special guides help you retrieve records quickly.

Figure **9-2.8**

Insurance companies may arrange records by policy number using a numeric file.

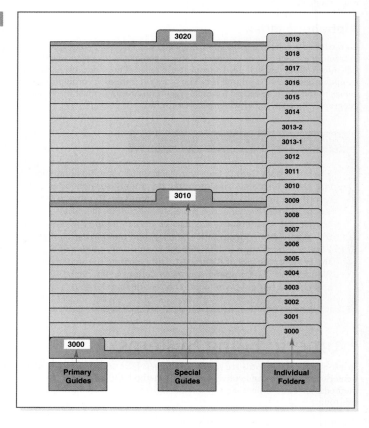

Individual Folders

In a numeric filing system, the caption on an individual folder is the number assigned to the person or organization whose records will be placed in the folder. An advantage to a numeric system is that it helps you keep records confidential. Scanning the numeric captions on folders will not tell a casual observer much about the contents.

CHAPTER 9: RECORDS MANAGEMENT SYSTEMS

Accession Log

To set up an individual folder, you first refer to an accession log, also called an accession file, book, or record. An accession log lists in numeric order the numbers already assigned. It also shows the name or subject related to each number. In Figure 9-2.9, you can see that the last number, 3877, was assigned to Global Security Systems. The next number you assign will be 3878. By keeping an accession log, you avoid assigning the same number to more than one name or subject. Such a log might be written by hand in some offices. In other offices, the accession log is kept using a computer database. Using a computer database allows you search for entries easily, either by number or by name.

accession log: list of numbers assigned in a numeric filing system

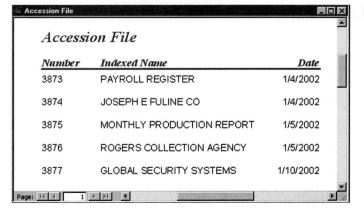

Figure **9-2.9**

This database accession log shows the number assigned to each name or subject in the file.

General Alphabetic File

In a numeric system, a general folder is not included behind each numeric guide. Instead, a separate alphabetic general file is used. Records that do not have an individual numeric folder are filed in the general alphabetic file by name or subject. When enough records related to one name or subject are collected, an individual numeric folder is created for that name or subject.

WORKPLACE CONNECTIONS

Today is Carlos's first day of work. Mimi Yung, Carlos's supervisor, briefed him on the filing system they use:

Carlos, the records in our department are confidential. We use a numeric filing system so that unauthorized people cannot locate specific records easily. To keep these files secure, we have a policy that allows only workers in our department to have access to the alphabetic index and the accession file.

Thinking Critically

Ask students to explain why it is necessary to keep an accession log. Have the students suggest problems that might arise if such a book were not kept or not used every time a file was created?

Points to Emphasize

In a numeric system, you do not provide a general folder behind each numeric guide. Instead, you maintain a separate alphabetic general file.

381

Topic 9-2: *Paper Records Systems*

A numeric file must have an alphabetic index. An alphabetic index is a list showing each name or subject in the file and the number or code assigned to it. When you must retrieve a record, you refer to the alphabetic index to learn the correct file folder number. If the accession log is kept in a computer database, this database can be searched by name. This file eliminates the need for a separate alphabetic index file. For records filed in the general alphabetic file, a *G* is entered in the number field. The letter indicates that the record is in the general alphabetic file. Fields can be included in the database for information such as mailing address and telephone number.

Figure **9-2.10**

A G *indicates that a record is stored in the general alphabetic file.*

Alphabetic Index	
Indexed Name	**Number**
ASPEN TILE COMPANY	3871
BLUMENTHAL ROSS A	G
CANYON CLEANERS	3872
CENTREX SYSTEMS	G
GLOBAL SECURITY SYSTEMS	3877
JOSEPH E FULINE CO	3874
MONTHLY PRODUCTION REPORT	3875
PAYROLL REGISTER	3873
ROGERS COLLECTION AGENCY	3876

Terminal-Digit and Middle-Digit Filing Systems

Sometimes in a numeric filing system numbers can be quite long. A social security number, for instance, is nine digits. Some insurance policy numbers might be fifteen or more digits. To improve the accuracy of filing in numeric filing systems, terminal-digit or middle-digit numbering methods are often used.

Terminal-Digit Filing

Terminal-digit filing is a kind of numeric filing in which the last two or three digits of each record number serve as the primary division under which a record is filed. Numbers are assigned consecutively, just as in numeric filing. However, they are read from *right to left* in small groups beginning with the terminal (final) group of numbers.

Record numbers are divided into three groups of two or three digits each. If numbers have too few digits for three equal groups, zeros are added to the *left* of each number. These groups of digits are called primary, secondary, and tertiary (third). The right (terminal) group of digits is primary, the middle group is secondary, and the left group is tertiary. The primary number (right group) is used as the number of the file section, drawer, or shelf. The secondary number (middle group) is used for the guide. The tertiary number (left group) is the folder/record number. Just as in regular numeric filing, an alphabetic index file is used.

382

CHAPTER 9: RECORDS MANAGEMENT SYSTEMS

Middle-Digit Filing

Middle-digit filing is a method of numeric filing in which the middle two or three digits of each record number are used as the primary division under which each record is filed. Numbers are assigned consecutively; however, for filing, numbers are read from *middle to left to right.*

Just as in terminal-digit filing, groups of digits are identified as primary, secondary, or tertiary. In this system, the middle group is primary, the left group is secondary, and the right group is tertiary. Drawer, file, or shelf numbers are from the primary (middle) group. Guide numbers are from the secondary (left) group. Folder numbers are from the tertiary (right) group. As in other types of numeric filing, an alphabetic index file is used.

Chronologic Filing Systems

In a **chronologic file**, records are filed according to date. Chronologic files can help you keep track of tasks you need to complete each day. A desk calendar and a tickler file are two kinds of chronologic files used for this purpose.

chronologic file: records arranged according to date

You may also use chronologic filing in combination with name, subject, geographic, or numeric systems. In these situations, individual folders are all coded in the normal way of that system. However, records within the individual folder are organized by date. Usually the most recent document is placed at the front of the folder.

Points to Emphasize

In middle-digit filing, numbers are assigned consecutively; however, they are read from middle to left to right.

Points to Emphasize

A tickler file, which students studied previously in Chapter 7, is a type of chronologic file. (Students will create a tickler file using invoice payment dates in Chapter 9 Activity 1.)

Topic Review 9-2

REVIEWING THE TOPIC

1. What are the three parts of a filing system?
2. What is the difference between indexing a record and coding a record?
3. Why are guides used in a filing system?
4. Describe an advantage of using color-coded labels.
5. Where should the tabs on primary guides be located? Why?
6. Name three frequently used alphabetic filing systems.
7. Why do you need an alphabetic index file in a geographic or numeric filing system?
8. What is an accession log or file? Why is it necessary to use an accession log?
9. In what direction are the numbers read in a terminal-digit filing system? In a middle-digit filing system?
10. When would you most often use a chronologic file?

THINKING CRITICALLY

For three months you have worked in the office of Davis Rider, Inc. a company with 12 employees. When you began the job, your supervisor, Ms. Davis, told you that you would be generally in charge of the files as well as having other duties. Although everyone has access to the files, she explained that you need to make sure the files are neat and that materials do not stack up.

Although the task seemed simple when Ms. Davis explained it to you, it has become a source of frustration. Some employees remove records and do not return them for several weeks. Other employees open file drawers and place folders on top of the other folders instead of inserting them in their proper places. Needless to say, the files are not being managed well. Because you are generally in charge of the files, you are being held accountable for the situation.

1. What steps could you take regarding your own work habits to help correct this problem?
2. What steps could you ask others to take to help correct this problem?

REINFORCING ENGLISH SKILLS

Using *it's* and *its* incorrectly is a common writing mistake. *It's* is a contraction of *it* and *is* or *has*. *Its* is a possessive pronoun. To help you know which term to use, ask yourself: "Could I substitute the words 'it is' or 'it has' in the sentence and have it make sense?" If you can, use *it's*; if not, use *its*. Key or write the following eight sentences, inserting either *it's* or *its*, whichever is appropriate.

1. You need to put the folder back in ____ place.
2. ____ time to remove the inactive files from active storage.
3. He replied, " ___ necessary to charge out each record."
4. This folder has lost ____ label.
5. ____ been returned to the files.
6. Please let me know when ____ ready.
7. The company improved ____ image.
8. ____ on the top shelf of the bookcase.

Topic 9-2 : ACTIVITY 1

Accession Log and Alphabetic Index

DATABASE
RECORDS MANAGEMENT

You work for Philips Associates, a company in Miami, Florida. To help keep the records confidential, a numeric filing system is used. You have been asked to create a database file to serve as both an accession log and an alphabetic index.

1. Open the *Access* file *CH09 Files Index* from the data files. This file contains information about the names of people and organizations in a numeric file.

2. Open the Names List table. The personal and company names, along with addresses and telephone numbers, have already been entered in the table. In the Indexed Name field, key the name as it would be indexed for filing on a paper record. (Review the alphabetic indexing rules in Figure 9-2.5 on pages 375 and 376.)

3. Create a query using the Names List table. Include only the Number and Indexed Name fields. Sort the data in the report by the Number field in descending order. In the Criteria row for the Number field, key **Not G.** Save the query using the name **Accession Log** and print the query results table. What number will be assigned to the next company or business for which an individual numeric folder is created?

385

Topic Review

Teaching Tips

After students write the sentences, give them the correct answers.

Teaching Tips

Remind students to refer to Figure 9-2.5 in the textbook or Reference Guide Section F in the *Student Activities and Simulations* workbook if they have questions about how to index names. Review the purpose of an accession log, an alphabetic index, and a general alphabetic file in a numeric filing system.

4. Create a report named **Alphabetic Index** using the Names List table. Include only the Indexed Name and Number fields. Sort the data in the report in ascending order by the Indexed Name field. Adjust the format as needed for an attractive report and print the report.

5. Create a query named **General File** using the Names List table. The query results should show the Indexed Name and Number fields for all the people or companies whose records should be stored in the general alphabetic file. Sort the names in alphabetic order. Print the query results.

6. Keep this database for use in a later activity.

Expand the Concept

Discuss with students how record numbers that are to be sorted in terminal-digit or middle-digit order might be entered in a database. For example, each part (group of digits) of the number might be stored in a separate field to facilitate sorting.

RECORDS MANAGEMENT

Topic **9-2**   ACTIVITY 2

Numeric Filing

Numeric filing systems are widely used in businesses. Practice your numeric filing skills in this activity.

1. List the 16 numbers below, arranging them in order for a consecutive numeric filing system. Ignore the spaces in the numbers for this step.

2. List the 16 numbers below, arranging them in order for a terminal-digit numeric filing system. Spaces in the numbers indicate the number groups.

3. List the 16 numbers below, arranging them in order for a middle-digit numeric filing system. Spaces in the numbers indicate the number groups.

786	67	1258	231	55	2187
303	99	2891	189	40	2891
947	28	6314	287	29	6314
502	64	9284	502	64	9485
786	67	1269	287	40	2756
303	89	2977	647	28	6325
502	63	8922	287	29	2341
946	40	2891	303	52	2977

CHAPTER REVIEW 9

Summary

In this chapter, you learned about the equipment, procedures, and supplies used in paper filing systems. As an office worker, you will probably be involved in some aspect of records management. Review the following key points from this chapter:

- A records management system is used to organize, store, retrieve, remove, and dispose of records.
- You may be called on to manage records on various media such as paper, magnetic or optical disks, and microfilm. Storage equipment and supplies should be chosen with specific storage media in mind.
- Removing a record from the files and noting information about the record is called charging out.
- Microimaging systems reduce documents to photos a fraction of their original size to fit on microfilm.
- An imaging system converts documents to electronic data that can be read by a computer.
- Costs are involved with managing records. These costs may include buying equipment and supplies, leasing storage space, and paying office workers to file and retrieve records.
- Records are categorized as vital, important, useful, or nonessential.
- The phases of the record life cycle include creation or collection, distribution, use, maintenance, and disposition.
- A retention schedule identifies how long types of records should be kept.
- A disaster recovery plan provides procedures to be followed in case of an event that results in a partial or total loss of records.
- In a paper filing system, records are stored in folders. These folders are labeled and organized according to a records management system.
- Records can be organized alphabetically by name, by subject, or by geographic location. Records can also be organized using numbers or dates.
- An accession log lists in numeric order the numbers already assigned and the name or subject related to each number.
- An alphabetic index is a list showing each name or subject in the file and its corresponding number, code, or geographic identifier used for filing.

Teaching Tips

Have students review the key terms by using the Flashcards available on *The Office* Web site.

Teaching Tips

Explain to students how to calculate the payment date for invoices. A common mistake in this process is counting the invoice date instead of beginning with the next day. Remind students to refer to Figure 9-2.5 in the textbook or Reference Guide Section F in the *Student Activities and Simulations* workbook if they have questions about how to index names.

Key Terms

accession log	floppy disk	medium or media
alphabetic file	folder	microfiche
archive	geographic file	micrographics
caption	guide	numeric file
charging out	hard disk	record
chronologic file	imaging system	records disposition
coding	indexing	records management
digitized	label	system
filing	magnetic media	retention schedule
flash drive	magnetic tape	subject file

RECORDS MANAGEMENT

Chapter 9 ACTIVITY 1

Tickler File

You work in the Accounts Payable Department in a small company. One of your duties is to determine payment dates for invoices to take advantage of discounts offered by vendors. You then file the invoices by payment date in a tickler file. You check the tickler file each day to see what invoices should be paid in the next couple of days. This ensures that payments are made within the discount periods and saves money for the company.

1. Determine the payment dates for each invoice shown on page 389 according to terms given. For example, terms *2/10, net 30* mean that a 2 percent discount may be taken if the invoice is paid within 10 calendar days of the invoice date. If the invoice is dated June 1, the payment date would be June 11. Terms *net 30* mean no discount is available, and the invoice should be paid in 30 days.

2. Determine the filing order of the invoices, arranging the invoices chronologically by payment date. If more than one invoice has the same payment date, arrange them alphabetically by company name. Refer to the alphabetic indexing rules in Figure 9-2.5 on pages 375 and 376.

3. For checking purposes, indicate the order of the invoices by listing their item numbers.

388

CHAPTER 9: RECORDS MANAGEMENT SYSTEMS

ITEM	COMPANY NAME	INVOICE DATE	TERMS
1.	Centrex Systems	May 18	2/10, net 30
2.	James Office Supply	June 6	1/10, net 30
3.	Frank Brothers, Inc.	May 22	1/10, net 30
4.	Caldwell Industries	July 2	2/10, net 30
5.	Baker and Sons	June 9	1/10, net 30
6.	Rodriguez and Parker	June 9	net 30
7.	Ralston, Inc.	July 2	1/10, net 30
8.	Ace Plumbing	May 18	2/10, net 30
9.	5 Star Producers	July 2	1/10, net 30
10.	Paragon Cable	June 6	2/10, net 30
11.	All State Products	May 18	net 30
12.	Freedom Motors	May 2	net 30
13.	Franklin Associates	May 22	1/10, net 30
14.	Rodgers Design	June 30	1/10, net 30
15.	Bakersfield Market	May 20	net 30

Chapter 9 ⋮ ACTIVITY 2

DATABASE
RECORDS MANAGEMENT

Sorting Records Geographically

Businesses such as publishers, mail-order houses, radio and television advertisers, and real estate agencies often file records geographically. Practice sorting records geographically in this activity.

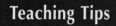

1. Open the database *CH09 Files Index* that you edited in Topic 9-2 Activity 1, which contains records for Philips Associates.

2. Create a query named **Geographic Index** using the Names List table. Show the City and Indexed Name fields in the query results. Sort the records first by city and then by indexed name in ascending order. Print the query results table.

Teaching Tips

Review how to create an *Access* query and how to sort records in a query by two fields.

Supplemental Activity

Have students complete the Chapter 9 Supplemental Activity, Folder Labels, available on *The Office* Web site.

Assessment

Assess student learning using the Chapter 9 test available on the *IRCD* and in *ExamView®* format.

© GETTY IMAGES/PHOTODISC

CHAPTER 10

Managing Records

Office records are stored on a variety of media. These media have different storage requirements. For example, magnetic media must be protected from magnetic sources that could erase or change the stored data. Equipment and supplies specially designed to protect magnetic media should be used. Storage equipment and supplies also are available for microforms as well as for paper records. All records that relate to a particular topic are often stored together. For example, a CD that contains a report and the paper copy of the report may be placed in a folder together.

This chapter describes the procedures, equipment, and supplies available to help you manage various forms of records efficiently. Because copies of paper records are often needed, reprographics is discussed. Managing electronic records and microforms is covered in the second topic.

390

Online Resources

- O *The Office* Web site:
  Data Files
  Vocabulary Flashcards
  Sort It Out, Filing Paper
    Records
  Chapter 10 Supplementary
    Activity
- O Institute of Certified Records
    Managers
  5818 Molloy Road
  Syracuse, NY 13211
- O Search terms:
  records management
  records retention
  storage media
  micrographics
  imaging systems
  reprographics
  copyright law

Topic 10-1

objectives

O Explain how to prepare
records for filing

O Apply efficient filing
procedures

O Describe the use of requisition forms and OUT
guides in charging-out
records

O Describe how inactive
files are moved and
stored

O Describe storage
plans for vital records
protection

O Identify copier features
and operating procedures

Wherever you work, whether in a small company or a large one, you probably will store some records on paper. Even in offices where magnetic media and microforms are used, certain paper (hard copy) records are needed. For this reason, you should understand how to maintain paper files. Once you have a clear understanding of how to manage these files, you can easily adapt this knowledge to managing records stored on other media.

In this topic, you will learn about preparing paper records for storage. You will study methods for locating and removing records and entire folders. You also will learn about the equipment used to copy and store paper records.

Preparing Records for Storage

Before filing a record for the first time, you need to prepare it properly for storage. By doing so, you speed up the filing process and increase filing accuracy. Follow these five steps to prepare paper records for storage:

1. Collect the records.
2. Inspect the records.
3. Index/code the records.
4. Cross-reference the records, if needed.
5. Sort the records.

*Office workers must be familiar
with the procedures for managing
paper files.*

© BILL ARON/PHOTOEDIT

391

Topic 10-1: *Managing Paper Records*

Getting Started

While teaching this chapter, you will want to introduce students to real-world records management systems. To achieve this goal, you may want to take students to local companies that have effective records management systems to see how workers use and manage files in a business environment.

Points to Emphasize

Paper is a major medium of storing records. Even in offices where magnetic media, optical media, and microforms are used extensively, paper records are still used for many records.

Supplemental Activity

To involve students in actively managing records, you may want to have them complete a filing practice set as a supplement to this text because it offers such extensive instruction in records management. Students could work on the practice set one day a week in class for a period of time, or they could complete the practice set as a homework assignment that you offer help with on certain days.

Collect Records

Throughout the workday, you will collect records that need to be filed. Place these records in a certain place such as a tray labeled *TO BE FILED.* Then at scheduled times, such as after lunch or at the end of the day, prepare the records for storage. You will not need to index, code, or cross-reference records that have been filed before. You will still need to inspect and sort them, however, before they can be refiled.

Inspect Records

When preparing records for storage, inspect each record by following these procedures:

release mark: an official approval to file a record

- When a record is being filed for the first time, look for a **release mark.** The initials of someone authorized to release the record, written on the record, often serve as the release mark.
- Remove all paper clips or rubber bands from the records.
- Staple all related materials together.
- Repair any torn records with transparent tape.
- Attach small records to a full sheet of paper so that they will not be lost or crumpled in the file. You could copy the small record onto a full page instead—unless the original must be kept.

Index and Code Records

You index a record by deciding how to identify it for filing purposes. The name, subject, geographic location, or number used to identify a record is called the filing segment. The name or subject most likely to be used in asking for the record is the one to be used for storage. On outgoing letters, the name of the recipient (company or person if no company is shown) is usually the most important. On incoming letters, the name of the sender (company or person if no company is shown) is the usually the most important.

You should code the record using the filing segment. Coding a record allows you to tell quickly how to file a record by glancing at it. You will file the record the same way each time it must be refiled. Records may be coded by hand, the conventional method, or by bar coding.

Conventional Coding

Some companies prefer that you code records with a blue, nonreproducing pencil. If you must copy the record, the code markings will not copy. To code a record indexed by subject, geographic location, or number, write the filing segment in the upper-right corner of the record. Coding a record indexed by individual or company name involves three steps:

1. Identify the filing segment. Underline or circle the name the first time it appears on the record. If the name is not contained in the record, write it in the upper-right corner.
2. Identify the indexing units of a name. For example, there are three indexing units in the name "Grady P. Hill." Use slash marks to divide the filing segment into separate indexing units:
   Grady / P. / Hill

CHAPTER 10: MANAGING RECORDS

3. Number the units in proper indexing order according to alphabetic indexing rules. For example, individual names are filed alphabetically by last names, not by first names. Therefore, in the case of Grady P. Hill, you would number the indexing units this way:

2	3	1
Grady /	P. /	Hill

Figure 9-2.5 on pages 375 and 376 presents alphabetic indexing rules for names. Refer to these rules as needed when indexing records. Figure 10-1.1 shows a record properly indexed and coded.

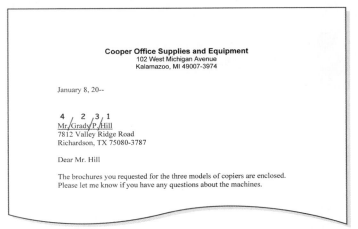

Cooper Office Supplies and Equipment
102 West Michigan Avenue
Kalamazoo, MI 49007-3974

January 8, 20--

4 2 3 1
Mr./Grady/P./Hill
7812 Valley Ridge Road
Richardson, TX 75080-3787

Dear Mr. Hill

The brochures you requested for the three models of copiers are enclosed. Please let me know if you have any questions about the machines.

Figure 10-1.1

This copy of an outgoing letter has been indexed and coded for filing.

Bar Coding

A **bar code** is a pattern of vertical lines of varying widths that contains coded data that can be read by a scanner. The scanner is also called a reader or tracker. A bar code can be printed on a label and attached to an item such as a file folder or box. Bar code labels can be printed on labels as needed, or preprinted labels may be purchased. The advantage of using preprinted labels is that an office worker will not accidentally assign the same bar code to two files.

When bar codes are used, indexes and logs as discussed in Chapter 9 are replaced by an automated indexing and tracking system. In a bar-code system, a code on a record is scanned into an electronic tracking system. This process is much the same as how product prices are scanned at a register in a store. The computer will add the date and time the record is filed or retrieved. When an item is refiled, the computer identifies the date and time of the return. Using bar codes allows less margin for human error, and fewer files are lost.

bar code: a pattern of vertical lines of varying widths that contains coded data that can be read by a scanner

Bar codes can be used to track files.

© THE SMEAD MANUFACTURING COMPANY

Cross-Reference Records

cross-reference: a record that gives the alternate name or subject by which a record may be requested and the name or subject by which the record is filed

A **cross-reference** is prepared when a record may be requested by more than one name or subject. For example, in Figure 10-1.2, the record may be indexed by the name of the company sending the letter or by the subject of the letter. In this case, you would first index and code the record by the name or subject of primary importance. This name is *Star Wholesale Groceries* (the name of the company sending the letter). Then you would code the name or subject of secondary importance. This topic is *SPRING BONANZA OF VALUES* (the subject of the letter). Note that you code the subject by underlining it, numbering the indexing units, and placing an X in the margin. The X is a signal that the record is cross-referenced under that particular subject.

A record may be requested by a variation of the name under which it is filed. For example, a letter filed under the name *Bird and Casey Associates* might be requested as *Casey and Bird Associates*. In this case, you would write the cross-reference caption on the document followed by an X. You would then index and code the cross-reference name on the letter and prepare a cross-reference sheet.

Cross-Reference Sheet

A cross-reference sheet includes information about the record and is filed in the cross-referenced folder. The following information is recorded on the cross-reference sheet as shown in Figure 10-1.3.

- The name or subject under which the record was cross-referenced
- The date of the item
- A brief description of the record
- The location of the record in the files
- The name of the authorized person who released the record and the date it was released

394

CHAPTER 10: MANAGING RECORDS

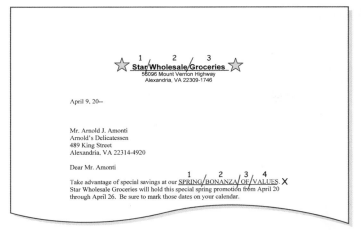

The sheet shown in Figure 10-1.3 would be filed in the SPRING BONANZA OF VALUES folder. The record shown in Figure 10-1.2 would be filed in the STAR WHOLESALE GROCERIES folder.

Copies of Records

Some companies do not use cross-reference sheets. Instead, they copy the original record and place the copy in the cross-referenced folder. This speeds retrieval because a complete copy of the record is available at each location. Making a copy may take the same or less time than completing a cross-reference sheet. If you use this method, be sure to code the copy for cross-referencing so you will file it in the proper folder. Procedures for copying records and information about copying equipment are presented later in this topic.

```
               CROSS-REFERENCE SHEET


Name or (Subject)  Spring Bonanza of Values
_____

Date of Item   April 9, 20--
Regarding    Annual spring promotion, special savings
_____

                     SEE

(Name) or Subject   Star Wholesale Groceries
_____

Authorized by  Glenda AcKinclose      Date  4 / 21 /--
```

Ask students how they can tell that the record in Figure 10-1.2 has been cross-referenced. (They should identify the X in the right margin of the letter.) Next, ask them under what name this letter has been cross-referenced. (They should say, "SPRING BONANZA OF VALUES.") Finally, ask them why that name was chosen. (They should understand that it is the subject of the letter.)

What is a disadvantage of making a copy of a record to place in an alternate filing location rather than using a cross-reference sheet? (If the record is several pages long, it will use more space in the file cabinet than a single cross-reference sheet.)

395

Topic 10-1: *Managing Paper Records*

Thinking Critically

Ask students to differentiate between a cross-reference guide and a cross-reference sheet. (They should explain the different uses for the two as well as the differing appearances.)

Teaching Tips

To involve students actively in filing, you may want to place a stack of random correspondence (appropriately depersonalized) on a desk in the classroom and have students see how quickly they can accurately sort the correspondence alphabetically, chronologically, or numerically.

For Discussion

What two purposes does sorting serve?

Cross-Reference Guides

If a permanent cross-reference is desired, you will need to prepare a cross-reference guide using a stiff board the same size as a file folder. A cross-reference guide might be needed when a company changes its name. You would label a fresh folder using the new company name and place in it all materials from the old folder. Then you would replace the old folder with a permanent cross-reference guide. The cross-reference guide should show the necessary retrieval information on the tab. The guide remains in the file as long as the name or subject is still active.

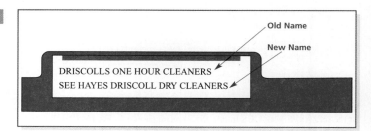

Figure 10-1.4

Prepare a permanent cross-reference guide for a company that changes its name.

When to Cross-Reference

As a general rule, you should cross-reference a record if doing so will save you time when you need to retrieve the item later. Too many cross-references, however, will make finding files more difficult. Follow any company guidelines that are provided to help you know when to make a cross-reference.

You usually will make cross-references only for records filed in name or subject filing systems. Geographic and numeric filing systems have alphabetic indexes that lead you directly to the item you need.

Sort Records

After you have coded the records and created the needed cross-references, you are ready to sort the records. **Sorting** is the process of arranging the records alphabetically or numerically before placing them in the folders.

sorting: arranging records alphabetically or numerically

Sorting serves two important purposes. First, it saves filing time. Because records are in proper sequence, you are able to move quickly from file drawer to file drawer as you place the records in folders. Second, if records are requested before you file them, you can find them quickly.

CHAPTER 10: MANAGING RECORDS

Charlotte Running-Bear is training Henry Davis, a new office worker. This afternoon they are preparing the records collected that day for storage. They have already indexed, coded, and cross-referenced the records that had never been filed before. Henry thinks they are ready to place the records in the folders. But Charlotte explains they have one more step to complete first.

Charlotte: "Henry, we need to sort these records alphabetically before we file them."

Henry: "It will take forever to sort this stack of records. Let's just file them in the order they are in now."

Charlotte: "Sorting doesn't take that long. First, we'll rough sort."

Henry: "What does that mean?"

Charlotte: "It means we'll group all the A records together, all the B records together, and so forth. Then we'll fine sort. That means we'll place all the A records in alphabetic order, then all the B records, and so on."

Charlotte and Henry quickly sort the records and begin to file. Their supervisor, Ms. Sanchez, approaches them and asks a question.

Ms. Sanchez: "Charlotte, I placed the Norris letter in the TO BE FILED tray, but I need it again. Have you filed it yet?"

Charlotte: "No, Ms. Sanchez. We've only filed up to the Cs."

Charlotte flips through the records, which are in alphabetic order, and quickly retrieves the Norris letter. Ms. Sanchez takes the letter and leaves.

Charlotte: "Well, Henry, now can you see why I believe sorting is worth the time it takes?"

Filing Paper Records

Office workers should set aside time each day to file. Many other tasks may seem more important than filing. However, filing records each day so they can be found quickly when needed is important. If you have followed the five steps for preparing records for storage, you can file the records quickly by following these steps:

1. Locate the proper file drawer by reading the drawer labels.
2. Search through the guides in the drawer to locate the needed alphabetic or numeric section.
3. If an individual folder has been prepared for the record, place the record in the folder. Place the front of the record facing the front of the folder and the top of the record at the left side. Place records in an individual folder according to date, with the most recent date in front.

397

Topic 10-1: *Managing Paper Records*

Points to Emphasize

Do not underestimate the importance of filing. You should allocate time each day to file just as you would allocate time to do any other office task.

Set aside time
each day to file
paper records.

© GETTY IMAGES/PHOTODISC

4. If no individual folder is available, file the record in the general folder for that section. Arrange records in a general folder alphabetically by name or subject. If there are two or more records for the same name or subject, they are arranged according to date with the most recent in front.

Using Special Folders

Some companies use special folders as well as general and individual folders. A special folder is a type of general folder that is used for a variety of purposes. For example, you may remove all the records coded *Smith* from the general folder and place them in a special folder. This procedure permits material filed under *Smith* to be found more quickly. You also may prepare special folders to collect information about a particular subject or project, such as *ARMA Convention Travel Plans*. You arrange records alphabetically in a special folder. Within each group of names or subjects, arrange the records by date.

Avoiding Overcrowded Files

Never allow folders to become overcrowded. Usually, a folder has score lines at the bottom. Creasing the score lines widens the folder and allows it to hold more records. A folder should not contain more than an inch of filed material. When a folder becomes too full, subdivide the records into two or more folders. The labels of each should reflect the contents of the new folders. For example, they could be labeled by date or subject.

Be sure to examine general folders often so that you can prepare individual and special folders when necessary. Do not fill a file drawer completely. You should have enough room in the drawer to move the folders easily.

Points to Emphasize

Never accumulate in a folder more than one inch of filed material. An overcrowded folder is unmanageable and should be subdivided into two or more folders.

398

CHAPTER 10: MANAGING RECORDS

398

CHAPTER 10: MANAGING RECORDS

Storage Equipment

Equipment and supplies for filing paper records are plentiful. Each business must decide what system works best to fit its filing needs. The following descriptions will give you a general idea of the equipment that is available for paper files and the best uses of each.

Vertical file cabinets contain one to five drawers. Of this kind of system, five-drawer cabinets provide the most filing space for the amount of floor space used. Vertical file cabinets must be arranged so there is space in front of each one to allow drawers to be opened fully.

Lateral file cabinets are common storage equipment. Lateral files are made in a variety of drawer heights, widths, and depths to fit different office needs. Fully opened drawers in such a cabinet do not open as far out into the room as do drawers in a vertical file cabinet.

Horizontal (flat) files are used to store large paper documents. Examples of such documents include advertising layouts, product drawings, and land surveys.

Both vertical file cabinets and shelf files are used in some offices.

Storage drawers are stackable file drawers that work like traditional vertical files. These drawers come in a variety of heights, widths, and depths. Some storage drawers, often used for temporary storage, are made of cardboard; others are made of metal.

Shelf files store records on open shelves instead of in drawers. They come in a wide variety of sizes. Records on open shelves can be removed easily. Shelf filing is most appropriate for filing and retrieving entire folders and is ideally suited for numeric filing systems. Because folders on open shelves are readily visible, many companies use color-coded folder labels to improve filing efficiency. Bar coding may be used with shelf filing systems. Shelf files are generally the most efficient and modern system.

399

Topic 10-1: *Managing Paper Records*

Open shelf files provide easy access to files.

Mobile files are shelf files that have many shelves but only one aisle. The shelves are arranged next to each other on a track. To form the aisle in front of the desired shelf, the shelves are moved along the track manually or electronically. Mobile files take up less floor space than either fixed shelf files or cabinets holding the same number of records.

Storage boxes are fiberboard cartons that are often used to hold files temporarily while moving them. These boxes are also used by some companies for the storage of inactive files.

Retrieving Paper Records

Once records are in active storage, they may be retrieved and refiled many times. Charge-out procedures help workers keep track of records when they are removed from the files.

Requisition Forms

Many companies that use central files have a staff of trained workers who file and retrieve records. In companies using this arrangement, other office workers do not have direct access to the files. To retrieve records, workers must submit a **requisition form**. This form has space for all the charge-out information needed, such as:

- A description or file number of the record
- The name and contact information of the person taking the record
- The current date
- The date the record is to be returned

requisition form: a document that has space for charge-out information for a record

CHAPTER 10: MANAGING RECORDS

Thinking Critically

Ask students what types of records might be best suited to storage in mobile files.

For Discussion

Ask students what problems might arise if a company had no formal procedures for retrieving records and simply allowed any worker to remove records or an entire folder at any time.

Teaching Tips

You may want to obtain from a local office supply store requisition forms, OUT guides, and OUT folders so that students can conduct a hands-on examination of the materials they are reading about.

Requisition information might also be kept in a database program. If you work in the central files, you will keep a copy of each requisition form or record. When a record has not been returned by the expected date, you need to take appropriate follow-up action. This is an important part of managing records. A records manager also may use requisition forms to analyze how often files are used and which records are most active.

OUT Guides

When you remove a record from the files, you should replace it with a record of the charge-out information. This can be done by using an out guide. An out guide is a sheet of thick cardboard that has the word *OUT* printed on the tab. On some OUT guides, you write the charge-out information on ruled lines. On other OUT guides, there is a pocket where you insert a completed requisition form. You usually use OUT guides when individual records within a folder are removed.

Figure **10-1.5**

An OUT guide may replace a folder that has been removed from the file.

OUT			
NUMBER, NAME, OR SUBJECT	CHARGE OUT DATE	NAME OF BORROWER	DUE DATE
Forest Park Florist	4/22/--	Ruth Carson	5/4/--
Spanish Village Apartments	6/5/--	Jerry Ahmed	5/14/--

OUT Folders

An OUT folder is used when an entire folder is removed from the file. When an OUT folder is used, you may temporarily file additional records in the OUT folder until the regular folder is returned.

WORKPLACE CONNECTIONS

When Lakisha removed the Brandon-Mills folder from the files, she provided the charge-out information on the printed lines of an OUT folder. Later, when Chin Lu was filing, he placed two letters in the Brandon-Mills OUT folder. If Lakisha had not provided the OUT folder, Chin Lu would not have been able to file the two letters. This way, Chin Lu could file the records. Lakisha then would insert those records into the Brandon-Mills folder when she returned it to the files.

For Discussion

Ask students when it is necessary to use an OUT guide and when it is necessary to use an OUT folder. (Students should be able to explain that an OUT guide is used when a record is removed and an OUT folder is used when a folder is removed.)

Removing Records from Active Storage

A retention schedule identifies which records should be removed from active storage and on which dates. Records that are placed in inactive storage usually are put into cardboard or fiberboard storage files. The boxes are sturdy and provide a place to identify the contents. Some storage boxes can be stacked, saving storage space. Color-coded storage boxes can help you locate inactive records quickly. As discussed in Chapter 9, some companies store inactive records in off-site locations, which range from rented storage space to underground vaults.

© GETTY IMAGES/PHOTODISC

Inactive records may be stored in cardboard or fiberboard boxes.

Protecting Vital Records

Vital records are those that are important to maintaining the operations or fulfilling the legal obligations of an organization. There are numerous methods of storage that can be used to protect vital records:

- Multisite storage. If a company has two or more locations, it may choose to keep duplicates of vital records at each location.
- Planned dispersing. Some companies use a secure vital records storage center and have a plan to disperse records there on a regular basis.
- Duplication. A number of organizations place vital records in microforms that are placed in a disaster-proof facility.
- Vaulting. Some businesses have special fire-resistant vaults, safes, or filing cabinets in which they store vital records. Other companies use an off-site facility with such protection.

Any combination of these methods may be used. Because the cost involved in storing vital records can be significant, records should be reviewed regularly. Those that are no longer of use should be removed and destroyed.

Copying Paper Records

Reprographics is the process of making copies of graphic images, such as printed documents. It also includes other image processing such as scanning images into computer files. Reprographics plays an important role in managing records. Paper is commonly used for storing documents and for sharing information with others. Copies of paper records are often needed at both the use and maintenance phases of the record life cycle.

Businesses have different needs for reprographic services. The needs depend on the size of the company and the types of documents to be copied. Some large businesses have a reprographics or copying center. In this setting, you would prepare the original from which the copies are to be made. You would use special forms to give detailed copying instructions to workers in the copying center. The company may set a minimum number of copies that will be made by the copying center. Smaller copying jobs are handled by individual employees using small copiers located throughout the business.

Small organizations do not usually have a copying center. In this setting, workers are responsible for preparing the original and making the copies. Even many larger organizations have done away with their copying centers. Instead, copiers are placed throughout the office areas.

Office Photocopiers

Photocopiers, often simply called copiers, produce copies directly from an original document. The original can be handwritten, printed, or drawn. The quality of the copy is good if the machine is in good condition and the original is of high quality. Many copiers reproduce onto one or both sides of a sheet of paper. They can copy onto letterhead paper, mailing labels, bond paper, and colored paper. Some machines copy in color as well.

reprographics: the process of making copies of graphic images, such as printed documents

© MICHAEL MALYSZKO/TAXI

Many businesses have small copiers located throughout the offices for employee use.

Copiers/Printers

Copier/printers, sometimes called intelligent copiers, can receive, transmit, store, print, and copy data. These devices can produce copies from sources such as a computer file, graphic scanners, or even pictures. For example, you may key material at your computer and then send the file to a copier/printer at a nearby location. The copies will then be printed.

Copier/printers can use specific print fonts, justify lines, number pages, or insert graphics within the text material. These machines can merge data from various electronic sources. They can also share data with other copier/printers.

© CORBIS

Files can be sent electronically to a copier/printer.

Copier Classifications and Features

Copiers can be classified according to their capacity: low, mid, high, and duplicating. Copier capacity is usually determined by two factors: speed and volume. Speed is often stated in copies produced per minute. Volume is often stated in copies produced per month. As an office worker, you should select the best copier for the task at hand when more than one machine is available to you.

Maria is a new employee. Her supervisor, Lana, is explaining to her the features and capacities of each copier available for her use. Lana emphasizes that choosing an appropriate copier for each copying job is very important. She hands Maria two copying jobs. One is a ten-page proposal requiring one photocopy. The other is a 55-page report requiring 6 photocopies. Lana asks Maria to choose the copiers that will complete each job most efficiently. On the basis of what Maria has learned about the company's copiers, she knows it is most efficient to copy the 10-page proposal on the low-capacity copier and the 55-page report on the high-capacity copier.

Special features designed to meet specific copying needs are available on many copiers. Many of the copiers found in offices have several of the features listed in Figure 10-1.6, which are only a few of those available.

Common Copier Features

Automatic duplexing	Allows the user to copy on both sides of the paper, saves paper and postage costs
Automatic image shift	Creates a margin on one or both sides of the copy paper to allow space for three-hole punching or for binding the copies
Book copy mode	Allows the user to copy both pages of an open book or magazine onto the front and back of a single sheet of copy paper
Image enlargement and reduction	Allows the user to make a copy larger or smaller than the original document
Sorter	Collates the copies, arranging the copies in order or in sets
Automatic document feed	Feeds the originals into the machine
Self-diagnosis feature	Detects common problems (a paper jam, for example) and displays words or symbols to alert the user
Automatic exposure control	Adjusts the darkness or lightness of copies after sensing the density of the original
Copy counter	Allows the user to select the number of copies to be made
Roll feeding	A roll of continuous-feed paper allows copies of varying sizes to be made at one time. The paper is cut by the machine to match the sizes needed.
Job recovery	Allows an interrupted print job to be started again at the place where the user stopped the job
Color	Color images on the original are reproduced on the copies

Figure **10-1.6**

You will want to be familiar with the common features of copiers found in your office.

Thinking Critically

What might be the consequences of routinely using a small copier for large copying jobs for which a heavy-duty machine would be more appropriate?

For Discussion

Which of the features listed in Figure 10-1.6 would likely be found on a small convenience copier? On a heavy-duty copier?

405

Topic 10-1: *Managing Paper Records*

Points to Emphasize

All employees are expected to follow closely the recommendations of the vendor or manufacturer and company guidelines when using copier supplies in order to control costs.

Operating Procedures

Failure to follow proper copying procedures can increase copying costs. If a company has copiers located throughout the building, copier misuse may occur more often than if copying is done by only a few employees in a copying center. Employees who do not know how to operate the equipment properly may damage the copier or misuse supplies.

WORKPLACE CONNECTIONS

When Antonio found that there was no paper in the copier, he added two reams to the paper bin. Before he had run three copies, the machine was jammed. He was upset and sought help from Robin, a coworker. When Robin checked the paper bin, she said, "You haven't inserted the paper under the guides correctly." Antonio responded, "Oh, is there a special way to place the paper in the bin?" Robin then showed Antonio how the paper should be placed in the bin so that it will be guided into the copier correctly.

Office employees need to be knowledgeable about the proper use and selection of reprographic supplies. You will find that the selection of paper, toner, and other materials can significantly affect the cost of making copies and the operation of the machines. All employees are expected to follow closely the recommendations of the vendor or manufacturer and company guidelines when using copier supplies in order to control costs.

An occasional paper jam is easily cleared by an employee familiar with the equipment.

© MICHAEL NEWMAN/PHOTOEDIT

Companies often take steps to help control copying costs and procedures. Companies with large copying needs may use a central copying center. This helps the company control the number of copies made and allows workers to make the best use of the equipment. Companies often allocate copying costs to the individual or department requesting the copies. Devices that monitor copier use may be placed on the copiers located throughout the offices. A common copier control procedure is a copier log book. More commonly, a computerized log is used. The log is based upon a code or card used by each employee or department. When a copier log book is used, employees record information for each copy job, such as the employee name, department, and the number of copies made. This data is recorded automatically when a code or card is used.

Many companies post guidelines for employees who use copiers near each copier. As a responsible employee, you should follow these general guidelines:

- Follow company policy regarding the maximum number of copies to be made at copiers. Large copier needs are best handled through a central copying center, when available.

- Be aware of copying costs when planning to use the copier. Use the copier's economy features, such as duplexing. Do not make more copies than you need.

- Comply with **copyright laws**. Copyright laws describe those documents that cannot be legally copied. Some documents should not be copied at their original size and with the intent to represent the original. Examples of these documents are money, postage stamps, birth certificates, passports, draft cards, and drivers' licenses. Many books and other documents may also be copyrighted and should not be reproduced.

- Do not use company resources to make copies for personal use.

- Follow good housekeeping rules. Always clean up the area after you have completed your copying project. Deal with any copier problems, such as a paper jam, or notify the appropriate person of the problem.

- Practice common courtesy when using the copier. If you have a long copy job and another worker needs a priority copy, stop at a convenient point and let the other person have access to the machine. If you need a few copies and someone else is near the end of a long copying job, wait until the other person is finished to make your copies.

copyright laws: regulate what documents or other information can be legally copied

Challenge Option

Ask students to write a response to the following scenario.

You are working for a company that gives you a code for the copier so that a count can be kept for your department's use of the machine. One day, without thinking, you begin to copy and discover that no code is needed to make the machine work. The counter/processor is obviously broken. You have some originals of a poster for a charity event that need to be copied. You were going to stop at a copier service center on the way home to make the copies. Would you now copy them on the office machine? Why or why not?

Student answers should explore the ethics of the situation. Students should understand that this unauthorized use is a form of stealing.

407

Topic 10-1: *Managing Paper Records*

REVIEWING THE TOPIC

1. List the five steps involved in preparing paper records for storage.
2. What is the purpose of a release mark?
3. Describe the process for coding a record indexed by name.
4. Why is it necessary to cross-reference some records?
5. Give two reasons for sorting records before filing them.
6. How should you arrange records in an individual folder?
7. What is a special folder, and how might it be used?
8. Why are shelf files the overall optimal filing equipment?
9. Under what circumstances might a requisition form be used?
10. What is the difference between an OUT guide and an OUT folder?
11. In what phases of the record life cycle are paper documents often reproduced?
12. Name and describe four common copier features.
13. Name three ways companies may attempt to control copying costs.
14. What information is typically recorded in a copier log?
15. List three general guidelines for copier use.

THINKING CRITICALLY

Personnel Services, Inc. is a small agency that places workers in both permanent and temporary jobs. The office is staffed by two placement officers and one office support worker, Eileen. Although Eileen is a competent office worker, she sometimes gets behind in her filing. This morning one of the placement officers, Mr. Thomas, said to her, "I can't even see the top of the filing cabinet because it's so cluttered with file folders. Don't you think you should take time to file them?" Eileen thought to herself, "I don't even have time to take a coffee break during the day. When am I going to find time to file all these folders?"

1. Why do you think Eileen puts filing so low on her priority list of things to do?
2. How might she find time to file and fulfill her other duties as well?

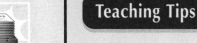

REINFORCING ENGLISH SKILLS

For written messages to be clear to the reader, commas must be used correctly. Test your skill in using commas in the sentences below. Key or write each sentence and insert commas in the correct positions.

1. Records can be organized alphabetically numerically and chronologically.
2. You will however be responsible for preparing paper records for storage.
3. As a general rule you should cross-reference a record if doing so will save you time when you need to retrieve it later.
4. Before filing a record for the first time you need to prepare it properly for storage.
5. Records may be coded by hand or bar coding may be used to code records.
6. At scheduled times such as after lunch or at the end of the day prepare the records for storage.
7. Bar code labels can be printed on labels as needed or preprinted labels may be purchased.
8. Too many cross-references however will make finding files more difficult.
9. If sorted records are requested before you file them you can find them quickly.
10. "Well Marcus now you see why sorting records is worth the time it takes."

RECORDS MANAGEMENT

Topic 10-1 ACTIVITY 1

Code and Cross-Reference Letters

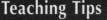

Paper records, such as letters, must be indexed and coded properly before filing. A cross-reference should be prepared when a record may be requested under a different name than the one it is filed under. Practice coding letters and preparing cross-reference sheets in this activity.

1. Open and print the PDF file *CH10 Letters* from the data files. This file contains six letters to be coded and two blank cross-reference sheets.
2. Index and code each letter for filing. You work at Star Satellite Systems, so the letters with this company name in the letterhead are outgoing letters. The other letters are incoming letters. See Figure 10-1.2 for an example of a coded letter.
3. The letter to Anne Ashby and the letter from William Abbott require cross-references. Code cross-reference captions and prepare cross-reference sheets for these letters. See Figure 10-1.3 for an example cross-reference sheet. Which of these letters might require a permanent cross-reference guide?

409

Topic Review

PRESENTATION
RESEARCH
TEAMWORK
WORD PROCESSING

Topic **10-1**   ACTIVITY 2

Reprographics Equipment Presentation

Schools, companies, libraries, government offices, and other organizations have reprographics equipment to help employees complete tasks efficiently. In this activity, you will research how this equipment is used at a local organization and report your findings to the class.

1. Work in a team with three or four other students to complete this activity.

2. With the members of your team, visit one of these local organizations as assigned by your instructor: school, library, business, government office, or copy center (any business that provides copying services for a fee).

3. Ask to see the various types of reprographics equipment used at the organization. Take note of the location and features of the equipment. Note the types of supplies used and the procedures or controls used.

4. Prepare a presentation about the reprographics equipment available at the organization. In the presentation, give the name and a brief description of the organization your team visited. For each piece of equipment, give the brand name, location, and features. Discuss the intended use of the machine—for small-size copying jobs, moderate-size copying jobs, or large jobs. Describe the types of supplies you saw in use or readiness. Discuss any controls or other procedures used (such as monitoring devices and copy logs).

5. Prepare appropriate visuals for use in your presentation. Identify the content each team member will present. Practice your presentation as a team.

6. Deliver your presentation to the class.

7. Write a thank-you letter to the organization you visited from your team. Thank the organization for allowing you to visit, and mention some information that you found particularly interesting or helpful in creating your presentation.

Topic 10-2

objectives

- Explain how to store records on magnetic media
- Describe supplies used to store and organize magnetic and optical media
- Explain why databases are useful in businesses
- Describe ways to organize microforms
- Explain how computer-assisted retrieval systems are used to speed record retrieval

As an office worker, you will need to know how to store and access information recorded on magnetic media, optical disks, and microforms. Unlike paper records, records stored on these media are not readable by simply looking at the media. These records must be accessed via a computer or a microfilm reader. For this reason, managing these media with great care is important.

Companies that keep many records for a long time may use microforms to store inactive records. Some companies use this medium for active records as well. As an office worker, you should know how these records are created and maintained. You may also need to know how to use computer-assisted retrieval systems.

Records Management Software

Records management software is a computer program that allows electronic control of records. Records can be tracked from receipt or creation, through processing, storage, and retrieval, to disposal. The advantage of such a system is that it allows records management tasks to be performed with limited personnel. Records management software is a tool that helps companies manage records efficiently.

Some records management programs are used with a computer network. This use allows the entire company to have access to records search and retrieval features. Thus, a reduced number of records clerks is required. Some software can also perform the library-like function of retrieving

records management software: computer program that allows electronic tracking and control of records

Records stored on magnetic or optical media must be accessed using a computer.

Topic 10-2: *Managing Magnetic, Optical, and Microfilm Media*

411

Teaching Tips

To familiarize students with magnetic, optical, and microimaging media, you may want to invite a product representative to your classroom to demonstrate the media and equipment. Be aware that a store owner may be more willing than a sales person to give her or his time because the latter may work strictly on commission. If a field trip is possible, you may wish to take the class to visit a company in your area that uses these media.

Teaching Tips

You may want to obtain various samples of magnetic, optical, and microimaging media from manufacturers' representatives to display in the classroom. Samples should include floppy disks, CDs, DVDs, flash drives, tapes, microfilm, microfiche, and aperture cards.

Points to Emphasize

Use of records management software allows companies to have fewer records management personnel.

records. This feature reduces the need for human management of requisition records. Records management software performs the functions such as:

- Tracking records from creation/reception to destruction
- Tracking stored records, whether on-site or off-site
- Creating and maintaining a retention schedule
- Archiving and managing record archives
- Identifying and managing vital records as part of a disaster recovery program

Storing Files on Magnetic and Optical Media

secondary storage: storage media or devices outside the internal memory of a computer system

Storage media used for data stored outside of a computer is referred to as auxiliary or **secondary storage**. Each collection of related data that is treated as a unit is called a file. Floppy disks, hard drives, flash drives, CDs, and DVDs are common media used for secondary storage. Because CDs and DVDs can hold many more records than a floppy disk, these media are a good choice for archiving records. They are also good for active records that do not need to be updated often.

The internal storage medium for most computer systems is a hard drive. The hard drive is used to store programs that run the system and data files. Many companies use secondary storage to make backup copies of files or for freeing hard drive space of files that are not used regularly. Files stored on the system should be examined periodically. Inactive files should be saved onto a secondary storage medium and then deleted from the internal memory of the system.

Converting Records to Electronic Form

For many large businesses, storing all records on paper is not practical. Decisions must be made about which records can be stored in other forms. Many records can be stored as electronic files on hard drives or CDs and DVDs. When planning to convert records, several questions must be answered. What computer system will be used? What files will be on individual hard drives or network drives? What records will be stored on secondary media, and which media will be used? Converting to electronic form or updating current electronic records systems involves several stages, as shown in Figure 10-2.1.

Storing Electronic Files

Electronic files must be assigned to a folder or directory and given a name so they can be identified and accessed when needed. Some operating systems limit the length of a filename to eight characters. Other systems allow longer, more descriptive names to be used. Some systems allow you to add a three-character extension (such as "doc" for document) to further identify your file. Many programs automatically add the three-character extension. Filenames should reflect the type of data stored in the file. For example, the name assigned to a mailing list file could be *Maillist* or *Austin TX Mailing List*.

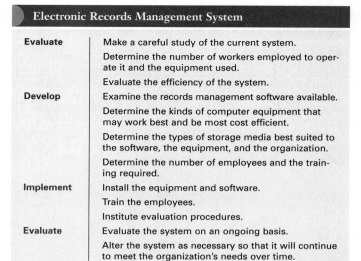

Electronic Records Management System   Figure **10-2.1**

Evaluate	Make a careful study of the current system.
	Determine the number of workers employed to operate it and the equipment used.
	Evaluate the efficiency of the system.
Develop	Examine the records management software available.
	Determine the kinds of computer equipment that may work best and be most cost efficient.
	Determine the types of storage media best suited to the software, the equipment, and the organization.
	Determine the number of employees and the training required.
Implement	Install the equipment and software.
	Train the employees.
	Institute evaluation procedures.
Evaluate	Evaluate the system on an ongoing basis.
	Alter the system as necessary so that it will continue to meet the organization's needs over time.

The following guidelines may be used in storing electronic files:

- Create folders to group related files. When a large number of files accumulate in the folder, move files into two or more new folders.
- Give each file a unique name even if it is stored in a different folder than a file with a similar name.
- Use abbreviations that are commonly recognized, for example, *Dept* for department or *Proj* for project.
- If your system allows the use of long file names, use as many characters as needed to make identifying the file easy.
- Use numbers or dates to label versions of a file. For example, your fourth letter to the Accounting Department might be labeled *AcctDpt4* or *Acct Dept Letter 4-2-06*.
- Use the default file extension or allow the program to assign the extension. For example, all word processing documents created with *Word* might use the file extension *doc*. If you use some versions of the *Microsoft Windows* operating system, you may not see file extensions. This setting can be changed in the software.

You must understand the system of drives and folders on your computer or network to store and retrieve files efficiently. The filename alone may not be enough information to retrieve the file quickly. You need to know the drive and folder name where the file is stored. This information is called the **file path**. Figure 10-2.2 shows a list of files and folders in the Abbott Project folder on the C: drive (hard drive) of a computer. The Abbott Project folder contains several subfolders. Individual files are shown for a schedule, a project summary, and a press release. File extensions are shown in this figure. You may or may not see file extensions on your system depending on the options set in the software.

file path: the complete location designation for an electronic file

As a general office worker (who does not specialize in records management), which of the steps shown in Figure 10-2.1 are you most likely to be involved with?

Discuss the type of filenames (short or long) and the naming conventions that apply to the computers or networks students use for this class.

413

Topic 10-2: *Managing Magnetic, Optical, and Microfilm Media*

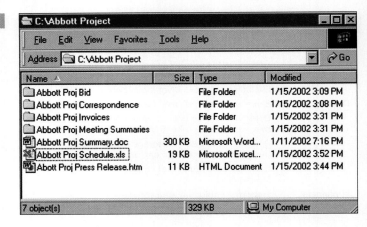

Figure **10-2.2**

This directory shows several folders and individual files.

Companies may have policies that tell how files should be organized on secondary storage media. For example, will all letters be stored in one folder or directory? All mailing lists in another? All business forms in another? Will various files related to one project be stored in the same folder? Will documents be stored in chronological order? By the name of the creator? By the name of the department? The type of records management system a company uses will determine how and where files will be stored.

Storage media can be organized alphabetically or numerically. Each disk, tape, drive, CD, or DVD should be labeled so that it can be located quickly. Captions should give the information to help find records quickly. Often, the labels are color coded to indicate how long the data on the media should be kept.

Making Backup Copies

Data files can be expensive to create again or replace if they become damaged and are no longer usable. Loss of important data files, such as customer, payroll, and personnel records, can cause serious problems for a company. A backup copy of each file, disk, or tape should be made if loss of the data would have serious consequences. Backing up a hard drive, tape, or disk means making a copy of all the data onto another storage medium. Backing up a file means making a copy of an individual file onto a different tape, disk, or drive.

Software programs can be expensive to replace if damaged. Store the original disks or CDs in a safe location after the programs have been loaded onto the computer. If the programs come preloaded on the computer, original disks may not be included. Make backup copies of the programs for use in restoring the software if the programs on the computer should become damaged.

In many companies, each office worker has a computer for his or her sole use. Often these computers are linked together in a local area network. They may also be linked to a wide area network of computers. In some cases, files may be backed up automatically to a network location. In other cases, each employee is responsible for backing up her or his own files.

Thinking Critically

What problems can arise when employees do not properly label magnetic and optical media used to store files?

414

Make a backup copy of important data files.

© DICK LURIA/TAXI/GETTY IMAGES

Most computer operating systems provide easy-to-follow procedures for making backup copies on tapes and disks. Research and practice the backup or copy commands for your particular system if you are not familiar with them. Backup disks should be labeled in the same manner as their original, perhaps with the word *Backup* added to the label. Backup copies of tapes and disks should be stored in a separate, safe location. A CD label is shown in Figure 10-2.3.

Figure **10-2.3**

This CD is properly labeled with the contents and date.

Petro-Davis Company

Wilson Project Budget
12/31/--
Windows XP Excel 2002

What information is stored on the disc shown in Figure 10-2.3? What application software was used? What operating system software was used?

415

Topic 10-2: *Managing Magnetic, Optical, and Microfilm Media*

password: series of letters, numbers, or symbols used to identify a user and gain access to a computer system

Controlling File Security

The security of files stored electronically is a concern to you as an office worker. You would not want a competitor to have access to a customer mailing list or a sales report that you keyed. Some companies use security measures such as access logs and **passwords**. These measures allow only authorized employees to access certain files. Employees in some companies are required to change passwords frequently. Choose passwords carefully so others cannot easily guess your password. For example, do not use variations of family members' names or birthdates or a favorite sport or hobby as a password. Choose a series of meaningless letters and numbers instead. Do not leave your password in a location where others can access it easily, such as taped to your monitor or under your keyboard. Store your password in a safe place.

Take steps to safeguard files when in use. For example, clear a document from the computer screen when you take a break or leave your computer for other reasons. Log off the computer network before leaving your computer so others cannot use your computer to access files. Do not send files containing confidential information as e-mail attachments. Store disks in a concealed location rather than on the surface of your workstation. Store disks with highly confidential information in a locked cabinet or drawer.

Many companies have a policy manual that outlines the procedures for handling files. In addition to security and backup procedures, such a manual often includes policies regarding:

- E-mail
- Downloaded files
- Internal audits for proper use and storage of files
- Retention schedules
- Accessing or storing files at home or other off-site locations

Storing Magnetic and Optical Media

Magnetic and optical media require special care to protect the valuable data they contain. Magnetic media, such as floppy disks, hard drives, and flash drives, must be protected from extreme heat or cold, moisture, dust, and magnetic fields. Optical media, such as CDs and DVDs, should be protected from dust, moisture, and rough surfaces that may scratch the disk. Being aware of these possible hazards can help you protect the media that you handle and organize.

Disk Storage

Floppy disks, DVDs, and CDs can be organized and stored in a variety of ways. The way selected will depend on the number of items you need to store. How often the records are used is also an important factor to consider in choosing how to store the disks. Many companies color code the labels to speed the storage and retrieval process.

416

FOCUS ON . . .

Protecting Online Records

Online records may be stored on a single computer or a computer network. Records are stored online so they may be accessed quickly. Security procedures are needed to protect online records from destruction, damage, theft, or misuse.

Damage to online records can result from mistakes made by workers. For example, an employee may delete the wrong file or incorrect data may be keyed in a database record. Employee training can help reduce these types of errors. Restricting access to only certain users can also help protect online records.

Online records can be destroyed or misused by employees. Dishonest employees may access records to steal data such as product designs. Unauthorized users, called **hackers**, may access a computer network to steal data. They might also create computer viruses that can destroy records. A virus can also be loaded by an unsuspecting employee using an infected file. A virus is dangerous because it can copy itself and may quickly use all of the computer's memory. The virus may delete important data or cause the computer to stop working. Some viruses can transmit across networks and avoid security systems.

To protect online records, companies back up data regularly. This process prevents the data from being lost if online records are damaged. Backup copies of records are stored in a safe location. Companies commonly issue passwords to employees. These passwords must be used to access the computer network. Passwords should be chosen carefully and stored in a secure location.

Companies use software and equipment called firewalls in an effort to prevent unauthorized use of a computer network. All messages entering or leaving the network pass through the firewall. The firewall blocks those messages that do not meet security standards. Programs are also available that can detect attempts at unauthorized access or other attacks on a computer system.

Antivirus software is designed to detect computer viruses and can destroy many viruses as well. Antivirus software can be set up to scan each file loaded on the computer or network to check for viruses. Antivirus software must be updated regularly to be effective because new viruses are created on an ongoing basis.

As an office worker, you have an important role to play in protecting online records. Security procedures are effective only if used correctly by employees. Regularly back up online records. Choose passwords carefully and store them where others cannot read them. Use antivirus software to scan all files loaded onto your computer. Update the software regularly. Follow all company procedures you are given for protecting online records.

For Discussion

Ask students to share experiences they have had or read about where online records or files were accessed by unauthorized users.

Teaching Tips

Discuss with students the system of passwords, firewalls, or other security measures used by your school to protect access to data.

Disks are often filed in plastic boxes, cases, or trays designed to protect them. Within the case are guides to create sections in the case and make storage and retrieval simpler. Disks may be stored in plastic pockets designed to fit a ring binder or folder. Each disk is protected by the pocket into which it slides. Some plastic pockets can hold hard copy as well as disks. Others are designed to allow disks to be placed in a standard paper file.

hacker: a person who accesses a computer or network without proper permission or approval

417

Topic 10-2: Managing Magnetic, Optical, and Microfilm Media

Colored labels on jewel cases can be used to help organize CDs.

Reel Tape Storage

Reels of tape are stored in round, protective cases. These cases are usually hung for easy access or stored on wire racks. Sometimes the cases have handles or hooks that allow the reels to be attached to frames or cabinets. Other times the cases rest on a backward-slanting shelf. Labels on the protective cases can be color coded for easy reference.

Database Management Systems

electronic database: a collection of records accessible by computer

A database is any collection of related records. An **electronic database** is a collection of records stored and retrieved by computer. These databases are useful because thousands of records can be searched in only a few seconds. Searching the same number of records stored on paper would take a long time. In many companies, workers can get data from a database by using a computer network. This prevents the need to have the same data stored in each department or work group.

A database management system (DBMS) organizes large numbers of records in a database. A major advantage of a DBMS is that data can be compared and shared among the tables in the database. For example, the Internal Revenue Service uses a DBMS to compare data on a person's current income tax return with data on past tax returns. Another advantage of a DBMS is data security. Access to parts of the database can be limited to authorized employees who have been issued passwords.

A DBMS helps users keep database records up to date. Suppose you work in a company that uses a DBMS to manage its personnel and payroll records. If an employee's last name changes, you need to make the change only in the personnel record. The system will automatically update the payroll record.

CHAPTER 10: MANAGING RECORDS

Points to Emphasize

Database software enables you to search thousands of records in seconds to locate alphabetic, numeric, and alphanumeric data (25521W, for example). Such software allows you to create reports that contain records with matching data as well.

Expand the Concept

Organizations collect large amounts of data that office workers and managers may want to access in different ways. The strength of a database management system is that it enables the user to select, sort, calculate, and retrieve data according to her or his particular needs.

Lao Ji works for The Supply Closet, which sells office supplies. The company's database management system contains a master record for each customer. When Lao Ji inputs data for a customer order, he simply enters the customer name in the customer order form screen. Other customer data such as the customer number, address, and available credit amount are completed by the DBMS. This data is stored in the customer master record. Lao Ji can create the customer order quickly and accurately because he does not need to key the customer number and address. He can also see whether the customer has enough available credit to cover the order.

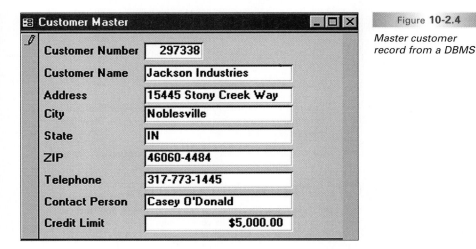

Figure **10-2.4**

Master customer record from a DBMS

Image Processing Systems

Image processing is an effective way to store documents that must be seen in their original form to verify information. An image processing system uses software and special equipment, including scanners and optical disks, to store an exact copy of a paper document. The images may be very complex. Sound files may be used to provide comments about the images. These systems are like huge electronic filing cabinets linked together. They allow the user to quickly access and review the images of documents. A computer is used to display a document on the screen or to print a hard copy of it.

419

Topic 10-2: *Managing Magnetic, Optical, and Microfilm Media*

Optical disks are an important part of image processing systems. Optical disks offer large storage capacity and can be stored in a retrieval system called a jukebox. A jukebox contains many disks and allows records to be retrieved quickly. Jukeboxes can be linked together, which further increases storage capacity.

WORKPLACE CONNECTIONS

Sharmane is a customer service supervisor at a savings and loan company. All questions and comments from customers regarding their mortgage accounts are directed to her. The company stores all its customer accounts on optical disks. Sharmane is describing the features of the image processing system to Dewey, a new employee.

Sharmane: "Our new image processing system lets me retrieve documents quickly. When customers call with questions about a mortgage payment, I just key the customer's account number at my computer. The system quickly locates the account and displays it on my screen. I can even get a printout if I want."

Dewey: "That's certainly efficient."

Sharmane: "Right! Before, locating document files took so long that I'd have to tell customers that I'd call them later after I'd pulled the folder."

Organizing Microforms

In a paper system, you file individual records in folders. You label each folder so that you can identify the contents and file the folder correctly. A microform is similar to a folder because it contains many records. Microforms should be labeled and organized so that they can be retrieved easily. How you label and organize the microforms will depend on the particular filing system used in your organization. Records may be filed by name, number, subject, or location.

A microfiche is a sheet of film containing several rows of images. At the top of each microfiche (or fiche) is space to label the contents of that particular sheet. The caption on a sheet is similar to the caption used on a folder in a paper filing system. Microfiche labels are frequently color coded for easy retrieval.

Microfiche is the microform commonly used for active (frequently used) storage. Fiche can be stored efficiently in panels. These panels are pages of paper or vinyl that have several slots into which you insert the microfiche. The slots are deep enough to protect the fiche, yet shallow enough to allow the caption to be read easily. Microfiche can also be stored in trays or file cabinets where guides and color-coded labels are used to organize them.

Roll microfilm is kept in protective cases or boxes. A label is attached to the case or box to identify the records. The roll is filed with other rolls in a drawer or cabinet according to the filing system used.

The most commonly used aperture card contains only one record or image. Captions can be printed along the top edge of the card. The cards can be filed much as you would file and retrieve paper records. Aperture cards are often housed in trays.

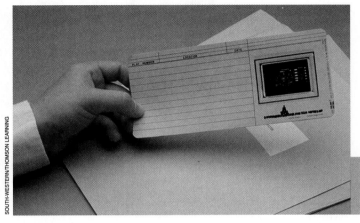

SOUTH-WESTERN/THOMSON LEARNING

The identifying information printed on an aperture card is used in storage and retrieval.

Retrieving Records on Microfilm

To find a record on microfilm, you must know on which roll, fiche, or aperture card the record is stored. If the record is on roll microfilm or microfiche, you also must know the specific location of the record on the film. An index lists an address for each microfilm record. The first step in retrieving a record is to consult the index to find the location of that record. Next, a reader is used to view the record. A full-sized hard copy of the record can be printed if needed.

Computer-assisted retrieval (CAR) is the process of locating records on film by using computer-stored indexes. A simple CAR system uses a computer and a reader/printer. You use the computer to print or display the index to find the record location. Then you manually locate and load the proper microform into the reader.

You may want to arrange for students to visit a company or library where they can see how records stored on microfilm are retrieved.

Advanced CAR systems use computer software to maintain an index that is similar to an electronic database. An advantage of a database index is that you can search for a record by name, subject, or date. The address of the needed record will be displayed on the screen. Then you place the microform into the reader/printer and view the record.

Some CAR systems automatically locate the correct image and display it on the reader screen by using a film autoloader. These systems allow microform records to be viewed from remote locations via a computer network.

A microform reader can be used to view and print records.

REVIEWING THE TOPIC

1. What is the advantage of records management software?
2. What functions does records management software perform?
3. List three guidelines to follow when naming files for electronic storage.
4. When labeling individual disks or tapes, what descriptive information should appear on the labels?
5. Why should you make backup copies of disks and tapes?
6. List four steps you can take to safeguard electronic files when in use.
7. Why are databases useful to businesses?
8. What is one major advantage of using optical disk storage?
9. Describe how microforms may be stored.
10. How are records retrieved using a simple CAR system?

INTERACTING WITH OTHERS

You and two of your coworkers, Gloria and Paula, are working late one evening. All the other employees have gone for the day. During a brief break, Gloria says to you: "I hear the company is about to close some pretty big real estate deals. You know the access code for the financial database. Let's look and see what's going on." Paula agrees, saying, "Sure! No one else is here. What difference will it make? We won't tell anyone you let us see the information."

1. How would you react in this situation? What would you say to your coworkers?
2. What might be the consequences of accessing and sharing this confidential information with coworkers?

REINFORCING MATH SKILLS

1. Your company estimates that it takes you 20 minutes less to file each day using folders with color-coded file labels than using folders without them. Calculate how many hours the use of color-coded file labels saves you each week (5 working days), each month (4 weeks), and each year (50 weeks). Show your calculations.
2. Eight file folders have captions with *Randolph* as the first indexing unit, six folders have *Reynolds* as the first unit, and two folders have *Rogers* as the first unit. One hundred and thirty folders are filed under the letter *R.* Of the total R folders, calculate what percentage are *Randolph* folders, what percentage are *Reynolds* folders, and what percentage are *Rogers* folders. Round your answers to the nearest whole percentages. Show your calculations.

Teaching Tips

Review with students the guidelines for naming electronic files found in this topic. Emphasize that the plan for naming files should be consistent and simple.

RECORDS MANAGEMENT

Topic **10-2** | A C T I V I T Y 1

Organizing Electronic Files

Electronic files must be named and organized properly to make them easy to retrieve. You have recently begun a new job working with three executives in the accounting firm Carson Associates. Several files that were created by the person who previously had this job are stored on your computer. However, no clear organization or consistent file names have been used. You must organize the existing files. You will also create a plan for naming and organizing the files you will store in the future. The plan should be simple and clear so that someone unfamiliar with your files, such as one of the executives or a temporary worker, could easily find a particular file.

1. You have quickly scanned the contents of the files on your computer and made notes about what each file contains. Open and print the PDF file *CH10 Files* from the data files. This file contains the information you noted about the files.

2. Review the guidelines for naming electronic files found in this topic. Then create a plan that includes folders and subfolders that will let you quickly find files about a particular topic for any of the three executives. Outline your plan showing the structure and names of main folders and subfolders so that it would be easy for someone else to understand.

3. Create a plan for naming files that will be consistent and simple. Write a brief description of your plan. For each file currently on your computer (as listed on the printout), key the current file name. Then key the file path (main folder and any subfolders in which the file will be stored) and the new name you will give the file. Assume that the computer is set to show file extensions.

   Example: Star bid 1.doc C:\Stone\Bids\Stardust Bid 6-23.doc

4. Show the structure of your new file system. Arrange the folder names and new file names in groups to show each main folder, each subfolder within each main folder, and each new file name within a main folder or subfolder.

5. Keep all your notes and a copy of your file structure and file names for use in a later activity.

CHAPTER 10: MANAGING RECORDS

Topic 10-2 : ACTIVITY 2

Electronic Files Index

In this activity, you will continue your work at Carson Associates. You created a file organization and naming plan in Topic 10-2 Activity 1. Now you will create a computer index to track the electronic records and their retention dates.

1. Create a new database named *CH10 Index*. Create a table named **Files Index.** Include the following text fields in the table: Filename, File Path, Date, Originator, Key Content, Category, Active Storage, and Inactive Storage. Make the Filename field the primary key.

2. Use the list of new filenames and paths you created in Topic 10-2 Activity 2. Create a record in your database for each file.

   - Enter the filename in the Filename field, for example, Stardust Bid 6-23.doc.
   - Enter the path for the file in the File Path field, for example, C:\Stone\Bids.
   - Enter the date of the file in the Date field.
   - Enter the name of the executive for whom the file was created in the Originator field.
   - Enter a few words that indicate what the record relates to in the Key Content field, for example, cover letter for bid.
   - Enter the type of record, such as letter, report, spreadsheet, presentation, or database, in the Category field.
   - Enter the retention period for which the document will be kept in active online storage on your computer in the Active Storage field. See the list below to determine retention periods.
   - Enter the retention period for which the document will be kept in inactive storage (on a disk) in the Inactive Storage field.

Retention Periods		
Category	Active Storage	Inactive Storage
Bank reconciliations	3 years	Permanent
Bids and related correspondence	1 year	4 years
Client database	Permanent	
Correspondence	1 year	4 years
Financial statements (balance sheets and income statements)	3 years	Permanent
Invoices	2 years	7 years
Presentations	1 year	2 years

425

Topic Review

Teaching Tips

Students must use the filenames and folder structure created in Topic 10-2 Activity 1 to complete this activity. Review how to create a new database, how to create a database table and enter data, and how to create a query.

3. Create a query named **Files by Originator.** Base the query on the Files Index table. Show the Originator, Filename, File Path, Date, and Key Content fields in the query results table. Sort the records in ascending order, first by the Originator field, then by the File Name field. Print the query results table.

4. Assume six months have gone by since you created your electronic records index. You would have created many more files during this time. Mr. Stone asks you to find any records related to taxes for Beal Tires. Create a query named **Beal Tires** to find this information. Base the query on the Files Index table. Display the Filename, File Path, Date, Originator, and Key Content fields in the query results. Sort the records by the Filename field. Print the query results.

CHAPTER REVIEW 10

Summary

In this chapter, you learned about managing records. Records may be stored on paper and other media. Reprographics was discussed as part of the use and maintenance phases of the record life cycle. Review the following key points:

- Five steps are involved in preparing paper records for storage. These steps are collecting, inspecting, indexing/coding, cross-referencing, and sorting.
- Vertical and lateral file cabinets are often used to house folders. Shelf files are overall the optimal choice for housing folders.
- Supplies such as requisition forms, OUT guides, and OUT folders are used to manage records efficiently.
- A retention schedule identifies which records should be removed from active storage and on which dates.
- Methods of storage that can be used to protect vital records include multisite storage, planned dispersing, duplication, and vaulting.
- Copiers are found in a typical business office and are used by almost all employees.
- Businesses may have a copying center to handle large copying jobs and other copiers for use with small copying jobs.
- Electronic copier/printers can receive, transmit, store, print, and copy data.
- Measures used to control copier use include monitoring devices, copy logs, user guidelines, and copying centers.
- Many businesses store records on magnetic disks, drives, and tapes. These media must be carefully labeled and organized.
- A company that has many records to maintain may use a database. A database management system simplifies and speeds up the retrieval process by organizing large numbers of records.
- Image processing systems allow users to view images of documents. The images may be stored on optical disks.
- Electronic files should be organized for easy retrieval. Many companies use secondary storage to back up files and free hard drive space.
- Companies use measures such as backing up data, password access, firewalls, and antivirus software to protect online records.

427

Chapter Review

427

Chapter Review

Key Terms

bar code	hacker	reprographics
copyright laws	password	requisition form
cross-reference	records management	secondary storage
electronic database	software	sorting
file path	release mark	

RECORDS MANAGEMENT

Chapter **10** ACTIVITY **1**

Alphabetic Filing

Applying standard alphabetic indexing rules correctly is essential for effective records management. In this activity, you will apply rules for alphabetic indexing as you index and code names of individuals and organizations. You will also arrange the records in filing order for an alphabetic file.

1. Open and print the PDF file *CH10 Names* from the data files. You have reviewed 60 pieces of correspondence that are to be filed in an alphabetic name file. You have identified the filing segment (name) to use for filing each document. These filing segments are shown on the printout.

2. Review the alphabetic indexing rules in Figure 9-2.5 on page 375 or in *Reference Section F* in your *Student Activities and Simulations* workbook.

3. For each filing segment on the printout, code the name by placing slash marks between the units. Number the indexing units above the name. Refer to Figure 10-1.1 on page 393 for an example of a coded name.

4. If you were filing the actual documents, you would sort them in alphabetic order before going to the filing cabinets to file the documents. Sort the coded names on the printout in alphabetic order as you would sort documents. Prepare a list of the document numbers as they are arranged in alphabetic order to submit to your instructor.

DATABASE
RECORDS MANAGEMENT
WORD PROCESSING

Chapter **10** ACTIVITY **2**

Electronic Files Backup

In this activity, you will continue your work at Carson Associates. In Topic 10-2 Activity 2, you created a computer index to track the electronic records and their retention dates. You will use the index to identify files to be moved to secondary storage. You will also determine the filing order for the backup disks.

1. Assume you created your records index on August 10 of the current year. Now assume that 13 months have gone by since that date when the index was created. You need to find all records that have been in active storage longer than the time shown on the retention schedule. In this situation, records with *1 year* in the Active Storage field would

428

be ready for transfer to inactive storage. Create a query based on the Files Index table. Name the query **Files to Transfer.** Show the Originator, Filename, File Path, Category, Active Storage, and Inactive Storage fields in the query results. Sort the query results by the Filename field. Key *1 year* in the Criteria row for the Active Storage field. Run the query and print the query results table.

2. Decide how to group these records shown in the query results for transfer to inactive storage on disks. How many disks will be used? Which files will be placed on each disk? Key and print a list of the files that will be saved on each disk.

3. Key a label to place on each backup disk. Each label should list the originator, the contents of the disk, the date the backup disk is created, and how long the files should be retained. See the example label below. Also indicate the operating system and software used to create the records. See your original notes about the files for this information.

```
Stone
Presentations

Backup Created: 9/10/--
Retention: 2 years:

Windows XP
Microsoft PowerPoint 2003
```

4. You will store the disks containing backup files in a plastic storage container. You have decided to arrange the disks alphabetically first by originator and then by subject. Arrange the disk labels in the order in which the disks would be arranged according to your plan.

5. Print the labels. (Print on plain paper if labels are not available.)

After completing all the chapters in Part 3, complete the Part 3 simulation, At Work at Maple Valley Chamber of Commerce. The simulation is found in the Student Activities and Simulations *workbook.*

429

Chapter Review

Supplemental Activity

Have students complete the Chapter 10 Supplemental Activity, Copier Log, available on *The Office* Web site.

Assessment

Assess student learning using the Chapter 10 test available on the *IRCD* and in *ExamView®* format.

PART 4

Mail and Telecommunication Systems

OBJECTIVES

- Apply procedures for handling incoming and outgoing mail

- Respond to incoming calls and place outgoing calls effectively

- Describe the equipment, technology, and procedures for common forms of telecommunications

Fast, efficient, and effective communications are critical for the success of most businesses. Whether you communicate with coworkers and customers around the corner or around the world by mail, telephone, fax, e-mail, or other electronic means, your ability to handle communications effectively is a valuable skill. You will build your communication skills as you study Part 4, Mail and Telecommunication Systems.

430

© GETTY IMAGES/PHOTODISC

CHAPTER 11

Processing Mail

Workers frequently send written messages to coworkers as well as to people outside the company. Mail must be processed efficiently so that these messages are not delayed. The size of a company and the type of equipment available affect the procedures used for processing incoming and outgoing mail. In a small company, one worker may handle incoming and outgoing mail. In a large company, a full-time mailroom staff often uses specialized equipment to process mail. Even in large companies, workers outside the mailroom may have certain mail-handling duties.

In this chapter, you will learn procedures for processing incoming and outgoing mail in both small and large companies. You also will learn about the equipment available to process mail.

431

Topic 11-1

objectives

- Sort and distribute incoming mail
- Open, separate, and annotate incoming mail
- Document the receipt of mail
- Refer, route, and prioritize mail

INCOMING MAIL PROCEDURES

Office workers often need to act promptly in response to items received in the mail. They may need to deposit checks, fill orders, or pay invoices. They may read literature, review reports, and answer correspondence. Mail must be accurately sorted and promptly distributed to the appropriate people. This prompt delivery is necessary so actions can be taken without delay. In this chapter, you will learn how to handle incoming mail from outside the company, as well as inter-office mail.

You may be responsible for sorting and distributing incoming mail for the entire company or just for handling your own mail. You may help your coworkers process their mail after another worker has distributed it. Your role in processing incoming mail will depend on the size of the company, the volume of incoming mail, and your job duties.

Sorting and Distributing Mail

Mail for various people and departments is delivered to a company. Most companies want all mail sorted quickly and delivered promptly. Express mail, registered mail, and insured mail may be delivered immediately on receipt. The delivery of such letters usually takes priority over the processing of other mail. The method used for sorting mail will vary depending on the size of the company and how it is organized.

In Small Companies

In a small company, you can easily sort the mail at your workstation. Making a stack of mail for each employee or department makes delivery quicker. In a small company, one person may process incoming mail as well as perform other office tasks.

To distribute the mail, you hand deliver each stack of mail to the appropriate person or department. If you have several stacks or bundles of mail to deliver, you may need to carry them in a pouch, alphabetized expanding folder, lightweight mail basket, or mail cart as you make your rounds through the office. You should arrange the bundles according to the route you will take.

When Ted finishes sorting the mail, he places rubber bands around each stack, creating a separate bundle for each worker. Then he places the bundles in a mail cart in the order he will deliver them. Because Angela Duncan's workstation is his first stop, Ted places her mail bundle at the front of the cart. Using this procedure, Ted distributes the mail quickly.

The mail clerk delivers mail at regularly scheduled times during the workday.

In Large Companies

Many large companies have mailrooms. A mailroom is an area where large volumes of incoming mail are processed. Mailrooms are easily accessible to postal workers who deliver the mail to the company. You are likely to find specialized equipment to aid mailroom workers in handling the mail.

Opening Envelopes and Packages

In some companies, mailroom workers open all the mail (except envelopes marked *Personal* or *Confidential*) before delivering it. An electric envelope opener often is used for opening envelopes. An electric envelope opener trims a narrow strip off one edge of each envelope. The amount trimmed off is very small so that there is little risk that the contents of the envelope will be damaged. To reduce the chances of cutting the contents, tap each envelope on the table before placing it in the opener, so the contents will fall away from the edge that you are trimming. Take care when opening packages and boxes not to damage the contents.

433

Topic 11-1: *Incoming Mail Procedures*

For Discussion

Why is it important for a mail clerk to sort and deliver the mail with careful attention to detail? Do you think that it is acceptable for employees to receive personal mail at work? Why or why not?

Teaching Tips

Business and office magazines often have advertisements with photographs of mailroom equipment. You may want to collect samples and have a student committee design a bulletin board display that provides students with an idea of what they might find in the mailroom of a large company.

This mailroom worker is sorting incoming mail from the post office and from private mail services.

Points to Emphasize

Mailroom and other office workers should take appropriate precautions related to handling mail to protect their health and safety.

Expand the Concept

Have students ask family and friends what procedures are used for distributing mail at their places of employment. Are the procedures similar to the examples listed here? If not, how do they differ?

Safety Precautions

Office workers should take care to protect themselves against dangerous substances that might be present in envelopes or packages received via mail. Wearing gloves and a face mask can provide some protection from airborne substances that might be dangerous. When handling mail, avoid touching your face and mouth to help prevent the transfer of germs. Wash your hands with disinfectant soap after handling mail. The United States Postal Service recommends that you do not handle a piece of mail that you suspect is dangerous.

According to the Centers for Disease Control and Prevention (CDC), "Characteristics of suspicious packages and letters include inappropriate or unusual labeling, strange return address or no return address, postmarks from a city or state different from the return address, excessive packaging material, and others. If a package appears suspicious, it should not be opened. The package should be handled as little as possible. The room should be vacated and secured promptly and appropriate security or law enforcement agencies promptly notified."[1] For more information, access the CDC Web site. A link is provided to the site on *The Office* web site.

Sorting Mail

A wide variety of sorting units are used to sort the mail. Each compartment is labeled with the name of an individual or department within the organization. To sort the mail, you place each piece of mail in the appropriate compartment.

Companies with a huge amount of incoming mail have found that they can save time and effort by using a rotary sorting unit. The unit turns easily, and the worker can remain in one place as he or she sorts the mail.

[1]"Update: Investigation of Bioterrorism-Related Anthrax and Interim Guidelines for Exposure Management and Antimicrobial Therapy, October 2001," Centers for Disease Control and Prevention, http://www.cdc.gov/mmwr/preview/mmwrhtml/mm5042a1.htm (accessed September 27, 2005).

Distributing Mail

Once the mail has been sorted, it is ready for distribution. Procedures for delivering mail within the organization vary from company to company. For example:

- A worker from each department comes to the mailroom to pick up the department's mail.
- A mailroom employee carries the mail in a basket or cart from the mailroom to the departments.
- An automated delivery system transports mail to the various departments. This robot-like cart follows a chemical path on the floor and is programmed to stop at certain locations throughout the building. Employees can then pick up incoming mail and deposit outgoing mail.

© 2003 PITNEY BOWES INC. USED BY PERMISSION.

In some companies, an employee delivers mail to each department.

Handling Incoming Mail

Some office workers are asked to process the mail before giving it to their coworkers. Some workers may simply separate and open the mail. Other workers may be expected to annotate, route, or prioritize correspondence.

In handling your own mail or mail for others, you may have access to confidential information. This information may be related to business plans or products, employee records, or customer profiles. You will be expected to take steps to protect this confidential information. You may be asked to sign a confidentiality agreement.

435

Topic 11-1: *Incoming Mail Procedures*

Sarah is an employee in the Office of Housing at a state university. She has access to sensitive and personal information about residents. Sarah has been directed not to disclose any of the information she has access to while employed by the university. If she fails to comply with the confidentiality agreement she signed when she was hired, she could be fired from her job.

© YANG CHINA TOURISM PRESS. LIU/IMAGE BANK/GETTY IMAGES

Opening Mail

If the mail is not opened when it reaches you, use a letter opener to open all envelopes. (See Safety Precautions on page 434.) When you are opening mail for coworkers, do not open envelopes marked *Personal* or *Confidential*. If you mistakenly open such an envelope, write on it, "Sorry, opened by mistake," and add your initials. Check the outside of each envelope carefully before you open it to avoid making that error.

As you remove the contents from the envelopes, be sure to verify that all enclosures referred to in the letter are actually enclosed. If an enclosure is missing, you should note in the margin of the letter that it is missing. Notify the sender of the missing enclosure right away, especially if it is a check, money order, cash, or stamps.

Check each letter for the signature and the address of the sender before you discard the envelope. If either is missing on the letter, attach the envelope to the back of the letter. The envelope usually has a return address on it. Sometimes the envelope is stapled to a document because the mailing date may be important.

Record the current date on each item received. In some cases, recording the time the item was received may also be helpful. This can be done with a pen or pencil, a rubber stamp, or a time-stamp machine.

Separating and Annotating Mail

As you inspect the mail, put the letters that you will answer or handle yourself in one stack and those that will be handled by a supervisor or coworkers in another stack. You may be able to handle communications that could be answered by a form letter, circular, or advertisement. Requests for catalogs or price lists can also be handled this way. However, your supervisor may wish to see all inquiries that are received.

annotate: write comments related to the content of a message

To help with answering mail, you may want to underline or **annotate** the correspondence. Using good judgment is necessary here, however, because too many marks on a letter can be distracting.

First, underline the key words and phrases in the correspondence that will aid in understanding the content quickly. Note the key phrases underlined in Figure 11-1.1 on page 438. Then determine the answers to questions in

CHAPTER 11: PROCESSING MAIL

FOCUS ON . . .

Protecting Confidential Information

Confidential information is data that is private or secret. Release of such data could cause harm to the business or its employees, clients, or customers. Businesses may have several types of confidential data. Inside information is data about the company that has not yet been released to the public. Examples are plans to open a new plant or merge with another company. Proprietary information is data about the company's products or services. An example is the formula or design for a product. Private information about employees and customers, such as salaries or credit card numbers, is often stored in company files. Usually, only those employees who need the data to do their jobs are allowed to see confidential information.

As an office worker, you may come in contact with confidential information as you process the mail, prepare documents, or handle records. The following guidelines will help you keep business information confidential:

- **Know your supervisor's preferences.** Know what information you should and should not give to visitors or callers. When your supervisor is not in the office, know who is to be allowed in your supervisor's office or who can use your supervisor's computer.

- **Follow your company's mail procedures.** Place confidential mail in a folder or in a secure location where it will be seen only by the intended recipient. Do not send confidential information by fax or e-mail. Use overnight mail services if speed is a consideration.

- **Secure your workstation.** Take precautions to keep others from reading confidential information from your computer screen. Turn over confidential mail or papers or place them in a drawer when you leave your desk—even for a few moments. At the end of the day, secure papers in a locked desk or file cabinet. Shred confidential documents rather than placing them in your wastebasket.

- **Protect written documents.** Use a folder or an envelope to conceal documents if you carry documents to another office. If you transport confidential documents outside the office, lock them in a briefcase or in the trunk of your car. If you use a briefcase, always keep it in your possession.

- **Reduce electronic information loss.** Use password sign-on and sign-off procedures and change your password frequently. Be alert to remove printouts from the printer when you finish the print job, particularly if the printer is shared with others. Make backup copies of confidential files and place them in a secure location.

Points to Emphasize

An office worker should discuss possible situations that may arise involving confidential information with a supervisor so the worker will know the proper steps to take when the situation occurs.

the message. Where appropriate, make related comments on the document. Write the clearly worded answers and/or comments in legible handwriting in the margin, on a note (paper or electronic) placed on the correspondence, or on a photocopy of the correspondence. Note the annotations on the letter shown in Figure 11-1.1.

437

Topic 11-1: *Incoming Mail Procedures*

Russell White and Brothers Lumber Company
3000 Winchester Avenue
Ashland, KY 41101-0077

December 5, 20--

DEC 8, 20-- 11:30 AM

Ms. Michele R. Carrel
Ashland Computerland, Inc.
405 Laurel Avenue
Ashland, KY 41101-0800

Dear Ms. Carrel

Copy sent to Mr. Ortiz.

Our new <u>computer system was installed on November 26,</u> and we were impressed with the efficiency of your installation team. The hardware and software are installed and working well. Feedback from the end-users has been positive.

Ed Ortiz, your installation team director, advises that we need to add one more workstation to maximize the use of the computer network. <u>Please add another PC2-2020 workstation to our order.</u>

Prepared Inv. 22892 on 12/9.

Mr. Ortiz also reminded us to make plans for our unit director, <u>Mary Ann Park,</u> to attend your <u>end-user workshop on January 6-10.</u> Ms. Park is eager to attend, and we know that this additional education will allow her to help us use our network more effectively. Please <u>send Ms. Park a registration form</u> for the workshop.

Registration form sent.

Sincerely

Harold G. White

Harold G. White, Manager

dc

Figure **11-1.1**

The date-time stamp, underlined words and phrases, and annotations make a quick response easier.

Copies of previous correspondence, reports, and other related documents might help in responding to the mail. For example, you may attach the file copy of a letter written to Ms. Park to the reply you receive from her. Or you might retrieve a folder related to an inquiry from the files and place it with the incoming letter.

Documenting Receipt of Mail

You should keep a record of items you expect to receive under separate cover (in another envelope or package) to be sure that you receive them. You might create a spreadsheet or database table to record the current date, the item expected, the date you expect to receive the item, and the person or company who will send the item. A field or column might be included to record the date the item is received. If you handle mail for several people, you would include the name of the person expecting the item. Check the table at least twice a week to see which items have not been received. Then take follow-up action on delayed mail. If you handle mail only for yourself, you might simply enter a reminder in your desktop utility software, such as *Microsoft Outlook*, to alert you on the date the mail is expected. Figure 11-1.2 shows such as entry.

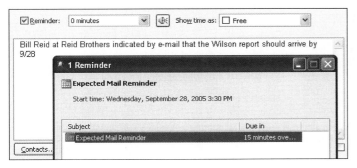

Figure **11-1.2**

Keep a reminder of incoming mail you expect to receive.

Whether you process incoming mail in a small company or in the mailroom of a large company, you should keep track of the receipt of mail sent by special postal services or private mail services. For example, you should record the receipt of certified, insured, registered, or express mail. You might use a printed form or record information in a database table as shown in Figure 11-1.3.

Item	For	From	City	State	Date	Time
Insured Package	B. Rudd	T. J. McIntosh	St. Louis	MO	4-5-02	3:20 p.m.
Special Delivery Package	S. Nowell	Bates Mfg. Co.	Memphis	TN	4-6-02	9:15 a.m.
Registered Letter	J. Jones	Ken Stewart	Des Moines	IA	4-9-02	10:45 a.m.
Express Mail Package	W. Yeager	Haskins Associates	Erie	PA	4-12-02	3:15 p.m.

Figure **11-1.3**

Use a mail register to document the receipt of special mail.

Topic 11-1: *Incoming Mail Procedures*

For Discussion

Ask students to refer to Figure 11-1.2. Then ask students: What expected mail item does the reminder refer to? By what date is the item expected? From whom is the item expected?

Points to Emphasize

Whether you process incoming mail in a small company or in the mailroom of a large company, you should document the receipt of mail sent by special postal services.

referral slip: a document that accompanies items sent to another person and indicates a requested action

You or your supervisor may decide to refer certain items to an assistant or associate to handle. To help with this process, a **referral slip** is attached to the item. The referral slip shown in Figure 11-1.4 lists a series of instructions from which to choose. A check mark is used to indicate the specific instruction to be followed.

Figure 11-1.4

Mail is often forwarded to an associate for action.

REFERRAL SLIP

Date _9/18/--_

TO _Alice Leary_

Refer to the attached material and
☐ Please note
☐ Please note and file
☐ Please note and return to me
☐ Please mail to_____
☐ Please note and talk with me
　　this a.m._____ p.m._____
☐ Please answer, sending me a copy
☑ Please write a reply for my signature
☐ Please handle
☐ Please have ____ photocopies made for

☐ Please sign
☐ Please let me have your comments
☐ Please RUSH, immediate action desired
☐ Please make follow-up for _____

REMARKS _Letter should go out no later than 9/25._

Signed _Ross Darlington_

When action is requested of another individual, you should keep a record of the referral. You should note the date the item was referred, the name of the person to whom it was referred, the subject, the action to be taken, and a follow-up date if one is necessary.

Often more than one person in the company should read items, such as correspondence and important magazine articles. You may be asked to make a copy for each person who should read the item, or you may be asked to route the item through the office. To do so, attach a **routing slip**, which is similar to a referral slip, to the item. Indicate with check marks the individuals who should read the item.

routing slip: a document attached to an item that shows the names of individuals to whom the item should be sent

prioritize: place in order of importance

Prioritizing Mail

Incoming mail should be **prioritized** for further processing. As a general rule, mail is categorized in the order of its importance. The following arrangement is usually satisfactory, moving from the top to the bottom of the stack:

1. Urgent messages, such as documents received by fax or overnight delivery, that require prompt attention
2. Personal and confidential letters
3. Business letters, memos, or other correspondence of special importance
4. Letters containing checks or money orders

CHAPTER 11: PROCESSING MAIL

440

5. Other business letters
6. Letters containing orders
7. Letters containing bills, invoices, or other requests for payment
8. Advertisements
9. Newspapers and magazines
10. Packages

ROUTING SLIP

FROM:

Ryan Talbert

_____**Information Services Department**

DATE: *3/25*

TO:	Date Forwarded
___Everyone	_____
___R. Bernardin	_____
✓ R. Carlson	*3/25*
___M. Carrell	_____
___J. Fouch	_____
✓ J. Hensen	*3/25*
___C. Hickman	_____
___H. Iwuki	_____
✓ S. Lansing	*3/26*
___M. Lucky	_____
___C. Tesch	_____
✓ R. Williams	*3/27*

Please:
___Read and keep in your files
___Read and pass on
___Read and return to me
✓ Read, route, and return to me

Figure **11-1.5**

A routing slip is attached to mail to be distributed to others.

For Discussion

In Figure 11-1.5, from whom was the item routed? What action was requested of the individuals receiving the item?

WORKPLACE CONNECTIONS

Roberta Diaz is the receptionist in a small real estate agency. Her duties include sorting and prioritizing mail for several coworkers. Roberta noticed that 25 to 50 percent of the mail received by the agency each day was advertisements and "junk" mail. She decided to write to the Direct Marketing Association, a trade group of telephone and mail marketers. She requested that the company's name be removed from national mailing lists. Now Roberta has many fewer ads to handle and can sort the mail more quickly each day.

441

Topic 11-1: *Incoming Mail Procedures*

Thinking Critically

What are examples of mail items that should be forwarded to business travelers while away from the office? What are examples of mail items that would be considered "routine" and could wait to be handled until the traveler is back in the office?

synopsis: general overview or summary

Handling Mail While Away from the Office

Technology makes it possible to receive and forward important mail and messages for immediate action while away from the office. In this way, business matters are not delayed, and deadlines are not missed. You will need to decide which mail should be forwarded and which mail should be held for action after returning to the office. The following guidelines may be helpful in keeping track of incoming mail for your supervisors or coworkers who are away from the office:

- Maintain a mail register as described on page 439.
- Communicate with the traveler immediately if important, unexpected action seems required.
- Refer routine mail to others who can respond.
- Answer mail yourself if it is within your area of responsibility.
- Send a synopsis of received mail (or a copy of the mail log) if the traveler is on an extended business trip.
- After the mail has been prioritized, store it in an appropriate place.

Effective processing of the incoming mail helps keep the office running smoothly while the traveler is away and saves time for the traveler upon returning to the office.

REVIEWING THE TOPIC

1. What is interoffice mail?
2. What three factors affect your role in processing incoming mail?
3. Describe safety precautions office workers can take to protect themselves against dangerous substances that might be present in envelopes or packages received via mail.
4. What equipment is used in mailrooms to process incoming mail?
5. What should you do if you open a confidential letter by mistake?
6. When you remove the contents from an envelope, what should you verify?
7. How might your annotating a letter save your supervisor time?
8. What is the purpose of keeping a record of expected mail?
9. Give an example of when a routing slip might be used.
10. What is the generally accepted order for prioritizing incoming mail?

INTERACTING WITH OTHERS

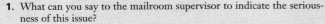

You work as an administrative assistant at Halbrook, Inc. One of your duties is to sort, open, and annotate mail for three executives. Letters that are not marked *Confidential* are normally opened by the staff in the central mail room. Ms. Santiago, one of the executives you assist, often receives correspondence that contains confidential information regarding acquiring and developing new products. She has requested that her letters not be opened in the mail room. You have discussed this issue with the mailroom supervisor on two occasions. However, her letters continue to arrive at your department opened. You suspect that some of the letters have been removed from the envelopes and replaced in them.

1. What can you say to the mailroom supervisor to indicate the seriousness of this issue?
2. What are some possible reasons why your request has not been honored?
3. What steps should you take if talking with the mailroom supervisor again does not result in the letters arriving unopened?

443

Topic Review

Teaching Tips

If the students are using the *Student Activities and Simulations* workbook, instruct them to complete the review activity for this topic.

For Discussion

Have students share their responses to the questions with the class.

Teaching Tips

Give students the correct answers after they complete the activity.

Teaching Tips

Have students share the reasons for the sort order used with the class.

REINFORCING MATH SKILLS

1. Based on records kept by the mailroom supervisor, about 3,000 pieces of incoming mail are sorted and distributed each month in your company. Additionally, the volume of mail is expected to increase by 6 percent next year. How many pieces of mail will be processed this year? How many more pieces of mail will be processed next year than will be processed this year?

2. An envelope has been prepared for each address on a mailing list of 18,000 names. The mailing machine can feed, seal, meter stamp, count, and stack 200 envelopes a minute. Of the 18,000 envelopes being processed, 20 percent are being sent to Minnesota, 30 percent to Wyoming, 15 percent to Wisconsin, and 35 percent to Nebraska. How long it will take to process all the envelopes using the mailing machine? How many envelopes will be sent to each state?

WORD PROCESSING

Topic 11-1 : **ACTIVITY 1**

Sort Incoming Mail

You work in the general office of Sperling Enterprises. Because your supervisor receives a large amount of mail of different types, she has asked you to prioritize it prior to delivering it to her.

1. Key the list of the mail items shown below.

2. Arrange the list of mail items in order of priority. (Begin the list with the most important and continue to the least important.)

- Personal letter from Michelle Jackson
- Overnight package from Hancock Associates
- Letter containing an order from Jackie Yung
- Advertisement for office furniture
- Newspaper
- Interoffice memo from coworker Paula Flores
- Fax from Karl Shelton, at Shelton Brothers
- Business letter of special importance from Norman Steel of Steel, Inc.
- *PC Magazine*
- Letter containing a bill from Office Depot
- Letter containing a check from Howard Supply Company
- Fax from David Foster of Foster Insurance
- Business letter from Maria Lopez of Quality Leasing

444

CHAPTER 11: PROCESSING MAIL

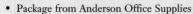

- Package from Anderson Office Supplies
- Advertisement from Media Plus
- *Business Week* magazine
- Letter containing a bill from Jackson Electric Company
- Letter containing a check from Susan Patrick
- Letter containing an order from Dan Alvarez
- Business letter from Creative Calendars, Inc.

Topic **11-1** : ACTIVITY 2

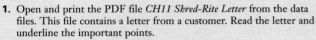

COMPOSITION
WORD PROCESSING

Annotate Letter and Compose Reply

You work for Shred-Rite Shredder Company, a retailer for office and personal paper shredders. Your supervisor, Ms. Wanda Albertson, is the customer service manager. You often annotate mail and compose replies for her signature.

1. Open and print the PDF file *CH11 Shred-Rite Letter* from the data files. This file contains a letter from a customer. Read the letter and underline the important points.

2. Open and print the PDF file *CH11 Shred-Rite Invoice* from the data files. This file contains a copy of the customer invoice. Review the invoice and then annotate the customer's letter with appropriate comments.

3. Compose a reply to the customer for your supervisor's signature. Assume the letter will be printed on company letterhead. Tell the customer how the problem will be corrected and express regret for the customer's inconvenience. Examine your letter for the five Cs of effective writing.

4. Submit the customer's letter with your annotations, the invoice, and your reply to your supervisor (instructor).

Create a bulletin board display using the best examples of annotated letters from students.

OUTGOING MAIL PROCEDURES

objectives

- Prepare outgoing mail
- Identify the classes of domestic mail
- Explain the various services provided by the USPS
- Identify address and packaging requirements
- Describe services provided by private mail delivery companies

A company may send several types of mail to those outside the company. For example, you may be asked to send purchase orders to customers. Letters may be sent to businesses. Advertisements may be sent to potential customers. Preparing outgoing mail properly is important for prompt delivery.

You probably have prepared letters and envelopes for mailing. You may have calculated and affixed proper postage. Companies have developed specific procedures for completing these tasks in order to handle outgoing mail efficiently.

The way outgoing mail is processed will depend on the size of your company and the procedures adopted by the company. If you work in a small office, you probably will be responsible for all the details involved with processing outgoing mail. If you work in the mailroom of a large company, however, you may weigh and seal mail, apply postage, and mail envelopes that have been prepared by workers in other departments.

The United States Postal Service (USPS) processes millions of pieces of mail each day. Businesses all across the country use the varied services of the USPS. Letters, financial reports, invoices, manuscripts, newsletters, and merchandise are examples of items delivered by the USPS. In some cases, the items are destined for delivery in the same city. In other cases, the items are delivered to an individual in a city halfway around the world.

courier service: a private mail delivery company

Local, national, and worldwide private mail delivery companies, sometimes called **courier services**, also deliver envelopes and packages. Most delivery services guarantee their delivery times. You also may send mail through an interoffice mail system. As an office worker, you need to know the mailing options available to you. This topic will help you learn about procedures for processing outgoing mail.

Processing Outgoing Mail

In a small company, an office worker may process all the outgoing mail, as well as handle other office tasks. In a large company, however, mail tasks may be divided between mailroom workers and workers in other areas. In a large company, the extent of mail-handling duties will be determined by company policy and the worker's specific job.

446

Students may be surprised by the variety of ways outgoing mail can be sent. They also may be unaware that so many services are available from the U.S. Postal Service (USPS). To help students understand the content of this topic, you may want them to search the index of the yellow pages to determine the types of mail and shipping companies in your area. Students could also view Web sites or obtain brochure/bulletins from the USPS and private companies that explain the range of services provided.

Expand the Concept

Discuss with students the private mail companies that serve your area. Encourage students to visit the Web sites for these companies to see the services offered.

Teaching Tips

Discuss with students the times when the USPS delivers and picks up mail at your school.

The USPS picks up and delivers mail to some organizations twice a day. In other organizations, a postal carrier may come to the office in the morning, and an office worker may take outgoing mail to a post office or a USPS mailbox in the afternoon. You need to know the scheduled times for pickup so you can have the mail ready on time. The USPS recommends mailing as early in the day as possible for the fastest service.

© DAVID YOUNG-WOLFF/PHOTOEDIT

Many private mail carriers pick up and deliver mail to business locations.

447

Topic 11-2: *Outgoing Mail Procedures*

Folding and Inserting Mail

Once a document is ready to mail, it is a good idea to give it a final check before inserting it in the envelope. Be sure that:

- Copies have been made, if necessary.
- Letters have been signed.
- Your initials appear below the signature on any letter you have signed for a supervisor or coworker.
- All enclosures noted at the bottom of a letter are actually enclosed in the envelope.
- The address on the envelope agrees with the address on the letter.
- The nine-digit ZIP code appears on the last line of both the envelope address and the return address.

You usually will insert documents into standard or window envelopes. Folding business documents correctly to fit into envelopes is a simple but important task. You should take care that the creases are straight and neat. A document should be inserted in an envelope so that it will be in a normal reading position when it is removed from the envelope and unfolded.

Standard Envelopes

The size for a standard envelope used for business letters is $9\frac{1}{2}$" × $4\frac{1}{8}$" (No. 10). Figure 11-2.1 shows how to fold a letter and insert it into a No. 10 envelope. The enclosures that accompany a document should be folded with the document and inserted so that they will come out of the envelope when the document is removed.

Figure **11-2.1**

Follow these steps to fold an 8½" × 11" sheet to insert into a No. 10 envelope.

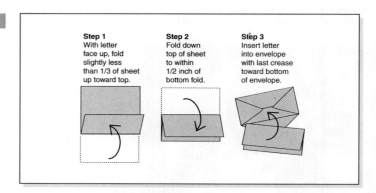

Step 1
With letter face up, fold slightly less than 1/3 of sheet up toward top.

Step 2
Fold down top of sheet to within 1/2 inch of bottom fold.

Step 3
Insert letter into envelope with last crease toward bottom of envelope.

Window Envelopes

A window envelope has a see-through panel on the front of the envelope. A window envelope eliminates the need to address an envelope because the address on the letter or form is visible through the window. The address on the letter or form must be positioned so that it can be seen through the window after the letter is folded and inserted into the envelope. Figure 11-2.2 shows how to fold a letter and insert it into a No. 10 window envelope.

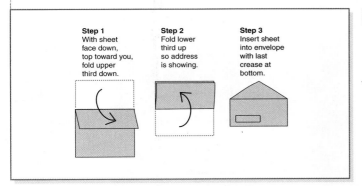

Step 1
With sheet face down, top toward you, fold upper third down.

Step 2
Fold lower third up so address is showing.

Step 3
Insert sheet into envelope with last crease at bottom.

Figure **11-2.2**

Follow these steps to fold an 8½″ × 11″ sheet to insert into a No. 10 window envelope.

Business forms are available in a variety of custom sizes. Special size envelopes are used to match the forms. When using special size forms and envelopes, make sure the mailing address shows properly in the envelope window.

Sealing and Weighing Envelopes

Envelopes must be sealed before they are mailed. When you need to seal more than one or two envelopes, you probably will want to use a moist sponge or moistener. Mail processing equipment that can insert letters into envelopes and seal the envelopes is available. If your office processes large mailings frequently, this equipment can save valuable time.

WORKPLACE CONNECTIONS

Alberto prepares several letters for mailing each morning. To quickly seal many envelopes at once, he spreads about ten envelopes on a table or desk. He places the letters address-side down, flap open, one on top of the other, with the gummed edges showing. Next, Alberto brushes over the gummed edges with a sponge or moistener. Starting with the top envelope, he quickly folds the flaps down one at a time until all the envelopes are sealed.

449

Topic 11-2: *Outgoing Mail Procedures*

Points to Emphasize

The enclosures that accompany a document should be folded with the document and inserted so that they come out of the envelope when the document is removed.

Thinking Critically

Moisteners and electronic postage scales are items designed to help office workers process outgoing mail efficiently. Ask students to name two additional items that help simplify the process of preparing outgoing mail.

Each piece of outgoing mail must be weighed accurately so you can apply the proper amount of postage. Electronic scales are available that automatically calculate the correct amount of postage for each piece of mail. You simply place the item to be mailed on the scale and indicate which postal class you wish to use. The amount of the postage is displayed on a small screen. When postal rates change, you update the scale with the new rates.

An electronic postage scale

© MICHAEL NEWMAN/PHOTOEDIT

Stamping Mail

Postage must be paid for all mail before it is delivered by the USPS. You may purchase postage stamps in sheet, booklet, or rolled form. Rolled stamps often are used in business because they can be placed quickly on envelopes and packages and they are less likely than individual stamps to be lost or damaged.

The post office sells envelopes and stamped cards (postcard size) that already have the correct postage printed on them. You can buy them one at a time or in quantity. Stamped cards may be purchased in single or double form. The double form is used when a reply is requested on the attached card.

Printing Postage for Mail

postage meter: a machine that prints postage in the amount needed

A **postage meter** is a machine that prints postage in the amount needed. The meter prints the postage either directly onto the envelope or onto a label that you apply to the envelope or package. You can use the numeric keys on the postage meter to set it to print postage for a letter weighing one ounce and easily reset it to print postage for a letter weighing three ounces. The postage meter prints the date as well as the postage amount. Always be sure the correct date is set on the meter. Some meters also print a business slogan or advertisement next to the postmark. Because metered mail is already dated and postmarked, it can be processed faster than stamped mail.

For Discussion

What form of stamps (sheet, booklet, or roll) would be most convenient for office use?

Thinking Critically

What internal control is provided by the use of a postage meter rather than rolls of stamps? What is the potential efficiency of using a postage meter instead of rolls of stamps?

An electronic postage meter prints the postmark and the postage.

For some postage meters, you take the meter with you to the post office to buy postage. A postal worker will reset the meter for the amount of postage purchased. As you use the postage meter, the meter setting decreases, showing you how much postage remains. Do not let the postage get too low before buying more. The meter locks when the postage runs out.

Several companies offer postage meters that allow you to purchase postage online. The user connects the meter, which contains a modem, to a standard phone line. Using a keypad, the user indicates the amount of postage to be purchased. The meter is updated, and the user is billed for the cost of the postage.

The USPS has authorized several companies to sell postage on the Internet. Users can access the Web site for one of these companies and subscribe to a postage service plan. The user receives computer software and, with some plans, a postage scale. The software allows the user to print a postmark and the appropriate amount of postage on an envelope or label using any computer printer. A graphic, such as the company logo, or text can be also be printed on the envelope or label.

Handling Volume Mailings

A volume mailing involves sending the same items to many people at the same time. For example, a marketing research company may send a questionnaire to all residents in a city asking about products, such as televisions or breakfast cereals. Companies doing volume mailings may qualify for reduced postage rates. To qualify for reduced postage rates, mailings must be prepared according to current USPS mailing regulations and standards.

Address labels may be used for volume mail items or the items may be addressed individually. Many companies use computer-generated mailing lists. Mailing lists for volume mail may contain addresses for customers, subscribers, or those who live in certain geographic areas. Mailing lists should always be current. Delete, correct, and add addresses as soon as you learn about changes.

Expand the Concept

Have students ask their family and friends what the procedures are for processing outgoing mail at their places of employment.

451

Topic 11-2: *Outgoing Mail Procedures*

Supplemental Activity

Instruct students to create a database of the names and addresses of all students in the class and generate a mailing list of labels from the database.

The post office recommends having the words *FORWARDING AND ADDRESS CORRECTION REQUESTED* printed on all envelopes. Then the post office will forward mail with an old address to the new address. For a small fee, the post office will send you a card giving the new address. Some of the advantages of using computer-generated mailing lists include the ability to:

- Quickly retrieve, change, or delete addresses
- Easily avoid duplicate addresses
- Select addresses from a master list to create a smaller list for a special mailing
- Print letter addresses and salutations on form letters as well as address labels

WORKPLACE CONNECTIONS

William Flag works in the Human Resources Department of a small company. He prepares volume mailings to employees, such as salespeople, who are not located at the company's home office. Benefits information, policy changes, and new procedures must be sent to these employees. Until recently, William keyed the address and printed an envelope for each employee each time a mailing was prepared. He soon realized that he was repeating work needlessly.

William decided to create a database to include the name, address, and other relevant data for each employee. He also created an envelope document and a mailing label document. He can merge data from the database with these documents. Now when William needs to prepare a mailing, he simply enters any updates in the database and completes the merge. Envelopes and labels are printed quickly and correctly.

Specialized mailing equipment is available to totally automate the process of preparing volume mailings. Some machines can print personalized letters and matching envelopes. The machines also fold the letters, insert the letters and any enclosures in the envelopes, and seal the envelopes. Postage can also be applied by machine.

Large companies may use equipment that can fold and insert documents, seal envelopes, weigh mail, and apply postage to speed mail processing.

© 2003 PITNEY BOWES INC. USED BY PERMISSION.

Address Requirements for Automated Handling

The USPS uses high-speed electronic mail-handling equipment in many of its postal centers. This equipment includes optical character readers and bar code sorters. An **optical character reader (OCR)** is electronic equipment that quickly scans or "reads" the address on an envelope. A bar code that relates to the scanned address is printed at the bottom of the envelope.

During the sorting process, the bar codes are "read" by a bar code sorter, and the mail is quickly routed to its proper destination. Not all postal centers are equipped with OCR equipment and bar code sorters; therefore, not all mail you receive will have a printed bar code on the envelope.

If the optical character reader is unable to read an address, the envelope is routed to a manual letter-sorting machine. This, of course, increases the processing time. Some of the reasons why an OCR may be unable to read an address are listed below. Use care when preparing mail to avoid these problems that may slow delivery of the mail.

optical character reader (OCR): electronic equipment that scans or "reads" text in a form that can be used by computers

- The address is handwritten.
- The address is not printed in the proper format.
- The envelope is too small or too large for the OCR equipment to handle. (To avoid this problem, use rectangular envelopes no smaller than $3\frac{1}{2}'' \times 5''$ and no larger than $6\frac{1}{8}'' \times 11\frac{1}{2}''$.)
- The address is not within the OCR read area.
- The complete address is not visible through the panel of a window envelope.

453

Topic 11-2: Outgoing Mail Procedures

For Discussion

Discuss the list of items that may slow the delivery of mail. Emphasize the importance of using the format for addresses recommended by the USPS.

ZIP Codes

To ensure prompt delivery of your mail, always use the nine-digit ZIP code, if known, to help with mail delivery. The first three digits of the ZIP code indicate a major geographic area or post office. The next two digits designate a local post office. A hyphen and the four digits that follow help the post office sort the mail more specifically. The first two digits after the hyphen indicate a delivery sector. A sector is several blocks within a city, a group of streets, several office buildings, or another small geographic area. The last two digits represent a delivery segment, which can indicate one side of a street, one floor in an office building, or specific departments in a firm.

ZIP code directories for both the five-digit and nine-digit codes can be purchased from the post office. If a directory is not available in the office where you work, you can call the post office to obtain a particular ZIP code. You can search for ZIP codes on the USPS Web site.

Address Format

The address should be printed clearly on the envelope or label for each item that is mailed. The characters should be dark, even, and clear. The address should be printed according to the following guidelines:

- Block the left margin of the address.
- Use all capital letters and omit all marks of punctuation (except the hyphen in a nine-digit ZIP code).
- Use the standard two-letter abbreviation for the state for domestic mail.
- Add the delivery point ZIP + 4 bar code on the envelope for domestic mail, if your software has this capability.
- For international addresses, place the foreign postal code, if known, on the same line as the city or town name. Place the city or town name and the province or state name on the next line after the street address information. Place the name of the foreign country in capital letters on the last line of the address. (On mail to Canada, the location of the country name and postal code are interchangeable.)

The post office has an approved list of abbreviations for states, cities, and other words commonly used in addresses. Always use the two-letter state abbreviations with the ZIP code in domestic addresses. Use other approved abbreviations if the address is too long to fit on a label.

Figure **11-2.3**

MS EMMA JO BERMAN
132 CANNON GREEN TOWERS APT 6A
SANTA BARBARA CA 93105-2233

Use the proper
address format,
abbreviations, and
postal codes for
addresses.

MR ARTURO FUENTES
VICE PRESIDENT MARKETING
ROSSLYN WHOLESALE COMPANY
1815 N LYNN STREET
ARLINGTON VA 22209-6183

MS JOYCE BROWNING
2045 ROYAL ROAD
LONDON WIP 6HQ
ENGLAND

MS HELEN SAUNDERS
1010 CLEAR STREET
OTTAWA ON K1A0B1
CANADA

MR JACQUES MOLIERE
RUE DE CHAMPAIGN
06570 ST PAUL
FRANCE

State and Territory Abbreviations

Alabama	AL	Illinois	IL	Nebraska	NE	South Carolina	SC
Alaska	AK	Indiana	IN	Nevada	NV	South Dakota	SD
Arizona	AZ	Iowa	IA	New Hampshire	NH	Tennessee	TN
Arkansas	AR	Kansas	KS	New Jersey	NJ	Texas	TX
California	CA	Kentucky	KY	New Mexico	NM	Utah	UT
Colorado	CO	Louisiana	LA	New York	NY	Vermont	VT
Connecticut	CT	Maine	ME	North Carolina	NC	Virgin Islands	VI
Delaware	DE	Maryland	MD	North Dakota	ND	Virginia	VA
District of Columbia	DC	Massachusetts	MA	Ohio	OH	Washington	WA
Florida	FL	Michigan	MI	Oklahoma	OK	West Virginia	WV
Georgia	GA	Minnesota	MN	Oregon	OR	Wisconsin	WI
Guam	GU	Mississippi	MS	Pennsylvania	PA	Wyoming	WY
Hawaii	HI	Missouri	MO	Puerto Rico	PR		
Idaho	ID	Montana	MT	Rhode Island	RI		

Figure **11-2.4**

USPS two-letter
state and territory
abbreviations

455

Topic 11-2: *Outgoing Mail Procedures*

Can you name five items that should be sent first class? What is the minimum charge for first-class mail weighing up to one ounce? What is the charge for each additional ounce over one ounce?

Classes of Domestic Mail

Domestic mail is distributed by the USPS within the United States and its territories (such as Puerto Rico, the Virgin Islands, and Guam). Domestic mail is divided into various classes. Some of these classes are described in the following paragraphs.

First-Class

First-class mail is commonly used for items such as letters, bills, postcards, checks, money orders, and business reply mail. A minimum amount is charged for all first-class mail weighing up to one ounce. An additional charge is made for each additional ounce or fraction of an ounce. If you

Various classes of domestic mail are sorted by postal workers each day.

© MARY KATE DENNY/PHOTOEDIT

are sending material in an oversized envelope that does not bear a preprinted FIRST CLASS notation, print or stamp FIRST CLASS on the envelope. Mail that weighs over 13 ounces must be sent as priority mail to receive handling comparable to first-class mail.

Priority Mail

Priority mail offers one- to three-day service to most domestic addresses. The maximum weight for priority mail is 70 pounds. Priority mail items must measure 130 inches or less in combined length and girth. Priority mail envelopes, boxes, and labels are available at no charge at post offices. If other envelopes or boxes are used, mark them *PRIORITY MAIL.* The amount of postage for priority mail envelopes or packages over one pound are based on the weight of the item and its destination. A flat-rate envelope is also available. Any amount of material that fits in the flat-rate priority mail envelope provided by the USPS may be mailed for one price.

Express Mail

Express mail is the fastest service offered by the USPS, with one- to two-day delivery to most destinations. No extra fee is charged for Saturday, Sunday, or holiday delivery. All packages should use an *Express Mail* label. The maximum weight for express mail is 70 pounds. Express mail items must measure 130 inches or less in combined length and girth. Express mail envelopes, boxes, and labels are available at no charge at post offices. The amount of postage for express mail is based on weight. A flat-rate envelope is also available. Any amount of material that fits in the flat-rate express mail envelope provided by the USPS may be mailed for one price. Insurance up to $100 is provided at no additional cost. Additional insurance may be purchased.

The United States Postal Service and many private companies offer express mail services.

457

Topic 11-2: *Outgoing Mail Procedures*

For Discussion

What items might be sent by standard mail? How are the rates for standard mail determined?

Points to Emphasize

Registered mail provides the most secure service offered by the USPS. First-class and priority mail may be registered.

Periodicals

Approved publishers and registered news agents may mail items such as newspapers and magazines at the periodicals rates of postage. To do so, you need authorization from the USPS, must pay a special fee, and must mail in bulk lots (volume mailings). Other rates, such as first-class or standard mail, must be used when periodicals are mailed by the general public.

Standard Mail

Standard mail is used primarily to advertise products and services. Advertising brochures and catalogs often are sent standard class. Mailings must contain at least 200 pieces or weigh 50 pounds to qualify for standard mail rates. Each item must weigh less than 16 ounces and be marked with a correct ZIP code. Sorting and postage restrictions apply.

Parcel Post

Parcel post may be used for small and large packages, thick envelopes, and tubes. The rates are based on the weight of the item and the distance it must travel to be delivered. Packages may weigh 1 to 70 pounds and measure up to 130 inches in combined length and girth.

Follow these guidelines when preparing packages for mailing.

- Select a box that is strong enough to protect the contents.
- Leave space for cushioning inside the carton. Cushion package contents with shredded or rolled newspaper, bubble wrap, or other packing material. Pack tightly to avoid shifting.
- Always use tape that is designed for shipping, such as pressure-sensitive or reinforced tape. Do not use wrapping paper, string, masking tape, or cellophane tape.
- Put the delivery and return addresses on one side only of the package. Place a return address label inside the package.

Special Postal Services

In addition to the regular delivery services, special postal services also are available. You must pay a fee for each of these special services. As a worker who processes outgoing mail, you need to know the different services that are available so you can choose the one best suited to your company's mailing needs. Some of the services available are described in this section.

Registered or Insured Mail

Registered mail provides the most secure service offered by the USPS. Mail can be registered to give protection against loss or damage of valuable documents or items. First-class and priority mail may be registered. Insurance is provided for items valued up to a maximum of $25,000. Additional handling charges apply for items valued at more than $25,000. You will be given a receipt showing that the post office has accepted your registered mail for transmittal and delivery. For an additional fee, you may obtain a return receipt to prove that the mail was delivered.

Insured mail provides insurance coverage of up to $5,000 for items lost or damaged in the mail. Insured mail is available for merchandise sent at first-class or priority mail rates and some packages. A receipt is issued to the sender of insured mail. You should keep the receipt on file until you know that the insured mail has arrived in satisfactory condition. If an insured parcel is lost or damaged, the post office will reimburse you for the lesser of the value of the merchandise or the amount for which it was insured.

Proof of Mailing or Delivery

An inexpensive way to obtain proof that an item was mailed is to purchase a certificate of mailing. The certificate is not proof of delivery; it serves only as proof that the item was mailed.

If you want proof of mailing and delivery, send the item by certified mail. Certified mail provides a receipt for the sender to use as proof of mailing. A certified mail receipt is shown in Figure 11-2.5. A record of delivery is maintained by USPS. For an additional fee, a return receipt may be requested to provide proof of delivery.

Delivery confirmation services may be purchased at the time of mailing. Customers can learn the delivery status of the item by accessing the USPS Web site or by calling 1-800-222-1811. Other options are available for large, bulk mailings.

Figure **11-2.5**

Certified mail receipt

For Discussion

What service may be used to provide inexpensive proof that an item was mailed? What service may be used to provide a record of delivery of mail?

459

Topic 11-2: *Outgoing Mail Procedures*

Points to Emphasize

COD charges must be prepaid by the seller. These charges are often passed on to the customer and are collected along with the price of the item.

Supplemental Activity

Assign one or more foreign cities to each student. Ask students to research proper address formats for their cities, as well as the appropriate postage for a first-class letter mailed to their cities.

For Discussion

In addition to the USPS, many companies also use private courier and delivery services. Discuss the private services that are available in the local community. Ask the students to consider what local companies are likely to be the primary users of such services.

COD Mail

A company may send merchandise to a buyer and collect payment for the item when it is delivered. Mail sent in this manner is referred to as COD (collect on delivery). The seller may obtain COD service by paying a fee in addition to the regular postage. Because fees and postage must be paid in advance by the seller, the seller often specifies that the total COD charges to be collected from the buyer include the postage and the collect-on-delivery fee. The maximum amount collectible on one package is $1,000. If the company you work for did not order an item that arrives COD, do not accept the package.

International Mail

Many companies send mail to other countries. A company may have branch offices or customers in countries throughout the world. Postage for letters and postal cards mailed to other countries are higher than for domestic mail, and the mail weights are limited. For current rates and weight limitations, contact your local post office or access the USPS Web site.

Global express delivery for letters and packages is available to many countries from specified post offices. Rates vary by weight and destination country. Overseas packages must be packed very carefully to ensure safe delivery.

customs: government taxes or duties on imported items

Customs forms are required when you send letter packages, small packets, and parcels that are subject to taxes to international destinations. The specific customs form is governed by the type of mail, the weight of the item, and the regulations of the country to which the mail is sent. Individual countries may restrict or prohibit certain articles. Specific information about restrictions for individual countries and about the forms required for mailing is listed in the *International Mail Manual*. This publication is available online at the USPS Web site. A hard copy may be ordered. For customs information, contact the U.S. Customs Service.

Private Courier/Delivery Service

Many companies sometimes use a private courier service rather than the USPS. A private service is often used when a guaranteed delivery time is required. Most cities are served by several private mail delivery companies. Check under *Delivery Service* in the yellow pages of the telephone directory for a listing of companies in your area. You will want to ask about services and fees to identify the delivery company that best meets your needs.

You must prepare a delivery form to accompany the package that includes information such as:

- Your name, address, and phone number
- The recipient's name, address, and phone number
- The class of delivery service
- The weight of the package
- The current date
- The payment method or account number

If you use the delivery company often, the company may provide you with forms that are preprinted with your name, address, and account number. Completing the entire delivery form accurately is essential for prompt delivery. Private mail services do not deliver to a post office box. Many delivery companies have Web sites that allow you to track packages that have been sent using the delivery company.

DHL Worldwide Express is a popular private mail delivery company.

Interoffice Mail

In a small company, processing interoffice mail may involve hand delivering a memo from one worker to another. In a large company, however, interoffice mail is collected from the departments. The mail is sorted in the mailroom and then sent to employees. Interoffice mail envelopes usually differ in color and size from envelopes used for mail going outside the company. That way, interoffice mail will not be sent to the post office accidentally.

Interoffice mail envelope

Telegrams

telegram: message sent using the private mail service Western Union

A **telegram** is a message sent using the private mail service Western Union. Telegrams can be sent anywhere in the United States. You can send a telegram by entering data on the Western Union site.

Messages will be delivered by courier service on the next business day if received by Western Union by 6 p.m. EST. Messages received after 6 p.m. EST will be delivered on the second business day. Telegram messages sent to Alaska or Hawaii take two or three business days for delivery. Charges for telegrams can be found on the Western Union Web site.

REVIEWING THE TOPIC

1. How does the procedure for mailing an item in a window envelope differ from that for a standard envelope?

2. Give two examples of items that might be sent in a volume mailing.

3. What is the function of a postage meter? Describe two methods for adding more postage to the meter when it runs low.

4. What is an optical character reader (OCR)? List three reasons why an OCR might not be able to read the address on an envelope.

5. Describe the recommended address format for mail items.

6. Name and briefly describe three of the classes of domestic mail.

7. What kinds of items may be mailed using priority mail? What is the maximum weight allowed for a priority mail package? What is the maximum width and girth for a priority mail package?

8. What are two inexpensive USPS special services that can be used for proof of mailing?

9. Under what circumstances would you use COD mail? What is the maximum amount collectible on one COD package?

10. Why should interoffice mail be placed in envelopes distinctly different from those used to send mail by the postal service?

INTERACTING WITH OTHERS

You work in an office where the mail is picked up by postal workers twice a day, at 10:30 a.m. and 2:45 p.m. Monday afternoon you receive a call from the regional vice president in a branch office. He needs six copies of the company's annual report by Wednesday. If the reports are in the 2:45 p.m. mail today, they will be delivered on Wednesday. You gather the annual reports, place them in a large envelope, and take them to the mailroom. You explain to Glenna, a mailroom worker, that the envelope must go with the 2:45 p.m. mail pickup. Glenna says she understands.

Later in the day, you call Glenna to verify that the annual reports were sent. Glenna sheepishly replies that she was on break at 2:45. When she returned, she noticed that the postal carrier had overlooked the envelope. The annual reports were not mailed.

1. You are very annoyed that the envelope was not mailed. Should you tell Glenna how you feel? If so, what should you tell her? Should you report this incident to Glenna's supervisor? How can you and Glenna work together to solve this problem?

2. The reports still need to be sent. How would you suggest that Glenna mail the reports so that they reach the vice president by Wednesday?

463

Topic Review

Teaching Tips

Give students the corrections that should be made after they have completed the activity.

REINFORCING ENGLISH SKILLS

1. Key the text that describes the U.S. Postal Inspection Service shown below.
2. Correct all errors in spelling, grammar, and word usage.

> The U.S. Postal Inspection Serviec is the law enforcment branch of the U.S. Postal Service. Postal inspectors investigate any crime in which the U.S. Mail is used to further a scheme, whether they originated in the mail, by telephone, or on the Internet. The use of the U.S. Mail is what makes it a mail fraud issue. Some important areas of jurisdition include:
>
> - Assaults and threats that occurr while postal employees is performing official duties
> - Distribution of child pornography and other crimes exploiting childs through the mail
> - Distributing narcotics or other controlled substances thru the mail
> - Forgged, altered, or counterfieted postage stamps or postal money orders
> - Delay of delivery or destructin are theft of mail
> - Mail that contains threats of kidnapping, physical injury, or injury too the property or reputations of others
> - Money laundering—attempts to conceal the proceeds of ilegal acts through monetary transactions

Teaching Tips

Assist students with using the postage calculator features found on the USPS Web site.

INTERNET
RESEARCH
WORD PROCESSING

Topic **11-2**   ACTIVITY 1

Calculate Postage

You work in a small office. You need to determine the correct postage for various items you have been given to mail.

1. Determine the amount of postage needed to mail each item listed below step 2 using the USPS. Use your town as the mailing location in figuring the postage. Consult current USPS rate charts available in print from your local post office or online at the USPS Web site. A link to the USPS Web site is found on *The Office* Web site.

2. Create a document that lists the items to be mailed and the correct postage for each item.

- A package weighing 4¾ pounds to be sent parcel post to Ann Arbor, Michigan
- A letter weighing three ounces to be sent by express mail to Camden, Maine
- A 12-ounce package containing a printed report to be sent by first-class mail to Santa Barbara, California
- A two-ounce letter to be sent by first-class, certified mail to Denver, Colorado
- A ten-ounce letter to be sent to a local bank

Topic 11-2 : ACTIVITY 2

INTEGRATED DOCUMENT
RESEARCH
SPREADSHEET
TEAMWORK
WORD PROCESSING

Compare Delivery Services

You have been asked to compare rates for the USPS and two private mail delivery services for mailing several types of items. Work with a classmate to complete this activity.

1. Identify two private mail delivery companies that serve your area.
2. Research the cost of mailing the items listed below step 4 using the USPS and the two private mail delivery services. Create a bar graph that compares the cost of mailing the six-ounce envelope to Tampa, Florida, using next-day delivery for two private mail delivery services. Adjust the scale of the graph, if necessary, to show the data clearly.
3. Create a memo form to include your company's name, Parnell Products, Inc., and the appropriate headings. Write a short memo report to your supervisor, Jeremy Waters, to report your findings.
   - Recommend the mail service that should be used for routine mailings and the service that should be used for items that must have guaranteed overnight or second-day delivery.
   - Introduce and include the graph you created in your report.
   - Determine whether each service has a system available for customers to track packages that have been mailed. Research mailing time deadlines, any special packaging requirements, and drop-off or pickup locations for each service. Consider these factors when making your decisions.
   - Give reasons to support your recommendations.

4. Attach a table to your report that gives the mailing cost for each item below for each of the three services.

Items to be mailed:

- A package weighing 10 pounds to be sent to Chicago, Illinois, which you would like to arrive within about 10 days (Delivery time is not critical.)
- A letter weighing six ounces sent to Tampa, Florida, which must arrive the next business day (Delivery time is critical.)
- A 12-ounce envelope to Santa Barbara, California, which must arrive within two working days (Delivery time is critical.)
- A four-ounce letter to Denver, Colorado, which you would like to arrive with seven working days (Delivery time is not critical.)
- A ten-ounce letter to be sent to a local business, which you would like to arrive within three or four days (Delivery time is not critical.)

Summary

In this chapter, you learned the procedures for processing both incoming and outgoing mail. You should be knowledgeable about the following key points:

- An office worker's mail-related tasks will depend on the size of the company, the volume of mail handled, and the job duties.
- Electric envelope openers, rotary units for sorting mail, and automated delivery systems help speed mail processing.
- First-class, priority, express, and standard are examples of classes of domestic mail. Special postal services are available such as registered mail, insured mail, and certified mail.
- To speed the processing of outgoing mail, some companies use electronic postage scales, postage meters, and equipment for addressing, labeling, folding, and inserting mail.
- The USPS uses electronic equipment such as optical character readers and bar code sorters to speed mail to its destination. You can help speed the process by following USPS address format guidelines and by using nine-digit ZIP codes.
- Special considerations for address formats, different postage rates, and customs regulations apply to international mail.
- Many companies sometimes use a private mail delivery service rather than the USPS.
- Interoffice mail envelopes usually differ in color and size from envelopes used for mail going outside the company. This difference helps avoid accidentally mixing in-house and outside mail.

Key Terms

annotate	postage meter	routing slip
courier	prioritize	synopsis
customs	referral slip	telegram
optical character reader (OCR)		

DATABASE
DESKTOP PUBLISHING

Chapter **11** ACTIVITY 1

Mailing List and Flyer

You work as an office assistant at Chaparral Coffee Company. Your supervisor approaches your workstation with this request:

Please create a flyer to send to all our current customers with our next catalog mailing. The flyer will contain an introductory half-price offer for two new products—our Dessert Coffee Assortment gift box and our Classic Delight package. Our new customer referral program is getting off to a good start. We have received 14 referrals thus far. Use this list to create a database for these prospective customers. Print labels from the list and send each person our catalog and the new product flyer.

1. Open the PDF file *CH11 Chaparral* from the data files. This file contains information about the new products and a list of prospective customers.

2. Use your desktop publishing skills to design a flyer to introduce the two new products. Explain that these two new products will be available at half their regular price for a limited time. Use the current date through two months from the current date as the time for the special offer. Include the company name and address information and appropriate graphics on the flyer.

3. Create a database named *CH11 Customers*. Create a table named **Customers** to contain the names and addresses of the prospective customers. Create appropriate fields. Enter data using the all caps, no punctuation format recommended by the USPS and the two-letter state abbreviations in the addresses.

4. Use the Labels Wizard to create mailing labels. Sort the addresses by state. Print the mailing labels. Use plain paper if labels are not available.

INTERNET
RESEARCH
WORD PROCESSING

Chapter **11** ACTIVITY 2

ZIP Code Update

Your company sends several volume mailings each quarter using standard mail. Periodically, an automated check for correct ZIP codes is performed. During the last check, the computer identified ten addresses that may have incorrect ZIP codes.

1. Find and record the correct ZIP code for each address on the list on page 469. Use a printed ZIP code directory or access the USPS Web site to find current ZIP code information. A link to the USPS Web site is found on *The Office* Web site.

CHAPTER 11: PROCESSING MAIL

2. Key a list of the addresses using the correct ZIP codes for each address.

1800 AUGUSTA CT LEXINGTON KY 40555-2860	1133 N DEARBORN ST CHICAGO IL 60690-2783
8701 TOWN PARK DR HOUSTON TX 88036-2614	11115 N NEBRASKA AVE TAMPA FL 36312-5748
2006 CENTRAL AVE ALBANY NY 17205-4500	8730 N HIMES AVE TAMPA FL 33618-8355
8500 KELLER DR LITTLE ROCK AR 72402-2356	7203 N FLORIDA AVE TAMPA FL 33694-4835
174 MAIN ST BANGOR ME 14401-6401	2730 BRANDY DR COLUMBUS OH 44232-5303

Supplemental Activity

Have students complete the Chapter 11 Supplemental Activity, Mail Report, available on *The Office* Web site.

Assessment

Assess student learning using the Chapter 11 test available on the *IRCD* and in *ExamView®* format.

469

Chapter Review

© GETTY IMAGES/PHOTODISC

CHAPTER 12

Telephone Systems and Procedures

The telephone plays a key role in communicating at work. Data, text, images, and video as well as voice can be transmitted across the country or around the world using telephone channels. Mobile phones allow users to place calls easily from many locations away from the office.

You will use the telephone and related technologies for sharing information at work. As these technologies change, you must learn about new equipment and features that are available. In this chapter, you will become familiar with telephone equipment and services. You will learn to use effective telephone procedures and become aware of available telephone technology.

Online Resources

O *The Office* Web site:
   Data Files
   Vocabulary Flashcards
   Sort It Out, Telephone
      Procedures
   Chapter 12 Supplementary
      Activity
O Search terms:
   facsimile
   online telephone directory
   smart phone
   telecommunications
   telephony
   video conference

470

objectives

Office workers often need to share information with others quickly and reliably. This information is often shared using telecommunications technology. **Telecommunications** is the electronic transfer of data over a distance. This data can be in the form of voice, video, text, or images. You are very familiar with the most popular telecommunications device ever invented—the telephone. Because voice transmission by telephone is a common form of telecommunications, the technology is often simply called telephone technology.

New telephones and systems are being equipped with features to meet the ever-changing variety of user wants and needs. Some widely used systems and equipment will be discussed in this chapter. However, technology is rapidly changing. Office workers must be prepared to become acquainted with new telephone features and equipment as they become available.

Transmitting Data Using Telephone Channels

Telephone technology allows workers to send information across the country or around the world. When you place a telephone call or transfer data to a remote computer, the data usually travels over telephone channels. The data may travel as either **analog** or **digital** signals. Many companies are replacing older analog lines with digital lines. Digital signals can transmit large quantities of data at speeds much faster than analog signals. This means your electronic message (a letter, a long report, or a chart) is received quickly and reliably. Data that can be read by a computer is in digital form.

Some communications systems use only analog signals. They require a device called a **modem** to send digital data. This device is used to convert the digital data into analog signals that can be transmitted over telephone channels. A modem can be an internal device installed inside the computer case. It can also be an external device that is attached to the computer.

Satellites play an important part in worldwide telecommunications systems. Satellites send voice, video, and other data in the form of microwave signals. A communications **satellite** is a data relay station that orbits the earth. A satellite dish is a data relay station that remains stationary, on earth. Data from your telephone or computer may travel through telephone lines to a satellite dish. From a satellite dish, data can be sent to an orbiting satellite. The orbiting satellite transmits the data to another satellite dish in another part of the world. Data from the second satellite dish may travel through telephone lines to the receiving telephone or computer.

- O Describe how data are transmitted using telephone channels
- O Define telephony and list features offered by telephony technology
- O Describe the purpose and features of a centralized telephone system
- O Discuss types of mobile phones available
- O List common features of telephones and telephone systems
- O Discuss procedures for telephone use, such as participating in conference calls and leaving voice mail messages
- O Describe procedures for effective use of fax messages

telecommunications: electronic transfer of information over a distance

analog: transmitted by a signal that corresponds to a physical change such as sound

digital: stored or transmitted by a process using groups of electronic bits of data

modem: a conversion device for digital and analog data

satellite: a data relay station that orbits the earth

471

Topic 12-1: *Telephone Technology and Services*

Getting Started

Today's workers must be able to use a variety of communications equipment. They must possess strong communications skills to be able to handle the demands of increased interactions with others. Encourage students to observe different ways in which all types of information are being transmitted when they visit banks, libraries, airports, shopping malls, and other places. Throughout the presentation of this chapter, highlight the importance of the role of the worker in ensuring effective use of new technology.

Teaching Tips

The Internet provides a wealth of information about telecommunications. Encourage students to visit the Web sites of major telephone service providers to gather the most up-to-date information about equipment, special features, rates, and emerging telephony technologies.

Points to Emphasize

Innovations in transmission of all types of data continue to increase the speed and the quality of communicating across distances.

For Discussion

Explain how a modem works. The modem connected to the sending computer converts the digital signals to analog signals so that the information can be sent over the analog telephone lines. When the analog signals reach their destination, a modem at that location converts the telephone line's analog signals to digital signals that the receiving computer can use.

471

© CORBIS

Telecommunications technology enables us to communicate globally.

WORKPLACE CONNECTIONS

Chin must send a price quote from his office in Miami to a customer in London. Using an e-mail attachment, he sends the price list to London in minutes. That data travels via a worldwide satellite communications network. The customer reviews the quote and sends Chin an order by return e-mail. This time savings allows Chin to receive and fill the customer's order quickly.

Telephony

telephony: integration of computer and telephone technologies

As technology changes, businesses are using new equipment and procedures to improve communications. The integration of computer and telephone technologies is called **telephony**. In a modern communications system, a computer may be used to control and access telephone functions. Such a system may also allow users to access computer functions by telephone. Telephony technology offers features such as:

- Two-way video, audio, and computer communications that let callers open, view, and edit computer files and send notes to each other as they talk
- Computer software that lets users manage telephone activity at a personal computer
- Caller ID service that allows the user to see the number of the caller and allows incoming calls to be screened—whether from within or outside the company

472

CHAPTER 12: TELEPHONE SYSTEMS AND PROCEDURES

- Conference calling that can be placed by using names from the user's computer phone directory
- Access to the Internet and World Wide Web
- Management of all voice, fax, or e-mail messages with either a touch-tone phone or a personal computer
- Multimedia tutorials that help users learn how to use advanced system features

Telephony technology allows two-way video and audio communications.

Some businesses take advantage of current technology by using voice over Internet protocol (VoIP). **VoIP**, also called Internet voice, allows users to make telephone calls using a high-speed Internet connection instead of standard telephone channels. A traditional telephone with an adaptor or a computer with a modem is used to place calls. The voice signal is changed to a digital signal. The digital signal travels over the Internet. The signal is then changed back into voice and delivered to the receiving phone or computer. Some VoIP services allow users to call only other people who have the same service. However, other services allow users to call anyone.

An advantage of using VoIP is that it can help a business save money. The business can use a broadband Internet connection and other equipment that is already in place for sending data to make phone calls. The business may be able to reduce or even cancel the services purchased from a standard telephone company. Some VoIP providers offer plans that allow unlimited local and long-distance calls to anywhere in the United States for one set fee. Also, some VoIP providers offer features such as caller ID, call waiting, and voice mail at no added charge. These services are often an extra charge when purchased from standard telephone companies.

VoIP: a technology that allows users to make telephone calls using a high-speed Internet connection instead standard telephone channels

For Discussion

Ask students whether they have any experience in using VoIP to place a phone call. Ask students to describe magazine or television ads that they have seen for VoIP.

473

Topic 12-1: *Telephone Technology and Services*

A disadvantage of using VoIP is that service may be lost during a power outage. Problems with the company's network or high-speed Internet connection may also mean that service will be disrupted. Backup power supplies and network servers can be used to help avoid these problems.

Using the 911 emergency number with VoIP from remote locations is also a concern. When the emergency 911 number is called using a standard telephone line, the 911 service can find the location from which the call is placed. If the caller is using VoIP, the 911 service may not be able to find the location of the caller. A VoIP call may be placed from any location with a high-speed Internet connection.

Voice Communication Systems

The telephone is an important tool for sharing information for businesses. In a small company, the telephone system may be as simple as having one or two telephone lines for the company. In other companies, the telephone system may include many lines and be integrated with a computer system.

Centralized Telephone Systems

Centralized telephone systems route calls coming into and going out of an organization. All calls in a centralized system are handled by a single computer or operator switchboard that routes calls to the requested location. Older systems required the assistance of a human switchboard operator to answer and transfer calls. Some systems that are handled by computer give callers the option of speaking to a human operator.

automated attendant: computerized system for handling telephone calls

Many telephone systems in businesses today are answered by an **automated attendant**. An automated attendant is a computerized system for handling telephone calls. When an incoming call is answered by an automated attendant, a recorded message is played. Messages vary depending on company needs. However, the message usually instructs the caller to dial the extension number of the person being sought. It may provide the caller with various menu options. Callers make selections using the telephone number keypad. Some systems also allow users to select menu options by speaking a word or term into the receiver. A computer will identify the spoken command and perform the chosen action. This feature is called speech recognition. Additional messages may then instruct and direct the caller.

The option of speaking with a person is no longer always a choice for the caller. However, many companies continue to offer an option to speak with a person to provide better service for customers. Some callers prefer to talk with a person rather than with a computer. Other callers may not have a touch-tone phone, which is usually required for the automated system.

Many callers have adjusted to computerized systems. However, some callers become frustrated with systems that seem to block human contact. Businesses must deal with these complaints and do their best to meet callers' needs and preserve goodwill.

Some callers become frustrated with computerized automated attendants.

Mobile Telephones

Mobile telephones are an important tool commonly used for both personal and business communications. Mobile phones use wireless, radio frequencies to transmit data across geographic areas called cells. These phones are also called **cellular telephones** or cell phones. When you dial a mobile telephone number, the radio signal "switches" from cell to cell until the right number is reached. Mobile service providers furnish the user with the transmission. Because modern cell phones use digital technology, they are sometimes referred to as digital phones.

cellular telephone: a mobile device that uses wireless, radio frequencies to transmit data across geographic segments

Cell phones are designed to be portable, lightweight, and small. You may use them in your car or carry them in your briefcase to use wherever you are. In some areas, cell phones may not be close enough to a transmission tower to receive a signal. A *no signal* message may be displayed to indicate that a call cannot be made from that location.

A camera phone (or camphone) is a mobile phone that has a built-in camera. This device can be used to take photographs and send these images to other phones. The user may be able to connect the phone to a computer to download pictures for printing or storage.

In Chapter 3 you learned about handheld computers called PDAs (personal digital assistants). These small, portable computers are used to track appointments, record contact data, take notes, access e-mail, and perform many other tasks. A device that combines the features of a PDA and a mobile phone is called a **smart phone**. With a smart phone, users have one device (rather than two) to handle calls and manage data. Some smart phones have a small keyboard on the outside of the device. Other smart phones have an on-screen keyboard and use handwriting recognition. When buying a smart phone, the user should be aware of the device's operating system and additional programs available that can be loaded onto the device.

smart phone: a device that combines the features of a mobile phone and a PDA

475

Topic 12-1: *Telephone Technology and Services*

Mobile telephones allow workers to keep in touch with the office wherever they are.

Travelers may need to call their offices or customers while flying. Some airplanes are now equipped with telephones that are available for use by passengers for placing calls. Telephones may be positioned at passenger seats or at a location made available by the flight staff. Because these telephones work while in flight, they are sometimes called airphones.

Pagers

pager: electronic device that alerts the user of the need to respond by telephone

Pagers are very small devices that alert the user of the need to respond by telephone to whomever has sent the signal or "page." Early pagers got the attention of the user with audio beeper signals. They became known as "beepers" because of the sounds they made. Today's pagers use a variety of signals such as vibrations, voice, and digital readout. The recipient of the signal should respond as soon as possible by finding the nearest telephone to call the number on the readout or to call the office.

Smart phones combine the features of mobile phones and handhelds.

Common Features of Telephone Systems

Many features are available that allow users to customize a telephone. Different features are available on different telephones or systems. A user's manual is generally provided. The manual gives steps for using the features available. To activate call forwarding, for example, you may be instructed to tap the * (asterisk, or "star") and 4 keys, listen for a tone, dial the number to which you want all incoming calls routed, and hang up. Your incoming calls will then be forwarded and will ring at that number. Figure 12-1.1 lists common features of telephones or systems.

Conference Calls

At times it may be necessary to place calls that will have three or more participants speaking at different locations. These calls are known as conference calls. Conference calls may be handled in several ways: with the user's own equipment, operator-dialed service, or dial-in service.

Common Telephone Features and Services

Figure **12-1.1**

Feature	Description
Auto redial	Redials automatically the last number dialed when the user presses a key
Call block	Restricts callers from making toll calls or calls for which an extra charge is made
Call forwarding	Sends calls automatically to another telephone number
Caller ID	Records or displays the telephone number of the caller
Call queuing or camp on	Re-establishes the connection after a busy signal when both parties are free
Call return	Allows users to press a code number, such as *69, to dial the number of the last incoming call
Call waiting	Signals an incoming call is waiting while a call is in progress
Conferencing	Allows the user to set up conversations with three or more people at the same time
Memory	Allows the user to store numbers and then dial a number with one button
Speakerphone	Allows the user to speak into a microphone on the telephone rather than the handset
Camera phone	Allows the user to transmit pictures at the same time as voice
E-mail access	Allows users to send and receive e-mail messages
Internet access	Allows users to access Web sites
Text messaging	Allows users to send text messages on mobile phones
Application programs	Allows users to perform various tasks on smart phones

477

Topic 12-1: *Telephone Technology and Services*

With some company telephone systems, users may be able to place a conference call. No outside help is needed from a telephone company service provider. The person setting up the call lets all those who will take part know the time to expect the call. At the appointed time, the user calls each person in turn and adds them to the call, following the appropriate steps for the phone system.

With operator-dialed service, a long-distance operator handles the setup and connections. After you inform the operator of the date, time, time zone, and estimated length of the call, the operator does the following:

- Informs all participants of the time that the conference call will take place
- Makes all the necessary connections at the prescribed time
- Calls the roll to make sure all callers are connected
- Can provide specialized services such as a recording or written transcript of the conference, or a translator for those who do not understand the main language used

Dial-in service allows participants to call a special number at a prearranged time without operator assistance. They may call from any telephone rather than wait for an operator to call them at one specific number.

Successful conference calls require advance planning to ensure that all the necessary information and equipment are at hand. Follow these guidelines in planning a conference call:

- Inform all participants of the date, time, and proposed length of the call.
- Verify everyone's telephone number.
- Send any needed information or items for discussion to all participants in advance.
- Identify the objectives and intended outcomes of the call.
- If using a service provider, call in advance and give accurate numbers, names, date, time, and expected duration of the call.

A conference call involves several people at different locations.

Participating in a conference call requires use of your best communication skills. Think of the conference call as a type of meeting where you will both contribute to the conversation and listen to others. Follow these procedures during the call:

- Take roll. Call out names of all participants.
- Lead the call by presenting the agenda and conference guidelines.
- Have participants identify themselves when speaking.
- Speak clearly, spelling out difficult or unusual names and terms. Repeat numbers.
- Avoid interrupting other speakers. Only one person should speak at a time.
- Take notes of important points and comments.
- Apply good listening skills.
- Encourage discussion and participation from everyone.

Voice Mail Systems

Voice mail is a messaging system that uses computers and telephones to record, send, store, and retrieve voice messages. Voice messaging systems are popular because they eliminate the problems of time lost in playing "telephone tag." Most voice mail systems operate 24 hours per day. They are an important communications tool.

voice mail: a messaging system that uses computers and telephones to record, store, and retrieve voice messages

Telephone push buttons are used to access the features of a voice mail system.

© GETTY IMAGES/PHOTODISC

Points to Emphasize

Identify yourself each time you speak during a conference call unless the call involves only three or four people who know each other well.

For Discussion

What is meant by "telephone tag"? How does it interfere with efficiency in an organization? How is voice mail different from simply recording a message on an answering machine?

Supplemental Activity

Instruct students to record appropriate voice mail messages using a tape recorder. Let them evaluate each other's messages for voice quality, appropriate identification, ample instructions for the caller, and overall professionalism.

Teaching Tips

Invite a representative from a local company that sells voice mail systems to speak to the class about the features of their systems and special training programs they may conduct for new users.

FOCUS ON . . .

Voice Mail

Voice mail is a computerized voice messaging system. It has many features that can be modified to meet individual needs. A standard personal computer, a special voice processing card, and voice software are needed. Both the sender and the receiver use the telephone push buttons to activate and use the features of voice mail.

Because of the convenience and efficiency of voice mail, its use has become widespread in business. Still, with all its advantages, voice mail does not replace human contact. Follow proper procedures to ensure that the negatives of voice mail are reduced and the full benefits are realized. When using your voice mail system:

- Prepare a message that presents you as a professional and delivers appropriate information and instructions to the caller. Include your name, department, and other necessary information. Give instructions as to how to get immediate assistance if the caller cannot wait for you to return the call.

- Record the message yourself. Speak clearly and distinctly. Pronounce words correctly and use correct grammar.

- If you are going to be out of the office for one or more days, refer callers to another worker who can provide help while you are away, if appropriate.

- Check your voice mail several times a day. Return all calls as soon as possible.

- Answer your telephone when you are at your desk unless you have visitors in your office or are involved in an important work project. Do not let voice mail answer your phone for you the majority of the time when you are at your desk.

Follow these procedures when leaving messages for others on their voice mail systems.

- Leave your name, telephone number, company, and a brief reason for your call. Make your message neither too lengthy nor too brief. You want the person you called to have enough information to return your call promptly and efficiently.

- Speak slowly and distinctly. Spell out any difficult names (your name, your company's name).

- Do not communicate bad news or negative statements in the voice message. Wait until you actually speak with the person to give negative information.

Each user of a voice messaging system has a voice mailbox. A voice mailbox is a space reserved in a computer to hold recorded voice messages. A caller leaves a voice message that is recorded by the computer. The message is held in storage until the recipient of the message chooses to access it. Unless a message is deleted, it remains in storage and can be accessed later for reference. Some of the voice mail features that may be used by companies include:

- Long-term incoming message storage
- Message prioritizing

480

CHAPTER 12: TELEPHONE SYSTEMS AND PROCEDURES

- Ability to broadcast recorded messages to multiple or all users of the system
- Creation of multiple greetings that can be selected as needed

Videoconferencing

Videoconferencing is communicating with people at two or more locations using two-way voice and video data. A special conference room equipped with microphones, television cameras, and screens is used to conduct meetings in which data, text, voice, and documents may be exchanged.

videoconferencing: communicating with people at two or more locations using two-way voice and video data

WORKPLACE CONNECTIONS

Will Flowers, Director of Sales, is located in Detroit. Will called a meeting with local managers, managers located at headquarters in San Francisco, and a third group of managers located at a branch in Hong Kong. Using videoconferencing, they could see and hear each other. Will wrote on an electronic whiteboard as he discussed sales projections. Will's notes from the board appeared on a video monitor at the remote locations. The data were sent and later printed for the managers at each location. This meeting was very cost effective when compared to the expense and time that would be required for all the managers to travel and meet in one location.

Video conferences, sometimes called Web conferences, may also be conducted by computer. In a Web conference, people communicate using private computer networks or the Internet. These conferences are sometimes called virtual meetings. The user's computers must have speakers, microphones, video cameras, and the appropriate software. See Chapter 8, Meetings and Travel, for more information about Web conferencing.

© FISHER/THATCHER/STONE

Video conferences allow people at different locations to see and hear each other and exchange information electronically.

Features for Impairments

Special telephone equipment and services are available for the visually or hearing impaired. Features that enable the blind, deaf, hard of hearing, or speech disabled to communicate on the telephone with others include text telephone (TTY) and the telebraille telephone (TB). With these services, a person serves as an interpreter between the hearing person and the deaf or blind person. The interpreter may be an employee of a telephone company or of a state or other agency that provides assistive services. The messages are relayed by the interpreter by typing the spoken words, which are relayed to the TTY or TB user. The blind person reads the **Braille**; the deaf person reads the screen.

Braille: a system that enables the blind to read by feeling a pattern of raised dots

Other features for impaired callers include:

- Large-button phones
- Headsets or speakerphones for hands-free operation
- Speech amplifiers to make voices louder
- Loud bells and flashing light indicators to signal incoming calls

Specialized equipment and services are available for telephone users with impairments.

© GOODSHOOT/SUPERSTOCK

facsimile: a technology used to send images (text, photographs, drawings) using telephone or VoIP channels

Facsimile Technology

Facsimile technology, often called fax, sends images (text, photographs, drawings) using telephone or VoIP channels. A fax machine works by combining scanning technology with telephone technology. The sending machine scans a page and encodes (electronically "takes a picture of") the data to be sent. The data are transmitted over telephone channels to a receiving fax. Within seconds, the document is received.

Fax machines are easy to use and are commonly found in offices. A company may have one or several fax machines. Portable models may be used to send documents while workers are away from the office. Fax machines are also found in some homes for personal use. They provide an inexpensive, fast way to send and receive information.

Fax machine to fax machine is not the only method of sending documents as images. An image can also be sent from a computer directly to a fax machine or another computer. The computer must have a fax card and software to control the process.

Features

Fax machines offer many features. Among the more common features are:

- Laser or full-color printing
- Store-and-forward capability
- Automatic dialing and redialing if the receiving number is busy
- Automatic answering
- Automatic document feed
- Activity-reporting of date, time, and number of pages sent and received
- Small screens that display messages such as data about sending and errors or problems with the system
- Security features

The automatic answering feature makes fax systems almost self-operating. Many users leave their machines on 24 hours a day, unattended, for receiving messages.

Fax machines speed the process of sending and receiving messages.

© GETTY IMAGES/PHOTODISC

Most fax machines are easy to use; however, features and procedures vary from office to office and machine to machine.

483

Topic 12-1: *Telephone Technology and Services*

Teaching Tips

Explain that fax cover sheets with large black areas are not desirable because they take longer to fax (costing more if the user pays for online time by the minute). They also require longer to print for the receiver. A simple cover sheet or a note placed in the top margin of the first page of the fax is faster to send and more economical.

Expand the Concept

Instead of fax transmittal sheets, many fax users include the transmission data in a special header at the top of the document. This is the usual practice when faxing a document from a PC to a fax machine.

Teaching Tips

Give students photocopies of one or more telephone billing statements. Together, examine each statement to find the service provider used for long distance calls. Discuss the long distance rates, extended local area rates, special services, and all types of charges shown.

Procedures

Procedures for using fax machines vary from office to office and from machine to machine. Many procedures depend on the sending and receiving equipment to be used. When you send a fax, include a cover sheet or note with the following information:

- Current date
- Total pages being sent, including the cover sheet
- Name, company, fax number, and address of the recipient of the message
- Name, company, address, telephone number, and fax number of the sender
- Subject of the document or message
- Special remarks as needed

Check the accuracy of your count of the number of pages to be sent and the number of pages you recorded on the cover sheet. Confirm the number carefully before dialing the fax number of the recipient. Enter your name, department, date, and number of pages sent or other required data on a fax log sheet if one is used in your office.

After all pages have been sent, your fax machine will let you know that the transmission has been completed. You may hear a series of beeps or a message may be displayed telling you that your message has been received at the location you dialed. If a report form is printed, attach it to the fax cover sheet and return it with the original materials to the sender. In Figure 12-1.2, the report includes the date, start time of the message, fax number dialed, number of pages sent, and time used to transmit pages. Note that the results are reported as "OK," the transmission was successful.

Telephone Equipment and Service Providers

Telephones and systems may be purchased from many vendors. A variety of equipment is available and varies in price. Some vendors will customize features to meet user needs. Some vendors will also conduct training and offer product support after the sale.

When purchasing mobile phones, the phones should be tested in the areas where they will be used often. If the areas do not receive a strong signal, users may have trouble making calls. Some companies allow users to borrow a mobile phone for a short trial period before purchasing a phone. This allows the user to test the phone in various areas.

A local telephone company provides services to users within a set local area. A business may have no choice as to which company to use for local service through standard telephone channels. Companies can choose a long-distance company and optional features. Companies can also choose whether to use standard telephone service, VoIP, or a combination of both types of service. A wide variety of features and pricing plans is available. Companies should carefully compare services and prices when choosing a telephone service provider. For mobile phones, the service area and roaming charges are important considerations when choosing a provider.

CHAPTER 12: TELEPHONE SYSTEMS AND PROCEDURES

Figure **12-1.2**

*Fax cover sheet and
transmission report*

Nouveau Investment Company
800 Elm Avenue
Mt. Vernon, NY 10500-3113
Fax # 914-555-9626
Telephone # 914-555-9692

FAX

To:	John Mayfield	**From:**	Sherman Kuntz
Fax:	513-555-6956	**Pages:**	3
Phone:	513-555-6988	**Date:**	March 9, 20--
Re:	Quarterly Report	**Time:**	11:35 a.m.

Comments:

Please review this report and send me your comments.

FAX TRANSMISSION REPORT

DATE	START TIME	REMOTE TERMINAL	MODE	TIME	RESULTS	TOTAL PAGES
Mar 09	11:38	513-555-6956	G3ST	02 min 02 sec	OK	03

For Discussion

In Figure 12-1.2, who is sending this fax? Who is receiving the fax? What information is being transmitted? What information does the transmission report tell the sender?

485

Topic 12-1: Telephone Technology and Services

Topic Review 12-1

REVIEWING THE TOPIC

1. Describe the role satellites play in transmitting data over telephone channels.
2. What is the purpose of a modem?
3. What is telephony? List three features that may be found in a telephony system.
4. How does using VoIP to place a call differ from using regular telephone lines?
5. What is the main function of a centralized telephone system? Describe how an automated attendant works.
6. What is a cellular phone? What is a smart phone?
7. List and describe three common features of telephones or telephone systems.
8. What procedures should you follow when participating in a conference call?
9. What procedures should you follow when creating a greeting message for your voice mail? What procedures should you follow when leaving messages for others on their voice mail systems?
10. What special telephone equipment and services are available for the visually or hearing impaired?
11. What information should be included on a fax cover sheet?
12. Why should a business compare services and prices when choosing a telephone service provider?

INTERACTING WITH OTHERS

Your sales team member, Jeremy, is letting voice mail answer his phone the majority of the time, even when he is at his desk. You and Jeremy share sales and service duties for several accounts. Your clients have complained to you that Jeremy seems never to be at his desk. Also, they complain that he takes several days to answer their voice mail messages. You realize that this is a problem situation. What should you do?

1. Should you inform your supervisor about Jeremy's voice mail procedures? Why or why not?
2. Should you apologize to clients for Jeremy's poor voice mail habits? Why or why not?
3. Should you tell clients to call you instead of Jeremy? Why or why not?
4. What could you say to Jeremy about the clients' complaints to encourage him to handle his voice mail messages following professional procedures?

REINFORCING ENGLISH SKILLS

Your knowledge of punctuation rules will be helpful as you prepare written messages on the job. Ten sentences follow that will reinforce your ability to use proper punctuation marks. Write or key each sentence, inserting the proper punctuation.

1. She faxed a report from Cheyenne Wyoming to Tucson Arizona
2. Our telephone bill was credited with two months interest
3. Did you place the call to Jeorge my friend from Mexico City
4. On Tuesday January 23 we began using our new computerized telephone system
5. To qualify for a position you must have a years experience using a computer telephone system
6. Showing you our new voice mail system was a pleasure we have a training session planned for all new users
7. We prefer using voice mail for recording messages not an answering machine
8. Conferencing lets you set up conversations with three four or more people at the same time
9. A speakerphone allows hands free speaking capabilities
10. Is the toll free number an 800 or an 888 number

Topic 12-1 | ACTIVITY 1

COMPOSITION
WORD PROCESSING

Fax Procedures

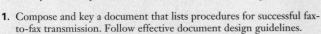

You work at the headquarters of Prudent Development Corporation. Your supervisor, Janet Naisbitt, asks you to prepare a well-designed one-page list of common procedures to be followed for successful fax transmissions. The procedures list is to be faxed to the office manager at the Denver branch. She also wants you to compose a short memo to include with the procedures.

1. Compose and key a document that lists procedures for successful fax-to-fax transmission. Follow effective document design guidelines.

2. Create a memo form for the company using appropriate headings. Compose a memo to Ed Stoddard, Office Manager. In the memo, explain that this list is to be distributed to all fax users at the Denver location. Also, ask him to write any additions or comments on the list and return it to you within three days.

487

Topic Review

Teaching Tips

Give students the correct answers after they have completed the activity.

Teaching Tips

Have students work in teams of two to review each other's documents and offer suggestions for improvement.

3. Create a fax cover sheet to send with the memo and the fax procedures document. Use the cover sheet in Figure 12-1.2 as an example, or use a fax cover sheet template from your word processor software.

> **Your company's information:**
> Prudent Development Corporation, 8700 Martin Luther King Blvd., Austin, TX 78765-0800
> Fax number: 512-555-0139
> Telephone number: 512-555-0142
>
> **Mr. Stoddard's information:**
> Prudent Development Corporation in Denver, CO
> Fax number: 303-555-0102
> Telephone number: 303-555-0122

COMPOSITION
WORD PROCESSING

Topic **12-1** ACTIVITY 2

Voice Mail Messages

You are the manager for the Accounting Department at Ryan Associates. While you were away from the office on a trip recently, you called several employees in your department. You noticed that the voice mail messages used by some department members were not very helpful and did not sound professional. You have decided to give department members suggestions for improving their messages and to provide sample messages.

1. Review the guidelines for effective voice mail messages found in this topic.

2. Compose a memo or an e-mail message to the Accounting Department from you. Use the current date and an appropriate subject line. (If you are using e-mail, save and print the message. Do not actually send the e-mail.)

3. In the memo or e-mail, mention tactfully that the voice mail messages used by some department members could be improved. Explain reasons why department members should record an effective voice mail message to be heard by persons reaching their voice mail. Discuss why they should leave effective messages for others. Include guidelines for effective voice mail messages in the memo or e-mail. Include a sample message that you might record for persons reaching your voice mail. Also include a sample message you might leave when you reach another person's voice mail. Ask department members to prepare and record effective and professional voice mail messages.

488

CHAPTER 12: TELEPHONE SYSTEMS AND PROCEDURES

objectives

○ Describe and apply skills required to make a favorable first impression over the telephone

○ Apply telephone techniques and procedures to handle incoming calls courteously and efficiently

○ Plan calls and use tools such as printed and computerized directories

○ Describe procedures to place local and long-distance domestic and international calls

○ Describe techniques for controlling telephone costs

A company may receive and place many calls each day. Workers talk with others both inside and outside the company to discuss common concerns, to place orders, or to request information. Messages must be taken and recorded either manually or electronically. Telephone calls are often less time consuming than a memo, a letter, or even an e-mail message.

All office workers should use proper techniques when answering or placing calls. When you place a call to a business, your first impression of the company is often based on how you are treated by the person answering your call. If the person is courteous and interested in helping you, you probably form a good impression of the company. If the person is abrupt, rude, or unwilling to help, you probably form a negative impression. When you answer the telephone or place an outgoing call, you may be making an initial customer contact. You will want to give callers a positive impression by what you say and how you say it.

To help control telephone costs, companies must choose carefully from the equipment and services that are available. Office workers should be aware of the local and long-distance services available in the office. In this topic, you will learn to create a good first impression when using the telephone. You will practice proper techniques and procedures for placing and receiving telephone calls.

Making a Favorable First Impression

When you handle telephone calls at work, you are representing your company. To the individual who is calling, you are the company. To create a positive image, you should develop good communication skills. Your voice, pronunciation, grammar, and vocabulary, as well as your attitude, contribute to the impression you make when using the telephone.

Your Voice

When you talk with others in person, you make them feel welcome by smiling and perhaps by shaking hands. You show interest and alertness by making eye contact with them during the conversation. When you talk by telephone, however, all you have to convey interest and courtesy is your voice. Elements of your voice that you must pay attention to include tone, pace, and volume.

The tone of your voice refers to the changes in pitch used to emphasize words and to get your meaning across to the listener. You have, no doubt, listened to speakers who talked in a monotone. Paying attention is difficult

489

Topic 12-2: *Effective Telephone Communications*

You represent your organization every time you place or answer a call.

when someone is speaking in a monotonous voice. The listener may become bored or may perceive the speaker as indifferent or inattentive. Vary the tone of your voice to express feelings and emphasis of ideas but avoid using extremes. An animated voice reflects interest in the caller and helps you achieve successful communication. Avoid speaking in a very high-pitched voice, a very low-pitched voice, or with an up-and-down, "singsong" manner.

Pace is the rate or speed of speech. The rate at which you talk to someone on the telephone can affect the ability of the listener to understand your message. If you speak too rapidly, the listener may not hear all the information. This is true especially if the information is technical or detailed. On the other hand, if you speak too slowly, the listener may become bored, insulted, or inattentive.

Consider the listener when determining a proper pace for speech. You may be speaking with people from different parts of your nation and with people from countries all over the world. You may be conversing with people who, even though they speak the same language as you, have speech patterns and regional dialects that are different from your own. You must learn to adjust your pace to fit the needs of the listener.

Extremes in volume should be avoided when speaking on the telephone. Do not shout or speak so softly that the listener cannot hear what you are saying. Control the volume of your voice so that you are speaking neither too loudly nor too softly. Speak directly into the telephone receiver or mouthpiece.

Your Speaking Skills

Your voice and speaking skills are put to the test when you speak on the telephone. Speaking skills such as word pronunciation, grammar, and vocabulary usage affect the impression you give over the phone. Although you may have a pleasant tone, a good pace, and a well-modulated voice, communication is difficult if the person you are speaking with cannot understand your words.

Pronunciation

Correct pronunciation of words is essential for understanding. Proper enunciation is also important. When you **enunciate** effectively you pronounce words clearly and distinctly. For example, you should say *what do you* instead of *whaddaya*, and you should say *going to* instead of *gonna*. Always enunciate word endings such as *ing*, *ed*, possessives, and plurals.

enunciate: pronounce words clearly and distinctly

You will find that many people speak with a regional accent. An accent involves a certain rhythm, speed, and pronunciation of vowels that is native to a particular region. You probably have an accent even though you may not be aware of it. If you find that you have trouble communicating because of an accent, several strategies can help you succeed:

- Pronounce words correctly and enunciate clearly.
- Speak slowly, but not so slowly that you insult or annoy the caller.
- Avoid long words, complicated phrases, or long sentences.
- If you are unsure of any word's pronunciation, look it up in the dictionary.

© GETTY IMAGES/PHOTODISC

Your voice and speaking skills help you create a positive impression over the phone.

Grammar

Although some rules of grammar are relaxed for spoken communications, you should follow basic grammar standards. Doing so will help you project a favorable impression of yourself and your company. Avoid use of slang or regional expressions that may not be widely known or understood, especially if the call is an international one. Other people may use terms that you do not recognize. When you do not understand an expression or phrase, always ask for an explanation.

Vocabulary

You should strive to improve your professional and personal vocabulary. You can learn new terms that relate to your position or your company. You can also learn words that will help you express your feelings, ideas, and needs. Remember that clear and courteous communication is always your goal. Avoid using trendy, slang expressions in formal business communications. State your ideas simply without using highly technical terms or lengthy words.

Many companies deal directly with clients, customers, or suppliers from other countries. Your company may even be an international one whose owners or headquarters are located outside the United States. Learn some simple courtesy phrases to use when speaking with international callers. Your attempts at learning and using some simple, basic phrases will be appreciated by foreign callers. Using these terms will help you make a favorable impression. Keep a list of basic phrases along with their translations and pronunciations. Practice them and make sure that you are saying them correctly.

Your Attitude

When you speak to someone over the telephone, all you have is your voice to give information and express your feelings. Even though you may not be seen by the person with whom you are speaking, your attitude is reflected in your speech and tone of voice. Any boredom, anger, or indifference you are feeling may be obvious to the person on the line. On the other hand, a smile and an upbeat, caring attitude are also clearly projected to the person with whom you are speaking. You should put any negative feelings aside and respond to the caller with a sincere, positive attitude.

Incoming Telephone Calls

Handling incoming telephone calls requires skill in using proper telephone techniques and effective procedures. When answering the telephone, you usually do not know who is calling or what the caller wants. Your work may be interrupted, or you may have a visitor in your office. You should know how to handle a variety of situations and take care of caller requests, needs, and problems.

Expand the Concept

With the increase in international organizations, most workers have to deal with clients from other countries, or perhaps they are working for a company with foreign ownership. Not only will they find it advantageous to learn several common phrases in the language of those with whom they must communicate, but also knowledge of the customs of that country will increase effectiveness in their business dealings.

For Discussion

Body language is a major factor when communicating with someone in person. Discuss how body language cannot be observed when speaking on the telephone. Ask students how they can convey a positive attitude when speaking on the telephone.

Proper Telephone Techniques

You now know that your voice, your speaking skills, and your attitude all affect a caller's impression of you and your company. Your call may be an initial customer contact—the first time the customer has spoken with someone at your company. How well you handle the call may determine, at least in part, whether the customer will do business with your company. Using proper telephone techniques will help you make a positive impression.

Answer Promptly

Answer all incoming calls promptly and pleasantly. If possible, answer the telephone after the first ring. When you reach for the receiver, also pick up a pen or pencil and a notepad or message form. You must be ready to take notes or a message.

When you reach for the receiver, have a pen and pad ready to take notes.

© CORBIS

Identify Yourself

Many companies use automated telephone systems that answer the calls and route them to the requested person. In this case, you may not need to identify your company when you answer a call. However, if you are the person to whom all incoming calls are routed, you should identify first the company, then yourself.

A telephone conversation cannot begin until the caller knows that the correct number, department, or person has been reached. Following are examples of improper and proper telephone answering responses.

Improper: "Hello," or "Yes?" (*These greetings do not give any identification of the person or of the company.*)

Improper: "Hello, hold please." (*This greeting does not give any company identification to the caller. Also, abruptly placing the caller on hold is rude and abrasive.*)

493

Topic 12-2: *Effective Telephone Communications*

Point out to students the consequences of passing callers off to other workers. Ask students if they have ever experienced aggravation when a call was transferred several times.

Improper: "Good morning. International Electronics. Our company is number one in the field of international electronics products sales and service. Pat Lopez speaking. May I be of help to you?" (This greeting is too long and distracting.)

Proper: "Good morning. International Electronics, Pat Lopez." (Use this greeting when you are answering an outside call.)

Proper: "Marketing Department, Leon DiMarco." (Use this greeting when you are answering an inside or outside call in a company where all calls are routed through a switchboard operator or an automated attendant that has already identified the company.)

Proper: "Ms. Yamaguchi's office, Lisa Stein." (Use this greeting when you are answering the telephone for a coworker.)

Assist the Caller

Your job is to help the caller as efficiently as you can. Never assume that you know what the caller wants. Instead, listen attentively to the caller's questions and comments. If you know that it will take several minutes to find the information needed for the call, do not keep the caller waiting. Explain the situation to the caller and offer the choice of being placed on hold or hanging up and receiving a return call. Follow through on any promise you make to return a call.

Make sure that you give accurate information to callers. If you do not know the answer to a question, admit it. Either tell the caller that you will obtain the information and call back, or offer to transfer the call to someone who can answer the question. Avoid passing off a caller to someone else if there is any way that you can be of help yourself.

Have reference materials handy to assist callers.

Conclude the Call

As a general rule, the person who places a call is the one who should end the call and hang up first. If you follow this rule, you avoid making the caller feel as if the conversation has been "cut off" before he or she was ready to hang up.

Use the caller's name as you end the conversation. For example: "Yes, Ms. O'Toole, I will be sure to mail you a copy of our latest catalog today," or, "Thank you for calling, Mr. Haliz. I will be sure to give Ms. Schmidt the information." Such a practice personalizes the conversation.

Effective Telephone Procedures

As you answer incoming calls, you need to handle many tasks efficiently. You may be requested to screen calls, give information, or take messages. You may need to place a caller on hold, transfer calls, handle disconnected calls, and deal with difficult callers. Effective procedures make managing each of these situations easier.

Plan to place and receive calls on a mobile phone at appropriate times and places. Do not use your mobile phone in an area where you will disturb other people. Meetings, movies, concerts, and restaurants are examples of places where using mobile phones can disturb others. Do not discuss confidential information in a public area. Do not use a mobile phone while driving a car, as this may distract your attention from driving.

Screening Calls

In some offices, you may be asked to **screen calls**. Screening incoming calls is a procedure used to determine who is calling and, at times, the purpose of the call. For example, your supervisor may instruct you to screen calls and take a message from all salespeople who call. You may inform the caller that you will relay the message; however, do not promise a return call. Your supervisor may be in an important meeting and ask you not to interrupt except for certain callers. Screening can save you and the caller time because you may be able to help the person yourself or transfer the call immediately to another person.

When screening calls, find out who is calling. Be tactful, yet direct. To learn the caller's name, ask questions such as "May I say who is calling?" or "Who is calling, please?"

Sometimes callers refuse to give their names. If your company requires you to identify each caller by name before transferring the call, you must be courteous, yet firm. Explaining the policy to the caller will usually encourage the caller to give you his or her name. Even if the caller becomes rude or still refuses to tell his or her name, you should at all times be courteous. Remain firm, however, in following the company's policies.

screen calls: determine who is calling and the purpose for each call

For Discussion

Why would some employers have a policy that no calls are to be screened?

Placing a Caller on Hold

At times, you must place a caller on hold while you answer another call. A telephone caller who is on hold is still connected but waiting for the other person to come back on the line. Ask the first caller if you may place him or her on hold. Then answer the second call. Ask permission to place the second caller on hold while you complete your conversation with the first caller.

Sometimes you will need to place a caller on hold while you look up information to answer a question. Politely inform the caller that you are placing him or her on hold. If you think several minutes will be needed to find the answer, ask if you should call back or if the caller would prefer to hold. When a caller is on hold, check back frequently to reassure the caller that he or she has not been forgotten.

Transferring Calls

Calls are usually transferred when the caller has reached a wrong extension or has a request that can be handled more effectively by another person. The caller may request the transfer, or you may determine that the transfer is necessary. Always tell the caller why the transfer is necessary. For example, you may say:

"I'm going to transfer your call to Mr. Rosen. He will be able to provide you with the information you need."

You may prefer to place the caller on hold while you speak with the person to whom you intend to transfer the call. This will allow you to confirm that this person can help the caller and to introduce the caller for screening purposes. Calls can sometimes become accidentally disconnected during a transfer. You may wish to give the caller the extension number or name of the person to which the call is being transferred. Then if the call is accidentally disconnected, the caller can reach the appropriate person or extension when he or she calls again.

For Discussion

Under what circumstances might a caller respond, "No, you may not place me on hold!"? How would you respond?

Points to Emphasize

Transfer calls carefully to avoid disconnecting the caller. Always tell the caller the person or extension the call is being transferred to.

Transfer a call carefully to avoid disconnecting the caller.

Handling a Disconnected Call

Occasionally, you will be disconnected while you are talking on the telephone or while you are waiting on hold. In general, the person who placed the call should call back immediately after the disconnection. That person has the telephone number of the party being called and should, therefore, be able to redial the call quickly.

The caller should report a disconnected long-distance call to the telephone company. Depending on the telephone company used, an adjustment may be made in the long-distance charge.

Giving Information

You may take calls for a manager or coworkers who are out of the office. In these situations, you must tactfully tell the caller that the person is not available and offer to take a message or assist the caller yourself. When coworkers are unavailable to receive calls, give the caller enough information to explain the person's absence. However, do not give unnecessary or sensitive details.

Improper	*"Ms. Fox has a hair appointment this afternoon."*
Improper	*"Ms. Fox had to pick up her son from school."*
Improper	*"Mr. Chandler is playing golf with a prospective client."*
Proper	*"Ms. Fox is out of the office until tomorrow morning. May I take a message or ask her to call you?"*
Proper	*"Mr. Chandler is in a meeting this afternoon and won't be available the rest of the day. May I take a message or ask him to return your call?"*

For Discussion

What are some examples of information that should not be given to a caller regarding the location or activities of the person the caller wishes to speak to?

497

Topic 12-2: *Effective Telephone Communications*

Taking Messages

In many companies, the use of voice mail eliminates some of the need for taking written messages. Even with voice mail, it will be necessary for you to record information for yourself such as the caller's name, telephone number, and purpose of the call.

Message forms are usually available in offices for recording telephone messages. When you record a message, it is essential that it is accurate and complete. Verify names and telephone numbers by reading back the information to the caller. Ask for accurate spellings of names if you are in doubt. Key or write the message carefully. If the message is handwritten, make sure that your handwriting is legible so you do not waste time rewriting it later or fail to be able to read it. Each message should include the following data:

- Date and time of the call
- Name of the caller with the caller's company (Check spellings of any names about which you are uncertain.)
- Caller's telephone number, including area code if it is a long-distance call (Remember to repeat the number for verification.)
- Details of the message
- Your name or initials

Figure 12-2.1

Record information on message forms legibly and accurately.

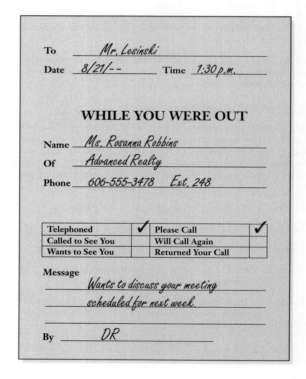

| To | Mr. Lesinski |
| Date | 8/21/-- | Time 1:30 p.m. |

WHILE YOU WERE OUT

Name _Ms. Rosanna Robbins_

Of _Advanced Realty_

Phone _606-555-3478_ Ext. 248

Telephoned	✔	Please Call	✔
Called to See You		Will Call Again	
Wants to See You		Returned Your Call	

Message
Wants to discuss your meeting scheduled for next week.

By _DR_

Your office may have software that can be used to complete an electronic message. Using a computer message offers these advantages:

- Less time is needed to key a message than to write it.
- The number of lost messages is reduced because messages can be transferred immediately to the intended receiver.
- Printed message forms are not needed.

Each computer message you key should include the same basic information as a handwritten message. As you key the message, make sure that is accurate and complete. Verify all names and numbers. The current date and time may be entered automatically by the system into the onscreen form, or you may need to enter this information. The message may be transferred to the receiver's computer screen by keying in the correct extension number. A reminder or some form of electronic notation will appear on the receiver's screen showing that a message is waiting. In some offices, e-mail is used to record and forward telephone messages.

For Discussion

What are the advantages and disadvantages of using a computer to prepare messages?

WORKPLACE CONNECTIONS

Answering the telephone in an appropriate manner and taking accurate messages is important for effective telephone communications. Notice how the office worker answering this call gives enough information to satisfy the caller but does not give inappropriate information.

Office Worker: "Hello. Mr. Lesinski's office. Jan House speaking."

Caller: "May I please speak with Mr. Lesinski? This is Rosanna Robbins from Advanced Realty."

Office Worker: "I'm sorry, Ms. Robbins, but Mr. Lesinski is out of the office until Thursday. I'm Mr. Lesinski's assistant. Could I help you, or may I ask him to call you when he returns?"

Caller: "Yes. Please ask him to call me at 606-555-0178, extension 248, regarding our meeting scheduled for next week."

Office Worker: "Thank you, Ms. Robbins. To confirm, your number is 606-555-0178, extension 248. I will give Mr. Lesinski the message."

Handling Difficult Callers

On occasion you may receive calls from persons who are angry, unreasonable, rude, or demanding. These calls may be few, but they can be very stressful. You must control yourself and remain professional when dealing with difficult callers. Your goal is to diffuse the situation and to maintain goodwill with the caller, if possible. Follow these guidelines when dealing with difficult telephone callers.

- Try to resolve the matter if possible. Usually the caller just wants the company to solve a problem or fix a mistake. Do not hesitate to apologize to the caller for any problems or inconveniences that have been experienced.
- Always present a helpful, positive, and sincere attitude even in an adverse situation.
- If the caller is personally abusive to you or uses profanity, end the conversation quickly after identifying the caller and recording relevant information about the call.
- Remain outwardly calm and do not display defensive behavior. Usually, the caller is not upset with you but with the company or its actions. Do not take the caller's anger personally.

Handling Personal Telephone Calls

Follow your company's policy regarding making or receiving personal telephone calls at work. Many companies permit a limited number of personal calls. Other companies discourage personal calls. Workers may be expected to use a pay phone located in the building and make calls during break times. Generally, brief urgent or emergency calls are permitted. Long or frequent personal calls are typically not considered acceptable at work.

Outgoing Telephone Calls

As with incoming telephone calls, outgoing calls may be made to a person outside or inside the company. Calls may be interoffice, local, or long distance. You should understand the process and procedures for placing all outgoing calls. Your goal is efficiency and economy.

Planning Calls

Every call you make requires some preparation and planning. Most calls may be simple; however, others may require detailed planning. When preparing for any call, confirm the name and number of the person you are calling. Identify clearly the main purpose of the call. Outline briefly the points you want to cover during the call. Gather other information or items you need to have available before making the call, such as:

- Dates and times of any meetings or planned events that relate to the call
- Documents that relate to the topic discussed
- Questions that you want to ask
- Pen and paper or your computer to take notes during the call

Outline the points you want to cover before placing a call.

Plan to place and receive calls on a mobile phone at appropriate times and places. Do not use your mobile phone in an area where you will disturb other people. Meetings, movies, concerts, and restaurants are examples of places where using mobile phones can disturb others. Confidential information should not be discussed in a public area. Do not use a mobile phone while driving a car as this may distract your attention from driving.

Time Zones

Be aware of time zone differences when placing long-distance calls. Note the current time in the location you are calling. Avoid calling when the time is before or after business hours or during lunch at that location. The continental United States and parts of Canada are divided into five standard time zones: Atlantic, Eastern, Central, Mountain, and Pacific. As you move west, each zone is one hour earlier. For example, when it is 1 p.m. in Washington, DC (Eastern zone), it is noon in Dallas (Central zone), 11 a.m. in Denver (Mountain zone), and 10 a.m. in Los Angeles (Pacific zone). If you are in San Diego and need to speak to a coworker in the New York City office, you will need to place the call before 2 p.m. Pacific time. Otherwise, the New York office may be closed because it will be 5 p.m. (Eastern time). A time zone map of the United States is included in most telephone directories. Web sites, such as Maps.com, display the current time in all U.S. time zones as well as providing a time zone map.

Twenty-four time zones are used throughout the world. To place a call to London, England, all you have to do is to dial the following sequence of numbers: 011 (international access code) + 44 (country code) + 71 (city code) + seven-digit phone number. Consult the International Calling or similar section of your local telephone directory for country codes.

With the increasing need to place international calls comes the need to determine the best time to place them. Problems arise when the countries are in time zones so far away that in order to reach a client, you must make the call in the middle of the night. Discuss how companies are overcoming this "time barrier" to communications with technology such as e-mail.

501

Topic 12-2: *Effective Telephone Communications*

If a caller is located in a time zone to which it is impossible for you to call during your regular business hours, you may have to make the call after your normal work time. If you make frequent international calls, you may want to keep a copy of a world time zone map at hand.

WORKPLACE CONNECTIONS

Sula works for Castor Imports. The company recently began doing business with a company in Mexico. Sula has tried to phone her contact at the company, Pedro Martinez, several times. Sula and Pedro cannot seem to find one another in the office. Sula usually calls Pedro between 1 p.m. and 2 p.m. when she returns from lunch. Pedro is always out. Pedro returns Sula's calls between 5 p.m. and 6 p.m. and finds that she is not in. Sula and Pedro need to learn about one another's customs and work schedules. For example, in Mexico during the hours of noon to 3 p.m., many offices are closed. Workers return at 3 p.m. and often remain in the office until 7 p.m. or 8 p.m. In the United States, the typical office work day ends at 5 p.m. Understanding these customs will help Sula and Pedro find a time to talk that is convenient for both of them.

Using Directories

Many resources are available for you to use when planning a call. Your local telephone company publishes a yearly directory. Local as well as national organizations publish a variety of business and professional directories. National telephone directories are available on CD, and directory information is available on the Internet. You should become familiar with the wide range of information contained in these resources.

Local Directories

Local telephone companies usually provide directories to their customers free of charge. You may want to find the telephone number of a business or individual in your local area. You can usually find the number in the white pages of the local directory. If you are searching for a particular service or product, you may find the number in the yellow pages section of the directory. You should become familiar with all sections of the local telephone directory. Typical directories contain the sections discussed in the following paragraphs.

Telephone directories with names of persons, businesses, and organizations arranged alphabetically are referred to as *white pages*. The front section of most directories is actually a user's guide for the directory itself and a "how-to" guide for the telephone services consumer. Some of the information you will find here includes types of telephone services provided by the company, local emergency numbers, and directions for making many types of calls. You should read and become very familiar with this section.

CHAPTER 12: TELEPHONE SYSTEMS AND PROCEDURES

Telephone numbers for local businesses can be found in the local telephone directory.

The next section of the local telephone directory contains names, addresses, and telephone numbers of businesses, government agencies, and individuals in your city. In some locations, the white pages may be divided into two sections. The first section lists personal names and numbers only while the second section lists only business names and numbers. Sometimes these sections are each contained in separate books. When personal and business numbers are divided, another section called the *blue pages* also may be included. The blue pages serve as an easy reference for locating telephone numbers of government offices and other helpful numbers such as those of the chamber of commerce, consumer protection agencies, and weather service.

A type of directory called the *yellow pages* contains an alphabetic listing of businesses arranged according to the services they provide or the products they sell. For example, if you want to find names and telephone numbers of businesses in the area that might cater your company's 50th anniversary dinner, you would look under *caterers* in the yellow pages.

Personal and Company Directories

You should make a list of all numbers that you call often. You may be able to program a limited number of frequently dialed numbers into your telephone. Your company may provide you with a directory of employees working at a particular location. A portion of a sample directory is shown in Figure 12-2.2 on page 504. The directory may also include procedures for using features of the telephone system. Tips for proper telephone techniques as well as how the company wants you to identify yourself and your department may also be included.

Figure **12-2.2**

Create a directory for telephone numbers you call frequently.

TELEPHONE DIRECTORY

Andersen Realty	606-555-8841
Burnett, Conley	606-555-3487
Captain J's Boat Shop	606-555-5698
Cash, Susan E.	513-555-8339
Century One Realtors	606-555-7722
Dautrich, Ela	606-555-7489
Estes, Sandra	513-555-4985
Guzzeta, Freia	270-555-3934
Habeeb, Mo	606-555-3519
Park, Kim	606-555-5681
Perez, Juan	606-555-2248

Electronic Directories

The types of data contained in the paper directories can also be accessed using a computer. National telephone directories can be purchased on CD. Several Web sites provide telephone numbers for individuals and businesses. Some sites also provide other services such as reverse lookup or a directory for toll-free numbers. Reverse lookup service allows users to enter a telephone number and find the person or company to which the number is assigned.

Directory Assistance

If you are unable to locate a telephone number, call the directory assistance operator for help. Dial 411 for a local directory assistance operator. For long-distance directory assistance, dial 1, the area code, and 555-1212. A directory assistance operator will ask you what city you are calling. Be prepared to supply the operator with as much information as possible about the person or business for which you need the number. Be prepared to give the correct spelling and street address if known. After giving the information, there will be a pause; then you will hear the number repeated twice. Make a note of the number for future reference. Because you may be charged for using directory assistance, use this service only as needed, not as a convenience.

Long-Distance Service

Long-distance calls are made to numbers outside the service area of your local telephone company. The time of day the call is placed, the length of the call, and type of long-distance service used may affect the cost of the call. Long-distance carriers provide a variety of pricing plans. The consumer or company chooses a long-distance provider. You may want to find out about the varied long-distance programs and prices available before selecting a carrier. Your local telephone directory may list several long-distance carriers and their numbers. You may also visit these companies' Web sites to learn of pricing and special offers and regulations.

Direct-Dial Calls

Direct-dial calls, also called station-to-station calls, are those placed without assistance from an operator. To make a direct-dial call, first dial 1, which gives you access to a long-distance line. Then dial the area code and the number you are trying to reach. Charges for these calls begin as soon as the telephone is answered. If you make a direct-dial call and the person you need to speak with is unavailable, your company still will be charged for the call.

Direct-dial calls are placed without assistance from an operator.

© CORBIS

Specialized Long-Distance Calls

Specialized long-distance calls are more expensive than those you dial direct. Person-to-person, collect, credit card, and conference calls are all types of special long-distance calls.

Person-to-person calls are an expensive type of operator-assisted calls. To place a person-to-person call, dial 0 (zero), the area code, and the telephone number of the individual or business you are calling. When you have finished dialing, you will be asked what type of call you wish to place, such as a person-to-person or collect call. You will say "person-to-person call" and will then be asked to supply the name of the person you are calling. Pronounce the name clearly and accurately. You may have to spell it for clarity.

person-to-person call: an operator-assisted, long-distance call which must be paid for only if the called person is reached

Charges for the call begin only after the person you have requested is on the line. If that person is not available, you will not be charged for the call. If you must call repeatedly before reaching the person, or if it takes the person several minutes to get to the phone, this type of call may be less expensive than a direct-dialed call. You do not pay until you begin speaking with the person you have indicated.

Topic 12-2: *Effective Telephone Communications*

Thinking Critically

In Topic 12-1, students learned about videoconferences. Have students explain how videoconferences and telephone conferences differ. How are they the same?

collect call: an operator-assisted, long-distance call paid for by the party being called

The charges for a **collect call** are billed to the telephone number being called, not to the number from which the call was placed. To place a collect call, dial 0 (zero), the area code, and the telephone number. You will be asked what type of call you are placing. Speak clearly into the phone, answering "collect." You will then be asked to give your name. Once again, speak very clearly and distinctly into the phone. The call will be completed, and the recipient will be asked whether or not the call and the charges will be accepted. People who travel for a business may find it necessary to make collect calls to their offices. Customers or clients may be invited to call collect.

A conference call is placed when it is necessary to talk with persons at several different locations at the same time. With some telephone systems, you can use special features to arrange these calls yourself. In many cases, conference calls are set up in advance with a conference operator. To place a conference call with this type of assistance, dial the number of this specialized service. You can obtain this number from your long-distance service provider or dial the operator and request a conference call. Be prepared to give the names, telephone numbers, and locations (cities and states) of the participants as well as the exact time the call is to be placed. At that time, the operator will call you and indicate that the other parties are on the line. Review the tips for planning and carrying out conference calls that were presented in Topic 12-1 in this chapter.

For people who travel frequently for business or pleasure, telephone credit cards can be very practical. The user is able to charge telephone calls to the credit card. A special PIN (personal identification number) is issued to the cardholder for security. The PIN number is entered using the telephone keypad. Some telephones, such as those found in airports, are specially equipped to read a magnetic card number when the credit card is slid through a slot.

prepaid phone card: card purchased in advance and used to pay for a certain number of minutes of phone use

Another type of phone card that is often used by travelers is a **prepaid phone card.** This card is purchased in advance and used to pay for a certain number of minutes of phone use. The user receives a PIN number and a toll-free access number. The phone system will inform you of the amount of calling time remaining for the card. Prepaid phone cards may be purchased in many locations such as airports and convenience stores and from your long-distance carrier.

Toll-Free Service

As a convenience to customers who call long-distance, a company may subscribe to toll-free service for callers. This discounted service applies to incoming calls only. No charge is made to the caller. For toll-free numbers, users dial 800 or 888 rather than an area code. To determine whether a company in the United States has a toll-free number, dial 1-800-555-1212 and give the company name. Several Web sites provide a lookup service for toll-free numbers. The Internet 800 Directory is an example of a site that offers this service. To find other sites, search the Internet using the phrase *lookup service for toll-free numbers.*

As with other telephone services, rate plans and regulations for toll-free service plans vary widely. Compare price plans and features from several companies to find the plan that will be most cost-effective for your company.

For Discussion

Why do you think hotel chains, airlines, and rental car companies offer toll-free numbers to their customers? Toll-free services are now available for home use through some service providers. What are the advantages for the home user?

© LISETTE LE BON/SUPERSTOCK

Prepaid phone cards are convenient for business travelers.

Controlling Telephone Costs

As an office worker, you will be expected to help control telephone costs. Some guidelines to follow for controlling telephone costs and improving efficiency are listed below.

- Use direct dialing most of the time. Make more specialized, expensive types of calls only when necessary.
- Plan your calls so the time spent during a long-distance or any other call is used efficiently.
- If possible, call when long-distance rates are least expensive.
- Notify the operator immediately after reaching a wrong number so you can receive credit for the call.
- Be an informed consumer of telephone services. Compare rate plans and promotional offerings.
- Learn how to use the equipment and features of your telephone system.

What are some steps office workers can take to help control telephone costs?

REVIEWING THE TOPIC

1. What factors influence the first impression you make when you respond to a telephone call?
2. Why should you use the caller's name as the conversation ends?
3. What information should you record when taking a telephone message or retrieving telephone messages from your voice mailbox?
4. What should you do if you have placed a caller on hold and you think several minutes will be needed for you to locate the requested information?
5. What questions might you ask to learn a caller's name?
6. Give three suggestions for handling difficult telephone callers.
7. Describe information found in a white pages telephone directory. How are organizations listed in a yellow pages telephone directory? For what purposes are the blue pages telephone directory used?
8. Name the five time zones into which the continental United States and parts of Canada are divided.
9. List five examples of information that may be needed before making a call.
10. Describe the procedure for dialing a domestic, long-distance direct-dial call.
11. Describe the procedure for dialing an international, long-distance direct-dial call.
12. List three guidelines for controlling telephone costs.

THINKING CRITICALLY

You are employed in a growing computer sales and service business, Hooser's Computer Corner. Several calls are received daily for the fifteen sales associates, seven service technicians, and four office services employees. The owner is considering the purchase of an automated attendant telephone system. The office manager, Ms. Lin Wong, would like to hear your suggestions before deciding whether to purchase a system. You are aware of both advantages and disadvantages of using these systems. What do you recommend?

1. Make a list of the pros and cons of using an automated attendant at Hooser's Computer Corner.
2. Prepare a memo or e-mail message to Lin Wong. Include your list of pros and cons. Give your recommendation as to whether or not you think the company should install an automated attendant. Give reasons for your recommendation.

508

508

REINFORCING MATH SKILLS

You work for Carrlson-Greer, which has offices in Seattle, Houston, and St. Louis. You are responsible for monitoring the costs of the various forms of telecommunications used by the company. As part of your analysis, prepare a table showing the monthly long-distance telephone charges for each regional office for a period of six months.

1. Prepare a spreadsheet to record and calculate the telephone charges. Key the company name as the main title of the spreadsheet. Key **Long-Distance Charges for Regional Carriers** under the company name.

2. Key **Months, Seattle, Houston, St. Louis,** and **Totals** as the column heads. Key the data for each office for each month as shown below step 4.

3. Enter formulas to calculate:
   - Total charges for the three offices for each month
   - Total charges for each regional office for the six-month period
   - Total charges for the six-month period for all regional offices
   - The average monthly charges for each regional office
   - The average monthly charges for all offices

4. Format the spreadsheet so it is attractive and easy to read. Print the spreadsheet.

Months	Seattle	Houston	St. Louis
January	$201.56	$58.67	$250.78
February	190.45	75.34	277.56
March	175.66	68.90	265.19
April	188.34	92.51	281.40
May	205.22	61.61	275.37
June	199.29	74.27	259.39

Topic 12-2 : ACTIVITY 1

DATABASE

Company Telephone Directory

As a special project, you will create a directory of employees for your office at the Home and Hearth Insurance Agency. The information will be contained in a database that can be accessed and updated easily.

1. Open and print the PDF file *CH12 Directory* from the data files. This file contains the information for the directory.

Teaching Tips

Give students the correct answers after they have completed the activity.

Teaching Tips

Assist students with sorting the database using two fields.

2. Create a new database file named *CH12 Phone Directory*. Create a table named **Directory** with the following text fields: Name, Title, Department, and Extension. Make the Extension field the primary key.

3. Enter records for all the workers at your location using data from the printout.

4. Sort the records in alphabetical order by last name and print the directory showing all fields.

5. Sort the records in alphabetical order first by department and then by last name. Print the directory showing all fields.

INTERNET
RESEARCH
WORD PROCESSING

Topic **12-2** | A C T I V I T Y   2

Directory Research

Telephone directories provide a wealth of information for your use in planning telephone communications and locating people and services. Use your local telephone directory or online directories to find the information requested. Key and print your answers.

1. Number of the nearest Federal Bureau of Investigation office

2. Number to call to report telephone problems on your line

3. Number to call if you have questions about your telephone bill

4. List of the first three digits of the telephone numbers in your local calling area

5. List of all area codes for Illinois, Colorado, and Washington, D.C.

6. The time zones for Nashville, TN; Prince Edward Island, Canada; Seattle, WA; and Wichita, KS

7. The country codes for dialing the following countries: Japan, Mexico, Kenya, and Greece

8. Number for your state's motor vehicle department

9. Number for the local public schools

10. Subject in the yellow pages where you would find:
   - Agencies that supply temporary office workers
   - A vision center that sells eyeglasses
   - A service station that will change your car's oil
   - A company that will repair your computer
   - A company that sells voice mail equipment
   - A doctor who specializes in eye surgery

CHAPTER REVIEW 12

Summary

Telecommunications plays a vital role in business affairs. Because the technology changes rapidly, office workers should keep abreast of new services and equipment. Read the following key points to review what you learned in this chapter:

- Office workers rely on telecommunications technology to share information quickly and reliably. This information may be in the form of text, images, or video as well as voice.
- A modem can be used to convert the digital data into analog signals that can be transmitted over telephone channels.
- Satellites play an important part in worldwide telecommunications systems.
- The integration of computer and telephone technologies is called telephony. Telephony technology offers many features useful to businesses.
- VoIP, also called Internet voice, allows users to make telephone calls using a high-speed Internet connection instead standard telephone channels.
- Centralized telephone systems route calls coming into and going out of an organization. An automated attendant is a computerized system for handling telephone calls.
- Mobile telephones are an important tool commonly used for both personal and business communications. Camera phones and smart phones are variations of mobile phones.
- A conference call is one that has three or more participants speaking at different locations. Conference calls may be handled in several ways: with the user's own equipment, operator-dialed service, or dial-in service.
- Voice mail is a messaging system that uses computers and telephones to record, send, store, and retrieve voice messages.
- Specialized telephone equipment and services are available for individuals with speech and sight impairments.
- Facsimile technology, often called fax, sends images (text, photographs, drawings) using telephone or VoIP channels.
- A variety of telephones and systems may be purchased from many vendors. Companies should carefully compare services and prices when choosing a telephone service provider.
- When you answer or place a call for your organization, you immediately make an impression on the other person.
- Workers should use proper techniques and procedures so that all incoming and outgoing calls are handled professionally and efficiently.

Have students review key points from the chapter by completing the Sort It Out game on *The Office* Web site.

- Plan an outgoing call before placing it to make sure all the points you want to discuss are included.
- Information needed for placing calls is contained in a variety of print and electronic directories.
- You can help control telephone costs by using direct-dial calls, planning outgoing calls, and placing calls when rates are least expensive.

Key Terms

analog	facsimile	smart phone
automated attendant	modem	telecommunications
Braille	pager	telephony
cellular telephone	person-to-person call	videoconferencing
collect call	prepaid phone card	voice mail
digital	satellite	VoIP
enunciate	screen calls	

COMPOSITION
TEAMWORK
WORD PROCESSING

Chapter 12 : A C T I V I T Y 1

Telephone Conversations

Role-playing telephone conversations will help you develop your telephone skills. For the role-playing activities, work with another member of your class. Rotate in each situation between being the caller and being the person answering the telephone.

1. Open and print the PDF file *CH12 Phone* from the data files. This file describes several dramatic situations that you will role play.

2. After you have read each dramatic situation, work with your teammate to prepare a script. Compose the dialog that each person might say in this situation and print a copy for each of you.

3. Practice the telephone conversations. If you have a tape recorder available, record the call. Evaluate yourself and your teammate using the form provided in the data file.

4. Present your call to the class or another team. Have classmates complete an evaluation form for each presentation. Your classmates will also be acting out the situations and you will complete forms to evaluate them.

Long-Distance Rates Comparison

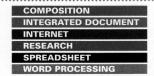

COMPOSITION
INTEGRATED DOCUMENT
INTERNET
RESEARCH
SPREADSHEET
WORD PROCESSING

Your company, Dee-Lite's Chocolates, is dissatisfied with its current long-distance service provider. Prices have risen on domestic calls over the last six months. The company remains open 24 hours a day, seven days a week to meet the demands of a growing market for its gourmet chocolates. Long-distance telephone calls are placed all during the seven-day work period.

Tina has researched several plans and recorded the domestic rates for long distance calls. You will complete the research by finding rate plans for two additional long distance carriers. You will use your spreadsheet software to find the average rates for each plan. You will also copy the spreadsheet table into a document with your recommendation for which plan to choose.

1. Create a spreadsheet sheet titled **TELEPHONE RATES COMPARISON.** Key Tina's data shown below.

Provider	Plan Name	Day Rate	Evening Rate	Weekend Rate
E-CON-O-ME	All-4-U	$0.10	$0.10	$0.10
VARI-PLAN	Ten Plan	0.10	0.10	0.10
EAGLE LINE	Wings	0.11	0.09	0.08
VALU-COM	Circle	0.12	0.08	0.08
BL&T	Makes Cents	0.14	0.08	0.07

2. Complete the research for this project. Use the Internet or other resources to find rates charged by at least two telephone service providers for long-distance calls within the United States. Record rate amounts for the same times as shown for the companies Tina researched. Key the data into your spreadsheet.

3. Key the column heading **Average** at the right of the spreadsheet. Enter formulas to average each company's day, evening, and weekend rates. Save the spreadsheet file as *CH12 Rates.*

4. Create a memo to Murray Washford from you. Use the current date and an appropriate subject line. Give your recommendation for the telephone service provider the company should choose. Point out the reasons for your choice. Include the rate comparison table from the spreadsheet in the memo to support your position.

5. Check the document for format and content. Save the file as *CH12 Rates Memo.* Print the document.

After completing all the chapters in Part 4, complete the Part 4 simulation, At Work at Buckhorn Mountain Outfitters. The simulation is found in the Student Activities and Simulations *workbook.*

Chapter Review

Teaching Tips

Students may complete this activity using only the data given if you do not want them to spend time researching additional companies.

Supplemental Activity

Have students complete the Chapter 12 Supplemental Activity, Research Online Directories, available on *The Office* Web site.

Assessment

Assess student learning using the Chapter 12 test available on the *IRCD* and in *ExamView®* format.

P A R T 5

Personal and Career Development

OBJECTIVES

- Plan for entry into the workplace and for career development

- Describe and develop personal characteristics valuable at work

- Discuss and develop the basic attitudes that support organizational goals

- Interact effectively with others at work

Success at work is based on a combination of skills and personal qualities. Both will prove important in finding a job and advancing your career. You will want to understand how to search for a job and how to present your credentials and yourself. You need to know what the expectations are as you begin work. Companies seek employees at all levels who are good team players. They want workers who are cooperative, responsible, and focused on meeting company goals. Part 5, Personal and Career Development, focuses on you as a worker and how you interact with others to secure a position and perform satisfactorily.

514

© DIGITAL VISION

CHAPTER 13

Planning and Advancing Your Career

You have had many opportunities to consider the types of tasks common to many jobs. You may have made a firm decision about your choice for an initial job or career. On the other hand, you may be planning full-time study for awhile and postponing a decision about your first full-time job. Regardless of your present plans, you will find it valuable to understand what is generally involved in getting a job.

In this chapter, you will become acquainted with various ways of learning about jobs. You will also learn how to respond to these career opportunities. Use your study of this material to become aware of your own interests and begin developing career goals. You can feel confident about finding a job and advancing your career when you have learned about effective job search and career planning strategies.

515

Topic 13-1

objectives

- Identify the factors to consider when planning a career strategy
- Discuss the role of a career goal in your planning
- Describe the steps in planning a job search
- Prepare a resume
- Prepare for an interview
- Explain what generally is expected of an interviewee

AN EFFECTIVE JOB SEARCH

While studying this textbook, you have learned that many jobs require office-related and information-related skills. At this point, you may be planning to:

- Begin work full time
- Begin work full time while pursuing further education on a part-time basis
- Begin work part time and become a full-time student in college or some other training or educational program
- Be a full-time college student with no plans for present full-time work

Regardless of your plans, you will find the information in this topic helpful for understanding how to enter the job market.

career goals: desired achievements related to work such as jobs, education, or work experience

career strategy: plans to meet career goals

interview: meeting to question or evaluate, as for a job applicant

Thinking Ahead About Careers and Jobs

Whatever your present plans for employment or further education, you should consider your long-term **career goals**. You might wonder why someone who is considering a first job should be thinking beyond that job. Thinking ahead may help you choose a first job that is closely related to long-term interests. Thinking ahead to what you see as a career goal and planning realistic steps to meet that goal is known as a **career strategy**. With a career goal in mind, you can evaluate beginning job offers in relation to that goal.

WORKPLACE CONNECTIONS

Christine works part-time in a large company in downtown Denver during her senior year in high school. She would like to be a secondary school teacher and plans to work full time for at least two years while she studies education at a local college. Then she plans to become a full-time student. The manager where she works has suggested that because she wants to be a teacher, she might like to work full time in their Human Resources Department and help the director of their extensive training programs. After an **interview** in the Human Resources Department, Christine was offered a position. She is looking forward to beginning her new full-time position in late July.

© BLUESTONE PRODUCTIONS/ SUPERSTOCK

516

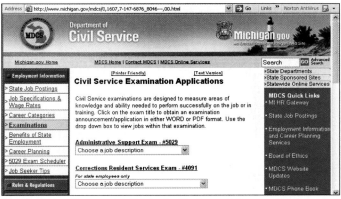

Source: Michigan Department of Civil Service. http://www.michigan.gov/mdcs/ 0,1607,7-147-6876_8046—,00.html (accessed October 17, 2005).

Figure **13-1.3**

Many government employees must pass civil service examinations.

Personal Inquiry

If you want to work for a particular company, you may want to write a carefully worded letter asking about job possibilities. In your letter, you should explain the reason for your interest in being an employee. Describe the kind of job you want and briefly outline your qualifications. You need not include a resume with your letter of inquiry, but you may want to state that you will be happy to forward a detailed resume.

Preparing a Resume

A resume, also called a data sheet or vita, is a concise, well-organized presentation of your qualifications for a job. The employer usually will see your resume before interviewing you. Your resume should make a positive impression on the reader. A resume should be accurate in every detail.

A resume usually has several categories: personal information, job interest, education, work experience, and references (or a statement about availability of references). You may want to include additional categories, such as computer competencies, extracurricular activities, or scholastic honors when appropriate. As a general rule, list the most important information first. Refer to Figure 13-1.4 on page 522 as you read about common resume categories.

- **Personal Information.** List your contact information clearly at the beginning of your resume. This information should include your name, mailing address, and telephone number. If you have an e-mail address or fax number, list those also. You need not provide information such as age, date of birth, or marital status.
- **Job Interest.** Briefly state the job for which you are applying. An employer will then be able to see how your qualifications relate to specific job openings.

Thinking Critically

What should you learn about an organization before you make an inquiry about a job?

Thinking Critically

Why do you think applicants are not required to provide information about their age and marital status?

521

Topic 13-1: *An Effective Job Search*

What volunteer experiences have you had that could be listed on your resume?

Valerie Gomez
3467 Mandelin Drive
Albuquerque, NM 87112-0341
(505) 555-0130

Job Interest

An administrative assistant position in an historical museum or college.

Education

Will graduate from Southwest High School, May, 20--
Grade Point Average: 3.57
Class Standing: 34th in class of 329

Related courses:

American History
Keyboarding
Computer Skills
Office Procedures

Special skills:

Keyboarding: 65 words per minute
Good command of Microsoft Office: Word, Excel, Access
Historical research experience in local libraries

School activities:

Vice President of American Historical Club
Member of Student Council

Work Experience

Assistant to the librarian of the historical archives in the Albuquerque Public Library. (Part-time during school year; full time during the past two summers.)

Student assistant to school librarian during first two years in high school.

References

Provided upon request.

Figure **13-1.4**

A resume presents an applicant's job qualifications.

522

- **Education.** List the name and address of your high school and the graduation date or anticipated date. List the courses you completed that prepared you for the job market. You may also include any scholastic honors or awards you have earned. You may want to show any extracurricular activities in which you participated, such as membership in special interest clubs.
- **Work Experience.** List in chronological order the jobs you have had, beginning with the most recent one. For each job, include the name and address of the organization, your job title, a brief description of the tasks performed, and the beginning and ending dates of your employment. If your job experience is limited, include part-time positions as well as any volunteer work you performed. Be sure to indicate clearly the work you did as a volunteer.
- **References.** References are persons who know your academic ability and/or work skills and habits and are willing to recommend you to employers. List references on your resume or include a note stating that references will be provided on request. When you list a reference, be sure to include a complete name, job title, address, and telephone number for each one. Generally, three references are considered sufficient. Ask permission before using a person as a reference on an application or in an interview with an employer.

reference: a person who knows your work abilities, skills, and habits and is willing to recommend you to employers

Because there is no standard resume format, an employer may consider your resume to be an example of your ability to organize data in a useful and meaningful form. The form in which you submit your resume will influence the content and format of the data. You should create a traditional hard copy resume. A hard copy resume formatted for ease of scanning may be required for some jobs. An electronic resume saved in a file format that can be posted online or sent by e-mail is also needed.

A hard copy resume for traditional use should be attractive and easy to read. Limit a hard copy resume to one page, or use a second page only if needed to list complete work history. Do not crowd text on the page. Use bold to emphasize categories of information and a leave blank line between categories. Print your resume on a laser printer or have it photocopied on high-quality paper. Whichever method you use, be sure the copies are clean with clear, sharp print.

Many companies and employment agencies receive hundreds or thousands of resumes each year. These resumes are often scanned and converted to electronic files. When a company has a job opening, the resume database is searched for key words or terms that relate to the qualifications for that job. To improve the chances that your resume will be readable after it has been scanned, keep the format simple. Do not use fancy fonts, bold type, bullets, rule lines, or a complicated layout with tables or columns of text. An attractively formatted hard copy resume that may make a good first impression on a person may be difficult for a computer to read. Keep the language simple and use key terms that are likely to match the description for the job you seek. For example, an accountant might use terms such as *month-end close* or *general ledger entries* in a list of duties at a previous job. Key terms are often nouns or noun phrases. Use terms such as *project supervisor* instead of *supervised projects*. If you do not know whether your hard copy resume will be scanned, call the company to which you are sending the resume and ask for this information.

Points to Emphasize

The appearance of your resume tells a great deal about you. Ask students: Why are applicants not invited for interviews when their resumes contain misspelled words or grammatical errors?

Thinking Critically

A beginning worker stated under Job Interest on his resume, "I'll do anything." Ask students to evaluate using that statement on a resume.

Show students job boards and demonstrate how to use job agents.

FOCUS ON . . .

Online Job Search and Resume

When you conduct a job search online, you may choose to search only one or two job boards or many job boards and company Web sites. The wider your search, the better your chances are of finding the job you want. Because new jobs may be posted daily, you should search for jobs frequently. Many job boards provide intelligent agents, often called **job scouts** or job agents, that can aid in this process. Simply indicate your search criteria for jobs, such as job titles and geographic locations, and the search frequency you desire (daily, weekly). The job scout will search for jobs that meet your criteria.

When jobs are located by your job scout, you will receive an e-mail containing links to the job postings. You can review these job postings and apply for the jobs that interest you. For some jobs, you can apply online by posting your resume and completing a job application form. For other jobs, you can apply by sending a hard copy resume and letter of application.

Just as job seekers search online for jobs, employers search online for prospective employees. Employers may search resumes that have been posted online at job boards or submitted via e-mail or a company Web site using search terms that reflect the skills and qualifications they seek in job applicants. Preparing your electronic resume in a format that can be easily searched for key terms will increase your chances of being selected as a job candidate by an employer. Follow these guidelines when preparing electronic resumes:

- Use default fonts and font sizes. Save the resume as a plain ASCII text file (also called Text Only by some pro-

grams). ASCII text is simply words without any special formatting and can be read by many programs. Keeping the format simple will increase the chances that your electronic resume will be readable at the many different sites where you may choose to post or send it.

- When submitting an electronic resume via e-mail, send the resume as an attachment only if you know the company's e-mail system can handle attachments. If you are not sure, place the resume in the body of the e-mail message instead.

- Keep the resume fairly short, although you do not need to limit it to a single printed page as is recommended for hard copy resumes. The computer can search two pages almost as quickly as one page.

- Include contact information and identify the type of job you seek as you would on a hard copy resume.

- Use concise, specific terms that describe your work experience, skills, and education or training. For example, say "Proficient with Microsoft Word" instead of "I have had training and work experience using word processing software."

- When posting a resume for a specific job, use the same terms for a particular skill or other requirement in your resume as are used in the job description or announcement. (Do not misrepresent your qualifications, however.)

- Use a professional, positive tone for the resume. Be sure all information is current and accurate.

You may decide to prepare several versions of your resume. For example, when submitting a resume for a particular job, you can use the title of that job in the job interest section of your resume. If you know the company scans hard copy resumes, use a simple format that will scan well. If the resume is to be posted online or sent by e-mail, use a file format that will be readable on other computers. Computer programs are available to provide guidance and allow you to create a resume in an appropriate format for many different jobs and situations.

job scout: computer program that works independently to retrieve and deliver job information

Writing a Letter of Application

A letter of application introduces you to an prospective employer and requests an interview. A letter of application that accompanies a resume should be an original, not a photocopy. The tone of the letter should appeal to the reader. Its content should be concise and informative. Remember, the reader is interested in you only in terms of your qualifications for a job in the company. An example letter of application is shown in Figure 13-1.5 on page 526. These guidelines will aid you in writing a letter of application:

- When submitting a hard copy letter, address the letter to a person, not to a department or position. If you do not have the name of the person to whom your letter should be addressed, call the company to ask for the name and title. When submitting a letter of application online, you may not be able to address the letter to a specific person. Follow the directions on the Web site.
- Explain in the first paragraph the reason for the letter. State specifically the position in which you are interested.
- Briefly indicate why you believe you are qualified for the position. Refer to specific classes, work experience, and/or interests you have that you believe are related to the position. Indicate that a resume is enclosed or also being transmitted to provide more details about your qualifications.
- In a final paragraph, request an interview.
- Limit your letter to a single printed page (or about the equivalent of a printed page for online letters of application).

The Interview

Companies may interview several candidates before hiring someone for a position. Successful interviewing is a critical step in securing a job.

Prepare for an Interview

Prepare carefully for each interview you accept. Consider how you will present your qualifications and interests to the interviewer. Anticipate questions and think about how you will respond to them. Learn about the company. What are the company's primary products or services? Does the company have branch offices? Is the company owned publicly or privately? What do your family and friends know about the firm? If the company has a Web site, review the site to learn about the company. If you prepare well, you will approach the interview with confidence, increasing your chances of making a favorable impression on the interviewer.

525

Topic 13-1: *An Effective Job Search*

Points to Emphasize

A letter of application should always be an original—not a photocopy. The letter should be written in a professional tone.

Thinking Critically

If a resume states the type of job the applicant is interested in and gives the complete background of education and work experience, why is an interview necessary?

For Discussion

Identify a local company known to students. Ask them: What questions would you ask a friend who works at (company name) in order to learn more about the company before an interview?

For Discussion

How did the applicant learn about the job for which she is applying? Why should this information be included in the letter?

3467 Mandelin Drive
Albuquerque, NM 87112-0341
May 10, 20--

Ms. Gretchen T. Wellington
Director, Hansen Historical Center
356 Front Street
Albuquerque, NM 87102-0356

Dear Ms. Wellington:

Your job opening for a library assistant came to my attention through my school librarian, Ms. Eva Elison. Please consider me as an applicant for the position. I am very interested in working in an organization that is involved in historical research.

I am currently completing my senior year at Southwest High School. I also work about ten hours each week at the Albuquerque Public Library. My work there is in the historical archives under the direction of Ms. Sarah Forman. A copy of my resume is enclosed to give you more details about my education and experience.

Please consider granting me an interview to discuss employment opportunities with your center. You may telephone me at 555-0130. Because I am at school or work most of the day, please leave a message; I will return your call as soon as possible.

Sincerely,

Valerie Gomez

Valerie Gomez

Enclosure: Resume

Figure **13-1.5**

A letter of application requests a job interview.

526
CHAPTER 13: PLANNING AND ADVANCING YOUR CAREER

Make a Good First Impression

At an interview, you usually do not know the person who will interview you. Your appearance and manner will influence the interviewer's first impression of you. A day or two before the interview, plan what you will wear. Consider dressing in clothes that are appropriate and at the same time comfortable. Generally, you should choose conservative, businesslike attire. Even though you may know that employees in the organization dress casually at most times, dress in business attire for an interview. Your manner should be polite and professional. Be friendly, but not overly familiar with people you meet at the company.

WORKPLACE CONNECTIONS

Joe Chin was excited about his interview at a local garden design and landscape company. He arrived for the interview on time, answered all the questions clearly, and expressed his interest in working for the company. When a letter arrived thanking Joe for his interest and telling him that another candidate had been hired, he was very disappointed. A few days later Joe had lunch with Roberto, a friend who works at the company. "Do you know why someone else was chosen for the job instead of me?" he asked. "If I did something wrong in the interview, I would really like to know so I can improve before my next interview." "Well," said Roberto, "I did hear the manager comment once that he thinks everyone should dress in professional business attire for an interview." "Oh," said Joe. "Then I definitely made a poor decision when I showed up in khakis and a polo shirt. I thought I should dress like the workers I have seen at the company." Joe learned the hard way that appearance can influence an interviewer's impression of a candidate.

Anticipate Questions

You will be asked a number of questions during the interview. Some are likely to be ones that are commonly asked in such a situation. Others may be unique to the interview. Some common questions and requests are listed below.

- Why does this job interest you?
- What courses did you study that you found most interesting? Why?
- What do you believe are your strongest qualifications for this job?
- What school activities or previous work experience required you to work in groups? On your own?
- How do you evaluate your participation in group activities?
- Why do you think you would enjoy working in our company?
- What are your career goals at this time?
- What new skills or knowledge do you want to acquire?

For Discussion

What about a student's typical school attire is likely to be inappropriate for a job interview?

Expand the Concept

Ask students to provide answers to the common questions as part of a class discussion. Instruct them to evaluate which of the several answers seem best.

527

Topic 13-1: *An Effective Job Search*

Thinking Critically

What might an interviewer conclude about an applicant who asks only about vacations, sick days allowed, and pay increases?

Points to Emphasize

Consider the traffic conditions or possible delays that are likely during the time of day you will be traveling to an interview.

For Discussion

An applicant told the receptionist: "I don't need to fill out this application form; I have prepared a resume." Was this statement a proper one for the applicant to make?

In the United States, laws have been passed to safeguard a person's right to equal opportunity for employment. Questions regarding age, marital status, ethnic background, religious beliefs, and physical and emotional disabilities (unless job related) are not considered appropriate and may be illegal for many jobs. If you are asked questions on these matters, you may wish to respond simply: "I prefer not to answer that question." You can, of course, answer such a question if you wish. You might also respond with a question such as "Why do you ask?" This response may cause the interviewer to explain the work-related issue that prompted the question.

Prepare Questions

Interviewers sometimes ask: "Do you have any questions about the company or the position?" While you are preparing for the interview, you may want to list any questions that come to mind. Some would naturally pertain to the job for which you are applying: "How much orientation is provided for the job?" "How often are employees evaluated?" "Are there promotional opportunities for which employees may apply?" "Has the company established standards for the tasks related to the job in which I am interested?"

Other questions cover a broad range of subjects, such as the company's mission statement, product lines, and employee benefits. Do not make salary and benefits the main focus of your questions. Ask questions that will help the interviewer focus on the contributions you can make to the company.

Arrive on Time

Arrive at the interview shortly before the scheduled time. You will want to be calm and collected when you are called into the interviewer's office. If you are not familiar with the location of the interview, you may want to visit the site in advance. Note how much time you should allow to arrive on schedule. Consider the traffic conditions or possible delays that are likely during the time of day you will be traveling to the interview. Once you arrive, use a visitor parking space in the company parking lot if available. You may need to give your name and the purpose of your visit to a security guard to be admitted to the parking lot or building. Parking lots and garages in downtown or other business areas are often crowded during business hours. Allow ample time to find a parking space and walk to the company location if necessary.

Complete an Application Form

employment application: form that provides information about a job applicant

A receptionist may greet you and ask you to fill out an **employment application** form. Complete the form carefully in neat, legible handwriting. Glance over the entire application to see what information is requested in each section before you begin writing. Read each question carefully and completely before answering.

Note every item included and do not leave blanks on an application. You should indicate with an N/A (not applicable) any item that does not apply to you such as military service, for example. The interviewer then knows that you have read the question. Take a copy of your resume with you as a source for details as you complete the application. Often the interviewer will read the application form before turning to your resume.

528

Participate Attentively

A common procedure is for the receptionist to introduce you to the interviewer. You should extend your hand for a firm handshake and look directly at the interviewer in a friendly, calm manner.

Being a little nervous at a job interview is natural, especially at your first interview. Instead of dwelling on your uneasiness, concentrate on what the interviewer asks and tells you. Remember that the interview is a two-way communication process. The interviewer is learning about you, and you are learning about the job and the company.

When you attend an interview, do the following:

- Dress appropriately.
- Greet the interviewer with a smile and a firm handshake.
- Remain standing until you are asked to have a seat.
- Use good posture when sitting or standing.
- Listen attentively and answer questions honestly and clearly.
- Use correct grammar.
- Exhibit a positive attitude.
- Ask questions about the company and its products or services.
- Make eye contact with the interviewer frequently.

When you attend an interview, do not do the following:

- Bring a friend or relative with you.
- Display nervousness by tapping a pencil, twirling your hair, or other annoying habits.

Greet the interviewer with a smile and a firm handshake.

529

Topic 13-1: An Effective Job Search

Expand the Concept

Engage the class in several instances of introducing an interviewer to an interviewee.

For Discussion

Review the list of things not to do when you attend an interview. Discuss why doing each of these things is not appropriate.

- Use poor posture or chew gum.
- Answer questions with "yeah," "nope," or "uh-huh."
- Misrepresent your strengths or accomplishments.
- Criticize past employers or teachers.
- Ask questions only about salary and benefits.
- Stand at the door after the interview is over and continue to talk.

The interviewer will write an evaluation of the interview in which judgments are recorded about key factors such as:

- Appearance
- Voice and language usage
- Knowledge and skills
- Effectiveness in working with others
- Attitude toward work and learning
- Self-confidence
- Flexibility
- Job interest

Follow Up

Review the interview in your mind and jot down notes to yourself about its good points and its weak points. Think of questions that you do not believe you answered well or that you failed to understand. Review this information later before your next interview.

Write a brief follow-up letter to thank the interviewer for talking with you. Indicate again your interest in the job and how you believe you are qualified for the position. A follow-up letter shows your willingness to follow through after a meeting. If the interviewer does not communicate with you within the time period mentioned at the interview, call and express your continued interest in the position.

If you receive a job offer and decide to take the job, you should accept in writing. If you have determined that you are not interested in the job, you should write a brief letter stating your decision and expressing thanks for the offer.

Documenting Your Job Search

You may find a job in a relatively short time if there are many job openings in your field of interest in the community where you seek employment. Job searches sometimes require a considerable amount of time, however. You may have to make changes in your strategy and in your job expectations before you find a job.

Maintain a job search diary of your activity. Indicate clearly the date, time, company name, and complete names of all persons with whom you talked. Indicate the communication you receive after each meeting, phone call, or message with someone related to getting a job. This information will be helpful if you are called for a second interview or interview for another job with the same company at a later time. A sample job search diary is shown in Figure 13-1.6.

Job Title:	Order Entry Clerk
Company Name:	MBA Manufacturing
Address:	P.O. Box 235
	Somerset, KY 42501
Phone:	(606) 555-0127
Contact Person:	Robin McCrae, Office Manager

Date	Contact	Comments
6/2	Mailed letter and resume	See attached job ad and copies of letter and resume
6/15	Phone message from Robin McCrae	
6/16	Returned phone call	Interview scheduled for 6/20 at 9 a.m. at company offices in Governor's Hill Office Park
6/20	Interview	Interview went well. Training provided for order entry system. Flexible hours. Expect to hear from Robin within two weeks.
6/21	Sent follow-up letter	Expressed continued interest. See attached copy of letter.

Figure **13-1.6**

A job search diary

Why is keeping a job search record like the one shown in Figure 13-1.6 important?

REVIEWING THE TOPIC

1. How might thinking ahead to a career goal help an individual think about a first full-time job?
2. Why is career planning unlikely to be a once-in-a-lifetime task?
3. Identify some questions that a person with a career goal is likely to be able to answer.
4. What are some attitudes employees will find appealing when considering applicants who have not yet established career goals?
5. Where can you learn of job opportunities?
6. What information should be included on your resume?
7. What is the purpose of a letter of application?
8. Describe appropriate planning for a job interview.
9. What are some factors that an interviewer will probably evaluate about a job applicant?
10. What content should be included in a follow-up letter written after an interview?

THINKING CRITICALLY

1. Assume that you are ready to begin full-time employment. Identify the type of job you will seek. Choose a job you are qualified for. Describe these factors related to the job:
   - Typical titles for this job
   - Typical tasks or activities associated with this job
   - Typical wages or salary for this job in your area
   - Education, skills, and experience required for the job
2. Describe how your education, skills, or experience qualify you for this job. Describe an experience that shows your ability to work successfully in a team.
3. Open the PDF file *CH13 Application*. This file contains a sample job application. Complete the form assuming you are applying the job identified in step 1.
4. Prepare written responses for the sample interview questions below:
   a) How did you learn about this job opening?
   b) What skills or experience do you have that best qualify you for this job?

c) Where you do want to be in your career five years from now?

d) What is your greatest accomplishment?

e) Why should I hire you rather than another applicant with comparable skills?

f) How would your current employer or teacher describe your job performance and attitude?

REINFORCING MATH SKILLS

You have been offered two jobs—one as an appliance salesperson and one as an office assistant. Use your math skills to help you evaluate the jobs and make a decision about which one to accept.

1. Read the information about each job below. What you can expect your gross pay less the deduction for health insurance coverage to be per year for each job?

2. Which job would you choose and why? Consider your job interests and the locations of the jobs in addition to salary and health insurance costs.

Sales Position in an Appliance Store

Your base salary will be $960 per pay period (1 month). You will also receive a 5 percent commission on the price of items you sell during the pay period. The store manager says you can expect to sell around $4,000 in merchandise in an average month. This amount can vary widely, however, and will depend on your selling skills. The deduction from your paycheck for health insurance will be $125 per pay period. The job is close to your home, and you can ride the public bus to work.

Office Assistant

As an office assistant, you will work 80 hours per pay period (two weeks) and receive $8 per hour. Your deduction for health insurance will be $50 per pay period. The company is located 20 miles from your home and is not accessible by bus.

Topic Review

Teaching Tips

You may need to help students identify jobs for which they are qualified. Ask students to work with a classmate to review and improve the letter of application and the resume each student prepares.

Teaching Tips

Ask students to work with a classmate to review the follow-up letter. Students should determine whether letters use the *you* approach, include appropriate information, and are formatted correctly.

COMPOSITION
RESEARCH
WORD PROCESSING

Topic 13-1 ACTIVITY 1

Application Letter and Resume

In this activity, you will prepare a letter of application for a job and a resume.

1. Identify a job for which you are qualified. Identify at least one organization where a position is open for the job you have chosen or there is some possibility that such a job might become available.

2. Prepare a letter of application to an organization where the job you seek exists. If a job opening currently exists, apply for that particular job. If not, express your interest in working for the company in the position you have chosen. Ask to be considered when an opening becomes available. See Figure 13-1.5 on page 526 for an example letter.

3. Prepare a resume to include with your letter. See Figure 13-1.4 on page 522 for an example resume. Include complete information for three references on a separate page attached to the resume.

COMPOSITION
WORD PROCESSING

Topic 13-1 ACTIVITY 2

Follow-up Letter and Job Search Diary

Writing a follow-up letter after an interview and preparing a job search diary are important steps in a job search. Practice these skills in this activity.

1. Assume that you have completed an interview for a job. You may use the job you chose in Topic 13-1 Activity 1 or a different job. Write a follow-up letter to thank the interviewer and to express your continued interest in the job.

2. Begin documenting your job search. Create a table similar to the one shown in Figure 13-1.6 on page 531. Record information related to this job and the one from the previous activity if a different job was used.

THE FIRST JOB AND BEYOND

When you begin a new job, you will have a great deal to learn about the company and how it operates. As you think ahead about your first full-time job, you may have questions such as the following:

- What will they expect me to be able to do immediately?
- Will I be able to learn everything I should know about this job?
- Will my coworkers be willing to help me?

Employers expect to provide new employees with an introduction to the company and to new jobs. Employees who understand their jobs and the total company are more likely to be successful in their work and contribute to achieving company goals.

objectives

- Describe typical ways organizations provide orientation for new employees
- Explain the responsibility for self-evaluation of performance
- Identify resources for continuous improvement of an employee's knowledge and skills
- Explain effective ways of facing job changes

Introduction to a New Job

In some instances, a job introduction or orientation is done informally by the employee's supervisor or manager. In other instances, the job introduction is provided in a formal, organized manner. Formal orientation programs are scheduled for a particular time and include a series of presentations or meetings. These programs are common in large organizations, where a number of new employees may begin their jobs at the same time.

WORKPLACE CONNECTIONS

A large bank in downtown Charlotte, North Carolina, provided a job orientation on the first day of work for 25 new employees. At the morning sessions, new employees learned about the company's mission and activities. After lunch, the 25 new employees had small group meetings with managers in the departments where they would be working.

Informal orientation programs are common in smaller organizations where fewer employees are likely to begin their new jobs at the same time. Generally, an informal program is directed by the new employee's immediate supervisor or by an experienced coworker. This person often has a checklist to guide the explanations during the orientation. Some of these topics and activities are likely to be included:

- Goals and policies of the organization
- The company's organization chart and key personnel

535

Topic 13-2: *The First Job and Beyond*

Expand the Concept

What value is there in orientation sessions scheduled several weeks after new employees have been on the job?

- Employment forms (such as the Form W-4 shown in Figure 13-2.1)
- Employee benefits provided
- Completion of forms related to benefits such as health care or retirement plans
- Company policies related to ethics, safety, and security
- Personnel policies, including performance evaluations
- Policies and procedures that guide the new employee's responsibilities

Orientation does not always end with the program offered on the first day of work. Sometimes additional meetings are scheduled after employees have had several weeks of experience in their new positions.

Cut here and give Form W-4 to your employer. Keep the top part for your records.

Form **W-4**

Department of the Treasury
Internal Revenue Service

Employee's Withholding Allowance Certificate

▶ Whether you are entitled to claim a certain number of allowances or exemption from withholding is subject to review by the IRS. Your employer may be required to send a copy of this form to the IRS.

OMB No. 1545-0010

2005

1 Type or print your first name and middle initial
Jeffrey C.
Last name
Hunter

2 Your social security number
321 22 4697

Home address (number and street or rural route)
45 Newland Place

3 ☐ Single ☑ Married ☐ Married, but withhold at higher Single rate.
Note. If married, but legally separated, or spouse is a nonresident alien, check the "Single" box.

City or town, state, and ZIP code
Matawan, NJ 07747-6321

4 If your last name differs from that shown on your social security card, check here. You must call 1-800-772-1213 for a new card. ▶ ☐

5 Total number of allowances you are claiming (from line **H** above **or** from the applicable worksheet on page 2) | **5** | 1
6 Additional amount, if any, you want withheld from each paycheck | **6** $ -0-
7 I claim exemption from withholding for 2005, and I certify that I meet **both** of the following conditions for exemption.
- Last year I had a right to a refund of **all** federal income tax withheld because I had **no** tax liability **and**
- This year I expect a refund of **all** federal income tax withheld because I expect to have **no** tax liability.
If you meet both conditions, write "Exempt" here | ▶ | **7**

Under penalties of perjury, I declare that I have examined this certificate and to the best of my knowledge and belief, it is true, correct, and complete.

Employee's signature
(Form is not valid unless you sign it.) ▶ *Jeffrey C. Hunter*

Date ▶ *July 5, 20- -*

8 Employer's name and address (Employer: Complete lines 8 and 10 only if sending to the IRS.) | 9 Office code (optional) | 10 Employer identification number (EIN)

For Privacy Act and Paperwork Reduction Act Notice, see page 2.

Cat. No. 10220Q

Form **W-4** (2005)

Figure **13-2.1**

Form W-4 documents tax withholding information.

Learning on the Job

As a new employee, realize that your supervisor is aware that you do not know everything that the job may require. Learning on the job is expected and is considered a part of your job. Some of the learning is guided by an experienced person, and some is done on your own.

As a new worker, you can expect to be given specific information about the tasks you will complete. The company may have a clearly stated job description of what you are to do, or you may be in a newly created position. In the latter case, just a general description of your duties may exist. An employee's actual work duties and tasks may differ from the job description because the job has changed but the description has not yet been updated.

A new employee will often find that coworkers are generous in providing help related to job tasks. They understand that a knowledgeable coworker is going to be a valuable asset to the unit or department. You will quickly realize which of your coworkers are most likely to want to answer questions you might have.

References and Resources

When you begin a new job, make a point to become acquainted with basic references available to you. Some of these references may be accessed using your computer, while some may be in print. Some of the references you may have are listed below.

- A company manual or employee handbook of policies and procedures
- A complete organization chart
- A calendar of events and a company newsletter
- An annual report if the company is publicly owned
- A directory of all personnel with phone numbers and possibly e-mail addresses

Companies have developed a wide range of materials to aid employees. You will want to learn what company databases and network or intranet resources are available for your use. An example of an online employee handbook is shown in Figure 13-2.2 on page 538. If your company has a library or resource center, spend some time getting acquainted with the range of information that you can access. Your department may subscribe to magazines, newspapers, or databases that are useful to you in your job.

Evaluation of Employee Performance

Many companies have a plan for evaluating employee performance and discussing the results with the employee at least once a year. A company may have several reasons for doing performance evaluations, also called **performance reviews** or appraisals. Information from performance reviews may be used in determining pay increases, promotions, employee disciplinary actions, or dismissals. Evaluations help identify employee strengths and areas for improvement. Setting goals for the employee to accomplish in the coming evaluation period and beyond is often a part of the evaluation process.

performance review:
evaluation of an
employee's work

Figure **13-2.2**

*Some companies
provide an employee
handbook on the
company intranet.*

Employee Handbook

This Employee Handbook is an outline of your privileges and obligations as an
employee and should be your primary reference. When you have questions
about policies or procedures outlined in this manual, refer them to your manager
or contact the Human Resources Department. Choose a link to learn more
about the company's policies and procedures.

- Attendance
- At-Will Employment
- Company Overview and Mission
- Compensation and Employee Benefits
- Confidentiality Policy
- Drug and Alcohol Policy

Although a formal evaluation may be completed only once a year, effective
managers provide feedback about employee performance throughout the
year. In a work situation where managers and employees talk regularly about
job performance, the performance review will bring no big surprises for the
employee.

Companies expect workers to be competent and perform their jobs satisfactorily. Some factors commonly considered in a employee evaluations
include:

- Job knowledge and skills
- Quality of performance
- Quantity of work completed
- Initiative and judgment
- Cooperation and teamwork
- Flexibility and adaptability
- Adherence to schedules and deadlines
- Accomplishment of goals set previously

New workers are given a period of time for learning their jobs. The trial
period typically lasts three to six months. The length of the trial period is
determined by the complexity of the job and the level of skills needed by the
employee. Employees often receive their first formal evaluation at the end
of the trial period. Future evaluations follow the company's normal evaluation schedule.

Ways of Evaluating Employees

Companies use varying methods to evaluate workers. In some companies,
evaluation practices may be informal. Little, if any, information may be
recorded in the personnel file of the employee. In such companies, the manager may write an appraisal of each employee at designated times. Generally, the employee signs the appraisal to indicate that it was read and may
add comments to the document.

Other companies use clearly stated employee evaluation procedures with carefully developed appraisal forms. In a traditional approach, employees are evaluated by a manager or supervisor. In some cases, a manager, coworkers, and the employee may all contribute to the evaluation. This approach, sometimes called a 360-degree evaluation, is becoming more popular. This is because some people think getting feedback from several people in different positions (the employee's circle of contacts) gives a better picture of an employee's overall performance.

Performance evaluations are rated or scored in a variety of ways. Using a checklist, where skills and traits are listed and points awarded for each area, is a popular method. Using this method, the employee's performance is compared to reasonable standards. Ideally, all employees in a unit or department could receive high scores using this method.

Ranking employees in a unit or department from highest to lowest is an evaluation method used by some companies. Using this method, the evaluator compares employees to one another, and all employees cannot receive high scores.

With a forced distribution method, employees are assigned scores that fall into preselected categories. For example, the evaluation procedures might state that a certain percent of employees will receive scores that fall in a particular category, as shown in Figure 13-2.3. As with the ranking method, all employees cannot receive acceptable scores with this method.

Figure **13-2.3**

Forced Distribution Scoring Method

Excellent	10 percent of employees
Good	20 percent of employees
Satisfactory	40 percent of employees
Poor	20 percent of employees
Unacceptable	10 percent of employees

Whatever the scoring method used, employee performance is usually compared to standards for acceptable work. For example, standards based on keystrokes, lines, or pages may be the basis for determining the productivity of an employee doing word processing. Often, standards are specified per hour or per day. Devices that keep track of such factors as keystrokes and lines may allow for detailed monitoring of output of many employees, especially those who work in factories and in offices where there are repetitive tasks. Standards for some evaluation categories, such as teamwork or responsibility, may be more subjective. Manager or coworker observations of employee behavior may be used to judge performance for these categories.

For Discussion

Which method of scoring a performance evaluation do you think is most fair to the employee? Most useful to the company?

benchmarks: standards used for comparisons such as job performance

Evaluating Your Own Performance

To progress in your job, you will want to ask yourself: "How well am I doing my job?" Such an evaluation might be scheduled to be completed about a month before the evaluation by your manager. The following steps should be helpful in your evaluation:

1. List the skills, tasks, and goals that relate to your position. For this step, a copy of the performance appraisal form used or your job description will be useful.

2. Think carefully about your work behavior, either daily for one week or one day each week for four or five weeks.

3. Record any instances of very effective or poor performance, indicating the date of each entry.

4. Assess what you have written at the end of your review period. Note especially instances of poor performance. Consider what you might change to improve your performance.

5. Compare your own evaluation with the one given you by your manager or supervisor. Reconsider your own evaluation in relation to that given by your manager or supervisor and make appropriate changes in how you assess yourself.

Continuous Improvement

Your performance evaluation can be used to guide your efforts toward continuous improvement in your work. The evaluation may point out areas for improvement or ways that you can become more productive. Consider these points as you strive for continuous improvement in your job:

- Simplify; eliminate needless steps in doing tasks.
- Follow an organized approach to completing each task. Do not think of *getting organized* as a separate activity.
- Consider the overall scope of a new project and set realistic estimates of the time and work required to meet deadlines.
- Think critically about the information you receive in various forms such as reports, letters, and e-mail messages. Keep what has value and discard that which does not.

CHAPTER 13: PLANNING AND ADVANCING YOUR CAREER

- Document steps or other information related to tasks and activities such as meetings or projects for later reference.
- Prioritize tasks and complete them in order of importance, keeping deadlines in mind.

Carefully evaluate documents you receive to determine which ones to save.

© GETTY IMAGES/PHOTODISC

WORKPLACE CONNECTIONS

Tonya, an administrative assistant, commented about her program of continuous improvement:

Instead of simply performing my normal tasks as I have always done them, I am now carefully thinking about how I do my work. What a revelation! For example, I never realized why my desk, which is clean at the beginning of each day, becomes a mess by midday. By observing my behavior, however, I know exactly what causes this problem—my failure to return material to its proper place when I no longer need it. I am now making a effort to modify my behavior so I can be more productive.

Promotional Possibilities

Although you may be content with your present job, remember to consider the future. While focusing primarily on your current job, also consider what you can do to prepare for future jobs, some of which may be **promotions**.

promotion: advancement in rank, grade, or position

Figure **13-2.4**

Review your company's job openings to learn about promotional possibilities.

Human Resources

Current Job Openings

Choose a department below to view current job openings for that department.

Corporate Communications
Finance & Accounting
Legal Services
Human Resources
Information Technology
Manufacturing, Warehousing, & Shipping
Marketing, Sales, & Support

Your company may post job openings in company bulletins, in local newspapers, or on the company Web site. An example of job postings on a company Web site is shown in Figure 13-2.4. These job postings may provide information about higher-level jobs. You may deal with people at varying levels of the company. You may be able to learn, in informal ways, about qualifications required for various jobs. Learning about higher-level positions in your company can help you decide whether you would want to work in one of these positions.

Beginning workers may find limited opportunities to move into jobs at higher levels within their companies. If you find yourself in such a situation, you may need to look elsewhere for higher-level jobs. Investigate various jobs to learn what types of positions relate to your interests and experiences. Learn the educational and experience requirements for the jobs in which you are interested. Then you can create a plan for acquiring the education, skills, and work experience you need for the job you want. Professional and trade organizations and their publications can help you build your qualifications for jobs in your career area. Programs offered by local schools, colleges, or community organizations can also help you improve your job skills.

Professional and Trade Associations

People with common work interests often belong to professional or trade associations. These groups provide programs and activities designed to help improve work skills and knowledge. Internet resources and local libraries will help you become acquainted with those available. Your company's Human Resources Department may have information about organizations that you may wish to join.

Your company may subscribe to magazines and newspapers related to the company's business. Check the resources of your local libraries and search the Web to become acquainted with what is available in print and electronic format.

For Discussion

The range of interests in the class will determine relevant discussion of professional and trade organizations. Activities of local chapters of professional and trade organizations that are reported in newspapers and on television can be used to introduce students to what is available. Resources on the World Wide Web will also be valuable for extending awareness of what is available.

Educational Resources

Think about skills you would like to acquire or improve to become a more effective worker. For example, you may want learn new software programs or become more effective at public speaking. You can probably find educational resources to help you develop these skills. Consider programs offered by a local public school system through adult education or by a local college or university. Many courses are also offered via the Internet.

Changing Jobs

A typical worker changes jobs several times during his or her career. A job change may be the worker's choice or it may be caused by events beyond the worker's control. Companies sometimes change their structures as they strive to grow and accomplish their goals. Companies are bought and sold, merged with other companies, relocated to other geographic areas, or **downsized**. A company may also fail or go out of business. These changes may mean that workers are promoted or transferred to different jobs, asked to move to another city, laid off temporarily, or dismissed from their jobs.

downsize: reduce, as in decreasing the number of workers in an organization

Job Termination

Being dismissed from a job can be an emotionally upsetting and stressful experience, even when you are dismissed through no fault of your own. You may have some prior warning that the dismissal may happen, or you may have no warning at all. Try to remain calm and professional during the job termination process.

Depending on the size and policies of the company, dismissal procedures may vary widely. Typically, you will be given a written notice or letter stating that you are dismissed from the company's employ. The letter may state the reason for the dismissal. You should receive a final paycheck on or shortly after your dismissal. You may also be paid for items such as unused vacation or sick days.

© CORBIS

An exit interview can be helpful to both the company and the departing employee.

543

Topic 13-2: *The First Job and Beyond*

For Discussion

Why would individuals consider changing jobs when they are successful in their present jobs?

Points to Emphasize

Try to remain calm and professional during the job termination process whether you are being dismissed or leaving the job by your choice.

You may be asked to attend a meeting, sometimes called an exit interview. The meeting may be with your supervisor or someone from the Human Resources Department. In this meeting, the reasons for your dismissal and the status of any continuing benefits may be discussed. You may be asked questions about how you think the company could improve operations. Company procedures that you think are effective may also be discussed.

You will be expected to return items such as company keys, credit cards, security badges, or access cards. Your manager or a coworker may escort you to your desk or work area to collect personal items and then out of the building. If the company's dismissal procedures are less formal, you may be allowed to leave on your own, taking time to say good-bye to coworkers.

Remember that while one company may no longer need your services, others are likely to need them. You may wish to ask your supervisor to give you a letter of recommendation or allow you to list him or her as a reference when you look for a new job. When employees lose their jobs for reasons such as downsizing or a move to a new location, the company may provide assistance in helping workers find other jobs. Some companies use outplacement services. These services are organizations that provide counseling and other services to help workers find new jobs.

severance pay: payment made to an employee being dismissed from a job

Companies typically provide **severance pay** to workers who lose their jobs through no fault of the employees. One or two weeks' pay for each year a worker has been employed at the company is a typical severance payment. Workers who are dismissed because of poor job performance or a serious violation of company policies, such as theft or harming or threatening a coworker, usually do not receive severance pay.

You may decide to leave your job at a company for a variety of reasons. You might move to a different city. You might complete training or education that qualifies you for a higher-level job. You might find better pay or more opportunity for advancement at a different company. You will want to take advantage of good job opportunities. Be aware, however, that a record of changing jobs too often (sometimes called *job hopping*) may make a negative impression on prospective employers. As a general rule, plan to stay in any full-time job you accept for at least one year. If you have changed jobs frequently, have an explanation for the frequent changes prepared to discuss in interviews.

resignation letter: a document stating the intention to end employment as of a certain date

When possible, give the company at least two weeks' notice when quitting a job. Always submit a formal **resignation letter**. The letter should be written to your immediate supervisor and should use a polite, professional tone. Keep the letter short and simple. In the first paragraph, ask your manager to accept your resignation from your job (state the job title) as of a particular date. Indicate that you are willing to do whatever you can to organize material or document procedures to help another worker assume your duties. In the second paragraph, thank the manager for the opportunity to work for the company and wish the company continued success. You need not give a reason for your resignation.

When you leave a company's employ, you may retain some of the benefits of having worked for the company. For example, if you were employed by the company for several years, you may draw benefits from a pension or retirement plan. Keeping health insurance coverage when changing jobs is a serious concern for many workers. COBRA (Consolidated Omnibus Budget

For Discussion

For what reasons might an employee's job be terminated other than poor performance by the employee?

Teaching Tips

Discuss severance pay with students. Give examples from the local community of companies that have provided severance pay to employees.

Points to Emphasize

Giving the company at least two weeks' notice before leaving a job allows the company time to find a replacement to take over the job when you leave.

For Discussion

Why is COBRA an important benefit for many workers?

© ADAM SMITH/SUPERSTOCK

COBRA makes keeping health insurance coverage easier when changing jobs.

Reconciliation Act) is a law that gives employees the right to continue health insurance coverage for at least 18 months after leaving the company. The employee must have been covered while employed. The worker must pay the cost of the insurance coverage. However, the cost will be at the company's group rate. This cost is usually lower than the cost an individual would pay for purchasing insurance.

Job Portfolio

A **job portfolio** is a file containing documents, work samples, and information related to employment. A job portfolio can be very helpful when applying for a new job or being interviewed. Keep items such as the following in your job portfolio:

job portfolio: file containing documents and information related to employment

- Copies of your resume in hard copy and electronic formats
- Sample letters of application and thank-you letters
- Your job search diary that includes job search activities and contact persons
- Copies of any awards or honors you have received
- Letters, notes, and other items related to your work
- Programs and newsletters that report your participation in school or community activities
- School transcript of courses completed
- Diplomas and certificates of completion of courses
- A detailed work history (job descriptions, evaluations, and related information about earlier full-time positions and about your current position)
- Samples of your work or pictures and descriptions of projects or work completed

As you begin full-time employment or continue your education, continue to broaden your awareness of jobs and career possibilities. Update your job portfolio frequently to reflect new skills, talents, and experiences.

At this point, what materials have you prepared that are appropriate to include in a job portfolio?

545

Topic 13-2: *The First Job and Beyond*

REVIEWING THE TOPIC

1. Why is orientation provided for new employees?
2. What general references will aid a new employee in learning about the company?
3. List five of the factors generally considered in an employee evaluation.
4. Describe the steps employees might follow in evaluating their own performance.
5. How can an employee learn about promotional opportunities in the company?
6. What types of changes in an organization may lead to a worker changing jobs?
7. What topics are usually discussed at an exit interview?
8. What services are provided by outplacement firms?
9. What is a typical amount for a severance payment?
10. What is *job hopping*, and what impression may it give a prospective employer?
11. What does COBRA provide employees?
12. What types of information or documents should be included in a job or career portfolio?

MAKING DECISIONS

Bill and Yoshi both accepted full-time jobs in a local company where they had worked during the summers for the last two years. They received information about when they should report for their first day of work and about the first day's schedule of orientation meetings. Bill called Yoshi and said, "Yoshi, did you see the schedule for orientation on Monday, our first day at work? Don't you think we can skip most of the day? I'd say we should plan to arrive at three o'clock when we will learn from our managers what exactly they want us to do on our jobs. Why should we waste our time hearing about things we already know? What do you think?"

1. What types of important information are likely to be presented at the orientation meeting?
2. What impression will the employer have of Bill and Yoshi if they do not attend the orientation meeting?
3. The orientation meeting is being held during regular working hours. Do Bill and Yoshi have a right to decide not to attend this work activity? What might be the result of not reporting for work?

546

THINKING CRITICALLY

When you begin a job, you will be asked to complete employment-related forms. Critical thinking will be required as you make decisions about issues related to federal tax withholding allowances.

1. Open and print the PDF file *CH13 FW4* from the data files. This file contains an Employee's Withholding Allowance Certificate, commonly called a W-4 Form. (This form is current for 2005. Your instructor may give you a form for the current year or instruct you to download a current form from the Internal Revenue Service Web site.)

2. Assume that you are single and have no children or other dependents. Read the instructions on the form and complete the Personal Allowance Worksheet section of the form. Then complete the Employee's Withholding Allowance Certificate portion of the form, which you would give to your employer for use in withholding federal taxes from your pay. See Figure 13-2.1 on page 536 for a sample completed certificate.

3. Read the Privacy and Paperwork Reduction Notice on the second page of the form. What will failure to provide a properly completed form result in?

Topic 13-2 ACTIVITY 1

COMPOSITION
WORD PROCESSING

Letter of Resignation

You have worked for Hinkle Trucking as an administrative assistant for four years. You have accepted a new job, and you must resign from your current position.

1. Write a letter of resignation to your manager, Mr. Juan Alverez. Use the current date for your letter and make the date of your resignation two weeks from today. The company address is 24 Motor Way, Ferguson, KY 42502-0024.

2. Because this is a personal business letter, print the letter on plain paper. Include your return address on the two lines above the letter date. Assume your address is 34 Apple Street, Ferguson, KY 42502-8834. Format the letter in block style with open punctuation.

3. Review your letter for the five Cs of effective correspondence. Remember to use the *you* approach. Proofread carefully and correct all errors. Print the letter.

Teaching Tips

You may wish to provide copies of the *Occupational Outlook Handbook* for use in this activity or have students access the *Handbook* online at the Bureau of Labor Statistics Web site.

INTERNET
RESEARCH
WORD PROCESSING

Topic **13-2** ACTIVITY 2

Research Resources for Training or Education

When you enter the workforce, you may not have the skills or education needed for the job you have chosen as your career goal. In many careers, a worker may hold an entry-level job while gaining further education or experience to prepare for a higher-level job. In this activity, you will research resources available for career training and education.

1. Identify a job in a career area that interests you, but for which you are not currently qualified.

2. List the qualifications for this job. You may find the required skills, education, and work experience for the job by reading job advertisements or job descriptions found in newspapers. You can also find information on job boards or in job postings on company Web sites. The *Occupational Outlook Handbook*, available online at the Bureau of Labor Statistics Web site, gives information about training and other requirements for many jobs.

3. Identify resources that will help you gain the education or skills needed for this job. Consider colleges, universities, vocational/technical schools, adult education programs, professional associations, and private training companies. Many schools have Web sites that provide a list of courses available. Remember that many colleges offer courses via the Internet, so do not limit the resources to those available in your local area. List each school or organization you identify and the program or course available that relates to this job.

548

CHAPTER 13: PLANNING AND ADVANCING YOUR CAREER

CHAPTER REVIEW 13

Summary

Conducting an effective job search is critical in securing a job that matches your interests and skills. Proper orientation to a new job and continuous efforts to improve your performance can aid in your success and lead to opportunities for promotion. Realistic self-evaluation and planning to secure needed education, training, and experience are important in carrying through your long-term career strategy. Review the following points related to these concepts:

- A career strategy is thinking ahead to a career goal and considering your first job in relation to that goal.
- A number of sources are available that may help you locate jobs. These sources include friends, relatives, former employers, placement services, sites on the World Wide Web, newspapers, employment agencies, and government job announcements.
- A carefully prepared resume and a letter of application will give your qualifications for a job.
- An interview is your opportunity to convince the interviewer that you have the education, skills, experience, and attitudes to be successful in the job. You may be asked to complete a job application when you arrive for an interview.
- A follow-up letter should be sent after an interview to thank the interviewer and to express continued interest in the job.
- A job diary will be helpful if you are called for a second interview or interview for another job with the same company at a later time.
- Learning on the job is expected and is considered a normal part of your total orientation. Some of the learning is guided by an experienced person, and some is done on your own.
- Information from performance reviews may be used in determining pay increases, promotions, employee disciplinary actions, or dismissals and in setting goals for the employee.
- Evaluating your own performance is important to your effectiveness on the job.
- Striving for continuous improvement can help you be more productive in your present position and may lead to promotional opportunities.
- Professional and trade associations, college, universities, and other organizations provide many opportunities for individuals to improve their work skills and knowledge.
- Job changes are common in today's business world. A job change may be the worker's choice or the company's choice.

Teaching Tips

Have students review key points from the chapter by completing the Sort It Out game on *The Office* Web site.

- Job termination procedures may vary widely. Typically, you will be given a written notice stating that you are dismissed from the company's employ and the reason for the dismissal. You may be asked to attend an exit interview.
- When possible, give the company at least two weeks' notice when quitting a job. Always submit a formal resignation letter.
- Keep items such as your resume, job search diary, work history, diplomas, work samples, and other related information in your job portfolio.

Key Terms

benchmarks	interview	performance review
career goals	job board	promotion
career strategy	job description	reference
downsize	job portfolio	resignation letter
employment application	job scout	resume
	letter of application	severance pay

COMPOSITION
RESEARCH
WORD PROCESSING

Chapter 13 : ACTIVITY 1

Changing Jobs Interview

You can learn a great deal from talking with people about their experiences with a job search and beginning a new job. In this activity, you will interview someone who has changed jobs recently.

1. Identify someone who began a new job within the past year, preferably in a field in which you are interested.

2. Interview this person asking the questions below. Prepare a written report to summarize your findings. Include the name of the person you interviewed in your report.
   - What are the organization's name and the nature of the organization's business?
   - What is your job title?
   - How did you learn about the job?
   - What were the key questions you were asked during your interview for the job?
   - What did you find appealing about the job offer?
   - Has the job turned out to be as you thought it would be?
   - How were you introduced to your job tasks and duties? Was any type of training provided?
   - What challenges have you faced in adjusting to the new job?

3. Write a thank-you letter to the person you interviewed. Thank the person for helping you and mention a couple of points from the interview that you found particularly interesting or unexpected. Mail one copy of the letter and give another copy to your instructor.

550

CHAPTER 13: PLANNING AND ADVANCING YOUR CAREER

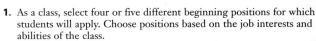

COMPOSITION
TEAMWORK
WORD PROCESSING

Role Playing Job Interviews

The interview is a critical step in a job search. In this activity, you will role-play being the applicant interviewed and being the person interviewing an job applicant.

1. As a class, select four or five different beginning positions for which students will apply. Choose positions based on the job interests and abilities of the class.

2. In teams of two, identify one person to play the interviewer and the other to play the applicant. For the interview, choose one of the positions identified earlier.

3. As the interviewer, develop a list of questions related to this particular job. Also write questions that will reflect attitudes related to responsibility, initiative, creative thinking, and ethics.

4. As the applicant, develop a resume to show your qualifications and interests related to this job. Develop a list of questions you plan to ask the interviewer about the job. Anticipate questions that you expect to be asked during the interview and plan your answers.

5. Conduct (role play) the interview. As the interviewer, complete an evaluation form for the applicant. (Open and print the PDF file *CH13 Interview* from the data files. This file contains the evaluation form.) As the applicant, respond to the questions asked as though you were actually taking part in a real interview. Review the evaluation completed by the interviewer to learn about areas for improvement.

6. Working in the same team or another as assigned by your teacher, switch roles. Repeat the interview preparation and role playing.

Adapt this activity, as needed, depending on the time you have available for role-playing interviews.

Have students complete the Chapter 13 Supplemental Activity, Research Job Scouts, available on *The Office* Web site.

Assess student learning using the Chapter 13 test available on the *IRCD* and in *ExamView®* format.

CHAPTER 14

Working with Others

The workplace is different today from what it was even a decade ago. New technology, organizational structures, and procedures have brought about some of the changes. However, one aspect remains the same—the way people interact. The personal qualities considered essential for work have not changed. They continue to reflect respect for oneself and others.

In this chapter, you will consider yourself as an individual at work who interacts with other workers. You will be introduced to personal qualities critical for success in the workplace. You will learn about the importance of working effectively with others.

Online Resources

○ *The Office* Web site:
   Data Files
   Vocabulary Flashcards
   Sort It Out, Conflicts at Work
   Chapter 14 Supplementary
     Activity
○ Search terms:
   business dress code
   business etiquette
   confidentiality
   conflict resolution
   employment discrimination
   sexual harassment
   work ethic

552

objectives

- Describe aspects of personality that are critical for effective performance at work
- Explain the attitudes that contribute to the success of organizations
- Describe expectations related to your appearance and manners at work

To work is to interact with other people. Even those who work at home interact with others. The character of each person in a group influences how effectively the group will work together. In fact, an employee identified as having *good character* is one who has a deep commitment to behaving appropriately.

Employers expect office workers to be reliable, productive, and cooperative. They also expect employees to learn new skills or knowledge that are needed for success on the job. This chapter focuses on personal attitudes and behaviors that help workers be successful.

In the business world, people are expected to behave in ways that others think are honorable and fair. Even though employees may be acting on behalf of a company, they have personal responsibility for their actions. They are expected to respect the rights of others. Employees should remember that they influence the nature and quality of their own work environment by their actions.

Your Personality at Work

Each individual is unique. The combination of traits that distinguishes one person from another is called **personality**. Your personal traits influence how you think, what you say, and how you respond to demands in your daily life. What is remarkable about your personality is that, to a far greater extent than many realize, you have control of who you are and what you believe. This means that you can make changes in your personality.

personality: patterns and qualities of behavior and attitudes of an individual

Character

The basic values and principles that are reflected in the way you live your life are referred to as **character**. Your parents, relatives, friends, or teachers have probably talked with you about issues such as character and **ethics**. This discussion, therefore, is not a new topic for you. You may want to use this opportunity, though, to review or reconsider some basic concepts related to character.

character: reputation, values, or principles as shown by behavior

ethics: a system of moral standards or values

At the core of your character is what you believe about **integrity**. Honesty and trustworthiness are synonyms for integrity. Individuals with integrity are valuable at work because they can be trusted to use the resources of the company only for company purposes.

integrity: honesty, sincerity, being of sound moral principle

553

Topic 14-1: *Personal Qualities at Work*

For Discussion

How do students exhibit reliability? How will these behaviors and habits transfer to the world of work?

WORKPLACE CONNECTIONS

Consider what might happen when a person lacks integrity. An executive, Linda Wong, confessed to embezzling funds. She and a vendor agreed on a scheme to take money from the company. The vendor issued invoices that overbilled the company. Linda processed the invoices as if they were legitimate. Then the vendor shared the money resulting from the overbilling with Linda. In a period of five years, the two had taken $6 million from the company. After the scheme was uncovered, Linda was sentenced to prison time.

Think what would happen in a company if many people acted dishonestly. Such behavior could cause a company to fail in a short time. Fortunately, most employees are honest and would not steal funds that belong to their companies. In its annual report, one major U. S. company described the importance of integrity as follows:

Highest Standards of Integrity: *We are honest and ethical in all our business dealings, starting with how we treat each other. We keep our promises and admit our mistakes. Our personal conduct ensures that our company's name is always worthy of trust.*

reliable: dependable or trustworthy

Another important part of character is reliability. Being **reliable** means that you will do what you agreed to do or what you can reasonably be expected to do in your job. You will not ignore your duties or dismiss them as unimportant. Company managers cannot constantly watch over employees to see that they do assigned tasks. Companies depend on the reliability of their employees.

Companies rely on employees to stay on task, even when unsupervised.

© STOCKDISC

Walt and Ricardo work from midnight to 8 a.m. in a 24-hour photocopying center. A supervisor rarely comes by to check on what they are doing. However, neither would ever think of closing the office for an hour and going off to an all-night diner. As Walt said: "I chose to work this late shift because I love the freedom and independence I have. I would never take my responsibilities lightly. I want my employer to know I can be counted on to complete my work without supervision."

Self-Acceptance

At the core of your personality is your attitude toward yourself. Experts in the field of mental health stress the value of accepting yourself. They have shown that you cannot change your personality without self-acceptance, which requires a realistic and honest view of who you are. To help bring about change in areas of your personality:

- Be honest with yourself. Do not deceive yourself about your behavior and beliefs. Admit your weaknesses and acknowledge your strengths.
- Understand that you are a unique individual. You share many of the same wants, needs, and fears of others. Remember that although others may not appear to have the problems you face, they usually have problems of their own.
- Believe in your own worthiness, while respecting the uniqueness of others. Regardless of your failings, you are worthy. Every human being is. Self-acceptance means that you are willing to accept your faults but still have a feeling of confidence and a sense of security. For example, you are not shattered by constructive criticism.

WORKPLACE CONNECTIONS

Kimberly admired a classmate, Susanne, who seemed carefree yet earned the top grades in her classes. Kimberly was certain that Susanne did not study but lived an easy life. One afternoon, Kimberly asked Susanne to join her in a game of tennis during the weekend. Kimberly was stunned when Susanne said to her: "I'd love to join you, but I spend most of my weekend studying. Would you ask me again when school ends?" An awareness of how others meet their obligations and how they make choices can help you to understand how much individuals are alike.

Points to Emphasize

Being candid with oneself is not always easy. Although individuals may know the flaws in their personality, they may find it painful to acknowledge them, even to themselves.

Maturity

A person in our society is expected to behave in a mature way by the end of adolescence. Of course, many young people show maturity earlier. A mature person has the emotional and mental qualities that are considered normal to a socially adjusted adult. To be mature means that you see beyond the moment and understand the consequences of your choices. A mature person considers the rights of others and makes decisions based on such understanding.

You are mature when you are willing to:

- Accept criticism or disappointment tactfully
- Acknowledge that you do not know or understand something
- Admit that you made a mistake
- Learn from your mistakes
- Face your weaknesses and determine how to overcome them
- Be considerate of others
- Demonstrate respect for differences of individuals
- Be objective and honest in your relationships with others
- Value the worth of every person and do not act superior to another person

A mature person can accept criticism or disappointment tactfully.

© GETTY IMAGES/PHOTODISC

Attitudes that Support Quality Performance

The attitudes that support quality performance at work include a strong belief in the work ethic, willingness to help in achieving company goals, and a desire to learn. You will want to develop these attitudes to increase your chances for success on the job.

The Work Ethic

As you have learned, high productivity and effective use of resources are common goals of businesses. Productivity depends in part on the **work ethic** of employees. Work ethic is a general term that combines a deep belief in the value of work in one's life and a willingness to meet the demands of work. Persons with a strong work ethic value both tangible and intangible rewards of work. Tangible rewards, such as pay and benefits, are important to most workers. Persons without a strong work ethic may not place much value on intangible rewards, such as enjoyment of the work performed or pride in a job well done. Persons with a strong work ethic tend to define job satisfaction differently from those without a strong work ethic.

Workers in the United States have long been credited with a strong work ethic. A positive attitude toward work, willingness to work overtime, and low error rates all reflect a strong work ethic. Companies looking for new locations want to be assured that employees in the area are willing to work hard to meet company goals.

work ethic: a system of values in which purposeful activity is of central importance

Participation and Cooperation

At the heart of cooperativeness is the willingness to participate in what needs to be done to achieve a goal. You may have heard someone say, "We would have missed our deadline if everyone hadn't chipped in and helped."

Many companies develop job descriptions for each job in the company. Given the changing nature of business, however, workers often need to perform tasks not included in their job descriptions. A positive attitude and a willingness to be helpful are critical at such a time.

WORKPLACE CONNECTIONS

Sam is a manager in one of the finest jewelry stores in the United States. Managers are not salespersons. Yet, Sam is likely to be assisting customers through much of a very busy shopping day. Sam pays no attention to the typical end of his working day. He stays on the job through the closing time for the store. He realizes that at a busy time, the most important task is assisting customers.

For Discussion

What are some tangible rewards of work? What are some intangible rewards of work? Are both important? Why or why not?

Points to Emphasize

A job description is helpful in knowing what is generally expected of an employee; however, workers are often asked to complete tasks not specifically listed in their job descriptions.

557

Topic 14-1: *Personal Qualities at Work*

557

Topic 14-1: *Personal Qualities at Work*

Learning

Work procedures can change often. Some changes may be needed to adapt to new technology. Other changes may be needed to adapt to produce new products or offer new services. As companies change, managers cannot always know what new skills each employee needs to learn. Companies expect workers to be independent learners. As an office worker, you are expected to show a willingness to learn and to improve your understanding or your skills that relate to your job.

Strive to be aware of new technology and methods that relate to your field. Industry magazines and professional organizations are good sources of information. Tell your employer about opportunities for training that will improve your job performance. The company may be willing to pay the cost of such training for you and other workers.

Impressions Influence Others

Your appearance affects how others think of you. People often form judgments on limited evidence such as a first impression. Appropriate dress and proper personal hygiene are important for making a good impression on others. Annoying habits and speaking in a manner that is not appropriate can create a poor impression.

Your appearance should convey responsibility and good taste.

© GETTY IMAGES/PHOTODISC

Dress

If you dress appropriately for work, others may be more likely to think that you are giving proper attention to your job duties. If your appearance is sloppy, others may think that your work is also sloppy and that you are probably not an efficient employee.

To illustrate appropriate business attire, you may want to use photos from current publications, such as full-page advertisements that show individuals in typical work attire. Some photos from leisure magazines might also be shown as a basis for noting attire that is not appropriate for business offices.

Dress considered appropriate for work varies somewhat from company to company. Some companies are specific about what they consider proper dress for work. Others expect new employees to determine appropriate dress from noting how the majority of other workers dress. If you work in a company that does not state its dress code, dress attractively in a businesslike manner. You want your appearance to show good taste and suggest that you are a responsible employee.

WORKPLACE CONNECTIONS

Kathy comes to work in messy jeans and running shoes. She thinks she is a good employee and that how she dresses is not important as long as she does a good job. Gail comes to work in a business suit and pumps with a low heel. She, too, thinks she is a good employee. Gail, however, thinks that how she dresses helps her project a professional image. What will a new executive meeting each of these two young women think about the value of each one to the company? The executive is likely to question Kathy's effectiveness in interacting with customers.

Annoying Habits

Annoying habits, such as throwing back your head to get your hair out of your eyes or drumming your fingers on a desk, can create a poor impression. These habits can have a negative effective on your interactions with coworkers. Over time, some people develop facial expressions that do not express how they feel. For example, an individual may appear to be frowning when frowning has nothing to do with how the person feels. Certain facial expressions seem to happen in an automatic fashion—they have become habits. Coworkers may think that you are unhappy or disagree with what they are saying or doing because of your expression.

Workers often must interact within a relatively small area. Many workers may share an open space, with only limited partitions to define workspaces for individuals. Conversations can be easily overheard in this type of office setting. When you are speaking by telephone or with a coworker, adjust the volume of your voice so that you speak to that person only. Do not speak so loudly that you disrupt or annoy others who are working near you.

Consider your behavior and identify what you believe might be annoying to others. Ask a trusted friend or coworker to help you identify any habits you have that others may find annoying. Make a decision to stop annoying behavior and follow through with your decision.

For Discussion

To what extent is "casual Friday" allowed in the businesses in our town? If students are acquainted with a local bank or municipal or state office, ask them to describe what they believe is appropriate attire for employees in such an organization.

For Discussion

As you interact with others, what annoying habits have you noticed? How do you modulate your voice so only the person with whom you are talking hears you?

559

Topic 14-1: *Personal Qualities at Work*

Basic Work Manners

You have been learning about manners since you were a child. You may recall a parent saying to you, "Do not eat while you are talking; keep your elbows off the table," or "Shake hands with Mr. Norris, who has come for a visit." What you know about good manners will be valuable when you interact with others at work. Only a limited number of points will be discussed here.

Introductions

In a meeting or other business situation, you may introduce individuals when you know both but they do not know each other. When you make an introduction, address the person of higher rank or age first. Then address the person of lower rank or age. For example, when introducing a new administrative assistant to the president of the company say: "Mrs. Carstairs, this is Miss Joy Pablo, our new office assistant. Miss Pablo, this is Mrs. Alma Carstairs, our company president." If the two people are from different companies or organizations, mention the affiliation. Use titles, such as Doctor, Major, or Reverend, if known. For example, say: "Dr. Tomas, this is Mr. Cary House of Ace Medical Supplies. Mr. House, this is Dr. Andy Tomas of Cumberland Area Hospital." When introducing a man and a woman of about the same age and rank, address the woman first. When introducing a customer to any member of your company, show courtesy for the customer by addressing the customer first.

Introductions should be made in a courteous manner.

© GETTY IMAGES/PHOTODISC

560

In general, extending your hand to another person when being introduced is considered a gracious gesture. A handshake should be firm yet not so strong that it causes pain. A limp handshake is often considered a sign that someone does not want to interact with others.

Electronic Etiquette

Remote ways of interacting with people require the use of good manners just as face-to-face meetings do. Use of voice mail, cellular phones, fax machines, and conference calls all offer opportunities to improve your relationship with others through the use of good manners.

Voice Mail

The manners that are considered appropriate when talking with someone in person should be extended to leaving a message by voice mail. The caller should be courteous and remember to leave a complete message:

- Speak slowly.
- Keep the message as brief as possible.
- Include your complete name and telephone number.
- Explain why a return call is essential, if that is the case.

Cellular Phones

Cellular phones allow workers to be "on the job" at all times. However, you should not use your cell phone during musical programs, lectures, films, in a crowded restaurant, or in other areas where your conversation will disrupt activities or annoy others. If you are using a cell phone at a conference, for example, you should move away from a place where others are talking. Do not discuss confidential business information when talking on your cell phone in a public area.

© GETTY IMAGES/PHOTODISC

Be careful not to disturb others when talking on a cell phone.

Topic 14-1: *Personal Qualities at Work*

Use your cellular phone in an appropriate way. Do not disturb others at programs or restaurants by talking loudly on your phone.

Speakerphones

When using a speakerphone, you may be in an area where others can hear the conversation. In this case, be sure the matter being discussed is not confidential. If you place the call, you should establish that the other person does not mind you using a speakerphone. When using a speakerphone, give your full attention to the caller. Do not attempt to do something else at the same time, even though your hands are free.

Fax Machines

In many offices, several workers share the same fax machine. Reading another person's incoming messages is considered impolite. When you find a message for someone else at the fax machine, you should read only to the point of identifying the recipient.

Conference Calls

Sensitivity to everyone taking part in a conference call is critical for the call to proceed without problems. When you begin to speak, identify yourself. Do not interrupt someone who is speaking. If you must step away from the call, do not put your line on hold if doing so will cause background music to play on the line.

General Courtesies at Work

Employees are expected to be aware of the responsibilities of their coworkers. Doing so means that you do not cause your coworkers to waste time. Conversations should generally be limited to matters of work during work time. Wait for breaks or lunchtime for personal talk. Employees often face deadlines. When seeking assistance from a coworker, first inquire if the time is appropriate for an interruption.

Equipment is often shared with coworkers. Employees should not monopolize equipment to the point of keeping others from completing tasks. For example, suppose you and a coworker are both waiting to use the copier. You arrived first at the copier and have a large copying job to complete. Your coworker needs to make only two copies. Offer to let your coworker use the copier first so he or she does not waste time waiting for you to complete your job. Be alert to the needs of those around you.

REVIEWING THE TOPIC

1. What are three characteristics or attitudes employers expect of employees?
2. What is personality? How can you change your personality?
3. What is character?
4. Explain the meaning of integrity and give examples of how integrity relates to office workers.
5. What characteristics indicate that a person is reliable?
6. What are some basic attitudes important to self-acceptance?
7. What does it mean for a person to have a strong work ethic?
8. Why should an employee give attention to his or her appearance?
9. Why should annoying habits at work be eliminated?
10. Describe some general courtesies at work that should be extended to others.

THINKING CRITICALLY

You must take a realistic look at your personality before you can determine ways to improve it. In this activity you will describe what you believe reflects your personality.

1. Assume that you are now a full-time employee and are making an assessment of yourself for your own benefit. Consider each of the factors listed below step 2.
2. For each of the factors listed below, key a brief description that provides a realistic statement of how you see yourself relative to the factor. Are you satisfied with your personality in each of these areas? If not, what steps can you take to change or improve in this area?

   - Integrity
   - Maturity
   - Reliability
   - Work ethic
   - Self-acceptance
   - Willingness to learn
   - Willingness to participate in achieving goals

Teaching Tips

Give students the correct answers after they have completed the activity.

REINFORCING MATH SKILLS

Employees in a large department were rated on the factors shown in the following table. The ratings were made on a scale from 1 to 5, with 5 being the best.

1. Compute the average score for each employee.

2. Compute the average score for the total group for each area.

3. Identify the areas where these employees as a group may need some further training.

Employee	Work Ethic	Partici- pation	Willingness to Learn	Appear- ance	Manners
Abbot, Roy	2	1	3	1	2
Abrams, Peter	4	4	5	2	2
Bryant, Silvia	1	1	1	3	2
Cooper, Rachel	5	4	4	4	5
Cordero, Allen	2	2	2	1	1
Dones, Carole	4	4	4	4	2
Herbik, Sheri	4	3	2	5	5
Kulpa, Rudy	5	5	4	5	5
Merena, Sam	4	5	5	4	5
Nang, Li	5	5	5	4	3
Ramsey, Nilda	3	2	4	1	2

Teaching Tips

Remind students to consult Section G of the Reference Guide in the *Student Activities and Simulations* workbook to review correct report format.

COMPOSITION
INTERNET
RESEARCH
WORD PROCESSING

Topic **14-1** | A C T I V I T Y 1

Business Dress Codes

Appropriate dress at work is important for making a good impression. The term *business attire* typically means a business suit or dress slacks and jacket for men. For women, business attire typically means a business suit or dress. Some companies use the term *business casual attire* to describe appropriate dress for work. This term, however, is not as clearly defined. In this activity, you will research and write a report on this topic.

1. Use the Internet or other reference sources to find current articles that discuss business casual dress. Read the articles and make notes about the main points discussed. Record complete information for each source: author, title of article, magazine or periodical name, date of publication, and Web site address if the article is found online.

564

CHAPTER 14: WORKING WITH OTHERS

2. Compose a short report describing business casual dress. Give examples of what is and what is not considered business casual dress. Include other information you may find from reading the articles. For example, when do companies allow business casual dress or when do they require formal business attire? Discuss the effect that business casual dress has on issues such as employee morale or productivity.

3. Format the report in unbound report style and include a page to list references at the end of the report.

Topic 14-1 : ACTIVITY 2

COMPOSITION
WORD PROCESSING

Tangible and Intangible Rewards of Work

Both tangible and intangible rewards of work will contribute to your job satisfaction. Which type of reward is most important to you? Identify and rank tangible and intangible rewards of work in this activity.

1. Create a list of ten or more tangible rewards of work, such as salary, stock options, company-paid life insurance, and so on.

2. Create a list of ten intangible rewards of work, such as a feeling of pride in work done well, the enjoyment of socializing with coworkers, or a feeling that your work contributes to the well-being of others.

3. Think about a job or career that interests you. Place the name of this job or career at the top of your two lists. Rank the tangible and intangible rewards you have listed in order of their importance to you.

4. Key a paragraph that explains how the job or career you identified in step 3 will allow you to experience the tangible and intangible rewards of work.

565

Topic Review

HUMAN RELATIONS AT WORK

- O Explain what effective interaction with others at work means
- O Describe appropriate responses in handling conflicts at work
- O Assess your ability to work with others
- O Identify some of the basic laws and regulations that apply to the workplace

Employees must be willing to work with others in a cooperative, business-like manner. Workers are often not able to choose those with whom they work. Employers expect office workers to show respect for others, be willing to listen to others, and be committed to helping meet the goals of the company.

Interacting with Supervisors

Few people work totally alone or independently. Regardless of the position you hold, you will be reporting to someone. Even key executives report to a board of directors or to owners. In most companies, employees have someone who supervises and guides their work.

What You Can Expect from Your Supervisor

What you can expect from your supervisor will depend in part on your job position. Office workers who are not in a management position often report to someone in middle management. As you learned in Chapter 1, managers at this level direct the day-to-day activities of a company.

Effective managers want employees to be successful. Managers may explain to employees how various tasks relate to achieving the goals of the company. They may provide direction or set priorities of tasks or projects to be done by workers. In some situations, they assign tasks or projects to certain workers. In other situations, tasks are clearly associated with particular jobs. Informing employees of deadlines and quality standards for work are other tasks of managers.

Managers have varying ways of carrying through their tasks. Some managers have staff meetings frequently. Other managers seldom hold meetings. Instead they send e-mail messages or memos to employees. Some managers plan carefully schedules and projects and share the plans with all staff members. Others make decisions and communicate information on an as-needed basis.

Understanding your supervisor's work style will be helpful to you in meeting his or her expectations. The manager's personality, the nature of the work in the department, and the expectations of the manager's supervisor all affect the manager's work style. Some managers explain clearly how they will communicate and what they expect from employees. Others expect employees to determine from observations and comments what the manager expects.

© GETTY IMAGES/PHOTODISC

*A supervisor guides
members of the team.*

What Your Manager Expects from You

Managers expect employees to focus on their tasks even though there is no direct, immediate supervision throughout the workday. Increasingly, workers are given authority to make decisions on the basis of general instructions without review by a manager. Managers expect to have completed work on schedule. They expect employees to keep them informed of unexpected work developments or about problems with meeting deadlines.

Managers expect employees to evaluate their own work and take needed steps to ensure a high quality of work. Employees are expected to continue to improve skills and gain knowledge as needed in their jobs.

Managers expect employees to be willing to handle unplanned situations. At such times, regular assignments must be set aside to complete tasks that now have higher priority. Managers depend on the flexibility and willingness of staff to respond to new demands in a busy workplace.

Managers expect employees to be loyal to the company and to their work group or department. Being loyal means supporting the efforts of the company and workgroup. A loyal employee does not make unfavorable remarks about the company or workgroup outside the group. For example, several members of a department may have different ideas about plans for a new project. Each person may offer suggestions and criticisms of proposed plans. Once the manager or the group has made a decision about how to proceed, however, all members of the team are expected to do their best to make the plan successful.

Points to Emphasize

Managers expect employees to be reliable, to evaluate their own work, to handle unplanned situations, to exhibit loyalty to the department and the company, and to behave in an ethical manner.

567

Topic 14-2: *Human Relations at Work*

Managers expect employees to be loyal and behave in an ethical manner. However, no employer should expect employees to take part in illegal or immoral behavior. Many companies publish a code of ethics that employees are expected to follow. When you begin a new job, ask if the company has a code of ethics that you are to follow. Become familiar with the rules of the company so that you do not unknowingly break the rules. Some activities that might seem harmless in a personal setting may not be appropriate at work. For example, employees may be forbidden to accept gifts from vendors or others related to work.

Interacting with Coworkers

The extent to which you must work with others will vary. If you are a member of a project team, you may perform many tasks as a group. If you serve as a research assistant, you may spend much time alone following through on the tasks that are your responsibility.

Even though much of your work may be done independently, at times you will need to interact with others. You will interact because you have common needs for information, tasks that overlap, or joint responsibility for some common task.

A project team performs many tasks as a group.

Cooperation

Employees must work together to achieve the goals of a company. When a colleague from another department calls you, your response should be to want to provide the needed help or data (assuming the data is not confidential). When you work as part of a team, do your best to complete your part of the task and to contribute to the success of the team. For suggestions on how to work successfully in a team, refer to Chapter 2, page 54.

Expand the Concept

What attitudes about people in general will be helpful as you work with your colleagues?

For Discussion

A colleague calls for information; you are very busy attempting to meet a deadline that afternoon. The information is needed as soon as possible. What will you say to your colleague?

Carlos Ortiz works as a buyer of ingredients for a large candy company. He communicates frequently with the company's laboratories where new products are being developed. He attends meetings to hear comments about the ingredients for products. Carlos believes much of the success of his work depends on the cooperation he gets from the departments for which he buys ingredients.

Confidentiality

You will want to be sure you understand what aspects of your work are confidential. Revealing confidential data may cause harm to the company or its employees or customers. Information about plans of the business might seem routine. If the information reaches the company's competitors, however, the results could be disastrous. In some cases, information is confidential only for a period of time. Later, when decisions are firm, information that was earlier restricted may be widely distributed. For more information on protecting confidential information, refer to Chapter 11, page 437.

Valerie works in the Human Resources Department of her company. In her position, she meets the candidates for key management positions. She reviews resumes and assists the director in making decisions. She knows which candidates are invited to headquarters for interviews. Valerie understands that all aspects of the recruiting process must be kept confidential. She never reveals any hiring details. The director is grateful for Valerie's attitude.

Avoiding Gossip

Information is often shared informally in a company. The informal network by which employees share information is sometimes called the "grapevine." Some informal communication can be good. Employees are naturally interested in the plans and events that affect the company and its employees.

Unfortunately, rumors and gossip are also often spread by employees. Rumors are incomplete or false statements about people or situations. They may be harmful to the company or its employees. Think carefully about the information you share with others. Avoid discussing company plans or events that you do not know are correct or that may be confidential at the present time. Do not discuss personal issues or affairs of fellow employees.

Thinking Critically

What are some reasons individuals do not adhere to a promise to keep information confidential?

Thinking Critically

Key contributors to the "grapevine" are often popular. Why should an employee resist joining in the spreading of rumors and risk not being popular among coworkers?

569

Topic 14-2: *Human Relations at Work*

Gossiping is not appropriate in the workplace.

Points to Emphasize

All workers should accept the reality that mistakes occur and should accept responsibility for their mistakes.

Accepting Responsibility for Mistakes

People are not perfect; they make mistakes. You may have a firm goal to be sure that the facts you communicate to others are accurate and to use good judgment in making decisions. Even with your best efforts, however, you will still make mistakes.

When you make a mistake, accept responsibility for the error as soon as you realize it was made. Take steps to correct the error immediately so that coworkers will not make decisions or plans based on incorrect information. Explain what led to the error if you think doing so will help resolve the problem. Do not, however, subject your coworkers to a long list of excuses about why you made the mistake. If possible, offer a solution to whatever problem the mistake may have caused when you alert others to the mistake or problem. Learn from your mistakes whenever possible to help avoid making a similar error in the future. Never blame others for your mistakes.

WORKPLACE CONNECTIONS

The assistant curator at the County Historical Society, Debra, realized that she had given a staff member the wrong dates for an exhibition. When the staff member called, Debra was very busy completing a report and failed to check the calendar. She merely gave the dates as she recalled them. Later in the day, she realized that she gave the staff member the wrong dates. She called the staff member and confessed: "Marion, I gave you the wrong dates! I am sorry. I hope it isn't too late to give you the correct information."

Facing Conflicts at Work

A **conflict** is a disagreement, quarrel, or controversy. Because human beings are not perfect, those with whom you work will have a variety of weaknesses and problems—just as you do. At times, problems may arise that hurt relations among coworkers. Responsible employees take steps to deal with conflicts in a mature and constructive way. These strategies can be helpful in resolving conflicts at work:

conflict: disagreement, quarrel, or controversy

1. **Communicate.** Listen and talk with your coworkers to be sure you all have the same understanding of the situation. Consider everyone's concerns. Sometimes what seems like a problem can be merely a misunderstanding that is easily resolved by talking openly.

2. **Analyze the situation.** Determine the real or underlying problems that may be leading to the conflict. Try to resolve a conflict at the earliest stage possible so that a small problem does not become a big problem.

3. **Be objective.** Focus on the issue—not the person. Do not let your personal feelings for the people involved stand in the way of resolving the problem.

4. **Look inward.** Objectively examine your role in the situation. Are you contributing to the problem or to a solution? Be willing to admit your mistakes and apologize when your behavior or comments hurt others.

5. **Look for solutions.** Brainstorm with coworkers to find ways to resolve the conflict.

6. **Be diplomatic.** Explain how resolving the conflict is of benefit to others. Be tactful when suggesting possible solutions. Focus on finding a solution rather than on placing blame.

diplomatic: tactful in dealing with people

7. **Compromise.** When appropriate, be willing to make changes to help resolve a conflict.

compromise: give up demands or make changes to reach a settlement

Many employees spend 40 hours or more per week on the job. Making these hours as stress free as possible is to everyone's benefit. Remember that you do not have to be friends with your coworkers. You do, however, need to be able to work with them productively.

Conflict with Your Manager

You hope to have what is referred to as a "good working relationship" with your manager. However, there are times when the relationship may not be good. A misunderstanding about job assignments, seemingly unreasonable demands, or failure to talk about work goals can lead to conflicts.

Good managers are expected to be aware of what their staff members are doing and to assess the work assigned. However, when work demands are heavy, a manager may fail to think about your work. If you receive no feedback from your manager, you may assume the work is acceptable. Perhaps the manager, however, has simply been too busy to discuss the problems with you. This difference of opinion will be revealed at some point and may lead to conflict between the two of you. To avoid such a situation, actively seek feedback on your work regularly. Ask specific questions to see whether the quality and quantity of your work meet your manager's expectations.

For Discussion

What are some possible sources of conflicts with coworkers?

Thinking Critically

Why is trying to place blame for a problem often not a good step toward solving the problem? What is the difference between placing blame for a problem and determining the cause of a problem?

Thinking Critically

What attitudes toward others might be missing in a manager who is insensitive to the demands made on employees in the department? When do you think a manager is justified in believing that employees should figure out what they are expected to do?

571

Topic 14-2: Human Relations at Work

When given a new task or duty, ask questions to be sure you understand what is expected of you. If problems develop with your work that will cause missed deadlines or results different from what your manager expects, keep your manager informed as events happen. This will help avoid conflicts between you and your manager.

Discuss the quality of your work with your manager to avoid conflicts.

© ELEKTRAVISION/INDEX STOCK IMAGERY

Conflict Related to Ethical Behavior

Sometimes conflicts arise because workers have different values. Increasingly, companies have created codes of conduct or ethics for all employees to follow. Policy manuals, training sessions, or written materials are used to inform everyone of the rules. These rules are to be honored as employees work with each other as well as with vendors and customers.

You will want to become fully acquainted with the ethical rules that guide the company in which you work. You want to understand the rules clearly. You should not depend on the interpretations of your colleagues. Violating the company's code of ethics can lead to disciplinary measures or even dismissal from your job.

As an individual, you also have a code of ethics. This code is a system of moral values that help you decide what behavior is appropriate and what is not. At times, your sense of what is morally right may come into conflict with the behavior of coworkers or duties related to your job. For example, coworkers may make remarks about other employees that you find offensive. Your company may ask you to work on a religious holiday. You must use your own judgment to decide how to handle such a situation. Talking about the situation with your manager is usually a good first step. Many companies have policies and procedures in place that employees can use to resolve conflicts or report unethical behavior.

572

CHAPTER 14: WORKING WITH OTHERS

FOCUS ON . . .

Work/Life Balance

The term *work/life balance* is commonly used to describe the need workers have to balance work with other aspects of life. In the last 20 years, the number of women in the workforce has increased significantly. This change has created more families with two working parents. Single-parent families are also on the rise. Many of the activities formerly handled by a nonworking parent must now be handled by a working parent.

When you think about a career, consider how your choice will affect all aspects of your life. Different careers make different demands on workers and their families. Some jobs may require much travel, overtime, or a long commute that will reduce time for family or participating in other activities. In many jobs, taking time off to care for a sick child or pursue a personal interest is very difficult.

When employees do not have enough time to take care of their personal matters, they bring stress to the workplace and are less productive. Many companies address this problem by creating a workplace that is supportive of workers' needs. For exam-

ple, some companies have childcare facilities on-site or help pay for the cost of childcare. Other companies create positions with flexible work hours. Employees in these positions can choose to arrive and leave work earlier or later than the normal working hours to accommodate their schedules. Another alternative that might be offered is a compressed workweek. Employees might work ten hours a day for four days a week, then take the fifth day off. Some companies allow job sharing. This permits two part-time employees working different shifts to fulfill the duties of one full-time worker. Some companies provide benefits for part-time workers. Telecommuting on a part-time or full-time basis is a helpful option for some employees.

Companies find that employee loyalty increases when the company makes accommodations for workers' personal needs. Employees find that these accommodations contribute to their job satisfaction. When choosing an employer, consider whether the company fits your needs as well as whether you fit the needs of the company.

Understanding Relevant Laws and Regulations

Organizations in the United States must adhere to certain laws and regulations of federal, state, and local governments that relate to employment. Some of the laws and regulations that relate to employment and maintaining a safe work environment are discussed in this section.

If you have a problem related to an employment law or a regulation, you will find that generally the company has someone to whom you can direct the problem. If the problem is not resolved, report it to the closest office of the agency responsible for enforcing the particular law.

Thinking Critically

Why does the federal government of the United States support freedom from discrimination? In what way does such a law aid an individual? In what way does it aid the society in general?

Teaching Tips

Any current cases involving sexual harassment might be used for a brief discussion of the problems that arise from this type of discrimination.

Teaching Tips

Identify the agencies with local offices that provide workplace safety information. Students might volunteer to visit such offices to collect information to share with the class. Emphasize the critical role Human Resources personnel play in monitoring adherence to laws and regulations.

Fair Labor Standards

The Fair Labor Standards Act (FLSA) sets the minimum wages for employees covered by the law. Requirements related to overtime are also specified. The Equal Pay Act makes it unlawful to pay different wages to men and women where jobs are equal in skills required, effort, responsibility, and working conditions. The Equal Pay Act and other laws are enforced by the Equal Employment Opportunity Commission (EEOC).

Freedom from Discrimination

Title VII of the Civil Rights Act of 1964 makes it illegal to discriminate in employment on the basis of a person's race, color, religion, sex, or national origin. This is the principal federal employment discrimination law. Later acts outlaw discrimination against handicapped individuals; against women because of pregnancy, childbirth, or other related medical conditions; or against anyone 40 years or older on the basis of age.

Freedom from Sexual Harassment

sexual harassment: sexually directed, unsolicited, and unwanted actions or speech that creates a hostile work environment

Title VII of the Civil Rights Act of 1964 bans discrimination on the basis of gender. Sexual harassment is one form of gender discrimination. **Sexual harassment** is sexually directed, unsolicited, and unwanted actions or speech that creates a difficult and hostile work environment or unreasonably interferes with an individual's work performance. Both men and women can be the victims of sexual harassment. The harasser can be of the opposite sex or the same sex as the victim. The harasser can be a superior, a coworker, a customer, or another person who is not an employee.

Many companies include policies on sexual harassment in their employee handbooks. Such a policy usually states that the company will not tolerate sexual harassment and describes the procedures for reporting an incident of sexual harassment.

Safe and Healthy Workplace

The Occupational Safety and Health Act of 1970 was enacted to assure safe and healthful working conditions for working men and women in the United States. The Occupational Safety and Health Administration (OSHA) is a government agency responsible for enforcing this law. In addition to enforcement, OSHA provides research, information, education, and training in the field of occupational safety and health. Workplace consultations are available to businesses that want on-site help in establishing safety and health programs and identifying and correcting workplace hazards. More information is available on the OSHA Web site as shown in Figure 14-2.1.

CHAPTER 14: WORKING WITH OTHERS

Source: U.S. Department of Labor, Occupational Safety & Health Administration. http://www.osha.gov (accessed October 20, 2005).

Figure 14-2.1

OSHA has an extensive Web site to help employers and employees better understand how to comply with OSHA standards.

Unemployment Insurance

Unemployment insurance provides income for persons who have been dismissed from their jobs. To be eligible, individuals must have worked for a required time. The amount of benefit payments varies depending on the worker's wages paid during the previous year and the benefits of the particular state where the individuals worked.

The provisions and restrictions of this benefit vary from state to state. In some states, workers may be denied unemployment payments for quitting a job without good reason, being fired because of misconduct while on the job, or refusing to take a job while unemployed.

Social Security Act Benefits

The Federal Social Security Act of 1935, also known as the Federal Insurance Contribution Act (FICA), provides eligible workers with:

- Retirement income
- Benefits for spouses of retired or disabled workers
- Survivor benefits
- Disability benefits
- Health insurance

Eligible workers may start receiving reduced benefits at age 62. The age requirement for full benefits varies according to date of birth. Information on retirement benefits can be found on the Social Security Administration's Web site as shown in Figure 14-2.2. The employee pays in to this fund, and the payments are deducted from his or her paycheck. The employer is required to match the employee's contributions.

Expand the Concept

Discuss the rules and procedures related to unemployment insurance in your state. Many states have Web sites with information about the state's program.

575

Figure **14-2.2**

Information on full retirement age can be found on the Social Security Administration's Web site.

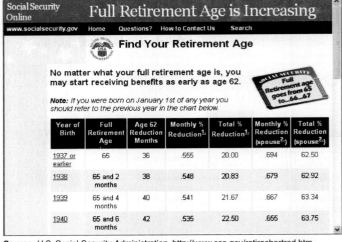

Source: U.S. Social Security Administration. http://www.ssa.gov/retirechartred.htm (accessed September 26, 2005).

CHAPTER 14: WORKING WITH OTHERS

REVIEWING THE TOPIC

1. Identify and describe skills and characteristics required to work effectively with others.
2. List three tasks or duties that managers typically perform related to workers who report to them.
3. Why does a manager want the employees in her or his department to be successful?
4. Describe four behaviors or characteristics managers expect of office workers.
5. Why is employee loyalty important to a business?
6. Explain the meaning of confidentiality as it relates to office work.
7. Why should an employee avoid gossiping?
8. What steps can an employee take to resolve conflicts that arise at work?
9. What is the purpose of the Fair Labor Standards Act?
10. Why is freedom from discrimination important in the workplace?
11. Define sexual harassment in the workplace and give an example of speech or behavior that would likely be considered sexual harassment.
12. List three benefits provided to workers by the Social Security Act.

INTERACTING WITH OTHERS

Peg, Jeff, and Marco were having lunch when the conversation turned to a fourth coworker, Sally, who was out ill that day. A week earlier, Sally had been told that she would not get the promotion she had expected. Sally was stunned by the news. She thought she was competent and handled all assignments she was given. When she told the unpleasant news to her three coworkers, she remarked: "How could they do this to me?" "Will you—my friends—tell me the truth?" Peg said: "Oh, Sally, don't make this a big deal. In a few months they will call you in to tell you that you have been promoted." Both Jeff and Marco agreed, and the topic shifted.

Now, a week later, the three felt somewhat guilty about avoiding Sally's question. What they concluded was that Sally was "too loud" for the next level of responsibility. They liked Sally, but she apparently did not realize that she just didn't seem to know when she should talk quietly, when she should just keep silent, and when she should shorten her explanations. Her friends think that Sally's shortcomings resulted in her not being promoted.

1. As her friend, what would you say to Sally in this situation? Should you tell her why you think she did not get the promotion even if you think her feelings will be hurt? Why or why not?

Teaching Tips

If the students are using the *Student Activities and Simulations* workbook, instruct them to complete the review activity for this topic.

For Discussion

Lead a class discussion using the questions posed in this activity. Ask students to tell tactful ways in which they could discuss this type of situation with a coworker.

continued

2. Suppose that you and Sally's other friends are wrong about why Sally did not get the promotion. Who should Sally ask to be sure she learns the real reasons why she was not promoted?

REINFORCING ENGLISH SKILLS

Companies have many different types of policies. These polices are often included in an employee handbook.

1. Key the workplace monitoring policy shown below. Correct errors in spelling, punctuation, and word usage.
2. Ask a classmate to review your work while you review his or her work. Make corrections based on the feedback you receive if needed.

Workplace Monitoring Policy

Effective Date: 10/26/20--

Workplace montoring will be conducted bye the company to ensure quality control, employee safety; building security, and customer satis-foction. Because the company is sensitive to the legitimate privacy rights of employees; every effort will be made too guaranty that work-place monitoring is done inn an ethical and respectful manner. Employ-ees should be aware of the following points related to this policy:

- Computers furnished two employees are the property of the com-pany. As such, computer usage and files may be monitored or accesssed.

- The company may conduct video survaillance of non-private workplace areas. Video monitoring is used to identify safety con-cerns; maintain quality control, detect theft and misconduct, and discourage or prevent acts of harrassment and workplace violence.

- Employees can request access to information gathered throught workplace monitoring that may impakt employment decisions. Access will be granted unless their is a legitimate business reason to protect confidentiality or an ongoing investigation.

578

Tell students the errors which should be corrected after they finish the activity.

Topic 14-2 : ACTIVITY 1

Encounter with a Manager

A staff assistant, Allen, had quietly taken on extra responsibilities when another assistant, Kay, was on an extended leave. By working extra hours and through lunch, he had just managed to do his regular work and the absent staff member's work, too. Near the end of Kay's leave, his manager stopped by Allen's desk and said: "Because you are handling both jobs so well, I'm going to recommend that Kay be assigned to another department. We really don't need him." At that point, the manager walked away.

Allen was stunned. Up to this time, he had not commented about what he was doing. He assumed that his manager was aware of the extraordinary efforts he had made to do both jobs. Allen has asked to meet with his manager to discuss the situation.

1. Assume you are Allen. Describe clearly in two or three sentences what you want the outcome of the meeting with your manager to be.
2. Compose a list of the main points you will make in the meeting with your manager in an effort to achieve the outcome you want.
3. What kinds of supporting materials might you take to the meeting to support your points?
4. Describe the attitude with which you will approach this meeting.
5. What might you (Allen) have done during the past few weeks to help avoid the conflict you now face with your manager?

Topic 14-2 : ACTIVITY 2

Research Sexual Harassment Policies

To combat sexual harassment in the workplace, many companies adopt a sexual harassment policy. This policy usually defines sexual harassment, gives examples of inappropriate behavior and speech, and outlines a procedure for filing complaints. In this activity, you will find an example of such a policy for two organizations.

1. Access the Internet. Use a search engine to find sites that give the sexual harassment policy of an organization. Search using the term *sexual harassment policy*.
2. Access at least two sites and read the sexual harassment policy provided. Make notes about the main points discussed. Record complete information for each source: Web site name, Web site address, and the date you accessed the site.
3. Write a short report that gives your findings. Include a definition of sexual harassment as shown on one Web site. Describe how the two policies differ and how they are alike, especially in procedures for reporting cases of harassment.

Topic Review

Teaching Tips

Have two students role-play the meeting between Allen and his manager. Ask the other students to comment on what might have been said differently after the role-play activity is finished.

Teaching Tips

Many universities and government agencies and some companies post their sexual harassment polices on their Web sites. You may wish to give students some guidance on which Web sites to use for this activity. This will allow common points of reference when discussing the policies.

CHAPTER REVIEW 14

Have students review key points from the chapter by completing the Sort It Out game on *The Office* Web site.

Summary

The personal qualities that individuals bring with them to the workplace and the nature of working with others are the topics of this chapter. Review these key points from the chapter:

- Most workers, even those who work at home, interact with others. The character of each person in a group influences how effectively the group will work together.
- Your personal traits and character influence how you think, what you say, and how you respond to others. Your responses influence your success at work.
- Self-acceptance is necessary if an individual wants to make personality changes.
- A strong belief in the work ethic, willingness to help in achieving company goals, and a desire to learn are attitudes that support quality work.
- Your appearance affects how others think of you. Appropriate dress and proper personal hygiene are important for making a good impression on others.
- Workers should try to eliminate behavior that may be annoying to others.
- Workers are expected to use good manners that promote pleasant interactions with others.
- Employees need to become acquainted with the expectations and work style of their managers.
- Employees must work together to achieve the goals of a company.
- Employees should understand that some aspects of work may be confidential.
- Workers should avoid spreading rumors; they may be harmful to the company or its employees.
- Workers should accept responsibility for mistakes they make and try to correct any resulting problems.
- Conflicts arise at work, but willingness to face them candidly can lead to resolutions.
- Laws and regulations related to work should be understood by all employees.

Key Terms

character	ethics	sexual harassment
compromise	integrity	work ethic
conflict	personality	
diplomatic	reliable	

Chapter 14 : ACTIVITY 1

COMPOSITION
INTERNET
RESEARCH
WORD PROCESSING

Report on Unethical Behavior in Business

Companies expect employees to behave in an ethical manner. The public expects companies to behave in an ethical manner. When ethics are disregarded, the company or the public often suffers. In this activity, you will do research to find examples of unethical behavior in business.

1. Search the Internet or other resources. Find an article that describes unethical behavior by a company or a person in business. Copy or print the article, if possible. Take notes of the important facts and points made in the article. Record complete source information for the article.

2. Write a short report using your research. Begin by explaining what is meant by ethical behavior. Then describe the unethical behavior from the article you found. Explain what happened to the company or the public as a result of the unethical behavior. Add your personal comments regarding the incident. Include the reference information for the article at the end of your report.

3. Format the report in unbound report style. Proofread and correct all errors before printing the report.

Have students review the key terms by using the Flashcards available on *The Office* Web site.

Remind students to consult Section G of the Reference Guide in the *Student Activities and Simulations* workbook to review correct report format.

Compare Job Opportunities

Choosing a job that provides the tangible and intangible rewards of work that you desire will increase your job satisfaction. In this activity, you will evaluate two job opportunities and decide which one you would choose, considering both tangible and intangible benefits.

1. Open and print the PDF file *CH14 Jobs* from the data files. This file contains information about two jobs. Read the description for each job. Identify tangible and intangible rewards for each job. Also identify any factors that you think are negative about each job.

2. Write a paragraph that identifies the job you would choose. Explain what tangible and intangible factors made you choose this job. Describe any factors that you think are negative about the job you chose.

GLOSSARY

A

accession log a list of numbers assigned in a numeric filing system

accounts payable short-term debts a company owes

accounts receivable short-term debts owed to a company by others, such as its customers

action plan a description of tasks to be completed

adjournment an ending or closing

agenda a document that contains the information for a meeting such as the participants and topics to be discussed

alphabetic file records arranged and stored according to the letters of the alphabet

analog transmitted by a signal that corresponds to a physical change such as sound

annotate write comments related to the content of a message

appendix a section of a report that provides detailed or supplementary data

aptitude a natural ability or talent

archive keep permanently in inactive files

assertive positive or confident in a persistent way

assets goods and property owned

audience listeners or recipients of a message

audio sound that can be heard by the human ear

audit verify or check facts or procedures

automated attendant a computerized system for handling telephone calls

B

balance sheet a report that presents the financial condition of a company as of a specific date

bank reconciliation a report used to compare bank and company account records

bar code a pattern of vertical lines of varying widths that contains coded data that can be read by a scanner

bar graph a chart used to show comparisons

benchmarks standards used for comparisons such as job performance

biases prejudices

body language posture, body movements, gestures, and facial expressions that serve as nonverbal communication

bonding insurance for financial loss due to employee theft or fraud

Braille a system that enables the blind to read by feeling a pattern of raised dots

brainstorm offer ideas or suggestions

budget a plan for allocating resources

bullets small graphics, such as circles or diamonds, used to draw attention to a line of text

C

caption a notation on a file guide, folder, or drawer that indicates the contents

career goals desired achievements related to work such as jobs, education, or work experience

career strategy plans to meet career goals

carpal tunnel syndrome a repetitive strain injury that occurs when stress is placed on the hands, wrists, or arms

CD compact disk, a type of storage device for electronic data that can be read by a computer

cellular telephone a mobile device that uses wireless, radio frequencies to transmit voice across geographic segments

character reputation, values, or principles as shown by behavior

charging out removing a record from the file and recording related information

charter a written grant of rights from a government, as to form a corporation

check a written order to a bank to make payment against the depositor's funds in that bank

chronologic file records arranged according to date

chronologically arranged in order of time

code of ethics moral standards or values and related behavior; also called code of conduct

coding marking a record to indicate how it is indexed for filing

collect call an operator-assisted, long-distance call paid for by the party being called

colloquialism informal language used among a particular group

commission payment based on the price of items sold

compensated paid

comprehension the ability to understand concepts or material that has been read

compromise give up demands or make changes to reach a settlement

computer virus a destructive program loaded onto a computer and run without the user's knowledge

confidential private or secret in nature

confirmation number a series of characters (often text and numbers) associated with a reservation

conflict a disagreement, quarrel, or controversy

consensus a common agreement or mutual understanding

consulate a person appointed by a government to serve its citizens and business interests in another country

continuous improvement being alert at all times to ways of working more productively

controller an employee who oversees company finances

cooperative willing to act or work with others for a common purpose

copyright laws regulations covering what documents or other information can be legally copied

corporation a business organized under the laws of a particular state for which a charter was secured

courier service a private mail delivery company

credibility authority, reliability

credit permission to pay later for goods or services

cross-reference a record that gives the alternate name or subject by which a record may be requested and the name or subject by which the record is filed

customs government taxes or duties on imported items

D

data mining a process in which a software program searches for significant patterns in data

data processing collecting, organizing, analyzing, and summarizing data

debit card a kind of bank card that allows the cost of purchases to be automatically deducted from the cardholder's bank account

deductions items that reduce gross pay

demographic data statistics that describe a population such as age or race

desktop publishing producing high-quality printed documents that include both text and graphics

detection system devices and alarms that sense and signal a change in the condition of an area

digital stored or transmitted by a process using groups of electronic bits of data

digitized converted to a form that can be read by a computer

diplomatic tactful in dealing with people

direct deposit placing money in a bank account by electronic means rather than issuing a check

diversity reflected in a workforce with people from a wide range of ethnic and cultural backgrounds

documentation source information for quotations or material adapted from other sources

downsize reduce, as in decreasing the number of workers in an organization

draft a rough or preliminary version of a written message

DVD digital video disk, a type of storage device for electronic data that can be read by a computer or a player connected to a TV or stereo

E

e-commerce business conducted electronically, as in making purchases or selling products via the World Wide Web

electronic database a collection of records accessible by computer

electronic funds transfer (EFT) exchange of money by sending bank records via a computer network

electronic imaging converting paper documents to pictures stored and displayed via computer

electronic ticket a document and receipt that contain ticket information received in electronic form

e-mail the electronic transfer of messages using computers and software

embassy the offices of an ambassador in a foreign country

emergency procedures steps to follow in time of trouble or danger

employee empowerment enabling employees to make decisions

employment application a form that provides information about a job applicant

endorsement a signature of a payee on the back of a check authorizing a bank to cash or deposit the check

enunciate pronounce words clearly and distinctly

enunciation pronouncing words clearly

ergonomics the study of the effects of the work environment on the health of workers

ethics a system of moral standards or values

etiquette standards for proper behavior

evacuation a mass departure or flight, the clearing of an area

expense financial cost; fee; charge

extranet an information network like an intranet, but partially available to select outside users

ezine electronic magazine available on the World Wide Web

F

facsimile a technology, commonly called fax, that sends images (text, photographs, and drawings) using telephone or VoIP channels

file path the complete location designation (drive and folders) for an electronic file

file transfer protocol a tool that allows files to be uploaded to or downloaded from a remote computer

filing the process of storing records in an orderly manner within an organized system

firewall software and hardware designed to prevent unauthorized users from gaining access to a computer or network

fiscal year a 12-month period used for financial accounting purposes

flash drive an external storage device for computer data

flexible able to adapt or change as necessary

floppy disk a portable magnetic medium used to store small amounts of computer data

folder a durable container used to hold papers in a file

font a style or design for a set of type characters

footer information that appears below the body text at the bottom of document pages

forge imitate or counterfeit for illegal purposes

format an arrangement or layout, as of text on a page

Fortune 500 companies the 500 largest companies listed in *Fortune* magazine

fraud intentional deception to cause a person or business to give up property (assets) or some lawful right

freelancer an independent contractor who works for others, usually on a project-by-project basis

G

general managing handling work time and tasks efficiently, creating and monitoring schedules, and tracking and reporting the progress of tasks or projects

geographic file records arranged according to locations

global marketplace buying and selling of goods or services throughout the world

goodwill a friendly feeling or attitude

gross salary money earned before any deductions are made

group dynamics the way people interact and communicate within a group

guide a heavy cardboard sheet that creates divisions in a file

H

hacker a person who accesses a computer or network without proper permission or approval

handout a printed document used to summarize or provide details, as for a presentation

hard disk a magnetic medium used to store electronic data that can be read by a computer

hardware the physical parts of a computer or related equipment

header information that appears above the body text on pages of a document

hoteling assigning temporary office workspace to workers as needed

HTML hypertext markup language, authoring language used for World Wide Web and intranet documents

hypertext highlighted, underlined, or contrast-colored words or images that, when clicked, take the user to another location

I

imaging system converts documents to electronic form

income statement a report that details the results of business operations for a certain period of time

incompatible unable to work together

indexing deciding how to identify each record to be filed

inflection tone of voice

information data or facts that have been summarized or organized into a meaningful form

information management organizing, maintaining, and accessing records or data

information processing putting facts or numbers into a meaningful and useful form

initiative the ability to act or think without prompting or guidance

innovation a new method or idea

integrity honesty, sincerity, being of sound moral principle

interactive involving the user or receiver, exchanging information

interactive voice response a recorded message accessed and directed by the user to provide or record information

internal control a method used by a business to safeguard assets

Internet a public, worldwide computer network made up of smaller, interconnected networks that spans the globe

Internet service provider a company that sells access to the Internet

interview a meeting to question or evaluate, as for a job applicant

intonation the rise and fall in voice pitch

intranet a communications network within an organization that is meant for the use of its employees or members

itinerary a document giving detailed plans for a trip

J

job board a Web site that provides job listings and allows persons seeking employment to post resumes

job description a listing of the duties and tasks of a job and information about the work environment and the skills, experience, and education required for the job

job portfolio a file containing documents, work samples, and information related to employment

job scout a computer program that works independently to retrieve and deliver job information

K

kerning adjusting the space between characters in text

L

label a strip of paper attached to a file drawer or folder with a caption identifying the contents

letter of application a letter expressing interest in a job and requesting an interview

liabilities debts

line graph a chart used to display trends that emerge over a period of time

local area network a group of connected computers that are close to each other

M

magnetic media disks or tapes used to store documents electronically

magnetic tape a storage medium for computer and other electronic data

mailing list a directory of Internet user addresses

media materials or means used to communicate

medium or media material(s) or form(s) on or in which information may be stored

microfiche a small rectangular sheet of microfilm that contains a series of records arranged in rows and columns

micrographics converts documents to very small photographs for storage on microfilm

microwave transmission radio waves that carry data

minutes a written record of meeting proceedings and decisions

mobile office an office temporarily located at a particular site or that can move from place to place

modem a device that allows computer data to be transmitted via the telephone system, a conversion device for digital and analog data

modular workstation a work area made up of parts (wall panels, storage areas, desktop surfaces) that can be put together in various ways

modulated adjusted to a proper level

motion a proposal formally made in a meeting

N

negative message a communication that will be disappointing to the recipient

negligence failure to use a reasonable amount of care resulting in damage

net pay final earnings amount after all deductions

netiquette guidelines for proper behavior when communicating online, derived from *network* and *etiquette*

neutral message a communication that simply relays facts; neither positive nor negative

newsgroup a publication of online articles and messages related to a certain topic

nonterritorial workspace an area not assigned to a specific person or task

non-words spoken sounds such as "uhh" and "ah"

numeric file records arranged by numbers

O

objections reasons to disapprove or reject ideas

objectively in a detached manner without bias or prejudice

office a place in which the affairs of a business, professional person, or organization are carried out

online available in electronic format such as on the Internet or an intranet

optical character reader (OCR) electronic equipment that scans or "reads" text in a form that can be used by computers

optical character recognition (OCR) reading text printed on paper and translating the images into words that can be saved in a computer file and edited

overhead business costs not directly related to a product or service sold

overtime hours worked beyond the standard number in a workweek

owner's equity the owner's share of the worth of a firm; capital

P

pager an electronic device that alerts the user of the need to respond by telephone

pagination the process of dividing a document into individual pages for printing

parliamentary procedures guides for conducting meetings

partnership a business that is not incorporated and has two or more owners

passive voice a style of writing in which the subject is acted upon rather than performing the action

passport an official U.S. government document that grants permission to travel outside the United States

password a series of letters, numbers, or symbols used to identify a user and gain access to a computer system

payee a person to whom a check is written

payroll a list of employees and amount of salary or wages due to each

performance review evaluation of an employee's work, also called performance evaluation or performance appraisal

personal digital assistant (PDA) handheld computer with programs for storing contact information, scheduling appointments, and other tasks

personality patterns and qualities of behavior and attitudes of an individual

person-to-person call an operator-assisted, long-distance call that must be paid for only if the called person is reached

persuasive message a communication designed to convince the recipient

petty cash money kept on hand for paying small expenses

pie chart a graph showing how a part contributes to the whole

positive message a communication of good news or agreement

postage meter a machine that prints postage in the amount needed

prejudgments conclusions reached before having full information

prepaid phone card a card purchased in advance and used to pay for a certain number of minutes of phone use

preventive maintenance servicing equipment and replacing parts to prevent failure

priorities a listing of items in order of importance

prioritize place in order of importance

procrastinate delay intentionally, put off

proficiency the ability to perform at a satisfactory level

profile a description or picture

profit monetary gain; advantage

project management program software with advanced features for planning large or long-term tasks

projection an estimate or guess about the future based on known data

promotion an advancement in rank, grade, or position

proofreading checking a document carefully for errors or omissions

proprietary information privately owned information, such as a design or formula, also called intellectual property

protocol generally accepted customs or rules

Q

quorum the minimum number of members that must be present to conduct business at a meeting

quotation an excerpt from a different source

R

record data in forms such as text, numbers, images, or voice that is kept for future reference

records disposition moving records to permanent storage or destroying records

records management software computer program that allows electronic tracking and control of records

records management system a set of procedures used to organize, store, retrieve, and dispose of records

reference a person who knows your work abilities, skills, and habits and is willing to recommend you to employers

references sources of information, as in preparing a report

referral slip a document that accompanies items sent to another person and indicates a requested action

relational database a software program that allows the user to link data from a number of database files or tables to find information or generate reports

release mark an official approval to file a record

reliable dependable, trustworthy

reprographics the process of making copies of graphic images, such as printed documents

requisition form form that has space for charge-out information for a record

resignation letter a document stating the intention to end employment as of a certain date

resolution the number of dots per inch (dpi) in printed text or images

resume a document that presents job qualifications such as training, skills, and work experience

retention schedule a list of how long each type of record should be kept

revenue income, money, or other gain received

routing slip a document attached to an item that shows the names of individuals to whom the item should be sent

S

sales channel a method of marketing products such as through retail stores or catalogs

satellite a man-made object placed in orbit around the Earth containing electronic devices for relaying communications data

screen calls determine who is calling and the purpose for each call

second indicate formally the support of a motion

secondary storage storage media or devices outside the internal memory of a computer system

severance pay a payment made to an employee being dismissed from a job

sexual harassment sexually directed, unsolicited, and unwanted actions or speech that create a hostile work environment or unreasonably interferes with an individual's work performance

slang informal language

smart phone a device that combines the features of a mobile phone and a PDA

software programs containing instructions for a computer

sole proprietorship a business owned by one individual, also called single proprietorship

sorting arranging records alphabetically or numerically

spam electronic junk mail, advertisements, or other messages not requested by the recipient and often sent in a mass mailing

speech recognition software computer programs that allow voice input, also called *voice recognition software*

storyboarding recording and organizing ideas, as for a presentation

subject file records arranged by topic

surge suppressor an electrical outlet that controls unexpected sharp increases in electricity

synopsis a general overview or summary

T

telecommunications the electronic transfer of data over a distance

telecommute the practice of working and communicating with others from a remote location

teleconference a meeting of people in different locations conducted using telecommunications equipment

telegram a message sent using the private mail service Western Union

telephony the integration of computer and telephone technologies

tickler file notes or records arranged by date for keeping track of future actions

time management planning to gain control over how time is spent

tone a style or manner of writing or speaking that shows a certain attitude

total quality management establishing and maintaining high standards in how work is done

transaction a business deal or agreement, exchange of data, or sale

transitions the motions used to move from one electronic slide to the next

travel expense report a document that lists expenses to be reimbursed such as for hotels and meals

U

USB flash drive a magnetic storage device for electronic data that can be read by a computer

V

vaccination an injection given to produce immunity to a disease

vendor a seller of goods or services

videoconferencing communicating with people at two or more locations using two-way voice and video data

virtual office the capability to perform work activities away from a traditional office setting

visa a permit granted by a foreign government for a person to enter its country

vocabulary a collection of words

voice mail a messaging system that uses computers and telephones to record, store, and retrieve voice messages

VoIP Voice over Internet protocol, also called Internet voice, allows users to make telephone calls using a high-speed Internet connection instead of standard telephone channels

voucher a document that provides information and approval to make a payment

W

white space the area of a printed page that is empty, having no text or images

wide area network a group of connected computers that are separated by long distances

word processing producing written documents such as letters or reports by using software programs and computers

work ethic a system of values in which purposeful activity is of central importance

work simplification the process of improving the procedures for doing work

workstation the physical area in which a worker performs a job

World Wide Web computers on the Internet that use and transmit HTML documents

INDEX

Confidential information, 15, 433, 437, 501, 569

Confirmation number, 331

Conflict, 571–572

Consensus, 316

Consolidated Omnibus Budget Reconciliation Act (COBRA), 544–545

Consulate, 338

Context, 117

Continuous improvement, 50–51, 540

Controller, 91

Conventional coding, 392–393

COO. *See* Chief operating officer

Cookies, defined, 103

Cooperation/cooperativeness, 49, 56, 57, 58, 557, 568

Copiers/printers, 404–405

Copying. *See* Paper records

Copyright laws, 407

Corporations, 16, 17, 24

Corrective internal control, 223

Correspondence. *See* Business correspondence

Costs, 360–361
  filing, 372
  telephone, 507

Counseling services. *See* School placement/counseling services

Courier service, 446

Creation/collection, in record life cycle, 361, 392

Credibility, 197

Credit, 223

Credit memorandum, 230

Cross-reference, for records, 394–396

CSI. *See* Computer Security Institute

Customer satisfaction, 49, 51, 52

Customs, 335–336, 460

D

Data, 94–95, 96, 103, 471
  attendance, 251
  backup copies for, 417

budget, 246, 247
collection of, 412
confidential, 437
demographic, 93
digitized electronic, 359
files for, 414
financial, 92
for telephone messages, 498
from government agencies, 93
hypertext, 99
in graphs/tables, 164–165
in marketing information systems, 91
managing, 72
micrographics systems and, 356
on Internet, 83, 154
on invoices, 224
on optical disks, 355–356
on tax returns, 418
paper directories and, 504
privacy and, 104
purchase order, 92
receiving/sending, 340
recording, 475
records and, 351
reminder systems and, 275
report, 152
resume, 523
security and, 85
storing, 77
transmitting, 471

Data mining, 94–95

Data privacy, 104

Data processing, 41

Data sheet. *See* Resume

Database management systems (DBMS), 418–419

Databases, 7, 137, 381
  defined, 418
  electronic, 94–95, 418
  incompatible, 72
  reading skills and, 115
  records and, 417
  relational, 94

requisition forms and, 401
software for, 279

Day planners. *See* Personal planners/day planners

DBMS. *See* Database management systems (DBMS)

DDOS attacks, 86

Deadlines, 152, 269, 271, 316, 541
  desk calendars and, 275
  meetings and, 320
  projects and, 273
  reminder systems and, 274
  tickler files and, 279

Debit card, 222

Dedicated/leased line, 82

Deductions, 251, 254–255

Delivery service. *See* Private courier/delivery service

Dell Computer Corporation, 252

Demographic data, 93

Department of Commerce, 19

Department of Labor, 35

Department of the Treasury, 19

Deposits, 227–229

Desktop publishing, 39, 144–146

Desktops, workstation area and, 285, 289, 293

Detection system, 300

Detective internal control, 222–223

Dial-up access, 84

Dial-up line, 82

Digital signals, 471, 475

Digital video disks (DVDs), 77, 94, 359
  optical storage media and, 355–356
  storage for, 412, 416–417

Diplomatic, 571

Direct deposit, 257

Direct service line (DSL), 82, 84

Direct-dial calls, 505

Directories, 502–504

Directory assistance, 504

Disaster Recovery Institute International, 365